BIOETHICS:

HEALTH CARE LAW AND ETHICS

Fifth Edition

Barry R. Furrow
Professor of Law and Director, Health Law Institute
Widener University

Thomas L. Greaney
Professor of Law
Co-Director, Center for Health Law Studies
Saint Louis University

Sandra H. Johnson
Tenet Chair in Health Care Law and Ethics,
Professor of Law in Health Care Administration and
Professor of Law in Internal Medicine
Saint Louis University

Timothy Stoltzfus Jost
Robert L. Willett Family Professor of Law
Washington and Lee University School of Law

Robert L. Schwartz
Professor of Law and Professor of Pediatrics
University of New Mexico

AMERICAN CASEBOOK SERIES®

THOMSON

WEST

American Casebook Series and West Group are trademarks registered in the U.S. Patent and Trademark Office.

COPYRIGHT © 1987, 1991 WEST PUBLISHING CO.

COPYRIGHT © 1997 WEST GROUP

COPYRIGHT © 2001 By WEST GROUP

© 2004 West, a Thomson business
     610 Opperman Drive
     P.O. Box 64526
     St. Paul, MN 55164–0526
     1–800–328–9352

ISBN 0–314–15406–X

To Donna Jo, Elena, Michael, Nicholas, Eva and Robert
B.R.F.

To Nancy, T.J., and Kati
T.L.G.

To Bob, Emily and Kathleen
S.H.J.

To Ruth, Jacob, Micah and David
T.S.J.

To Jane, Mirra and Elana
R.L.S.

This book is also dedicated to the memory of Nancy Rhoden and Jay Healey, great teachers, wonderful colleagues and warm friends.

*

Preface

Since the first edition of this book was published, no part of the American landscape has changed more that the American health care system. The system has been stressed by demographic changes, buffeted by the health care systems, winds of political change, and utterly transformed by social and economic developments. While the fundamental ethical principles underlying the study of bioethics have remained largely unchanged, their application by courts (and legislatures, and administrative agencies) has changed rather substantially. Until a few years ago virtually no one attained elective office because of her position on issues related to health care; now it is an important part of every politician's platform – with bioethics issues, ranging from stem cell research to control of bioterrorism to the distribution of health resources – front and center.

The fifth edition of this Bioethics casebook continues to use the broad organization that teachers and students found so helpful in the previous editions. As was the case in previous editions, we employ materials from a variety of sources. This book continues to contain the most significant and useful judicial opinions dealing with the issues of bioethics, drawn from the federal and state courts. The book also contains statutes, legislative history, administrative regulations, excerpts from contracts, international resources, and a host of other kinds of materials designed to bring the subject of health law to life in the classroom. It also contains many classroom-tested problems that should be helpful in encouraging reflection on bioethics issues. While many of the problems and other materials have been brought forward from earlier editions of this book, every section of this casebook has been rewritten and the organization of the text reflects new developments in American health care law and bioethics. The cases, statutes, regulations and other materials that have been carried forward have been edited to maintain their teaching value while assuring that they reflect problems faced by health lawyers coping with the health system in the twenty-first century. The notes are written to expose students to a range of the most subtle bioethics questions under discussion at the time of publication.

This Bioethics casebook is primarily drawn from a larger and more comprehensive casebook, Health Law (Fifth Edition). Because that larger volume is often used for more than one course at American law and medical schools, the authors thought it would be convenient for students who need access to only a part of that material to have the needed casebook sections available separately. In addition to its coverage of bioethics, Health Law (Fifth Edition) also includes a discussion of how we define illness and health and assess quality within the health care system, an analysis of ways in which the law can contribute to the promotion of the quality of health care (including materials on medical malpractice, its alternatives, and potential reforms), an evaluation of issues relating to access to health care and control of health care costs (including materials on both private and public financing mechanisms and the regulation of managed care), and an account of the role of the law in organizing the health care enterprise (including materials on different ways in which business of health care delivery can be organized, on the legal relationships among different players in the health care enterprise, on government regulation of the financial relationships of providers, and on the application of antitrust law to health care).

Chapter 1 of the Bioethics casebook, An Introduction to the Study of Ethics and Ethical Theory, is the only portion of the Bioethics book which does not appear in the Health Law casebook as well. Chapter 2 of Bioethics, Human Reproduction and Birth, appears as Chapter 16 of Health Law. Chapter 3 of Bioethics, Legal, Social and Ethical Issues in Human Genetics, is Chapter 17 of Health Law. Bioethics Chapter 4, Defining Death, and Chapter 5, Life and Death Decisions, appear as Chapters 18 and 19 of Health Law, and Chapter 6 of Bioethics, Regulation of Research Involving Human Subjects, is published as Chapter 20 of Health Law. Bioethics Chapters 7 and 8, Distributive Justice and the Allocation of Health Care Resources, and Public Health and Bioterrorism, are both drawn from Chapter 1 of the Health Law book, where they appear as sections IV and V. With the exception of page and chapter references, the materials in the Bioethics and Health Law casebooks are identical.

This casebook is designed to be a teachable book. We are grateful for the many comments and helpful suggestions that health law (and, especially, bioethics) teachers across the United States (and from elsewhere, too) have made to help us improve this new edition. We continue to present all sides of policy issues, not to evangelize for any political, economic or social agenda of our own. This task is made easier, undoubtedly, by the diverse views on virtually all policy issues that the several different authors of this casebook bring to this endeavor. A large number of very well respected health law teachers have contributed a great deal to this and previous editions by making suggestions, reviewing problems, or encouraging our more thorough investigation of a wide range of health law subjects. We are especially grateful to Charles Baron, Eugene Basanta, David Bennahum, Kathleen Boozang, Arnold Celnicker, Don Chalmers, Ellen Wright Clayton, Dena Davis, Ileana Dominguez-Urban, Stewart Duban, Margaret Farrell, David Frankford, Michael Gerhart, Joan McIver Gibson, Susan Goldberg, Jesse Goldner, Andrew Grubb, Art LaFrance, Diane Hoffman, Thomasine Kushner, Pam Lambert, Theodore LeBlang, Antoinette Sedillo Lopez, Lawrence Singer, Joan Krause, Aroop Mangalik, Leslie Mansfield, Thomas Mayo, Maxwell Mehlman, Alan Meisel, Vicki Michel, Frances Miller, John Munich, David Orentlicher, Vernellia Randall, Ben Rich, Arnold Rosoff, Karen Rothenberg, Mark Rothstein, Giles Scofield, Jeff Sconyers, Charity Scott, Ross Silverman, Loane Skene, George Smith, Sheila Taub, Michael Vitiello, Sidney Watson, Ellen Wertheimer, William Winslade and Susan M. Wolf for the benefit of their wisdom and experience.

We wish to thank those who provided support for our research and the preparation of the manuscript, including Blake Morant and the Frances Lewis Law Center, the Robert L. Willett family, Heather Bearden, Kelly Dineen, Kallie Dixon, Clara Fields, Karla Harris, Kathy Kunkel, Aaron McCullough, Vera Mencer, Jeanmarie Montney, Vinita Ollapally, Gloria Ortiz, Willow Whispering Cloud Parks, Cody Rogers, Matthew Vebele, Christopher Van Blarcum, and David Wertz. We all have special appreciation for the exceptional work done by Mary Ann Jauer at St. Louis University, and for the tremendous publication assistance provided by Staci Herr and Roxanne Birkel at Thomson West.

Finally, we wish to thank our deans, Douglas Ray, Jeffrey E. Lewis, Suellyn Scarnecchia, and David Partlett, and Department Chair Dr. Gerry Magill.

A note on editorial style: Elipses in the text of the quoted material indicate an omission of material within the quoted paragraph. Centered elipses indicate the omission of a paragraph or more; the first line following centered elipses may not be the first line of the next paragraph, and the last line preceding centered elipses may not be the last line of the preceding paragraph. Brackets indicate the omission of a citation without the omission of other materials. There is no acknowledgment of omitted footnotes. To the extent it is possible, the style of this casebook is consistent with the principle that legal writing form should follow function, and the function of this text is to help students understand health law.

BARRY R. FURROW
THOMAS L. GREANEY
SANDRA H. JOHNSON
TIMOTHY S. JOST
ROBERT L. SCHWARTZ

June, 2004

*

Acknowledgements

Annas, George J., Blinded by Bioterrorism: Public Health and Liberty in the 21st Century, 13 Health Matrix 33 (2003). Reprinted with permission of the author and Case Western Reserve University. Permission conveyed through Copyright Clearance Center, Inc.

Arras, John and Robert Hunt, Ethical Theory in the Medical Context, in J. Arras and N. Rhoden, Ethical Issues in Modern Medicine (3d ed. 1989). Copyright, 1989. Reprinted with permission.

Austin, C.R., Human Embryos: Debate on Assisted Reproduction (1989). Copyright 1989, Oxford University Press. Reprinted by permission of Oxford University Press.

Battin, Margaret, A Dozen Caveats Concerning the Discussion of Euthanasia in Netherlands, in the Lease Worst Death (1994). Copyright 1994, Oxford University Press. Reprinted by permission of Oxford University Press and the author.

Battin, Margaret, The Least Worst Death, 13 Hastings Center Report (2) 13 (April 1983). Copyright 1983, The Hastings Center. Reprinted with permission of the Hastings Center. Reprinted with permission of the Hastings Center and the author.

Bernat, James, Charles Culver and Bernard Gert, Defining Death in Theory and Practice, 12 Hastings Center Report (1) 5 (February 1982). Copyright 1982, the Hastings Center. Reprinted with permission of the Hastings Center and the authors.

Capron, Alexander Morgan and Leon Kass, A Statutory Definition of the Standards for Determining Human Death: As Appraisal and a Proposal, 121 U. Pa. L. Rev. 87 (1972). Copyright 1972, the University of Pennsylvania Law Review. Reprinted with permission of the University of Pennsylvania Law Review and William S. Hein & Co., Inc.

Cassel, Christine and Diane Meier, Morals and Moralism in the Debate Over Euthanasia and Assisted Suicide, 323 N. Eng. J. Med. 750 (1990). Copyright 1990, Massachusetts Medical Society. All rights reserved. Reprinted with permission of the Massachusetts Medical Society.

Center for Law and the Public's Health at Georgetown and John Hopkins University, The Model State Emergency Health Powers Act As of December 21, 2001. Reprinted with permission of the Center for Law and the Public's Health.

Council on Ethical and Judicial Affairs, The Use of Anencephalic Neonates as Organ Donors, 273 JAMA 1614 (1995). Copyright 1995, American Medical Association. All rights reserved. Reprinted with permission of American Medical Association.

Fletcher, Joseph, Indicators of Humanhood, 2 Hastings Center Report (5) 1 (November 1972). Copyright 1972, the Hastings Center. Reprinted with permission of the Hastings Center.

Fried, Terri et al., Understanding the Treatment Preferences of Seriously Ill Patients, 346 NEJ Med. 1061 (2002). Copyright 2002, Massachusetts Medical Society. All rights reserved. Reprinted with permission of the Massachusetts Medical Society.

Gostin, Lawrence O., The Model State Emergency Health Powers Act: Public Health and Civil Liberties in a Time of Terrorism, 13 Health Matrix 3 (2003). Reprinted with permission of Lawrence O. Gostin and Case Western Reserve University. Permission conveyed through Copyright Clearance Center, Inc.

Gostin, Lawrence O., Public Health Law: Power, Duty, Restraint. Copyright 2000, University of California Press. Reprinted with permission of the University of California Press,

Levy, Barry, Twenty-First Century Challenges for Law and Public Health, 32 Ind. L. Rev. 1149 (1999). Copyright 1999, Indiana Law Review. Reprinted with permission of the Indiana Law Review.

National Conference of Commissioners on Uniform State Laws, Uniform Anatomical Gift Act. Copyright 1977, National Conference of Commissioners on Uniform State Laws. Reprinted with permission of National Conference of Commissioners on Uniform State Laws.

National Conference of Commissioners on Uniform State Laws, Uniform Determination of Death Act. Copyright 1980, National Conference of Commissioners on Uniform State Laws. Reprinted with permission of National Conference of Commissioners on Uniform State Laws.

National Conference of Commissioners of Uniform State Laws, Uniform Health-Care Decisions Act. Copyright 1994, National Conference of Commissioners on Uniform State Laws. Reprinted with permission of National Conference of Commissioners on Uniform State Laws.

National Conference of Commissioners on Uniform State Laws, Uniform Parentage Act. Copyright 1973, 2000 and 2002, National Conference of Commissions on Uniform State Laws. Reprinted with permission of National Conference of Commissioners on Uniform State Laws.

National Conference of Commissioners on Uniform State Laws, Uniform Probate Code. Copyright, National Conference of Commissioners on Uniform State Laws. Reprinted with permission of National Conference of Commissioners on Uniform State Laws.

Report of the Ad Hoc Committee of the Harvard Medical School to Examine the Definition of Brain Death: A Definition of Irreversible Coma, 205 JAMA 85 (August 1968). Copyright 1968, American Medical Association. Reprinted with permission of the American Medical Association.

Report of the Committee of Inquiry into Human Fertilisation and Embryology (Cmnd 9314) (1984). Copyright 1984, Her Majesty's Stationery Office. Crown copyright is reproduced with the permission of the Controller of Her Majesty's Stationery Office.

Roth, Loren, Alan Meisel and Charles Lidz, Tests of Competency to Consent to Treatment, 134 Am. J. Psychiatry 279 (1977). Copyright 1977, the American Psychiatric Association. Reprinted with permission.

Rothenberg, Karen, New Perspectives for Teaching and Scholarship: The Role of Gender in Law and Health Care, 54 Md. L. Rev. 473 (1995). Copyright 1995, Karen Rothenberg. Reprinted with permission of Karen Rothenberg.

Ulrich, Lawrence P., Reproductive Rights of Genetic Disease, in J. Humber and R. Almeder, eds., Biomedical Ethics and the law. Copyright 1986, Kluwer/Plenum Publishers. Reprinted with permission.

Veatch, Robert, Correspondence—What it Means to be Dead, 12 Hastings Center Report (5) 45 (October 1982). Copyright 1982, the Hastings Center. Reprinted with permission of the Hastings Center.

Wolf, Susan M., Gender, Feminism and Death: Physician Assisted Suicide and Euthanasia, in S.M. Wolf, ed., Feminism and Bioethics: Beyond Reproduction (1996). Copyright 1996, Oxford University Press. Reprinted by permission of Susan M. Wolf and Oxford University Press.

*

Summary of Contents

Page

PREFACE --- v
ACKNOWLEDGEMENTS --- ix
TABLE OF CASES --- xxi

Chapter 1. An Introduction to the Study of Ethics and Ethical Theories --- 1

Chapter 2. Human Reproduction and Birth ----------------------------- 31
  I. When Does Human Life Become a "Person"? ------------------------ 32
  II. Medical Intervention in Reproduction ------------------------- 47
  III. Fetal Maternal Decisionmaking ------------------------------- 159

Chapter 3. Legal, Social and Ethical Issues in Human Genetics ------ 181
  I. Introduction --- 181
  II. Legal Responses -- 186

Chapter 4. Defining Death -- 209
  I. Introduction --- 210
  II. The Development of the "Brain Death" Definition ------------- 211
  III. The "Dead Donor" Rule and Expanding Classes of Organ Donors— Anencephalic Infants and "Non–Heart Beating" Donors ----------- 219
  IV. Religious and Other Objections to Definitions of Death: Letting The Patient Decide Which Definition to Use ---------------------- 236

Chapter 5. Life and Death Decisions ------------------------------- 238
  I. Introduction --- 238
  II. The United States Constitution and the "Right to Die" ------- 243
  III. The "Right to Die"—Patients With Decisional Capacity ------ 256
  IV. The "Right to Die"—Patients Without Decisional Capacity ---- 273
  V. The "Right to Die"—Children and Newborns ------------------- 341
  VI. Physician Assisted Death ---------------------------------- 365
  VII. Regulation of End–of–Life Care: The Case of Medical Marijuana ---- 398

Chapter 6. Regulation of Research Involving Human Subjects -------- 408
  I. The Nuremberg Code --- 408
  II. Regulation of Research Upon Human Subjects in the United States 410
  III. International Regulation of Research Involving Human Subjects ---- 444

Chapter 7. Distributive Justice and the Allocation of Health Care Resources—The Example of Human Organ Transplantation --- 450
  I. Introduction --- 450
  II. Rationing of Scarce Human Organs -------------------------- 455

Page

III. Increasing the Supply of Organs for Transplantation: The Impact of Legal Restraints ------- 461

Chapter 8. Public Health and Bioterrorism ------- **473**
  I. Introduction to Public Health Law ------- 473
  II. The Constitutional Foundation of Public Health Law ------- 476
  III. Forced Treatment, Isolation and Quarantine ------- 483
  IV. Bioterrorism and Public Health ------- 489

INDEX ------- 501

Table of Contents

Page

PREFACE --- v
ACKNOWLEDGEMENTS -- ix
TABLE OF CASES --- xxi

Chapter 1. An Introduction to the Study of Ethics and Ethical Theories --- 1
Joan Gibson, Thinking About the "Ethics" in Bioethics ---------------- 1
John Arras and Robert Hunt, Ethical Theory in the Medical Context ----- 6
Note on the Application of Ethical Theories in Law ------------------- 23
Note: New Theories of Bioethics Analysis and the Attack on "Principlism" ------ 23
Note on Codes of Ethics and Oaths ----------------------------------- 27
Oath of Hippocrates --- 27
Prayer of Maimonides -- 28
American Medical Association's Principles of Medical Ethics ---------- 29
Problem: Drafting a Professional Code of Ethics --------------------- 30

Chapter 2. Human Reproduction and Birth -------------------------- 31
Problem: Death During Pregnancy ------------------------------------- 31
I. When Does Human Life Become a "Person"? -------------------------- 32
  A. The Attributes of Personhood ---------------------------------- 33
     Joseph Fletcher, "Humanness," in Humanhood: Essays in Biomedical Ethics ------ 33
     Notes and Questions --- 36
     C.R. Austin, Human Embryos: The Debate on Assisted Reproduction --- 36
  B. Legal Recognition of The Beginning of Human Life -------------- 39
     1. Constitutional Recognition -------------------------------- 39
     2. Statutory Recognition ------------------------------------- 41
     3. Common Law Recognition ------------------------------------ 44
II. Medical Intervention in Reproduction ---------------------------- 47
  A. Limiting Reproduction --- 48
     1. Government Prohibitions on Reproduction ------------------- 48
     2. Contraception -- 49
     3. Abortion --- 50
        Roe v. Wade -- 51
        Notes and Questions -------------------------------------- 54
        Planned Parenthood of Southeastern Pennsylvania v. Casey ------- 57
        Stenberg v. Carhart -------------------------------------- 68
        Notes and Questions on Casey and Stenberg ---------------- 74
        Problem: The Partial Birth Abortion Ban Act of 2003 ------ 80
        Note: The Freedom of Access to Clinic Entrances Act of 1994 ------- 83
        Note: The Blurry Distinction Between Contraception and Abortion, and the Advent of Mifepristone (RU–486) ------- 85
     4. Sterilization -- 87
     5. Tort Remedies for Failed Reproductive Control: Wrongful Birth, Wrongful Life and Wrongful Conception ------- 91
        Smith v. Cote -- 91
        Notes and Questions -------------------------------------- 99

Page

B. Assisting Reproduction 104
   Problem: Reproductive Arrangements Go Awry 104
   1. Introduction 105
      a. The Process of Human Reproduction 105
      b. The Role of the Law 107
      c. Facilitating Reproduction and the Definition of the Family 107
   2. Artificial Insemination 109
      The Process of Artificial Insemination (or "Intrauterine Insemination") 109
      a. Artificial Insemination—Homologous (AIH) 109
      b. Artificial Insemination—Donor (AID) 110
         Uniform Parentage Act (1973) 110
         Uniform Parentage Act (2002) 111
         Notes and Questions 113
   3. In Vitro Fertilization, Egg Transfer and Embryo Transfer 116
      The Process of In Vitro Fertilization and Related Techniques 116
      Notes and Questions: The Status of the Parents 118
      Davis v. Davis 119
      Notes and Questions: The Status of the Embryo 126
   4. Surrogacy 129
      The Process of Surrogacy 129
      In the Matter of Baby M 130
      Notes and Questions 134
      Johnson v. Calvert 137
      Notes and Questions 143
      Prato–Morrison v. Doe 145
      Notes on Prato–Morrison v. Doe 149
      Uniform Parentage Act (2002) 150
      Notes and Questions 152
   5. Cloning 153
      Recommendations of the National Bioethics Advisory Commission (NBAC) with Regard to Cloning (1997) 155
      Note: Reproductive and Therapeutic Cloning and Stem Cell Research 158
      Bibliographical Note: Facilitating Reproduction 159
III. Fetal Maternal Decisionmaking 159
   Problem: Children Bearing Children 159
   In re A.C. 160
   Notes and Questions 166
   Guardianship of J.D.S. 173
   Notes and Questions 179
   Bibliographical Note 180

Chapter 3. Legal, Social and Ethical Issues in Human Genetics 181
  I. Introduction 181
 II. Legal Responses 186
   A. Privacy and Confidentiality of Genetic Information 189
      Safer v. Pack 189
      Notes and Questions 193
      Problem: All in the Family 194
   B. Discrimination Based on Genetic Traits 195
      1. Insurance 195
         Problem: Insurance Decisions 195
         Notes and Questions 196
      2. Employment 196
         Problem: Preventing Harms? 198
   C. Ownership of Genetic Information and Resultant Products 199
      Greenberg v. Miami Children's Hospital Research Institute 199

Page

Notes and Questions---- 204

Note on Government–Owned Biobanks and Joint Ventures for Commercial Development ---- 205

Problem: Creating the Treasure Trove ---- 207

Chapter 4. Defining Death ---- **209**

Problem: When Does Death Occur? ---- 209

I. Introduction ---- 210

Note: Religious Perspective on Death ---- 211

II. The Development of the "Brain Death" Definition ---- 211

A. History ---- 211

B. Uniform Determination of Death Act (1980) ---- 214

Note: Brain Death and Homicide Statutes ---- 215

C. Higher Brain Death ---- 217

III. The "Dead Donor" Rule and Expanding Classes of Organ Donors—Anencephalic Infants and "Non–Heart Beating" Donors ---- 219

A. Anencephalic Infants ---- 219

In re T.A.C.P. ---- 219

Council on Ethical and Judicial Affairs, American Medical Association, The Use of Anencephalic Neonates as Organ Donors ---- 222

Notes on the Use of Anencephalic Infants as Organ Donors ---- 226

In re Baby K ---- 228

Notes and Questions ---- 232

B. Non–Heart–Beating Donors ---- 233

Problem: Holy Central Hospital's Organ Harvesting Proposal ---- 233

Note ---- 235

IV. Religious and Other Objections to Definitions of Death: Letting The Patient Decide Which Definition to Use ---- 236

Chapter 5. Life and Death Decisions ---- **238**

I. Introduction ---- 238

Problem: Right to Die ---- 241

II. The United States Constitution and the "Right to Die" ---- 243

Cruzan v. Director, Missouri Department of Health ---- 243

Notes and Questions ---- 252

III. The "Right to Die"—Patients With Decisional Capacity ---- 256

Problem: The Christian Scientist in the Emergency Room ---- 256

A. The General Rule ---- 257

Bouvia v. Superior Court ---- 257

Notes and Questions ---- 261

Note: Countervailing State Interests ---- 264

Note: State Law Bases for a "Right to Die" ---- 267

B. The Right to Refuse Medical Treatment for Religious Reasons ---- 268

Application of the President and Directors of Georgetown College, Inc. ---- 269

Notes ---- 270

Public Health Trust of Dade County v. Wons ---- 271

Notes ---- 272

IV. The "Right to Die"—Patients Without Decisional Capacity ---- 273

A. Determining Decisional Capacity ---- 273

Problem: Determining the Decisional Capacity of a Dying Patient ---- 273

Loren H. Roth, Alan Meisel, and Charles W. Lidz, Tests of Competency To Consent to Treatment ---- 275

President's Commission for the Study of Ethical Problems in Medicine And Biomedical and Behavioral Research, Decisionmaking Capacity ---- 278

Notes and Questions ---- 279

B. Determining the Patient's Choice ---- 281

1. A Statutory Framework for Health Care Decision Making: Advance Directives and Surrogate Decisionmakers ---- 282

Uniform Health–Care Decisions Act ---- 282

                                                                Page
        Notes on Advance Directives --- 290
    2. Decisionmaking for Incompetent Patients in the Absence
        of a Governing Statute ------------------------------------ 297
        a. Discovering the Patient's Wishes---------------------- 297
            In re Eichner -- 297
            Note: Applying the Principle of Substituted Judgment -------- 299
            In re Conroy --- 300
            Notes and Questions --- 302
            Note: Choosing Futile Medical Care --------------------- 308
            Problem --- 310
        b. The Role of the Courts and the Burden of Proof in
            Cases Involving the Decision to Forego Lifesustain-
            ing Treatment -- 311
            Conservatorship of Wendland ------------------------------ 311
            Notes and Questions-- 321
        c. Disputes Among Family Members Acting as Decision
            Makers --- 327
            Guardianship of Schiavo ---------------------------------- 327
            Note on the Legal and Political History of the Schiavo Case 330
            *Note: Wendland, Schiavo and the Role of the Court in
            Making Health Care Decisions for Those Without Capaci-
            ty* --- 333
            Problem: Not Quite Persistent Vegetative State ------------- 335
    3. Making Health Care Decisions for Patients Who Have
        Never Been Competent----------------------------------- 336
        Superintendent of Belchertown State School v. Saikewicz--------- 336
        In re Storar--- 338
        Notes and Questions--- 340
 V. The "Right to Die"—Children and Newborns ---------------------- 341
    A. Children--- 341
        Problem: Choosing to Forgo Cancer Treatment ------------------- 341
        Newmark v. Williams --- 341
        Notes and Questions-- 347
    B. Newborns-- 351
        Problem: Newborn With Spina Bifida --------------------------- 351
        Note: Treating Seriously Ill Newborns ---------------------------- 352
        Miller v. HCA --- 355
        Notes and Questions-- 362
        Problem: Conjoined Twins -- 364
 VI. Physician Assisted Death --- 365
    A. The Constitutional Framework---------------------------------- 365
        Washington v. Glucksberg--- 365
        Vacco v. Quill-- 376
        Notes and Questions-- 379
    B. Legislation to Support Physician Assisted Death—"Death With
        Dignity" Initiatives-- 387
        The Oregon Death With Dignity Act------------------------------- 387
        *Oregon Department of Human Services, Office of Disease Prevention
        and Epidemiology, Fifth Annual Report on Oregon's Death with
        Dignity Act.* --- 392
        Notes and Questions-- 394
        Problem: Drafting Legislation ----------------------------------- 398
 VII. Regulation of End–of–Life Care: The Case of Medical Marijuana ----- 398
        United States v. Oakland Cannabis Buyers' Cooperative---------------- 398
        Notes and Questions -- 403
        Problem: Drafting Medical Marijuana Legislation------------------------- 407

Page

Chapter 6. Regulation of Research Involving Human Subjects --- 408
  I. The Nuremberg Code -- 408
    Nuremberg Code: Permissible Medical Experiments ---------------- 409
    Notes and Questions -- 410
  II. Regulation of Research Upon Human Subjects in the United States 410
    A. History -- 410
    B. Federal Regulation of Research ------------------------------ 412
      Problem: Is It Research? ----------------------------------- 412
      45 C.F.R. Part 46 -- 413
      Notes and Questions -- 420
    C. Research Regulation by Litigation: Protecting Vulnerable Subjects --- 422
      Grimes v. Kennedy Krieger Institute, Inc. ------------------ 422
      Notes and Questions -- 432
      Note on Regulations Restricting Research on Other Vulnerable Populations --- 434
      Note on Conflicts of Interest in Research ------------------ 437
      Problem: Conflicts or Not? --------------------------------- 439
    D. Reforming the System to Protect Research Participants ---------- 440
      Responsible Research: A Systems Approach to Protecting Research Participants -------------------------------------- 440
      Notes and Questions -- 444
  III. International Regulation of Research Involving Human Subjects ----- 444
    Declaration of Helsinki, Ethical Principles for Medical Research Involving Human Subjects --- 445
    Problem: The African and Asian AIDS Trials -------------------- 448
    Notes and Questions --- 448

Chapter 7. Distributive Justice and the Allocation of Health Care Resources—The Example of Human Organ Transplantation --- 450
  I. Introduction -- 450
  II. Rationing of Scarce Human Organs -------------------------------- 455
    Problem: Selecting an Organ Transplant Recipient -------------- 455
    Note: The Organ Procurement Transplant Network --------------- 456
      1. Geographic Distribution of Organs ----------------------- 456
      2. Listing Patients for Transplantation -------------------- 457
      3. Zero Antigen Mismatch and Disparate Impact by Race --------- 458
        Problem: Setting Priorities ---------------------------- 459
        Problem: State or Federal Control? --------------------- 460
  III. Increasing the Supply of Organs for Transplantation: The Impact of Legal Restraints --- 461
    Newman v. Sathyavaglswaran ----------------------------------- 461
    Notes and Questions --- 465
    Note: Market Solutions to Organ Shortages -------------------- 467
    Problem: Organ Donation From an Adolescent ------------------- 469
    Note: Organs from Living Donors ------------------------------ 470

Chapter 8. Public Health and Bioterrorism ----------------------- 473
  I. Introduction to Public Health Law ------------------------------- 473
    Barry Levy, Twenty–First Century Challenges for Law and Public Health --- 473
    Notes --- 475
    Problem --- 476
  II. The Constitutional Foundation of Public Health Law ------------- 476
    Jacobson v. Massachusetts ------------------------------------- 476
    Notes and Questions --- 480
    Problem --- 483

Page

III. Forced Treatment, Isolation and Quarantine ------------------------------ 483
   Tuberculosis Control Units, Ohio Code § 339.80–.89 (2003) --------------------- 484
   Notes and Questions -- 487
   Problem --- 488
IV. Bioterrorism and Public Health --- 489
   The Model State Emergency Health Powers Act ----------------------------------- 489
   Lawrence O. Gostin, The Model State Emergency Health Powers Act:
      Public Health and Civil Liberties in a Time of Terrorism --------------------- 494
   George J. Annas, Blinded by Bioterrorism: Public Health and Liberty in
      the 21st Century --- 496
   Notes -- 498

INDEX -- 501

Table of Cases

The principal cases are in bold type. Cases cited or discussed in the text are roman type. References are to pages. Cases cited in principal cases and within other quoted materials are not included.

AB, In re, 196 Misc.2d 940, 768 N.Y.S.2d 256 (N.Y.Sup.2003), 348, 364
A.C., In re, 573 A.2d 1235 (D.C.1990), **160,** 166, 167, 168, 179
Addington v. Texas, 441 U.S. 418, 99 S.Ct. 1804, 60 L.Ed.2d 323 (1979), 488
Adoption of (see name of party)
Advocacy Center for Persons With Diasabilities, Inc. v. Schiavo, 2003 WL 23305833 (M.D.Fla.2003), 332
Air Crash Disaster at Detroit Metropolitan Airport on Aug. 16, 1987, In re, 737 F.Supp. 427 (E.D.Mich.1989), 45, 46
Akron, City of v. Akron Center for Reproductive Health, Inc., 462 U.S. 416, 103 S.Ct. 2481, 76 L.Ed.2d 687 (1983), 57
Amadio v. Levin, 509 Pa. 199, 501 A.2d 1085 (Pa.1985), 44
American Academy of Pediatrics v. Heckler, 561 F.Supp. 395 (D.D.C.1983), 353
American Academy of Pediatrics v. Lungren, 51 Cal.Rptr.2d 201, 912 P.2d 1148 (Cal. 1996), 77
Angela M.W., State ex rel. v. Kruzicki, 209 Wis.2d 112, 561 N.W.2d 729 (Wis.1997), 170
Anonymous, In re Adoption of, 74 Misc.2d 99, 345 N.Y.S.2d 430 (N.Y.Sur.1973), 113
Application of (see name of party)
Armstrong v. Mazurek, 906 F.Supp. 561 (D.Mont.1995), 77
A Woman's Choice—East Side Women's Clinic v. Brizzi, 537 U.S. 1192, 123 S.Ct. 1273, 154 L.Ed.2d 1026 (2003), 78
A Woman's Choice—East Side Women's Clinic v. Newman, 305 F.3d 684 (7th Cir.2002), 78
A Woman's Choice—East Side Women's Clinic v. Newman, 132 F.Supp.2d 1150 (S.D.Ind. 2001), 78
A.Z. v. B.Z., 431 Mass. 150, 725 N.E.2d 1051 (Mass.2000), 127

Baby Boy Blackshear, In re, 90 Ohio St.3d 197, 736 N.E.2d 462 (Ohio 2000), 168
Baby Boy Doe, In re, 260 Ill.App.3d 392, 198 Ill.Dec. 267, 632 N.E.2d 326 (Ill.App. 1 Dist. 1994), 166, 167

Baby Doe, In re, 291 S.C. 389, 353 S.E.2d 877 (S.C.1987), 113
Baby K, Matter of, 16 F.3d 590 (4th Cir. 1994), **228,** 232, 233
Baby M, Matter of, 109 N.J. 396, 537 A.2d 1227 (N.J.1988), **130,** 134, 135, 136, 143, 153
Bader v. Johnson, 732 N.E.2d 1212 (Ind.2000), 100
Bailey v. Lally, 481 F.Supp. 203 (D.Md.1979), 436
Barnes v. State of Mississippi, 992 F.2d 1335 (5th Cir.1993), 76
Barry, In re Guardianship of, 445 So.2d 365 (Fla.App. 2 Dist.1984), 268
Bartling v. Superior Court, 163 Cal.App.3d 186, 209 Cal.Rptr. 220 (Cal.App. 2 Dist. 1984), 257, 261
Beal v. Doe, 432 U.S. 438, 97 S.Ct. 2366, 53 L.Ed.2d 464 (1977), 55
Becker v. Schwartz, 413 N.Y.S.2d 895, 386 N.E.2d 807 (N.Y.1978), 100
Belcher v. Charleston Area Medical Center, 188 W.Va. 105, 422 S.E.2d 827 (W.Va.1992), 349
Belsito v. Clark, 67 Ohio Misc.2d 54, 644 N.E.2d 760 (Ohio Com.Pl.1994), 143
Berman v. Allan, 80 N.J. 421, 404 A.2d 8 (N.J.1979), 100
Blouin v. Spitzer, 356 F.3d 348 (2nd Cir.2004), 299, 335
Bouvia v. County of Los Angeles, 195 Cal. App.3d 1075, 241 Cal.Rptr. 239 (Cal.App. 2 Dist.1987), 335
Bouvia v. Superior Court, 179 Cal.App.3d 1127, 225 Cal.Rptr. 297 (Cal.App. 2 Dist. 1986), **257,** 261, 262, 263, 264, 268, 307
Bowen v. American Hosp. Ass'n, 476 U.S. 610, 106 S.Ct. 2101, 90 L.Ed.2d 584 (1986), 354
Bowers v. Hardwick, 478 U.S. 186, 106 S.Ct. 2841, 92 L.Ed.2d 140 (1986), 56
Britell v. United States, 204 F.Supp.2d 182 (D.Mass.2002), 227
Brooks' Estate, In re, 32 Ill.2d 361, 205 N.E.2d 435 (Ill.1965), 271
Brophy v. New England Sinai Hosp., Inc., 398 Mass. 417, 497 N.E.2d 626 (Mass.1986), 261, 266, 299, 306, 307

Brown, In re, 294 Ill.App.3d 159, 228 Ill.Dec. 525, 689 N.E.2d 397 (Ill.App. 1 Dist.1997), 44, 179

Browning, In re Guardianship of, 568 So.2d 4 (Fla.1990), 291

Bryan v. Rectors and Visitors of University of Virginia, 95 F.3d 349 (4th Cir.1996), 232

Buck v. Bell, 274 U.S. 200, 47 S.Ct. 584, 71 L.Ed. 1000 (1927), 87, 88, 114, 182

Busalacchi, Matter of, 1991 WL 26851 (Mo. App. E.D.1991), 255, 256

Bush v. Schiavo, 866 So.2d 136 (Fla.App. 2 Dist.2004), 332

Bush v. Schiavo, 861 So.2d 506 (Fla.App. 2 Dist.2003), 332

Buzzanca v. Buzzanca, 72 Cal.Rptr.2d 280 (Cal.App. 4 Dist.1998), 144, 152

Care and Protection of Beth, 412 Mass. 188, 587 N.E.2d 1377 (Mass.1992), 340, 348

Carey v. Population Services, Intern., 431 U.S. 678, 97 S.Ct. 2010, 52 L.Ed.2d 675 (1977), 50

Chandler v. Hektoen Institute for Medical Research, 2003 WL 22284199 (N.D.Ill.2003), 432

Chenault v. Huie, 989 S.W.2d 474 (Tex.App.-Dallas 1999), 168

Christopher I., In re, 131 Cal.Rptr.2d 122 (Cal. App. 4 Dist.2003), 348, 349, 351

City of (see name of city)

C. M. v. C. C., 152 N.J.Super. 160, 377 A.2d 821 (N.J.Juv. & Dom.Rel.1977), 113

C (Minor), In re, [1989] 2 All E.R. 782 (C.A.), 355

Commissioner of Correction v. Myers, 379 Mass. 255, 399 N.E.2d 452 (Mass.1979), 267

Commonwealth v. _____ (see opposing party)

Compassion in Dying v. State of Washington, 79 F.3d 790 (9th Cir.1996), 379

Compassion in Dying v. State of Washington, 850 F.Supp. 1454 (W.D.Wash.1994), 379

Conant v. Walters, 309 F.3d 629 (9th Cir.2002), 405, 406

Connor v. Monkem Co., Inc., 898 S.W.2d 89 (Mo.1995), 46

Conroy, Matter of, 98 N.J. 321, 486 A.2d 1209 (N.J.1985), 267, **300**, 302, 303, 304, 305, 306, 307, 310, 323, 333

Conservatorship of Drabick, 200 Cal.App.3d 185, 245 Cal.Rptr. 840 (Cal.App. 6 Dist. 1988), 300

Conservatorship of Valerie N., 219 Cal.Rptr. 387, 707 P.2d 760 (Cal.1985), 88

Conservatorship of Wanglie, No. PX–91–283 (Minn.Dist.Ct.1993), 308, 309, 310

Conservatorship of Wendland, 110 Cal. Rptr.2d 412, 28 P.3d 151 (Cal.2001), 256, 300, **311**, 323, 326, 333

Cook County, Ill. v. United States ex rel. Chandler, 538 U.S. 119, 123 S.Ct. 1239, 155 L.Ed.2d 247 (2003), 432

Corbett v. D'Alessandro, 487 So.2d 368 (Fla. App. 2 Dist.1986), 307

Coveleski v. Bubnis, 535 Pa. 166, 634 A.2d 608 (Pa.1993), 47

Crum, In re Guardianship of, 61 Ohio Misc.2d 596, 580 N.E.2d 876 (Ohio Prob.1991), 350

Cruzan v. Director, Missouri Dept. of Health, 497 U.S. 261, 110 S.Ct. 2841, 111 L.Ed.2d 224 (1990), 56, 240, **243**, 253, 254, 255, 256, 265, 266, 267, 282, 291, 293, 296, 299, 303, 304, 305, 307, 323, 325, 334

Cruzan v. Harmon, 760 S.W.2d 408 (Mo.1988), 297

Curran v. Bosze, 141 Ill.2d 473, 153 Ill.Dec. 213, 566 N.E.2d 1319 (Ill.1990), 471

Custody of A Minor, 385 Mass. 697, 434 N.E.2d 601 (Mass.1982), 348

Davis v. Davis, 842 S.W.2d 588 (Tenn.1992), **119**

Davis, People v., 30 Cal.Rptr.2d 50, 872 P.2d 591 (Cal.1994), 42

DeGrella v. Elston, 858 S.W.2d 698 (Ky.1993), 268, 300

Diamond v. Chakrabarty, 447 U.S. 303, 100 S.Ct. 2204, 65 L.Ed.2d 144 (1980), 204

Diaz v. Tampa General Hospital, 2000 WL 1682918 (M.D.Fla.2000), 432

DiDonato v. Wortman, 320 N.C. 423, 358 S.E.2d 489 (N.C.1987), 47

D.K., Matter of, 204 N.J.Super. 205, 497 A.2d 1298 (N.J.Super.Ch.1985), 44

Doe v. Doe, 244 Conn. 403, 710 A.2d 1297 (Conn.1998), 144

Doe, Guardianship of, 411 Mass. 512, 583 N.E.2d 1263 (Mass.1992), 340

E.G., In re, 133 Ill.2d 98, 139 Ill.Dec. 810, 549 N.E.2d 322 (Ill.1989), 349

Eichner, In re, 438 N.Y.S.2d 266, 420 N.E.2d 64 (N.Y.1981), **297**, 322, 323, 324, 336

Eisenstadt v. Baird, 405 U.S. 438, 92 S.Ct. 1029, 31 L.Ed.2d 349 (1972), 50, 136

Estate of (see name of party)

Etkind v. Suarez, 271 Ga. 352, 519 S.E.2d 210 (Ga.1999), 100

Eulo, People v., 482 N.Y.S.2d 436, 472 N.E.2d 286 (N.Y.1984), 215, 216, 217

Farley v. Sartin, 195 W.Va. 671, 466 S.E.2d 522 (W.Va.1995), 46

Farrell, Matter of, 108 N.J. 335, 529 A.2d 404 (N.J.1987), 303

Ferguson v. City of Charleston, 532 U.S. 67, 121 S.Ct. 1281, 149 L.Ed.2d 205 (2001), 170

Ferguson v. City of Charleston, S.C., 186 F.3d 469 (4th Cir.1999), 170

Ferguson v. District of Columbia, 629 A.2d 15 (D.C.1993), 47

Ferrer v. Trustees of University of Pennsylvania, 573 Pa. 310, 825 A.2d 591 (Pa.2002), 433

Fletcher, Matter of, 141 Misc.2d 333, 533 N.Y.S.2d 241 (N.Y.Fam.Ct.1988), 168

Ford, People v., 221 Ill.App.3d 354, 163 Ill.Dec. 766, 581 N.E.2d 1189 (Ill.App. 4 Dist.1991), 42

Fosmire v. Nicoleau, 551 N.Y.S.2d 876, 551 N.E.2d 77 (N.Y.1990), 271

Gauntlett, People v., 134 Mich.App. 737, 352 N.W.2d 310 (Mich.App.1984), 436

Gentry v. Gilmore, 613 So.2d 1241 (Ala.1993), 47

Gildiner v. Thomas Jefferson University Hospital, 451 F.Supp. 692 (E.D.Pa.1978), 101

Gleitman v. Cosgrove, 49 N.J. 22, 227 A.2d 689 (N.J.1967), 100

Gordy, Matter of, 658 A.2d 613 (Del.Ch.1994), 300

Gray v. Romeo, 697 F.Supp. 580 (D.R.I.1988), 307, 335

Gray, State v., 62 Ohio St.3d 514, 584 N.E.2d 710 (Ohio 1992), 170

Greco v. United States, 111 Nev. 405, 893 P.2d 345 (Nev.1995), 100

Greenberg v. Miami Children's Hospital Research Institute, Inc., 264 F.Supp.2d 1064 (S.D.Fla.2003), **199**, 204, 205, 413

Greenville Women's Clinic v. Bryant, 222 F.3d 157 (4th Cir.2000), 77, 79

Gregg, United States v., 226 F.3d 253 (3rd Cir.2000), 84

Grimes v. Kennedy Krieger Institute, Inc., 366 Md. 29, 782 A.2d 807 (Md.2001), 420, 421, **422**, 432, 433, 437, 444

Griswold v. Connecticut, 381 U.S. 479, 85 S.Ct. 1678, 14 L.Ed.2d 510 (1965), 49, 50, 51

Grodin v. Grodin, 102 Mich.App. 396, 301 N.W.2d 869 (Mich.App.1980), 168

Guardianship of (see name of party)

Gursky v. Gursky, 39 Misc.2d 1083, 242 N.Y.S.2d 406 (N.Y.Sup.1963), 113

Hall, People v., 134 Misc.2d 515, 511 N.Y.S.2d 532 (N.Y.Sup.1987), 217

Hamlin, Matter of Guardianship of, 102 Wash.2d 810, 689 P.2d 1372 (Wash.1984), 333, 334

Harbeson v. Parke–Davis, Inc., 98 Wash.2d 460, 656 P.2d 483 (Wash.1983), 100

Harris v. McRae, 448 U.S. 297, 100 S.Ct. 2671, 65 L.Ed.2d 784 (1980), 55, 254

Hartke v. McKelway, 707 F.2d 1544, 228 U.S.App.D.C. 139 (D.C.Cir.1983), 101

Hayes, Matter of Guardianship of, 93 Wash.2d 228, 608 P.2d 635 (Wash.1980), 89, 90

HCA, Inc. v. Miller, 36 S.W.3d 187 (Tex.App.-Hous. (14 Dist.) 2000), 363

Head v. Colloton, 331 N.W.2d 870 (Iowa 1983), 471

Hecht v. Superior Court, 20 Cal.Rptr.2d 275 (Cal.App. 2 Dist.1993), 126

Hickman v. Group Health Plan, Inc., 396 N.W.2d 10 (Minn.1986), 103

Hill v. Colorado, 530 U.S. 703, 120 S.Ct. 2480, 147 L.Ed.2d 597 (2000), 85

Hollis v. Doerflinger, 2003 WL 21266788 (Tenn.Ct.App.2003), 47

Iafelice v. Zarafu, 221 N.J.Super. 278, 534 A.2d 417 (N.J.Super.A.D.1987), 354

Illinois Dept. of Corrections, People ex rel. v. Millard, 335 Ill.App.3d 1066, 270 Ill.Dec. 407, 782 N.E.2d 966 (Ill.App. 4 Dist.2003), 267

In re (see name of party)

International Union, United Auto., Aerospace and Agr. Implement Workers of America, UAW v. Johnson Controls, Inc., 499 U.S. 187, 111 S.Ct. 1196, 113 L.Ed.2d 158 (1991), 172

Jacobsen v. Marin General Hosp., 192 F.3d 881 (9th Cir.1999), 470

Jacobson v. Commonwealth of Massachusetts, 197 U.S. 11, 25 S.Ct. 358, 49 L.Ed. 643 (1905), **476**

Jamaica Hosp., Application of, 128 Misc.2d 1006, 491 N.Y.S.2d 898 (N.Y.Sup.1985), 166

James G. v. Caserta, 175 W.Va. 406, 332 S.E.2d 872 (W.Va.1985), 100

Jane L. v. Bangerter, 61 F.3d 1493 (10th Cir. 1995), 77

J.B. v. M.B., 170 N.J. 9, 783 A.2d 707 (N.J. 2001), 127

J.D.S., In re Guardianship of, 864 So.2d 534 (Fla.App. 5 Dist.2004), 44, **173**

Jefferson v. Griffin Spalding County Hospital Authority, 247 Ga. 86, 274 S.E.2d 457 (Ga. 1981), 167, 168

J (Minor), In re, [1990] 3 All E.R. 930 (C.A.), 355

Jobes, Matter of, 108 N.J. 394, 529 A.2d 434 (N.J.1987), 261, 303, 304, 307, 323

Johnson v. Calvert, 19 Cal.Rptr.2d 494, 851 P.2d 776 (Cal.1993), **137,** 143, 153

Johnson v. Ruark Obstetrics and Gynecology Associates, P.A., 327 N.C. 283, 395 S.E.2d 85 (N.C.1990), 47

Johnson v. State, 602 So.2d 1288 (Fla.1992), 170

Johnson v. Verrilli, 134 Misc.2d 582, 511 N.Y.S.2d 1008 (N.Y.Sup.1987), 47

Kass v. Kass, 673 N.Y.S.2d 350, 696 N.E.2d 174 (N.Y.1998), 126

Katskee v. Blue Cross/Blue Shield of Nebraska, 245 Neb. 808, 515 N.W.2d 645 (Neb.1994), 184

Keeler v. Superior Court, 87 Cal.Rptr. 481, 470 P.2d 617 (Cal.1970), 41

Kevorkian, People v., 447 Mich. 436, 527 N.W.2d 714 (Mich.1994), 381

K.I., In re, 735 A.2d 448 (D.C.1999), 348, 350, 354

Kline, State v., 155 Or.App. 96, 963 P.2d 697 (Or.App.1998), 90

Krischer v. McIver, 697 So.2d 97 (Fla.1997), 387

Kruzicki, State ex rel. Angela M.W. v., 209 Wis.2d 112, 561 N.W.2d 729 (Wis.1997), 170

Kurr, People v., 253 Mich.App. 317, 654 N.W.2d 651 (Mich.App.2002), 43, 44

Lai, People v., 131 A.D.2d 592, 516 N.Y.S.2d 300 (N.Y.A.D. 2 Dept.1987), 217

Lambert v. Wicklund, 520 U.S. 292, 117 S.Ct. 1169, 137 L.Ed.2d 464 (1997), 76

Lane v. Candura, 6 Mass.App.Ct. 377, 376 N.E.2d 1232 (Mass.App.Ct.1978), 281

Lawrence v. Texas, 539 U.S. 558, 123 S.Ct. 2472, 156 L.Ed.2d 508 (2003), 56, 137

Lee v. State of Oregon, 107 F.3d 1382 (9th Cir.1997), 395

Lenz v. L.E. Phillips Career Dev. Center, 167 Wis.2d 53, 482 N.W.2d 60 (Wis.1992), 268

L.H.R., In re, 253 Ga. 439, 321 S.E.2d 716 (Ga.1984), 348

Lininger v. Eisenbaum, 764 P.2d 1202 (Colo. 1988), 101

Longeway, In re Estate of, 133 Ill.2d 33, 139 Ill.Dec. 780, 549 N.E.2d 292 (Ill.1989), 267, 299

Long Island Jewish Medical Center, Application of, 147 Misc.2d 724, 557 N.Y.S.2d 239 (N.Y.Sup.1990), 350

Luff v. Hawkins, 551 A.2d 437 (Del.Super.1988), 47

Mack v. Mack, 329 Md. 188, 618 A.2d 744 (Md.1993), 256, 300

Maher v. Roe, 432 U.S. 464, 97 S.Ct. 2376, 53 L.Ed.2d 484 (1977), 55

Maher v. Yoon, 297 A.D.2d 361, 746 N.Y.S.2d 493 (N.Y.A.D. 2 Dept.2002), 47

Marciniak v. Lundborg, 153 Wis.2d 59, 450 N.W.2d 243 (Wis.1990), 102

Marriage of (see name of party)

Martin, In re, 450 Mich. 204, 538 N.W.2d 399 (Mich.1995), 256, 299, 302, 303, 324, 325

Mathews v. Eldridge, 424 U.S. 319, 96 S.Ct. 893, 47 L.Ed.2d 18 (1976), 487

Matter of (see name of party)

Mayfield v. Dalton, 109 F.3d 1423 (9th Cir. 1997), 207

McCollum v. CBS, Inc., 202 Cal.App.3d 989, 249 Cal.Rptr. 187 (Cal.App. 2 Dist.1988), 382

McConnell v. Beverly Enterprises–Connecticut, 209 Conn. 692, 553 A.2d 596 (Conn.1989), 267, 291, 307, 323

McDonald v. McDonald, 196 A.D.2d 7, 608 N.Y.S.2d 477 (N.Y.A.D. 2 Dept.1994), 143

McIntyre v. Crouch, 98 Or.App. 462, 780 P.2d 239 (Or.App.1989), 113

McKnight, State v., 352 S.C. 635, 576 S.E.2d 168 (S.C.2003), 43, 170

Mercy Hosp., Inc. v. Jackson, 62 Md.App. 409, 489 A.2d 1130 (Md.App.1985), 271

Merrill, State v., 450 N.W.2d 318 (Minn.1990), 42

Millard, People ex rel. Illinois Dept. of Corrections v., 335 Ill.App.3d 1066, 270 Ill.Dec. 407, 782 N.E.2d 966 (Ill.App. 4 Dist.2003), 267

Miller v. HCA, Inc., 118 S.W.3d 758 (Tex. 2003), **355**

Milton v. Cary Medical Center, 538 A.2d 252 (Me.1988), 47

Miskimens, State v., 22 Ohio Misc.2d 43, 490 N.E.2d 931 (Ohio Com.Pl.1984), 351

Mitchell, People v., 132 Cal.App.3d 389, 183 Cal.Rptr. 166 (Cal.App. 4 Dist.1982), 215

Morabito, People v., 151 Misc.2d 259, 580 N.Y.S.2d 843 (N.Y.City Ct.1992), 170

Morrison, United States v., 529 U.S. 598, 120 S.Ct. 1740, 146 L.Ed.2d 658 (2000), 84

National Organization for Women, Inc. v. Scheidler, 510 U.S. 249, 114 S.Ct. 798, 127 L.Ed.2d 99 (1994), 84

Newman v. Sathyavaglswaran, 287 F.3d 786 (9th Cir.2002), **461,** 465, 466

Newmark v. Williams, 588 A.2d 1108 (Del. Supr.1991), **341,** 347, 349, 350

New York v. United States, 505 U.S. 144, 112 S.Ct. 2408, 120 L.Ed.2d 120 (1992), 406

Nixon, Commonwealth v., 563 Pa. 425, 761 A.2d 1151 (Pa.2000), 350

Noah M., In re, 212 Cal.App.3d 30, 260 Cal. Rptr. 309 (Cal.App. 4 Dist.1989), 168

Norwood Hosp. v. Munoz, 409 Mass. 116, 564 N.E.2d 1017 (Mass.1991), 271

Oakland Cannabis Buyers' Co-op., United States v., 532 U.S. 483, 121 S.Ct. 1711, 149 L.Ed.2d 722 (2001), **398,** 405, 406, 407

Oakley, State v., 245 Wis.2d 447, 629 N.W.2d 200 (Wis.2001), 90

O'Grady v. Brown, 654 S.W.2d 904 (Mo.1983), 47

Ohio v. Akron Center for Reproductive Health, 497 U.S. 502, 110 S.Ct. 2972, 111 L.Ed.2d 405 (1990), 76

Oregon v. Ashcroft, 368 F.3d 1118 (9th Cir. 2004), 397

Oregon v. Ashcroft, 192 F.Supp.2d 1077 (D.Or. 2002), 397

Osborne, In re, 294 A.2d 372 (D.C.1972), 271

O'Toole v. Greenberg, 488 N.Y.S.2d 143, 477 N.E.2d 445 (N.Y.1985), 101

Parham v. J. R., 442 U.S. 584, 99 S.Ct. 2493, 61 L.Ed.2d 101 (1979), 347, 358

Pate v. Threlkel, 661 So.2d 278 (Fla.1995), 191, 194

Pemberton v. Tallahassee Memorial Regional Medical Center, Inc., 66 F.Supp.2d 1247 (N.D.Fla.1999), 167

People v. _____ (see opposing party)

People ex rel. v. _____ (see opposing party and relator)

Perry v. Saint Francis Hosp. and Medical Center, Inc., 886 F.Supp. 1551 (D.Kan.1995), 470

Pescinski, In re Guardianship of, 67 Wis.2d 4, 226 N.W.2d 180 (Wis.1975), 471

Peter, Matter of, 108 N.J. 365, 529 A.2d 419 (N.J.1987), 292, 303, 304, 307

Planned Parenthood of Cent. New Jersey v. Farmer, 165 N.J. 609, 762 A.2d 620 (N.J. 2000), 76

Planned Parenthood of Middle Tennessee v. Sundquist, 38 S.W.3d 1 (Tenn.2000), 77, 78

Planned Parenthood of Southeastern Pennsylvania v. Casey, 505 U.S. 833, 112 S.Ct. 2791, 120 L.Ed.2d 674 (1992), 23, 51, 55, **57,** 74, 78, 100, 126

Planned Parenthood of Southern Arizona, Inc. v. Woods, 982 F.Supp. 1369 (D.Ariz.1997), 77

Poelker v. Doe, 432 U.S. 519, 97 S.Ct. 2391, 53 L.Ed.2d 528 (1977), 55

Porter v. Lassiter, 91 Ga.App. 712, 87 S.E.2d 100 (Ga.App.1955), 46

Prato–Morrison v. Doe, 126 Cal.Rptr.2d 509 (Cal.App. 2 Dist.2002), 128, **145,** 153

President and Directors of Georgetown College, Inc., Application of, 331 F.2d 1000, 118 U.S.App.D.C. 80 (D.C.Cir.1964), **269,** 271, 273

Printz v. United States, 521 U.S. 898, 117 S.Ct. 2365, 138 L.Ed.2d 914 (1997), 406

Procanik v. Cillo, 97 N.J. 339, 478 A.2d 755 (N.J.1984), 100

Protection and Advocacy System, Inc. v. Presbyterian Healthcare Services, 128 N.M. 73, 989 P.2d 890 (N.M.App.1999), 295, 334, 340

Public Health Trust of Dade County v. Wons, 541 So.2d 96 (Fla.1989), **271**, 272, 273

Quackenbush, Matter of, 156 N.J.Super. 282, 383 A.2d 785 (N.J.Co.Prob.Div.1978), 280, 281

Quill v. Vacco, 80 F.3d 716 (2nd Cir.1996), 379

Quinlan, Matter of, 70 N.J. 10, 355 A.2d 647 (N.J.1976), 23, 267, 290, 304

R v. Senior, All E.R. 511 (1895–9), 271

Rademacher v. McDonnell Douglas Corp., 737 F.Supp. 427 (E.D.Mich.1989), 45, 46

Rahman v. Mayo Clinic, 578 N.W.2d 802 (Minn.App.1998), 470

Raich v. Ashcroft, 352 F.3d 1222 (9th Cir. 2003), 406

Raleigh Fitkin–Paul Morgan Memorial Hospital v. Anderson, 42 N.J. 421, 201 A.2d 537 (N.J.1964), 166, 271

Ramirez v. Health Partners of Southern Arizona, 193 Ariz. 325, 972 P.2d 658 (Ariz.App. Div. 2 1998), 470

Rasmussen v. Fleming, 154 Ariz. 207, 741 P.2d 674 (Ariz.1987), 268

Reinesto v. Superior Court of State In and For County of Navajo, 182 Ariz. 190, 894 P.2d 733 (Ariz.App. Div. 1 1995), 170

Remy v. MacDonald, 440 Mass. 675, 801 N.E.2d 260 (Mass.2004), 47

Renslow v. Mennonite Hospital, 67 Ill.2d 348, 10 Ill.Dec. 484, 367 N.E.2d 1250 (Ill.1977), 101

R.H., Matter of, 35 Mass.App.Ct. 478, 622 N.E.2d 1071 (Mass.App.Ct.1993), 340

Rhea v. Board of Education of Devils Lake Special School Dist., 41 N.D. 449, 171 N.W. 103 (N.D.1919), 482

Robak v. United States, 658 F.2d 471 (7th Cir.1981), 100

Roberts, People v., 211 Mich. 187, 178 N.W. 690 (Mich.1920), 380, 381

Roe v. Wade, 410 U.S. 113, 93 S.Ct. 705, 35 L.Ed.2d 147 (1973), 23, 39, 40, 41, 43, 50, 51, **51,** 54, 55, 56, 57, 59, 74, 100, 103, 179

Rutherford, United States v., 442 U.S. 544, 99 S.Ct. 2470, 61 L.Ed.2d 68 (1979), 56

Safer v. Estate of Pack, 291 N.J.Super. 619, 677 A.2d 1188 (N.J.Super.A.D.1996), **189,** 193, 194

Salerno, United States v., 481 U.S. 739, 107 S.Ct. 2095, 95 L.Ed.2d 697 (1987), 79

Sattler v. Northwest Tissue Center, 110 Wash. App. 689, 42 P.3d 440 (Wash.App. Div. 1 2002), 470

Satz v. Perlmutter, 379 So.2d 359 (Fla.1980), 334

Scheidler v. National Organization for Women, Inc., 537 U.S. 393, 123 S.Ct. 1057, 154 L.Ed.2d 991 (2003), 85

Schembre v. Mid–America Transplant Ass'n, 2003 WL 21692986 (Mo.App. E.D.2003), 470

Schenck v. Pro–Choice Network Of Western New York, 519 U.S. 357, 117 S.Ct. 855, 137 L.Ed.2d 1 (1997), 85

Schiavo, In re Guardianship of, 851 So.2d 182 (Fla.App. 2 Dist.2003), 330

Schiavo, In re Guardianship of, 780 So.2d 176 (Fla.App. 2 Dist.2001), **327,** 330, 333

S.H. v. D.H., 796 N.E.2d 1243 (Ind.App.2003), 76

Siemieniec v. Lutheran Gen. Hosp., 117 Ill.2d 230, 111 Ill.Dec. 302, 512 N.E.2d 691 (Ill. 1987), 100

Simat Corp. v. Arizona Health Care Cost Containment System, 203 Ariz. 454, 56 P.3d 28 (Ariz.2002), 55

66 Federal Credit Union v. Tucker, 853 So.2d 104 (Miss.2003), 46

Skinner v. State of Oklahoma, 316 U.S. 535, 62 S.Ct. 1110, 86 L.Ed. 1655 (1942), 88, 114

Smith v. Borello, 370 Md. 227, 804 A.2d 1151 (Md.2002), 47

Smith v. Columbus Community Hosp., Inc., 222 Neb. 776, 387 N.W.2d 490 (Neb.1986), 47

Smith v. Cote, 128 N.H. 231, 513 A.2d 341 (N.H.1986), **91,** 100, 101, 103

Smith v. Mercy Hosp. and Medical Center, 203 Ill.App.3d 465, 148 Ill.Dec. 567, 560 N.E.2d 1164 (Ill.App. 1 Dist.1990), 46

Smith, Matter of, 128 Misc.2d 976, 492 N.Y.S.2d 331 (N.Y.Fam.Ct.1985), 172

Sojourner T. v. Edwards, 974 F.2d 27 (5th Cir.1992), 75

Sorensen, People v., 68 Cal.2d 280, 66 Cal. Rptr. 7, 437 P.2d 495 (Cal.1968), 113

Spring, Matter of, 380 Mass. 629, 405 N.E.2d 115 (Mass.1980), 333

State v. _____ (see opposing party)

State ex rel. v. _____ (see opposing party and relator)

Stenberg v. Carhart, 530 U.S. 914, 120 S.Ct. 2597, 147 L.Ed.2d 743 (2000), 23, 51, 55, **68,** 74, 85

Storar, Matter of, 438 N.Y.S.2d 266, 420 N.E.2d 64 (N.Y.1981), 267, 336, **338,** 340

Strachan v. John F. Kennedy Memorial Hosp., 109 N.J. 523, 538 A.2d 346 (N.J.1988), 217

Strnad v. Strnad, 190 Misc. 786, 78 N.Y.S.2d 390 (N.Y.Sup.1948), 113

Strunk v. Strunk, 445 S.W.2d 145 (Ky.1969), 471

Summerfield v. Superior Court In and For Maricopa County, 144 Ariz. 467, 698 P.2d 712 (Ariz.1985), 47

Superintendent of Belchertown State School v. Saikewicz, 373 Mass. 728, 370 N.E.2d 417 (Mass.1977), 264, 265, **336,** 340

Surrogate Parenting Associates, Inc. v. Commonwealth ex rel. Armstrong, 704 S.W.2d 209 (Ky.1986), 129

Szekeres v. Robinson, 102 Nev. 93, 715 P.2d 1076 (Nev.1986), 101

T.A.C.P., In re, 609 So.2d 588 (Fla.1992), **219,** 226, 227, 228

Talty, State v., 2003 WL 21396835 (Ohio App. 9 Dist.2003), 90

Tavel, Matter of, 661 A.2d 1061 (Del. Supr.1995), 267

Taylor v. Kurapati, 236 Mich.App. 315, 600 N.W.2d 670 (Mich.App.1999), 100

T.D. v. New York State Office of Mental Health, 668 N.Y.S.2d 153, 690 N.E.2d 1259 (N.Y.1997), 436

Terrell v. Rankin, 511 So.2d 126 (Miss.1987), 47

Thornburgh v. American College of Obstetricians and Gynecologists, 476 U.S. 747, 106 S.Ct. 2169, 90 L.Ed.2d 779 (1986), 55

Turpin v. Sortini, 182 Cal.Rptr. 337, 643 P.2d 954 (Cal.1982), 100

United States v. _____ (see opposing party)

Vacco v. Quill, 521 U.S. 793, 117 S.Ct. 2293, 138 L.Ed.2d 834 (1997), 369, 370, 375, **376**

Walker v. Superior Court (People), 194 Cal. App.3d 1090, 222 Cal.Rptr. 87 (Cal.App. 3 Dist.1986), 351

Warren, Matter of, 858 S.W.2d 263 (Mo.App. W.D.1993), 308

Washington v. Glucksberg, 521 U.S. 702, 117 S.Ct. 2258, 138 L.Ed.2d 772 (1997), 240, 253, 254, 266, **365,** 369, 370, 375

Webster v. Reproductive Health Services, 492 U.S. 490, 109 S.Ct. 3040, 106 L.Ed.2d 410 (1989), 40, 55, 85

Welch, Commonwealth v., 864 S.W.2d 280 (Ky. 1993), 170

Welfare of Colyer, Matter of, 99 Wash.2d 114, 660 P.2d 738 (Wash.1983), 323

Westchester County Medical Center on Behalf of O'Connor, Matter of, 534 N.Y.S.2d 886, 531 N.E.2d 607 (N.Y.1988), 256, 292, 299, 321, 323

Wickard v. Filburn, 317 U.S. 111, 63 S.Ct. 82, 87 L.Ed. 122 (1942), 406

Wiersma v. Maple Leaf Farms, 543 N.W.2d 787 (S.D.1996), 46

Witbeck–Wildhagen, In re Marriage of, 281 Ill. App.3d 502, 217 Ill.Dec. 329, 667 N.E.2d 122 (Ill.App. 4 Dist.1996), 113

Witty v. American General Capital Distributors, Inc., 727 S.W.2d 503 (Tex.1987), 47

Women's Medical Professional Corp. v. Taft, 353 F.3d 436 (6th Cir.2003), 75

Women's Medical Professional Corp. v. Voinovich, 911 F.Supp. 1051 (S.D.Ohio 1995), 75

Wong Wai v. Williamson, 103 F. 1 (C.C.N.D.Cal.1900), 481

York v. Jones, 717 F.Supp. 421 (E.D.Va.1989), 126

Zehr v. Haugen, 318 Or. 647, 871 P.2d 1006 (Or.1994), 101

BIOETHICS:

HEALTH CARE LAW AND ETHICS

Fifth Edition

*

Chapter 1

AN INTRODUCTION TO THE STUDY OF ETHICS AND ETHICAL THEORIES

JOAN GIBSON, THINKING ABOUT THE "ETHICS" IN BIOETHICS[1]

At 4:30 on a Friday afternoon, you, as legal counsel for a 300–bed for-profit hospital, receive a telephone call from a physician, Dr. Smith, asking your advice. For some time she has been caring for a 37–year–old man, Mr. Jones, who is in the late stages of lung cancer which has metastasized to his bones. Dr. Smith predicts that Mr. Jones may live for another month or so if treatment is continued.

Treatment consists of chemotherapy (administration of drugs which slow the growth and spread of the cancer), and pain medication (injection of morphine which reduces, although does not eliminate, the pain Mr. Jones experiences). Mr. Jones also has a pacemaker to regulate his heart beat. Dr. Smith has just admitted Mr. Jones to the hospital, and Mr. Jones makes a request that he has made repeatedly in the past. Specifically, Mr. Jones requests that all chemotherapy be stopped and that the pacemaker be deprogramed immediately, so that his heart will malfunction and cause his death in a very short time. Dr. Smith has talked at length with Mr. Jones about his request and she is convinced that the patient is clear, determined and consistent in his wishes. You mention to Dr. Smith that a meeting with the hospital ethics committee might be of help, and she asks, "Why a committee just for **ethics**?"

Indeed, just what is meant by "ethics," especially as applied to health care decision making? There are a few ways to approach an answer to this question: first, we should define and distinguish certain terms that are used regularly in discussion; second, we should consider some of the processes used

1. This introduction was prepared by Dr. Joan Gibson, Director of the Health Sciences Ethics Program at the University of New Mexico. A portion of this Introduction first appeared in Virginia Trotter Betts, Margie Nicks Gale and Joan McIver Gibson, Ethical and Legal Issues, in D. Critchley and J. Mavrin, eds., *The Clinical Specialist in Psychiatric Mental Health Nursing: Theory, Research, and Practice* 453, 454 (1985).

in applied ethics and health care decision making; and finally, we should recognize some strengths and limitations of this enterprise generally.

DEFINITIONS

While the terms values, morals, and ethics are sometimes used interchangeably, in this introduction they will be defined and used as follows: *value* is, in the broad sense, the worth, goodness, or desirability of something, whether moral or non-moral, such as tidiness, efficiency, honesty, and compassion. *Morals,* or morality, refer to those traditions of belief about what is right or wrong in human conduct that develop, are transmitted, and are learned independently of rational, ethical inquiry. *Ethics* denotes that branch of philosophy or reasoned inquiry that studies both the nature of and the justification for general ethical principles governing right conduct.

Morality expresses society's basic instructions about what people may and may not do. Ethical theory, on the other hand, describes and justifies such traditions and is often divided into two quite separate areas: scientific and philosophical. The *scientific* branch of ethics gathers and reports accurate empirical information about existing moral beliefs, without evaluating the worth of moral judgments in any way. *Philosophical* ethics moves beyond and either evaluates important moral concepts (for example, freedom, justice, the good) and moral reasoning from a logical, as opposed to a psychological, perspective, or establishes theoretical justifications for what is right and wrong in human actions. These two subcategories of philosophical ethics are known, respectively, as metaethics and normative ethics.

Special mention ought to be made of one component of formalized moral tradition that is not necessarily the product of rational, ethical inquiry but which is, nevertheless, an important repository of and force for the moral beliefs of certain groups: codes of ethics. They constitute a kind of oath that affirms the highest ideals and standards of the profession and that exhorts individuals always to strive for these standards. They also provide rules for expected behavior and conduct, and they suggest, usually in general terms, certain ethical principles that professionals ought to consider when determining conduct. Professional codes are taken seriously and form an important expression of a profession's collective identity and mission at any given time. They are limited, however, in their effectiveness as rational tools for analyzing and resolving ethical issues and dilemmas; there is still a need for the more systematic, comprehensive, and internally consistent disciplines of scientific and philosophical ethics.

ETHICS AND PROCESS

A somewhat different definition of ethics focuses on one aspect of philosophical ethics: establishing theoretical justifications for what is right and wrong in human actions. Why ought/ought not Dr. Smith accede to Mr. Jones's wishes? Should deprogramming the pacemaker be evaluated in the same manner as stopping the chemotherapy? Indeed, it is asking "Why?" of specific moral value judgments, proffering good reasons in response to that question, and proceeding to ever more abstract reasons that characterize critical thinking generally.

For example, a comparison between the giving of good reasons in science, which is called "explanation," and the giving of good reasons in ethics, which is called "moral justification," reveals striking procedural similarities bordering on identity. Consider the following diagram:[2]

Science (As EXPLANATION)				Ethics (As MORAL JUSTIFICATION)	
↑ EXPLANATION From bottom to top	Theory Law Hypothesis Observation	↓ PREDICTION From top to bottom	↑ MORAL JUSTIFICATION	Theory Principle Rule Moral Value Judgment	↓ DECISIONS

WHY?

... did the pencil fall when dropped?

Because of the hypothesis that all objects fall when dropped. Why?

Because of the law of gravity, i.e., because objects with mass attract each other. Why?

Because of the theory of Newtonian Mechanics or General Relativity (which I will not try to describe here)

... should Mr. Jones's pacemaker *not* be deprogramed?

Because of the rule that you should never do an act that will kill another person. Why?

Because of the principle of nonmaleficence, i.e., you should never do something that will cause another harm. Why?

Because of the theory of (take your pick) Christianity, Judaism, Islam, Hinduism, Aristotelian virtue, Secular Humanism, Utilitarianism (and others which I will not try to describe here)

Of course, the right-hand column could have read:

... should Mr. Jones's pacemaker be deprogramed?

Because of the rule that you should always do what a patient wishes. Why?

Because of the principle of autonomy, i.e., every person ought to control his own body and mind. Why?

Because of the theory of (take your pick) . . . .

Answering the question "Why?" moving up the column under "Science" is known as explanation: the accounting for observed phenomena at levels of increased abstraction, generalization, and simplification. Moving down the

2. Adapted and expanded from T. Beauchamp and L. Walters, *Contemporary Issues in Bioethics* (5th ed. 2001).

column, once the "Why?"'s are answered, generates the power of prediction about future similar observations and phenomena.

And so it is with giving good reasons for individual moral value judgments, like whether Dr. Smith ought to accede to Mr. Jones's wishes. Answering the question "Why?" moving up the column under "Ethics" is known as moral justification. Moving down the column, once the "Why?"'s are answered, yields decisions about similar, future moral value judgments that must be made. Answering "Why?" (and thus moving up the column in either discipline) requires that reasons be elucidated and organized. Truth in science as well as in ethics derives not so much from discovering isolated, once-and-for-all answers, but rather from continually articulating, evaluating and revising the reasons one gives for the continually modified propositions one asserts and the consistently reevaluated judgments one makes. Extrapolating into the future (predicting and making decisions) is only as sound as the integrity of prior explanations and moral justifications. Does this sound a great deal like the process of the development of the common law? Is it any surprise that the courts have been at the forefront of our society's debates on bioethics?

How does all of this apply to the case of Mr. Jones and Dr. Smith? As we saw, Dr. Smith, when considering whether to stop chemotherapy, might say, "As a rule I believe that patient wishes ought to prevail." The first level of abstraction above specific moral value judgments is the level of rule-making, a level of generalization with which most people who justify moral decisions are familiar. It is the "Why?" asked of rules themselves and the move up to principles, however, that has engaged the energies of bioethicists over the past several decades. Why should Dr. Smith normally respect patients' wishes? Is there a harm that would arise if she were to deprogram Mr. Jones's pacemaker? Why should Dr. Smith normally avoid harm? What is her professional responsibility as a physician?

Biomedical ethics has assumed a kind of "principlist" orientation over the past 30 years, in which ethical principles, "at best ... operate primarily as checklists naming issues worth remembering when considering a biomedical moral issue."[3] Such a checklist of principles includes at least the following:

1. **Autonomy.** The principle that independent actions and choices of the individual should not be constrained by others.

2. **Non–Maleficence (Do No Harm)**. The principle that one has a duty not to inflict evil, harm, or risk of harm on others.

3. **Beneficence**. The principle that one has a duty to help others by doing what is best for them. Obviously, this principle is related to that of non-maleficence.

4. **Confidentiality**. The principle that when information is divulged by one person to another with the implicit promise that it will not be revealed to any other person that implicit promise should be respected.

5. **Distributive Justice**. The principle that benefits and burdens ought to be distributed equitably, that resources (especially scarce resources) ought to be allocated fairly, and that one ought to act in such a

3. K. Clouser and B. Gert, A Critique of Principlism, 15 J. Med. & Phil. 200 (1990).

manner that no one person or group bears a disproportionate share of benefits or burdens.

6. **Truth Telling (Honesty, Integrity)**. The principle that one ought to disclose all pertinent information about a person to that person.

There is also one "meta-principle" which is often invoked by those engaged in bioethics discussion, the principle of **Professional Responsibility**. This principle provides that the physician, as professional, has an obligation to observe the rules, principles and moral precepts governing relations with patients, colleagues, the profession as a whole, and the community at large.

CONCLUSION: STRENGTHS AND WEAKNESSES

Most people understand and accept the need for clear and systematic analysis of moral value judgments and decisions. Perhaps, though, our rigorous (and, some would say, narrow) principle-oriented bioethics needs major overhauling—an issue of special interest to those in the legal profession because the law still adheres to the principle-oriented approach with such tenacity. While clarity of thought, separation and identification of moral concepts and issues, and the development of a common language of ethics applied to health care decision making are some of the benefits that have accrued through this form of rigorous bioethics approach, challenges to this now "traditional" method of analysis are increasingly frequent. For an account of these challenges, see the Note on New Theories of Bioethics Analysis and the Attack on "Principlism" following the article on "Ethical Theory in the Medical Context," below.

Dr. Smith is fortunate enough to practice in a hospital whose ethics committee and legal counsel have taken the time to educate yourselves about ethics as a discipline (as well as about the law, about communication and interpersonal relations, about economics, about health policy in general, and about the role that various faiths play in health care decision making). While the discipline of ethics itself may not provide answers, solve knotty problems, or contribute to moral behavior, certainly practice that is tempered with such reflection, that is grounded in character and virtue, and that takes moral issues seriously, can make a moral difference.

But what is the ethical or moral source of the principles that seem to be universally invoked to resolve bioethics inquiries? Where do autonomy, beneficence, distributive justice, and other principles come from? Is there some basic theory of ethics that forms the basis of all bioethics discussions? Hardly. While these principles can be derived from a number of different fundamental ethical theories, the ones most of us depend upon most frequently—whether we know it or not—are utilitarianism, Kantian theory and natural law theory. It is worth spending a few moments reflecting upon those basic theories of ethics.

JOHN ARRAS AND ROBERT HUNT, ETHICAL THEORY IN THE MEDICAL CONTEXT[4]

J. Arras and N. Rhoden, *Ethical Issues in Modern Medicine*, (3d ed.) 6–28 (1989).

THE NEED FOR ETHICAL THEORY

* * * It is our contention that there is little hope of resolving ethical problems and little value in describing ethical dilemmas unless we are willing to engage in a serious inquiry into ethical theory. That is why much of the following discussion addresses itself to the conceptual foundations of predominant ethical alternatives. But before we turn to an examination of ethical theories, let us give brief consideration to two views about ethics that have acquired wide currency in recent times.

ETHICS AND CULTURE

Many see all ethical questions as relative to the attitudes and customs of the particular society in which they arise; that is, they believe that the rightness or wrongness of an action or practice cannot be determined apart from the cultural or societal context in which the action occurs. Moreover, according to this view, the moral quality of an action in a particular society is determined by consulting the attitudes held by the members of that society. We cannot, for example, simply ask whether infanticide of defective newborns is morally wrong; rather, we must ask the question in relation to a specific cultural context. We may then discover that infanticide, while quite wrong in the eyes of certain societies, is not only permissible, but even obligatory in others. To say that an action is wrong in a particular society is to say that it is disapproved of in that society; to say that it is right is to say that it meets with approval in that society.

Judgments of what is "right" or "wrong" on such a relativistic basis may be quite appropriate in discussing table manners and the like, but they are less appropriate, it would seem, in resolving moral issues. For one thing, this approach contains the puzzling implication that there could be *no sense* to the arguments of a moral reformer within a given society. Consider, for example, a society where slavery was an accepted institution. It would be silly for a reformer on this issue to argue (or even think) that slavery was wrong, if "wrong" meant "disapproved of by most people in that society." Does it not seem plausible to argue that something may be morally wrong in spite of the fact that one's society approves of it? * * * Moreover, relativism, if taken seriously, has the odd implication that all moral reflection and deliberation are in fact quite irrelevant. Take the all-too-frequent medical dilemma concerning whether it would be wrong to terminate the life of a patient who is slowly and painfully dying. Ethical relativism would not have us search for a solution based upon considerations of mercy nor would it ask us what we would do if we were in the patient's place. Rather, it would seem that ethical relativism would have us consult a sociologist, for our dilemma could only be resolved by discovering the prevailing societal attitudes. In turn, this points to another difficulty with ethical relativism—namely, that often there is no

---

4. For the most recent and unedited version of these materials, see Bonnie Steinbock, John Arras and Alex John London, Ethical Issues in Modern Medicine (6th edition 2003), which is an extraordinarily valuable bioethics textbook.

prevailing attitude regarding one course of action rather than another. The morally difficult cases—of the kinds that are occurring with more and more frequency in modern medicine—are those very cases on which society is likely to split. But we don't take this split as an indication that *there is no right or wrong* in these matters; rather, we take it as an indication that, for the moment at least, *we don't know* what is right and what is wrong in these cases.

Ethics and Feelings

Another viewpoint on ethics that one is liable to encounter nowadays maintains that morality is a matter of individual feelings and that, therefore, reasoning is inappropriate to the resolution of moral problems. It is difficult to state this view precisely, but it seems to hold that a right action is one with which a person feels comfortable or one that the person feels must be done and that an action is not wrong if one doesn't feel bad about it. Since people tend to have different feelings, this view further holds that right and wrong are relative to the particular individual. On this basis, it might be said that the performance of an abortion in the third trimester could be right for some women and wrong for others, depending on how the particular woman felt about it.

This view effectively assimilates moral judgments to judgments of taste; saying that a certain act may be "right for me but wrong for you" renders moral judgments analogous to comments such as "Lemon custard may taste good to me but bad to you." Hence, moral judgments that appeal to individual feelings would appear to be not so much judgments about some feature of an action or practice but, rather, reports of an agent's reactions or attitudes toward that action or practice. If this view is correct, ethical disagreements would seem pointless. What would be the point of arguing about ethical issues? Even more cogently, *what* would such an argument be? An attempt to convince a person that he was mistaken about his feelings—that is, that he didn't really have the feelings he thought he had? * * *

We do not deny a relationship between feelings and ethical decisions, for moral issues often, if not always, provoke deep emotional responses. But to assign feelings ultimate authority in these matters is, we think, to put the cart before the horse. Our feelings may provoke us to moral inquiry, but the inquiry does not terminate there.

We hope that the foregoing, of necessity brief, arguments, will suffice to indicate the inadequacy of attempts to resolve ethical issues by appeals either to prevailing attitudes or to individual feelings. It is our contention that, if answers to ethical issues are to be found, they are to be found through the development of a cogent and comprehensive ethical theory—a theory that will both explain the principles of morality and give us a guide to their application.

In the pages that follow, we shall examine two major ethical theories that have currency on the contemporary scene: *utilitarianism* and *Kantianism*. The former locates rightness and wrongness in the *consequences* of our behavior; the latter holds that the *principles* governing our behavior are of utmost importance. Finally, we shall turn our attention, albeit briefly, to the relationship between religion and ethics and particularly to the religious-philosophical viewpoint known as natural law ethics.

UTILITARIANISM

Jeremy Bentham (1748–1832) and John Stuart Mill (1806–1873) are generally credited with developing the first detailed and systematic formulation of the ethical theory known as utilitarianism. The heart of utilitarianism is "the greatest happiness principle," which, as Mill puts it, "holds that actions are right in proportion as they tend to promote happiness; wrong as they tend to produce the reverse of happiness." [ ] The *utility* of an action is determined by its tendency to promote or produce happiness; the *right* action among alternative actions in a situation is that which has the greatest utility (promotes the greatest happiness). Thus, for utilitarianism, the *good* is happiness and the *right* is that which promotes the good. Conversely, the wrongness of an action is determined by its "disutility," that is, its tendency to bring about unhappiness. Clearly, many actions will create both conditions—happiness for some parties and unhappiness for others. In such a case, the utilitarian ethic directs us to elect among available alternatives the one that results in the greatest net amount of happiness.

* * *

The two major forms of utilitarianism—*act-utilitarianism* and *rule-utilitarianism*—both provide criteria for assessing the moral quality of acts, albeit in different ways. Act-utilitarianism enjoins us to examine the effects of specific, individual acts on a case-by-case basis; rule-utilitarianism asks us to assess the effects of classes, or kinds, of actions. The difference between the two views can be illustrated by considering the situation of a ten-year-old boy with leukemia, who will probably die within the next six months. Question: Would or would it not be right to deceive him concerning the nature of his condition and prognosis? An act-utilitarian would seek to determine which alternative *in this particular case* would maximize happiness and/or minimize suffering. For certain children, and their families, the alternative with greater utility, and therefore the right thing to do, would be to tell the truth; for others, merciful deception would offer the greater utility and, therefore, be right. A rule-utilitarian, instead, would approach this situation by asking, "Which policy, *as a general rule,* would maximize happiness and/or minimize suffering?" If he concluded that the overall effects of following the rule "In cases such as this, tell the truth" would offer the greater utility, then the rule-utilitarian would say that truth telling is "right," irrespective of the specific situation. Conversely, if following the rule "In cases such as this, do *not* tell the truth" is deemed more beneficial, then deception would be seen as being "right." Again, both forms of utilitarianism employ the greatest happiness principle; but one applies it to particular actions, the other to classes of actions. [ ]

When we speak of utilitarianism later, we shall be speaking of act-utilitarianism unless we specify otherwise. We do this not only because this kind of utilitarianism seems to us to be the more frequently encountered of the two but also because it presents the clearest alternative to Kantian ethics, which is discussed later in this Introduction. Moreover, many of the features of, as well as objections to, act-utilitarianism are common to both forms.

FEATURES OF UTILITARIANISM

As we indicated earlier, the ethical outlook of utilitarianism is based on the *consequences* of actions. For this reason, it is called a *teleological* theory (from the Greek word *telos,* which means "end"). This view holds that the relevant question in assessing the moral quality of an action (or of a set of alternative actions) is "What will be the results?" Utilitarianism's focus on actions and their results allow us to make the familiar distinction between a person's character and the rightness or wrongness of his or her acts in a given situation. For example, as a result of sincerely held religious beliefs, a doctor might refuse a request for abortion made by a woman who had contracted rubella during pregnancy. Now, many people might think that the doctor's decision was a wrong one—that refusing to perform an abortion was the wrong thing to do—even though they would be disinclined to impugn the doctor's character. The utilitarian approach allows us to make the distinction between a person's acts and his or her character and to acknowledge what seems to be a familiar fact of moral experience—that even sincere and well-intentioned persons may sometimes do the wrong thing. (This example is not meant to prejudge the moral issues of abortion; it simply illustrates a certain distinction that is commonly made in moral discussions.)

* * *

Since most, if not all, actions have both "short-term" and "long-term" consequences, it is important to note that utilitarianism—which is so focused on consequences—seeks to gauge the utility of an action in accordance with its overall effects, both in terms of all the parties affected and with regard to its consequences over time. Thus, even though utilitarianism is concerned with alleviating suffering, it does not follow that a utilitarian would always seek any available means to reduce physical pain—for example, in a case in which administering a potent pain-killing drug would alleviate immediate suffering at the cost of creating even greater, long-term suffering as a result of addiction. (Naturally, when addiction is not an issue—say, in the last stages of a terminal illness—utilitarianism would call for any measures that would most effectively alleviate suffering.) Utilitarianism, therefore, espouses a prudent moral doctrine, one that requires us to think carefully about what we shall do and to consider not only the immediate effects of our actions but also their long-term consequences.

* * *

OBJECTIONS TO UTILITARIANISM

Even if one were moved to adopt the utilitarian position * * *, one could not ignore a number of difficulties concerning this theory. These difficulties can be generally formulated as two distinct objections: (1) utilitarianism is unworkable, and (2) utilitarianism is inadequate.

Utilitarianism Is Unworkable. The first of these objections may be pressed on a variety of fronts, three of which are discussed here.

a. The concept of happiness, it may be argued, is so unclear as to be unusable. Can we really agree on a definition of happiness? Probably not; and if we can't, how can utilitarianism deliver on its promise to provide us with an objective basis for discovering what is right, when its central concept remains undefined?

In response, the utilitarian may agree that we cannot supply an adequate (verbal) definition for the term "happiness," but, he or she might say, it doesn't follow that we don't understand that word. Consider words such as "pain," "blue," and "sweet." You may not be able to adequately define them verbally, but if you have had the relevant experiences, you know what they mean. Moreover, there is no strong reason to suppose that your understanding of them is different, at least not significantly different, from that of other people. By analogy, we may not be able to define "happiness" verbally, but we *do* know what it means, and we needn't suppose (as the objection suggests) that each of us means something different by this term. * * *

b.   Closely related to argument (a) is the objection that, although we may very often know what circumstances will be conducive to happiness, we cannot be sure that our actions will produce those circumstances.

* * *

To this the utilitarian may respond that, indeed, there are times when our lack of empirical knowledge makes us unable to tell what is the right thing to do; there are even times when our best efforts may, because of ignorance, lead us to do that which turns out to be grossly wrong. But the utilitarian would probably add * * * that we must keep in mind that most of the time we do know what will make people happy (if we could bring it about) and we also know what the effects of our actions will be. * * *

c.   Finally, it may be held that utilitarianism is unworkable because the pleasure or happiness (alternatively, suffering or unhappiness) of one person and that of another are *incommensurable*. If this is so, if these conditions can't be measured and compared in some way, it would seem that utilitarianism, like so many other doctrines, is "nice in theory, but won't work in practice."

* * *

It may not be wholly satisfactory, but perhaps the best response [is] an appeal to common experience and judgment, similar to the one made under (b) earlier. We do after all, whether or not we are utilitarians, make comparisons between people concerning happiness. And we usually have no difficulty in telling when one person is happier, or suffering more, than another. Is it really very often a problem for a nurse to discern which of two patients is in greater distress (physical *or* mental) and therefore in greater need of comfort and attention? At times, of course, we may be unable to tell, and at other times we may even be mistaken, but this occasional inability or these occasional mistakes are no good reason to be suspicious about such judgments in general.

* * *

Utilitarianism Is Inadequate. The second major objection to utilitarianism is that it is an inadequate approach—specifically, that utilitarianism alone cannot account for some of our basic moral attitudes and presuppositions. A correlative, and more serious, charge holds that utilitarianism sometimes yields judgments that conflict with fundamental moral beliefs.

For example, utilitarianism does not seem to recognize the fact that we create special moral ties between ourselves and others through various voluntary associations. If, for example, X borrows five dollars from Y, then X is obligated to Y, and it would be wrong for X not to return the money to Y, *even if* more overall happiness would result from X giving the five dollars to someone else. Because of its emphasis on consequences, utilitarianism is often termed a "forward-looking" ethic. However, as this example demonstrates, in order to determine what is right, we often have to look "backward" and take into account our obligations and debts. If we wish to be moral, we can't simply forget the past; for the rightness or wrongness of what we do now is, in part, determined by what we have done before. The extent to which utilitarianism fails to countenance that fact may be a measure of its inadequacy.

Furthermore, as the objection goes, utilitarianism fails to account for the fact that we often value certain acts not because they maximize happiness (for sometimes they don't) but simply because they are just and fair. Worse yet, utilitarianism can even approve actions that conflict with basic concepts of justice and fairness. One could envisage that applying the principle of the greatest happiness for the greatest number of people might lead us to condone—or even accept as "right"—situations in which some members of society become "sacrificial lambs" to serve the interest of the majority. For example, one could readily postulate an economic system based on slavery of a minority that would produce the greatest happiness for the greatest number. As John Rawls (a philosopher whose views will be discussed later) has argued, there is something wrong with a moral theory that would allow us even to consider slavery, regardless of whether slavery would indeed satisfy the principle of the greatest happiness.

The utilitarian might respond to this cluster of objections by first asking that we closely reexamine the facts of each case. He could argue that utilitarianism *does* acknowledge that we stand in special moral relationships to certain people as a result of our past actions—actions such as promises, agreements, and assumptions of positions of responsibility. But he would argue that, ultimately, even those "special relationships" are founded on considerations of utility, and hence they can, in exceptional circumstances, be overridden on utilitarian grounds. Thus, utilitarian theory would hold that a doctor has a greater obligation to see patient A, with whom she has made an appointment, than to see patient B, who has just come in off the street. However, if patient A requires a routine examination and B requires emergency treatment, then utilitarianism (and common sense) would maintain that the doctor has a greater obligation to see patient B.

Regarding the value we place on certain acts simply because they are just and fair, the utilitarian would say that we value the fair and equal treatment of others because we know that such treatment has positive utilitarian consequences for us. (It requires no great exercise of imagination to picture the ever-present anxiety produced in a society in which one can't depend on receiving fair treatment.) Our moral practices such as telling the truth, keeping promises, honoring confidences, and respecting each other's liberty are indeed valuable. But they are valuable not per se, but because adherence to them tends to increase the sum of happiness. Hence, there is a *prima facie* case to be made for abiding by such practices. Moreover, the utilitarian would say, there is a legitimate presumption that failure to adhere to such practices will have negative consequences: either the undermining of the practices themselves or at least the undermining of people's faith that the practices will be adhered to by others.

In short, the utilitarian sees that the value of traditional moral practices resides in their tendency to maximize happiness. But the utilitarian does not make the unlikely claim that, given a set of alternative actions, the one with greatest utility will *always* be one that is just or fair. And when faced with a conflict between justice and utility, the utilitarian will favor the latter.

RULE–UTILITARIANISM

Many people, although attracted to the greatest happiness principle, object to utilitarianism precisely because it does tolerate conflicts with justice and other basic moral practices such as telling the truth and keeping promises. *Rule-utilitarianism* may be seen as one attempt to counter this objection. Rule-utilitarianism maintains that adherence to moral rules is a prime directive but holds that we should adopt moral rules that are governed by the greatest-happiness principle. Thus, to determine whether an action is right, the rule-utilitarian would have us ask, "Does this conform to a rule the general practice of which would result in the greatest net amount of happiness?"

How does this concept compare with act-utilitarianism, which we have just been discussing? Since we do not always have the time (or, for that matter, the need) to calculate the respective utilities of the alternatives before us, the sensible act-utilitarian may, as a matter of convenience if not of necessity, govern his behavior by such general ethical principles as telling the truth and keeping one's promises, whose observance is most likely to maximize utility. This policy is analogous to that of following certain general strategies in sports ("Punt on fourth down," "Hit to your opponent's backhand," "Take only high-percentage shots"), which are not guaranteed to produce optimum results, but barring unusual circumstances, are most likely to. The act-utilitarian, however, like an athlete or a coach, will always be willing to depart from these rules if the particular circumstances warrant it. The rule-utilitarian, instead, makes the greatest happiness principle the test for the *rules* he adopts, but not for particular acts. The acts are tested by the rules. Hence, a rule-utilitarian will not condone making exceptions to the rules, even if the exception would promote more happiness in a particular case.

* * *

KANTIAN ETHICAL THEORIES

As we have seen, utilitarians are primarily concerned with raising the quality of our lives; they hold that we are morally obligated to increase well-being and to decrease the amount of pain and suffering in the world. These are also the goals of every physician, nurse, and biomedical researcher. Although considerations of utility are extremely important in the resolution of disputes in biomedical ethics and ethics in general, many ethical philosophers have argued that utilitarianism—which restricts its attention to the maximizing of benefits—cannot provide us with a completely adequate moral philosophy.

One major ethical viewpoint, known as Kantianism from its most illustrious exponent, Immanuel Kant (1724–1804), affirms that utilitarianism cannot account for some of our most prized and strongly felt moral intuitions. Mill focused on the consequences of an act and defined right actions as those that maximize the good (that is, happiness)—a "teleological" position. Kant, instead, argued that consequences do not make an action right or wrong; rather, it is the principle upon which an agent acts that is the morally decisive factor. We call Kant's position a *deontological* ethical theory (from the Greek word *deon,* which means "that which is binding, duty"). * * *

For Kant, an act is moral only if it springs from what he calls a "good will"—that is, a will governed by a rational moral principle. Mill claims that happiness is the only thing that is desirable in itself; Kant holds that a good will is the only thing that is good without qualification. All other traits, such as moderation, self-control, and intelligence, are good only when they exist in conjunction with a good will. For example, intelligence may be used to eradicate poverty or to plunder the public coffers, depending on the presence or absence of good will. Moreover, the desirability of good will is seen by Kant as independent of its ability to achieve desirable results. Kant states that even if our good will is thwarted at every turn, "it would still shine like a jewel for its own sake as something which has its full value in itself." [ ]

But what does it mean to have a good will? It means to act on the basis of a sense of *duty,* as opposed to acting on the basis of inclination.

* * *

Kant's supreme principle of morality is his famous "categorical imperative": "I ought never to act except in such a way that I can also will that my maxim should become a universal law." [ ] This principle is Kant's supreme test for the morality of our acts. The principle is completely formal; it lacks specific content, yet it is supposedly applicable to every possible action. How can such a seemingly abstract and forbidding principle be applied to concrete moral situations? Indeed, what does the ability to universalize a moral principle have to do with morality?

At the risk of oversimplifying somewhat, Kant's categorical imperative may be compared to the golden rule, "Do unto others as you would have them do unto you"; alternatively, "Do not do unto others what you would not have them do unto you." Both formulations of the golden rule and Kant's imperative demand that we treat others as moral equals and that we recognize the equality of other persons by permitting other to act as we do when they occupy a position similar to ours. * * * Kant's categorical imperative is predicated on the principle of the moral equality of all persons, and it holds that the test of right action is that it can be universalized without violating the recognized equality of all human beings. * * *

APPLYING THE CATEGORICAL IMPERATIVE

Let us see how this principle can be put to work. Imagine a researcher who desperately needs subjects for what he knows to be a highly dangerous but highly promising experiment. Since potential subjects would refuse to participate if they were fully informed of all the dangers involved, the researcher assures them that the experiment is perfectly safe. The researcher could be said to be acting on the principle, "Whenever your research is imperiled by the reluctance of human subjects to participate in it, it is permissible to make false promises to them." Does this principle pass the test established by Kant; that is, could one will that it become a universal law? Obviously not, for if it became a universally recognized law that all researchers make false promises to potential subjects in the interest of scientific progress, the very notion of making such promises would cease to make sense. One could not will that the researcher's principle become a universal law because such a law would be self-defeating.

It is essential to note, in this connection, that Kant's argument is not based on the actual or probable consequences of our actions. He is not asking about the overall *utility* of transforming a principle into a universal law; rather, he is pointing out that some principles cannot be universalized without involving their author in contradictions. As we indicated in our example, a universal principle of false promise making contradicts the very notion of promise making. This is not a purely logical contradiction (a world without promises is at least conceivable), but it is a *practical* contradiction since, in order for the notion of a false promise to make any sense, there must be a general practice of making and keeping promises. Therefore, if making false promises becomes a universal law (if *everyone always* made false promises), then promise making itself becomes meaningless; correlatively, if promise making lacks meaning, so must the notion of promising *falsely*. Thus, when Kant points out our inability to generalize certain principles, he is referring to a practical contradiction—his focus is still on principles rather than on the probable consequences of our actions.

We have seen that we cannot even think about elevating certain principles (maxims) to the level of universal laws without creating a contradiction. There exists another class of principles that are impossible for a rational person to will into universal laws, yet they involve no such internal inconsistency. For example, it is perfectly conceivable to entertain the principle "Never contribute to the well-being of others"—a principle that is even conceivable as a universal law. [ ] However, Kant claims that it would be impossible for us to *will* that everyone's behavior be governed by such a principle. Why? Because we can't will something that would thwart our own ends. And surely a universal principle of nonassistance would thwart our own ends, for it is certain that at some time we ourselves shall require assistance, and therefore we cannot rationally will as universal law a principle that would deprive us of that assistance.

* * *

DUTIES AND RIGHTS

There are two categories of obligations or duties related to the two classes of principles just discussed: a "perfect duty" and an "imperfect duty." A perfect duty is violated when the principle of our action cannot be universalized without contradiction (for example, the principle of making false promises). An imperfect duty is violated when the principle of our action cannot be willed as a universal law for reasons pertaining to our nature (for example, the principle of nonassistance). [ ]

A perfect duty is one that can *never* be right for us to violate. To say that we have a perfect duty to refrain from unjustly harming another person means that no interest, inclination, or utilitarian consideration could ever justify treating a person as a mere means to an end. An example of an imperfect duty is the duty to contribute to the well-being of others. To say that the duty of benevolence is "imperfect" is to say that it is not constantly and universally binding; that is, we are not obligated or duty-bound to help everyone all the time. This is not to say that we are not still morally obligated to be benevolent; rather, it says that inclination can play a legitimate role in determining whom to aid and when to aid them.

In order to round out this Kantian analysis of moral relations, we should note that perfect duties are matched by perfect rights; specifically, the perfect duty to refrain from violating the liberty or integrity of others is matched by a corresponding *right* to be free from such violation. (Kant sees this right as being perfect, or absolutely binding, since it cannot be overridden by utilitarian considerations.) The symmetry of duties and rights does not obtain in the case of imperfect duties, which do not seem to generate any corresponding rights. For example, although we have a duty of beneficence toward others, ordinarily it does not follow that others have a right to our generosity. Thus, if we donate money to the Red Cross, we may discharge our duty of beneficence, but that donation does not accord the Red Cross any right to that money or any future donations that we might wish to make to another charity.

In sum: Kantian ethics holds that the categorical imperative is the supreme principle of morality, the ultimate test of moral action. Actions may fail this test in two ways: either because the principle behind our action is intrinsically inconsistent and, therefore, self-defeating or because the principle—if made a universal law—would serve to thwart our own ends. Kantian ethics defines two types of duties related, respectively, to the two classes of actions just discussed: perfect and imperfect duties, or moral obligations. Finally, Kantian ethics state that perfect duties are matched by rights held by others and that imperfect duties generate no corresponding rights.

RESOLVING CONFLICTING DUTIES

Kant's distinction between different *kinds* of duty leads us to consider one of the most forceful and persistent objections to Kantian ethical theory—its alleged inability to deal effectively with the existence of conflicting ethical duties. Most of our moral difficulties involve the presence of more than one duty; indeed, the presence of two or more conflicting duties is often the source of our moral difficulties. We are frequently forced to choose between, say, obedience to the law and obedience to the pursuit of justice (as in problems involving civil disobedience) or between the amelioration of suffering and the prolongation of life (a problem created by the development of pain-relieving, life-shortening drugs). Now, when faced with such conflicting duties, we must confront the problem of *ranking* our various and conflicting moral commitments. If we are to act morally, we must choose among the conflicting moral demands, and the rightness of our choice will rest upon our ability to structure or coordinate the various ethical duties involved. Can Kant's theory assist us in the resolution of such conflicts? Many critics deny that it can and therefore state that Kant's theory must be replaced with, or at least supplemented by, utilitarian standards. Let us see for ourselves.

Suppose that X will soon die unless she receives an organ transplant. Y, a terminally ill patient, is the only available potential donor, and a transplant operation would kill her because of her generally weakened condition. If a transplant operation is not performed, both women will soon die; if the operation is performed, X can be saved at Y's expense. Would a transplant operation at this time be morally acceptable without Y's permission? Some utilitarians might approve of the operation on the ground that one life saved is better than none; a Kantian, however, would no doubt condemn such an action on the ground that it would violate Y's right to control the use of her own body, and he would base his argument on the aforementioned distinction between perfect and imperfect duties and rights. In this case, the physician can only discharge his *imperfect duty* to help X by violating Y's *perfect right* to the control over her own body.

* * *

[But] it is not at all obvious that perfect duties should always have priority over imperfect duties. Suppose that you have promised to meet a friend for lunch. (You have incurred a perfect duty—the fidelity to promises.) En route to the restaurant, you encounter a man who urgently needs your help in getting to the hospital. (You are faced with an imperfect duty— benevolence.) Clearly you cannot discharge the imperfect duty of benevolence without violating the perfect duty to keep promises, and yet who would say that you act wrongly in escorting the man to a doctor? This example indicates that some imperfect duties should occasionally take precedence over perfect duties. [In addition, Kant's theory may not help us in dealing with conflicting perfect duties.]

RESPECT FOR PERSONS

[Kant also recognized another formulation of the categorical imperative, which he called the formula of the "end in itself":] "Act in such a way that you always treat humanity, whether in your own person or in the person of any other, never simply as a means, but always at the same time as an end." [ ]

This formulation of Kant's imperative draws a radical moral distinction between *things* and *persons*. According to Kant, things possess a "market value" (their worth consists precisely in the uses to which they can be put); but persons alone possess dignity, or intrinsic worth, which cannot be reduced to a market value. * * *

KANTIANISM AND MEDICAL ETHICS

Kantian theory has profound and far-reaching implications for medical ethics. For example, its insistence that the patient/subject be treated as a person—that is, as an autonomous rational agent * * *—provides a coherent theoretical framework for the so-called "consent requirement," wherein research subjects are asked to consent to be the subjects of experiments only after they have been fully and effectively informed about the probable consequences of the experiment. Failure to inform subjects of potential experimental hazards * * * provides us with a clear example of using another person merely as a means to an end. Thus, the consent requirement, which is designed not only to protect people from harm but also to protect their status as moral beings capable of choosing for themselves, would seem to be firmly grounded in Kantian ethics.

Let us now consider how a Kantian moral perspective might prompt us to redefine the relationship between physician and patient. Take the Hippocratic injunction to "benefit and do no harm to the patient." This maxim assumes that the physician should decide his or her actions according to utilitarian calculations of benefit and harm. Moreover, it places the physician in the role of a parent who decides and the patient in the role of a child who (presumably) must accept the decision. To the extent to which this model of the doctor-patient relationship represents a faithful mirror image of current reality (at least as it is depicted on television), the physician may be ignoring the moral autonomy of the patient. Concern for the patient's "own good" could cause a physician to override the explicit value preferences of his or her patient. The standard of utility, coupled with the parental model of the physician implicit in the maxim "benefit and do no harm to the patient," could easily justify withholding the truth from dying cancer patients and bearers of fatal genetic diseases. Even more seriously, it could justify coercing adult members of religious sects, such as the Jehovah's Witnesses, to undergo therapies forbidden by their own moral codes. Although such lying and coercion might well maximize overall utility, many persons would condemn such practices as assaults upon the moral integrity and dignity of the patients in question.

In place of the utilitarian model of the physician-patient relationship, a Kantian moralist would recommend what [one philosopher] has termed a "contractual model"—a model that affirms the moral autonomy of both parties to the agreement. Governed by such a model, the physician would regard the patient as a responsible human being who is capable of making major decisions concerning his or her life. The patient, on the other hand, would respect the conscience of the physician and would not demand that the physician violate his or her own ethical and professional standards. Such a relationship between doctor and patient, which has been characterized by [one theologian, Paul Ramsey] as a "covenant" relationship, sets up demands that differ markedly from the demands of utility. As Ramsey puts it, "*Justice, fairness, faithfulness, canons of loyalty,* the *sanctity* of life, *hesed, agape,* or *charity* are some of the names given to the moral quality of attitude and of action owed to all men by any man who steps into a covenant with another man. . . . " [ ] A covenantal relationship demands a kind of moral reciprocity that is foreign to a utilitarian model. Both parties to a covenant are bound by certain moral obligations, and each has a duty to honor the freedom and dignity of the other. Although such a covenant might be exceedingly difficult to implement in the day-to-day practice of medicine, achieving the ideals of mutuality, freedom, and shared responsibility implicit in it is certainly worth the struggle. [ ]

A KANTIAN THEORY OF JUSTICE

The idea of a covenant, or contract, between moral agents is fundamental to a Kantian theory of justice. In his book, *A Theory of Justice,* John Rawls * * * developed a highly acclaimed deontological theory of justice based on the notion of a hypothetical social contract between free, equal, and rational persons. His theory is worth describing here because it is offered explicitly as a Kantian alternative to utilitarianism.

For Mill, justice was only a part, albeit the most important part, of a larger concept of social utility; he refused to concede that the claims of justice could challenge those of utility or that justice had any value in itself apart from its ability to maximize the aggregate social welfare. Consequently, Mill's conception of the just society demanded laws and basic social institutions that achieve the greatest possible satisfaction of desire for the population taken as a whole. According to classical utilitarianism, it does not matter precisely how such satisfactions are distributed among the members of society, so long as the net sum is maximized.

* * *

Rawls offers instead a social contract wherein free and rational persons choose principles of justice from the standpoint of what he considers to be an "original position" of equality and under a "veil of ignorance" regarding their social and economic status in society, their natural assets, and even their specific conception of the good. Unlike some other proponents of a social contract, Rawls does not ask us to believe that society was originally formed by means of such a contract; he stipulates a contract simply as a purely hypothetical methodological construct designed to generate principles of justice acceptable to all rational persons. By hypothetically stripping the contracting parties of any "knowledge" concerning their social and economic differences, by returning them to what he considers to be their original equality, and by stressing their rationality, Rawls is attempting to create an initial situation that all the parties will regard as being fair and in which all parties are able to freely choose principles of justice. Hence the name of his theory, "justice as fairness."

* * *

Perhaps the most remarkable difference between utilitarianism and "justice as fairness" concerns their respective theories of the "good" and the "right" and how these important moral concepts are related. Utilitarian theories define the good independently of the right; first the good is defined as happiness, then the right is defined as that which maximizes happiness. Because justice is defined as a function of utility, it cannot limit the claims of utility. Justice is not desirable for its own sake but only insofar as it serves to advance maximum social welfare. Rawls, instead, sees the concepts of right and justice as preceding the concept of the good. [ ] He states that, in order for desires (concepts of the good) to have any value or to be taken into account in our calculations, they must accord with the principles of justice. Thus, the utilitarian would at least have to take into account the desires of a sadist to observe the suffering and deprivation of others, while for Rawls such desires would have absolutely no weight.

Rawls's conception of justice is thus very Kantian in nature. Both theories are concerned primarily with justice and the right, as opposed to a focus on happiness; both consider respect for the person as having priority over virtues of benevolence. Kant's commitment to the moral equality of all persons is expressed in the demand of the categorical imperative for universality; Rawls's commitment to this same ideal is reflected both in the design of the original position (which assumes a basic equality) and in his requirement that the principles chosen in that position be acceptable to *all* of the contracting parties. Rawls's attempt to construct an ethic of mutual respect between free and rational persons is indeed a worthy continuation of the Kantian tradition in moral and political philosophy.

* * *

THE LIMITS OF KANTIAN INDIVIDUALISM

It is no wonder that Kantian ethical theories have achieved predominance in the field of bioethics. Although some stouthearted moralists still proclaim their allegiance to the tradition of Bentham and Mill, many people have come to regard the Kantian emphasis on individual rights as a necessary corrective to the crude tendency of utilitarianism to sacrifice the individual for the greater good of the many. The Kantian conception of rights as trumps against the claims of social utility has thus played a very important role in our thinking and legislating concerning the moral status of experimental subjects. No matter what the proposed gains, we refuse on Kantian grounds to enlist persons as cannon fodder in the war against disease.

Moreover, the Kantian emphasis on the moral sovereignty of the individual strongly appeals to the individualistic ethos of our culture. By cleaving to the dictates of reason and the categorical imperative, the Kantian subject detaches herself from the moral authority of God, nature, and society. So long as the Kantian moral agent violates no one's rights, she is free to choose her own values and way of life. As a rational legislator of the moral law, each individual remains free to set her own course, unencumbered by anyone else's conceptions of the good life, virtue, or social obligations. Paternalism, the limitation of freedom for the individual's "own good," remains the original Kantian sin.

Notwithstanding the depth of the Kantian understanding of the moral life and its demonstrated fruitfulness in many areas of bioethics, this outlook exhibits distinct limitations which require further discussion. In this section we shall argue that the individualistic orientation of Kantian ethics renders it less and less applicable to the emerging problems of biomedical ethics, and that its relative lack of concern for the social context of individual rights can lead to untoward moral consequences.

The Inadequacy of (Some) Right Claims. While the Kantian themes of moral sovereignty and respect for persons have indeed effected a radical change in the basic structure of the doctor-patient relationship—replacing the paternalistic "priestly" model with a contractual approach—this change has done nothing to alter the essentially individualistic perspective of biomedical ethics. Although the moral and legal balance of power has shifted somewhat in the direction of the patient, medical ethics has remained largely preoccupied with "microlevel" issues bearing on the dilemmas of the individual practitioner. As Daniel Callahan * * * pointed out, this standard view of medical ethics has "presumed as its model that of one physician treating one patient, the necessity for some qualified or expert individual to make a final choice, and the general belief that there could be no fixed answers to specific moral dilemmas." [ ]

* * *

While single-minded appeals to rights as trumps may have succeeded in protecting the moral status of Jehovah's Witnesses and experimental subjects during the last decade, a similar strategy will most likely prove insufficient in the upcoming debates over health policy. What is the best health care delivery system compatible with the demands of justice, our political and economic traditions, and the constraints of a stagnant economy? What, if anything, should be done to address the current inequities in access to health services between urban and rural areas? Should the bulk of our health care resources go towards preventing disease or providing basic care for the many, or should we rather continue the present trend toward more "high-tech" medicine for the acutely ill few? * * * Clearly, a mere appeal to individual rights will not answer all the tough questions raised by these and other problems. * * *

The Inappropriateness of (Some) Right Claims. Although utilitarianism is not ordinarily based on a study of worldly facts, it nevertheless presupposes certain things about the world and human nature. For example, it assumes that certain actions will regularly produce certain good or bad consequences, and that moral agents are capable of calculating the probable effects of their actions. Likewise, while Kant emphatically repudiated any taint of the factual in the formulation of his ethical theory, he had to assume that moral agents are free from the causal determinism that reigns in the world of Newtonian physics. If people are not free to choose to do their duty, how could Kant assert that they *ought* to so choose?

* * *

As we have seen, a number of important moral concepts cascade out of the Kantian theory of moral autonomy. Our capacity to choose our own values and establish our own life plans is the source of the Kantian moral right to self-determination, which, in turn, establishes the moral and legal right of patients to informed consent. These rights and their progeny have played a decisive role in many of the bioethical controversies of the last decade, including the debates surrounding abortion, truth telling, human experimentation, behavior control, and treatment refusal. In many instances, the invocation of these rights has seemed to many to be entirely appropriate and unobjectionable—the protection of human subjects in research is perhaps the best example—but this should not lead us to conclude that their application is always and everywhere appropriate.

An obviously inappropriate instance of invoking the right to self-determination comes from the area of treatment refusal. Suppose that a patient enters the emergency room screaming from the pain inflicted by severe burns. The attending physicians conclude that, although her burns are serious, she will recover if given immediate and sustained treatment. Suddenly the patient, on the verge of shock, rebuffs the efforts of the medical staff on the ground that she has a right to "die with dignity." Clearly, in this sort of case it would be wrong for the medical staff to honor the claimed right to refuse treatment. Not only is the woman mistaken in her belief that she is about to die regardless of treatment, but her capacity for self-determination has itself been substantially impaired or temporarily eclipsed by her recent trauma. To honor her refusal would be tantamount to treating an incompetent person as though she were competent, with morally disastrous results.

RELIGION AND NATURAL LAW

Before closing, it seems appropriate that we make some mention of the role that ~~religious beliefs and/or attitudes~~ often have in the discussion of ethical issues. We are not suggesting that "religious ethics" is one among competing ethical theories in the sense that utilitarianism and Kantianism are; religious beliefs do not, in general, seem to imply any one particular ethical orientation. * * * Perhaps [the] disparity of ethical views within a single religious context can be explained by saying that, although there are certainly ethical directives inherent in religious belief, such directives are sufficiently vague as to be subject to quite different interpretations. Clearly, religious belief provides many people with a powerful motive to lead a moral life. And certainly there are religious beliefs that would rule out some approaches to ethical issues. One presumes, for example, that no sincere Christian or Jew would maintain that it is morally permissible to act always and only with regard to one's own self-interest. But it does seem that the ethical directions provided by religion require "filling out" or specification * * *.

There are some religious groups that seem to be more unified in their ethical views than others; one thinks particularly of Roman Catholic moral thought, which, generally speaking, seems more characterized by agreement than by disagreement. Roman Catholic ethics deserves our attention here for two reasons. First, it has a well-developed body of thought dealing specifically with medical-moral problems, and for centuries the Catholic church has addressed itself to such problems, with the result that it has had considerable influence on what are now prevailing medical-moral attitudes (even among many non-Catholics), as well as on legal doctrine regarding a wide range of biomedical ethical issues. Second, the Catholic tradition includes an alternative ethical theory—known as natural law ethics—that provides principles for interpreting the general ethical directives of the Christian faith. [ ]

NATURAL LAW THEORIES
* * *

Catholic theologians conceive of ~~natural law as the law inscribed by God into the nature of things—as a species of divine law~~. According to this conception, the Creator endows all things with certain potentialities or tendencies that serve to define their natural end; the fulfillment of a thing's natural tendencies constitutes the specific "good" of that thing. The natural tendency of an acorn is to become an oak. But what is the natural potential, or tendency, of human beings? In order to answer this question, the natural law theorist fastens onto an attribute that he regards as distinctively human, as separating human beings from the rest of worldly creatures—that is, the ability to live according to the dictates of reason. Other creatures can fulfill their potential merely by "doing what comes naturally"; human beings can fulfill their potential (that is, become truly human) only by exercising their intelligence or reason. Natural law is said to bind us all because we all share a common human essence. Thus, natural law ethics is characterized by its rationalism and by its commitment to ethical objectivity.

By means of deductive reasoning, natural law ethics systematically proceeds from moral precepts to practical conclusions. The most general moral precept of the natural law is "do good and avoid evil" (moral evil must always be avoided, no matter what the cost). Consequently, the commission of an evil deed, such as the murder of an innocent person, can never be condoned, even if it is intended to advance the noblest of ends.

THE PRINCIPLE OF DOUBLE EFFECT

To be properly implemented, the basic precept to do good and avoid evil often requires subsidiary principles. One such principle, the principle of *double effect,* is used to analyze the morality of actions that involve more than one effect. For example, administering a drug that eases the pain of a dying cancer patient may also weaken his condition and hasten his death; thus, the same action produces a good effect (the decrease in pain) as well as a bad effect (the decrease in life expectancy). How should such actions be analyzed from a moral viewpoint? If we are morally bound to avoid evil, even as a means to a good end, then are we not also bound to consider the use of such medicines as immoral in spite of the good that they do?

According to * * * one authoritative source, [ ] actions based on the principle of double effect can be justified only if they satisfy all of the following three conditions: (1) the evil must not be the means of producing the good effect, (2) the evil may not be "directly" intended, and (3) there must be a proportionate reason for performing the action, in spite of its evil consequences. The fine distinctions implicit in these three conditions can be used to justify the use of pain-relieving drugs that also shorten life. In the first place, a physician who administers such drugs does not effect alleviation of the patient's suffering by means of weakening his condition; thus, the evil effect is not a means to the desired end. Second, the intent of administering the drug is to ease the patient's excruciating pain, not to weaken or kill him. The adverse effect of the drug is only willed "indirectly"; we "directly" intend to aid the patient. Finally, with a patient whose days are already numbered, relief from terrible pain can be considered "a proportionate reason" for an action that decreases life expectancy. Thus, we can see that the principle of double effect can be a useful tool for justifying an action that may entail a bad effect.

* * *

Although many people reject natural law ethics because they cannot accept the metaphysical presuppositions on which it is based, one may still find within it a number of distinctions and approaches that are both useful and insightful. Moreover, it is interesting to note that references to the "natural" hold a strong appeal—even for those who do not believe in a god and who would reject the concept of a divine moral law. For example, many people who lack any religious commitment find morally objectionable some of the "unnatural" procedures that are being tested and developed in current biomedical research, such as work designed to perfect in vitro fertilization and "test-tube babies." Similar objections are raised concerning certain techniques for prolonging life * * *, which are seen as interfering with natural processes. Whether such positions can be worked into a consistent ethical view is, of course, a moot point since there may be a serious problem in drawing the line between what we call "natural" and "unnatural."

Note on the Application of Ethical Theories in Law

As you read the legal material in the following chapters, ask yourself which theories are consistent with the judicial opinions in cases implicating bioethics. What was the ethical basis of the decision of the Cruzan family to seek authority to terminate Nancy Cruzan's treatment? What was the ethical basis of the Missouri Supreme Court's majority opinion? How is the ethical framework that appears to support the Missouri majority different from that which supports the dissents in the Missouri Supreme Court? How is it different from those ethical frameworks that appear to support the majority and the dissenting opinions in the United States Supreme Court? Do any of the United States Supreme Court opinions appear to be based in utilitarianism? In Kantian analysis? In natural law? Do any of the Justices appear to have been influenced by Rawls's *A Theory of Justice?* In what way? How do the different ethical theories applied by different actors in the Cruzan case play out in the context of physician assisted death?

What is the ethical structure that holds up Justice Blackmun's majority opinion in *Roe v. Wade?* To what extent is the three-judge opinion in *Planned Parenthood of Southeastern Pennsylvania v. Casey* or any of the opinions in *Stenberg v. Carhart* consistent with the approach to ethical analysis taken in *Roe v. Wade?* Do the supporters of the Partial Birth Abortion Ban Act of 2003 disagree with the ethical analysis of the abortion cases, or with the factual analyses to which that analysis is applied? What are the implications of the different ethical theories for the development of procedures designed to facilitate reproduction— procedures like artificial insemination, in vitro fertilization, gestational surrogacy, and cloning? What do the different ethical theories tell us about health care reform and the distribution of health care resources? Are there some bioethics issues that would be resolved if this society were to agree on a common theory of ethics? Do the different potential applications of the different theories of ethics have any implications for institutional ethics committees or committees designed to review research on human subjects?

Finally, as you read the subsequent chapters, ask yourself how ethical theory should be manifested in law.

Note: New Theories of Bioethics Analysis and the Attack on "Principlism"

Over the past decade many bioethics scholars have started to question the application of the traditional principle-based ethical analysis as unnecessarily narrow. Not everything, they argue, can be parsed into manifestations of autonomy, beneficence, distributive justice, and the few other secondary principles (including non-maleficence, confidentiality and truth telling) that have been the hallmarks of bioethics debate ever since the National Commission for the Protection of Human Subjects and Behavioral Research issued its Belmont Report, the *Quinlan* case was decided, and Tom Beauchamp and James Childress published the first edition of their enormously influential *Principles of Biomedical Ethics*, all in the late 1970s. Not all theories can be neatly classified as utilitarian, Kantian, or natural law in origin, the critics point out. There have been a number of candidates advanced to replace the formally principled approach to bioethics. Among the contenders are:

1. Narrative bioethics. This theory suggests that we can learn a great deal from hearing the stories of those involved in bioethics disputes. Essentially, the argument is that if we hear the narrative of the participants—if we hear them tell their stories—we will realize what the proper ending to the stories should be. When we listen to the story of a family dealing with someone who is in the process of dying, it is suggested, we will realize what should happen next. A good story will tell us more about physician assisted death, for example, than any rendering of pure ethical theory ever could. The power of literature in helping us think about ethical issues demonstrates the value of this approach.

2. Virtue bioethics. This return to Aristotelian virtue ethics suggests that we can tell what ought to be done under any particular set of circumstances by asking what a truly good person—a virtuous person—would do under those circumstances. Some scholars believe that the great intuitive appeal of narrative bioethics stems from its origin in virtue ethics. In any case, the significance of the views of respected physicians or beloved clergyman is often independent of the logic of those views; we sometimes are convinced of the virtue of the position because of the person advocating it.

3. Ethics of caring. This form of bioethics reasoning, which is sometimes considered a branch of feminist bioethics, requires that we analyze the strength of important relationships among human beings and evaluate how the resolution of bioethical dilemmas will affect those relationships. This approach stresses the caring, personal role of medicine, and distinguishes that role from medicine's more purely scientific curing role. This approach to bioethics reasoning would require we look at the whole web of relationships created by a "surrogate mother" contract, for example.

4. Religious bioethics. There has also been a renaissance of the application of religious reasoning to bioethics dilemmas. Sometimes religious bioethics looks very much like traditional principled bioethics, but with religiously defined principles replacing the more secular mantra of autonomy, beneficence and justice. Sometimes, however, spiritual approaches to bioethics problems look much more like the approach taken by those who subscribe to the ethics of caring. Given the very wide range of religious views in our society, it is hardly surprising that the religiously based bioethics of different groups bear almost no relationship to each other—except in the source of the principles they adopt. Indeed, there is as great a range of opinions among religiously based Protestant bioethics scholars, or orthodox and reform Jews, or liberal and conservative Islamic writers, as among all bioethicists.

5. Casuistry. This form of decision making is based in the notion that each bioethics case must be separately evaluated with the realization that the indiscriminate application of general principles and overarching rules sometimes leads to ethically unsound moral value judgments. For example, a casuist confronted with the question of whether it is appropriate to deprogram a patient's pacemaker at that patient's request would ask whether the deprogramming is more like the removal of life sustaining medical treatment from a competent adult (which is now generally permitted) or more like the purposeful commission of an act which directly causes the death of the patient (which is now generally forbidden). In fact, one example of casuistry is the common law system. Not surprisingly, lawyers have been particularly comfortable with this form of practical, case based reasoning.

6. Pragmatism. The pragmatic approach to bioethics decision making has substantial overlap with other approaches, especially casuistry. Pragmatists argue that we ought to respect the fact that different people apply different forms of ethical analysis in different cases, and that we should bring our practical knowledge to the resolution of dilemmas in bioethics.

7. Law and economics theory. This form of analysis applies traditional economic models to bioethics issues. It generally supports the private, rather than governmental, resolution of disputes in bioethics. Law and economics scholars are skeptical about the paternalistic role government plays when it regulates for any purpose other than to assure that individuals can freely and fairly enter private agreements to order their own lives. Law and economic theorists tend to take libertarian positions—favoring the authority of competent adults to make virtually any uncoerced decisions concerning medical treatment.

8. Critical race theory. This approach suggests that there is much to be learned about bioethics dilemmas by looking to the distinctively different perspectives brought to these issues by those with different racial and cultural backgrounds, and by evaluating the issues against the background of race relations and cultural domination within the society. We could not do a serious evaluation of research involving human subjects during this century without taking notice of how racism manifested itself in abuses in medical laboratories across the world, for example.

9. Feminist bioethics. Probably the most important scholarly development in bioethics over the past five years has been the development of a substantial literature in feminist bioethics. There is a wide diversity within feminist bioethics, however, and the term is used in a host of different ways. One legal scholar has provided a brief account of the leading forms of feminism that have been applied to deal with issues in bioethics:

> Liberal feminism is based on a belief in formal gender equality, particularly in the economic and political arenas. Since women possess the same capabilities as men, women should be entitled to equal rights, equal employment opportunities, and equal pay. Under this equality model gender classifications are highly suspect because they reflect and reinforce stereotypes that fail to treat men and women as individuals, without regard to gender. Liberal feminists have focused primarily on eliminating state imposed gender distinctions and on preventing the state from limiting individual choice. While liberal feminism has been quite successful in expanding political and economic opportunities available to white, middle class, women, it has been criticized for ignoring the constraints of race and class and for adopting an assimilation model that benefits women only if they act like men.
>
> While liberal feminism emphasizes the essential sameness of men and women, cultural or relational feminism focuses on their differences. Cultural feminism is grounded in the work of Carol Gilligan and other contemporary psychologists who suggest that men and women speak in a "different" voice. These theorists argue that men on average tend to analyze problems in terms of abstract rules and competing rights and to emphasize the importance of autonomy. Women, by contrast, tend to be more contextual in their analysis of problems and to place more emphasis on preserving personal relationships and on maintaining connections between and among individuals. Cultural feminists argue that many traditional legal doctrines and practices are based on male values of autonomy and abstraction and fail to value the positive "feminine" concerns of responsibility, relationship, and essential connectedness experienced in the mother-child relationship. Many cultural feminists have sought to promote a positive vision of a female ethic of care, rather than a morality of rights. For example, cultural feminists have suggested that the law look for alternatives to the traditional adversary paradigm including alternative dispute resolution mechanisms. In a similar view, they suggest that courts apply a feminist ethic of care in negligence law.

Dominance or radical feminism also arose in large part in response to the perceived inadequacies in liberal feminist theory. Like cultural feminists, Catherine MacKinnon, the major proponent of dominance theory, argues that men and women are different, but that these differences largely reflect the societal fact that women are subordinate and men are dominant. According to dominance theorists, it is this inequality in power to which the law must respond. Moreover, since the primary source of women's oppression is private power, particularly the threat of sexual violence, the solution is not—as liberal feminists often claim—less state interventions, but more. Dominance feminists argue, for example, that the legal system should abandon its traditional "hands-off" attitude toward violence in the family and move more aggressively to protect women from abusive power of men in the private sphere. * * * Thus, whereas liberal feminists have argued primarily on expanding women's choices, and cultural feminists attempted to reform legal rules to reflect women's real experiences and affirm women's values, radical feminists have argued that law should address the harms to women that arise from conduct of other private actors, particularly men, and particularly with respect to sex and violence.

Postmodern feminism rejects the assumptions and generalizations at the core of the other feminist theories. Since no objective reality can describe the "essential" woman, postmodern feminists embrace the particular "situated" realities of all individual women. Postmodernists encourage feminists to consider real life experiences influenced by each women's race, class, age and sexual orientation. Critical legal feminist scholars have incorporated themes of postmodernism by rejecting abstract universal theory and embracing the need for a social policy that provides practical and just solutions to real life problems.

Karen Rothenberg, New Perspectives for Teaching and Scholarship: The Role of Gender in Law and Health Care, 54 Md. L. Rev. 473 (1995).

Of Course, this list of nine alternative approaches to bioethics is hardly comprehensive, and there is a great deal of overlap among these and other approaches. Most of us act on the basis of several different theories of bioethics whenever we address a bioethics issue. For a very good, brief account of the significance of many of these theories, see Tom Beauchamp and James Childress, *Principles of Medical Ethics* (5th ed. 2001). A good bibliography for many of these approaches is provided in the thorough footnotes to Susan M. Wolf, Shifting Paradigms in Bioethics and Health Law: The Rise of a New Pragmatism, 20 Am. J. L. & Med. 395 (1994).

On the role of narrative in bioethics, see Hilde Lindemann Nelson, Stories and Their Limits: Narrative Approaches to Bioethics (1997), and for the role of narrative in legal analysis generally, see Daniel A. Farber and Suzanna Sherry, Telling Stories Out of School: An Essay on Legal Narratives, 45 Stan. L. Rev. 807 (1993). For one account of the new casuistry written by the same person who prepared the summary of ethical theories that you just read, see John Arras, Principles and Particularity: The Role of Cases in Bioethics, 69 Ind. L. J. 983 (1994). For two examples of the application of the principles of law and economics to bioethics, see Richard Posner, The Ethics and Economics of Enforcing Contracts of Surrogate Motherhood, 5 J. Contemp. Health L. & Pol. 21 (1989), and Roger Blair and David Kaserman, The Economics and Ethics of Alternative Cadaveric Organ Procurement Policies, 8 Yale J. Reg. 403 (1991). For a perspective on the role of race in bioethics issues, see *African–American Perspectives on Biomedical Ethics* (Harley Flack and Edmund Pellegrino, eds., 1992). For an account of race and health that incorporates critical race analysis of health issues, see Vernellia Randall's website on Race, Healthcare and Law at http://academic.udayton.edu/health/05bioethics/bioethics02.htm (visited June 1, 2004).

There is a wealth of writing on feminist bioethics. Several excellent articles are found in two collections, *Feminist Perspectives in Medical Ethics* (Helen Bequaert Holmes and Laura Purdy, eds., 1992), and *Feminism and Bioethics: Beyond Reproduction* (Susan Wolf, ed., 1996). See also R. Tong, Feminist Approaches to Bioethics: Theoretical Reflection and Practical Application (1997) and R. Tong, G. Anderson and A. Santos, Globalizing Feminist Bioethics: Cltural Responses (2000). A good account of the role of feminism in health care ethics is also found in Leslie Bender, Teaching Feminist Perspectives on Health Care Ethics and Law: A Review, 61 U. Cin. L. Rev. 1251 (1993).

Note on Codes of Ethics and Oaths

For the last few millennia, individuals and professional groups have attempted to distinguish themselves from others by adopting and applying principles which define ethically appropriate conduct in their professional roles. Sometimes these principles are accepted by individual professionals by the taking of an oath—a promise—to adhere to them, as in the case of the oath taken by followers of Hippocrates (and many doctors even today). Sometimes these oaths are expressed as contracts, promises, or even prayers, as in the case of the Prayer of Maimonides. Sometimes professional groups, such as the American Medical Association, simply announce those principles that ought to apply to their membership, as they did in the Principles of Medical Ethics. As you read the oath, prayer and set of principles which follow, ask yourself some questions about them. Are oaths, prayers, principles, pledges and codes truly statements of ethics, or are they statements of professional convention and etiquette? Are they statements of fundamental principles, or parts of a contract among health care providers and between health care providers and their patients? Do they give rise to reasonable expectations among providers? Among patients? For the whole society? Which ethical theories are reflected in each of these documents? Does any one of them have any utilitarian element? Why is the utilitarian theory—so popular among philosophers and American courts—so little represented in these statements?

Should any of these statements be enforceable in law? Should they be enforceable in some other way? Does it make sense to approve and accept these statements but maintain them as unenforceable exhortations? As you read the material in the rest of this casebook, ask yourself whether the expectations of these oaths and codes have been accepted by the courts, formally or informally, whether they have been rejected by the courts, or whether they have been ignored by the courts.

OATH OF HIPPOCRATES

I swear by Apollo the physician, and Aesculapius and Health, and All-heal, and all the gods and goddesses, that, according to my ability and judgment, I will keep this Oath and this stipulation—to reckon him who taught me this Art equally dear to me as my parents, to share my substance with him, and relieve his necessities if required; to look upon his offspring in the same footing as my own brothers, and to teach them this Art, if they shall wish to learn it, without fee or stipulation; and that by precept, lecture and every other mode of instruction, I will impart a knowledge of the Art to my own sons, and those of my teachers, and to disciples bound by a stipulation and oath according to the law of medicine, but to none other. I will follow that system of regimen which, according to my ability and judgment, I consider for the benefit of my patients, and abstain from whatever is deleterious and mischievous. I will give no deadly medicine to anyone if asked, nor suggest any such counsel; and in like manner I will not give to a woman a pessary to produce abortion. With purity and with holiness I will pass my life and practice my Art. I will not cut persons laboring under the stone, but will leave this to be done by men who are practitioners of this work. Into whatever houses I enter, I will go into them for the benefit of the sick, and will abstain from every voluntary act of mischief and corruption; and, further, from the seduction of females, or males, of freemen or slaves. Whatever, in connection with my professional practice, or not in connection with it, I see or hear, in the life of men, which ought not to be spoken of abroad, I will not divulge, as reckoning that all such should be kept secret. While I continue to keep this Oath un-violated, may it be granted to me to enjoy life and the practice of the Art, respected by all men, in all times. But should I trespass and violate this Oath, may the reverse be my lot.

PRAYER OF MAIMONIDES

Almighty God, Thou has created the human body with infinite wisdom. Ten thousand times ten thousand organs hast Thou combined in it that act unceasingly and harmoniously to preserve the whole in all its beauty—the body which is the envelope of the immortal soul. They are ever acting in perfect order, agreement and accord. Yet, when the frailty of matter or the unbridling of passions deranges this order or interrupts this accord, then forces clash and the body crumbles into the primal dust from which it came. Thou sendest to man diseases as beneficent messengers to foretell approaching danger and to urge him to avert it.

Thou has blest Thine earth, Thy rivers and Thy mountains with healing substances; they enable Thy creatures to alleviate their sufferings and to heal their illnesses. Thou hast endowed man with the wisdom to relieve the suffering of his brother, to recognize his disorders, to extract the healing substances, to discover their powers and to prepare and to apply them to suit every ill. In Thine Eternal Providence Thou hast chosen me to watch over the life and health of Thy creatures. I am now about to apply myself to the duties of my profession. Support me, Almighty God, in these great labors that they may benefit mankind, for without Thy help not even the least thing will succeed.

Inspire me with love for my art and for Thy creatures. Do not allow thirst for profit, ambition for renown and admiration, to interfere with my profession, for these are the enemies of truth and of love for mankind and they can lead astray in the great task of attending to the welfare of Thy creatures. Preserve the strength of my body and of my soul that they ever be ready to cheerfully help and support rich and poor, good and bad, enemy as well as friend. In the sufferer let me see only the human being. Illumine my mind that it recognize what presents itself and that it may comprehend what is absent or hidden. Let it not fail to see what is visible, but do not permit it to arrogate to itself the power to see what cannot be seen, for delicate and indefinite are the bounds of the great art of caring for the lives and health of Thy creatures. Let me never be absent-minded. May no strange thoughts divert my attention at the bedside of the sick, or disturb my mind in its silent labors, for great and sacred are the thoughtful deliberations required to preserve the lives and health of Thy creatures.

Grant that my patients have confidence in me and my art and follow my directions and my counsel. Remove from their midst all charlatans and the whole host of officious relatives and know-all nurses, cruel people who arrogantly frustrate the wisest purposes of our art and often lead Thy creatures to their death.

Should those who are wiser than I wish to improve and instruct me, let my soul gratefully follow their guidance; for vast is the extent of our art. Should conceited fools, however, censure me, then let love for my profession steel me against them, so that I remain steadfast without regard for age, for reputation, or for honor, because surrender would bring to Thy creatures sickness and death.

Imbue my soul with gentleness and calmness when older colleagues, proud of their age, wish to displace me or to scorn me or disdainfully to teach me. May even this be of advantage to me, for they know many things of which I am ignorant, but let not their arrogance give me pain. For they are old and old age is not master of the passions. I also hope to attain old age upon this earth, before Thee, Almighty God!

Let me be contented in everything except in the great science of my profession. Never allow the thought to arise in me that I have attained to sufficient knowledge, but vouchsafe to me the strength, the leisure and the ambition ever to extend my knowledge. For art is great, but the mind of man is ever expanding.

Almighty God! Thou hast chosen me in Thy mercy to watch over the life and death of Thy creatures. I now apply myself to my profession. Support me in this great task so that it may benefit mankind, for without Thy help not even the least thing will succeed.

AMERICAN MEDICAL ASSOCIATION'S PRINCIPLES OF MEDICAL ETHICS

(2001)

PREAMBLE

The medical profession has long subscribed to a body of ethical statements developed primarily for the benefit of the patient. As a member of this profession, a physician must recognize responsibility to patients first and foremost, as well as to society, to other health professionals, and to self. The following Principles adopted by the American Medical Association are not laws, but standards of conduct which define the essentials of honorable behavior for the physician.

PRINCIPLES OF MEDICAL ETHICS

I.   A physician shall be dedicated to providing competent medical care, with compassion and respect for human dignity and rights.

II.   A physician shall uphold the standards of professionalism, be honest in all professional interactions, and strive to report physicians deficient in character or competence, or engaging in fraud or deception, to appropriate entities.

III. A physician shall respect the law and also recognize a responsibility to seek changes in those requirements which are contrary to the best interests of the patient.

IV. A physician shall respect the rights of patients, colleagues, and other health professionals, and shall safeguard patient confidences and privacy within the constraints of the law.

V. A physician shall continue to study, apply, and advance scientific knowledge, maintain a commitment to medical education, make relevant information available to patients, colleagues, and the public, obtain consultation, and use the talents of other health professionals when indicated.

VI. A physician shall, in the provision of appropriate patient care, except in emergencies, be free to choose whom to serve, with whom to associate, and the environment in which to provide medical care.

VII. A physician shall recognize a responsibility to participate in activities contributing to the improvement of the community and the betterment of public health.

VIII. A physician shall, while caring for a patient, regard responsibility to the patient as paramount.

IX. A physician shall support access to medical care for all people.

Problem: Drafting a Professional Code of Ethics

You are legal counsel to several medical professional organizations, including organizations of physicians, nurses, and health care administrators, and you have been asked to draft codes of ethics for these organizations. From whom would you seek advice as you began such a drafting process? What information would you need? Draft an appropriate code of ethics for any one of these professions, and also draft an oath (or affirmation) the professionals should take upon becoming a member of the organization.

Chapter 2

HUMAN REPRODUCTION AND BIRTH

The rights, obligations, privileges, and relationships previously described in this book are generally rights, obligations, privileges, and relationships of people. But who ought to be recognized as a person, subject to the principles that apply to persons, and not to human limbs, individual cells, hair pieces, animals, disembodied souls, hospitals, state legislatures or other entities? While a fertilized ovum is life in some form, so is a single still-functioning liver cell taken from the body of a person who died yesterday. Is there a difference in these two entities? When does a person, entitled to formal legal respect as such, come into existence? When does one who is so defined go out of existence? The obvious answers—at the point of life and at the point of death—are fraught with ambiguities that can be resolved only through an analysis of medicine, ethics, law, social history, anthropology, theology and other disciplines which seek to answer the basic questions of human existence. Physicians and lawyers have been deeply involved in determining when life begins and when it ends, and it is therefore appropriate to consider these issues in this text. The first portion of this chapter deals with the definition of human life; the definition of death is taken up in the next chapter.

Physicians and lawyers have also been deeply involved in developing and defining new forms of procreation, and in determining the role that society ought to play in limiting and facilitating reproduction. Issues surrounding contraception, genetic screening (and control and protection of those involved in this process), sterilization, abortion, the social allocation of the cost of failed reproduction, potential fetal-maternal conflicts, and government intervention to preserve sexuality (in outlawing practices that result in genital mutilation, for example) have all been addressed by law-makers, in either a judicial or legislative forum. In addition, such forms of facilitating reproduction as artificial insemination, *in vitro* fertilization, ovum transfer and surrogacy have also been addressed in legal fora. The second portion of this chapter examines the interdisciplinary debate that has given rise to legal intervention that may result in limiting or facilitating reproduction.

Problem: Death During Pregnancy

Ms. Baggins was carrying a fetus in the twenty-fifth week of gestation when the automobile she was driving was struck by a truck racing away from a convenience store and pursued by a city police car. The driver of the truck, who was unlicensed and highly intoxicated, was attempting to escape after committing an armed robbery at the convenience store when the collision occurred. The truck struck the driver's door of Ms. Baggins's car and flung her through the passenger window onto the ground about thirty feet from the car. The chasing police officer arrested the intoxicated driver, who was subsequently charged with armed robbery, driving while intoxicated, and driving without a license. The police officer did not call for medical help for Ms. Baggins, and no ambulance came for her until a passing motorist called the fire department. The ambulance arrived to find her unconscious.

When Ms. Baggins arrived at the hospital, physicians immediately provided her cardiopulmonary support. An examination revealed that the fetus she was carrying had suffered serious cranial injuries which could result in severe brain dysfunction if the child were born alive. Tests done about 24 hours after Ms. Baggins's admission to the hospital indicated no spontaneous activity in any part of her brain. Physicians have determined that maintaining Ms. Baggins on the cardiopulmonary support systems would provide the only chance for the fetus to be born alive.

Ms. Baggins was widowed in the fifth month of her pregnancy, two months ago. Her only living relatives are her two sisters, whom she despises. In fact, to avoid the possibility that they might inherit some of her wealth, last month she executed a will leaving all of her property to "my children, and, if I have none at the time of my death, to the National Abortion Rights League and the American Eugenics Society."

What actions should the hospital staff take in this case? Should Ms. Baggins be maintained on cardiopulmonary support, or should she be removed?

Consider the medical, social, political and legal (both civil and criminal) consequences of your actions as you read this chapter.

I. WHEN DOES HUMAN LIFE BECOME A "PERSON"?

This society has had difficulty defining who is a "person." In part, this arises out of the different and inconsistent purposes for which we seek a definition. The "person" from whom we wish to harvest a kidney for transplantation is likely to be different from the "person" who is protected by the Fourteenth Amendment, federal civil rights laws, and various other federal and state laws. Even when the purpose of the definition is settled—as when we seek to know who is a person able to bring an action under state tort law—there is no consensus on when the status of "personhood" first attaches. The most obvious definition of personhood is a recursive one: a human being (and, thus, a "person") is the reproductive product of other human beings. Even if we accept this "human stock" definition of person, however, the inquiry remains open. Does that human stock become a person, for tort law or other purposes, upon conception? Upon quickening? Upon viability? Upon birth? A year after birth? Upon physical maturity?

The definition of "person" is not limited to various stages in the development of human stock. "Personhood" could commence upon ensoulment, upon the development of self concept, upon the development of a sense of personal history, or upon the ability to communicate through language. The resolution of the question appears to require a resort to first principles.

In the vast majority of cases, it is not difficult to distinguish a person from something else. You are easily distinguishable from your arms, your dog, your insurance company and your gold bust of Elvis, as close as you may feel to each of them. The most difficult questions tend to arise at the very beginning and at the very end of human life. Just as you may be able to identify the fact that you were in love, but not be able to identify exactly when it began, or the moment when it ended, the beginnings and the endings of "personhood" are the fuzzy portions.

There are limits to what may reasonably be considered a "person," even when we limit our consideration to human stock. No one suggests that anything independent of the unified sperm and ovum, or its consequences, ought to be considered a person. A great many religious groups consider "personhood" to attach at conception. Aristotle viewed the development of the person as a three stage process, going from vegetable (at conception), to animal (in utero), to rational (sometime after birth). For many centuries, Christian theology fixed the point of "immediate animation" when the fetus was "ensouled" as forty days after conception for males and eighty days after conception for females. St. Thomas Aquinas determined that the ensoulment took place at the time of quickening, usually fourteen to eighteen weeks after conception, and his determination had a very substantial effect on the development of the common law in England and in this country. Recently some philosophers have suggested that "personhood," at least to the extent that it includes a right to life, depends on attributes that are not likely to be developed until sometime after birth. For example, Michael Tooley, a philosopher, defends infanticide on the grounds that it is indistinguishable from abortion and that neither constitutes the improper killing of a human being because there can be no human being until the being possesses a concept of itself as a continuing subject of experiences and other mental states, and recognizes that it is such a continuing entity. Professor Tooley suggests that this occurs sometime after birth, perhaps many weeks after birth. M. Tooley, *Abortion and Infanticide* (1983).

The most comprehensive set of attributes of personhood has been developed by Joseph Fletcher, a bioethicist. Consider his fifteen criteria, described below, and determine whether some or all of them can be used to properly define who is your colleague in personhood and who is not. Consider whether the fact that many of these criteria disqualify fetuses, newborns, and the seriously developmentally disabled affects their acceptability as standards. Further, does the fact that some animal or some man-made machine might eventually fulfill all of these criteria cause you to doubt their validity? What are the consequences of our failure to define a cloned person, a highly intelligent and communicative ape, or a robot as a "person" in terms of our conceptions of "democracy" and "slavery," for example?

A. THE ATTRIBUTES OF PERSONHOOD

JOSEPH FLETCHER, "HUMANNESS," IN HUMANHOOD: ESSAYS IN BIOMEDICAL ETHICS

12–16 (1979).

Synthetic concepts such as human and man and person require operational terms, spelling out the which and what and when. Only in that way can we get down to cases—to normative decisions. There are always some people who prefer to be visceral and affective in their moral choices, with no desire to have any rationale for what they do. But ethics is precisely the business of rational, critical reflection (encephalic and not merely visceral) about the problems of the moral agent—in biology and medicine as much as in law, government, education, or anything else.

To that end, then, for the purposes of biomedical ethics, I now turn to a *profile of man* in concrete and discrete terms.* * * There is time only to itemize the inventory, not to enlarge upon it, but I have fifteen positive propositions. Let me set them out, in no rank order at all, and as hardly more than a list of criteria or indicators, by simple title.

1. Minimum Intelligence

Mere biological life, before minimal intelligence is achieved or after it is lost irretrievably, is without personal status.

2. Self-awareness

* * *

3. Self-control

If an individual is not only not controllable by others (unless by force) but not controllable by the individual himself or herself, a low level of life is reached about on a par with that of a paramecium. * * *

4. A Sense of Time

* * *

5. A Sense of Futurity

How "truly human" is any man who cannot realize there is a time yet to come as well as the present? Subhuman animals do not look forward in time; they live only on what we might call visceral strivings, appetites. Philosophical anthropologies (one recalls that of William Temple, the Archbishop of Canterbury, for instance) commonly emphasize purposiveness as a key to humanness. Chesterton once remarked that we would never ask a puppy what manner of dog it wanted to be when it grows up. * * *

6. A Sense of the Past

* * *

7. The Capability to Relate to Others

Interpersonal relationships, of the sexual-romantic and friendship kind, are of the greatest importance for the fullness of what we idealize as being truly personal. * * *

8. Concern for Others

Some people may be skeptical about our capacity to care about others (what in Christian ethics is often distinguished from romance and friendship as "neighbor love" or "neighbor concern"). * * * But whether concern for others is disinterested or inspired by enlightened self-interest, it seems plain that a conscious extra-ego orientation is a trait of the species * * *.

9. Communication

Utter alienation or disconnection from others, if it is irreparable, is dehumanization. * * *

10. Control of Existence

It is of the nature of man that he is not helplessly subject to the blind workings of physical or physiological nature. He has only finite knowledge, freedom, and initiative, but what he has of it is real and effective. * * *

11. Curiosity

To be without affect, sunk in *anomie,* is to be not a person. Indifference is inhuman. Man is a learner and a knower as well as a tool maker and user. * * *

12. Change and Changeability

To the extent that an individual is unchangeable or opposed to change, he denies the creativity of personal beings. It means not only the fact of biological and physiological change, which goes on as a condition of life, but the capacity and disposition for changing one's mind and conduct as well. Biologically, human beings are developmental: birth, life, health, and death are processes, not events, and are to be understood progressively, not episodically. All human existence is on a continuum, a matter of becoming. * * *

13. Balance of Rationality and Feeling

* * * As human beings we are not coldly rational or cerebral, nor are we merely creatures of feeling and intuition. It is a matter of being both, in different combinations from one individual to another. * * *

14. Idiosyncrasy

The human being is idiomorphous, a distinctive individual. * * * To be a person is to have an identity, to be recognizable and callable by name.

15. Neocortical Function

In a way, this is the cardinal indicator, the one all the others are hinged upon. Before cerebration is in play, or with its end, in the absence of the synthesizing function of the cerebral cortex, the person is nonexistent. Such individuals are objects but not subjects. This is so no matter how many other spontaneous or artificially supported functions persist in the heart, lungs, neurologic and vascular systems. Such noncerebral processes are not personal. * * * But what is definitive in determining death is the loss of cerebration, not just of any or all brain function. Personal reality depends on cerebration and to be dead "humanly" speaking is to be excerebral, no matter how long the body remains alive.

Notes and Questions

1. Which attributes does Fletcher consider to be necessary for personhood? Are any sufficient? Would you add any others to his list? Is there any underlying principle that describes the fifteen attributes selected by Fletcher? Are they all really a subset of the first?

2. Which attributes of personhood, if any, does Ms. Baggins or her fetus possess?

3. Dr. Fletcher commenced a serious debate over whether the persons protected by law ought to be defined in terms of attributes we wish to protect or in terms of the human stock from which the person is created. Both forms of definition may be valuable for different purposes. We provide some rights to people because they possess many or all of the attributes that distinguish human beings. The right to make medical decisions, based on the autonomy of individuals, is not accorded to those without some "minimum intelligence." On the other hand, we provide minimally adequate housing, food, medical care, and other necessities for those of human stock, even when they do not meet some of Dr. Fletcher's criteria, and even when we do not provide those same benefits to others, (e.g., animals) who fail the same criteria. In the end, the Fletcher propositions may be useful in determining some of the rights of persons and the "human stock" definition may be helpful in determining others. Just as property is often described as a bundle of rights, it may turn out that "personhood" is a bundle of rights that need to be separated out and individually analyzed.

4. As we saw earlier, even the adoption of a "human stock" definition does not answer the question of when that human stock becomes a person. What is the attribute of the human stock that makes it a person—genetic uniqueness? Responsiveness? The potential to be born? The appearance of a human being? Consider the following list of the alternative medical points of personhood.

C.R. AUSTIN, HUMAN EMBRYOS: THE DEBATE ON ASSISTED REPRODUCTION

22–31 (1989).

When does a person's life really begin?

* * * Probably most people who were asked this question would answer "at fertilization" (or "conception"). Certainly, several interesting and unusual things happen then—it is really the most *obvious* event to pick—but for biologists the preceding and succeeding cellular processes are *equally* important. Nevertheless, "fertilization" continues to be the cry of many religious bodies and indeed also of the august World Medical Association, who, in 1949, adopted the Geneva Convention Code of Medical Ethics, which contains the clause: "I will maintain the utmost respect for human life from the time of conception." So we do need to look more closely at this choice, for a generally acceptable "beginning" for human life would be a great help in reaching ethical and legal consensus.

In the first place human *life,* as such, obviously begins before fertilization, since the egg or oocyte is alive before sperm entry, as were innumerable antecedent cells, back through the origin of species into the mists of time. A more practical starting point would be that of the life of the human *individual,* so it is individuality that we should be looking for, at least as one of the essential criteria. Now the earliest antecedents of the eggs, as of sperm, are the primordial germ cells, which can be seen as a group of distinctive little entities migrating through the tissues of the early embryo. When they first become recognizable, they number only about a dozen or two, but they multiply fast and soon achieve large numbers, reaching a peak of 7–10 million about 6 months after conception. Then, despite continued active cell division, there is a dramatic decline in the cell population, which has tempted people to suggest that some sort of "selection of the fittest" occurs, but there is no good evidence in support of this idea; nor is there any good reason to look for individuality in that mercurial population. In due course, the primordial germ cells, while still undergoing cell divisions, settle down in the tissues of the future ovary, change subtly in their characteristics, and thus become oogonia; and then, soon after birth, *cell division ceases,* the cells develop large nuclei and are now recognizable as primary oocytes. From now on, there are steady cell losses but no further cell divisions * * *; it is the same entity that was a primary oocyte, becomes a fertilized egg, and then develops as an embryo. The primary oocytes are very unusual cells, for they have the capacity to live for much longer than most other body cells; the *same* oocytes can be seen in the ovaries of women approaching the menopause—cells that have lived for about 40 years or longer. And it is with the emergence of the primary oocytes that we can hail the start of *individuality.* Then, in those oocytes that are about to be ovulated, the first meiotic division takes place—another important step, for the "shuffling" of genes that occurs at that point bestows *genetic uniqueness* on the oocyte. So both individuality and genetic uniqueness are established before sperm penetration and fertilization; these processes have distinctly different actions—providing the stimulus that initiates cleavage and contributing to biparental inheritance. Thus, the preferred choice for the start of the human individual should surely be the formation of the primary oocyte, but there is certainly no unanimity on this score.

Passing over now the popularity of fertilization, for many people it is instead the emergence of the embryonic disc and primitive streak that most appeals as the stage in which to identify the start of "personhood" (one or more persons, in view of the imminent possibility of twinning), and there is much to support this opinion. Here, for the first time, are structures that are designed to have a different destiny than *all the rest of the embryo*—they represent the primordium of the fetus, and the developmental patterns of embryo and fetus progressively diverge from this stage onwards. An additional point is that this new emergence is not inevitable, for in around one in two-thousand pregnancies the embryo grows, often to quite a large size, but there is no fetus; the clinical conditions are known as blighted ovum, dropsical ovum, hydatidiform mole, etc. Evidence suggests that hydatidiform mole is attributable to fertilization of a faulty egg, the embryo developing only under the influence of the sperm chromosomes.

At the time of appearance of the embryonic disc, and shortly beforehand, the process of implantation is occurring, and this is considered by many to have special significance in relation to embryonic potential—so far as we know, implantation cannot occur once the development of the embryo has passed the stage when interaction with * * * the uterus normally takes place.

But despite all that has been said, there are still many folk who remain unconvinced—is the being at this stage sufficiently "human" to qualify as the start of a person? After all, the disc is just a collection of similar cells, virtually undifferentiated, poorly delineated from its surroundings, about a fifth of a millimetre long, non-sentient, and without the power of movement. It is in no way a "body" and it does not bear the faintest resemblance to a human being—*and* the soul cannot enter yet, for the disc may yet divide in the process of twinning, and the soul being unique is indivisible. Also, it is argued that we should be looking for some spark of personality, and a moral philosopher has proposed that some sort of responsiveness is an essential feature.

One of the earliest succeeding changes in the direction of humanness could be the development of the heart primordium, and soon after that the beginnings of a circulatory system; the first contractions of the heart muscle occur possibly as early as day 21, with a simple tubular heart at that stage, and in the fourth week a functional circulation begins. With the heart beats we have the first movements initiated within the embryo (?fetus) and thus in a way the first real "sign of life." The conceptus is now about 6 mm long. During the fifth and sixth weeks, nerve fibres grow out from the spinal cord and make contact with muscles, so that at this time or soon afterwards, a mechanical or electrical stimulus might elicit a muscle twitch; this is important for it would be the first indication of sentient existence—of "responsiveness." At this stage, too, the embryo could possibly feel pain. But, still, some would find cause to demur: only an expert could tell that this embryo/fetus, now 12–13 mm in length, with branchial arches (corresponding to the "gill-slits" in non-mammalian embryos), stubby limbs, and a prominent tail, is human. A marginally more acceptable applicant is the fetus at 7½ weeks, when the hands and feet can be seen to have fingers and toes, and thereafter physical resemblance steadily improves; also at this time, a special gene on the Y-chromosome (the "testis-determining factor" or TDF) is switched on, and the fetuses that have this chromosome, the males, proceed thenceforward to develop *as* males, distinguishable from females.

At about 12 weeks, electrical activity can be detected in the brain of the fetus, which could signal the dawn of consciousness. Here, we would seem to have a very logical stage marking the *start* of a person, for the cessation of electrical activity in the brain ("brain death") is accepted in both medical and legal circles as marking the *termination* of a person—as an indication that life no longer exists in victims of accidents or in patients with terminal illnesses. Around the fourth or fifth month of pregnancy, the mother first experiences movements of the fetus ('quickening'), which were regarded by St. Thomas Aquinas as the first indication of life, for he believed that life was distinguished by two features, knowledge and movement; moreover, it would seem logical that the fetus would move when the *animus* (life or soul) took up residence.[1] * * *

At about 24 weeks, the fetus reaches a state in which it can commonly survive outside the maternal body, with assistance. * * * Just which stage marks the start of a person's life is a matter of personal opinion. Much of the foregoing argumentation may seem to some people difficult to comprehend, especially if they have not had formal training in biology, and to others may even seem irrelevant, in view of the firm line taken by many church authori-

---

1. The modern equivalent would be at about day 21, when the heart begins to beat.

ties. But it really is important that we should try to reach a consensus on just when a person's life should be held to begin, for the decision does have important practical consequences—it directly affects the rights of other embryos, of fetuses, and of people.

B. LEGAL RECOGNITION OF THE BEGINNING OF HUMAN LIFE

The law is increasingly forced to confront the question of when rights and privileges of persons attach to fetuses and young children. While children have always been treated differently from adults in the law, those fundamental common law and constitutional rights that uniformly extend to both competent and incompetent adults also have been extended to children from the time of birth. Courts have had greater difficulty determining which rights, if any, attach to a fetus.

The trend over the past twenty years has been for states to expand the common law rights of the fetus and to recognize that the fetus can be an independent victim for purposes of the criminal law. For example, most states now permit a tort action to be filed by an estate of a stillborn child. Just fifteen years ago, the vast majority of states required that the child be born alive before any right to sue would attach. Similarly, many states now extend the protection of their homicide law to fetuses; several years ago that extension was very unusual. The extent of any constitutional protection of fetuses is far less certain.

1. *Constitutional Recognition*

While the Supreme Court has never formally determined when a fetus becomes a "person" for constitutional purposes, it has not been able to completely avoid that question despite its several attempts to finesse it. Indeed, some commentators thought that the matter was finally resolved in the watershed case of Roe v. Wade, 410 U.S. 113, 93 S.Ct. 705, 35 L.Ed.2d 147 (1973), in which the Supreme Court was called upon to determine whether a fetus was a person for purposes of the protections of the Fourteenth Amendment. While *Roe v. Wade* will be considered in some greater detail below, it is significant to know that the Court held that the term "person," at least as that term appears in the Fourteenth Amendment, was not intended to encompass the fetus. After reviewing over 2,000 years of the history of abortion the Court addressed the question directly:

> The appellee and certain amici argue that the fetus is a "person" within the language and meaning of the Fourteenth Amendment. In support of this, they outline at length and in detail the well-known facts of fetal development. If this suggestion of personhood is established, the appellant's case, of course, collapses, for the fetus' right to life is then guaranteed specifically by the Amendment. The appellant conceded as much on reargument. On the other hand, the appellee conceded on reargument that no case could be cited that holds that a fetus is a person within the meaning of the Fourteenth Amendment.
>
> The Constitution does not define "person" in so many words. Section 1 of the Fourteenth Amendment contains three references to "person." The first, in defining "citizens," speaks of "persons born or naturalized in the United States." The word also appears both in the Due Process

Clause and in the Equal Protection Clause. "Person" is used in other places in the Constitution: in the listing of qualifications for Representatives and Senators, Art I, § 2, cl 2, and § 3, cl 3; in the Apportionment Clause, Art I, § 2, cl 3;[2] in the Migration and Importation provision, Art I, § 9, cl 1; in the Emolument Clause, Art I, § 9, cl 8; in the Electors provisions, Art II, § 1, cl 2, and the superseded cl 3; in the provision outlining qualifications for the office of President, Art II, § 1, cl 5; in the Extradition provisions, Art IV, § 2, cl 2, and the superseded Fugitive Slave Clause 3; and in the Fifth, Twelfth, and Twenty-second Amendments, as well as in §§ 2 and 3 of the Fourteenth Amendment. But in nearly all these instances, the use of the word is such that it has application only postnatally. None indicates, with any assurance, that it has any possible prenatal application.[3]

* * *

All this, together with our observation * * * that throughout the major portion of the 19th century prevailing legal abortion practices were far freer than they are today, persuades us that the word "person," as used in the Fourteenth Amendment, does not include the unborn. * * * 410 U.S. at 156–157, 93 S.Ct. at 728–729.

The Supreme Court recognized that there were protectable interests beyond those specified in the Constitution and determined:

[W]e do not agree that, by adopting one theory of life, Texas may override the rights of the pregnant woman that are at stake. We repeat, however, that the state does have an important and legitimate interest in preserving and protecting the health of the pregnant woman * * *, and that it has still *another* important and legitimate interest in protecting the potentiality of human life. 410 U.S. at 162, 93 S.Ct. at 731.

Thus, a state may be able to define and protect rights in the fetus, but these are not the Fourteenth Amendment rights of "persons."

Of course, the continued viability of *Roe v. Wade* itself has been called into question continually since 1973. See section II, below. In Webster v. Reproductive Health Services, 492 U.S. 490, 109 S.Ct. 3040, 106 L.Ed.2d 410 (1989), the Supreme Court reviewed a Missouri statute that restricted the availability of abortions in several ways. In addition, that statute included a preamble that defined personhood:

1.   The general assembly of this state finds that:

2. We are not aware that in the taking of any census under this clause, a fetus has ever been counted.

3. When Texas urges that a fetus is entitled to Fourteenth Amendment protection as a person, it faces a dilemma. Neither in Texas nor in any other State are all abortions prohibited. Despite broad proscription, an exception always exists. The exception contained in Art 1196, for an abortion procured or attempted by medical advice for the purpose of saving the life of the mother, is typical. But if the fetus is a person who is not to be deprived of life without due process of law, and if the mother's condition is the sole determinant, does not the

Texas exception appear to be out of line with the Amendment's command?

There are other inconsistencies between Fourteenth Amendment status and the typical abortion statute. It has already been pointed out [ ] that in Texas the woman is not a principal or an accomplice with respect to an abortion upon her. If the fetus is a person, why is the woman not a principal or an accomplice? Further, the penalty for criminal abortion specified by Art 1195 is significantly less than the maximum penalty for murder prescribed by Art 1257 of the Texas Penal Code. If the fetus is a person, may the penalties be different?

(1) the life of each human being begins at conception;

(2) unborn children have protectable interests in life, health, and well being; * * *

2. * * * the laws of this state shall be interpreted and construed to acknowledge on behalf of the unborn child at every stage of development, all the rights, privileges, and immunities available to other persons, citizens, and residents of this state, subject only to the Constitution of the United States, and decisional interpretations thereof. * * *

3. As used in this section, the term "unborn children" or "unborn child" shall include all unborn child or children or the offspring of human beings from the moment of conception until birth at every stage of biological development. * * *

Vernon's Ann.Mo.Stat. § 1.205. This preamble was attacked on the grounds that it was beyond the constitutional authority of the state legislature to define personhood, at least to the extent that the definition extended personhood to pre-viable fetuses. The Supreme Court sidestepped that question by concluding that the preamble was nothing more than a state value judgment favoring childbirth over abortion, and that such a value judgment was clearly within the authority of the legislature.

There are two separate constitutional issues that surround the definition of person. First, is there a definition of "person" for purposes of the Constitution? Second, do the substantive provisions of the Constitution put any limit on the way that *states* may define "person" for any other purpose? Could each state define "person" differently for constitutional purposes? States effectively did so before the Thirteenth Amendment, of course. Could the definition of "person" for constitutional purposes be different from that definition for other purposes?

2. Statutory Recognition

As Justice Blackmun pointed out in *Roe v. Wade,* courts have generally considered killing a fetus to be substantially different from killing a person who was born alive. This is reflected in the different penalties that usually attach to feticide and other forms of homicide and the fact that feticide itself has been distinguished from murder or manslaughter in most jurisdictions. Over the past several years, however, some states have made the penalties for feticide commensurate with the penalties for homicide, and several have promulgated new homicide statutes that explicitly include fetuses as those whose death may give rise to homicide prosecutions. Most commonly, these statutes seek to impose the homicide penalty on one who kills an "unborn child," although the California statute provides:

Murder is the unlawful killing of a human being, *or a fetus,* with malice aforethought.

Cal. Penal Code Sec. 187(a). The words "or a fetus" were added to the statute in 1970 in reaction to a California Supreme Court decision, Keeler v. Superior Court, 2 Cal.3d 619, 87 Cal.Rptr. 481, 470 P.2d 617 (1970), which defined "human being" as a person born alive.

The statutes which do not distinguish between viable and nonviable fetal victims of a homicide have been unsuccessfully attacked on due process and equal protection grounds in at least three states. The due process attack is two pronged. First, criminal defendants argue that the statutes violate their due process rights because they apply even when the perpetrator (and, for that matter, the pregnant woman) do not know of the existence of the pregnancy. As the Minnesota court said in rejecting such an argument, though, "[t]he fair warning rule has never been understood to excuse criminal liability simply because the defendant's victim proves not to be the victim the defendant had in mind." State v. Merrill, 450 N.W.2d 318, 323 (Minn.1990). Second, defendants argue that terms like "unborn child" are unconstitutionally vague because it is uncertain when a conceptus, embryo or fetus becomes an "unborn child." As an Illinois appellate court pointed out, the statute "only requires proof that whatever the entity within the mother's womb is called, it had life, and, because of the acts of the defendant, it no longer does." People v. Ford, 221 Ill.App.3d 354, 163 Ill.Dec. 766, 777, 581 N.E.2d 1189, 1200 (1991).

The defendant's equal protection argument is based in the failure of the statutes to distinguish between viable and nonviable fetuses. Defendants have argued that the state makes an improper distinction when it treats some who end the life of a nonviable fetus as murderers, while others, including the pregnant woman herself and her doctor, who are protected by the Constitutionally recognized right to an abortion, are not treated as murderers. This argument has also failed to garner a majority in any state. See State v. Merrill, supra, and People v. Ford, supra.

The California statute was upheld and applied to both nonviable and viable fetuses by a divided court in People v. Davis, 7 Cal.4th 797, 30 Cal.Rptr.2d 50, 872 P.2d 591 (1994), where the Court found that the history of applying the statute only when the victim was a viable fetus required that it be applied to cases where the victims were nonviable fetuses only prospectively, and not to the case before it. The dissent argued that the majority's application of the statute to nonviable fetuses "will make our murder law unique in the nation in its severity: it appears that in no other state is it a capital offense to cause the death of a nonviable and invisible fetus that the actor neither knew nor had reason to know existed." 30 Cal.Rptr.2d at 79, 872 P.2d at 620. For an excellent survey of the way state laws now deal with feticide, an account of those that criminalize only the killing of a viable fetus and those that also criminalize the killing of a nonviable fetus, and a survey of punishments imposed on those whose acts result in the death of a fetus, see People v. Davis, 30 Cal.Rptr.2d at 79–83, 872 P.2d at 621–623 (Mosk, J. dissenting).

In State v. Merrill, supra, the majority distinguished human life from "personhood," and determined that the feticide statute was designed to protect human life, not persons. Could the legislature also protect other forms of human life—human blood cells, for example—in the same way that it has decided to protect "nonperson" human life in this case, or is the potential personhood of the embryo fundamental to the majority's decision that the statute's protection of human life is constitutional?

Do you agree with the decisions in Merrill, Ford and Davis? Whose interests were really at stake in those cases? To what extent should these courts depend upon the interests of the pregnant woman, and to what extent should the courts depend on the interests of the embryo or fetus in deciding these cases?

In her dissent in the Merrill case, Justice Wahl argues that Roe v. Wade forbids a state from treating a nonviable fetus like a person, at least for purposes of the criminal law. How strong is that argument? For purposes of the homicide law, is there any reason to draw a line between a viable and a nonviable fetus if the mother of each intends to carry the fetus in utero to term? If not, why have so many states decided to criminalize only the killing of a viable fetus? Might it be that at the point of viability the fact of pregnancy is likely to be obvious to the assailant? Are any purposes of the criminal law served by application of a feticide statute to a case (like the Merrill case) in which neither the pregnant woman nor the assailant knew of the pregnancy?

The Supreme Court of South Carolina found a woman guilty of "child abuse resulting in death" of her stillborn child as a consequence of her prenatal use of cocaine. State v. McKnight, 352 S.C. 635, 576 S.E.2d 168 (2003). Could the court apply the same criminal statute if the cocaine use resulted in the termination of the mother's pregnancy after the fetus was viable? What if the fetus was not yet viable? What if the illegal drug use resulted in a fertilized ovum not properly implanting in the mother's uterus? Would the 20 year sentence handed down in this case constitute cruel and unusual punishment in any of these cases?

In 2002 the question of the status of the fetus for purposes of the criminal law arose in very different circumstances. Jaclyn Kurr was convicted of voluntary manslaughter when she knifed to death the father of the 17–week fetuses (there were twins) that she was carrying. In the midst of a fight over cocaine use, the father, who had a history of violently attacking Ms. Kurr, came at her and punched her twice in the stomach. She told him not to hit her any more because she was "carrying his babies." As he came at her again, she stabbed him. Although Michigan law recognizes that one may use deadly force in defense of another, the trial court refused her request for an instruction on "defense of others" on the grounds that the fetus was nonviable, and thus could not be an "other" for purposes of Michigan law.

The Michigan Court of Appeal reversed and held that "an individual may indeed defend a fetus from such an assault and may use deadly force if she honestly and reasonably believes the fetus to be in imminent danger of death or great bodily harm." People v. Kurr, 253 Mich.App. 317, 654 N.W.2d 651, 656 (2002). The court based its decision on the state policy of fetal protection that was explicit in Michigan's 1998 Fetal Protection Act.

> We conclude that in this state, the defense should also extend to the protection of a fetus, viable or nonviable, from an assault against the mother, and we base this conclusion primarily on the fetal protection act adopted by the Legislature in 1998. * * *
>
> *The plain language of these provisions shows the Legislature's conclusion that fetuses are worthy of protection as living entities as a matter of public policy.* * * * Moreover, in enacting the fetal protection act, the Legislature did not distinguish between fetuses that are viable, or capable of surviving outside the womb, and those that are nonviable. In fact, the Legislature used the term "embryo" as well as the term "fetus" [in the

relevant statutory sections.] * * * . This definition clearly encompasses nonviable fetuses. Moreover, the legislative analysis of the act indicates that, in passing the act, the Legislature was clearly determined to provide criminal penalties for harm caused to nonviable fetuses during assaults or negligent acts against pregnant women. [ ]

Because the act reflects a public policy to protect even an embryo from unlawful assaultive or negligent conduct, we conclude that the defense of others concept does extend to the protection of a nonviable fetus from an assault against the mother. We emphasize, however, that the defense is available *solely* in the context of an assault against the mother. Indeed, the Legislature has *not* extended the protection of the criminal laws to embryos existing outside a woman's body, i.e., frozen embryos stored for future use, and we therefore *do not* extend the applicability of the defense of others theory to situations involving these embryos.

People v. Kurr, 654 N.W.2d at 654 (italics in original).

The question of the statutory recognition of the fetus as a person has also arisen in litigation over whether state statutes allow for the appointment of a guardian (or a guardian ad litem) for a fetus. For a sense of the deep symbolism attached to such an appointment by all sides in the debate, see the last case in this chapter, Guardianship of J.D.S., 864 So.2d 534 (Fla. App. 2004). See also In re D.K., 204 N.J.Super. 205, 497 A.2d 1298 (1985)(interpreting rules rather than statutes) and In re Brown, 294 Ill. App.3d 159, 228 Ill.Dec. 525, 689 N.E.2d 397 (1997).

3. *Common Law Recognition*

The debate over the common law recognition of the personhood of the fetus has been waged primarily over whether a fetus may recover under state wrongful death and survival statutes. Until recently courts were divided over whether such actions would be permitted only if the decedent were born alive, or whether such actions would be permitted if the decedent had reached the point of viability, even though the decedent was not born alive. In Amadio v. Levin, 509 Pa. 199, 501 A.2d 1085 (1985), the court listed the five reasons courts had traditionally articulated for limiting such actions to children born alive:

First, the Court surmised that the real objective of such a lawsuit was to compensate the parents of the deceased child for their emotional distress, and that since parents already had the ability in their own right to institute such an action, it would only be duplication to permit parents to file a second action on behalf of the estate of the child.

Second, because wrongful death actions are derivative, and since the Court refused to acknowledge that a stillborn child was an individual under the wrongful death or survival statutes, it was concluded that the Acts were not intended to provide for recovery by the estate of a stillborn child.

Third, extending causes of actions to the estates of stillborn children was felt to increase problems of causation and damages.

Fourth, the prior cases arose out of an era when most jurisdictions did not permit the filing of such actions. * * *

Fifth, it was reasoned that since only children born alive may take property by descent under our Intestate Laws, the Court assumed that the Legislature had already limited the creation of causes of actions to those instances where the existence or estate of a child was recognized by the laws of intestacy.

That court rejected those five arguments and determined that the live birth requirement was an arbitrary line that served no purpose of the wrongful death and and survival statute:

> Today's holding merely makes it clear that the recovery afforded the estate of a stillborn is no different than the recovery afforded the estate of a child that dies within seconds of its release from its mother's womb. In view of the current attitude throughout our sister states to let the representatives of the stillborn's estate prove their losses, it would be illogical to continue to deny that such claims could be established, when we permit them for the child that survives birth for an instant.

Others more influenced by the arguments over abortion urged that such actions should be recognized for another reason: the fetus is, they argued, a full human being entitled to all protections accorded to all other human beings. Those who opposed recovery on behalf of fetuses who were not born alive argued that there was no genuine loss that was being compensated in such cases, and that the real reason for permitting the recovery was to allow plaintiffs a greater chance at a larger recovery—i.e., a pro-plaintiff bias.

Many courts now distinguish between a viable and a pre-viable fetus for purposes of recovery under wrongful death and survival statutes. Is such a distinction justifiable? If a fetus becomes a "person" for purposes of commencing a tort action only upon viability, the court must address several questions when it hears a tort action commenced on behalf of a fetus. First, what is the legally relevant moment when the fetus must be viable for that fetus to possess a cause of action—is it the time of the injury or the time of the tortious action? Second, when is a fetus viable as a general matter? Is this a matter of law or fact? Third, was the plaintiff-fetus viable at the legally relevant time in the instant case?

All of these questions were before the court upon a motion for summary judgment in In re Air Crash Disaster at Detroit Metropolitan Airport on August 16, 1987, Rademacher v. McDonnell Douglas Corporation, 737 F.Supp. 427 (E.D.Mich.1989), an action brought on behalf of the fetus of a flight attendant killed in an air crash. The District Court determined that Michigan law would permit recovery on behalf of the fetus only if the fetus were "viable at the time of the injury." Further, the court rejected evidence that fetuses could be viable as early as twenty weeks, and adopted the "generally accepted *Roe [v. Wade]* proposition that viability occurs at twenty-four weeks." Finally, the court concluded:

> [The plaintiff] submits a sonogram report from July 13, 1987, which concludes that the "[e]stimated gestational age is 15.8 +/- 2 weeks." The fatal accident involving Northwest Flight 255 occurred five weeks later.

Therefore, on the date of the accident the * * * fetus was 20.8 weeks old +/- 2 weeks. Therefore, the fetus was, at most, 22.8 weeks old. * * *

Thus, the subject fetus in this case was nonviable as a matter of law [and has no cause of action under Michigan law].

The *Rademacher* case also discusses the irony in allowing the estate of a fetus to recover damages even if the tortious act was committed at a time when the mother could have chosen to abort the fetus. The court suggests that while a mother's interest in terminating a pregnancy may outweigh a state's interest in maintaining the life of a pre-viable fetus, a third party's interest does not overcome both the state's and the mother's interest in continuing the pregnancy. Is this distinction sound? Is there any place for abortion jurisprudence in analyzing the propriety of tort liability for the death of a fetus?

In fact, is there any reason to draw the line for recovery at viability? Why not just permit a wrongful death recovery on behalf of a fetus of any gestational age, from the moment of conception? While this was generally uncharted territory before the 1990s, in the middle of that decade three states suddenly recognized such a cause of action. In Wiersma v. Maple Leaf Farms, 543 N.W.2d 787 (S.D.1996), the South Dakota court, in response to a certified question, announced that the wrongful death statute permitted an action on behalf of a first trimester fetus who was alleged to have been miscarried as a result of salmonella in a frozen dinner consumed by the decedent-fetus's mother. The court treated the case as a simple one of statutory construction: the statute allowed actions on behalf of an "unborn child," and that term was unqualified. The dissent argued that such a term was necessarily ambiguous, and thus it needed to be interpreted. As the dissenting justice pointed out, "The heart of the issue, in my opinion, is whether an action for wrongful death can stand where no sustainable life exists at the time of the negligent act." 543 N.W.2d at 794. Shortly before the South Dakota court rendered its opinion, courts in West Virginia and Missouri had allowed similar actions on behalf of nonviable fetuses. See Connor v. Monkem Co., 898 S.W.2d 89 (Mo.1995) and Farley v. Sartin, 195 W.Va. 671, 466 S.E.2d 522 (1995). Such actions also appear to be allowed in Illinois, see Smith v. Mercy Hosp. and Medical Center, 203 Ill.App.3d 465, 148 Ill.Dec. 567, 560 N.E.2d 1164 (1990) and, after quickening, in Mississippi and Georgia. 66 Federal Credit Union v. Tucker, 853 So.2d 104 (Miss. 2003) and Porter v. Lassiter, 91 Ga.App. 712, 87 S.E.2d 100 (1955).

Consider the Baggins problem above. Would the estate of Ms. Baggins or the estate of her fetus have a tort action against a police department that negligently failed to seek medical assistance for her? Suppose Ms. Baggins is declared dead and then gives birth to a child who lives for two days. Should Ms. Baggins's estate be distributed to the beneficiaries listed in her will, or might her sisters be able to argue successfully that her child inherited her estate, and that they were the heirs of that child? Would your answer be different if Ms. Baggins were declared dead and the fetus were subsequently stillborn? What if Ms. Baggins died before the fetus were even viable? Should any of these distinctions make a legal difference?

A host of cases have considered the issue of whether a wrongful death action may be brought on behalf of a fetus who dies in utero. Among those that have allowed such actions for *viable* fetuses are DiDonato v. Wortman, 320 N.C. 423, 358 S.E.2d 489 (1987); Luff v. Hawkins, 551 A.2d 437 (Del.Super.1988); Summerfield v. Superior Court, 144 Ariz. 467, 698 P.2d 712 (1985); O'Grady v. Brown, 654 S.W.2d 904 (Mo.1983); See also Johnson v. Ruark Obstetrics, 327 N.C. 283, 395 S.E.2d 85 (1990) (permitting recovery for physician's failure to treat maternal diabetes which resulted in the death of a viable fetus) and Terrell v. Rankin, 511 So.2d 126 (Miss.1987) (also permitting a wrongful death action on behalf of a viable fetus for whose mother the physician prescribed medicine for symptoms typical of pregnancy up to the eighth month without ever diagnosing the pregnancy itself). See also Hollis v. Doerflinger, 2003 WL 21266788 (Tenn. App. 2003) (addressing insurance coverage). In New York and Maryland, at least, because a fetus is not a legal person, it is considered a part of the mother for tort law purposes. Thus, an injury to the fetus may be compensable as an injury to the mother. See Smith v. Borello, 370 Md. 227, 804 A.2d 1151 (2002) and Johnson v. Verrilli, 134 Misc.2d 582, 511 N.Y.S.2d 1008 (1987), modified, 139 A.D.2d 497, 526 N.Y.S.2d 600 (1988).

For cases which have not permitted wrongful death recovery for the death of a fetus in utero, see Smith v. Columbus Community Hospital, Inc., 222 Neb. 776, 387 N.W.2d 490 (1986) (dissent suggests that the live birth requirement is inconsistent with the developing theories of causation), Witty v. American General Capital Distributors, Inc., 727 S.W.2d 503 (Tex.1987) (while not a person, a fetus is not a chattel either; thus, mother cannot recover for negligent destruction of a chattel), Milton v. Cary Medical Center, 538 A.2d 252 (Me.1988) (majority depends upon legislative history to show that wrongful death statute intended to include only children born alive; dissent would find power in the courts to interpret the statute in matters unanticipated by the legislature when it first promulgated it). Recently in New York, the Appellate Division confronted a case in which the mother of a stillborn fetus attempted to show that the fetus had some brain activity before the stillbirth to justify an award of damages for the pre-stillbirth pain and suffering of the fetus. The court rejected the argument, maintaining the New York position that "no cause of action lies to recover damages on behalf of a stillborn fetus." Maher v. Yoon, 297 A.D.2d 361, 746 N.Y.S.2d 493 (2002). For an interesting twist on this debate see Remy v. MacDonald, 440 Mass. 675, 801 N.E.2d 260 (2004), where the court found that a pregnant woman owed no duty of care in tort law to her fetus, who sustained injuries as a result of an automobile accident before birth.

Among the courts that have rejected wrongful death actions on behalf of nonviable fetuses are Gentry v. Gilmore, 613 So.2d 1241 (Ala.1993), Ferguson v. District of Columbia, 629 A.2d 15 (D.C.App.1993), and Coveleski v. Bubnis, 535 Pa. 166, 634 A.2d 608 (1993). For a complete account of the cases that have considered this issue, see Sheldon R. Shapiro, Annotation, Right to Maintain Action or to Recover Damages for Death of Unborn Child, 84 ALR3d 411 (1978, and supplements).

II. MEDICAL INTERVENTION IN REPRODUCTION

The law has been invoked regularly to order the relationships of private individuals and to constrain government to its appropriate role with regard to the limitation of reproduction. The law has also been engaged to regulate medical interventions designed to facilitate reproduction, such as artificial insemination, ovum and embryo transfer, in vitro fertilization, and surrogacy. While the propriety of legal intervention in these matters will undoubtedly remain a matter of dispute, the sexual nature of the issues, as well as their novelty and moral complexity, is likely to cause society to maintain a high interest in regulating them. This section of this chapter is not intended to be a comprehensive analysis of all of these questions; many related issues are discussed elsewhere in this text or in other courses. It is the purpose of this section of this chapter to provide structure to those issues surrounding procreation and reproduction that are likely to be of special concern to attorneys representing health care professionals, institutions and their patients.

A. LIMITING REPRODUCTION

1. *Government Prohibitions on Reproduction*

Is there a role for the government in prohibiting reproduction, at least in some circumstances? To control population growth, as China has attempted to do? To serve political, economic, or environmental goals? For eugenic purposes? Dr. Joseph Fletcher has argued that there is a moral obligation to prevent the birth of genetically diseased or defective children, and a failure to carry out that obligation to those children "who would suffer grievously if conceived or born * * * would be tantamount to rejecting the whole notion of preventive medicine, sanitation, environmental protection law, and all the other ways in which we express our obligation to the unborn." Consider the following argument and determine whether it is strong enough to overcome the potential abuses inherent in allowing the government to determine who can reproduce, and under what circumstances.

> My fundamental commitment is that survival of the human species is a good and that it is a good of such importance and value that it can be accredited as a right. From this I deduce that individuals and social units have the concomitant obligation to pursue courses of actions that will foster and protect the right of the species' survival. Among these acknowledged and traditional courses of action is general health care. One segment of that health care involves the protection of the population from the transmission of identifiable, seriously deleterious genes and from debilitating and costly (in terms of natural, economic and human resources) genetic disease which can neither be cured nor treated with any preservation of the quality of life and relative independence of the afflicted. Because individual human rights are negotiable according to their historical context, and because there is legal precedent for restricting the exercise of reproductive rights, those who are at high risk for passing on clearly identifiable and severely deleterious genes and debilitating genetic disease should not be allowed to exercise their reproductive prerogative.

E. Ulrich, Reproductive Rights and Genetic Disease, in J. Humber and R. Almender, Biomedical Ethics and the Law, 351, 360 (1976).

Of course, manipulation of the gene pool is not the only reason governments seek to regulate procreation. Because of the theological, ethical, and social values related to sexual conduct and its consequences, governments have often regulated techniques designed to limit reproduction. In the United States, legislatures and courts have often considered the propriety of contraception, sterilization, and abortion. Because these issues are considered in detail in constitutional law courses, they are only briefly addressed here.

2. *Contraception*

Historical and religious reasons explain why some states made the use of contraceptives a crime. The question of the propriety of those statutes reached the Supreme Court in Griswold v. Connecticut, 381 U.S. 479, 85 S.Ct. 1678, 14 L.Ed.2d 510 (1965). An official of the Planned Parenthood League of Connecticut and a Yale physician were charged with aiding and abetting "the use of a drug, medicinal article, or instrument for the purpose of preventing conception," a crime under Connecticut law, by providing contraceptives to a married couple. The Supreme Court reversed their conviction. Justice Douglas, writing for the Court, concluded:

> [S]pecific guarantees in the Bill of Rights have penumbras, formed by emanations from those guarantees that helped give them life and substance. Various guarantees create zones of privacy. The rights of association contained in the penumbra of the first amendment is one * * * the third amendment in its prohibition against the quartering of soldiers "in any house" in time of peace without the consent of the owner is another facet of that privacy. The fourth amendment explicitly affirms the right of the people to be secure in their persons, houses, papers, and effects against unreasonable searches and seizures. The fifth amendment in its self-incrimination clause enables the citizen to create a zone of privacy which government may not force him to surrender to his detriment. The ninth amendment provides "the enumeration in the constitution of certain rights will not be construed to deny or disparage others retained by the people."

> The present case * * * concerns a relationship lying within the zone of privacy created by several fundamental constitutional guarantees * * *.

> We deal with a right of privacy older than the Bill of Rights—older than our political parties, older than our school system. Marriage is a coming together for better or worse, hopefully enduring, and intimate to the degree of being sacred. It is an association that promotes a way of life, not causes; a harmony in living, not political faith; a bilateral loyalty, not commercial or social projects. Yet it is an association for as noble a purpose as any involved in our prior decisions.

381 U.S. at 484, 85 S.Ct. at 1681. Although a majority concurred in Justice Douglas's opinion, Chief Justice Warren and Justices Brennan and Goldberg based their determination on the Ninth Amendment. Justice Harlan based his concurrence entirely on the due process clause of the Fourteenth Amendment. Separately, Justice White concurred in the judgment and based his determination on the Fourteenth Amendment. Justices Black and Stewart dissented. Justice Black wrote:

> There is no single one of the graphic and eloquent strictures and criticisms fired at the policy of this Connecticut law either by the court's

opinion or by those of my concurring brethren to which I cannot subscribe—except their conclusion that the evil qualities they see in the law make it unconstitutional * * *

I like my privacy as well as the next one, but I am nevertheless compelled to admit the government has a right to invade it unless prohibited by some specific constitutional provision. For these reasons, I cannot agree with the court's judgment and the reasons it gives for holding this Connecticut law unconstitutional.

381 U.S. at 510, 85 S.Ct. at 1696. The *Griswold* case left open the question of whether this new right of privacy extended only to married couples or to single people as well. It also left open the question of whether it extended only to decisions related to procreation or whether it extended to all health care decisions. The first of these questions was answered in 1972 when the Court determined that a law that allowed married people, but not unmarried people, to have access to contraceptives violated the equal protection clause of the Fourteenth Amendment because there could be no rational basis for distinguishing between married and unmarried people in permitting access to contraceptives. The Court suggested that "if the right of privacy means anything, it is the right of the individual, married or single, to be free from unwarranted government intrusion into matters so fundamentally affecting a person as a decision whether to bear a child." Eisenstadt v. Baird, 405 U.S. 438, 453, 92 S.Ct. 1029, 1038, 31 L.Ed.2d 349 (1972). In Carey v. Population Services International, 431 U.S. 678, 97 S.Ct. 2010, 52 L.Ed.2d 675 (1977), the Supreme Court confirmed that since *Griswold* declared it unconstitutional for a state to deny contraceptives to married couples, and *Eisenstadt* declared it unconstitutional for a state to distinguish between married couples and unmarried people in controlling access to contraceptives, a state was without authority to ban the distribution of contraceptives to any adult.

More recently governments have been faced with the prospect of whether some "contraceptives" that work by making implantation difficult (like the "morning after pill") are really contraceptives, subject to very limited government regulation, or agents of abortion, subject to far greater restriction and regulation (and, perhaps, prohibition). For a further discussion of this issue, see Note: The Blurry Distinction Between Contraception and Abortion and the Advent of Mifepristone (RU–486), below.

3. *Abortion*

The right to privacy discussed (and perhaps invented) in *Griswold* found its most significant articulation in Roe v. Wade, 410 U.S. 113, 93 S.Ct. 705, 35 L.Ed.2d 147 (1973), the abortion case. Imagine Justice Blackmun writing this opinion, going through medicine and history texts hoping to find out just when a person protected by the Fourteenth Amendment really did come into existence. Justice Blackmun, who had been counsel to the Mayo Clinic earlier in his legal career, was keenly aware of the medical consequences of his determination. A comparison of Justice Blackmun's approach to this problem and Justice Douglas's approach, which appears in his concurring opinion, suggests that Justice Blackmun viewed abortion as a medical problem, while Justice Douglas viewed it as a personal issue. In any case, *Roe v. Wade* clearly recognized a constitutionally based right of privacy which extended to personal procreative decisions. Further, this right was based on the due process clause of the Fourteenth Amendment, not the penumbras and emanations that formed the unstable foundation for *Griswold*. While *Roe* was increasingly narrowed during the 1980s, and while its death was often predicted, in 1992 the Court concluded that "the essential holding of *Roe v. Wade* should be retained and once again reaffirmed." *Planned Parenthood of Southeastern Pennsylvania v. Casey*, 505 U.S. 833, 112 S.Ct. 2791, 120 L.Ed.2d 674 (1992). In 2000 the Supreme Court narrowly decided "not [to] revisit those legal principles" and to reaffirm *Roe* and *Casey* yet one more time. *Stenberg v. Carhart*, 530 U.S. 914, 120 S.Ct. 2597, 147 L.Ed.2d 743 (2000). But what is the "essential holding" of *Roe* that was retained in *Casey* and applied in *Stenberg*?

ROE v. WADE

Supreme Court of the United States, 1973.
410 U.S. 113, 93 S.Ct. 705, 35 L.Ed.2d 147.

MR. JUSTICE BLACKMUN delivered the opinion of the Court.

* * *

We forthwith acknowledge our awareness of the sensitive and emotional nature of the abortion controversy, of the vigorous opposing views, even among physicians, and of the deep and seemingly absolute convictions that the subject inspires. One's philosophy, one's experiences, one's exposure to the raw edges of human existence, one's religious training, one's attitudes toward life and family and their values, and the moral standards one establishes and seeks to observe, are all likely to influence and to color one's thinking and conclusions about abortion.

In addition, population growth, pollution, poverty, and racial overtones tend to complicate and not to simplify the problem.

Our task, of course, is to resolve the issue by constitutional measurement, free of emotion and of predilection. We seek earnestly to do this, and, because we do, we have inquired into, and in this opinion place some emphasis upon, medical and medical-legal history and what that history reveals about man's attitudes toward the abortion procedure over the centuries. We bear in mind, too, Mr. Justice Holmes' admonition in his now-vindicated dissent in Lochner v. New York, 198 U.S. 45, 76, 49 L.Ed. 937, 25 S.Ct. 539 (1905):

"[The Constitution] is made for people of fundamentally differing views, and the accident of our finding certain opinions natural and familiar or novel and even shocking ought not to conclude our judgment upon the question whether statutes embodying them conflict with the Constitution of the United States."

* * *

The principal thrust of appellant's attack on the Texas statutes is that they improperly invade a right, said to be possessed by the pregnant woman, to choose to terminate her pregnancy. Appellant would discover this right in the concept of personal "liberty" embodied in the Fourteenth Amendment's Due Process Clause; or in personal, marital, familial, and sexual privacy said to be protected by the Bill of Rights or its penumbras, [ ]; or among those rights reserved to the people by the Ninth Amendment [ ]. Before addressing this claim, we feel it desirable briefly to survey, in several aspects, the history of abortion, for such insight as that history may afford us, and then to examine the state purposes and interests behind the criminal abortion laws.

VI

It perhaps is not generally appreciated that the restrictive criminal abortion laws in effect in a majority of States today are of relatively recent vintage. Those laws, generally proscribing abortion or its attempt at any time during pregnancy except when necessary to preserve the pregnant woman's life, are not of ancient or even of common-law origin. Instead, they derive from statutory changes effected, for the most part, in the latter half of the 19th century.

[The Court then reviewed, in great detail, ancient attitudes, the Hippocratic Oath, the common law, English statutory law, American Law, the position of the American Medical Association, the position of the American Public Health Association, and the position of the American Bar Association.]

VII

Three reasons have been advanced to explain historically the enactment of criminal abortion laws in the 19th century and to justify their continued existence.

[The first, Victorian sexual morality, is dismissed as an anachronism.]

A second reason is concerned with abortion as a medical procedure. When most criminal abortion laws were first enacted, the procedure was a hazardous one for the woman. * * * Thus, it has been argued that a State's real concern in enacting a criminal abortion law was to protect the pregnant woman, that is, to restrain her from submitting to a procedure that placed her life in serious jeopardy.

Modern medical techniques have altered this situation. Appellants and various amici refer to medical data indicating that abortion in early pregnancy, this is, prior to the end of the first trimester, although not without its risk, is now relatively safe. Mortality rates for women undergoing early abortions, where the procedure is legal, appear to be as low as or lower than the rates for normal childbirth. Consequently, any interest of the State in protecting the woman from an inherently hazardous procedure, except when it would be equally dangerous for her to forgo it, has largely disappeared. Of course, important state interests in the area of health and medical standards do remain. The State has a legitimate interest in seeing to it that abortion, like any other medical procedure, is performed under circumstances that assure maximum safety for the patient. * * *

The third reason is the State's interest—some phrase it in terms of duty—in protecting prenatal life.

* * *

It is with these interests, and the weight to be attached to them, that this case is concerned.

VIII

The Constitution does not explicitly mention any right of privacy. In a line of decisions, however, going back perhaps as far as [ ] 1891 the Court has recognized that a right of personal privacy, or a guarantee of certain areas or zones of privacy, does exist under the Constitution. In varying contexts, the Court or individual Justices have, indeed, found at least the roots of that right in the First Amendment, [ ] in the Fourth and Fifth Amendments, Terry v. Ohio, [ ] in the penumbras of the Bill of Rights, Griswold v. Connecticut, [ ] the Ninth Amendment, [ ] or in the concept of liberty guaranteed by the first section of the Fourteenth Amendment. [ ] These decisions make it clear that only personal rights that can be deemed "fundamental" or "implicit in the concept of ordered liberty," [ ] are included in this guarantee of personal privacy. They also make it clear that the right has some extension to activities relating to marriage, [ ] family relationships, [ ] and child rearing and education [ ].

This right of privacy, whether it be founded in the Fourteenth Amendment's concept of personal liberty and restrictions upon state action, as we feel it is, or, as the District Court determined, in the Ninth Amendment's reservation of rights to the people, is broad enough to encompass a woman's decision whether or not to terminate her pregnancy. The detriment that the State would impose upon the pregnant woman by denying this choice altogether is apparent. Specific and direct harm medically diagnosable even in early pregnancy may be involved. Maternity, or additional offspring, may force upon the woman a distressful life and future. Psychological harm may be imminent. Mental and physical health may be taxed by child care. There is also the distress, for all concerned, associated with the unwanted child, and there is the problem of bringing a child into a family already unable, psychologically and otherwise, to care for it. In other cases, as in this one, the additional difficulties and continuing stigma of unwed motherhood may be involved. All these are factors the woman and her responsible physician necessarily will consider in consultation.

On the basis of elements such as these, appellant and some amici argue that the woman's right is absolute and that she is entitled to terminate her pregnancy at whatever time, in whatever way, and for whatever reason she alone chooses. With this we do not agree. * * * [A] State may properly assert important interests in safeguarding health, in maintaining medical standards, and in protecting potential life. At some point in pregnancy, these respective interests become sufficiently compelling to sustain regulation of the factors that govern the abortion decision.

* * *

X

* * *

With respect to the State's important and legitimate interest in the health of the mother, the "compelling" point, in the light of present medical knowledge, is at approximately the end of the first trimester. This is so because of the now-established medical fact * * * that until the end of the first trimester mortality in abortion may be less than mortality in normal childbirth. It follows that, from and after this point, a State may regulate the abortion procedure to the extent that the regulation reasonably relates to the preservation and protection of maternal health. * * *

This means, on the other hand, that, for the period of pregnancy prior to this "compelling" point, the attending physician, in consultation with his patient, is free to determine, without regulation by the State, that, in his medical judgment, the patient's pregnancy should be terminated. If that decision is reached, the judgment may be effectuated by an abortion free of interference by the State.

With respect to the State's important and legitimate interest in potential life, the "compelling" point is at viability. This is so because the fetus then presumably has the capability of meaningful life outside the mother's womb. State regulation protective of fetal life after viability thus has both logical and biological justifications. If the State is interested in protecting fetal life after viability, it may go so far as to proscribe abortion during that period, except when it is necessary to preserve the life or health of the mother.

* * *

XI

To summarize and to repeat:

1. A state criminal abortion statute of the current Texas type, that excepts from criminality only a *lifesaving* procedure on behalf of the mother, without regard to pregnancy stage and without recognition of the other interests involved, is violative of the Due Process Clause of the Fourteenth Amendment.

(a) For the stage prior to approximately the end of the first trimester, the abortion decision and its effectuation must be left to the medical judgment of the pregnant woman's attending physician.

(b) For the stage subsequent to approximately the end of the first trimester, the State, in promoting its interest in the health of the mother, may, if it chooses, regulate the abortion procedure in ways that are reasonably related to maternal health.

(c) For the stage subsequent to viability, the State in promoting its interest in the potentiality of human life may, if it chooses, regulate, and even proscribe, abortion except where it is necessary, in appropriate medical judgment, for the preservation of the life or health of the mother.

* * *

Notes and Questions

1. There are few cases that have affected the American political landscape as much as *Roe v. Wade*. On January 22, 2003, many of those engaged in the abortion debates marked the thirtieth anniversary of this Supreme Court decision. Americans remain deeply divided on the issue, with polls showing the same split for the last fifteen years. For an interesting account of the celebrations and lamentations that attended the recognition that *Roe* had been law for three decades, see K. Zernike, Thirty Years After Roe v. Wade: New Trends But the Old Debate, New York Times, January 20, 2003, at A–1.

2. Justice Blackmun's Fourteenth Amendment analysis is not the only way that the Court could have reached this result. Justice Douglas, concurring, would have depended on the Ninth Amendment, as did the District Court. His approach would have recognized a far broader right of privacy:

> The Ninth Amendment obviously does not create federally enforceable rights. It merely says, "The enumeration in the Constitution, of certain rights, shall not be construed to deny or disparage others retained by the people." But a catalogue of these rights includes customary, traditional, and time-honored rights, amenities, privileges, and immunities that come within the sweep of "the Blessings of Liberty" mentioned in the preamble to the Constitution. Many of them, in my view, come within the meaning of the term "liberty" as used in the Fourteenth Amendment.

> *First is the autonomous control over the development and expression of one's intellect, interests, tastes, and personality.*

> *Second is freedom of choice in the basic decisions of one's life respecting marriage, divorce, procreation, contraception, and the education and upbringing of children.*

> *Third is the freedom to care for one's health and person, freedom from bodily restraint or compulsion, freedom to walk, stroll, or loaf.*

Consider how the subsequent history of abortion legislation and litigation might have been different had this less medical, much broader, definition of the right been accepted by the Court in 1973.

3. The Court's opinion stirred into action political forces opposed to abortion. They have encouraged state legislatures to seek creative ways to discourage abortions without running afoul of the requirements of *Roe v. Wade.* The Supreme Court at first resisted attempts to limit the underlying rights recognized in 1973, although the number of justices supporting that decision declined over time. *Roe* was reaffirmed more than a dozen times in its first decade, but by 1986 the 7–2 majority was down to 5–4, Thornburgh v. American College of Obstetricians and Gynecologists, 476 U.S. 747, 106 S.Ct. 2169, 90 L.Ed.2d 779 (1986), and by 1989 the Court appeared to be evenly divided, with Justice O'Connor unwilling to confront the issue. Webster v. Reproductive Health Services, 492 U.S. 490, 109 S.Ct. 3040, 106 L.Ed.2d 410 (1989). *Roe* was revived in Planned Parenthood of Southeastern Pennsylvania v. Casey, 505 U.S. 833, 112 S.Ct. 2791, 120 L.Ed.2d 674 (1992), and in this revived form, by the narrowest of majorities, it remains the governing law. Stenberg v. Carhart, 530 U.S. 914, 120 S.Ct. 2597, 147 L.Ed.2d 743 (2000).

4. *Roe v. Wade* has been vigorously criticized, both as a matter of policy and a matter of law. While Congress has not taken action to promulgate a constitutional amendment allowing states to prohibit abortions, government funding for abortions has been limited and the restrictions on the use of government funds for abortions have generally been upheld by the courts. In 1977, the Supreme Court upheld state statutes and Medicaid plans that refused to fund nontherapeutic abortions as well as a city's determination that its hospitals would not provide nontherapeutic abortions. Beal v. Doe, 432 U.S. 438, 97 S.Ct. 2366, 53 L.Ed.2d 464 (1977); Maher v. Roe, 432 U.S. 464, 97 S.Ct. 2376, 53 L.Ed.2d 484 (1977); Poelker v. Doe, 432 U.S. 519, 97 S.Ct. 2391, 53 L.Ed.2d 528 (1977). Three years later in Harris v. McRae, 448 U.S. 297, 100 S.Ct. 2671, 65 L.Ed.2d 784 (1980), the Supreme Court upheld the Hyde amendment, which provided that federal funds could not be used for virtually any abortion. Some states have continued to provide entirely state-funded Medicaid abortions. Simat Corp. v. Arizona Health

Care Cost Containment System, 203 Ariz. 454, 56 P.3d 28 (2002)(reviewing, in detail, the state court decisions that have considered this issue).

5. There were two legal lines of attack on the Supreme Court's decision in *Roe v. Wade*. The first argued that the Supreme Court had returned to the unhappy Lochnerian days of substantive due process, during which the Court acted as if it were free to make social policy without regard to legal or constitutional restrictions. Of course, the authors of the Fourteenth Amendment were not confronted with abortion as a political and social issue, and the intent of the framers with regard to this particular question is not likely to be helpful in resolving this issue. While the Fourteenth Amendment has been broadly interpreted, *Roe v. Wade* and the subsequent abortion cases are among the few examples of the application of a "right to privacy" that arise out of that amendment. The Supreme Court has refused to extend this right of privacy to other areas, even within the health care system. See United States v. Rutherford, 442 U.S. 544, 99 S.Ct. 2470, 61 L.Ed.2d 68 (1979) (no privacy right to use an unproven cancer drug). In the first right to die case considered by the Court, none of the Justices even used the word "privacy" to describe the underlying constitutional right; instead they depended upon the apparently more limited "liberty interest" explicitly mentioned in the Fourteenth Amendment. Cruzan v. Director, Missouri Dept. of Health, 497 U.S. 261, 110 S.Ct. 2841, 111 L.Ed.2d 224 (1990). See Chapter 19. In 1986 the Supreme Court explicitly rejected the application of the right of privacy to protect those engaging in homosexual conduct in Bowers v. Hardwick, 478 U.S. 186, 106 S.Ct. 2841, 92 L.Ed.2d 140 (1986), and, in a strictly legal, conceptual sense, *Roe v. Wade* appeared to be a derelict on the waters of the law.

The vitality of the doctrine of substantive due process was suddenly revived when the Court overturned Bowers in 2003. In Lawrence v. Texas, 539 U.S. 558, 123 S.Ct. 2472, 156 L.Ed.2d 508 (2003), the Court announced that those who engaged in homosexual conduct are protected from criminal action by the state of Texas by the right to privacy, which itself is firmly rooted in the Due Process Clause of the Fifth and Fourteenth Amendments. Justice Kennedy, for the Court, used sweeping language to address this issue:

> The case does involve two adults who, with full and mutual consent from each other, engaged in sexual practices common to a homosexual lifestyle. The petitioners are entitled to respect for their private lives. The State cannot demean their existence or control their destiny by making their private sexual conduct a crime. Their right to liberty under the Due Process Clause gives them the full right to engage in their conduct without intervention of the government. "It is a promise of the Constitution that there is a realm of personal liberty which the government may not enter." [citing Casey, which follows this Note] The Texas statute furthers no legitimate state interest which can justify its intrusion into the personal and private life of the individual.

> Had those who drew and ratified the Due Process Clauses of the Fifth Amendment or the Fourteenth Amendment known the components of liberty in its manifold possibilities, they might have been more specific. They did not presume to have this insight. They knew times can blind us to certain truths and later generations can see that laws once thought necessary and proper in fact serve only to oppress. As the Constitution endures, persons in every generation can invoke its principles in their own search for greater freedom.

156 L.Ed.2d at 525–526. Has the power of arguments based in substantive due process, which had been on the wane for thirty years after Roe v. Wade, suddenly been restored, or will Lawrence be limited to its own facts? Does the fact that the

opinion was written by Justice Kennedy, who also wrote the scathing dissent in the Stenberg case, below, suggest that the substantive due process right defined in Lawrence will not be broad enough to encompass decisions relating to abortion?

The second line of attack on *Roe v. Wade* focused on the opinion's scientific foundation. *Roe v. Wade* made two kinds of distinctions. First, it identified that point at which it became more dangerous to abort than to bear the child; second, it identified that point at which the fetus was viable. The court identified those points as occurring at the end of the first and second trimesters. As the science of obstetrics improves and safer techniques of abortion are developed, the first point is being moved back, closer to the time of delivery, and the second point is being moved forward, closer to the time of conception. It is now quite safe to have an abortion long after the end of the first trimester, and a fetus may be viable before the end of the second trimester. Should the Supreme Court stick to its scientifically justifiable points (the point of increased danger and the point of viability), which would create an ambiguity because it changes with the latest medical developments, or should it stick with the arbitrary first and second trimester timelines, which are easy to apply, even though they are no longer supported by science? The Court attempted to answer this question in City of Akron v. Akron Center for Reproductive Health, Inc., 462 U.S. 416, 103 S.Ct. 2481, 76 L.Ed.2d 687 (1983), and finally reconsidered the trimester division altogether in 1992.

PLANNED PARENTHOOD OF SOUTHEASTERN PENNSYLVANIA v. CASEY

Supreme Court of the United States, 1992.
505 U.S. 833, 112 S.Ct. 2791, 120 L.Ed.2d 674.

JUSTICE O'CONNOR, JUSTICE KENNEDY, and JUSTICE SOUTER announced the judgment of the Court and delivered the opinion of the Court with respect to Parts I, II, III, V–A, V–C, and VI, an opinion with respect to Part V–E, in which JUSTICE STEVENS joins, and an opinion with respect to Parts IV, V–B, and V–D.

I.

Liberty finds no refuge in a jurisprudence of doubt. Yet 19 years after our holding that the Constitution protects a woman's right to terminate her pregnancy in its early stages, [ ] that definition of liberty is still questioned.
* * *

At issue in these cases are five provisions of the Pennsylvania Abortion Control Act of 1982. * * * The Act requires that a woman seeking an abortion give her informed consent prior to the abortion procedure, and specifies that she be provided with certain information at least 24 hours before the abortion is performed. [ ] For a minor to obtain an abortion, the Act requires the informed consent of one of her parents, but provides for a judicial bypass option if the minor does not wish to or cannot obtain a parent's consent. [ ] Another provision of the Act requires that, unless certain exceptions apply, a married woman seeking an abortion must sign a statement indicating that she has notified her husband of her intended abortion. [ ] The Act exempts compliance with these three requirements in the event of a "medical emergency," which is defined in the Act. [ ] In addition to the above provisions regulating the performance of abortions, the Act imposes certain reporting requirements on facilities that provide abortion services. [ ]

* * *

After considering the fundamental constitutional questions resolved by *Roe*, principles of institutional integrity, and the rule of stare decisis, we are led to conclude this: the essential holding of *Roe v. Wade* should be retained and once again reaffirmed.

It must be stated at the outset and with clarity that *Roe's* essential holding, the holding we reaffirm, has three parts. First is a recognition of the right of the woman to choose to have an abortion before viability and to obtain it without undue interference from the State. Before viability, the State's interests are not strong enough to support a prohibition of abortion or the imposition of a substantial obstacle to the woman's effective right to elect the procedure. Second is a confirmation of the State's power to restrict abortions after fetal viability, if the law contains exceptions for pregnancies which endanger a woman's life or health. And third is the principle that the State has legitimate interests from the outset of the pregnancy in protecting the health of the woman and the life of the fetus that may become a child. These principles do not contradict one another; and we adhere to each.

II.

* * *

Men and women of good conscience can disagree, and we suppose some always shall disagree, about the profound moral and spiritual implications of terminating a pregnancy, even in its earliest stage. Some of us as individuals find abortion offensive to our most basic principles of morality, but that cannot control our decision. Our obligation is to define the liberty of all, not to mandate our own moral code. The underlying constitutional issue is whether the State can resolve these philosophic questions in such a definitive way that a woman lacks all choice in the matter, except perhaps in those rare circumstances in which the pregnancy is itself a danger to her own life or health, or is the result of rape or incest. * * * Abortion is a unique act. It is an act fraught with consequences for others: for the woman who must live with the implications of her decision; for the persons who perform and assist in the procedure; for the spouse, family, and society which must confront the knowledge that these procedures exist, procedures some deem nothing short of an act of violence against innocent human life; and, depending on one's beliefs, for the life or potential life that is aborted. Though abortion is conduct, it does not follow that the State is entitled to proscribe it in all instances. That is because the liberty of the woman is at stake in a sense unique to the human condition and so unique to the law. The mother who carries a child to full term is subject to anxieties, to physical constraints, to pain that only she must bear. That these sacrifices have from the beginning of the human race been endured by woman with a pride that ennobles her in the eyes of others and gives to the infant a bond of love cannot alone be grounds for the State to insist she make the sacrifice. Her suffering is too intimate and personal for the State to insist, without more, upon its own vision of the woman's role, however dominant that vision has been in the course of our history and our culture. The destiny of the woman must be shaped to a large extent on her own conception of her spiritual imperatives and her place in society.

* * *

While we appreciate the weight of the arguments made on behalf of the State in the case before us, arguments which in their ultimate formulation conclude that *Roe* should be overruled, the reservations any of us may have in reaffirming the central holding of *Roe* are outweighed by the explication of individual liberty we have given combined with the force of stare decisis. We turn now to that doctrine.

III.

A.

[In this section, the court discussed the conditions under which it is appropriate for the Court to reverse its own precedent.]

So in this case we may inquire whether *Roe's* central rule has been found unworkable; whether the rule's limitation on state power could be removed without serious inequity to those who have relied upon it or significant damage to the stability of the society governed by the rule in question; whether the law's growth in the intervening years has left *Roe's* central rule a doctrinal anachronism discounted by society; and whether *Roe's* premises of fact have so far changed in the ensuing two decades as to render its central holding somehow irrelevant or unjustifiable in dealing with the issue it addressed.

* * *

The sum of the precedential inquiry to this point shows *Roe's* underpinnings unweakened in any way affecting its central holding. While it has engendered disapproval, it has not been unworkable. An entire generation has come of age free to assume *Roe's* concept of liberty in defining the capacity of women to act in society, and to make reproductive decisions; no erosion of principle going to liberty or personal autonomy has left *Roe's* central holding a doctrinal remnant; *Roe* portends no developments at odds with other precedent for the analysis of personal liberty; and no changes of fact have rendered viability more or less appropriate as the point at which the balance of interests tips. Within the bounds of normal stare decisis analysis, then, and subject to the considerations on which it customarily turns, the stronger argument is for affirming *Roe's* central holding, with whatever degree of personal reluctance any of us may have, not for overruling it.

B.

[The Court next distinguished the rule in the abortion cases from the rules in *Lochner* and the "separate but equal" cases, two areas in which the Supreme Court did reverse its well settled precedents this century. The Court also explained that it should not expend its political capital and put the public respect for the Court and its processes at risk by reversing *Roe*.]

IV.

From what we have said so far it follows that it is a constitutional liberty of the woman to have some freedom to terminate her pregnancy. We conclude that the basic decision in *Roe* was based on a constitutional analysis which we cannot now repudiate. The woman's liberty is not so unlimited, however, that from the outset the State cannot show its concern for the life of the unborn, and at a later point in fetal development the State's interest in life has sufficient force so that the right of the woman to terminate the pregnancy can be restricted.

* * *

We conclude the line should be drawn at viability, so that before that time the woman has a right to choose to terminate her pregnancy. We adhere to this principle for two reasons. First, as we have said, is the doctrine of stare decisis. * * *

The second reason is that the concept of viability, as we noted in *Roe,* is the time at which there is a realistic possibility of maintaining and nourishing a life outside the womb, so that the independent existence of the second life can in reason and all fairness be the object of state protection that now overrides the rights of the woman. * * *

The woman's right to terminate her pregnancy before viability is the most central principle of *Roe v. Wade.* It is a rule of law and a component of liberty we cannot renounce.

* * *

Yet it must be remembered that *Roe v. Wade* speaks with clarity in establishing not only the woman's liberty but also the State's "important and legitimate interest in potential life." [ ] That portion of the decision in *Roe* has been given too little acknowledgment and implementation by the Court in its subsequent cases. Those cases decided that any regulation touching upon the abortion decision must survive strict scrutiny, to be sustained only if drawn in narrow terms to further a compelling state interest. [ ] Not all of the cases decided under that formulation can be reconciled with the holding in *Roe* itself that the State has legitimate interests in the health of the woman and in protecting the potential life within her. In resolving this tension, we choose to rely upon *Roe,* as against the later cases.

* * *

We reject the trimester framework, which we do not consider to be part of the essential holding of *Roe.* [ ] Measures aimed at ensuring that a woman's choice contemplates the consequences for the fetus do not necessarily interfere with the right recognized in *Roe,* although those measures have been found to be inconsistent with the rigid trimester framework announced in that case. A logical reading of the central holding in *Roe* itself, and a necessary reconciliation of the liberty of the woman and the interest of the State in promoting prenatal life, require, in our view, that we abandon the trimester framework as a rigid prohibition on all previability regulation aimed at the protection of fetal life.

* * *

The fact that a law which serves a valid purpose, one not designed to strike at the right itself, has the incidental effect of making it more difficult or more expensive to procure an abortion cannot be enough to invalidate it. Only where state regulation imposes an undue burden on a woman's ability to make this decision does the power of the State reach into the heart of the liberty protected by the Due Process Clause.

* * *

Roe v. Wade was express in its recognition of the State's "important and legitimate interests in preserving and protecting the health of the pregnant woman [and] in protecting the potentiality of human life." [ ] The trimester framework, however, does not fulfill *Roe's* own promise that the State has an interest in protecting fetal life or potential life. *Roe* began the contradiction by using the trimester framework to forbid any regulation of abortion designed to advance that interest before viability. [ ] Before viability, *Roe* and subsequent cases treat all governmental attempts to influence a woman's decision on behalf of the potential life within her as unwarranted. This treatment is, in our judgment, incompatible with the recognition that there is a substantial state interest in potential life throughout pregnancy. [ ]

The very notion that the State has a substantial interest in potential life leads to the conclusion that not all regulations must be deemed unwarranted. Not all burdens on the right to decide whether to terminate a pregnancy will be undue. In our view, the undue burden standard is the appropriate means of reconciling the State's interest with the woman's constitutionally protected liberty.

* * *

A finding of an undue burden is a shorthand for the conclusion that a state regulation has the purpose or effect of placing a substantial obstacle in the path of a woman seeking an abortion of a nonviable fetus. A statute with this purpose is invalid because the means chosen by the State to further the interest in potential life must be calculated to inform the woman's free choice, not hinder it. And a statute which, while furthering the interest in potential life or some other valid state interest, has the effect of placing a substantial obstacle in the path of a woman's choice cannot be considered a permissible means of serving its legitimate ends. * * *

Some guiding principles should emerge. What is at stake is the woman's right to make the ultimate decision, not a right to be insulated from all others in doing so. Regulations which do no more than create a structural mechanism by which the State, or the parent or guardian of a minor, may express profound respect for the life of the unborn are permitted, if they are not a substantial obstacle to the woman's exercise of the right to choose. [ ]

[The Justices then summarized their new undue burden test:]

(a) To protect the central right recognized by *Roe v. Wade* while at the same time accommodating the State's profound interest in potential life, we will employ the undue burden analysis as explained in this opinion. An undue burden exists, and therefore a provision of law is invalid, if its purpose or effect is to place a substantial obstacle in the path of a woman seeking an abortion before the fetus attains viability.

(b) We reject the rigid trimester framework of *Roe v. Wade*. To promote the State's profound interest in potential life, throughout pregnancy the State may take measures to ensure that the woman's choice is informed, and measures designed to advance this interest will not be invalidated as long as their purpose is to persuade the woman to choose childbirth over abortion. These measures must not be an undue burden on the right.

(c) As with any medical procedure, the State may enact regulations to further the health or safety of a woman seeking an abortion. Unnecessary health regulations that have the purpose or effect of presenting a substantial obstacle to a woman seeking an abortion impose an undue burden on the right.

(d) Our adoption of the undue burden analysis does not disturb the central holding of *Roe v. Wade,* and we reaffirm that holding. Regardless of whether exceptions are made for particular circumstances, a State may not prohibit any woman from making the ultimate decision to terminate her pregnancy before viability.

(e) We also reaffirm *Roe's* holding that "subsequent to viability, the State in promoting its interest in the potentiality of human life may, if it chooses, regulate, and even proscribe, abortion except where it is necessary, in appropriate medical judgment, for the preservation of the life or health of the mother." [ ]

* * *

V.

* * *

A.

Because it is central to the operation of various other requirements, we begin with the statute's definition of medical emergency. Under the statute, a medical emergency is "that condition which, on the basis of the physician's good faith clinical judgment, so complicates the medical condition of a pregnant woman as to necessitate the immediate abortion of her pregnancy to avert her death or for which a delay will create serious risk of substantial and irreversible impairment of a major bodily function." [ ]

Petitioners argue that the definition is too narrow, contending that it forecloses the possibility of an immediate abortion despite some significant health risks.

[The Justices accepted the Court of Appeals interpretation of the statute, which assured that "abortion regulation would not in any way pose a significant threat to the life or health of a woman," and determined that the definition imposed no undue burden on a woman's right to an abortion.]

B.

We next consider the informed consent requirement. [ ] Except in a medical emergency, the statute requires that at least 24 hours before performing an abortion a physician inform the woman of the nature of the procedure, the health risks of the abortion and of childbirth, and the "probable gestational age of the unborn child." The physician or a qualified nonphysician must inform the woman of the availability of printed materials published by the State describing the fetus and providing information about medical assistance for childbirth, information about child support from the father, and a list of agencies which provide adoption and other services as alternatives to abortion. An abortion may not be performed unless the woman certifies in writing that she has been informed of the availability of these printed materials and has been provided them if she chooses to view them.

* * *

To the extent [our prior cases] find a constitutional violation when the government requires, as it does here, the giving of truthful, nonmisleading information about the nature of the procedure, the attendant health risks and those of childbirth, and the "probable gestational age" of the fetus, those cases go too far, are inconsistent with *Roe's* acknowledgment of an important interest in potential life, and are overruled. * * * If the information the State requires to be made available to the woman is truthful and not misleading, the requirement may be permissible.

We also see no reason why the State may not require doctors to inform a woman seeking an abortion of the availability of materials relating to the consequences to the fetus, even when those consequences have no direct relation to her health. * * * As we have made clear, * * * we permit a State to further its legitimate goal of protecting the life of the unborn by enacting legislation aimed at ensuring a decision that is mature and informed, even when in so doing the State expresses a preference for childbirth over abortion. In short, requiring that the woman be informed of the availability of information relating to fetal development and the assistance available should she decide to carry the pregnancy to full term is a reasonable measure to insure an informed choice, one which might cause the woman to choose childbirth over abortion. This requirement cannot be considered a substantial obstacle to obtaining an abortion, and, it follows, there is no undue burden.

* * *

All that is left of petitioners' argument is an asserted First Amendment right of a physician not to provide information about the risks of abortion, and childbirth, in a manner mandated by the State. To be sure, the physician's First Amendment rights not to speak are implicated, [ ] but only as part of the practice of medicine, subject to reasonable licensing and regulation by the State. We see no constitutional infirmity in the requirement that the physician provide the information mandated by the State here.

The Pennsylvania statute also requires us to reconsider the holding [ ] that the State may not require that a physician, as opposed to a qualified assistant, provide information relevant to a woman's informed consent. [ ] Since there is no evidence on this record that requiring a doctor to give the information as provided by the statute would amount in practical terms to a substantial obstacle to a woman seeking an abortion, we conclude that it is not an undue burden. Our cases reflect the fact that the Constitution gives the States broad latitude to decide that particular functions may be performed only by licensed professionals, even if an objective assessment might suggest that those same tasks could be performed by others. [ ] Thus, we uphold the provision as a reasonable means to insure that the woman's consent is informed.

Our analysis of Pennsylvania's 24–hour waiting period between the provision of the information deemed necessary to informed consent and the performance of an abortion under the undue burden standard requires us to reconsider the premise behind the decision in *Akron I* invalidating a parallel requirement. In *Akron I* we said: "Nor are we convinced that the State's legitimate concern that the woman's decision be informed is reasonably served by requiring a 24-hour delay as a matter of course." [ ] We consider that conclusion to be wrong. The idea that important decisions will be more informed and deliberate if they follow some period of reflection does not strike us as unreasonable, particularly where the statute directs that important information become part of the background of the decision. * * *

Whether the mandatory 24-hour waiting period is nonetheless invalid because in practice it is a substantial obstacle to a woman's choice to terminate her pregnancy is a closer question. The findings of fact by the District Court indicate that because of the distances many women must travel to reach an abortion provider, the practical effect will often be a delay of much more than a day because the waiting period requires that a woman seeking an abortion make at least two visits to the doctor. * * *

These findings are troubling in some respects, but they do not demonstrate that the waiting period constitutes an undue burden. We do not doubt that, as the District Court held, the waiting period has the effect of "increasing the cost and risk of delay of abortions," [ ] but the District Court did not conclude that the increased costs and potential delays amount to substantial obstacles. * * *

We are left with the argument that the various aspects of the informed consent requirement are unconstitutional because they place barriers in the way of abortion on demand. Even the broadest reading of *Roe*, however, has not suggested that there is a constitutional right to abortion on demand. [ ] Rather, the right protected by *Roe* is a right to decide to terminate a pregnancy free of undue interference by the State. Because the informed consent requirement facilitates the wise exercise of that right it cannot be classified as an interference with the right *Roe* protects. The informed consent requirement is not an undue burden on that right.

C.

Pennsylvania's abortion law provides, except in cases of medical emergency, that no physician shall perform an abortion on a married woman without receiving a signed statement from the woman that she has notified her spouse that she is about to undergo an abortion.

* * *

This information and the District Court's findings reinforce what common sense would suggest. In well-functioning marriages, spouses discuss important intimate decisions such as whether to bear a child. But there are millions of women in this country who are the victims of regular physical and psychological abuse at the hands of their husbands. Should these women become pregnant, they may have very good reasons for not wishing to inform their husbands of their decision to obtain an abortion. Many may have justifiable fears of physical abuse, but may be no less fearful of the consequences of reporting prior abuse to the Commonwealth of Pennsylvania. Many may have a reasonable fear that notifying their husbands will provoke further instances of child abuse; these women are not exempt from [the] notification requirement. Many may fear devastating forms of psychological abuse from their husbands, including verbal harassment, threats of future violence, the destruction of possessions, physical confinement to the home, the withdrawal of financial support, or the disclosure of the abortion to family and friends. * * *

The spousal notification requirement is thus likely to prevent a significant number of women from obtaining an abortion. It does not merely make abortions a little more difficult or expensive to obtain; for many women, it will impose a substantial obstacle. We must not blind ourselves to the fact that the significant number of women who fear for their safety and the safety of their children are likely to be deterred from procuring an abortion as surely as if the Commonwealth had outlawed abortion in all cases.

Respondents attempt to avoid the conclusion that [the spousal notification provision] is invalid by pointing out that it imposes almost no burden at all for the vast majority of women seeking abortions. * * * Respondents argue that since some of [the 20% of women who seek abortions who are married] will be able to notify their husbands without adverse consequences or will qualify for one of the exceptions, the statute affects fewer than one percent of women seeking abortions. For this reason, it is asserted, the statute cannot be invalid on its face. [ ] We disagree with respondents' basic method of analysis.

The analysis does not end with the one percent of women upon whom the statute operates; it begins there. Legislation is measured for consistency with the Constitution by its impact on those whose conduct it affects. * * * [A]s we have said, [the Act's] real target is narrower even than the class of women seeking abortions * * *: it is married women seeking abortions who do not wish to notify their husbands of their intentions and who do not qualify for one of the statutory exceptions to the notice requirement. The unfortunate yet persisting conditions * * * will mean that in a large fraction of the cases * * *, [the statute] will operate as a substantial obstacle to a woman's choice to undergo an abortion. It is an undue burden, and therefore invalid.

* * *

[The spousal notification provision] embodies a view of marriage consonant with the common-law status of married women but repugnant to our present understanding of marriage and of the nature of the rights secured by the Constitution. Women do not lose their constitutionally protected liberty when they marry. * * *

D.

* * *

Our cases establish, and we reaffirm today, that a State may require a minor seeking an abortion to obtain the consent of a parent or guardian, provided that there is an adequate judicial bypass procedure. [ ] Under these precedents, in our view, the [Pennsylvania] one-parent consent requirement and judicial bypass procedure are constitutional.

The only argument made by petitioners respecting this provision and to which our prior decisions do not speak is the contention that the parental consent requirement is invalid because it requires informed parental consent. For the most part, petitioners' argument is a reprise of their argument with respect to the informed consent requirement in general, and we reject it for the reasons given above. Indeed, some of the provisions regarding informed consent have particular force with respect to minors: the waiting period, for example, may provide the parent or parents of a pregnant young woman the opportunity to consult with her in private, and to discuss the consequences of her decision in the context of the values and moral or religious principles of their family. [ ]

E.

[The Justices upheld all of the record keeping and reporting requirements of the statute, except for that provision requiring the reporting of a married woman's reason for failure to give notice to her husband.]

VI.

Our Constitution is a covenant running from the first generation of Americans to us and then to future generations. It is a coherent succession. Each generation must learn anew that the Constitution's written terms embody ideas and aspirations that must survive more ages than one. We accept our responsibility not to retreat from interpreting the full meaning of the covenant in light of all of our precedents. We invoke it once again to define the freedom guaranteed by the Constitution's own promise, the promise of liberty.

* * *

[In addition to those parts of the statute found unconstitutional in the three-justice opinion, Justice Stevens would find unconstitutional the requirement that the doctor deliver state-produced materials to a woman seeking an abortion, the counseling requirements, and the 24–hour waiting requirement. His concurring and dissenting opinion is omitted. Justice Blackman's opinion, concurring in the judgment in part and dissenting in part, is also omitted.]

CHIEF JUSTICE REHNQUIST, with whom JUSTICE WHITE, JUSTICE SCALIA, and JUSTICE THOMAS join, concurring in the judgment in part and dissenting in part.

The joint opinion, following its newly-minted variation on stare decisis, retains the outer shell of *Roe v. Wade*, [ ] but beats a wholesale retreat from the substance of that case. We believe that *Roe* was wrongly decided, and that it can and should be overruled consistently with our traditional approach to stare decisis in constitutional cases.

* * *

The end result of the joint opinion's paeans of praise for legitimacy is the enunciation of a brand new standard for evaluating state regulation of a woman's right to abortion—the "undue burden" standard. As indicated above, *Roe v. Wade* adopted a "fundamental right" standard under which state regulations could survive only if they met the requirement of "strict scrutiny." While we disagree with that standard, it at least had a recognized basis in constitutional law at the time *Roe* was decided. The same cannot be said for the "undue burden" standard, which is created largely out of whole cloth by the authors of the joint opinion. It is a standard which even today does not command the support of a majority of this Court. And it will not, we believe, result in the sort of "simple limitation," easily applied, which the joint opinion anticipates. [ ] In sum, it is a standard which is not built to last.

In evaluating abortion regulations under that standard, judges will have to decide whether they place a "substantial obstacle" in the path of a woman seeking an abortion. [ ] In that this standard is based even more on a judge's subjective determinations than was the trimester framework, the standard will do nothing to prevent "judges from roaming at large in the constitutional field" guided only by their personal views. [ ]

* * *

The sum of the joint opinion's labors in the name of stare decisis and "legitimacy" is this: *Roe v. Wade* stands as a sort of judicial Potemkin Village, which may be pointed out to passers by as a monument to the importance of adhering to precedent. But behind the facade, an entirely new method of analysis, without any roots in constitutional law, is imported to decide the constitutionality of state laws regulating abortion. Neither stare decisis nor "legitimacy" are truly served by such an effort.

* * *

JUSTICE SCALIA, with whom the CHIEF JUSTICE, JUSTICE WHITE, and JUSTICE THOMAS join, concurring in the judgment in part and dissenting in part.

* * *

The States may, if they wish, permit abortion-on-demand, but the Constitution does not require them to do so. The permissibility of abortion, and the limitations upon it, are to be resolved like most important questions in our democracy: by citizens trying to persuade one another and then voting. As the Court acknowledges, "where reasonable people disagree the government can adopt one position or the other." [ ] The Court is correct in adding the qualification that this "assumes a state of affairs in which the choice does not intrude upon a protected liberty," [ ]—but the crucial part of that qualification is the penultimate word. A State's choice between two positions on which reasonable people can disagree is constitutional even when (as is often the case) it intrudes upon a "liberty" in the absolute sense. Laws against bigamy, for example—which entire societies of reasonable people disagree with—intrude upon men and women's liberty to marry and live with one another. But bigamy happens not to be a liberty specially "protected" by the Constitution.

That is, quite simply, the issue in this case: not whether the power of a woman to abort her unborn child is a "liberty" in the absolute sense; or even whether it is a liberty of great importance to many women. Of course it is both. The issue is whether it is a liberty protected by the Constitution of the United States. I am sure it is not. I reach that conclusion not because of anything so exalted as my views concerning the "concept of existence, of meaning, of the universe, and of the mystery of human life." [ ] I reach it for the same reason I reach the conclusion that bigamy is not constitutionally protected—because of two simple facts: (1) the Constitution says absolutely nothing about it, and (2) the longstanding traditions of American society have permitted it to be legally proscribed.

* * *

I am certainly not in a good position to dispute that the Court has saved the "central holding" of *Roe*, since to do that effectively I would have to know what the Court has saved, which in turn would require me to understand (as I do not) what the "undue burden" test means. * * * I thought I might note, however, that the following portions of *Roe* have not been saved:

- Under *Roe*, requiring that a woman seeking an abortion be provided truthful information about abortion before giving informed written consent is unconstitutional, if the information is designed to influence her choice [ ]. Under the joint opinion's "undue burden" regime (as applied today, at least) such a requirement is constitutional [ ].

- Under *Roe,* requiring that information be provided by a doctor, rather than by nonphysician counselors, is unconstitutional [ ]. Under the "undue burden" regime (as applied today, at least) it is not [ ].

- Under *Roe*, requiring a 24-hour waiting period between the time the woman gives her informed consent and the time of the abortion is unconstitutional. Under the "undue burden" regime (as applied today, at least) it is not [ ].

- Under *Roe*, requiring detailed reports that include demographic data about each woman who seeks an abortion and various information about each abortion is unconstitutional [ ]. Under the "undue burden" regime (as applied today, at least) it generally is not [ ].

* * *

STENBERG v. CARHART

Supreme Court of the United States, 2000.
530 U.S. 914, 120 S.Ct. 2597, 147 L.Ed.2d 743.

JUSTICE BREYER delivered the opinion of the Court.

We again consider the right to an abortion. We understand the controversial nature of the problem. Millions of Americans believe that life begins at conception and consequently that an abortion is akin to causing the death of an innocent child; they recoil at the thought of a law that would permit it. Other millions fear that a law that forbids abortion would condemn many American women to lives that lack dignity, depriving them of equal liberty and leaving those with least resources to undergo illegal abortions with the attendant risks of death and suffering. Taking account of these virtually irreconcilable points of view, aware that constitutional law must govern a society whose different members sincerely hold directly opposing views, and considering the matter in light of the Constitution's guarantees of fundamental individual liberty, this Court, in the course of a generation, has determined and then redetermined that the Constitution offers basic protection to the woman's right to choose. *Roe v. Wade*; *Planned Parenthood of Southeastern Pa. v. Casey*.[ ] We shall not revisit those legal principles. Rather, we apply them to the circumstances of this case.

Three established principles determine the issue before us. We shall set them forth in the language of the joint opinion in Casey. First, before "viability * * * the woman has a right to choose to terminate her pregnancy."

Second, "a law designed to further the State's interest in fetal life which imposes an undue burden on the woman's decision before fetal viability" is unconstitutional. An "undue burden is * * * shorthand for the conclusion that a state regulation has the purpose or effect of placing a substantial obstacle in the path of a woman seeking an abortion of a nonviable fetus."

Third, " 'subsequent to viability, the State in promoting its interest in the potentiality of human life, may, if it choose, regulate, and even proscribe, abortion except where it is necessary, in appropriate medical judgment, for the preservation of the life or health of the mother.' "

We apply these principles to a Nebraska law banning "partial birth abortion." The statute reads as follows:

> "No partial birth abortion shall be performed in this state, unless such procedure is necessary to save the life of the mother whose life is endangered by a physical disorder, physical illness, or physical injury, including a life-endangering physical condition caused by or arising from the pregnancy itself."

The statute defines "partial birth abortions" as:

> "an abortion procedure in which the person performing the abortion partially delivers vaginally a living unborn child before killing the unborn child and completing the delivery."

It further defines "partially delivers vaginally a living unborn child before killing the unborn child" to mean

> "deliberately and intentionally delivering into the vagina a living unborn child, or a substantial portion thereof, for the purpose of performing a procedure that the person performing such procedure know will kill the unborn child and does kill the unborn child."

The law classifies violation of the statute as a "Class III felony" carrying a prison term of up to 20 years, and a fine of up to $25,000. It also provides for the automatic revocation of a doctor's license to practice medicine in Nebraska.

We Hold that this statute violates the Constitution.

* * *

[The Court next described two kinds of medical procedures used to perform abortions, the dilation and evacuation ("D & E") and dilation and extraction ("D & X") procedures. The D & E is the most common previability second trimester abortion procedure, and sometimes the safest procedure available for the mother. The D & X procedure is the one commonly referred to as "partial birth abortion." The D & E procedure includes] (1) dilation of the cervix; (2) removal of at least some fetal tissue using nonvacuum instruments; and (3) (after the 15th week) the potential need for instrumental disarticulation or dismemberment of the fetus or the collapse of fetal parts to facilitate evacuation from the uterus.

* * *

[The D & X procedure, on the other hand, includes:]

1. deliberate dilatation of the cervix, usually over a sequence of days;

2. instrumental conversion of the fetus to a footling breech;

3. breech extraction of the body excepting the head; and

4. partial evacuation of the intracranial contents of a living fetus to effect vaginal delivery of a dead but otherwise intact fetus[ ]

* * *

The question before us is whether Nebraska's statute, making criminal the performance of a "partial birth abortion," violates the Federal Constitution, as interpreted in *Planned Parenthood of Southeastern Pa. v. Casey* * * * and *Roe v. Wade* * * *. We conclude that it does for at least two independent reasons. First, the law lacks any exception " 'for the preservation of the * * * health of the mother.' " *Casey*. Second, it "imposes an undue burden on a woman's ability" to choose a D & E abortion, thereby unduly burdening the right to choose abortion itself.

* * *

In sum, using this law some present prosecutors and future Attorneys General may choose to pursue physicians who use D & E procedures, the most commonly used method for performing previability second trimester abortions. All those who perform abortion procedures using that method must fear prosecution, conviction, and imprisonment. The result is an undue burden upon a woman's right to make an abortion decision. We must consequently find the statute unconstitutional.

JUSTICE STEVENS, with whom JUSTICE GINSBURG joins, concurring.

Although much ink is spilled today describing the gruesome nature of late-term abortion procedures, that rhetoric does not provide me a reason to believe that the procedure Nebraska here claims it seeks to ban is more brutal, more gruesome, or less respectful of "potential life" than the equally gruesome procedure Nebraska claims it still allows. Justice Ginsburg and Judge Posner have, I believe, correctly diagnosed the underlying reason for the enactment of this legislation—a reason that also explains much of the Court's rhetoric directed at an objective that extends well beyond the narrow issue that this case presents. The rhetoric is almost, but not quite, loud enough to obscure the quiet fact that during the past 27 years, the central holding of *Roe v. Wade*, has been endorsed by all but 4 of the 17 justices who have addressed the issue. That holding—that the word "liberty" in the Fourteenth Amendment includes a woman's right to make this difficult and extremely personal decision—makes it impossible for me to understand how a State has any legitimate interest in requiring a doctor to follow any procedure other than the one that he or she reasonably believes will best protect the woman in her exercise of this constitutional liberty * * *.

JUSTICE O'CONNOR, concurring.

* * *

First, the Nebraska statute is inconsistent with *Casey* because it lacks an exception for those instances when the banned procedure is necessary to preserve the health of the mother.

* * *

The statute at issue here * * * only excepts those procedures "necessary to save the life of the mother whose life is endangered by a physical disorder, physical illness or physical injury." * * * This lack of a health exception necessarily renders the statute unconstitutional.

* * *

Second, Nebraska's statute is unconstitutional on the alternative and independent ground that it imposes an undue burden on a woman's rights to choose to terminate her pregnancy before viability. Nebraska's ban covers not just the dilation and extraction (D & X) procedure, but also the dilation and evacuation (D & E) procedure, "the most commonly used method for performing previability second trimester abortions."

* * *

It is important to note that, unlike Nebraska, some other States have enacted statutes more narrowly tailored to proscribing the D & X procedure alone. Some of those statutes have done so by specifically excluding from their coverage the most common methods of abortion, such as the D & E and vacuum aspiration procedures.

* * *

[A] ban on partial birth abortion that only proscribed the D & X method of abortion and that included an exception to preserve the life and health of the mother would be constitutional in my view.

* * *

JUSTICE GINSBURG, with whom JUSTICE STEVENS joins, concurring.

* * *

[As] Chief Judge Posner commented, the law prohibits the [partial birth abortion] procedure because the State legislators seek to chip away at the private choice shielded by *Roe v. Wade*, even as modified by *Casey*.

* * *

Again, as stated by Chief Judge Posner, "if a statute burdens constitutional rights and all that can be said on its behalf is that it is the vehicle that legislators have chosen for expressing their hostility to those rights, the burden is undue."[ ]

* * *

CHIEF JUSTICE REHNQUIST, dissenting.

I did not join the joint opinion in *Casey*, and continue to believe that case is wrongly decided. Despite my disagreement with the opinion, the *Casey* joint opinion represents the holding of the Court in that case. I believe Justice Kennedy and Justice Thomas have correctly applied Casey's principles and join their dissenting opinions.

JUSTICE SCALIA, dissenting.

I am optimistic enough to believe that, one day, *Stenberg v. Carhart* will be assigned its rightful place in the history of this Court's jurisprudence beside *Korematsu* and *Dred Scott*. The method of killing a human child—one cannot even accurately say an entirely unborn human child—proscribed by this statute is so horrible that the most clinical description of it evokes a shudder of revulsion.... The notion that the Constitution of the United States, designed, among other things, "to establish Justice, insure domestic Tranquility, ... and secure the Blessings of Liberty to ourselves and our Posterity," prohibits the States from simply banning this visibly brutal means of eliminating our half-born posterity is quite simply absurd.

* * *

In my dissent in *Casey*, I wrote that the "undue burden" test made law by the joint opinion created a standard that was "as doubtful in application as it is unprincipled in origin," * * * "hopelessly unworkable in practice," * * * "ultimately standardless," * * * . Today's decision is the proof.* * *

While I am in an I-told-you-so mood, I must recall my bemusement, in *Casey*, at the joint opinion's expressed belief that *Roe v. Wade* had "call[ed] the contending sides of a national controversy to end their nation division by accepting a common mandate rooted in the Constitution," and that the decision in *Casey* would ratify that happy truce. It seemed to me, quite to the contrary, that "Roe fanned into life an issue that has inflamed our national politics in general, and has obscured with its smoke the selection of Justices to this Court in particular, ever since"; and that, "by keeping us in the abortion-umpiring business, it is the perpetuation of that disruption, rather than of any Pax Roeana, that the Court's new majority decrees." * * *

JUSTICE KENNEDY, with whom THE CHIEF JUSTICE joins, dissenting.

For close to two decades after *Roe v. Wade*, the Court gave but slight weight to the interests of the separate States when their legislatures sought to address persisting concerns raised by the existence of a woman's right to elect an abortion in defined circumstances. When the Court reaffirmed the essential holding of *Roe*, the central premise was that the States retain a critical and legitimate role in legislating on the subject of abortion, as limited by the woman's right the Court restated and again guaranteed. *Planned Parenthood of Southeastern Pa. v. Casey* [ ]. The political processes of the State are not to be foreclosed from enacting laws to promote the life of the unborn and to ensure respect for all human life and its potential. * * *

The Court's decision today, in my submission, repudiates this understanding by invalidating a statute advancing critical state interests, even though the law denies no woman the right to choose an abortion and places no undo burden upon the right. The legislation is well within the State's competence to enact. Having concluded Nebraska's law survives the scrutiny dictated by a proper understanding of *Casey*, I dissent from the judgment invalidating it.

* * *

Casey is premised on the States having an important constitutional role in defining their interests in the abortion debate. It is only with this principle in mind that Nebraska's interests can be given proper weight. The state's brief describes its interests as including concern for the life of the unborn and "for the partially-born," in preserving the integrity of the medical profession, and in "erecting a barrier to infanticide."

* * *

Courts are ill-equipped to evaluate the relative worth of particular surgical procedures. The legislatures of the several States have superior factfinding capabilities in this regard. In an earlier case, Justice O'CONNOR had explained that the general rule extends to abortion cases, writing that the Court is not suited to be "the Nation's ex officio medical board with powers to approve or disapprove medical and operative practices and standards throughout the United States." * * * "Irrespective of the difficulty of the task, legislatures, with their superior factfinding capabilities, are certainly better able to make the necessary judgments than are courts." Nebraska's judgment here must stand.

* * *

The Court fails to acknowledge substantial authority allowing the State to take sides in a medical debate, even when fundamental liberty interests are at stake and even when leading members of the profession disagree with the conclusions drawn by the legislature.

* * *

JUSTICE THOMAS, with whom THE CHIEF JUSTICE and JUSTICE SCALIA JOIN, DISSENTING.

In 1973, this Court struck down an Act of the Texas Legislature that had been in effect since 1857, thereby rendering unconstitutional abortion statutes in dozens of states. *Roe v. Wade*. As some of my colleagues on the Court, past and present, ably demonstrated, that decision was grievously wrong. . . . Abortion is a unique act, in which a woman's exercise of control over her own body ends, depending on one's view, human life or potential human life. Nothing in our Federal Constitution deprives the people of this country of the right to determine whether the consequences of abortion to the fetus and to society outweigh the burden of an unwanted pregnancy on the mother. Although a State may permit abortion, nothing in the Constitution dictates that a State must do so.

* * *

The majority assiduously avoids addressing the actual standard articulated in *Casey*—whether prohibiting partial birth abortion without a health exception poses a substantial obstacle to obtaining an abortion. And for good reason: Such an obstacle does not exist. There are two essential reasons why the Court cannot identify a substantial obstacle. First, the Court cannot identify any real, much less substantial, barrier to any woman's ability to obtain an abortion. And second, the Court cannot demonstrate that any such obstacle would affect a sufficient number of women to justify invalidating the statute on its face.

* * *

We were reassured repeatedly in *Casey* that not all regulations of abortions are unwarranted and that the States may express profound respect for fetal life. Under *Casey*, the regulation before us today should easily pass constitutional muster. But the Court's abortion jurisprudence is a particularly virulent strain of constitutional exegesis. And so today we are told that 30 States are prohibited from banning one rarely used form of abortion that they believe to border on infanticide. It is clear that the Constitution does not compel this result.

Notes and Questions on Casey and Stenberg

1. How, exactly, is a court to apply the Supreme Court's "undue burden" test of *Casey*? In finding whether a state law "has the purpose or effect of placing a substantial obstacle in the path of a woman seeking an abortion of a nonviable fetus," is the Court really proposing a two-part (purpose and effect) analysis? How is the court expected to divine the purpose of such an act? From the terms of the law? From formal legislative statements of the purpose? Are many state legislatures likely to promulgate enacting clauses declaring that their purpose is to unduly burden those who seek to abort nonviable fetuses? It may be even more difficult for a court to evaluate the effect of a statute which limits or conditions access to abortions. Of course, we know that a state law has the effect of establishing an "undue burden" when it puts a "substantial obstacle" in the path of a woman seeking to abort a nonviable fetus, but how much does that advance the inquiry? Is an obstacle substantial because it imposes a serious limitation on any identifiable woman, or because it affects a large number of women, or because it affects a large percentage of the cases in which women would seek abortions?

Unlike in Roe v. Wade, though, in which the Court dealt with virtually absolute bans on abortion, in Casey the Court faced several narrow regulations on abortion that had been promulgated by the Pennsylvania legislature, and it thus was required to apply its test to a series of articulated restrictions. These included the requirement that particular state-mandated information be provided to the pregnant woman before the abortion is performed, the requirement that the information be provided by a physician, a 24 hour waiting period between the receipt of the information and the pregnant woman's formal consent to the abortion (and thus a "two-step" procedure), the requirement that a minor get parental consent (with a judicial bypass procedure to avoid that requirement in some cases), and various state reporting requirements, none of which were found to constitute "undue burdens," at least in Pennsylvania on the evidence presented to the Court in 1992. On the other hand, the Court did find that a spousal notification requirement did constitute an undue burden (as did any reporting requirement related to that notification requirement), and the Court struck that down.

Thus, in Casey the Supreme Court provided a template that could be used by lower courts in evaluating the constitutional sufficiency of abortion legislation. It also provided a template that could be used by state legislatures in determining what kinds of legislation would be likely to withstand constitutional attack. Between 1973 and 1992 many state legislatures had attempted to impose the most restrictive abortion laws arguably permitted. Since 1992 few have gone beyond what is clearly permitted in Casey, although legislatures have tested the limits of Casey by promulgating partial birth abortion bans and, more recently, new forms of funding restrictions. Why have the state legislatures become comparatively restrained? Is it because the standard of Casey really is clearer than the standard of Roe? Is it because the pro-life forces in these states have grown weary of further judicial battles? Is it because the pro-choice forces have decided to focus on making those abortions that are legal actually available to those who seek them? Is it because those provisions found to be constitutional in Casey are, in fact, the very provisions that have the strongest political support anyway? Is it because both sides in this battle have moved on to other issues of the day (including physician assisted death)?

Some of the most recent state legislative battles have been over the allocation of resources, including family planning and Medicaid resources. Some address proposed substantive changes in the law, though. For example, a handful of states have passed legislation requiring insurers to charge a separate and identifiable premium if a health insurance policy will cover abortion procedures, and more state legislatures are expected to debate this kind of legislation in the next couple of years. Since 2002 pro-choice advocates have also gone on the offensive in some state legislatures. Instead of merely opposing new restrictions on abortion, in some states advocates are supporting legislation that would make some procedures more easily available. For example, some state legislatures have debated proposals that would effectively require hospital emergency rooms to have emergency contraception available for women who have been assaulted. Whether such "emergency contraception" constitutes abortion remains a controversy.

In those few cases where state legislatures have insisted on going far beyond what Pennsylvania did in Casey, the courts have had no trouble striking down the statutes by applying the "undue burden" test. See, e.g. Sojourner T. v. Edwards, 974 F.2d 27 (5th Cir.1992), cert. denied, 507 U.S. 972, 113 S.Ct. 1414, 122 L.Ed.2d 785 (1993)(statute would have outlawed all abortions except to remove a dead fetus, to save the life of the pregnant woman, or, if performed in the first trimester only, if the pregnancy was a result of rape or incest); Women's Medical Professional Corporation v. Voinovich, 911 F.Supp. 1051 (S.D.Ohio 1995) (preliminary injunction against statute that would, inter alia, ban all postviability abortions, even if the mother's life were at stake).

2. If you live in one of the nearly thirty states that had statutes restricting partial birth abortions at the time Stenberg was decided in 2000, review your state statute. How does it compare with the statute before the Court in Stenberg, and with the Partial–Birth Abortion Ban of 2003, which follows this note? Is it constitutional under the principle supplied by Casey and applied in Stenberg? In her opinion in Stenberg, Justice O'Connor does provide a description of the form of partial birth abortion ban that would meet constitutional muster; a statute that made an exception to preserve the life and health of the mother and included a ban only on the D & X procedure (and permitted the D & E procedure) would be acceptable in constitutional terms. Is there any other justice who shares this view? If this view is held only by Justice O'Connor (and announced by her in a concurring opinion), is it appropriate to call it a part of the holding of Stenberg?

In late 2003 a split panel of the Sixth Circuit upheld Ohio's new Partial–Birth Abortion statute which made "partial birth feticide" a second degree felony. Ohio Rev. Code Ann. section 2919.15.1(D). The statute provides:

> * * * [N]o person shall knowingly perform a partial birth procedure on a pregnant woman when the procedure is not necessary, in reasonable medical judgment, to preserve life or health of the mother as a result of the mother's life or health being endangered by a serious risk of substantial and irreversible impairment of a major bodily function.

A "serious risk of the substantial and irreversible impairment of a major bodily function" is defined in the statute as "any medically diagnosed condition that so complicates the pregnancy of the woman as to directly or indirectly cause the substantial and irreversible impairment of a major bodily function." What does this mean? What conditions might be included? What conditions might be excluded? Must the Stenberg-approved health exception defer to the doctor's judgment in every case, or can the state require that there be a "substantial" health risk before a partial birth abortion is permitted? See Women's Medical Professional Corporation v. Taft, 353 F.3d 436 (6th Cir. 2003).

3. *Consent and Notification Requirements.* There remain, of course, other kinds of regulation with uncertain constitutional status, too. It is now clear that it does not violate the United States Constitution for minors to be required to obtain the consent of a parent to an abortion, as long as the state permits a court (or, perhaps, an appropriate administrative agency) to dispense with that requirement under some circumstances. The Supreme Court has never determined if a two-parent consent requirement (with a proper judicial bypass provision) would pass constitutional muster, however. See Barnes v. Mississippi, 992 F.2d 1335 (5th Cir.1993), cert. denied, 510 U.S. 976, 114 S.Ct. 468, 126 L.Ed.2d 419 (1993)(upholding two-parent consent requirement because involvement of both parents will increase "reflection and deliberation" on the process, and if one parent denies consent the other will be able to go to court in support of the child) and S.H. v. D.H., 796 N.E.2d 1243 (Ind. App. 2003)(family court judge cannot require consent of both parents before an abortion is performed, even if the divorced parents have joint custody). The Supreme Court has suggested that a state requirement of mere parental notification (rather than consent) requires a judicial bypass, and lower courts have generally assumed that it does. Ohio v. Akron Center for Reproductive Health, 497 U.S. 502, 110 S.Ct. 2972, 111 L.Ed.2d 405 (1990). One state supreme court has found that a parental notification requirement violates the state constitution's equal protection clause when it is imposed only on those who seek abortions, not on pregnant children making other, equally medically risky, reproductive decisions. Planned Parenthood of Central New Jersey v. Farmer, 165 N.J. 609, 762 A.2d 620 (2000).

It is not entirely clear what constitutional standard a court must apply in a "bypass" case. Is the court required to waive consent or notification (1) if it finds that the minor is sufficiently mature that she should be able to make the decision herself, or (2) if it finds that if she seeks consent from (or notifies) her parents she will be subject to abuse, or (3) if it finds that it is in her best interest to have the abortion, or (4) if it finds that it is in her best interest not to be required to notify, or get consent from, her parent, or (5) some combination of all of these? The Supreme Court has determined that a statute that provides for the waiver of parental consent or notification when a court determines that an abortion is in the best interest of the minor is constitutionally sufficient. Further, the Court has announced that "a judicial bypass procedure requiring a minor to show that *parental notification is not* in her best interests is equivalent to a judicial bypass procedure requiring a minor to show that *abortion without notification* is in her best interests * * *." Lambert v. Wicklund, 520 U.S. 292, 297, 117 S.Ct. 1169, 137 L.Ed.2d 464 (1997) (per curiam).

If the statute does include a substantively constitutional bypass provision, what kind of procedural conditions may be placed on a bypass case? May the petitioner be required to prove her case by clear and convincing evidence? Is she entitled to counsel? Is she required to have a special guardian appointed for purposes of the litigation? Can the state require an expedited hearing? Can it allow the court to refuse an expedited hearing? Can it require the petition be filed within a very short time after the commencement of the pregnancy? Can it limit appeals by those who unsuccessfully seek judicial bypass?

The debate for and against consent and notification requirements reveals an even deeper debate about the current role of the family in contemporary life. While most agree that a teenager's abortion should be a decision made in consultation with her parents, that belief rests upon several assumptions. First, it assumes that the family dynamics are such that the daughter's disclosure will not trigger domestic violence or other forms of family abuse. Second, it assumes that the daughter lives within a traditional nuclear family, or can readily reach her biological parents. Finally, and most critically, it assumes that parents will act in the daughter's best interest. Some of these assumptions may, sadly, be based upon an idealized view of contemporary family life. While many children are brought up in healthy families, as Justice Kennard of the California Supreme Court has pointed out, "[n]ot every pregnant adolescent has parents out of the comforting and idyllic world of Norman Rockwell." American Academy of Pediatrics v. Lungren, 51 Cal.Rptr.2d 201, 224, 912 P.2d 1148, 1171 (1996)(Kennard, J., dissenting).

Those who support these consent and notification statutes offer many stories of girls who had abortions secretly and now regret not discussing it with their parents. Those who oppose these statutes offer stories about girls who committed suicide rather than go through the notification procedures. Is this anecdotal evidence offered by both sides of much value? Could respectable research data on these issues be developed? Why do you think it has not been developed in any reliable way? Does it seem ironic that under a consent or notification statute a court could declare a pregnant minor to be too immature to proceed without parental consultation, and thus order her to become a mother?

Whatever may be the uncertain status of the details surrounding parental consent and notification, it is now well established that spousal consent and spousal notification requirements are unconstitutional, even if the notification is done by the physician or someone else rather the pregnant woman. See Jane L. v. Bangerter, 61 F.3d 1493 (10th Cir.1995). One state legislature attempted to get around constitutional limitations on spousal consent by permitting the abortion without such consent but providing for the civil liability of those physicians who perform these abortions without that consent. This approach was found to be indistinguishable from requiring spousal consent, and thus unconstitutional, in Planned Parenthood of Southern Arizona v. Woods, 982 F.Supp. 1369, 1380 (D.Ariz.1997). Is the civil liability provision of the Partial Birth Abortion Ban of 2003 (see Problem, below) on any firmer Constitutional ground than the Arizona statute?

4. *Regulation of Medical Procedures.* As a general matter, courts have been reluctant to uphold statutory limitations on abortion procedures against arguments that those limitations—usually designed to increase the chance that an abortion procedure will result in a live birth—impose additional health risks on the pregnant woman. As the debate over partial-birth abortion suggests, the Constitutional contours of such limitations remain indefinite. One state supreme court has determined that a requirement that second trimester abortions be performed in a hospital violated the state constitution, which was read to be more protective of abortion rights than the United States constitution. See Planned Parenthood of Middle Tennessee v. Sundquist, 38 S.W.3d 1 (Tenn.2000). But see Greenville Women's Clinic v. Bryant, 222 F.3d 157 (4th Cir. 2000) (upholding rigid South Carolina licensing requirements for facilities where abortions are performed).

Courts have had little trouble with a requirement that only physicians, not physicians' assistants or others, perform abortions, because the authority granted with professional licenses is a matter state law. See Armstrong v. Mazurek, 906 F.Supp. 561 (D.Mont.1995). Such licensing requirements are seen as ways of protecting the pregnant woman, not imposing an undue burden on her decision to have an abortion.

5. *Two-trip Requirements.* When a state imposes a waiting period between the time the pregnant woman is provided the information that is to be the basis of her informed consent to an abortion and the medical procedure itself, it may, de facto, be requiring that the pregnant woman make two trips to the medical facility where the abortion is to be performed. In Casey the Court announced that a 24–hour waiting period did not constitute an unconstitutional undue burden. In *A Woman's Choice—East Side Women's Clinic v. Newman*, 132 F.Supp.2d 1150 (S.D.Ind.2001), a trial court threw out an Indiana statute that required face-to-face counseling with a woman at least eighteen hours before that woman could be provided an abortion. Effectively, this statute imposed a two trip requirement on women seeking an abortion. The Indiana law was very similar to a provision of the Pennsylvania law that was upheld in *Casey,* but the Indiana federal court still found that it would place an undue burden on those seeking abortions. In reaching its conclusion, the court depended on post-*Casey* empirical studies that demonstrated that similar laws in Utah and Mississippi cut down the abortion rate in those states by ten percent.

The Seventh Circuit reversed in *A Woman's Choice—East Side Women's Clinic v. Newman*, 305 F.3d 684 (7th Cir.2002), finding that those studies were insufficient to support the trial court's conclusions. The Court of Appeals also noted that there was an emergency exception to the eighteen hour requirement. The United States Supreme Court denied certiorari in *A Woman's Choice—East Side Women's Clinic v. Brizzi*, 537 U.S. 1192, 123 S.Ct. 1273, 154 L.Ed.2d 1026 (2003).

The Tennessee Supreme Court determined that imposing what amounts to a three day waiting period violated the state constitution's protected right of privacy. See Planned Parenthood of Middle Tennessee v. Sundquist, 38 S.W.3d 1 (Tenn.2000).

Could the in-person, fully informed, two-visit consent process can also be required of a pregnant girl's parents who are required to give consent under a state law requiring such consent?

6. *Other Informed Consent Requirements.* In Casey the Court upheld a statute that requires that a state-approved packet of material be given to the pregnant woman as a part of the informed consent process, and that the consent process be obtained by the physician, not by anyone else. The only requirement Casey appears to put on the distributed material is that it contain information that is true. In early 1996 a couple of epidemiological studies arguably suggested a very weak relationship between having an abortion and the subsequent risk of developing breast cancer and the severity of that cancer. Subsequent reports cast doubt on this relationship. See P.A. Newcomb, B. E. Storer, M. P. Longnecker et al., Pregnancy Termination in Relation to Risk of Breast Cancer, 275 JAMA 283 (1996). May states require that physicians inform potential abortion patients that "there is a correlation between abortion and the risk of breast cancer?" May states require that patients be provided the information about this correlation even if they do not require that patients be told of the different, but significantly higher, risks of ordinary pregnancy? Could the state require that a woman attend a short course on fetal development as a condition of having an abortion? See a graphic movie dealing with that same subject? Talk to other women who have had abortions? Speak with adoptive couples?

7. Could a state ban abortions for certain purposes? Pennsylvania considered outlawing abortion for gender selection (i.e., because the parents thought that the fetus was the "wrong" sex); could they legally do so? Could the state outlaw

abortion if it is used as a primary method of birth control? As a method for controlling the genetic makeup of a child? If it could do so legally, how would it do so as a practical matter?

8. Under Casey, the "undue burden" test appears to require a factual inquiry; the question is whether a state law, as a matter of fact, imposes a substantial obstacle on the path of a woman seeking to abort a previable fetus. Is it possible to attack a state abortion statute on its face under Casey, or must the plaintiff meet some evidentiary burden by proving the fact of the substantial obstacle? Might the same statutory provisions that were constitutional in Casey be found unconstitutional in some other state? Might a "two-trip" requirement be unconstitutional in a state where patients of the state's only clinic are harassed after they make a visit to the clinic? Is each statutory restriction in each state subject to litigation that depends upon the environment surrounding abortion in that state?

In United States v. Salerno, 481 U.S. 739, 107 S.Ct. 2095, 95 L.Ed.2d 697 (1987), the United States Supreme Court found that a statute would survive a facial constitutional attack unless it could be shown that it would operate unconstitutionally under any conceivable set of circumstances. Is that test relevant in evaluating state statutory regulation of abortion? Is that test inconsistent with the "undue burden" test of Casey? Which standard should courts apply in evaluating that legislation? The circuits continue to be split on whether the restrictive Salerno test applies in this area (a position taken by two circuits) or whether Casey provides an alternative and less strict test (a position taken by five circuits). See Greenville Women's Clinic v. Bryant, 222 F.3d 157 (4th Cir. 2000)(applying the Salerno standard). See also Ruth Burdick, The Casey Undue Burden Standard: Problems Predicted and Encountered, and the Split Over the Salerno Test, 23 Hastings Const. L. Q. 825 (1996).

9. Some believe that the ultimate disappearance of abortion practice will be the result of the fact that medical schools and residency programs are discontinuing training in abortion techniques because offering that training is not worth the political cost. Should all Obstetrics and Gynecology training programs include, at the very least, some exposure to the abortion process, or may a medical school decide that it will not provide that training because it finds the practice of abortion morally unacceptable? Should students who find such practice abhorrent be able to opt out of that training? Are there constitutional implications to the removal of abortion from the medical school curriculum at a state university, or from the list of procedures done at a teaching hospital? See Barbara Gottlieb, Sounding Board, 332 JAMA 532 (1995).

10. Neighboring states often have very different laws regulating abortion, and women from one state may go to another state to take advantage of what they consider a favorable law. May a state prohibit a woman from crossing a state line to obtain an abortion that would be illegal in the first state? In 1996 a New York jury convicted a woman of "interfering with the custody of a minor," a felony, for taking a 13 year old pregnant girl from Pennsylvania (which requires parental consent) to New York (which does not) to obtain an abortion. See David Stout, Guilty Verdict for Enabling Girl to Have An Abortion, *New York Times*, Oct. 31, 1996, A–8.

11. There may be some basic value issues upon which the pro-choice and pro-life partisans agree. While pro-choice supporters argue that an abortion should be among the choices of a pregnant woman, no one views an abortion as a happy event. Both sides would be pleased if society reached a point where there were no

need for abortions. Similarly, while some pro-life supporters believe that every fetus is entitled to be born alive, many recognize that there are some times when the mother's interest does trump that of the fetus—when the mother's life is at stake, for example, and, perhaps, when the pregnancy is a result of rape or incest—and many recognize that the quality of life of the fetus is a relevant consideration. Very few people oppose early abortions of anencephalic fetuses, for example, or early abortions of other fetuses who are virtually certain to be stillborn or to die within the first few minutes of birth. Both sides may also support expanded state funding for prenatal care and post-natal care, each of which may make abortion a less attractive alternative to pregnant women. Is there a common ground that could give rise to some kind of generally acceptable state policy on abortion, at least in some states? If pro-choice partisans and pro-life partisans were to sit with you and enumerate their common concerns, would there be some basic issues and basic principles upon which they would agree?

12.   There has been a great deal of writing about abortion law. Some recent and provocative articles include Aimee Gauthier, Stenberg v. Carhart: Have the States Lost Their Power to Regulate Abortion?, 36 N. Eng. L. Rev. 625 (2002), Martin Guggenheim, Minor Rights: The Adolescent Abortion Cases, 30 Hofstra L. Rev. 589 (2002), David Cruz, The Sexual Freedom Cases: Contraception, Abortion, Abstinence and the Constitution, 35 Harv. Civ. Rts.-Civ. Lib. L. Rev. 299 (2000), and Melanie Price, The Privacy Paradox: The Divergent Paths of the United States Supreme Court and State Courts on Issues of Sexuality, 33 Ind. L. Rev. 863 (2000). For a comparative approach to some of these issues, see Timothy Stoltzfus Jost, Rights of Embryos and Foetuses in Private Law, 50 Am. J. Comp. L. 633 (2002).

Problem: The Partial Birth Abortion Ban Act of 2003

On November 5, 2003, the following federal statute was enacted:

18 U.S.C. § 1531. Partial-birth abortions prohibited

(a) Any physician who, in or affecting interstate or foreign commerce, knowingly performs a partial-birth abortion and thereby kills a human fetus shall be fined under this title or imprisoned not more than 2 years, or both. This subsection does not apply to a partial-birth abortion that is necessary to save the life of a mother whose life is endangered by a physical disorder, physical illness, or physical injury, including a life-endangering physical condition caused by or arising from the pregnancy itself. * * *

(b) As used in this section—

(1) the term "partial-birth abortion" means an abortion in which the person performing the abortion—

(A) deliberately and intentionally vaginally delivers a living fetus until, in the case of a head-first presentation, the entire fetal head is outside the body of the mother, or, in the case of breech presentation, any part of the fetal trunk past the navel is outside the body of the mother, for the purpose of performing an overt act that the person knows will kill the partially delivered living fetus; and (B) performs the overt act, other than completion of delivery, that kills the partially delivered living fetus; and

(2) the term "physician" means a doctor of medicine or osteopathy legally authorized to practice medicine and surgery * * *.

(c) (1) The father, if married to the mother at the time she receives a partial-birth abortion procedure, and if the mother has not attained the age of 18 years at the time of the abortion, the maternal grandparents of the fetus, may in a civil action obtain appropriate relief, unless the pregnancy resulted from the plaintiff's criminal conduct or the plaintiff consented to the abortion.

(2) Such relief shall include—

(A) money damages for all injuries, psychological and physical, occasioned by the violation of this section; and

(B) statutory damages equal to three times the cost of the partial-birth abortion.

(d) (1) A defendant accused of an offense under this section may seek a hearing before the State Medical Board on whether the physician's conduct was necessary to save the life of the mother whose life was endangered by a physical disorder, physical illness, or physical injury, including a life-endangering physical condition caused by or arising from the pregnancy itself.

(2) The findings on that issue are admissible on that issue at the trial of the defendant. Upon a motion of the defendant, the court shall delay the beginning of the trial for not more than 30 days to permit such a hearing to take place.

(e) A woman upon whom a partial-birth abortion is performed may not be prosecuted under this section, for a conspiracy to violate this section * * *.

In passing this statute, Congress made particularized findings to justify their action. In particular, the Congress found and declared the following:

(1) A moral, medical, and ethical consensus exists that the practice of performing a partial-birth abortion—an abortion in which a physician deliberately and intentionally vaginally delivers a living, unborn child's body until either the entire baby's head is outside the body of the mother, or any part of the baby's trunk past the navel is outside the body of the mother and only the head remains inside the womb, for the purpose of performing an overt act (usually the puncturing of the back of the child's skull and removing the baby's brains) that the person knows will kill the partially delivered infant, performs this act, and then completes delivery of the dead infant—is a gruesome and inhumane procedure that is never medically necessary and should be prohibited.

(2) Rather than being an abortion procedure that is embraced by the medical community, particularly among physicians who routinely perform other abortion procedures, partial-birth abortion remains a disfavored procedure that is not only unnecessary to preserve the health of the mother, but in fact poses serious risks to the long-term health of women and in some circumstances, their lives. As a result, at least 27 States banned the procedure as did the United States Congress which voted to ban the procedure during the 104th, 105th, and 106th Congresses.

(3) In [Stenberg], the United States Supreme Court opined 'that significant medical authority supports the proposition that in some circumstances, [partial birth abortion] would be the safest procedure' for pregnant women who wish to undergo an abortion. Thus, the Court struck down the State of Nebraska's ban on partial-birth abortion procedures, concluding that it placed an 'undue burden' on women seeking abortions because it failed to include an exception for partial-birth abortions deemed necessary to preserve the 'health' of the mother.

(4) In reaching this conclusion, the Court deferred to the Federal district court's factual findings that the partial-birth abortion procedure was statistically and

medically as safe as, and in many circumstances safer than, alternative abortion procedures.

(5) However, substantial evidence presented at the Stenberg trial and overwhelming evidence presented and compiled at extensive congressional hearings, much of which was compiled after the district court hearing in Stenberg, and thus not included in the Stenberg trial record, demonstrates that a partial-birth abortion is never necessary to preserve the health of a woman, poses significant health risks to a woman upon whom the procedure is performed and is outside the standard of medical care.

* * *

(8) However, under well-settled Supreme Court jurisprudence, the United States Congress is not bound to accept the same factual findings that the Supreme Court was bound to accept in Stenberg under the 'clearly erroneous' standard. Rather, the United States Congress is entitled to reach its own factual findings—findings that the Supreme Court accords great deference—and to enact legislation based upon these findings so long as it seeks to pursue a legitimate interest that is within the scope of the Constitution, and draws reasonable inferences based upon substantial evidence.

* * *

(13) There exists substantial record evidence upon which Congress has reached its conclusion that a ban on partial-birth abortion is not required to contain a 'health' exception, because the facts indicate that a partial-birth abortion is never necessary to preserve the health of a woman, poses serious risks to a woman's health, and lies outside the standard of medical care. Congress was informed by extensive hearings held during the 104th, 105th, 107th, and 108th Congresses and passed a ban on partial-birth abortion in the 104th, 105th, and 106th Congresses. These findings reflect the very informed judgment of the Congress that a partial-birth abortion is never necessary to preserve the health of a woman, poses serious risks to a woman's health, and lies outside the standard of medical care, and should, therefore, be banned.

(14) [Here Congress declares, in great detail, based upon testimony received during extensive legislative hearings during the 104th, 105th, 107th, and 108th Congresses, the medical, ethical, legal and social problems with partial birth abortions, as defined by the statute. The Congress finds, in particular, that such abortions are dangerous to the mother, that they are never safer than other abortion procedures, and that they are "brutal and inhumane." Congress concludes its findings by determining that partial birth abortion "is never medically indicated to preserve the health of the mother; is in fact unrecognized as a valid abortion procedure by the mainstream medical community; poses additional health risks to the mother; blurs the line between abortion and infanticide in the killing of a partially-born child just inches from birth; and confuses the role of the physician in childbirth and should, therefore, be banned."]

Does the new federal statute meet the Constitutional test applied in Casey and Stenberg? Does it impose an undue burden on a woman seeking an abortion? Does the statute avoid the Constitutional infirmities of Stenberg? Does it adequately define the procedure? Does it adequately provide for the health of the mother? Are the extensive findings by Congress significant? Can Congress decide, on a divided vote on a contentious issue, that there is a "moral, medical, and ethical consensus" on an issue? In any case, did Congress have authority to promulgate this law? Under the commerce clause? Under some other provision of the Constitution?

Why do you think Congress provided for civil actions against those who perform partial-birth abortions in addition to criminal sanctions? Is it appropriate to allow such actions to be brought by the father of the aborted fetus? The maternal grandparents? Are there additional Constitutional problems that arise out of giving this authority to the father or grandparents, even if the pregnant woman actually consented to the abortion?

If you do not think that this statute is Constitutional, could you draft a statute that would ban partial-birth abortions in some circumstances and that would pass muster?

Note: The Freedom of Access to Clinic Entrances Act of 1994

In the 1990s the focus of the challenge to abortion practices was moving from the courts and the legislatures to medical clinics that provided abortion services. Often those clinics were the subject of protests, prayer vigils, or other demonstrations, and in a few cases violence resulted. Some employees of the clinics feared for their safety, and some were also concerned that patients coming to the clinics were being harassed and intimidated by those outside. Those participating in the demonstrations argued that they were doing nothing more than exercising their first amendment rights, and that they were doing their best to make the exercise of those rights effective by dissuading patients from having abortions. In response to some particularly egregious incidents of violence perpetrated against a few abortion clinics, Congress passed the Freedom of Access to Clinic Entrances Act of 1994 ("FACE"), which provides:

Whoever—

(1) by force or threat of force or by physical obstruction, intentionally injures, intimidates or interferes with or attempts to injure, intimidate or interfere with any person because that person is or has been, or in order to intimidate such person or any other person or any class of persons from, obtaining or providing reproductive health services; * * * (3) intentionally damages or destroys the property of a facility, or attempts to do so, because such facility provides reproductive health services * * * shall be guilty of a crime and fined or imprisoned.

18 U.S.C.A. section 248 (a). The statute provides longer prison terms and larger fines for repeat offenders and shorter prison terms and smaller fines for offenses "involving exclusively a nonviolent physical intrusion." 18 U.S.C.A. section 248(b). The term "reproductive health services" is expansively defined to include "medical, surgical, counseling or referral services * * * including services relating to * * * the termination of a pregnancy" whether those services are provided "in a hospital, clinic, physician's office, or other facility." 18 U.S.C.A. section 248(e)(5). In addition to its criminal sanctions, the Act provides for civil enforcement by the United States Attorney General and the attorneys general of

the states, and for civil damages of $5,000 per violation in lieu of actual damages, at the election of the plaintiff. 18 U.S.C.A. section 248(c)(1)(B).

The Act also extends the same protection that is accorded to those seeking access to clinics to those "seeking to exercise the First Amendment right of religious freedom at a place of religious worship." This additional protection was originally added by an amendment offered by Senator Hatch, who opposed the bill and thought (incorrectly) that this addition might kill it. The Act explicitly provides that it is not to be construed to prohibit any "expressive conduct" protected by the First Amendment, 18 U.S.C.A. section 248(d)(1). Eight circuits have found that Congress had authority to promulgate FACE against arguments that the statute exceeded the Congress's commerce clause powers; and one, United States v. Gregg, 226 F.3d 253 (3d Cir. 2000) (2–1 on the commerce clause issue), made that finding after considering the Supreme Court's restrictive reading of the commerce clause power in United States v. Morrison, 529 U.S. 598, 120 S.Ct. 1740, 146 L.Ed.2d 658 (2000), which found that Congress had no authority under the commerce clause to promulgate the civil liability provisions of the Violence Against Women Act ("VAWA") because the regulated acts were not commercial in nature. The majority in Gregg argued that Congress reasonably could have concluded that the statute was necessary to address the burden protesters were placing on the business operations of the abortion clinics, which were engaged in interstate commerce, and that FACE was thus distinguishable from VAWA. The dissent in the Gregg case argued that FACE applied to the non-economic acts of protesting abortion, not the business aspects of the operation of abortion clinics, and that FACE was indistinguishable from VAWA in this respect. The Supreme Court has not yet addressed the issue of the constitutionality of FACE.

This Act is not the only weapon provided to those who are concerned about the effects of demonstrations around clinics that perform abortions. Earlier in 1994 the United States Supreme Court declared that RICO could be applied against those who violate laws to blockade the clinics, and that created the possibility of substantial civil damage awards against organizations and individuals that encourage or participate in illegal conduct to limit the access of women to the clinics. National Organization for Women v. Scheidler, 510 U.S. 249, 114 S.Ct. 798, 127 L.Ed.2d 99 (1994). Both the Freedom of Access to Clinic Entrances Act and RICO were implicated in early 1999 when an Oregon federal court jury returned a verdict in excess of $107 million against twelve individuals, the American Coalition of Life Activists and the Advocates for Life Ministries, for maintaining a web site that threatened those who performed abortions. The site, called "The Nuremberg Files," listed physicians who performed abortions, drew lines through those who had been murdered, and listed those who had been wounded by would-be assassins in gray. The defendants also published Old West style "wanted" posters with the names and pictures of physicians who performed abortions. The defendants claimed a first amendment right to publish the web site and the wanted posters, and some first amendment analysts were concerned about the potentially chilling effect of such a large judgment on the publication of unpopular political views. The defendants also claimed that they had transferred their assets to be able to avoid paying any part of the judgment, although their unsubtle approach to the transfer is likely to hinder its legal success. See Sam Howe Verhook, Creators of Anti–Abortion Web Site Told to Pay Millions, New York Times, February 3, 1999.

Trial courts have also issued injunctions limiting abortion protesters where judges thought that was necessary to protect the rights of clinic patients. In

Schenck v. Pro–Choice Network, 519 U.S. 357, 117 S.Ct. 855, 137 L.Ed.2d 1 (1997) the Supreme Court upheld an injunction which created a 15–foot protected "bubble zone" around the doorways and driveways of a clinic offering abortion services, and it also upheld a limit on the number of people who could "counsel" a woman entering the clinic. The Court determined, further, that those trying to dissuade a patient from having an abortion could be required to desist when the patient asked them to do so, although the Court found that a moveable bubble zone that followed the patient as she entered the clinic would violate the free speech rights of pro-life protesters.

Three years later, in Hill v. Colorado, 530 U.S. 703, 120 S.Ct. 2480, 147 L.Ed.2d 597 (2000), decided the same day as Stenberg v. Carhart, the Supreme Court upheld a Colorado statute that prohibited any person within 100 feet of a health care facility's entrance door from knowingly coming within 8 feet of another person, without the consent of that person, to pass a "leaflet [or] handbill, to displa[y] a sign to, or [e]ngage in oral protest, education or counseling with that person * * *." The Court distinguished the larger moveable bubble zone in Schenck, and rejected the first amendment attack on the Colorado law. In dissent, Justice Scalia complained that the Colorado statute "enjoy[ed] the benefit of the 'ad hoc nullification machine' that the Court has set in motion to push aside whatever doctrines of constitutional law stand in the way of th[e] highly favored practice [of abortion]. * * * [T]oday's decision is not an isolated distortion of our traditional constitutional principles, but is one of many aggressively proabortion novelties announced by the Court in recent years." Justice Kennedy dissented separately, suggesting that the judgment of the Court "strikes at the heart of the reasoned, careful balance I had believed was the basis for the joint opinion in Casey."

The news has not been all bad for abortion protesters. In 2003 the Supreme Court determined that pro-life advocates do not obtain any property from another, and thus do not commit the federal crime of extortion under the Hobbs Act, when they use force or threats of force at abortion clinics to dissuade women from seeking abortion services. Whether the protesters had committed the crime of extortion was relevant to the underlying RICO claim filed by the National Organization of Women and others. *Scheidler v. NOW, Inc.*, 537 U.S. 393, 123 S.Ct. 1057, 154 L.Ed.2d 991 (2003).

Note: The Blurry Distinction Between Contraception and Abortion, and the Advent of Mifepristone (RU–486)

If contraception refers to any process designed to prevent a pregnancy, and abortion refers to any process designed to end an established pregnancy, then the point at which the process of contraception becomes the process of abortion is at the commencement of the pregnancy. There is some ambiguity, however, about when the pregnancy begins, just as there is some ambiguity about when "conception" takes place.

> The Missouri statute defines "conception" as "the fertilization of the ovum of a female by a sperm of a male," even though standard medical texts equate "conception" with implantation in the uterus occurring about six days after fertilization.

Webster v. Reproductive Health Services, 492 U.S. at 561, 109 S.Ct. at 3080 (Stevens, J., concurring in part and dissenting in part). When does the pregnancy begin? Does the fact that a large number of fertilized eggs—perhaps 50%—never implant, suggest that pregnancy does not begin until implantation? Is the fact that cells of the fertilized ovum are identical for about three days, and then begin to separate into differentiated cells that will become the placenta, on one hand, and cells that will become the embryo and fetus, on the other, relevant?

If there is to be a legal difference between contraception and abortion, the courts will have to determine when "conception" takes place and when a pregnancy begins. As Justice Stevens points out, some forms of what we now consider contraception are really devices designed to stop the fertilized egg from implanting in the uterus, not devices designed for avoiding fertilization of the egg in the first place.

> An intrauterine device, commonly called an IUD "works primarily by preventing a fertilized egg from implanting"; other contraceptive methods that may prevent implantation include "morning-after pills," high-dose estrogen pills taken after intercourse, particularly in cases of rape, and mifepristone (also known as RU 486), a pill that works "during the indeterminate period between contraception and abortion," low level estrogen "combined" pills—a version of the ordinary, daily ingested birth control pill—also may prevent the fertilized egg from reaching the uterine wall and implanting [ ].

492 U.S. at 563, 109 S.Ct. at 3081 (Stevens, J., concurring in part and dissenting in part). If the law recognizes a distinction between contraception and abortion, should the law also be required to define that point at which contraception becomes abortion? Justice Stevens suggests that we must depend upon a medical definition of pregnancy, because any alternative would constitute the legal adoption of a theological position and thus be a violation of the establishment clause of the First Amendment. Do you agree? Can you develop a coherent legal argument that the state may regulate abortion in any way it sees fit, but *may not* prohibit a woman's choice to stop a fertilized ovum from reaching her uterus and implanting?

There are several reasons that contraception might be distinguished from abortion as a matter of law. Historically, one significant factor has been that the highly invasive and comparatively risky surgical nature of abortion has contrasted so substantially with the medical nature of contraception, which depends on the use of pills or relatively simple devices. This distinction has proven evanescent as mifepristone, the "abortion pill" formerly known as RU–486 and distributed in the United States as Mifeprex, has become available. Mifepristone stops the production of progesterone, which is necessary to allow for implantation and the maintenance of the pregnancy. Once the mifepristone has been successfully used, the patient takes another drug to cause contractions and expel the embryonic tissue. This drug is now chosen by about half of the eligible women who have abortions in many countries in Europe, where it has been available since the early 1990s. This method of abortion is available only for the first seven weeks of pregnancy; about one-third of American abortions are performed during this time window. While its costs may be higher and its side effects may not be much better than those for surgical abortions, the availability of mifepristone was expected to make pregnancy terminations easier to obtain in rural (and other) areas where patients have less access to surgical interventions.

Although the FDA found the drug to be safe in 1996, it was not approved for distribution until late in 2000. Its distribution in the United States was then further held up by a number of problems, some stemming from the vitality of its political opposition. By early 2004 it was widely distributed and had been used by almost 200,000 women in the United States. In the vast majority of cases it was administered in a medical setting, and so it has not made pregnancy termination more available to those who cannot visit a clinic. It still accounts for a very small percentage—less than 10%—of abortions performed in the United States, although its use is increasing.

In late 2003 the safety of mifepristone was called into question when 18–year-old Holly Patterson died in an emergency room in California a week after taking the drug. Her death lead to a renewal of the debate over the propriety of the use of this drug, and the potential risks of the consequent medical (rather than surgical) abortion. As one commentator pointed out, writing about the Patterson case, mifepristone "has long had a symbolic significance transcending its medical use." Gina Kolata, Death at 18 Spurs Debate Over a Pill for Abortion, New York Times, September 24, 2003, at A–24.

In early 2004 the F.D.A. commissioner was considering the recommendation of two F.D.A. expert advisory committees that Plan B, an emergency contraceptive that acts to block both fertilization and implantation, be sold over the counter. Abortion opponents are split on the issue; it will decrease the need for other abortions, but it may constitute abortion itself. For a taste of the discussion around this issue, see Gina Kolata, Debate on Selling Morning–After Pill Over the Counter, New York Times, December 12, 2003, A–1. In 2004 one Texas pharmacist was fired for his refusal, on moral and religious grounds, to dispense the "morning after" pill to a victim of rape who had a prescription for it. She was forced to travel to another pharmacy to find the drug. See Pharmacist Fired for Denying "Morning After" Pill, CNN Thursday, February 12, 2004.

4. *Sterilization*

The sterilization of the mentally retarded has given rise to considerable discussion beginning with the development of the eugenics movement in the late 19th century. While there is no significant evidence that most forms of mental retardation are genetic and inheritable, there remains a residue of social support for the notion that this society can purify its gene pool by sterilizing those who would pollute it, such as the mentally retarded and criminals. The aim of the eugenics movement was confirmed by Justice Holmes in Buck v. Bell, 274 U.S. 200, 47 S.Ct. 584, 71 L.Ed. 1000 (1927), which dealt with an attempt by the State of Virginia to sterilize Carrie Buck, who had been committed to the State Colony for Epileptics and the Feeble Minded. The State was opposed on the grounds that the statute authorizing sterilization violated the Fourteenth Amendment by denying Ms. Buck due process of law and the equal protection of the law. Justice Holmes responded:

> Carrie Buck is a feeble minded white woman who was committed to the State Colony above mentioned in due form. She is the daughter of a feeble minded mother in the same institution and the mother of an illegitimate feeble minded child * * *.

> [The lower court found] "that Carrie Buck is the probable potential parent of socially inadequate offspring, likewise afflicted, that she may be sterilized without detriment to her general health and that her welfare and that of society will be promoted by her sterilization." * * * We have seen more than once that the public welfare may call upon the best citizens for their lives. It would be strange if it could not call upon those who already sapped the strength of the state for these lesser sacrifices, often not felt to be such by those concerned, in order to prevent our being swamped with incompetence. It is better for all the world if instead of

waiting to execute degenerate offspring for crime, or to let them starve for their imbecility, society can prevent those who are manifestly unfit from continuing their kind. The principle that sustains compulsory vaccination is broad enough to cover cutting the fallopian tubes. [ ] Three generations of imbeciles are enough.

* * *

The Supreme Court has never overturned the decision in *Buck v. Bell,* although it is of questionable precedential value today. Society's perception of the mentally incompetent has changed and, especially after the Nazi experience, arguments based upon eugenics are held in low regard. In fact, when Carrie Buck was discovered in the Appalachian hills in 1980, she was found to be mentally competent and extremely disappointed that throughout her life she was unable to bear another child.

The Supreme Court addressed eugenic sterilizations once more, in Skinner v. Oklahoma, 316 U.S. 535, 62 S.Ct. 1110, 86 L.Ed. 1655 (1942). The Court determined that the equal protection clause prohibited Oklahoma from enforcing its statute which required sterilizing persons convicted of repeated criminal acts, but only if the crimes were within special categories. White collar crimes were exempted from these categories, and the Supreme Court's determination was based on the state's irrational distinction between blue collar (sterilizable) and white collar (unsterilizable) crimes. The Court was asked to, but did not, overrule *Buck v. Bell.*

Recent programs to sterilize individual mentally retarded people have been based on the convenience of sterilization for the patient and his (or, virtually always, her) family. Some who have sought sterilization for the mentally retarded have been worried about the consequences of sexual exposure upon people who can barely cope with the minimal requirements of daily life; some have suggested that it would be much easier to care for patients, especially menstruating women, if they were sterilized; and others have suggested that sterilization might make it practical for mentally retarded people who would otherwise be institutionalized to live at home. Generally, courts have acted to protect the mentally retarded from sterilization if there is any less restrictive alternative that would serve the same interests.

Not all of the protection has come out of the judiciary, however. In California, for example, the Probate Code was amended to prohibit the sterilization of mentally retarded persons. This statute was challenged by the conservator of an incompetent mentally retarded woman who argued that the legislature had denied her a procreative choice that was extended to all other women in the community. She argued that to deny her the opportunity for a sterilization when there would be no other safe and effective method of contraception available to her would be to deny her important constitutionally protected rights. While a mentally retarded person may have a right not to be unfairly sterilized, she argued, she has a correlative right not to be unfairly and arbitrarily denied a sterilization (and thus an opportunity to satisfy her sexuality).

In Conservatorship of Valerie N., 40 Cal.3d 143, 219 Cal.Rptr. 387, 707 P.2d 760 (1985), the California Supreme Court upheld the challenge and threw out the statute:

True protection of procreative choice can be accomplished only if the state permits the court supervised substituted judgment of the conservator to be exercised on behalf of the conservatee who is unable to personally exercise this right. Limiting the exercise of that judgment by denying the right to effective contraception through sterilization to this class of conservatees denies them a right held not only by conservatees who are competent to consent but by all other women. Respondent has demonstrated neither a compelling state interest in restricting this right nor a basis upon which to conclude that the prohibition contained [in the statute] is necessary to achieve the identified purpose of furthering the incompetent's right not to be sterilized.

One justice wrote a particularly strong dissent:

Today's holding will permit the state, through the legal fiction of substituted consent, to deprive many women permanently of the right to conceive and bear children. The majority run roughshod over this fundamental constitutional right in a misguided attempt to guarantee a procreative choice for one they assume has never been capable of choice and never will be. * * *

The majority opinion opens the door to abusive sterilization practices which will serve the convenience of conservators, parents, and service providers rather than incompetent conservatees. The ugly history of sterilization abuse against developmentally disabled persons in the name of seemingly enlightened social policies counsels a different choice.

Rather than place an absolute prohibition upon the sterilization of the developmentally disabled as the California legislature attempted to do, most courts attempt to safeguard those who may be subject to sterilization by applying very strict procedural requirements to any proposed sterilization. For example, the standard that has been most often emulated is that provided in In re Guardianship of Hayes, 93 Wash.2d 228, 608 P.2d 635 (1980), where the court set out the procedural requirements simply and explicitly:

The decision can only be made in a superior court proceeding in which (1) the incompetent individual is represented by a disinterested guardian ad litem, (2) the court has received independent advice based upon a comprehensive medical, psychological, and social evaluation of the individual, and (3) to the greatest extent possible, the court has elicited and taken into account the view of the incompetent individual.

Within this framework, the judge must first find by clear, cogent and convincing evidence that the individual is (1) incapable of making his or her own decision about sterilization, and (2) unlikely to develop sufficiently to make an informed judgment about sterilization in the foreseeable future.

Next it must be proved by clear, cogent and convincing evidence that there is a need for contraception. The judge must find that the individual is (1) physically capable of procreation, and (2) likely to engage in sexual activity at the present or in the near future under circumstances likely to result in pregnancy, and must find in addition that (3) the nature and extent of the individual's disability, as determined by empirical evidence and not solely on the basis of standardized tests, renders him or her permanently incapable of caring for a child, even with reasonable assistance.

Finally, there must be no alternatives to sterilization. The judge must find that by clear, cogent and convincing evidence (1) all less drastic contraceptive methods, including supervision, education and training, have been proved unworkable or inapplicable, and (2) the proposed method of sterilization entails the least invasion of the body of the individual. In addition, it must be shown by clear, cogent and convincing evidence that (3) the current state of scientific and medical knowledge does not suggest either (a) that a reversible sterilization procedure or other less drastic contraceptive method will shortly be available or (b) that science is on the threshold of an advance in the treatment of the individual's disability.

The court recognized that there was "a heavy presumption against sterilization of an individual incapable of informed consent" and that the burden "will be even harder to overcome in the case of a minor incompetent * * *." Some have read the procedural requirements of *Hayes* as effectively removing the possibility of the sterilization of the developmentally disabled. Can you imagine a case that would meet the stiff "procedural" requirements of *Hayes?*

Recently courts and legislatures have considered interventions that are designed to provide sterilization or some form of castration as criminal punishments (or "treatment" for those disposed to criminal conduct). In State v. Kline, 155 Or.App. 96, 963 P.2d 697 (1998) the Oregon Court of Appeals found that a criminal defendant's right to procreate was not unconstitutionally abridged when he was ordered not to have children upon his conviction for mistreatment of children. In State v. Oakley, 245 Wis.2d 447, 629 N.W.2d 200 (2001), the Wisconsin Supreme Court upheld an order that a defendant not father additional children as a condition of his probation after conviction for intentional failure to pay child support, a felony. A similar "no procreation" order will be considered by the Ohio Supreme Court in 2004 in a father's appeal from a conviction for failing to pay child support for three of his children. Two months after this condition was imposed, the father married his girlfriend (with whom he had previously had two other children), and both the father and his wife claimed a right to procreation. State v. Talty, 2003 Ohio 3161 (App.2003), rev. gr., 100 Ohio St.3d 1469, 798 N.E.2d 405 (2003).

One group, Children Requiring a Caring Community (Crack), also called Project Prevention, is now offering a cash payment (most recently, $200) to any drug addict who can prove that he or she has been sterilized or put on some long term contraceptive. The group was started by a woman who adopted four children who had been affected by prenatal drug abuse, and the bounty is paid upon proof of both addiction (an arrest record or doctor's note will do) and sterilization. The organization does not pay for the sterilization or long-term contraception itself. For a description of the program see C.M. Vega, Sterilization Offer to Addicts Reopens Ethics Issue, New York Times, January 6, 2003, at A–1. Is there any ethical problem with this program? What is it? Who is being more paternalistic, those who want to encourage drug addicted people not to have children, or those who want to save these same poor, drug addicted people from considering this offer? Are there people our society should discourage from reproducing, or is that always improper? If so, are the drug addicted among those people? Are issues of race, ethnicity and gender relevant to your consideration of this issue? How?

For a history of sterilization of the developmentally disabled in this country, see Richard K. Sherlock and Robert D. Sherlock, Sterilizing the Retarded: Constitutional, Statutory and Policy Alternatives, 60 N.C.L.Rev. 943 (1982). For thoughtful discussion of sexuality in the developmentally disabled, see S.F. Haavik and K. Menninger, Sexuality, Law and the Developmentally Disabled Person (1981). For a more recent analysis of the various interest at stake in such cases, see R. Adler, Estate of C.W.: A Pragmatic Approach to the Involuntary Sterilization of the Mentally Disabled, 20 Nova L.Rev. 1323 (1996). For a discussion of "chemical castration" provisions that apply to convicted sex offenders, see William Winslade et al., Castrating Pedophiles Convicted of Sex Offenses Against Children: New Treatment or Old Punishment?, 51 SMU L.Rev. 349 (1998), and Karen Rebish, Nipping the Problem in the Bud: The Constitutionality of California's Castration Law, 14 N.Y.L. Sch. J. Hum. Rts. 507 (1998). For another review of the California statute—the first to actually require "chemical castration" in some cases—see Recent Legislation: Constitutional Law, 110 Harv. L. Rev. 799 (1997).

5. Tort Remedies for Failed Reproductive Control: Wrongful Birth, Wrongful Life and Wrongful Conception

SMITH v. COTE

Supreme Court of New Hampshire, 1986.
128 N.H. 231, 513 A.2d 341.

BATCHELDER, JUSTICE.

* * *

* * * Plaintiff Linda J. Smith became pregnant early in 1979. During the course of her pregnancy Linda was under the care of the defendants, physicians who specialize in obstetrics and gynecology. Linda consulted the defendants on April 8, 1979, complaining of nausea, abdominal pain and a late menstrual period. * * *

On August 3, 1979, nearly four months after the April visits, Linda underwent a rubella titre test at the direction of the defendants. The test indicated that Linda had been exposed to rubella. At the time the test was performed, Linda was in the second trimester of pregnancy.

Linda brought her pregnancy to full term. On January 1, 1980, she gave birth to a daughter, Heather B. Smith, who is also a plaintiff in this action. Heather was born a victim of congenital rubella syndrome. Today, at age six, Heather suffers from bilateral cataracts, multiple congenital heart defects, motor retardation, and a significant hearing impairment. She is legally blind, and has undergone surgery for her cataracts and heart condition.

In March 1984 the plaintiffs began this negligence action. They allege that Linda contracted rubella early in her pregnancy and that, while she was under the defendants' care, the defendants negligently failed to test for and discover in a timely manner her exposure to the disease. The plaintiffs further contend that the defendants negligently failed to advise Linda of the potential for birth defects in a fetus exposed to rubella, thereby depriving her of the knowledge necessary to an informed decision as to whether to give birth to a potentially impaired child. * * *

The plaintiffs do not allege that the defendants caused Linda to conceive her child or to contract rubella, or that the defendants could have prevented the effects of the disease on the fetus. Rather, the plaintiffs contend that if Linda had known of the risks involved she would have obtained a eugenic abortion.

The action comprises three counts, only two of which are relevant here. In Count I, Linda seeks damages for her emotional distress, for the extraordinary maternal care that she must provide Heather because of Heather's birth defects, and for the extraordinary medical and educational costs she has sustained and will sustain in rearing her daughter.

* * *

In Count III, Heather seeks damages for her birth with defects, for the extraordinary medical and educational costs she will sustain, and for the impairment of her childhood attributable to her mother's diminished capacity to nurture her and cope with her problems.

* * * [T]he Superior Court transferred to us the following questions of law:

"A. Will New Hampshire Law recognize a wrongful birth cause of action by the mother of a wilfully conceived baby suffering from birth defects[?]"

B.   If the answer to question A is in the affirmative, will New Hampshire law allow recovery in such a cause of action for damages for emotional distress, extraordinary maternal child care, and the extraordinary medical, institutional and other special rearing expenses necessary to treat the child's impairments?

C.   Will New Hampshire law recognize a cause of action for wrongful life brought by a minor child suffering from birth defects[?]

D.   If the answer to question C is in the affirmative, what general and specific damages may the child recover in such an action?"

* * *

We recognize that the termination of pregnancy involves controversial and divisive social issues. Nonetheless, the Supreme Court of the United States has held that a woman has a constitutionally secured right to terminate a pregnancy. *Roe v. Wade* [ ]. It follows from *Roe* that the plaintiff Linda Smith may seek, and the defendants may provide, information and advice that may affect the exercise of that right. The basic social and constitutional issue underlying this case thus has been resolved; we need not cover ground already traveled by a court whose interpretation of the National Constitution binds us. Today we decide only whether, given the existence of the right of choice recognized in *Roe,* our common law should allow the development of a duty to exercise care in providing information that bears on that choice.

For the sake of terminological clarity, we make some preliminary distinctions. A wrongful birth claim is a claim brought by the parents of a child born with severe defects against a physician who negligently fails to inform them, in a timely fashion, of an increased possibility that the mother will give birth to such a child, thereby precluding an informed decision as to whether to have the child. * * *

A wrongful life claim, on the other hand, is brought not by the parents of a child born with birth defects, but by or on behalf of the child. The child contends that the defendant physician negligently failed to inform the child's parents of the risk of bearing a defective infant, and hence prevented the parents from choosing to avoid the child's birth.

I. WRONGFUL BIRTH: CAUSE OF ACTION

We first must decide whether New Hampshire law recognizes a cause of action for wrongful birth. Although we have never expressly recognized this cause of action, we have considered a similar claim, one for "wrongful conception." In *Kingsbury v. Smith,* 122 N.H. 237, 442 A.2d 1003 (1982), the plaintiffs, a married couple, had had three children and wanted no more. In an attempt to prevent the conception of additional offspring, Mrs. Kingsbury underwent a tubal ligation. The operation failed, however, and Mrs. Kingsbury later gave birth to a fourth child, a normal, healthy infant. The plaintiffs sued the physicians who had performed the operation, alleging that in giving birth to an unwanted child they had sustained an injury caused by the defendants' negligence.

We held that the common law of New Hampshire permitted a claim for wrongful conception, an action "for damages arising from the birth of a child to which a negligently performed sterilization procedure or a negligently filled birth control prescription which fails to prevent conception was a contributing factor." We reasoned that failure to recognize a cause of action for wrongful conception would leave "a void in the area of recovery for medical malpractice" that would dilute the standard of professional conduct in the area of family planning. [ ]

In this case, the mother contends that her wrongful birth claim fits comfortably within the framework established in *Kingsbury* and is consistent with well established tort principles. The defendants argue that tort principles cannot be extended so as to accommodate wrongful birth, asserting that they did not cause the injury alleged here, and that in any case damages cannot be fairly and accurately ascertained.

* * *

* * * In general, at common law, one who suffers an injury to his person or property because of the negligent act of another has a right of action in tort. [ ] In order to sustain an action for negligence, the plaintiff must establish the existence of a duty, the breach of which proximately causes injury to the plaintiff. [ ]

The first two elements of a negligence action, duty and breach, present no conceptual difficulties here. If the plaintiff establishes that a physician-patient relationship with respect to the pregnancy existed between the defendants and her, it follows that the defendants assumed a duty to use reasonable care in attending and treating her. [ ] Given the decision in *Roe v. Wade,* we recognize that the "due care" standard, may have required the defendants to ensure that Linda had an opportunity to make an informed decision regarding the procreative options available to her. [ ] It is a question of fact whether this standard required the defendants, at an appropriate stage of Linda's pregnancy, to test for, diagnose, and disclose her exposure to rubella. The standard is defined by reference to the standards and recommended practices and procedures of the medical profession, the training, experience and professed degree of skill of the average medical practitioner, and all other relevant circumstances.

We note that this standard does not require a physician to identify and disclose every chance, no matter how remote, of the occurrence of every possible birth "defect," no matter how insignificant. [ ] If (1) the applicable standard of care required the defendants to test for and diagnose Linda's rubella infection in a timely manner, and to inform her of the possible effects of the virus on her child's health; and (2) the defendants failed to fulfill this obligation; then the defendants breached their duty of due care.

The third element, causation, is only slightly more troublesome. The defendants point out that proof that they caused the alleged injury depends on a finding that Linda would have chosen to terminate her pregnancy if she had been fully apprised of the risks of birth defects. The defendants argue that this hypothetical chain of events is too remote to provide the basis for a finding of causation.

We do not agree. No logical obstacle precludes proof of causation in the instant case. Such proof is furnished if the plaintiff can show that, but for the defendants' negligent failure to inform her of the risks of bearing a child with birth defects, she would have obtained an abortion. * * *

We turn to the final element of a negligence action, injury. Linda contends that, in bearing a defective child after being deprived of the opportunity to make an informed procreative decision, she sustained an injury. The defendants argue that, because both benefits (the joys of parenthood) and harms (the alleged emotional and pecuniary damages) have resulted from Heather's birth, damages cannot accurately be measured, and no injury to Linda can be proved. The defendants in effect assert that the birth of a child can never constitute an injury to its parents; hence, when an actor's negligence causes a child to be born, that actor cannot be held liable in tort.

We do not agree. We recognize * * * that in some circumstances parents may be injured by the imposition on them of extraordinary liabilities following the birth of a child. Under *Roe,* prospective parents may have constitutionally cognizable reasons for avoiding the emotional and pecuniary burdens that may attend the birth of a child suffering from birth defects. Scientific advances in prenatal health care provide the basis upon which parents may make the informed decisions that *Roe* protects. We see no reason to hold that as a matter of law those who act negligently in providing such care cannot cause harm * * *.

The defendants' emphasis on the inherent difficulty of measuring damages is misplaced. An allegation of "injury," an instance of actionable harm, is distinct from a claim for "damages," a sum of money awarded to one who has suffered an injury. We have long held that difficulty in calculating damages is not a sufficient reason to deny recovery to an injured party. [ ] Other courts have recognized that the complexity of the damages calculation in a wrongful birth case is not directly relevant to the validity of the asserted cause of action. [ ]

We hold that New Hampshire recognizes a cause of action for wrongful birth. Notwithstanding the disparate views within society on the controversial practice of abortion, we are bound by the law that protects a woman's right to choose to terminate her pregnancy. Our holding today neither encourages nor discourages this practice, [ ] nor does it rest upon a judgment that, in some absolute sense, Heather Smith should never have been born. We cannot (and need not, for purposes of this action) make such a judgment. We must, however, do our best to effectuate the first principles of our law of negligence: to deter negligent conduct, and to compensate the victims of those who act unreasonably.

II.   WRONGFUL BIRTH: DAMAGES

We next must decide what elements of damages may be recovered in a wrongful birth action. The wrongful birth cause of action is unique. Although it involves an allegation of medical malpractice, it is not (as are most medical malpractice cases) a claim arising from physical injury. It is instead based on a negligent invasion of the parental right to decide whether to avoid the birth of a child with congenital defects. When parents are denied the opportunity to make this decision, important personal interests may be impaired, including an interest in avoiding the special expenses necessitated by the condition of a child born with defects, an interest in preventing the sorrow and anguish that may befall the parents of such a child, and an interest in preserving personal autonomy, which may include the making of informed reproductive choices. [ ] The task of assessing and quantifying the tangible and intangible harms that result when these interests are impaired presents a formidable challenge.

Linda seeks compensation for the extraordinary medical and educational costs that she will sustain in raising Heather, as well as for the extraordinary maternal care that she must provide her child. In addition, she asks for damages for her "emotional distress, anxiety and trauma," which she claims is a natural and foreseeable consequence of the injury she has sustained, and hence should be included as an essential element in the calculation of general damages. We consider these claims for tangible and intangible losses in turn.

A.   *Tangible Losses*

The usual rule of compensatory damages in tort cases requires that the person wronged receive a sum of money that will restore him as nearly as possible to the position he would have been in if the wrong had not been committed. [ ] In the present case, if the defendants' failure to advise Linda of the risks of birth defects amounted to negligence, then the reasonably foreseeable result of that negligence was that Linda would incur the expenses involved in raising her daughter. According to the usual rule of damages, then, Linda should recover the entire cost of raising Heather, including both ordinary child-rearing costs and the extraordinary costs attributable to Heather's condition.

However, "few if any jurisdictions appear ready to apply this traditional rule of damages with full vigor in wrongful birth cases." [ ] Although at least one court has ruled that all child-rearing costs should be recoverable, most courts are reluctant to impose liability to this extent. A special rule of damages has emerged; in most jurisdictions the parents may recover only the extraordinary medical and educational costs attributable to the birth defects. In the present case, in accordance with the rule prevailing elsewhere, Linda seeks to recover, as tangible losses, only her extraordinary costs.

The logic of the "extraordinary costs" rule has been criticized. * * * The rule in effect divides a plaintiff's pecuniary losses into two categories, ordinary costs and extraordinary costs, and treats the latter category as compensable while ignoring the former category. At first glance, this bifurcation seems difficult to justify.

The disparity is explained, however, by reference to the rule requiring mitigation of tort damages. The "avoidable consequences" rule specifies that a plaintiff may not recover damages for "any harm that he could have avoided by the use of reasonable effort or expenditure" after the occurrence of the tort. Rigidly applied, this rule would appear to require wrongful birth plaintiffs to place their children for adoption. [ ] Because of our profound respect for the sanctity of the family, [ ] we are loathe to sanction the application of the rule in these circumstances. If the rule is not applied, however, wrongful birth plaintiffs may receive windfalls. Hence, a special rule limiting recovery of damages is warranted.

Although the extraordinary costs rule departs from traditional principles of tort damages, it is neither illogical nor unprecedented. The rule represents an application in a tort context of the expectancy rule of damages employed in breach of contracts cases. Wrongful birth plaintiffs typically desire a child (and plan to support it) from the outset. [ ] It is the defendants' duty to help them achieve this goal. When the plaintiffs' expectations are frustrated by the defendants' negligence, the extraordinary costs rule "merely attempts to put plaintiffs in the position they expected to be in with defendant's help." [ ]

Under this view of the problem, ordinary child-rearing costs are analogous to a price the plaintiffs were willing to pay in order to achieve an expected result. According to contract principles, plaintiffs "may not have a return in damages of the price and also receive what was to be obtained for the price." [ ] We note that expectancy damages are recoverable in other kinds of tort cases, [ ] and that contract principles are hardly unknown in medical malpractice litigation, which has roots in contract as well as in tort. [ ] In light of the difficulty posed by tort damages principles in these circumstances, we see no obstacle—logical or otherwise—to use of the extraordinary costs rule. [ ]

The extraordinary costs rule ensures that the parents of a deformed child will recover the medical and educational costs attributable to the child's impairment. At the same time it establishes a necessary and clearly defined boundary to liability in this area. [ ] Accordingly, we hold that a plaintiff in a wrongful birth case may recover the extraordinary medical and educational costs attributable to the child's deformities, but may not recover ordinary child-raising costs.

Three points stand in need of clarification. First, parents may recover extraordinary costs incurred both before and after their child attains majority. Some courts do not permit recovery of post-majority expenses, on the theory that the parents' obligation of support terminates when the child reaches twenty-one. [ ] In New Hampshire, however, parents are required to support their disabled adult offspring. [ ]

Second, recovery should include compensation for the extraordinary maternal care that has been and will be provided to the child. Linda alleges that her parental obligations and duties, which include feeding, bathing, and exercising Heather, substantially exceed those of parents of a normal child. One court has ruled that parents "cannot recover for services that they have rendered or will render personally to their own child without incurring financial expense." [ ] We see no reason, however, to treat as noncompensable the burdens imposed on a parent who must devote extraordinary time and effort to caring for a child with birth defects. * * * Avoiding these burdens is often among the primary motivations of one who chooses not to bear a child likely to suffer from birth defects. We hold that a parent may recover for his or her ministrations to his or her child to the extent that such ministrations:

(1) are made necessary by the child's condition;

(2) clearly exceed those ordinarily rendered by parents of a normal child; and

(3) are reasonably susceptible of valuation.

* * *

Third, to the extent that the parent's alleged emotional distress results in tangible pecuniary losses, such as medical expenses or counseling fees, such losses are recoverable. [ ]

B. Intangible Losses

Existing damages principles do not resolve the issue whether recovery for emotional distress should be permitted in wrongful birth cases. Emotional distress damages are not uniformly recoverable once a protected interest is shown to have been invaded. [The court discussed New Hampshire precedent which denied parents damages for emotional distress resulting from the death of their children.]

This case arises from a child's birth, not a child's injury or death. Nonetheless, we are struck by the parallels between the claims for emotional distress in [cases involving the death of children] and the claim before us. Moreover, we are mindful of the anomaly that would result were we to treat parental emotional distress as compensable. The negligent conduct at issue in [those cases] was the direct cause of injuries to or the death of otherwise healthy children. By contrast, in wrongful birth cases the defendant's conduct results, not in injuries or death, but in the birth of an unavoidably impaired child. It would be curious, to say the least, to impose liability for parental distress in the latter but not the former cases.

We also harbor concerns of proportionality. "[T]he unfairness of denying recovery to a plaintiff on grounds that are arbitrary in terms of principle may be outweighed by the perceived unfairness of imposing a burden on defendant that seems much greater than his fault would justify."

We hold that damages for emotional distress are not recoverable in wrongful birth actions. [ ]

III.   WRONGFUL LIFE

The theory of Heather's wrongful life action is as follows: during Linda's pregnancy the defendants owed a duty of care to both Linda and Heather. The defendants breached this duty when they failed to discover Linda's exposure to rubella and failed to advise her of the possible effects of that exposure on her child's health. Had Linda been properly informed, she would have undergone an abortion, and Heather would not have been born. Because Linda was not so informed, Heather must bear the burden of her afflictions for the rest of her life. The defendant's conduct is thus the proximate cause of injury to Heather.

This theory presents a crucial problem, however: the question of injury. * * *

In order to recognize Heather's wrongful life action, then, we must determine that the fetal Heather had an interest in avoiding her own birth, that it would have been best *for Heather* if she had not been born.

This premise of the wrongful life action—that the plaintiff's own birth and suffering constitute legal injury—has caused many courts to decline to recognize the claim. * * * As one court has written,

> "[w]hether it is better never to have been born at all than to have been born with even gross deficiencies is a mystery more properly to be left to the philosophers and the theologians. Surely the law can assert no competence to resolve the issue, particularly in view of the very nearly uniform high value which the law and mankind has placed on human life, rather than its absence."

Becker v. Schwartz, 46 N.Y.2d 401, 411, 386 N.E.2d 807, 812, 413 N.Y.S.2d 895, 900 (1978).

Moreover, compelling policy reasons militate against recognition of wrongful life claims. The first such reason is our conviction that the courts of this State should not become involved in deciding whether a given person's life is or is not worthwhile. * * *

* * *

The second policy reason militating against recognition of Heather's claim is related to the first.

> "[L]egal recognition that a disabled life is an injury would harm the interests of those most directly concerned, the handicapped. * * * Furthermore, society often views disabled persons as burdensome misfits. Recent legislation concerning employment, education, and building access reflects a slow change in these attitudes. This change evidences a growing public awareness that the handicapped can be valuable and productive members of society. To characterize the life of a disabled person as an injury would denigrate both this new awareness and the handicapped themselves." [ ]

The third reason stems from an acknowledgment of the limitations of tort law and the adjudicative process. Wrongful life actions are premised on the ability of judges and juries accurately to apply the traditional tort concept of injury to situations involving complex medical and bioethical issues. Yet this concept applies only roughly. In the ordinary tort case the *existence* of injury is readily and objectively ascertainable. In wrongful life cases, however, the finding of injury necessarily hinges upon subjective and intensely personal notions as to the intangible value of life. * * * The danger of markedly disparate and, hence, unpredictable outcomes is manifest.

In deciding whether to recognize a new tort cause of action, we must consider the "defendant's interest in avoiding an incorrect judgment of liability because of the court's incompetence to determine certain questions raised by application of the announced standard." [ ] Wrongful life claims present problems that cannot be resolved in a "reasonably sensible, even-handed, and fair" manner from case to case. [ ] As Chief Justice Weintraub of the Supreme Court of New Jersey recognized nearly twenty years ago, "[t]o recognize a right not to be born is to enter an area in which no one could find his way." *Gleitman v. Cosgrove*, 49 N.J. 22, 63, 227 A.2d 689, 711 (1967) (Weintraub, C.J., dissenting in part).

* * *

We recognize that our rejection of the [wrongful life action] is not without cost. In the future recovery of an impaired child's necessary medical expenses may well depend on whether the child's parents are available to assert a claim for wrongful birth. * * * But this cost is the price of our paramount regard for the value of human life, and of our adherence to fundamental principles of justice. We will not recognize a right not to be born, and we will not permit a person to recover damages from one who has done him no harm.

* * *

IV. CONCLUSION

We answer the transferred questions as follows:

A.   New Hampshire recognizes a cause of action for wrongful birth.

B.   The damages that may be recovered are the extraordinary medical and educational costs of raising the impaired child. Such damages should reflect costs that will be incurred both before and after the child attains majority, and should include compensation for extraordinary parental care. In addition, the mother may recover her tangible losses attributable to her emotional distress.

C.   New Hampshire does not recognize a cause of action for wrongful life.

* * *

Notes and Questions

1.   Although courts have used the terms in different ways over the past two decades, "wrongful birth", "wrongful life", and "wrongful conception" have come to describe identifiably different kinds of actions. An action for wrongful birth is one commenced by parents against a defendant whose negligence led to the birth of a child with birth defects. An action for wrongful life is one commenced by a child born with birth defects against a defendant whose negligence resulted in the birth of the child. An action for wrongful conception (or wrongful pregnancy) is an action brought by a healthy child or that child's parents against a defendant whose negligence (in performing a tubal ligation, for example) resulted in the

birth of the child. Is there any justification for distinguishing between "wrongful life," "wrongful birth," and "wrongful conception"? Are these distinctions based upon any real legal difference? An economic difference? A philosophical analysis? Social policy consequences?

Some courts have concluded that these labels "add nothing to the analysis, inspire[ ] confusion, and impl[y] that the court has adopted a new tort," when, in fact, the only relevant question is whether there has been medical malpractice. Bader v. Johnson, 732 N.E.2d 1212 (Ind.2000); see also Greco v. United States, 111 Nev. 405, 893 P.2d 345 (1995). Does it make any difference that these actions are denominated as "wrongful birth," "wrongful life" or "wrongful conception" cases rather than ordinary malpractice cases? Does it change the standard of care to be applied, the nature of the proof that must be offered by the parties, the application of the causation requirement, or the assessment of damages? See Mark Strasser, Misconceptions and Wrongful Births: A Call for a Principled Jurisprudence, 31 Ariz. St. L. J. 161 (1999).

2.   While wrongful birth cases were not initially well received by the judiciary, see Gleitman v. Cosgrove, 49 N.J. 22, 227 A.2d 689 (1967) (first "modern" wrongful birth action; recovery denied), only a few courts have refused to entertain such actions since *Roe v. Wade* was decided in 1973. As the *Smith* court pointed out,

> Two developments help explain the trend toward judicial acceptance of wrongful birth actions. The first is the increased ability of health care professionals to predict and detect the presence of fetal defects.

> *Roe v. Wade* and its progeny constitute the second development explaining the acceptance of wrongful birth actions.

513 A.2d at 345–346. Obviously, medicine's ability to do prenatal diagnosis will only improve. Is the Court's retreat in *Casey* from some of the implications of *Roe* relevant to the state recognition of wrongful birth actions? Ultimately, are such cases really founded on abortion law or tort law?

Among those decisions that have recognized wrongful birth actions are Siemieniec v. Lutheran Gen. Hosp., 117 Ill.2d 230, 111 Ill.Dec. 302, 512 N.E.2d 691 (1987), Berman v. Allan, 80 N.J. 421, 404 A.2d 8 (1979) (overruling *Gleitman*), James G. v. Caserta, 175 W.Va. 406, 332 S.E.2d 872 (1985), and Becker v. Schwartz, 46 N.Y.2d 401, 413 N.Y.S.2d 895, 386 N.E.2d 807 (1978). See also Robak v. United States, 658 F.2d 471 (7th Cir.1981). Two recent cases rejecting such actions are Taylor v. Kurapati, 236 Mich.App. 315, 600 N.W.2d 670 (1999) and Etkind v. Suarez, 271 Ga. 352, 519 S.E.2d 210 (1999)(adoption of such a cause of action is a matter for the legislature, not the courts).

3.   Wrongful life actions have been far less successful than wrongful birth actions, although the California, New Jersey and Washington courts have recognized wrongful life actions. See Turpin v. Sortini, 31 Cal.3d 220, 182 Cal.Rptr. 337, 643 P.2d 954 (1982), Procanik v. Cillo, 97 N.J. 339, 478 A.2d 755 (1984) and Harbeson v. Parke–Davis, Inc., 98 Wash.2d 460, 656 P.2d 483 (1983). To the extent that a wrongful life action seeks the same damages that could be recovered in a wrongful birth action, it hardly makes sense to allow one and not the other. In fact, in such cases permitting the wrongful life action simply has the effect of extending the statute of limitations, which is usually longer for an injured newborn than for an injured adult in medical malpractice cases. See Procanik v. Cillo, 97 N.J. 339, 478 A.2d 755 (1984) (justice requires allowing the wrongful life action because the wrongful birth action is barred by the statute of limitations). Despite this, most of the courts that have considered the issue have reached the

same result that was reached in New Hampshire; they permit wrongful birth actions but not wrongful life actions. See, e.g., Lininger v. Eisenbaum, 764 P.2d 1202 (Colo.1988), and Gildiner v. Thomas Jefferson Univ. Hosp., 451 F.Supp. 692 (E.D.Pa.1978).

There are several reasons that courts are reluctant to accept wrongful life actions. The first argument against such actions is that a defendant cannot have a duty to a putative plaintiff who did not exist at the time that the tortious action took place. Of course, the law does recognize such a duty under other circumstances. As John Robertson has pointed out, one would be liable to an injured party for a bomb planted in a newborn nursery and set to go off a year later; the fact that the injured party was not even conceived at the time the bomb was planted would not be dispositive. See also Renslow v. Mennonite Hosp., 67 Ill.2d 348, 10 Ill.Dec. 484, 367 N.E.2d 1250 (1977) (doctor liable to child born to a woman several years after the doctor negligently transfused the woman).

The second argument against permitting a child to sue the party whose negligence caused his birth is the presumption that being born is always better than not being born; one cannot have suffered damages because one was born alive. Do you agree? Is the general acceptance of "right to die" cases, discussed below in Chapter 19, a refutation of this "life is always better than the alternative" argument? The *Smith* court distinguished the "right to die" cases from the wrongful life cases quite directly:

> Simply put, the judiciary has an important role to play in protecting the privacy rights of the dying. It has no business declaring that among the living are people who never should have been born.

513 A.2d at 353.

Another argument raised against permitting wrongful life actions is that legal recognition of these lawsuits would constitute a social judgment that handicapped lives are worth less than other lives. Is the legal decision not to recognize wrongful life actions an appropriate way to indicate society's desire to respect the handicapped?

4.　Those wrongful conception cases brought by parents to recover the costs of a pregnancy have fared well in the courts. See, e.g., O'Toole v. Greenberg, 64 N.Y.2d 427, 488 N.Y.S.2d 143, 477 N.E.2d 445 (1985) (failed tubal ligation), Hartke v. McKelway, 707 F.2d 1544 (D.C.Cir.1983) (tubal cauterization). Only one state, Nevada, refuses to recognize such an action. See Szekeres v. Robinson, 102 Nev. 93, 715 P.2d 1076 (1986). On the other hand, wrongful conception cases seeking damages that include the cost of raising the healthy child have run into the same barriers that have faced wrongful life actions.

5.　The measure of damages is a significant legal issue in most wrongful birth, wrongful life, and wrongful conception cases. As a matter of general course, the courts have allowed special damages for the pregnancy itself in wrongful birth and wrongful conception cases, and they have permitted recovery of some child rearing costs, where those costs exceed the costs of raising a normal healthy child, in wrongful birth actions. Some courts deny any recovery of the cost of raising a healthy child on the rationale that a healthy child can never be an injury, as a matter of public policy. See O'Toole v. Greenberg, supra, and Hartke v. McKelway, supra. Other courts have fashioned a curious hybrid, allowing child-rearing costs but deducting a quantified estimate of the "benefit" of parenthood. A minority of courts allow child-rearing costs without any offset. See, e.g., Zehr v. Haugen, 318

Or. 647, 871 P.2d 1006 (1994) (allowing damages extending beyond the minority of the child).

In Marciniak v. Lundborg, 153 Wis.2d 59, 450 N.W.2d 243 (1990), an action to recover damages for a negligent sterilization that resulted in a normal healthy child, the public policy arguments for limiting recovery in such cases were enumerated and rejected:

> Defendants first argue that child rearing costs are too speculative and that it is impossible to establish with reasonable certainty the damages to the parents. We do not agree that the damages are too speculative. * * * [S]imilar calculations are routinely performed in countless other malpractice situations. Juries are frequently called on to make far more complex damage assessments in other tort cases. * * *
>
> Defendants next argue that because the costs of raising a child are so significant, allowing these costs would be wholly out of proportion to the culpability of the negligent physician. We find no merit in that contention. Admittedly, the cost of raising a child is substantial. However, the public policy of this state does not categorically immunize defendants from liability for foreseeable damages merely because the damages may be substantial.
>
> Defendants next argue that "awarding damages to the parents may cause psychological harm to the child when, at a later date, it learns of its parents' action for its wrongful birth thereby creating an 'emotional bastard.' "Again, we do not agree." The parents' suit for recovery of child rearing costs is in no reasonable sense a signal to the child that the parents consider the child an unwanted burden. The suit is for costs of raising the child, not to rid themselves of an unwanted child. They obviously want to keep the child. The love, affection, and emotional support any child needs they are prepared to give. But the love, affection, and emotional support they are prepared to give do not bring with them the economic means that are also necessary to feed, clothe, educate and otherwise raise the child. That is what this suit is about and we trust the child in the future will be well able to distinguish the two.
>
> Defendants also argue that allowing these costs would in some way debase the sanctity of human life, stating that "[T]he courts have been loath to adopt a rule, the primary effect of which is to encourage or reward the parents' disparagement of the value of their child's life." We do not perceive that the Marciniaks in bringing this suit are in any way disparaging the value of their child's life. They are, to the contrary, attempting to enhance it.
>
> Defendants further argue that allowing these costs would shift the entire cost of raising the child to the physician, thereby creating a new category of surrogate parent. This suit is not an attempt to shift the responsibility of parenting from the Marciniaks to the physician. The Marciniaks are assuming that responsibility. To equate the responsibility of parenting with the responsibility of paying for the costs of child raising is illogical.
>
> We do not agree that the refusal of the Marciniaks to abort the unplanned child or give it up for adoption should be considered as a failure of the parents to mitigate their damages. The rules requiring mitigation of damages require only that reasonable measures be taken. We do not consider it reasonable to expect parents to essentially choose between the child and the cause of action.

450 N.W.2d at 245–247.

Finally, the court decided not to apply the "benefit rule" that would allow an offset for the joy of having the child against the damages awarded:

We conclude that it is not equitable to apply the benefit rule in the context of the tort of negligent sterilization. The parents made a decision not to have a child. It was precisely to avoid that "benefit" that the parents went to the physician in the first place. Any "benefits" that were conferred upon them as a result of having a new child in their lives were not asked for and were sought to be avoided. With respect to emotional benefits, potential parents in this situation are presumably well aware of the emotional benefits that might accrue to them as the result of a new child in their lives. When parents make the decision to forego this opportunity for emotional enrichment, it hardly seems equitable to not only force this benefit upon them but to tell them they must pay for it as well by offsetting it against their proven emotional damages.

450 N.W.2d at 450. The cost of raising a healthy child is, in fact, less than the special damages sought in many other kinds of medical malpractice cases, and it is far less than those damages related to the medical care of a seriously ill newborn. See Comment, Wrongful Pregnancy: Child Rearing Damages Deserve Full Judicial Consideration, 8 Pace L.Rev. 313, 333–34 (1988).

6. Because wrongful birth, wrongful life and wrongful conception actions may expand the areas in which physicians are liable for malpractice, and because they implicate abortion, about half of the state legislatures have considered legislative resolutions of these issues. While one state has promulgated a statute allowing for wrongful birth and wrongful life actions, 24 Me.Rev.Stat.Ann. § 2931, several others have promulgated legislation forbidding both wrongful birth and wrongful life actions. Most have language similar to that adopted in Minnesota, which provides that "no person shall maintain a cause of action or receive an award of damages on the claim that but for the negligent conduct of another, a child would have been aborted." Minn.Stat.Ann. § 145.424(2). The Minnesota Supreme Court upheld that statute in an action brought by a thirty-four year old mother of a child born with Down's syndrome. The mother alleged that the physician defendant negligently discouraged her from undergoing a test which would have revealed the Down's syndrome and resulted in the abortion of the fetus. The court rejected the argument that the statute violated interests protected by *Roe v. Wade,* and that it violated the equal protection of the Fourteenth Amendment. First, the court decided that there was no state action alleged, and thus no constitutionally protected right at stake. Even if there were state action, the court concluded, the statute did not constitute a legally impermissible burden on the mother's right to seek an abortion. Three justices dissented, finding the statute to be an improper state interference with the mother's right to an abortion, Hickman v. Group Health Plan, Inc., 396 N.W.2d 10 (Minn.1986). For examples of other state legislation prohibiting wrongful birth and wrongful life actions, see Idaho Code Sec. 5–334, West's Ann. Ind. Code Sec. 34–1–1–11, Vernon's Ann. Mo. State. § 188.30.

7. There are a number of articles on the propriety of wrongful birth, wrongful life and wrongful conception actions. The seminal article in the field, and one that the court depended upon very heavily in *Smith v. Cote,* is Patrick Kelley, Wrongful Life, Wrongful Birth and Justice in Tort Law, 1979 Wash. U.L.Q. 919; See also Mark Strasser, Misconceptions and Wrongful Births: A Call for a Principled Jurisprudence, 31 Ariz. St. L. J. 161 (1999); Kelly Rhinehart, The Debate Over Wrongful Birth and Wrongful Life, 26 L. & Psych. Rev. 141 (2002); Michael Kelly, The Rightful Position in "Wrongful Life" Actions, 42 Hast. L.J. 505 (1991); John Robertson, Toward Rational Boundaries for Tort Liability to the Unborn: Prenatal Injuries, Preconception Injuries, and Wrongful Life, 1978 Duke L.J. 1401; Alexander Capron, Tort Liability in Genetic Counseling, 79 Colum.L.Rev. 618 (1979); Thomas Rogers, Wrongful Life and Wrongful Birth:

Medical Malpractice in Genetic Counseling and Prenatal Testing, 33 S.C.L.Rev. 713 (1982). The question of whether life can ever be "wrongful" is nicely discussed in Melinda A. Roberts, Distinguishing Wrongful from "Rightful" Life, 6 J. Contemporary Health L. & Policy 59 (1990). For a vigorous response to the new trend allowing full damages in wrongful conception cases, see Brett Simmons, Zehr v. Haugen and the Oregon Approach to Wrongful Conception; An Occasion for Celebration or Litigation? 31 Willamette L.R. 121 (1995). A good response to some specific legislation is found in Note, Wrongful Birth Actions: The Case Against Legislative Curtailment, 100 Harv.L.Rev. 2017 (1987) (arguing that statutory limitations infringe on parents' right to make informed procreative decisions). An interesting comparative law analysis of this issue is found in Anthony Jackson, Action for Wrongful Life, Wrongful Pregnancy and Wrongful Birth in the United States and England, 17 Loy. L.A. Int'l & Comp. L.J. 535 (1995).

B. ASSISTING REPRODUCTION

Problem: Reproductive Arrangements Go Awry

Avery and Bertha Carp wanted a child for years, but Avery proved infertile. Artificial insemination of Bertha also proved unsuccessful because her uterus is unable to maintain a fertilized ovum. A year ago they consulted Dr. Dominguez, a specialist in the treatment of infertility. He suggested *in vitro* insemination of Bertha's ovum, which could then be implanted in the womb of a surrogate. The Carps agreed, and Dr. Dominguez arranged to have fertile sperm delivered from Nobel Labs Incorporated for impregnation of one of Bertha's ova, which he surgically removed from her. He then implanted the fertilized ovum in the uterus of Ellen Featherstone, a healthy 25–year old single woman who was referred to Dr. Dominguez by Motherhood Incorporated, a surrogate mother brokering company. The Carps agreed to the selection of Ms. Featherstone, whom they had never met, and they agreed to pay Dr. Dominguez his fee of $15,000, and Motherhood Incorporated their administrative fee of $40,000, which included "all legal and medical expenses of carrying the child to term." Motherhood Incorporated agreed to pay the legal and medical fees incurred by Ms. Featherstone, and they agreed to pay her $15,000 to carry the child to term and then place the child for adoption with the Carps. The Carps agreed to adopt the child at birth, and Motherhood Incorporated agreed to hold the $40,000 in escrow until the adoption was complete.

One month ago the child, Gerald, was born with some serious problems. He is likely to be mildly developmentally disabled as a consequence of an automobile accident Ms. Featherstone suffered during the eighth month of the pregnancy, in which Gerald's skull was partially crushed *in utero*. The automobile accident was the result of Ms. Featherstone's negligence in going through a red light. In addition, the child is likely to develop mottled, discolored teeth as a consequence of the administration to Ms. Featherstone of tetracycline in the emergency room after the automobile accident. Discolored teeth is a well known consequence of the use of that antibiotic in pregnant women. Finally, the infant suffers from Von Willebrand disease, which is a form of hemophilia that is apparently the result of a genetic defect in the biological father. The defect could have been discovered before impregnation, but only through a genetic analysis of the sperm source. That analysis was not undertaken because the sperm, according to Nobel Incorporated, "came from a very healthy, very smart man, highly prolific with several healthy children; there was no indication that any further inquiry was necessary."

The Carps have refused to adopt the infant, and they have demanded a refund of the $40,000 from Motherhood's escrow agent. Motherhood Incorporated demands the $40,000. Ms. Featherstone is willing to keep the baby, as long as the Carps pay support, which they refuse. She is threatening a maternity action against Bertha and a contract action against Avery. The state child protective services agency is threatening to take the child into state custody.

Who are Gerald's parents? Who has what rights against whom? What kind of a contract would you have drawn as counsel to the Carps? Nobel Incorporated? Motherhood Incorporated? Ms. Featherstone? Dr. Dominguez? Which of those contracts, if any, would be enforceable?

1. Introduction

a. The Process of Human Reproduction

Those seeking medical help in facilitating reproduction do so because they want a child. The birth of a child requires the growth of a fetus in a woman's uterus. This, in turn, requires the implantation of a fertilized ovum (also called an egg or an oocyte) in the uterine wall. At least until the cloning of human beings is perfected, the ovum can implant in the uterine wall only if it has been fertilized by a sperm, a process which generally takes place in the fallopian tube.

Despite the development of a variety of techniques to accomplish this, most people still use coitus as the preferred process for initiating pregnancy. Typically, an ovum leaves a woman's ovary when the wall of follicular cells in which it has been residing breaks and it is carried upon a wave of escaping follicular fluid into the upper end of the fallopian tube; this process is called ovulation and it occurs once each menstrual cycle, usually between the ninth and fourteenth day. During this stage, if a man ejaculates semen which contains motile spermatozoa (sperm) into the woman's vagina, the sperm move (at a rate of a little less than five inches per hour) through her uterus and into her fallopian tubes. Although one ejaculation may contain a billion sperm pursuing the ovum, only a much smaller number reach the upper portion of the one fallopian tube that contains the freshly released ovum. An even smaller number of sperm actually reach the ovum. Of these, the first sperm head to embed in the outer wall of the ovum releases a substance that changes the ovum's outer wall, making it impermeable to other sperm. Sperm remain alive and capable of fertilization in the uterine environment for only about 48 hours after ejaculation. Because the ovum is estimated to have a fertilizable life of less than 24 hours after it is released from the ovary, the timing of fertilization is important.

Within a day, the fertilized ovum has divided twice, into a two- and then a four-celled "embryo," and it is here that we must pause to consider the impact that our language has on our conceptualization and therefore our law. The terminology of early pregnancy is rife with alternative phraseology. For example, a fertilized ovum/egg/oocyte is also called a "zygote," or a cluster of dividing "blastomeres" which eventually divide into a "blastocyst" or hollow cellular ball. Some will argue that because there is no differentiated living matter generated in forming the blastocyst (i.e., there are no fetal or placental cells yet), this division of cell material is not a constructive development of living substance. It is a process which does nothing to distribute particular developmental qualities to particular parts of a resulting fetus. On the other hand, it is the preliminary stage which makes it possible for the blastocyst cell ball to implant and use materials from the uterine wall to grow and develop into a fetus. Obviously, the fertilization of the ovum by the sperm begins the embryonic process, although some use the term "embryo" only to apply to later stages of development.

At any rate, whether it is called an embryo, a preembryo or something else, the fertilized ovum continues its migration through the fallopian tube toward the uterus. The fertilized and subdividing ovum arrives at the lower end of the fallopian tube, hesitating for about two days before being expelled into the uterus. This delay allows the uterine lining to build up for successful implantation. The implantation of this cell cluster is a complicated biological process that takes several days. Where the fertilized ovum cell cluster adheres to the uterine lining is variable, although there is less risk of some subsequent complications if implantation occurs in the upper half of the uterus.

Even when all other conditions are met, not all fertilized ova actually do implant and not all implanted ova survive until birth. About 50% of fertilized ova are expelled from the body before the woman has any reason to know that she is pregnant. Some of these spontaneous expulsions occur before implantation, and some occur during the first few days after the commencement of the implantation process.

There are several reasons that those who wish to raise children may not conceive them through this natural process. First, some are unable to participate in coital sexual relations, or choose not to participate in such relations. Others are infertile—that is, normal coitus does not result in a fertilized ovum that implants in the uterine wall and grows into a fetus and then a child. Although estimates vary, at least 10% of American couples are infertile. There are a variety of reasons for infertility. Some men do not produce sperm that is capable of fertilizing the ovum. Some women are unable to produce ova, for example, and others have fallopian tubes that cannot adequately accept ova to be fertilized, or do not permit the travel of fertilized ova to the uterus. In some cases, the "shell" around the ovum may not admit any sperm at all. In other cases, the ovum is successfully fertilized but the uterus is incapable of allowing for implantation of the fertilized ovum or of maintaining the implanted embryo through the pregnancy. In all of these cases, some form of intervention may allow those who could not become parents through unassisted coitus to achieve parenthood nonetheless.

The variety of problems that results in the need to assist reproduction give rise to a wide variety of alternative interventions. These interventions, in turn, require the involvement of a host of other people. A sperm source (who is not necessarily a sperm donor—he is usually a sperm vendor) is necessary where the problem is the lack of a man or a man's inability to produce physiologically adequate sperm; an ovum source is necessary where the problem is a woman's inability to provide a potentially fertile ovum; a uterus source (originally called a "surrogate mother," now more generally described as a "gestational mother") is necessary where a woman is unable or unwilling to carry the fertilized ovum through the pregnancy in her own uterus. Medical treatment of an ovum may allow it to be fertilized, and treatment of a fertilized ovum may allow it to be implanted. Sometimes a combination of these needs requires that there be a series of interventions to produce a pregnancy and a child. A woman may be unable to produce ova and unable to carry a fertilized ovum in her uterus, for example. There may be several options available to allow her to obtain both an ovum that can be fertilized (from an ovum source) and a uterus for the gestation of that fertilized ovum (from a surrogate).

b. The Role of the Law

The law's involvement in human reproduction has not been limited to evaluating the propriety of techniques used to avoid bearing children: the law is also involved in regulating processes designed to facilitate reproduction. These processes include AIH (artificial insemination-homologous: artificial insemination of a woman with the sperm of the person who is intended to be the biological and nurturing father, usually the husband), AID (artificial insemination-donor: artificial insemination of the woman with the sperm of someone who is presumed to have no continuing relationship with the child), IVF (*in vitro* fertilization: fertilizing an ovum outside of the uterus and then implanting it), embryo transfer, egg transfer, and gestational surrogacy (carrying a fetus expected to be raised by an identifiable person other than the pregnant woman). There are other techniques that may be applied to aid fertilization problems—such as full IVP (*in vitro* pregnancy) and cloning—but these are unlikely to be of much practical concern over the next few years. There are hundreds of thousands of children now alive in the United States who were conceived by AID; there are tens of thousands who are the result of *in vitro* fertilization, and (probably) thousands carried by surrogate mothers. Questions surrounding their legal status are real, substantial, and immediate.

It is not hard to imagine the variety of unusual legal relationships which can develop as a consequence of medical and non-medical reproductive techniques. It is possible to have a child who is the product of sperm from one source (whose sperm may be mixed with sperm from several sources), an ovum extracted from one woman, implanted in another, and carried for the benefit of yet another set of parents who intend to nurture the child from the time of its birth. Such a child would have two genetic parents, a gestational mother, and two contractual (or intended or nurturing) parents. Who ought to be treated as the legal parents? Should the others involved in the process have any rights whatsoever? For example, if the nurturing parents have the rights normally associated with parenthood, should any rights—visitation, for example—be extended to the gestational mother, or the genetic parents? Should we consider parenthood to be a bundle of rights, much as we have come to view property, and should these rights be separated out and split among several people, each of whom would share in the privileges and responsibilities of parental status? Is there a good reason to limit a child to two legal parents?

For the original descriptions of the taxonomies of relationships resulting from reproductive technology, see Alexander Capron, Alternative Birth Technologies: Legal Challenges, 20 U.Cal. Davis L.Rev. 679, 682 (1987) and Bernard Dickens, Reproduction Law and Medical Consent, 35 Toronto L.J. 255, 280 (1985).

c. Facilitating Reproduction and the Definition of the Family

We are so concerned about the use of new technology to facilitate reproduction in part because of its potential effect on family structure, and because any consequent change in family structure may also have an impact on social structure. Courts and legislatures have been tentative at best in actually defining what constitutes a "family" of the kind which we wish to preserve and protect. Perhaps this should not come as a surprise; others who have attempted to define "family" have not been any more successful. As R.D. Laing explained,

> [w]e speak of families as though we all knew what families are. We identify, as families, networks of people who live together over periods of time, who have ties of marriage and kinship to one another. The more one studies family dynamics, the more *un*clear one becomes as to the ways *family* dynamics compare and contrast with the dynamics of other groups not called families, let alone the ways families differ themselves. As with dynamics, so with structure (patterns, more stable and enduring than others): again, comparisons and generalizations must be very tentative.

R.D. Laing, The Politics of the Family and Other Essays, 3 (1971). Since 1971 American social living arrangements, and the consequent notions of the family, have become even more uncertain. Last century a society of extended families (which were extended both horizontally, to include near relatives, and vertically, to include near generations) was transformed through increased mobility, increased urbanization, and increased industrialization into a society of nuclear families, each family possessing an identifiable head of a household (generally the father) a mother, and children; the dog was optional.

Over the past few decades, this model of the family has been tested by many forces, including those that come from women's reassessment of their roles. Even greater changes have driven us from a society of nuclear families to a society of "constructed" families—designer families, really—where relationships between adults, and between adults and children, are arranged on an *ad hoc* basis or by agreement. Of course, these *ad hoc* arrangements may provide for a different relationship between children and their parents, and between these new social units and the state, than those which traditionally have been recognized in law. Further, while many of these new "constructed" families look very much like the families of a few decades ago, many do not. Many are one parent families, some include more than two parents and some include two parents of the same gender.

The law has struggled to deal with the social and medical developments that made these families possible with only limited success. While courts have been able to develop processes to accommodate the breakup of nuclear families—custody and support arrangements, primarily—neither the courts nor legislatures have done very well in developing institutions that are capable of dealing with these previously legally unrecognized families. Ultimately this society will call upon the law to define families, declare family relationships, and allocate power within families. The solutions to the problems thus raised will depend upon the answer to the question the law has not yet asked: why does this society recognize families? Why do we strive to protect families? Why are the institutions of government so interested in preserving and restoring the authority of families? These questions have been unanswered—indeed, unasked—by the law until now because the law has not been called to address them. However, social and medical changes over the last several years have forced these questions into the legal spotlight. This society must determine first, descriptively, the role families do play in society, and, second, prescriptively, the role they ought to play in this society.

As you read the rest of this section of this chapter, ask yourself whether the law reflects forethought and purpose behind its definitional conclusions (be they explicit or implicit). Is the law consistent in this area? Is it just? For the classic academic structure of these issues, see A. Skolnick and J. Skolnick, Family in Transition: Rethinking Marriage, Sexuality, Childbearing, and Family Organization (1971).

2. *Artificial Insemination*

The Process of Artificial Insemination
(or "Intrauterine Insemination")

Artificial insemination (now known commonly as "intrauterine insemination") is the placement of the semen in the vagina (or in the cervical canal or uterus) by means other than the penis. The sperm source produces semen through masturbation and ejaculation. The ejaculate is then put into a syringe and injected directly into the woman who intends to become pregnant. This process, using "fresh" semen, need not be a medical procedure; it can be done successfully at home by anyone who understands the underlying biological principles. Ideally, the insemination is done at about the time of ovulation, a time that can be determined with increasing accuracy through home ovulation prediction tests.

Medically performed artificial insemination now generally employs frozen semen rather than fresh semen. Although freezing semen permits subsequent tests upon the donor to determine the presence of any latent contaminant (HIV, for example, or, perhaps, a genetic defect), the freezing process is comparatively difficult and expensive. The semen is mixed with a preservative before it is frozen, and it must be carefully thawed before it is used. Once the semen is frozen, however, it is unlikely to undergo substantial deterioration; one estimate is that the risk of genetic mutation will double if the semen is kept frozen for 5,000 years. In 1990 one Seattle man successfully inseminated his wife with sperm he deposited in a New York sperm bank fourteen years earlier. The man, who became sterile after his deposit, had paid a fee each year to keep his deposit on ice. In 2004 an Israeli fertility clinic announced the birth of healthy twins from sperm that had been kept on ice for a dozen years. There is no reason to believe that the semen could not be kept in the freezer for hundreds of years; whether it should be is another question. As of early 2004, one leading sperm bank charged $385 to prepare a specimen for cryopreservation and between $335 (for one year) to $1820 (for ten years) for storage. There is also a $50 thawing charge.

There are hundreds of thousands of women artificially inseminated medically each year in the United States. The service is provided by thousands of doctors throughout the country. Frozen sperm costs a few hundred dollars per vial; preparation of fresh sperm costs about half of that. The total cost of artificial insemination, per cycle, may be less than $1,000.

a. *Artificial Insemination—Homologous (AIH)*

Virtually no legal questions have arisen surrounding the use of the sperm of a husband to inseminate his wife, even if the sperm is artificially injected into the vagina or cervical canal. Such a process may be used within a marriage to allow for processing of the semen to overcome low sperm count. In these cases, there is no question about the identity of the mother and the father of the child. While there are some religious objections to masturbation (which, obviously, is required) and to any process that alters the "natural" arrangement, AIH has now become well accepted as a social and medical matter, and it is not a matter of substantial legal concern.

b. Artificial Insemination—Donor (AID)

When the sperm is not that of the husband of the woman whose pregnancy results, the question of who ought to be considered the father of the resulting child may arise. For the most part this matter has been resolved by the adoption of the 1973 Uniform Parentage Act (adopted, at least in part, in one form or another; in most states), the Uniform Status of Children of Assisted Conception Act or another statute that serves the same purposes. In 2000 the original (1973) Uniform Parentage Act and the Uniform Status of Children of Assisted Conception Act were combined and rewritten in the form of a new (2000) Uniform Parentage Act, which was amended in 2002. As the Prefatory Note to the 2002 version explains, "[t]he amendments of 2002 are the end-result of objections lodged by the American Bar Association Section of Individual Rights and Responsibilities and the ABA Committee on the Unmet Legal Needs of Children, based on the view that in certain respects the 2000 version did not adequately treat a child of unmarried parents equally with a child of married parents." The portions of this new statute that deal with assisted reproduction have proven highly controversial, and as of early 2004 the new uniform act had been introduced in only one state legislature (Utah) and adopted in none.

UNIFORM PARENTAGE ACT

(1973).

* * *

§ 5. [Artificial Insemination.]

(a) If, under the supervision of a licensed physician and with the consent of her husband, a wife is inseminated artificially with semen donated by a man not her husband, the husband is treated in law as if he were the natural father of a child thereby conceived. The husband's consent must be in writing and signed by him and his wife. The physician shall certify their signatures and the date of the insemination, and file the husband's consent with the [State Department of Health], where it shall be kept confidential and in a sealed file. However, the physician's failure to do so does not affect the father and child relationship. All papers and records pertaining to the insemination, whether part of the permanent record of a court or of a file held by the supervising physician or elsewhere, are subject to inspection only upon an order of the court for good cause shown.

(b) The donor of semen provided to a licensed physician for use in artificial insemination of a married woman other than the donor's wife is treated in law as if he were not the natural father of a child thereby conceived.

* * *

§ 23.   [Birth Records.]

(a) Upon order of a court of this State or upon request of a court of another state, the [registrar of births] shall prepare [an amended birth registration] [a new certificate of birth] consistent with the findings of the court [and shall substitute the new certificate for the original certificate of birth].

(b) The fact that the father and child relationship was declared after the child's birth shall not be ascertainable from the [amended birth registration] [new certificate] but the actual place and date of birth shall be shown.

(c) The evidence upon which the [amended birth registration] [new certificate] was made and the original birth certificate shall be kept in a sealed and confidential file and be subject to inspection only upon consent of the court and all interested persons, or in exceptional cases only upon an order of the court for good cause shown.

UNIFORM PARENTAGE ACT

(2000, as amended in 2002).

* * *

§ 102.   DEFINITIONS.

(4) "Assisted reproduction" means a method of causing pregnancy other than sexual intercourse. The term includes:

(A) intrauterine insemination;

(B) donation of eggs;

(C) donation of embryos;

(D) in-vitro fertilization and transfer of embryos; and

(E) intracytoplasmic sperm injection.

* * *

§ 103.   SCOPE OF [ACT]; CHOICE OF LAW.

(a) This [Act] governs every determination of parentage in this State.

(b) The court shall apply the law of this State to adjudicate the parent-child relationship. The applicable law does not depend on:

(1) the place of birth of the child; or

(2) the past or present residence of the child.

(c) This [Act] does not create, enlarge, or diminish parental rights or duties under other law of this State.

* * *

§ 201.   ESTABLISHMENT OF PARENT–CHILD RELATIONSHIP.

(a) The mother-child relationship is established between a woman and a child by:

(1) the woman's having given birth to the child [, except as otherwise provided in [Article] 8, concerning gestational surrogacy];

(2) an adjudication of the woman's maternity; [or]

(3) adoption of the child by the woman * * *

(b) The father-child relationship is established between a man and a child by:

(1) an unrebutted presumption of the man's paternity of the child * * *;

(2) an effective acknowledgment of paternity by the man * * *;

(3) an adjudication of the man's paternity;

(4) adoption of the child by the man; [or]

(5) the man's having consented to assisted reproduction by his wife under [this Act] which resulted in the birth of the child * * *

ARTICLE 7—CHILD OF ASSISTED REPRODUCTION

§ 701. SCOPE OF ARTICLE.

This [article] does not apply to the birth of a child conceived by means of sexual intercourse [, or as the result of a gestational agreement as provided in [Article] 8].[For a discussion of section 8, see below]

§ 702. PARENTAL STATUS OF DONOR.

A donor is not a parent of a child conceived by means of assisted reproduction.

§ 703. PATERNITY OF CHILD OF ASSISTED REPRODUCTION.

A man who provides sperm for, or consents to, assisted reproduction by a woman as provided in Section 704 with the intent to be the parent of her child, is a parent of a resulting child.

§ 704. CONSENT TO ASSISTED REPRODUCTION.

(a) Consent by a woman, and a man who intends to be a parent of a child born to the woman by assisted reproduction must be in a record signed by the woman and the man. This requirement does not apply to a donor.

(b) Failure by a man to sign a consent required by subsection (a), before or after birth of the child, does not preclude a finding of paternity if the woman and the man, during the first two years of the child's life, resided together in the same household with the child and openly held out the child as their own.

* * *

§ 706. EFFECT OF DISSOLUTION OF MARRIAGE OR WITHDRAWAL OF CONSENT.

(a) If a marriage is dissolved before placement of eggs, sperm, or embryos, the former spouse is not a parent of the resulting child unless the former spouse consented in a record that if assisted reproduction were to occur after a divorce, the former spouse would be a parent of the child.

(b) The consent of a former spouse to assisted reproduction may be withdrawn by that individual in a record at any time before placement of eggs, sperm, or embryos. An individual who withdraws consent under this section is not a parent of the resulting child.

§ 707. PARENTAL STATUS OF DECEASED INDIVIDUAL.

If an individual who consented in a record to be a parent by assisted reproduction dies before placement of eggs, sperm, or embryos, the deceased individual is not a parent of the resulting child unless the deceased [individual] consented in a record that if assisted reproduction were to occur after death, the deceased individual would be a parent of the child.

Notes and Questions

1. What is the difference between the approach taken by the 1973 Uniform Parentage Act and the approach taken by the 2002 Act? In what kinds of cases would the application of the different Acts yield different parents?

Under the 2000 version of the Uniform Parentage Act, a child born of donor semen to an unmarried woman (or to a woman whose husband did not consent to the procedure) would have had no father. It was to avoid the creation of such a class of legally fatherless children that the Act was amended in 2002.

2. While the 2002 version of the Uniform Parentage Act applies in every case of assisted conception, it has not been adopted anywhere. On the other hand, the 1973 version, parts of which have been adopted in the majority of states, applies only if the woman who is inseminated is a wife (i.e., is married), if she proceeds with the consent of her husband and the procedure is carried out under the supervision of a licensed physician. If any of these conditions is not met, the statute is inapplicable and the common law will define the rights and interests of all of the parties. See Marriage of Witbeck–Wildhagen, 281 Ill.App.3d 502, 217 Ill.Dec. 329, 667 N.E.2d 122 (1996) (husband did not consent to wife's insemination; statute did not apply). Some common law cases have treated the source of the sperm to be the father, with all of the rights (including visitation) and obligations (including child support) that come with such a designation; others have not. Compare Gursky v. Gursky, 39 Misc.2d 1083, 242 N.Y.S.2d 406 (Sup.Ct. 1963) (child born of AID is illegitimate) with In re Adoption of Anonymous, 74 Misc.2d 99, 345 N.Y.S.2d 430 (Sur.Ct.1973). See also In re Baby Doe, 291 S.C. 389, 353 S.E.2d 877 (1987) (one who assists his wife's efforts to conceive by artificial insemination must be treated as the legal father of the resulting child); Strnad v. Strnad, 190 Misc. 786, 78 N.Y.S.2d 390 (Sup.Ct.1948) (husband of woman who receives AID with his consent has rights and obligations of father); People v. Sorensen, 68 Cal.2d 280, 66 Cal.Rptr. 7, 437 P.2d 495 (1968) (husband of wife impregnated by AID with his consent is liable for support of child) and C.M. v. C.C., 152 N.J.Super. 160, 377 A.2d 821 (1977) (natural father by AID liable for support). For an analysis of the sperm donor's constitutional rights to maintain a relationship with the child when the woman promised she would permit such a relationship, see McIntyre v. Crouch, 98 Or.App. 462, 780 P.2d 239 (1989), aff'd, 308 Or. 593, 784 P.2d 1100 (1989).

3. In addition to the moral arguments that are made against AIH, there are four additional arguments against the moral and social propriety of AID. First, some believe that it constitutes adultery. Second, the uncertainty of the screening of the sperm source in AID can provide for uncertainty in the health of the child, and the anonymity of the sperm source can impose upon the woman or her child unforeseen emotional consequences. Third, there is a worry that the availability of AID will reshape and dilute family structure, replacing the nuclear family with unusual and inappropriate combinations of adults and children. Finally, there is an argument that AID is inappropriate because if there is no limit on the number of times one man may donate sperm there may be a genetically unacceptably large number of "test tube" children who unknowingly have the same genetic father. This may lead to the dilution of the genetic pool of some communities. Do any of these arguments provide a good reason to prohibit the practice, or to regulate it?

4. Should a woman being inseminated be able to choose the man who will be the source of the sperm? At the least, should she be able to designate some of the attributes that she wishes the source of the sperm to possess? Alternatively, should the source of the sperm remain unknown to the child, the inseminated woman, and, perhaps, even the inseminating physician? Sperm banks do provide profiles of their various donors, and some issue catalogs of these profiles allowing their consumers to choose the profile that seems most appropriate. One "donor catalog" provides information on ethnicity, hair color and texture, eye color, height, weight, blood type, skin tone, years of education, and occupation (or major in college). Short (2 page) profiles, and longer (10 page) descriptions are available on all donors, and audio tapes are available for some. In addition to relevant health information, what kind of information, if any, about the sperm source ought to be provided to the woman who is going to be inseminated? In considering the appropriate policy for Britain, a government commission considered the American practice:

> It is the practice of some clinics in the U.S.A. to provide detailed descriptions of donors, and to permit couples to exercise choice as to the donor they would prefer. In the evidence there was some support for the use of such descriptions. It is argued that they would provide information and reassurance for the parents and, at a later date, for the child. They might also be of benefit to the donor, as an indication that he is valued for his own sake. A detailed description also offers some choice to the woman who is to have the child, and lack of such choice can be said to diminish the importance of the woman's right to choose the father of her child.

> The contrary view, also expressed in the evidence, is that detailed donor profiles would introduce the donor as a person in his own right. It is also argued that the use of profiles devalues the child who may seem to be wanted only if certain specifications are met, and this may become a source of disappointment to the parents if their expectations are unfulfilled.

Report to the Committee of Inquiry into "Human Fertilization and Embryology" (Cmnd 9314) (the "Warnock Commission") Paragraphs 4.19–20 (1984). The committee went on to recommend "that on reaching the age of 18 the child should have access to the basic information about the donor's ethnic origin and genetic health and that legislation be enacted to provide the right of access to this." *Id.* ¶ 4.21.

5. Should a determination of who will be inseminated be left to physicians who perform this procedure? A 1987 study found that over half of the physicians doing artificial insemination had rejected, or would be likely to reject, a request for artificial insemination from a potential recipient with any one of the following attributes: unmarried (and with no partner), psychologically immature, homosexual, welfare dependent, evidence of child abuse, evidence of drug abuse, evidence of alcohol abuse, history of serious genetic disorder, HIV positive, under 18 years old or criminal record. Office of Technology Assessment, Artificial Insemination Practice in the United States (1988). Does the determination by these physicians not to inseminate the poor or those with criminal records harken back to the era of *Buck v. Bell* and *Skinner v. Oklahoma,* when there was a presumption that wealth and criminal proclivity were inheritable, or do such screening processes merely suggest that the physicians, who can choose whom they will make parents, are determining which of the proposed patients are likely to be the best parents? Should a physician ever be required to perform artificial insemination in a case where she believes that the woman being inseminated is not capable of the physical, mental, financial or emotional obligations of motherhood?

Might there be additional problems if a state institution were to limit those who could be provided with assisted conception? What kinds of equal protection claims would you expect to be successful? Does the Americans with Disabilities Act require medical institutions to provide treatment for infertility if they provide other necessary medical treatment? Is infertility a disability?

6.   The ability to freeze and preserve sperm gives rise to the possibility that the father of a child conceived through artificial insemination could have died years before that child's birth. The Social Security Administration faced this issue when Nancy Hart applied for social security survivor's benefits on behalf of her daughter, Judith. After Nancy's husband, Edward Hart, was diagnosed with cancer, he arranged to preserve some of his sperm because of his fear that the necessary chemotherapy would render him sterile. In fact, the chemotherapy was unsuccessful, and he died. Shortly thereafter Judith was conceived, using the sperm left by Edward. The Social Security Administration originally refused to recognize Judith's claim to be Edward's survivor because under the law of Louisiana, where she lived, a child could not be recognized as an heir of a person who died before that child was conceived. In fact, the Social Security Administration had previously paid a similar claim that originated in Arizona, which imposes no restriction on recognizing a child as an heir. While Judith's case was pending in the district court, the Social Security Administration changed its approach and decided to pay this claim because, in the words of the Social Security Commissioner, "[r]ecent advances ... particularly in the field of reproductive medicine, necessitate a careful review of current laws ... to ensure that they are equitable in awarding social security payments in cases such as this." Girl Conceived After Dad Dies Gets Benefits, Chicago Tribune, March 12, 1996, at 12. For a more thorough discussion of this case see Ellen Garside, Posthumous Progeny: A Proposed Resolution to the Dilemma of the Posthumously Conceived Child, 41 Loy. L. Rev. 713 (1996).

Is sperm simply property that can be passed on like any other property upon death? Ought there be any limitation on the people to whom sperm can be willed or sold? Is a child born of sperm from a "father" who died years before an heir of that man? Is the only limitation upon that heir's opportunity to partake in the estate the statute of limitations? For the few of you who remember your first year property course very well, does this problem implicate the rule against perpetuities?

The Uniform Status of Children of Assisted Conception Act explicitly provided that one who died before implantation of his or her genetic contribution was not a parent of the "resulting child." The 2002 version of the Uniform Parentage Act, on the other hand, provides that an insemination of a woman by a man's sperm after his death does not render him a parent unless he "consented" to this in writing. Why did the drafters of Uniform Status of Children of Assisted Conception Act make such a policy choice? Why was it rejected—at least for fathers who provided consent in writing—by the drafters of the new Uniform Parentage Act? Are you satisfied with section 707 of the 2002 version of the Uniform Parentage Act? How would you redraft it?

7.   What is the tort liability that arises out of the provision of inadequate sperm for purposes of artificial insemination? Might the physician or the sperm bank be liable in negligence for inadequately screening the count, health and motility of the sperm? What is the standard of care for screening sperm? How would you find out? In any case, might the doctor or the sperm bank be strictly liable without negligence (on a products liability theory) for the provision of defective sperm?

Of course, the physician and the physician's staff could also be liable in negligence for failing to carry out properly the procedure or failing to adequately inform and counsel the woman to be inseminated about the risks, benefits and alternatives of the procedure.

Might there be a contract action against the physician or the sperm bank who deals commercially in the sale of sperm? If the sperm is sold to the woman who is to be inseminated, is it sold with any implied warranty—perhaps a warranty of fitness for a particular purpose—under the Uniform Commercial Code?

Could the sperm source himself be liable for providing defective sperm? What if the sperm source knew that his semen carried some venereal disease or that he had some unmanifested or secretly manifested genetic defect? Would he be liable as a manufacturer of a product? In negligence? For fraud? On some other theory?

3. *In Vitro Fertilization, Egg Transfer and Embryo Transfer*

The Process of *In Vitro* Fertilization and Related Techniques

In vitro (literally, "in glass") fertilization is a highly technical medical intervention. Unlike artificial insemination, it cannot be performed with instruments that one finds in a kitchen. In the normal *in vitro* case, an ovum that is ready to be released from the ovary is identified through laparoscopy or ultrasound and removed from the ovary by surgery or aspiration through a hollow needle. The ovum (or ova—there usually is an attempt to get more than one) is placed in a container with the appropriate amount of semen containing fertile sperm. Most medical programs in the United States will mix between 50,000 and several hundred thousand sperm with each ovum. The fertilized ovum is then placed in the woman's uterus, where it is permitted to implant and develop.

In the United States clinics conducting *in vitro* fertilization generally try to remove several eggs so that at least a few will be fertilized *in vitro* and can be replaced in the uterus. In some cases there is no fertilization or inadequate fertilization *in vitro,* and, thus, no return to the uterus, although fertilization occurs in most of the ova in which it is attempted. Where the ova comes from a younger woman, the fertilization rate generally will be particularly high. In a normal *in vitro* fertilization effort, there is between a 10% and 60% chance that a clinical pregnancy (i.e., implantation) will result. The rate of miscarriage for *in vitro* fertilization pregnancies is higher than the rate of spontaneous miscarriages in other pregnancies. The perinatal (i.e., birth) and neonatal (i.e., newborn) mortality rates for *in vitro* fertilization babies are also slightly higher than for others. Thus the fertilization and pregnancy rates are higher than the "take home baby" rate when these techniques are used.

Because the chances of success are substantially increased if several fertilized ova are returned to the uterus, and because of the high cost and physical burden of repeating the procedure, women undergoing *in vitro* fertilization are generally given drugs to increase the number of ova that become ripe and ready for release and fertilization in one cycle. While this "superovulation" increases the chances of successful fertilization and implantation, inducing ovulation itself may have adverse side effects. In addition, the simultaneous placement of multiple fertilized ova results in a higher rate of multiple births than in the rest of the population.

The medical cost of the ovum retrieval, fertilization and implantation process can exceed $15,000 per ovulation cycle. The drugs the prospective mother must take add another few thousand dollars each cycle. While many infertile couples are thus priced out of *in vitro* fertilization, it is the only process available to women whose fallopian tubes cannot accommodate the fertilization process, and thousands of happy and healthy children (and parents) have resulted from this process.

The development and common use of *in vitro* fertilization has given rise to several other related procedures and some variations on the original process. In gamete intra-fallopian transfer (GIFT) the ova are collected just as they would be for *in vitro* fertilization, but both the ova and the semen containing fertile sperm are then injected into the fallopian tubes, where fertilization takes place. In zygote intra-fallopian transfer (ZIFT), it is the zygote that is transferred. If the problem appears to be in the sperm penetration of the wall of the ovum, physicians may try Intracytoplasmic Sperm Injection (ICSI), in which a single sperm is injected into an ovum (at an additional cost of about $2,000). If the problem arises because the fertilized ovum cannot break free of its "shell" and implant in the uterus, physicians can use an "assisted hatching" (AZH) technique and cut into the "shell" (by the use of a hard object, a laser, or an acid solution) and render it more likely to implant (at an additional cost of over $1000).

In addition, it is possible to freeze an embryo, permitting evaluation of the genetic structure of the embryo before it is thawed and implanted. While the insertion of the fertilized ovum may be the most difficult portion of the procedure from a medical point of view, the removal of the ovum is often the most difficult process from the point of view of the woman. Thus, removing extra ova, fertilizing and freezing them, may save an additional retrieval process if the first insertion is unsuccessful.

When the ovum transferred to a woman comes from a source other than her own ovaries, the process will cost her more. The ovum source generally is paid between $3,000 and $12,000 dollars per retrieval; each retrieval usually results in several ova. One egg retrieval program charges the recipient $3,500 plus 10% of the egg donor fee.

For a list of current prices, fees and additional costs for IVF procedures at one multi-center clinic, see, *www.fertility-docs.com/fertility_fees.phtml,* which, as this casebook goes to press, is running a special on IVF services at $7800 (plus medications) for two cycles for young, healthy couples. For an account of the financial compensation available for egg vendors, see *www.eggdonor.com/edfinan.html,* which seeks women between 21 and 30 who are bright and attractive, have (or are pursuing) a college degree, are in excellent health, and have weight proportional to height. For a lively account of the journey of one Yale undergraduate who thought about becoming an egg vendor (at a substantial premium), see Jessica Cohen, Grade A: The Market for a Yale Woman's Eggs, The Atlantic Monthly, December 2002, at 74.

The legal issues that arise out of *in vitro* fertilization multiply when the fertilized ova are placed in a woman other than the one who produced them. In such a case, the pregnant woman is not the genetic mother of the child that she is carrying. Of course, the man expecting to raise the child may not be the genetic father either. Such a case may be a variant on gestational surrogacy, which is discussed below.

Notes and Questions: The Status of the Parents

1. *In vitro* fertilization using the ova of a woman into whom they are replaced and the sperm of that woman's husband should raise no more moral or legal questions, at least as to the status of the parents, than AIH. Is the essentially religious argument—that procreation should be a natural process and that the consequences of intervening are too serious and unknown for us to permit it—stronger in the case of the more highly medicalized *in vitro* fertilization than in the case of artificial insemination?

2. Analogously, *in vitro* fertilization using the ova supplied by the woman into whom it is replaced and the sperm of a man not her husband ought to be treated very much like AID, at least as regards the status of the parents. Is there any reason to give the sperm source greater (or lesser) rights as against the mother just because the fertilization process has been *in vitro* rather than *in vivo?*

3. The most difficult questions arise when the ova of one woman are placed in the uterus of another, whatever the source of the sperm. Under such circumstances, who is the mother? Perhaps the simplest case is where the ova of one woman is placed in the uterus of a second after it has been fertilized by the sperm of that second woman's husband, with the expectation of all parties that the pregnant woman and her husband will raise the child. In some respects, this is simply a gender reversed version of AID. Under what circumstances do any of the uniform acts apply to such cases?

Of course, providing an egg is not the same as providing sperm; retrieving the egg is far more invasive than retrieving the sperm. On the other hand, there is no male activity that is analogous, in time commitment, physical commitment, and emotional consequences, to carrying the pregnancy. Should that commitment and the fact that the fetus is nurtured by the pregnant woman's body make the pregnant woman the legal mother, whatever the source of the ovum? While there is a presumption that the woman from whose womb the baby emerges is that baby's mother, that presumption arose before there was any possibility that the source of the ovum and the source of the womb could be different women. Are there any circumstances in which you would want to treat the ovum source, rather than the pregnant woman, as the mother? Should a woman with fertile ova but no uterus who wishes to bear a child with her husband (or someone else) be able to enter a binding contract with another woman to have that second woman carry and give birth to her child for her? See the discussion of gestational surrogacy, below.

4. One consequence of the implantation of several embryos that were *fertilized in vitro* is that many of the embryos may continue to develop *in vivo*. While most multiple births pose no substantial problems to the mother or the neonatal siblings, sometimes the life or health of the mother (or some of the developing fetuses) can be preserved only if the number of fetuses that the mother is carrying is reduced. Under what circumstances is it appropriate to selectively reduce the number of fetuses being carried? Is the case of such selective reduction governed by the more general law applying to abortion, described above? Are there any ethical or legal concerns present in cases of selective reduction that are not present in other situations that might give rise to abortion? Are there any legal or ethical limitations on how the mother (or the family, or the doctor, or the court)

should choose which of two or more fetuses should be aborted to save the life or health of that fetus's mother or potential siblings?

5. The legal issues raised by embryo transfer are roughly the same as those raised by ovum transfer. The hardest questions do not relate to the status of the parents but, rather, to the status of the embryos themselves. The question of the status of frozen embryos first came to a state's highest court in 1992 in the context of a divorce of a couple undergoing *in vitro* fertilization.

DAVIS v. DAVIS

Supreme Court of Tennessee, 1992.
842 S.W.2d 588.

DAUGHTREY, J.:

This appeal presents a question of first impression, involving the disposition of the cryogenically-preserved product of in vitro fertilization (IVF), commonly referred to in the popular press and the legal journals as "frozen embryos." The case began as a divorce action, filed by the appellee, Junior Lewis Davis, against his then wife, appellant Mary Sue Davis. The parties were able to agree upon all terms of dissolution, except one: who was to have "custody" of the seven "frozen embryos" stored in a Knoxville fertility clinic that had attempted to assist the Davises in achieving a much-wanted pregnancy during a happier period in their relationship.

I. INTRODUCTION

Mary Sue Davis originally asked for control of the "frozen embryos" with the intent to have them transferred to her own uterus, in a post-divorce effort to become pregnant. Junior Davis objected, saying that he preferred to leave the embryos in their frozen state until he decided whether or not he wanted to become a parent outside the bounds of marriage.

Based on its determination that the embryos were "human beings" from the moment of fertilization, the trial court awarded "custody" to Mary Sue Davis and directed that she "be permitted the opportunity to bring these children to term through implantation." The Court of Appeals reversed, finding that Junior Davis has a "constitutionally protected right not to beget a child where no pregnancy has taken place" and holding that "there is no compelling state interest to justify [ ] ordering implantation against the will of either party." The Court of Appeals further held that "the parties share an interest in the seven fertilized ova" and remanded the case to the trial court for entry of an order vesting them with "joint control . . . and equal voice over their disposition."

Mary Sue Davis then sought review in this Court, contesting the validity of the constitutional basis for the Court of Appeals decision. We granted review, not because we disagree with the basic legal analysis utilized by the intermediate court, but because of the obvious importance of the case in terms of the development of law regarding the new reproductive technologies, and because the decision of the Court of Appeals does not give adequate guidance to the trial court in the event the parties cannot agree.

We note, in this latter regard, that their positions have already shifted: both have remarried and Mary Sue Davis (now Mary Sue Stowe) has moved out of state. She no longer wishes to utilize the "frozen embryos" herself, but wants authority to donate them to a childless couple. Junior Davis is adamantly opposed to such donation and would prefer to see the "frozen embryos" discarded. The result is, once again, an impasse, but the parties' current legal position does have an effect on the probable outcome of the case, as discussed below.

If we have no statutory authority or common law precedents to guide us [in this case], we do have the benefit of extensive comment and analysis in the legal journals. In those articles, medical-legal scholars and ethicists have proposed various models for the disposition of "frozen embryos" when unanticipated contingencies arise, such as divorce, death of one or both of the parties, financial reversals, or simple disenchantment with the IVF process. Those models range from a rule requiring, at one extreme, that all embryos be used by the gamete-providers or donated for uterine transfer, and, at the other extreme, that any unused embryos be automatically discarded. Other formulations would vest control in the female gamete-provider—in every case, because of her greater physical and emotional contribution to the IVF process, or perhaps only in the event that she wishes to use them herself. There are also two "implied contract" models: one would infer from enrollment in an IVF program that the IVF clinic has authority to decide in the event of an impasse whether to donate, discard, or use the "frozen embryos" for research; the other would infer from the parties' participation in the creation of the embryos that they had made an irrevocable commitment to reproduction and would require transfer either to the female provider or to a donee. There are also the so-called "equity models": one would avoid the conflict altogether by dividing the "frozen embryos" equally between the parties, to do with as they wish; the other would award veto power to the party wishing to avoid parenthood, whether it be the female or the male progenitor.

Each of these possible models has the virtue of ease of application. Adoption of any of them would establish a bright-line test that would dispose of disputes like the one we have before us in a clear and predictable manner. As appealing as that possibility might seem, we conclude that given the relevant principles of constitutional law, the existing public policy of Tennessee with regard to unborn life, the current state of scientific knowledge giving rise to the emerging reproductive technologies, and the ethical considerations that have developed in response to that scientific knowledge, there can be no easy answer to the question we now face. We conclude, instead, that we must weigh the interests of each party to the dispute, in terms of the facts and analysis set out below, in order to resolve that dispute in a fair and responsible manner.

* * *

IV.   THE "PERSON" VS. "PROPERTY" DICHOTOMY

One of the fundamental issues the inquiry poses is whether the preembryos in this case should be considered "persons" or "property" in the contemplation of the law. The Court of Appeals held, correctly, that they cannot be considered "persons" under Tennessee law * * *.

Nor do preembryos enjoy protection as "persons" under federal law. * * *

Left undisturbed, the trial court's ruling would have afforded preembryos the legal status of "persons" and vested them with legally cognizable interests separate from those of their progenitors. Such a decision would doubtless have had the effect of outlawing IVF programs in the state of Tennessee. But in setting aside the trial court's judgment, the Court of Appeals, at least by implication, may have swung too far in the opposite direction.

To our way of thinking, the most helpful discussion on this point is found not in the minuscule number of legal opinions that have involved "frozen embryos," but in the ethical standards set by The American Fertility Society, as follows:

> Three major ethical positions have been articulated in the debate over preembryo status. At one extreme is the view of the preembryo as a human subject after fertilization, which requires that it be accorded the rights of a person. This position entails an obligation to provide an opportunity for implantation to occur and tends to ban any action before transfer that might harm the preembryo or that is not immediately therapeutic, such as freezing and some preembryo research.

> At the opposite extreme is the view that the preembryo has a status no different from any other human tissue. With the consent of those who have decision-making authority over the preembryo, no limits should be imposed on actions taken with preembryos.

> A third view—one that is most widely held—takes an intermediate position between the other two. It holds that the preembryo deserves respect greater than that accorded to human tissue but not the respect accorded to actual persons. The preembryo is due greater respect than other human tissue because of its potential to become a person and because of its symbolic meaning for many people. Yet, it should not be treated as a person, because it has not yet developed the features of personhood, is not yet established as developmentally individual, and may never realize its biologic potential.

* * *

In its report, the Ethics Committee then calls upon those in charge of IVF programs to establish policies in keeping with the "special respect" due preembryos and suggests:

> Within the limits set by institutional policies, decision-making authority regarding preembryos should reside with the persons who have provided the gametes. . . . As a matter of law, it is reasonable to assume that the gamete providers have primary decision-making authority regarding preembryos in the absence of specific legislation on the subject. A person's liberty to procreate or to avoid procreation is directly involved in most decisions involving preembryos.[ ]

We conclude that preembryos are not, strictly speaking, either "persons" or "property," but occupy an interim category that entitles them to special respect because of their potential for human life. It follows that any interest that Mary Sue Davis and Junior Davis have in the preembryos in this case is not a true property interest. However, they do have an interest in the nature of ownership, to the extent that they have decision-making authority concerning disposition of the preembryos, within the scope of policy set by law.

V. THE ENFORCEABILITY OF CONTRACT

* * *

We believe, as a starting point, that an agreement regarding disposition of any untransferred preembryos in the event of contingencies (such as the death of one or more of the parties, divorce, financial reversals, or abandonment of the program) should be presumed valid and should be enforced as between the progenitors. This conclusion is in keeping with the proposition that the progenitors, having provided the gametic material giving rise to the preembryos, retain decision-making authority as to their disposition.

At the same time, we recognize that life is not static, and that human emotions run particularly high when a married couple is attempting to overcome infertility problems. It follows that the parties' initial "informed consent" to IVF procedures will often not be truly informed because of the near impossibility of anticipating, emotionally and psychologically, all the turns that events may take as the IVF process unfolds. Providing that the initial agreements may later be modified by agreement will, we think, protect the parties against some of the risks they face in this regard. But, in the absence of such agreed modification, we conclude that their prior agreements should be considered binding.

* * *

[In this case,] we are * * * left with this situation: there was initially no agreement between the parties concerning disposition of the preembryos under the circumstances of this case; there has been no agreement since; and there is no formula in the Court of Appeals opinion for determining the outcome if the parties cannot reach an agreement in the future.

* * *

VI. THE RIGHT OF PROCREATIONAL AUTONOMY

Although an understanding of the legal status of preembryos is necessary in order to determine the enforceability of agreements about their disposition, asking whether or not they constitute "property" is not an altogether helpful question. As the appellee points out in his brief, "[as] two or eight cell tiny lumps of complex protein, the embryos have no [intrinsic] value to either party." Their value lies in the "potential to become, after implantation, growth and birth, children." Thus, the essential dispute here is not where or how or how long to store the preembryos, but whether the parties will become parents. The Court of Appeals held in effect that they will become parents if they both agree to become parents. The Court did not say what will happen if they fail to agree. We conclude that the answer to this dilemma turns on the parties' exercise of their constitutional right to privacy.

* * *

[The Court found there was a right to individual privacy in both Federal and Tennessee State law, and that this right to individual privacy encompassed the right of procreational autonomy.]

For the purposes of this litigation it is sufficient to note that, whatever its ultimate constitutional boundaries, the right of procreational autonomy is composed of two rights of equal significance—the right to procreate and the right to avoid procreation. Undoubtedly, both are subject to protections and limitations.

The equivalence of and inherent tension between these two interests are nowhere more evident than in the context of in vitro fertilization. None of the concerns about a woman's bodily integrity that have previously precluded men from controlling abortion decisions is applicable here. We are not unmindful of the fact that the trauma (including both emotional stress and physical discomfort) to which women are subjected in the IVF process is more severe than is the impact of the procedure on men. In this sense, it is fair to say that women contribute more to the IVF process than men. Their experience, however, must be viewed in light of the joys of parenthood that is desired or the relative anguish of a lifetime of unwanted parenthood. As they stand on the brink of potential parenthood, Mary Sue Davis and Junior Lewis Davis must be seen as entirely equivalent gamete-providers.

It is further evident that, however far the protection of procreational autonomy extends, the existence of the right itself dictates that decisional authority rests in the gamete-providers alone, at least to the extent that their decisions have an impact upon their individual reproductive status. * * * [N]o other person or entity has an interest sufficient to permit interference with the gamete-providers' decision to continue or terminate the IVF process, because no one else bears the consequences of these decisions in the way that the gamete-providers do.

Further, at least with respect to Tennessee's public policy and its constitutional right of privacy, the state's interest in potential human life is insufficient to justify an infringement on the gamete-providers' procreational autonomy.

Certainly, if the state's interests do not become sufficiently compelling in the abortion context until the end of the first trimester, after very significant developmental stages have passed, then surely there is no state interest in these preembryos which could suffice to overcome the interests of the gamete-providers. The [Tennessee] abortion statute reveals that the increase in the state's interest is marked by each successive developmental stage such that, toward the end of a pregnancy, this interest is so compelling that abortion is almost strictly forbidden. This scheme supports the conclusion that the state's interest in the potential life embodied by these four- to eight-cell preembryos (which may or may not be able to achieve implantation in a uterine wall and which, if implanted, may or may not begin to develop into fetuses, subject to possible miscarriage) is at best slight. When weighed against the interests of the individuals and the burdens inherent in parenthood, the state's interest in the potential life of these preembryos is not sufficient to justify any infringement upon the freedom of these individuals to make their own decisions as to whether to allow a process to continue that may result in such a dramatic change in their lives as becoming parents. The unique nature of this case requires us to note that the interests of these parties in parenthood are different in scope than the parental interests considered in other cases. Previously, courts have dealt with the childbearing and child-rearing aspects of parenthood. Abortion cases have dealt with gestational parenthood. In this case, the Court must deal with the question of genetic parenthood. We conclude, moreover, that an interest in avoiding genetic parenthood can be significant enough to trigger the protections afforded to all other aspects of parenthood. The technological fact that someone unknown to these parties could gestate these preembryos does not alter the fact that these parties, the gamete-providers, would become parents in that event, at least in the genetic sense. The profound impact this would have on them supports their right to sole decisional authority as to whether the process of attempting to gestate these preembryos should continue. This brings us directly to the question of how to resolve the dispute that arises when one party wishes to continue the IVF process and the other does not.

VII. BALANCING THE PARTIES' INTERESTS

Resolving disputes over conflicting interests of constitutional import is a task familiar to the courts. One way of resolving these disputes is to consider the positions of the parties, the significance of their interests, and the relative burdens that will be imposed by differing resolutions. In this case, the issue centers on the two aspects of procreational autonomy—the right to procreate and the right to avoid procreation. We start by considering the burdens imposed on the parties by solutions that would have the effect of disallowing the exercise of individual procreational autonomy with respect to these particular preembryos.

Beginning with the burden imposed on Junior Davis, we note that the consequences are obvious. Any disposition which results in the gestation of the preembryos would impose unwanted parenthood on him, with all of its possible financial and psychological consequences. The impact that this unwanted parenthood would have on Junior Davis can only be understood by considering his particular circumstances, as revealed in the record.

Junior Davis testified that he was the fifth youngest of six children. When he was five years old, his parents divorced, his mother had a nervous breakdown, and he and three of his brothers went to live at a home for boys run by the Lutheran Church. Another brother was taken in by an aunt, and his sister stayed with their mother. From that day forward, he had monthly visits with his mother but saw his father only three more times before he died in 1976. Junior Davis testified that, as a boy, he had severe problems caused by separation from his parents. He said that it was especially hard to leave his mother after each monthly visit. He clearly feels that he has suffered because of his lack of opportunity to establish a relationship with his parents and particularly because of the absence of his father.

In light of his boyhood experiences, Junior Davis is vehemently opposed to fathering a child that would not live with both parents. Regardless of whether he or Mary Sue had custody, he feels that the child's bond with the non-custodial parent would not be satisfactory. He testified very clearly that his concern was for the psychological obstacles a child in such a situation would face, as well as the burdens it would impose on him. Likewise, he is opposed to donation because the recipient couple might divorce, leaving the child (which he definitely would consider his own) in a single-parent setting.

Balanced against Junior Davis's interest in avoiding parenthood is Mary Sue Davis's interest in donating the preembryos to another couple for implantation. Refusal to permit donation of the preembryos would impose on her the burden of knowing that the lengthy IVF procedures she underwent were futile, and that the preembryos to which she contributed genetic material would never become children. While this is not an insubstantial emotional burden, we can only conclude that Mary Sue Davis's interest in donation is not as significant as the interest Junior Davis has in avoiding parenthood. If she were allowed to donate these preembryos, he would face a lifetime of either wondering about his parental status or knowing about his parental status but having no control over it. He testified quite clearly that if these preembryos were brought to term he would fight for custody of his child or children. Donation, if a child came of it, would rob him twice—his procreational autonomy would be defeated and his relationship with his offspring would be prohibited.

The case would be closer if Mary Sue Davis were seeking to use the preembryos herself, but only if she could not achieve parenthood by any other reasonable means. We recognize the trauma that Mary Sue has already experienced and the additional discomfort to which she would be subjected if she opts to attempt IVF again. Still, she would have a reasonable opportunity, through IVF, to try once again to achieve parenthood in all its aspects—genetic, gestational, bearing, and rearing.

Further, we note that if Mary Sue Davis were unable to undergo another round of IVF, or opted not to try, she could still achieve the child-rearing aspects of parenthood through adoption. The fact that she and Junior Davis pursued adoption indicates that, at least at one time, she was willing to forego genetic parenthood and would have been satisfied by the child-rearing aspects of parenthood alone.

VIII. CONCLUSION

In summary, we hold that disputes involving the disposition of preembryos produced by in vitro fertilization should be resolved, first, by looking to the preferences of the progenitors. If their wishes cannot be ascertained, or if there is dispute, then their prior agreement concerning disposition should be carried out. If no prior agreement exists, then the relative interests of the parties in using or not using the preembryos must be weighed. Ordinarily, the party wishing to avoid procreation should prevail, assuming that the other party has a reasonable possibility of achieving parenthood by means other than use of the preembryos in question. If no other reasonable alternatives exist, then the argument in favor of using the preembryos to achieve pregnancy should be considered. However, if the party seeking control of the preembryos intends merely to donate them to another couple, the objecting party obviously has the greater interest and should prevail.

But the rule does not contemplate the creation of an automatic veto, and in affirming the judgment of the Court of Appeals, we would not wish to be interpreted as so holding.

For the reasons set out above, the judgment of the Court of Appeals is affirmed, in the appellee's favor. This ruling means that the Knoxville Fertility Clinic is free to follow its normal procedure in dealing with unused preembryos, as long as that procedure is not in conflict with this opinion.

Notes and Questions: The Status of the Embryo

1. In fact, the Knoxville Fertility Clinic could not "follow its normal procedure in dealing with unused preembryos" because its normal procedure was to provide those preembryos to infertile couples—a procedure that would have been in conflict with the opinion. On rehearing directed to this issue, the Tennessee court looked to the report of the American Fertility Society's Ethics Committee, which authorizes the preembryos to be donated for research purposes (which would require the consent of both of the Davises) or to be discarded. See Davis v. Davis, Order on Petitions to Rehear (Sup. Ct. Tenn., Nov. 23, 1992).

2. The court suggests that the state interest in assuring that the embryo is implanted and allowed to develop cannot be sufficiently compelling to overcome a gamete-provider's right to avoid parenthood because, by analogy, "the state's interest does not become sufficiently compelling in the abortion context until the end of the first trimester, after very significant developmental stages have passed...." Is the analogy to the abortion context a persuasive one? In the same year in which this case was decided, the United States Supreme Court reconsidered the value of drawing trimester lines in Planned Parenthood of Southeastern Pennsylvania v. Casey, supra section II(A). As a Constitutional matter, could a state now have an interest in protecting fertilized ova that would be sufficiently compelling to overcome the interests of one or both of the gamete providers?

3. The court describes several different rules that could be applied in these disputes over the status and control of extracorporeal fertilized ova or pre-embryos. One of the alternatives is to treat the pre-embryos as personal property and apply the common law of property to them; another would be to treat those pre-embryos as if they were children entitled to protection of the state law. Each view has some legal support. In York v. Jones, 717 F.Supp. 421 (E.D.Va. 1989), a federal district court treated frozen embryos prepared in the course of infertility treatment as property that would be subject to the ordinary law of bailment; thus, the court required the infertility program where they were developed (the bailee) to transfer them to a new program selected by the progenitors. In Hecht v. Superior Court, 16 Cal.App.4th 836, 20 Cal.Rptr.2d 275 (1993), the California Court of Appeal found that the probate court could distribute a decedent's frozen sperm, concluding that it was property subject to disposition upon death. In Louisiana, on the other hand, disputes between those who want to control the disposition of pre-embryos are resolved by applying the "best interest of the pre-embryo" standard. See La. Stat. Ann. Rev. section 14:87:2.

4. The New York Court of Appeals followed a path close to that taken in Davis v. Davis when it concluded that the parties to assisted reproduction are bound by an unambiguous agreement which states the parties mutual intent as to the disposition of cryogenically preserved pre-embryos. In Kass v. Kass, 91 N.Y.2d 554, 673 N.Y.S.2d 350, 696 N.E.2d 174 (1998), the Court of Appeals applied the provisions of the informed consent document signed by both progenitors when their infertility treatment commenced. This document declared that the clinic would use any frozen pre-embryos for research in the event that the progenitors could not agree on their disposition. The court thus affirmed the Appellate Division, which had reversed the trial court's determination that after fertilization the disposition of genetic material was exclusively in the hands of the mother, who possessed all of the rights over the frozen embryo that she would possess over a fetus developing in her body.

The two courts to confront this issue most recently have expressly rejected the notion that the prior agreement of the progenitors should always govern the disposition of frozen embryos. In A.Z. v. B.Z., 431 Mass. 150, 725 N.E.2d 1051 (2000), the Massachusetts Supreme Judicial Court was faced with an agreement that provided that if the intended parents were to become separated, the frozen embryos then available would be given to one of the parents for implantation. In that case, though, the application of that agreement would have forced the former husband to become a parent against his will, and this, the court concluded, would be contrary to public policy. The court explained that, "forced procreation is not an area amenable to judicial enforcement." In J.B. v. M.B., 170 N.J. 9, 783 A.2d 707 (2001) the Supreme Court of New Jersey addressed a contested claim that the parties to an IVF contract had agreed to bring all of the frozen embryos to life. The court determined that the parties would not normally be bound by a prior IVF agreement that would now require one of those parties to become a parent against that person's will.

In Davis and Kass, the enforceable prior agreements provided for the destruction of frozen embryos rather than their implantation; in A.Z. and J.B., the agreement would have resulted in the creation of a child (and, of course, parents). Is that distinction sufficient to explain the difference in the outcomes of these cases? Could there be other bases for distinguishing the decisions of the courts in Tennessee and New York, on one hand, and Massachusetts and New Jersey, on the other?

5. Given the difference in the burden of retrieval processes, should the ovum source (who went through an invasive surgical procedure, following sometimes debilitating hormone therapy) have greater say in the disposition of the frozen embryo than the sperm source (who went into the next room with a cup)? Would it violate principles of equal protection to do so? The American Medical Association would treat each progenitor equally:

> The gamete providers should have an equal say in the use of their pre-embryos and, therefore, the pre-embryos should not be available for use by either provider or changed from their frozen state without the consent of both providers. The man and woman each has contributed half of the pre-embryo's genetic code. In addition, whether a person chooses to become a parent and assume all of the accompanying obligations is a particularly personal and fundamental decision. Even if the individual could be absolved of any parental obligations, he or she may have a strong desire not to have offspring. The absence of a legal duty does not eliminate the moral duty many would feel toward any genetic offspring.

Policy E–2.141. Frozen Pre–Embryos.

6. All of the cases suggest that the result in a frozen embryo disposition case might be different if the party who wished to bring the frozen embryo to life were otherwise infertile, and would have no other way to become a parent. Justice Verniero, concurring in the J.B. case, pointed out that "the same principles that compel the outcome in this case would permit an infertile party to assert his or her right to use a preembryo against the objections of the other party, if such use were the only means of procreation. In that instance, the balance arguably would weigh in favor of the infertile party absent countervailing factors of greater weight." What count as be "countervailing factors of greater weight"? The J.B. majority didn't seem so certain that the result would be different if the one seeking to use the embryo were otherwise infertile, saying, "[w]e express no opinion in respect of a case in which a party who has become infertile seeks use of stored preembryos against the wishes of his or her partner, noting only that the

possibility of adoption also may be a consideration, among others, in the court's assessment."

7. What is the warden of the freezer to do with frozen embryos whose contributors cannot agree upon their disposition? Can they be destroyed, or sold to the highest bidder when the storage fee remains unpaid? If one of the parties who contributed to the embryos dies, does that party's interest pass to the other?

Only a few states have dealt with this issue legislatively, and they have done so idiosyncratically; in Louisiana a pre-zygote must be implanted while in Florida there must be a written document describing the parties' dispositional intent. In 1990 the United Kingdom enacted the Human Fertilization and Embryology Act, which provides that unused pre-embryos are to be destroyed five years after they are created unless there are contrary instructions from the progenitors. Australia has employed similar rules since 1984, and Germany has outlawed freezing of embryos altogether. The American Medical Association Council on Ethical and Judicial Affairs has proposed that intended parents be encouraged to express their intent with regard to the disposition of frozen embryos, but that such an expression not be mandatory on physicians. The intended parents would be able to implant them, thaw (and thus destroy) them, permit research upon them, or donate them to another woman. They would be prohibited from selling them, however.

8. If you were employed by a clinic to draft a form contract that would provide for the disposition of excess or unneeded frozen pre-embryos, how would you write it? If you were a patient seeking treatment at a clinic, how would you want it written? What provisions would a contract written by counsel for the patients and the counsel for the providers, negotiating at arms length, include?

9. The new reproductive technologies of *in vitro* fertilization and embryo cryopreservation can give rise to a host of different kinds of liability. Of course, the physician and medical institution could be liable in an ordinary medical malpractice case for negligently performing the procedure. Would the duty of due care extend to the fetus as well as the parents? Would it extend to a fetus not born alive? To an aborted fetus? Negligently freezing an ovum or embryo, or negligently thawing it and thus destroying or damaging it, would also subject the appropriate professionals to malpractice liability.

Presumably, an ovum source would also be liable in contract to the same extent as would a sperm source. Any warranty that would come with an ovum would be analogous to that which would come with sperm, and the nature of any such warranty under the U.C.C. could depend upon whether the ovum is a good or a service.

The value of cryogenically preserved fertilized pre-embryos (or ova) may also make them targets for theft; clinic employees (or others) may be tempted to provide excess genetic material to those who need it without seeking consent from the original progenitors. Indeed, during the late 1990s that kind of redirection of ova apparently became fairly common at the University of California–Irvine's fertility clinic, where at least fifteen children were born as a result of the use of ova from women who had not consented to their transfer. For a wonderful account of the problems created by this misconduct, see Alice Noble–Allgire, Switched at the Fertility Clinic: Determining Maternal Rights When a Child is Born from Stolen or Misdelivered Genetic Material, 64 Mo. L. Rev. 517 (1999). One of the consequences of this redirection of ova is also discussed in Prato–Morrison v. Doe, below at page 145. What kinds of civil, criminal and administrative liability could arise out of these occurrences? As clinic counsel, what could you do to limit the chance of this happening?

4. *Surrogacy*

The Process of Surrogacy

Surrogacy may be the least technological of reproductive technologies. It is also the oldest; Genesis tells of Abraham's servant Hagar bearing a child to be raised by the genetic father, Abraham, and his wife Sarah. Genesis 16:1–16. Surrogacy is that arrangement in which a woman carries a child to term intending at the initiation of the pregnancy for another woman to raise the child as the social mother. As was the case with Hagar, fertilization may take place through normal coitus. It also may be a consequence of artificial insemination, *in vitro* fertilization or embryo transfer. While the genetic father is often the husband of the woman who expects to raise the child as its mother, that need not be the case. While the genetic mother is often the pregnant woman, that is not required either; an arrangement in which the pregnant woman is not the source of the ovum is called gestational surrogacy. It is possible to take the sperm from one source, the ovum from another and place the subsequently developed embryo in the uterus of a third person.

Although there is some debate about whether surrogacy ought to be considered a "medical treatment" for infertility, it provides the only way for a woman without a uterus to be the genetic mother of a child (through embryo transfer, for example), or to be the mother of a child whose genetic father is her husband (through artificial insemination of the surrogate with the husband's sperm). In addition, some women may choose to avoid pregnancy because it poses grave physical or emotional risk to them, or because it would be difficult for them to continue to work (or play) while pregnant.

It is hard to estimate the cost of the "average" surrogacy arrangement. In some cases the carrying mother is a friend or relative of the woman who expects to raise the child and seeks no compensation for her efforts. Other unrelated women may also be willing to act as surrogates for entirely altruistic reasons. Yet others engage in surrogacy for entirely economic reasons. A couple wishing to contract for a surrogate through a commercial service may pay in excess of $50,000 for the medical and legal fees, psychological services, egg donor fee, health insurance for the surrogate, and the fees (which may be denominated "expenses") of the surrogate herself. A surrogate is likely to be paid at least $15,000 for her labor. Legal fees for all parties range from a few thousand dollars to over $20,000. Potential surrogates (like ova and sperm vendors, surrogacy brokers, fertility clinics, and law offices providing infertility-related legal services) can be easily discovered, and their fees can be estimated, through a web search

Commercial surrogacy arrangements have given rise to a great deal of controversy. In some states the process itself has been challenged before any particular case has arisen on the grounds that commercial surrogacy constitutes baby selling *per se*. See, e.g., Surrogate Parenting Associates, Inc. v. Commonwealth ex rel. Armstrong, 704 S.W.2d 209 (Ky.1986). While the Uniform Parentage Act (2002) now includes an article recognizing surrogacy contracts and regulating them, no state has yet adopted that provision. On the other hand, as the Reporter's Note to the "gestational agreement" portion of that uniform act points out, "eleven states allow such agreements by statutes or caselaw; six states void such agreements by statute; eight states statutorily ban compensation to the gestational mother; and two states have judicially refused to recognize them." For a more detailed accounting, see the Appendix, Article 8, Uniform Parentage Act (2002). When there is no governing statute, a dispute between the parties will require the courts to determine the rights and responsibilities of all of those involved, and the propriety and enforceability of any contractual arrangements of the parties.

IN THE MATTER OF BABY M

Supreme Court of New Jersey, 1988.
109 N.J. 396, 537 A.2d 1227.

WILENTZ, C.J.:

In this matter the Court is asked to determine the validity of a contract that purports to provide a new way of bringing children into a family. For a fee of $10,000, a woman agrees to be artificially inseminated with the semen of another woman's husband; she is to conceive a child, carry it to term, and after its birth surrender it to the natural father and his wife. The intent of the contract is that the child's natural mother will thereafter be forever separated from her child. The wife is to adopt the child, and she and the natural father are to be regarded as its parents for all purposes. The contract providing for this is called a "surrogacy contract," the natural mother inappropriately called the "surrogate mother."

We invalidate the surrogacy contract because it conflicts with the law and public policy of this State. While we recognize the depth of the yearning of infertile couples to have their own children, we find the payment of money to a "surrogate" mother illegal, perhaps criminal, and potentially degrading to women. Although in this case we grant custody to the natural father, the evidence having clearly proved such custody to be in the best interests of the infant, we void both the termination of the surrogate mother's parental rights and the adoption of the child by the wife/stepparent. We thus restore the "surrogate" as the mother of the child. We remand the issue of the natural mother's visitation rights to the trial court, since that issue was not reached below and the record before us is not sufficient to permit us to decide it *de novo*.

We find no offense to our present laws where a woman voluntarily and without payment agrees to act as a "surrogate" mother, provided that she is not subject to a binding agreement to surrender her child. Moreover, our holding today does not preclude the Legislature from altering the current law, however, the surrogacy agreement before us is illegal and invalid.

I.

Facts

In February 1985, William Stern and Mary Beth Whitehead entered into a surrogacy contract. It recited that Stern's wife, Elizabeth, was infertile, that they wanted a child, and that Mrs. Whitehead was willing to provide that child as the mother with Mr. Stern as the father.

[The Court reviewed the facts of the case with excruciating detail, and then reviewed the lower court's holding that the contract was valid, but that placement of the child—called Melissa by the Sterns and Sara by Mary Beth Whitehead—should depend upon the best interest of the child.]

* * *

II.

Invalidity and Unenforceability of Surrogacy Contract

We have concluded that this surrogacy contract is invalid. Our conclusion has two bases: direct conflict with existing statutes and conflict with the public policies of this State, as expressed in its statutory and decisional law.

One of the surrogacy contract's basic purposes, to achieve the adoption of a child through private placement, though permitted in New Jersey "is very much disfavored." [ ] Its use of money for this purpose—and we have no doubt whatsoever that the money is being paid to obtain an adoption and not, as the Sterns argue, for the personal services of Mary Beth Whitehead—is illegal and perhaps criminal. * * * In addition to the inducement of money, there is the coercion of contract: the [natural mother's] irrevocable agreement, prior to birth, even prior to conception, to surrender the child to the adoptive couple. Such an agreement is totally unenforceable in private placement adoption. [ ] Even where the adoption is through an approved agency, the formal agreement to surrender occurs only *after* birth * * *, and then, by regulation, only after the birth mother has been counseled. * * * Integral to these invalid provisions of the surrogacy contract is the related agreement, equally invalid, on the part of the natural mother to cooperate with, and not to contest, proceedings to terminate her parental rights, as well as her contractual concession, in aid of the adoption, that the child's best interests would be served by awarding custody to the natural father and his wife—all of this before she has even conceived, and, in some cases, before she has the slightest idea of what the natural father and adoptive mother are like.

The foregoing provisions not only directly conflict with New Jersey statutes, but also offend long-established State policies. These critical terms, which are at the heart of the contract, are invalid and unenforceable; the conclusion therefore follows, without more, that the entire contract is unenforceable.

A. *Conflict with Statutory Provisions*

The surrogacy contract conflicts with: (1) laws prohibiting the use of money in connection with adoptions; (2) laws requiring proof of parental unfitness or abandonment before termination of parental rights is ordered or an adoption is granted; and (3) laws that make surrender of custody and consent to adoption revocable in private placement adoptions. [The court discusses the terms of the New Jersey statutes in each of these areas.]

B. *Public Policy Considerations*

The surrogacy contract's invalidity, resulting from its direct conflict with the above statutory provisions, is further underlined when its goals and means are measured against New Jersey's public policy. The contract's basic premise, that the natural parents can decide in advance of birth which one is to have custody of the child, bears no relationship to the settled law that the child's best interests shall determine custody.

* * *

This is the sale of a child, or, at the very least, the sale of a mother's right to her child, the only mitigating factor being that one of the purchasers is the father. Almost every evil that prompted the prohibition of the payment of money in connection with adoptions exists here.

* * *

In the scheme contemplated by the surrogacy contract in this case, a middleman, propelled by profit, promotes the sale. Whatever idealism may have motivated any of the participants, the profit motive predominates, permeates, and ultimately governs the transaction. The demand for children is great and the supply small. The availability of contraception, abortion, and the greater willingness of single mothers to bring up their children has led to a shortage of babies offered for adoption. [ ] The situation is ripe for the entry of the middleman who will bring some equilibrium into the market by increasing the supply through the use of money.

Intimated, but disputed, is the assertion that surrogacy will be used for the benefit of the rich at the expense of the poor. [ ] In response it is noted that the Sterns are not rich and the Whiteheads not poor. Nevertheless, it is clear to us that it is unlikely that surrogate mothers will be as proportionately numerous among those women in the top twenty percent income bracket as among these in the bottom twenty percent. [ ] Put differently, we doubt that infertile couples in the low-income bracket will find upper income surrogates.

* * *

The point is made that Mrs. Whitehead *agreed* to the surrogacy arrangement, supposedly fully understanding the consequences. Putting aside the issue of how compelling her need for money may have been, and how significant her understanding of the consequences, we suggest that her consent is irrelevant. There are, in a civilized society, some things that money cannot buy. * * *

The long-term effects of surrogacy contracts are not known, but feared— the impact on the child who learns her life was bought, that she is the offspring of someone who gave birth to her only to obtain money; the impact on the natural mother as the full weight of her isolation is felt along with the full reality of the sale of her body and her child; the impact on the natural father and the adoptive mother once they realize the consequences of their conduct. Literature in related areas suggests these are substantial considerations, although, given the newness of surrogacy, there is little information. [ ]

* * *

In sum, the harmful consequences of this surrogacy arrangement appear to us all too palpable. In New Jersey the surrogate mother's agreement to sell her child is void. Its irrevocability infects the entire contract, as does the money that purports to buy it.

III.

Termination

We have already noted that under our laws termination of parental rights cannot be based on contract, but may be granted only on proof of the statutory requirements. * * *

* * *

There is simply no [statutory] basis * * * to warrant termination of Mrs. Whitehead's parental rights. We therefore conclude that the natural mother is entitled to retain her rights as a mother.

IV.

Constitutional Issues

Both parties argue that the Constitutions—state and federal—mandate approval of their basic claims. The source of their constitutional arguments is essentially the same: the right of privacy, the right to procreate, the right to the companionship of one's child, those rights flowing either directly from the fourteenth amendment or by its incorporation of the Bill of Rights, or from the ninth amendment, or through the penumbra surrounding all of the Bill of Rights. They are the rights of personal intimacy, of marriage, of sex, or family, or procreation. Whatever their source, it is clear that they are fundamental rights protected by both the federal and state Constitutions. * * * The right asserted by the Sterns is the right of procreation; that asserted by Mary Beth Whitehead is the right to the companionship of her child. We find that the right of procreation does not extend as far as claimed by the Sterns. As for the right asserted by Mrs. Whitehead,[4] since we uphold it on other grounds (*i.e.*, we have restored her as mother and recognized her right, limited by the child's best interests, to her companionship), we need not decide that constitutional issue, and for reasons set forth below we should not.

* * * The right to procreate very simply is the right to have natural children, whether through sexual intercourse or artificial insemination. It is no more than that. Mr. Stern has not been deprived of that right. Through artificial insemination of Mrs. Whitehead, Baby M is his child. The custody, care, companionship, and nurturing that follow birth are not parts of the right to procreation; they are rights that may also be constitutionally protected, but that involve many considerations other than the right of procreation.

* * *

V.

Custody

[The court determined that it would be in the best interest of the child for custody to be awarded to the father, Mr. Stern.]

---

4. Opponents of surrogacy have also put forth arguments based on the thirteenth amendment, as well as the Peonage Act, 42 U.S.C.A. Section 1993 (1982). We need not address these arguments because we have already held the contract unenforceable on the basis of state law.

VI.

Visitation

The trial court's decision to terminate Mrs. Whitehead's parental rights precluded it from making any determination on visitation. [ ] Our reversal of the trial court's order, however, requires delineation of Mrs. Whitehead's rights to visitation.

[The court pointed out that Mrs. Whitehead was the legal and natural mother, and that she was entitled to be treated as such.]

* * *

* * *[T]he trial court should recall the touchstones of visitation: that it is desirable for the child to have contact with both parents; that besides the child's interests, the parents' interests also must be considered; but that when all is said and done, the best interest of the child is paramount.

We have decided that Mrs. Whitehead is entitled to visitation at some point, and that question is not open to the trial court on this remand. The trial court will determine what kind of visitation shall be granted to her, with or without conditions, and when and under what circumstances it should commence. * * *

* * *

Conclusion

This case affords some insight into a new reproductive arrangement: the artificial insemination of a surrogate mother. The unfortunate events that have unfolded illustrate that its unregulated use can bring suffering to all involved. Potential victims include the surrogate mother and her family, the natural father and his wife, and most importantly, the child. Although surrogacy has apparently provided positive results for some infertile couples, it can also, as this case demonstrates, cause suffering to participants, here essentially innocent and well-intended.

* * *

Notes and Questions

1.   Upon remand, the superior court determined that Mary Beth Whitehead Gould should have "unsupervised uninterrupted liberal visitation" with Baby M. Under the court's schedule, the visitations would be increased until they included a two-day (and one overnight) visit every other week, and an annual two-week visit. See 14 Fam.L.Rep. 1276 (1988).

2.   Most of the arguments against surrogacy are outlined in the opinion of the court in *Baby M.* Generally, these objections fall into three categories—those related to the contracting parties; those related to the child; and those related to the effect of the process on society as a whole.

The first argument generally advanced against surrogacy is that it exploits women who are willing to give or rent their bodies as vessels to carry other people's children. Could the inducement of payment for pregnancy cause a woman to consent to something that otherwise would be an unthinkable intrusion upon her body? Will the development of commercial surrogacy lead to a class of poor women who will become child bearers for wealthy women who do not want to spend the time or energy on pregnancy? Is it likely that the fact that there is a relationship between ethnicity and the distribution of wealth in this society mean that we will develop separate childbearing races and child-raising races?

Feminists are divided on this issue. Some are deeply offended by the overt use of the woman's body that is the whole goal of a surrogacy arrangement; others believe it is merely misguided paternalism that leads courts (and others) to conclude that women are incapable of deciding for themselves whether they should enter surrogacy contracts. Some economists argue that making surrogacy contracts unenforceable will merely lower the amount that is paid to surrogates. Thus, they suggest, making surrogacy contracts unenforceable is just another in a long history of allegedly protectionist regulations that restrict what a woman may choose to do with her body.

Some argue that surrogacy contracts ought to be prohibited or discouraged because they advance only the best interests of the contracting parties, not the best interest of the child. Normally in a custody dispute between those with claims as parents, the court will look to the best interest of the child in determining the appropriate placement. Enforcing a surrogacy contract is necessarily inconsistent with this principle. In addition, some believe that children who find out that they were carried by a surrogate will be injured by that discovery, and others argue that surrogacy contracts render children instruments for the use of parents, not ends in themselves, and that this is necessarily harmful for children.

Finally, some believe that the fabric of society as a whole is weakened by surrogacy arrangements, at least commercial ones. As Justice Wilentz points out in *Baby M,* there are some things that money cannot buy. How, exactly, does he define this class of things? Why does he conclude that surrogacy is one of them?

Perhaps a surrogacy contract, which is a contract to put one's body to work for the benefit of another, is nothing more than a form of slavery. Since the Thirteenth Amendment we have prohibited contracts for slavery, even if the contracting parties are all competent adults who are acting voluntarily. One argument for the Thirteenth Amendment is that in addition to whatever it offers those who might be or become slaves, society as a whole is better off if the status of "slave" is impossible for everyone. Are all people in this society—including those who would never participate in a surrogacy contract in any way—better off if the society simply eliminates surrogacy?

3.   Why would the analysis in *Baby M* be different if the arrangement were not one that involved the exchange of money? Which ethical and legal arguments depend upon the commercial nature of the arrangement, and which remain just as strong whether or not any money changes hands?

4.   In addressing one constitutional issue, Judge Wilentz announces that the "right to procreate very simply is the right to have natural children, whether through sexual intercourse or artificial insemination. It is no more than that." Why does he limit the right in this way? Why does he include artificial insemination, but not *in vitro* fertilization (even between husband and wife) among those actions protected by the constitutional "right to procreate"? How far do you think the "right to procreate" should go? Should it include *in vitro* fertilization? Egg transfer? Embryo transfer? Surrogacy? Cloning? In which of these circumstances might one person's "right to procreate" conflict with another's?

5. Surrogacy contracts are often condemned on the ground that they constitute baby selling, which is illegal in every state. There is confusion over the purpose of statutes that prohibit baby selling, though: they may be intended to protect parents from financial inducements to give up their children, or they may be intended to protect children from being reduced to the status of an ordinary commodity. Are baby selling statutes merely anachronisms left over from the 19th century practice of selling children into effective slavery? Should baby selling be prohibited? Why? Should surrogacy arrangements be governed by baby selling statutes?

6. There is no doubt that the remedy of specific performance is not available to those who offer some consideration in return for the surrogate's labor. For this reason, surrogacy contracts drafted by careful lawyers do not provide for any substantial payment to the surrogate until the baby is delivered to the commissioning party and the surrogate mother (and her husband, if necessary) relinquish their parental rights. There remains the risk that the surrogate mother will not relinquish her parental rights, and that it will be impossible to have a court order termination of those rights. Indeed, this was the case in *Baby M*. In such a case a sperm source who has commissioned the surrogate may find himself liable for child support (and eligible for visitation rights) for a child who bears no legal or physical relationship to his own wife. After *Baby M*, is there any way to draft a contract to avoid these consequences? *Should* there be a way to do so? The *Baby M* court appended to their opinion a copy of the surrogacy contract and the contract between Mr. Stern and the surrogacy agency. To see exactly what the court determined to be unenforceable, see 537 A.2d at 1265–1273.

7. One argument against the use of surrogacy arrangements is the legal uncertainty they cause. Is this a good argument when those uncertainties could be resolved by judicial or legislative action? While many have called for legislative action to prohibit surrogacy arrangements, others have called for legislative action to regulate such arrangements so that the legal uncertainties can be avoided. See the Uniform Parentage Act (2002), below, choosing the path of regulation over the path of prohibition.

Several state legislatures have taken up the invitation to legislate in this area. Some clearly permit the practice; some formally outlaw it; some even make participating in the process a felony. For a full description of the laws of all of the states pertaining to this issue, see Uniform Parentage Act (2002), Appendix to Article 8.

8. The technology for facilitating reproduction is not only of interest to married couples. Single men and women, and single sex couples, have a special need for this technology. The use of a surrogate is the only way that a single man could expect to have a child to whom he would be genetically related. Similarly, the use of artificial insemination may be an especially attractive way for a single woman, or a lesbian couple, to have a child. While the law has put no formal restriction on the availability of reproductive techniques, some physicians and hospitals are reluctant to provide the full range of infertility services to single people or non-traditional families. Local and state statutes restricting discrimination on the basis of sexual preference may provide avenues of relief for those gay and lesbian potential parents who are denied reproductive services. *Eisenstadt v. Baird,* which threw out a statute forbidding single people access to contraceptives under some circumstances in which they were available to married people, might suggest that the equal protection clause of the Fourteenth Amendment would also protect single people who are denied access to infertility treatment provided to married people by state hospitals and other state facilities. Might their arguments,

and the arguments of gays and lesbians who seek parenthood, be bolstered by the Supeme Court's newfound respect for the private lives of different kinds of families in Lawrence v. Texas, 539 U.S. 558, 123 S.Ct. 2472, 156 L.Ed.2d 508 (2003)?

9. Did the Baby M court depend upon the fact that Mary Beth Whitehead Gould was the genetic mother of the child, or the fact that she was the gestational mother of the child? Would the result be different if she were not the genetic mother? Consider the following case, where the gestational mother and the genetic mother are, in fact, different women.

JOHNSON v. CALVERT

Supreme Court of California, 1993.
5 Cal.4th 84, 19 Cal.Rptr.2d 494, 851 P.2d 776.

PANELLI, J:

* * *

Mark and Crispina Calvert are a married couple who desired to have a child. Crispina was forced to undergo a hysterectomy in 1984. Her ovaries remained capable of producing eggs, however, and the couple eventually considered surrogacy. In 1989 Anna Johnson heard about Crispina's plight from a coworker and offered to serve as a surrogate for the Calverts.

On January 15, 1990, Mark, Crispina, and Anna signed a contract providing that an embryo created by the sperm of Mark and the egg of Crispina would be implanted in Anna and the child born would be taken into Mark and Crispina's home "as their child." Anna agreed she would relinquish "all parental rights" to the child in favor of Mark and Crispina. In return, Mark and Crispina would pay Anna $10,000 in a series of installments, the last to be paid six weeks after the child's birth. Mark and Crispina were also to pay for a $200,000 life insurance policy on Anna's life.

The zygote was implanted on January 19, 1990. Less than a month later, an ultrasound test confirmed Anna was pregnant.

Unfortunately, relations deteriorated between the two sides. Mark learned that Anna had not disclosed she had suffered several stillbirths and miscarriages. Anna felt Mark and Crispina did not do enough to obtain the required insurance policy. She also felt abandoned during an onset of premature labor in June.

In July 1990, Anna sent Mark and Crispina a letter demanding the balance of the payments due her or else she would refuse to give up the child. The following month, Mark and Crispina responded with a lawsuit, seeking a declaration they were the legal parents of the unborn child. Anna filed her own action to be declared the mother of the child, and the two cases were eventually consolidated. The parties agreed to an independent guardian ad litem for the purposes of the suit.

The child was born on September 19, 1990, and blood samples were obtained from both Anna and the child for analysis. The blood test results excluded Anna as the genetic mother. The parties agreed to a court order providing that the child would remain with Mark and Crispina on a temporary basis with visits by Anna.

DISCUSSION

Determining Maternity Under the Uniform Parentage Act [of 1973]

* * * [W]e are left with the undisputed evidence that Anna, not Crispina, gave birth to the child and that Crispina, not Anna, is genetically related to him. Both women thus have adduced evidence of a mother and child relationship as contemplated by the [Uniform Parentage] Act [1973]. [ ] Yet for any child California law recognizes only one natural mother, despite advances in reproductive technology rendering a different outcome biologically possible.

We decline to accept the contention of amicus curiae * * * that we should find the child has two mothers. Even though rising divorce rates have made multiple parent arrangements common in our society, we see no compelling reason to recognize such a situation here. The Calverts are the genetic and intending parents of their son and have provided him, by all accounts, with a stable, intact, and nurturing home. To recognize parental rights in a third party with whom the Calvert family has had little contact since shortly after the child's birth would diminish Crispina's role as mother.

We see no clear legislative preference in [the statutory law] as between blood testing evidence and proof of having given birth.

* * *

Because two women each have presented acceptable proof of maternity, we do not believe this case can be decided without enquiring into the parties' intentions as manifested in the surrogacy agreement. Mark and Crispina are a couple who desired to have a child of their own genes but are physically unable to do so without the help of reproductive technology. They affirmatively intended the birth of the child, and took the steps necessary to effect in vitro fertilization. But for their acted-on intention, the child would not exist. Anna agreed to facilitate the procreation of Mark's and Crispina's child. The parties' aim was to bring Mark's and Crispina's child into the world, not for Mark and Crispina to donate a zygote to Anna. Crispina from the outset intended to be the child's mother. Although the gestative function Anna performed was necessary to bring about the child's birth, it is safe to say that Anna would not have been given the opportunity to gestate or deliver the child had she, prior to implantation of the zygote, manifested her own intent to be the child's mother. No reason appears why Anna's later change of heart should vitiate the determination that Crispina is the child's natural mother.

We conclude that although the Act recognizes both genetic consanguinity and giving birth as means of establishing a mother and child relationship, when the two means do not coincide in one woman, she who intended to procreate the child—that is, she who intended to bring about the birth of a child that she intended to raise as her own—is the natural mother under California law.[5]

* * *

5. Thus, under our analysis, in a true "egg donation" situation, where a woman gestates and gives birth to a child formed from the egg of another woman with the intent to raise the child as her own, the birth mother is the natural mother under California law.

The dissent would decide parentage based on the best interests of the child. Such an approach raises the repugnant specter of governmental interference in matters implicating our

Anna urges that surrogacy contracts violate several social policies. Relying on her contention that she is the child's legal, natural mother, she cites the public policy embodied in [the] Penal Code [ ], prohibiting the payment for consent to adoption of a child. She argues further that the policies underlying the adoption laws of this state are violated by the surrogacy contract because it in effect constitutes a prebirth waiver of her parental rights.

We disagree. Gestational surrogacy differs in crucial respects from adoption and so is not subject to the adoption statutes. The parties voluntarily agreed to participate in in vitro fertilization and related medical procedures before the child was conceived; at the time when Anna entered into the contract, therefore, she was not vulnerable to financial inducements to part with her own expected offspring. As discussed above, Anna was not the genetic mother of the child. The payments to Anna under the contract were meant to compensate her for her services in gestating the fetus and undergoing labor, rather than for giving up "parental" rights to the child. Payments were due both during the pregnancy and after the child's birth.

* * *

Finally, Anna and some commentators have expressed concern that surrogacy contracts tend to exploit or dehumanize women, especially women of lower economic status. Anna's objections center around the psychological harm she asserts may result from the gestator's relinquishing the child to whom she has given birth. Some have also cautioned that the practice of surrogacy may encourage society to view children as commodities, subject to trade at their parents' will.

We are unpersuaded that gestational surrogacy arrangements are so likely to cause the untoward results Anna cites as to demand their invalidation on public policy grounds. Although common sense suggests that women of lesser means serve as surrogate mothers more often than do wealthy women, there has been no proof that surrogacy contracts exploit poor women to any greater degree than economic necessity in general exploits them by inducing them to accept lower-paid or otherwise undesirable employment. We are likewise unpersuaded by the claim that surrogacy will foster the attitude that children are mere commodities; no evidence is offered to support it.

The argument that a woman cannot knowingly and intelligently agree to gestate and deliver a baby for intending parents carries overtones of the reasoning that for centuries prevented women from attaining equal economic rights and professional status under the law. To resurrect this view is both to foreclose a personal and economic choice on the part of the surrogate mother,

most fundamental notions of privacy, and confuses concepts of parentage and custody. Logically, the determination of parentage must precede, and should not be dictated by, eventual custody decisions. The implicit assumption of the dissent is that a recognition of the genetic intending mother as the natural mother may sometimes harm the child. This assumption overlooks California's dependency laws, which are designed to protect all children irrespective of the manner of birth or conception. Moreover, the best interests standard poorly serves the child in the present situation: it fosters instability during litigation and, if applied to recognize the gestator as the natural mother, results in a split of custody between the natural father and the gestator, an outcome not likely to benefit the child. Further, it may be argued that, by voluntarily contracting away any rights to the child, the gestator has, in effect, conceded the best interests of the child are not with her.

and to deny intending parents what may be their only means of procreating a child of their own genes.

* * *

Constitutionality of the Determination That Anna Johnson Is Not the Natural Mother

Anna argues at length that her right to the continued companionship of the child is protected under the federal Constitution.

* * *

Anna relies mainly on theories of substantive due process, privacy, and procreative freedom, citing a number of decisions recognizing the fundamental liberty interest of natural parents in the custody and care of their children. [ ] These cases do not support recognition of parental rights for a gestational surrogate.

Anna's argument depends on a prior determination that she is indeed the child's mother. Since Crispina is the child's mother under California law because she, not Anna, provided the ovum for the in vitro fertilization procedure, intending to raise the child as her own, it follows that any constitutional interests Anna possesses in this situation are something less than those of a mother. * * *

* * *

The judgment of the Court of Appeal is affirmed.

[ARABIAN, J., concurred with the majority's Uniform Parentage Act analysis, but would leave the issue of whether surrogacy contracts could be consistent with public policy to the legislature.]

KENNARD, J., dissenting.

When a woman who wants to have a child provides her fertilized ovum to another woman who carries it through pregnancy and gives birth to a child, who is the child's legal mother? Unlike the majority, I do not agree that the determinative consideration should be the intent to have the child that originated with the woman who contributed the ovum. In my view, the woman who provided the fertilized ovum and the woman who gave birth to the child both have substantial claims to legal motherhood. Pregnancy entails a unique commitment, both psychological and emotional, to an unborn child. No less substantial, however, is the contribution of the woman from whose egg the child developed and without whose desire the child would not exist.

For each child, California law accords the legal rights and responsibilities of parenthood to only one "natural mother." When, as here, the female reproductive role is divided between two women, California law requires courts to make a decision as to which woman is the child's natural mother, but provides no standards by which to make that decision. The majority's resort to "intent" to break the "tie" between the genetic and gestational mothers is unsupported by statute, and, in the absence of appropriate protections in the law to guard against abuse of surrogacy arrangements, it is ill-advised. To determine who is the legal mother of a child born of a gestational surrogacy arrangement, I would apply the standard most protective of child welfare—the best interests of the child.

* * *

Analysis of the Majority's "Intent" Test

Faced with the failure of current statutory law to adequately address the issue of who is a child's natural mother when two women qualify under the UPA, the majority breaks the "tie" by resort to a criterion not found in the UPA—the "intent" of the genetic mother to be the child's mother.

* * *

The majority offers four arguments in support of its conclusion to rely on the intent of the genetic mother as the exclusive determinant for deciding who is the natural mother of a child born of gestational surrogacy. Careful examination, however, demonstrates that none of the arguments mandates the majority's conclusion.

The first argument that the majority uses in support of its conclusion that the intent of the genetic mother to bear a child should be dispositive of the question of motherhood is "but-for" causation. Specifically, the majority relies on a commentator who writes that in a gestational surrogacy arrangement, " 'the child would not have been born but for the efforts of the intended parents.' "[ ] [But the resort to the "but-for" test derived from tort law is unprecedented and unjustified here.]

* * *

Behind the majority's reliance on "but-for" causation as justification for its intent test is a second, closely related argument. The majority draws its second rationale from a student note: " 'The mental concept of the child is a controlling factor of its creation, and the originators of that concept merit full credit as conceivers.' "[ ]

* * *

[This concept is taken from the law of intellectual property.] The problem with this argument, of course, is that children are not property. Unlike songs or inventions, rights in children cannot be sold for consideration, or made freely available to the general public.

Next, the majority offers as its third rationale the notion that bargained-for expectations support its conclusion regarding the dispositive significance of the genetic mother's intent. Specifically, the majority states that " 'intentions that are voluntarily chosen, deliberate, express and bargained-for ought presumptively to determine legal parenthood.' "

* * * But the courts will not compel performance of all contract obligations. [ ] The unsuitability of applying the notion that, because contract intentions are "voluntarily chosen, deliberate, express and bargained-for," their performance ought to be compelled by the courts is even more clear when the concept of specific performance is used to determine the course of the life of a child. Just as children are not the intellectual property of their parents, neither are they the personal property of anyone, and their delivery cannot be ordered as a contract remedy on the same terms that a court would, for example, order a breaching party to deliver a truckload of nuts and bolts.

* * *

The majority's final argument in support of using the intent of the genetic mother as the exclusive determinant of the outcome in gestational surrogacy cases is that preferring the intending mother serves the child's interests, which are " '[u]nlikely to run contrary to those of adults who choose to bring [the child] into being.' "[ ]

I agree with the majority that the best interests of the child is an important goal * * *. The problem with the majority's rule of intent is that application of this inflexible rule will not serve the child's best interests in every case.

* * *

The Best Interests of the Child
* * *

In the absence of legislation that is designed to address the unique problems of gestational surrogacy, this court should look not to tort, property or contract law, but to family law, as the governing paradigm and source of a rule of decision. The allocation of parental rights and responsibilities necessarily impacts the welfare of a minor child. And in issues of child welfare, the standard that courts frequently apply is the best interests of the child. [ ] This "best interests" standard serves to assure that in the judicial resolution of disputes affecting a child's well-being, protection of the minor child is the foremost consideration. Consequently, I would apply "the best interests of the child" standard to determine who can best assume the social and legal responsibilities of motherhood for a child born of a gestational surrogacy arrangement.

* * *

Factors that are pertinent to good parenting, and thus that are in a child's best interests, include the ability to nurture the child physically and psychologically [ ] and to provide ethical and intellectual guidance. [ ] Also crucial to a child's best interests is the "well recognized right" of every child "to stability and continuity." [ ] The intent of the genetic mother to procreate a child is certainly relevant to the question of the child's best interests; alone, however, it should not be dispositive.

* * *

In this opinion, I do not purport to offer a perfect solution to the difficult questions posed by gestational surrogacy; perhaps there can be no perfect solution. But in the absence of legislation specifically designed to address the complex issues of gestational surrogacy and to protect against potential abuses, I cannot join the majority's uncritical validation of gestational surrogacy.

I would reverse the judgment of the Court of Appeal, and remand the case to the trial court for a determination of disputed parentage on the basis of the best interests of the child.

Notes and Questions

1.   As was the case in *Baby M*, the gestating mother and the commissioning parents developed palpable animosity for each other in *Johnson v. Calvert*. In this case, Johnson argued that the Calverts failed to pay her adequately or treat her with respect. On the other hand, the Calverts argued that Johnson, who admitted to welfare fraud during the course of the pregnancy, was trying to extort money from them. To add a bit of complexity to this baffling case, Johnson also claimed that she was, in part, Native American, and thus subject to provisions of the Indian Child Welfare Act, which preempts state law.

Is the fact that the commissioning parents and gestating woman may develop such a deep-seated mutual hatred a reason to forbid these contracts absolutely, or a reason to regulate them?

2.   Are there identifiable principles upon which the majority in *Baby M* and the majority in *Johnson v. Calvert* disagree? Why is the California court so much less concerned than the New Jersey court about the pernicious social effects of surrogacy contracts? Which court do you think better predicts the consequences of such actions? Is the fact that *Johnson* involves gestational surrogacy relevant in the California court's evaluation of the pressure surrogacy contracts will have upon our social fabric?

3.   All of the justices agreed that the child could not have two mothers. Is this conclusion a good one? From the perspective of law? From the perspective of public policy? In these days of blended families, is the two parent (one father; one mother) family an anachronism? How could the court have dealt with the ultimate disposition of this case if it had decided that both Ms. Johnson and Ms. Calvert had maternal rights?

4.   In her dissenting opinion in Johnson v. Calvert, Justice Kennard depended very heavily upon the surrogacy provisions of the Uniform Status of Children of Assisted Conception Act, which allows states to choose between two options with regard to surrogacy: alternative A (which permits but heavily regulates surrogacy contracts, and which has been adopted by one state) and alternative B (which prohibits those contracts, and which has also been adopted in one state). Although this uniform act provided the starting point for discussions on the propriety of state recognition and regulation of surrogacy contracts, the paucity of states that adopted it suggests that it was not very well received.

5.   In McDonald v. McDonald, 196 A.D.2d 7, 608 N.Y.S.2d 477 (1994), another "true 'egg donation'" case, the New York Supreme Court, Appellate Division, determined that a woman who gestated a child produced through the fertilization of another woman's ovum with her husband's sperm was to be considered the mother of the child that resulted. The New York court depended heavily on the reasoning of *Johnson v. Calvert*. On the other hand, the Court of Common Pleas of Ohio rejected the *Johnson* reasoning in an uncontested case initiated to determine who was to be listed as the mother on the birth certificate in the case of gestational surrogacy. In Belsito v. Clark, 67 Ohio Misc.2d 54, 644 N.E.2d 760 (Comm.Pl.1994), the court determined that parentage was to be determined by genetic contribution, not by the intent-to-procreate of the parties to the original surrogacy agreement. The court found *Johnson* unpersuasive "for the following three important reasons: (1) the difficulty in applying the *Johnson* intent test; (2) public policy; and (3) *Johnson's* failure to recognize and emphasize

the genetic provider's right to consent to procreation and to surrender potential parental rights."

This issue has also arisen in the context of the child custody portion of a divorce case in which the child was born as a result of artificial insemination of a surrogate mother with the sperm of the husband. The child (fourteen at the time of the divorce) was raised by husband and wife, but the child bore no genetic relationship to the wife. Should the wife be entitled to parental rights upon divorce? Is her position weakened by the fact that she had never attempted to adopt the child? Should the court consider the case like any other custody dispute between biological parents, or should the court treat the case like one between the father and a legal stranger to the child? Should the court apply the best interest test in either case? See Doe v. Doe, 244 Conn. 403, 710 A.2d 1297 (1998).

6. While legal pundits were creating ultimate assisted conception hypotheticals in which the sperm from one person was joined with the ovum of a second and implanted in the womb of a third to be raised by a fourth and fifth, the real case arose in California in Buzzanca v. Buzzanca, 61 Cal.App.4th 1410, 72 Cal.Rptr.2d 280 (1998):

Jaycee was born because Luanne and John Buzzanca agreed to have an embryo genetically unrelated to either of them implanted in a woman—a surrogate—who would carry and give birth to the child for them. After the fertilization, implantation and pregnancy, Luanne and John split up, and the question of who are Jaycee's lawful parents came before the trial court.

Luanne claimed that she and her erstwhile husband were the lawful parents, but John disclaimed any responsibility, financial or otherwise. The woman who gave birth also appeared in the case to make it clear that she made no claim to the child.

The trial court then reached an extraordinary conclusion: Jaycee had no lawful parents. First, the woman who gave birth to Jaycee was not the mother; the court had—astonishingly—already accepted a stipulation that neither she nor her husband were the "biological" parents. Second, Luanne was not the mother. According to the trial court, she could not be the mother because she had neither contributed the egg nor given birth. And John could not be the father, because, not having contributed the sperm, he had no biological relationship with the child. We disagree. Let us get right to the point: Jaycee never would have been born had not Luanne and John both agreed to have a fertilized egg implanted in a surrogate.

The trial judge erred because he assumed that legal motherhood, under the relevant California statutes, could only be established in one of two ways, either by giving birth or by contributing an egg. He failed to consider the substantial and well-settled body of law holding that there are times when fatherhood can be established by conduct apart from giving birth or being genetically related to a child. The typical example is when an infertile husband consents to allowing his wife to be artificially inseminated. * * *

The same rule which makes a husband the lawful father of a child born because of his consent to artificial insemination should be applied here—by the same parity of reasoning that guided our Supreme Court in the first surrogacy case, Johnson v. Calvert [ ]—to both husband and wife. Just as a husband is deemed to be the lawful father of a child unrelated to him when his wife gives birth after artificial insemination, so should a husband and wife be deemed the lawful parents of a child after a surrogate bears a biologically unrelated child on their behalf. In each instance, a child is procreated because a medical procedure was initiated and consented to by intended parents. The only difference is that in this case—unlike artificial insemination—there is no reason to distinguish between husband and wife. We therefore must reverse the trial court's judgment and direct that a new judgment be entered, declaring that both Luanne and John are the lawful parents of Jaycee.

The California Court of Appeal, in a case which the California Supreme Court chose not to review, ultimately based its decision on a rather strained reading of the older Uniform Parentage Act. As the court pointed out,

> In the present case Luanne is situated like a husband in an artificial insemination case whose consent triggers a medical procedure which results in a pregnancy and eventual birth of a child. Her motherhood may therefore be established under this part [of the 1973 version of the Uniform Parentage Act], by virtue of that consent.

7. The Buzzanca court joined others in pleading that the legislature resolve these issues:

> Again we must call on the Legislature to sort out the parental rights and responsibilities of those involved in artificial reproduction. No matter what one thinks of artificial insemination, traditional and gestational surrogacy (in all its permutations), and—as now appears in the not-too-distant future, cloning and even gene splicing—courts are still going to be faced with the problem of determining lawful parentage. A child cannot be ignored. Even if all means of artificial reproduction were outlawed with draconian criminal penalties visited on the doctors and parties involved, courts will still be called upon to decide who the lawful parents really are and who—other than the taxpayers—is obligated to provide maintenance and support for the child. These cases will not go away.

> Courts can continue to make decisions on an ad hoc basis without necessarily imposing some grand scheme, looking to the imperfectly designed Uniform Parentage Act and a growing body of case law for guidance in the light of applicable family law principles. Or the Legislature can act to impose a broader order which, even though it might not be perfect on a case-by-case basis, would bring some predictability to those who seek to make use of artificial reproductive techniques. As jurists, we recognize the traditional role of the common (i.e., judge-formulated) law in applying old legal principles to new technology. [ ] However, we still believe it is the Legislature, with its ability to formulate general rules based on input from all its constituencies, which is the more desirable forum for lawmaking.

Do you agree? What values do you think you state legislature will bring to this kind of a task? Is your state legislature likely to write a statute that you would approve? Will the legislature be able to "settle" the issue in a way that the courts cannot? Might it be better for the courts (and the rest of society) to discuss and experiment with the issue of surrogacy before the legislature sets rules that will be hard to change?

8. These cases are difficult even when all of the actions are intentional. When there is institutional fraud involved, as was alleged in the next case, the interests of the parties, and the issues, may be different.

PRATO–MORRISON v. DOE
Court of Appeal of California, 2002.
103 Cal.App.4th 222, 126 Cal.Rptr.2d 509.

VOGEL, J:

* * *

FACTS

A.

In 1988, Donna Prato–Morrison and Robert Morrison were fertility clinic patients of the Center for Reproductive Health (CRH) at the University of

California at Irvine (UCI). As part of the *in vitro* fertilization process, the Morrisons' eggs and sperm were entrusted to CRH with the intent that the resulting embryos would produce the child they hoped to conceive. No pregnancy was achieved and the Morrisons ultimately abandoned their efforts on the assumption that any remaining genetic material would be destroyed by CRH.

B.

In the mid–1990's, UCI learned stealing "had occurred—human eggs were taken from one patient and implanted in another without the consent of the donor." [ ] The Morrisons (and many others) sued CRH, UCI, and the doctors involved in the "egg stealing." The Morrisons' case was settled by the payment of money—but only after the Morrisons learned through the discovery process that their genetic material might not have been destroyed, that Judith and Jacob Doe (who were also patients of the CRH fertility clinic) *might have* (without the Does' knowledge) received the Morrisons' eggs, sperm, or embryos, and that (in December 1988) Judith Doe had given birth to twin daughters, Ida and Rose. The Morrisons claim they are the twins' genetic parents.

C.

In 1996, the Morrisons filed a "complaint to establish parental relationship," naming the Does as defendants, alleging that the Morrisons are the "biological and legal parents" of the twins, and asking for custody, visitation rights, and an award of attorney's fees. Between 1996 and 1999, the Morrisons attempted to obtain blood tests and DNA samples from the twins but the Does refused to provide them and these "negotiations" ultimately failed.

In 1999, the Morrisons filed an amended complaint in which they abandoned their quest for custody but reasserted their demands for blood tests and for visitation. At the Morrisons' request, a hearing was set to determine the Morrisons' right (1) to obtain DNA tests and (2) to have a mental health professional appointed to help determine "the commencement, frequency, degree of contact or visitation" the Morrisons should have with the twins. * * *

In April 2000, the Does asked the trial court (1) to seal the records of this case; (2) to issue protective orders "to ensure the privacy of the children in this potentially high-profile litigation, and to preclude deliberate or accidental disclosure of the existence of this litigation and the [Morrisons'] claims ... to the children"; and (3) to quash the Morrisons' petition on the grounds (among others) that (a) the Does are the "presumed natural and legal parents" of the twins, and (b) the Morrisons lacked standing to pursue a parentage action or to compel blood or DNA testing. [ ]

In support of their motions, the Does submitted declarations establishing that since 1983 they have lived together continuously as husband and wife, that in addition to the twins they have two older children (one from Jacob's former marriage, the other together), and that the twins were conceived because the Does had "actively tried to conceive with medical assistance, intending to use Jacob's sperm and anonymously and voluntarily donated ova." Judith Doe "became pregnant by [her] husband," gave birth to the twins, and remains a "full time mother." Jacob Doe was "neither impotent nor sterile" at the time the twins were conceived or at the time they were born, and he is their father (as well as the father of the Does' two older children). When Judith Doe gave birth to the twins, the Does "knowingly and joyously received the twins into [their] home and family. [They] have adored [the twins and have] reared them in [the Does'] culture and religion. . . ." The Does "are the only parents that Ida and Rose have ever known." The Does objected to the release of any medical information to the Morrisons, pointed out that the Morrisons' claims had caused "great emotional stress" to the Does, and said the introduction of the Morrisons into the Does' "family life would be a monstrous intrusion."

In opposition to the Does' motion to quash, the Morrisons claimed they had standing to pursue this action because Donna Morrison is "a genetic mother." * * *

D.

At a hearing held in June 2000, the family law court sustained the Does' objections to the Morrison's evidence and found that the Morrisons had failed to establish their status as "interested parties" entitled to pursue a parentage action. The court nevertheless continued the matter to afford the Morrisons an opportunity to present additional evidence.

As "additional evidence," the Morrisons submitted an unredacted copy of the handwritten list and a declaration from Teri Ord—who stated that she was employed from 1986 through and including 1988 by AMI Medical Center as an "In Vitro Fertilization Biologist" in charge of "the embryology lab at that facility." In that capacity, she states, she "participated" in "transfers of genetic materials obtained by the doctors [at UCI] from fertility patients. According to laboratory records, Donna [Morrison] was an infertility patient at AMI . . . between March and May 1988, as was [Judith Doe]." Ord stated that, based on information contained in other clinical and laboratory records, she prepared the handwritten document in 1995 to show that, "between March and May of 1988, patient '[Judith Doe]' received sixteen eggs from patient '[Donna Morrison].' Twenty-one eggs were extracted from [Donna Morrison], and five transferred into [Donna Morrison's] own fallopian tubes. The remaining sixteen were transferred to [Judith Doe]," and the notations next to Judith Doe's name show that "a twin pregnancy resulted." (Emphasis added.) The Morrisons also submitted evidence that UCI's original clinical and laboratory records for its former patients were generally unavailable because they had been confiscated (in 1995) by the Federal Bureau of Investigation.

The Does objected to Ord's declaration and compilation as hearsay, and on the ground that it violated the Does' physician-patient privilege and their right to reproductive privacy. In October 2000, the family law court sustained the Does' evidentiary objections and granted their motion to quash. In April

2001, the court dismissed the Morrisons' action. The Morrisons appeal from the order of dismissal.

DISCUSSION

I.

The Morrisons contend their evidence is sufficient to establish Donna status as the genetic mother and, therefore, her standing to pursue a parentage action. We disagree.

"Any interested person may bring an action to determine the existence or non-existence of a mother and child relationship" [ ], but an unrelated person who is not a genetic parent is not an "interested person" within the meaning of [the relevant section]. [ ] The threshold question, therefore, is whether Ord's declaration and handwritten list were properly excluded by the trial court. If so, there is no evidence at all to suggest that Donna Morrison is the twins' genetic mother, or that either of the Morrisons is otherwise related to the twins.

The declaration and list were properly excluded as inadmissible hearsay that does not satisfy the requirements of the business record exception to the hearsay rule. As Ord concedes in her declaration, the list was compiled from other, non-identified clinical and laboratory records, and she does not attempt to establish her personal knowledge of the information stated on her list. She does not say she was a percipient witness to the transfers of genetic material, or that she made the entries in the original records. She admits the list was not made at or near the time of the events it purports to describe, but was in fact made almost eight years later. She offers no clue as to *why* the list was made. By Ord's own admission, her sources of information and method and time of preparation show a lack of trustworthiness and defeat the Morrisons' contention that the list comes within the business records exception to the hearsay rule. [ ]

To avoid this conclusion, the Morrisons contend the unavailability of the original records in itself makes Ord's statements and her list admissible. We disagree. When an original document is missing, secondary evidence offered to prove its content must be "otherwise admissible." [ ] Since the list and Ord's statements are inadmissible hearsay, they are not "otherwise admissible." * * *

Since Ord's declaration and list were properly excluded and since there is no other evidence suggesting a genetic link between the Morrisons and the Does' twins, the Morrisons had no standing to pursue their parentage action.

II.

The Morrisons contend they should be allowed to "discover" whether the twins were born "as a result of the theft of their genetic materials," and that their rights as alleged biological parents ought to trump the Does' rights as presumed parents. We disagree.

The Morrisons' "rights" were vindicated when they accepted an undisclosed amount of money to resolve their lawsuit against CRH, UCI, and the individuals involved in the misuse of the Morrisons' genetic materials. The rights still at issue are not the Morrisons' rights. They are the rights of the

Does and their twins to be free from the interference of strangers who have no standing to pursue their demands for blood tests or visitation rights, and the Morrisons cannot alter the focus of this issue by characterizing the Does' rights as mere privacy interests that may, under appropriate circumstances, give way to greater rights. [ ]

The trial court found, and we agree, that the dismissal of this action is in the best interests of the children. More to the point, we conclude that, had the Morrisons presented proof of a genetic link to the twins sufficient to establish their standing to pursue a parentage action, it would not be in the best interests of the twins to have the Morrisons intrude into their lives, or to be subjected to the blood tests and "mental health" evaluation suggested by the Morrisons. Because the twins are now almost 14 years old, their relationship with their presumed parents is considerably more palpable than the possibility of a new relationship with a previously unknown biological parent, and the Morrisons will not be allowed to disrupt the Does' "family in order to satisfy the [alleged] biological [parents'] unilateral desire, however strong, to turn their genetic connection into a personal relationship." [ ]

Simply put, the social relationship established by the Does and their daughters is more important to the children than a genetic relationship with a stranger.[ ][10]

The order of dismissal is affirmed. * * *

Notes on Prato–Morrison v. Doe

1. Should the Morrisons be recognized as "interested parties" under the California statute? How does the court know that the Morrisons are unrelated persons who are not "genetic parents" of the twins in the absence of DNA testing? Under the circumstances of this case, given the fraud of the fertility clinic, is there any other way that the Morrisons could develop admissible evidence of their genetic parentage? Shouldn't the production of some evidence—even if it is not admissible—be enough to justify the order of DNA testing? Why doesn't the court simply require the DNA testing, so that there will be no doubt as to the genetic parentage of the twins?

2. Why does the fact that the Morrisons accepted a damage award from the fertility clinic cut off their claims of parentage? Did that damage award amount to a purchase of the rights to the children by the clinic? Why should it have any effect on the relationship between the Morrisons and the Does (who were not a party to the Morrisons' lawsuit against the clinic)?

3. Would the result in this case be the same if the Morrisons had discovered the twins shortly after their birth, instead of eight years later? If they had discovered the mix-up during the pregnancy? Should the result be the same?

4. In the last full paragraph of the opinion the court refers to the "best interests of the children." Is the court applying the "bests interests" standard to resolve this case? Does this paragraph suggest that the Morrisons could not

---

10. We join the chorus of judicial voices pleading for legislative attention to the increasing number of complex legal issues spawned by recent advances in the field of artificial reproduction. Whatever merit there may be to a fact-driven case-by-case resolution of each new issue, some over-all legislative guidelines would allow the participants to make informed choices and courts to strive for uniformity in their decisions. (*In re Marriage of Buzzanca*[ ]; *Johnson v. Calvert*[ ].)

establish legal parentage to Ida and Rose even if they *could* produce proof—DNA evidence, for example—that they are the genetic progenitors of the twins, because that would not be in the twins' best interest? Is this an appropriate use of this standard?

5. How terrible would it be for Ida and Rose to find out that their social parents are not their genetic parents (or, at least, that their social mother is not their genetic mother)? Would it be worse for them to make this discovery than it is for adopted children who make this discovery? Might it be in their interest to get this information, or would the disruption of the Does' household be so harmful that it would outweigh any benefit to the girls?

6. The girls themselves were not represented in this litigation. Should the court have appointed a guardian ad litem to represent their interests? Could the court do that without telling them about the litigation, and thus undercutting the very status quo that the Does fought so hard to maintain?

UNIFORM PARENTAGE ACT

(2002).

ARTICLE 8—GESTATIONAL AGREEMENT

§ 801. GESTATIONAL AGREEMENT AUTHORIZED.

(a) A prospective gestational mother, her husband if she is married, a donor or the donors, and the intended parents may enter into a written agreement providing that:

(1) the prospective gestational mother agrees to pregnancy by means of assisted reproduction;

(2) the prospective gestational mother, her husband if she is married, and the donors relinquish all rights and duties as the parents of a child conceived through assisted reproduction; and

(3) the intended parents become the parents of the child.

(b) The man and woman who are the parents must both be parties to the gestational agreement.

(c) A gestational agreement is enforceable only if validated as provided in Section 803.

(d) A gestational agreement does not apply to the birth of a child conceived by means of sexual intercourse.

(e) A gestational agreement may provide for payment of consideration.

(f) A gestational agreement may not limit the right of the gestational mother to make decisions to safeguard her health or that of the embryos or fetus.

§ 802. REQUIREMENTS OF PETITION.

(a) The intended parents and the prospective gestational mother may commence a proceeding in the [appropriate court] to validate a gestational agreement.

(b) A proceeding to validate a gestational agreement may not be maintained unless:

(1) the mother or the intended parents have been residents of this State for at least 90 days;

(2) the prospective gestational mother's husband, if she is married, is joined in the proceeding; and

(3) a copy of the gestational agreement is attached to the [petition].

§ 803. HEARING TO VALIDATE GESTATIONAL AGREEMENT.

(a) If the requirements of subsection (b) are satisfied, a court may issue an order validating the gestational agreement and declaring that the intended parents will be the parents of a child born during the term of the of the agreement.

(b) The court may issue an order under subsection (a) only on finding that:

(1) the residence requirements of Section 802 have been satisfied and the parties have submitted to the jurisdiction of the court under the jurisdictional standards of this [Act];

(2) unless waived by the court, the [relevant child-welfare agency] has made a home study of the intended parents and the intended parents meet the standards of suitability applicable to adoptive parents;

(3) all parties have voluntarily entered into the agreement and understand its terms;

(4) adequate provision has been made for all reasonable health-care expense associated with the gestational agreement until the birth of the child, including responsibility for those expenses if the agreement is terminated; and

(5) the consideration, if any, paid to the prospective gestational mother is reasonable.

§ 804. INSPECTION OF RECORDS.

The proceedings, records, and identities of the individual parties to a gestational agreement under this [article] are subject to inspection under the standards of confidentiality applicable to adoptions as provided under other law of this State.

§ 805. EXCLUSIVE, CONTINUING JURISDICTION.

Subject to the jurisdictional standards of [Section 201 of the Uniform Child Custody Jurisdiction and Enforcement Act], the court conducting a proceeding under this [article] has exclusive, continuing jurisdiction of all matters arising out of the gestational agreement until a child born to the gestational mother during the period governed by the agreement attains the age of 180 days.

§ 806. TERMINATION OF GESTATIONAL AGREEMENT.

(a) After issuance of an order under this [article], but before the prospective gestational mother becomes pregnant by means of assisted reproduction, the prospective gestational mother, her husband, or either of the intended parents may terminate the gestational agreement by giving written notice of termination to all other parties.

(b) The court for good cause shown may terminate the gestational agreement.

(c) An individual who terminates a gestational agreement shall file notice of the termination with the court. On receipt of the notice, the court shall vacate the order issued under this [article]. An individual who does not notify the court of the termination of the agreement is subject to appropriate sanctions.

(d) Neither a prospective gestational mother nor her husband, if any, is liable to the intended parents for terminating a gestational agreement pursuant to this section.

§ 807. PARENTAGE UNDER VALIDATED GESTATIONAL AGREEMENT.

(a) Upon birth of a child to a gestational mother, the intended parents shall file notice with the court that a child has been born to the gestational mother within 300 days after assisted reproduction. Thereupon, the court shall issue an order:

(1) confirming that the intended parents are the parents of the child;

(2) if necessary, ordering that the child be surrendered to the intended parents; and

(3) directing the [agency maintaining birth records] to issue a birth certificate naming the intended parents as parents of the child.

(b) If the parentage of a child born to a gestational mother is alleged not to be the result of assisted reproduction, the court shall order genetic testing to determine the parentage of the child.

* * *

§ 808. GESTATIONAL AGREEMENT: EFFECT OF SUBSEQUENT MARRIAGE.

After the issuance of an order under this [article], subsequent marriage of the gestational mother does not affect the validity of a gestational agreement, her husband's consent to the agreement is not required, and her husband is not a presumed father of the resulting child.

§ 809. EFFECT OF NONVALIDATED GESTATIONAL AGREEMENT.

(a) A gestational agreement, whether in a record or not, that is not judicially validated is not enforceable.

(b) If a birth results under a gestational agreement that is not judicially validated as provided in this [article], the parent-child relationship is determined as provided in [Article] 2 [of the Uniform Parentage Act of 2000, which would denominate the gestational mother as the mother for all legal purposes].

(c) Individuals who are parties to a nonvalidated gestational agreement as intended parents may be held liable for support of the resulting child, even if the agreement is otherwise unenforceable. The liability under this subsection includes assessing all expenses and fees * * *

Notes and Questions

1. The drafters of the uniform act referred to the plea in *Buzzanca* for state legislative solutions to the legal problems that arise as a result of new assisted reproductive techniques. As a consequence of that—and other—judicial invitations to action, the drafters determined that the new Uniform Parentage Act should include a provision that permits and regulates surrogacy contracts despite the "strongly held differences on this subject." Unlike the Uniform Status of Children

of Assisted Conception Act promulgated twelve years earlier, the 2002 Uniform Parentage Act does not include an option A (permitting gestational agreements) and an option B (prohibiting them). In recognizing the comparatively frail support for statutes of this nature, however, the National Conference made the gestational agreement provisions of the Uniform Parentage Act optional because, it concluded, the other changes to the Uniform Parentage Act were "too * * * important * * * to jeopardize its passage because of opposition to this article."

2.   The Reporter's Notes to article 8 of the 2002 Uniform Parentage Act also express concern that "voiding or criminalizing gestational agreements will force individuals to find friendly legal forums for the process," and that this forum shopping will make the legal status of their children uncertain. Must states give full faith and credit to birth certificate notations made in other states? Could one state refuse to recognize the parent-child relationships that arise out of assisted reproduction performed in other states?

3.   What would have happened if the Article 8 of the Uniform Parentage Act (2002) had been adopted in the relevant states before *Baby M* and *Johnson v. Calvert* had been decided? Would those cases have been decided differently? Could the parties have obtained judicial approval of the gestational agreements in those cases? What would have happened in those cases if Article 8 were in place, but the contracts had not been judicially approved? Could the Uniform Parentage Act (2002) be applied in *Prato-Morrison v. Doe*?

4.   The new Uniform Parentage Act takes strong positions on a number of controversial issues: the drafters declare that surrogacy contracts are acceptable, that the surrogate may be compensated for her labor, that judicial approval is necessary before such an agreement can be enforced (and that non-approved contracts are not enforceable, but not illegal, either), and that the intending parents must undergo a home study that shows them "suitable" to be an adopting family. Is that the way those questions should be resolved? Would you redraft any particular portions of Article 8 of the Uniform Parentage Act (2002)?

5.   The legal approach to the regulation of gestational agreements (and to assisted reproduction more generally) depends on the legal perspective one brings to the enterprise. Family lawyers tend to view the process as analogous to adoption, and they ask how any proposed regulation ought to be different from the regulation that governs adoption. Health lawyers are more likely to see the process as the provision of a form of health care, and they ask how regulation designed to assure the quality of our health care system can best be applied to help "patients" in this area. Criminal lawyers are more likely to ask whether there is any aspect of assisted reproductive techniques that should be prohibited. In the end, is the creation of a child through the use of assisted reproduction techniques, including surrogacy, more like ordinary procreation (for which we do not require marriage, a home study, or advance judicial approval), adoption, or a regulated medical treatment?

5. *Cloning*

In early 1997 the world was stunned by the revelation that a Scottish laboratory had cloned a mammal—to be precise, a Finn Dorset sheep. Scientists achieved this by removing the nucleus from a sheep ovum, replacing it with the genetic material from the sheep to be cloned, and then reimplanting the genetically changed ovum back into the surrogate mother sheep. In fact, the one cloned sheep was the only success in almost 300 attempts, and scientists warned that the likelihood that this technology would be available for human beings remained, for the present, a few years away. Despite this, the bioethics community began a world-wide discussion on the consequences of cloning as a form of human reproduction.

Is it possible to talk about the creation of human beings through cloning as we talk about the creation of human beings through other processes of assisted reproduction? How are the questions raised by the existence of cloned human beings truly different from the questions raised by human beings created by other technically driven medical processes? Cloning requires in vitro manipulation (like in vitro fertilization) and then implantation in a womb (like surrogacy). Is it different from either of those two forms of assisted reproduction? Is cloning really a form of reproduction at all, or is it something different—perhaps, merely replication? Who counts as the parents of the cloned individual? Does it make sense to speak of a "mother" or "father," or must we limit ourselves to speaking of the cloned person's "antecedent" or "precursor"?

For generations, science fiction has raised fears of totalitarian regimes that can clone human beings for slave-like work for the benefit of the regime. Should this present a genuine worry to this society? Could cloning be appropriated by the state in support of a Nazi-like eugenics policy? A related worry is that a society could treat a newly cloned person as nothing more than the continuation of the source of its genetic material—or as a body parts source for the person who provided the genetic material. But wouldn't a cloned person have all of the rights of any other person? As some bioethicists argue, if our society were to treat cloned human beings as slaves or spare parts warehouses, the existence of cloning would be the least of our problems.

Would cloned people have the same relationship to each other that identical twins maintain? Identical twins have a common genetic make-up, as a clone and his source would, yet we treat those twins as separate human beings with separate lives and we have identified no social dislocation that arises out of their existence. Why should we be more worried about cloned human beings than about identical twins? In fact, because a cloned person and his source would be different ages, they would be likely to be raised in different environments, and thus to be less similar than identical twins. On the other hand, the number of identical twins is naturally limited, and there are very few identical triplets. We could, through cloning, create a much larger number of identical "siblings."

In any case, is there any justifiable reason for cloning a full human being? A few have been suggested. Suppose a child were dying of a disease that could be treated with a bone marrow transplant from a genetically identical donor, but such a donor could not be found. Might it be acceptable to clone the patient, and then, independently, determine if the newly replicated person ought to be a donor for his brother? Alternatively, suppose a couple has an infertility problem which makes it impossible for either of them to become a parent in the ordinary course of events. Should they be able to opt for cloning so that their child will be related to one of them? What if only one of the parents is infertile, and they want a child that does not require the potentially interfering involvement of a third party?

The National Bioethics Advisory Commission published a comprehensive and thoughtful report on the cloning of human beings within months of the revelation that it had been successfully performed on sheep. The report includes a useful description of the relevant scientific procedures as well as a fully annotated analysis of the ethical, theological, legal and policy issues. The Recommendations are reprinted here:

RECOMMENDATIONS OF THE NATIONAL BIOETHICS ADVISORY COMMISSION (NBAC) WITH REGARD TO CLONING (1997)

With the announcement that an apparently quite normal sheep had been born in Scotland as a result of somatic cell nuclear transfer cloning came the realization that, as a society, we must yet again collectively decide whether and how to use what appeared to be a dramatic new technological power. The promise and the peril of this scientific advance was noted immediately around the world, but the prospects of creating human beings through this technique mainly elicited widespread resistance and/or concern. Despite this reaction, the scientific significance of the accomplishment, in terms of improved understanding of cell development and cell differentiation, should not be lost. The challenge to public policy is to support the myriad beneficial applications of this new technology, while simultaneously guarding against its more questionable uses.

Much of the negative reaction to the potential application of such cloning in humans can be attributed to fears about harms to the children who may result, particularly psychological harms associated with a possibly diminished sense of individuality and personal autonomy. Others express concern about a degradation in the quality of parenting and family life. And virtually all people agree that the current risks of physical harm to children associated with somatic cell nuclear transplantation cloning justify a prohibition at this time on such experimentation.

In addition to concerns about specific harms to children, people have frequently expressed fears that a widespread practice of somatic cell nuclear transfer cloning would undermine important social values by opening the door to a form of eugenics or by tempting some to manipulate others as if they were objects instead of persons. Arrayed against these concerns are other important social values, such as protecting personal choice, particularly in matters pertaining to procreation and child rearing, maintaining privacy and the freedom of scientific inquiry, and encouraging the possible development of new biomedical breakthroughs.

As somatic cell nuclear transfer cloning could represent a means of human reproduction for some people, limitations on that choice must be made only when the societal benefits of prohibition clearly outweigh the value of maintaining the private nature of such highly personal decisions. Especially in light of some arguably compelling cases for attempting to clone a human being using somatic cell nuclear transfer, the ethics of policy making must strike a balance between the values society wishes to reflect and issues of privacy and the freedom of individual choice.

To arrive at its recommendations concerning the use of somatic cell nuclear transfer techniques, NBAC also examined long-standing religious traditions that often influence and guide citizens' responses to new technologies. Religious positions on human cloning are pluralistic in their premises, modes of argument, and conclusions. Nevertheless, several major themes are prominent in Jewish, Roman Catholic, Protestant, and Islamic positions, including responsible human dominion over nature, human dignity and destiny, procreation, and family life. Some religious thinkers argue that the use of somatic cell nuclear transfer cloning to create a child would be intrinsically immoral and thus could never be morally justified; they usually propose a ban on such human cloning. Other religious thinkers contend that human cloning to create a child could be morally justified under some circumstances but hold that it should be strictly regulated in order to prevent abuses.

The public policies recommended with respect to the creation of a child using somatic cell nuclear transfer reflect the Commission's best judgments about both the ethics of attempting such an experiment and our view of traditions regarding limitations on individual actions in the name of the common good. At present, the use of this technique to create a child would be a premature experiment that exposes the developing child to unacceptable risks. This in itself is sufficient to justify a prohibition on cloning human beings at this time, even if such efforts were to be characterized as the exercise of a fundamental right to attempt to procreate. More speculative psychological harms to the child, and effects on the moral, religious, and cultural values of society may be enough to justify continued prohibitions in the future, but more time is needed for discussion and evaluation of these concerns.

Beyond the issue of the safety of the procedure, however, NBAC found that concerns relating to the potential psychological harms to children and effects on the moral, religious, and cultural values of society merited further reflection and deliberation. Whether upon such further deliberation our nation will conclude that the use of cloning techniques to create children should be allowed or permanently banned is, for the moment, an open question. Time is an ally in this regard, allowing for the accrual of further data from animal experimentation, enabling an assessment of the prospective safety and efficacy of the procedure in humans, as well as granting a period of fuller national debate on ethical and social concerns. The Commission therefore concluded that there should be imposed a period of time in which no attempt is made to create a child using somatic cell nuclear transfer.

Within this overall framework the Commission came to the following conclusions and recommendations:

I.   The Commission concludes that at this time it is morally unacceptable for anyone in the public or private sector, whether in a research or clinical setting, to attempt to create a child using somatic cell nuclear transfer cloning. We have reached a consensus on this point because current scientific information indicates that this technique is not safe to use in humans at this time. Indeed, we believe it would violate important ethical obligations were clinicians or researchers to attempt to create a child using these particular technologies, which are likely to involve unacceptable risks to the fetus and/or potential child. Moreover, in addition to safety concerns, many other serious ethical concerns have been identified, which require much more widespread and careful public deliberation before this technology may be used.

The Commission, therefore, recommends the following for immediate action:

A continuation of the current moratorium on the use of federal funding in support of any attempt to create a child by somatic cell nuclear transfer.

An immediate request to all firms, clinicians, investigators, and professional societies in the private and non-federally funded sectors to comply voluntarily with the intent of the federal moratorium. Professional and scientific societies should make clear that any attempt to create a child by somatic cell nuclear transfer and implantation into a woman's body would at this time be an irresponsible, unethical, and unprofessional act.

II.   The Commission further recommends that:

Federal legislation should be enacted to prohibit anyone from attempting, whether in a research or clinical setting, to create a child through somatic cell nuclear transfer cloning. It is critical, however, that such legislation include a sunset clause to ensure that Congress will review the issue after a specified time period (three to five years) in order to decide whether the prohibition continues to be needed. If state legislation is enacted, it should also contain such a sunset provision. Any such legislation or associated regulation also ought to require that at some point prior to the expiration of the sunset period, an appropriate oversight body will evaluate and report on the current status of somatic cell nuclear transfer technology and on the ethical and social issues that its potential use to create human beings would raise in light of public understandings at that time.

III.   The Commission also concludes that:

Any regulatory or legislative actions undertaken to effect the foregoing prohibition on creating a child by somatic cell nuclear transfer should be carefully written so as not to interfere with other important areas of scientific research. In particular, no new regulations are required regarding the cloning of human DNA sequences and cell lines, since neither activity raises the scientific and ethical issues that arise from the attempt to create children through somatic cell nuclear transfer, and these fields of research have already provided important scientific and biomedical advances. Likewise, research on cloning animals by somatic cell nuclear transfer does not raise the issues implicated in attempting to use this technique for human cloning, and its continuation should only be subject to existing regulations regarding the humane use of animals and review by institution-based animal protection committees.

If a legislative ban is not enacted, or if a legislative ban is ever lifted, clinical use of somatic cell nuclear transfer techniques to create a child should be preceded by research trials that are governed by the twin protections of independent review and informed consent, consistent with existing norms of human subjects protection.

The United States Government should cooperate with other nations and international organizations to enforce any common aspects of their respective policies on the cloning of human beings.

IV.   The Commission also concludes that different ethical and religious perspectives and traditions are divided on many of the important moral issues that surround any attempt to create a child using somatic cell nuclear transfer techniques. Therefore, we recommend that:

The federal government, and all interested and concerned parties, encourage widespread and continuing deliberation on these issues in order to further our understanding of the ethical and social implications of this technology and to enable society to produce appropriate long-term policies regarding this technology should the time come when present concerns about safety have been addressed.

V.   Finally, because scientific knowledge is essential for all citizens to participate in a full and informed fashion in the governance of our complex society, the Commission recommends that:

Federal departments and agencies concerned with science should cooperate in seeking out and supporting opportunities to provide information and education to the public in the area of genetics, and on other developments in the biomedical sciences, especially where these affect important cultural practices, values, and beliefs.

Note: Reproductive and Therapeutic Cloning and Stem Cell Research

The controversy over cloning became more focused when Congress debated bills to outlaw the practice in 2002. While almost everyone now agrees that there is weak justification for *reproductive cloning*—i.e., cloning designed to create a human being—the propriety of *therapeutic cloning*—i.e., cloning designed to develop stem cells that would be useful in research and for treatment purposes—has a great deal more support.

Both forms of cloning may require somatic cell nuclear transfer, a process in which the nucleus of an unfertilized human ovum is removed and replaced with the nucleus from an adult cell. The resulting ovum cell, which has the full complement of human genetic material, is then stimulated so that it will divide and form a pre-embryo. In *therapeutic cloning*, some cells from the pre-embryo are removed for purposes of medical research or treatment. These stem cells have the potential to develop into almost any human cells, and they may be useful in repairing almost any human tissue. In *reproductive cloning*, the pre-embryo would be placed in a uterus to develop into a human being.

Because of the scientific promise shown by stem cell research many people who support legislation banning reproductive cloning vigorously oppose placing any limitation upon therapeutic cloning. However, because this research requires that a pre-embryo, which could develop into a human being, be the subject of research, the process is viewed by some as requiring an act that kills a potential human being.

Attempts to ban both therapeutic and reproductive cloning have been held up in Congress, which will consider the issue again in 2004. Those in Congress who support stem cell research have offered alternative bills, which would outlaw reproductive cloning but permit therapeutic cloning. President Bush has expressed his opposition to all forms of human cloning, and he has permitted federal funds to be used for stem cell research only when the research is done on stem cell lines already available—a scientific avenue that many therapeutic cloning advocates suggest has little promise. Five states (Arkansas, Iowa, Michigan, North Dakota and South Dakota) have banned all human cloning and the law in a sixth (Virginia) is unclear. Two states (California and New Jersey) have passed legislation that specifically permits and encourages therapeutic cloning. The United

States and several other countries are now seeking an international ban on both reproductive and therapeutic cloning through the United Nations.

Bibliographical Note: Facilitating Reproduction

There has been a great deal of useful writing on the techniques available for facilitating reproduction, and on the analyses of the ethical and legal issues that they create. See, e.g., Marsha Garrison, Law Making for Baby Making: An Interpretive Approach to the Determination of Legal Parentage, 113 Harv. L. Rev. 835 (2000), Janet Dolgin, The Family in Transition: From Griswold to Eisenstadt and Beyond, 82 Geo. L.J. 1519 (1994) and John Robertson, Embryos, Families and Procreative Liberty: The Legal Structure of the New Reproduction, 59 S.Cal. L. Rev. 939 (1986) For a good overview of some aspects of the genetic revolution, see Michael Malinowski, Choosing the Genetic Makeup of Children, 36 Conn. L. Rev. 125 (2003). For a particularly compelling account of the hopeless task of the Human Embryo Research Panel in determining the ethical status of the embryo, written by a member of that panel, see Alta Charo, The Hunting of the Snark: The Moral Status of Embryos, Right-to-Lifers, and Third World Women, 6 (2) Stan. L. & Pol. Rev. 11 (1995).

Many of the significant ethical issues in gestational surrogacy are discussed in Robin Fretwell Wilson, Uncovering the Rationale for Requiring Infertility in Surrogacy Arrangements, 29 Am.J.L. & Med. 337 (2003). The Summer, 1999 issue of the Loyola Law Review contains an interesting symposium on interdisciplinary examinations of the new reproductive technology. The November, 1995 issue of the Virginia Law Review features a symposium on new directions in family law, which includes Richard Epstein, Surrogacy: The Case for Full Contractual Enforcement, 81 Va. L. Rev. 2305 (1995) and a response, Margaret F. Brinig, A Maternalistic Approach to Surrogacy: Comment on Richard Epstein's "Surrogacy," 81 Va. L. Rev. 2377 (1995). For a good debate on baby selling and its logical consequences, see E. Landes and R. Posner, The Economics of the Baby Shortage, 7 J. Legal. Stud. 323 (1978) and J.R.S. Prichard, A Market for Babies?, 34 U. Toronto L. J. 341 (1984). For a discussion of issues that arise out of cloning, see Judith Daar, The Prospect of Human Cloning: Improving Nature or Dooming the Species?, 33 Seton Hall L. Rev. 511 (2003) and John Robertson, Two Models of Human Cloning, 27 Hofstra L. Rev. 609 (1999). For a helpful analysis of the problems that could arise when genetic material is accidentally (or intentionally) implanted in the wrong womb, and for an interesting solution to those problems, see Alice Noble–Allgire, Switched at the Fertility Clinic: Determining Maternal Rights When a Child is Born from Stolen or Misdelivered Genetic Material, 64 Mo. L. Rev. 517 (1999). For a critical analysis of many of these subjects, see Leslie Binder, Genes, Parents and assisted Reproductive Technologies: ARTs, Mistakes, Sex, Race and Law, 12 Colum. J. Gender & L. 1 (2003).

III. FETAL MATERNAL DECISIONMAKING *substituted judgment*

Problem: Children Bearing Children ✱

Elsie McIntosh is a fifteen year-old high school dropout in the fourth month of her first pregnancy. She lives at home with her mother, whose primary source of income is general assistance (i.e., state welfare) and food stamps. Elsie and her mother, who has been a desperate alcoholic for the past eight years, have spoken barely ten words in the past year. They live more like roommates than a mother-daughter family, and Elsie lives on her share of her mother's state aid, supplemented by a modest income from her own prostitution. Her prostitution has led to her arrest twice, and each of the arrests resulted in a night in juvenile detention, a morning in court, and a deferred finding of delinquency that was subsequently dismissed. Elsie has been a heavy drinker and a heavy user of crack cocaine for the past three or four years, and her drinking and cocaine use have continued during her pregnancy. She also occasionally uses heroin, and she smokes three packs of cigarettes a day. Elsie has received some health care (for an injury received in a knife fight with a customer) through the Big City HMO Clinic, the managed care organization to which she was assigned by the state Medicaid program. She felt that the health care professionals there treated her with disdain and she has not sought any prenatal care.

Knowing all of this, what should her state-assigned welfare worker do? If she were being seen by an obstetrician who knew all of this about Elsie, what should the obstetrician do? If this information about a patient were to come to the attention of a medical clinic legal counsel, what should that legal counsel do? If this information were to come to the attention of the district attorney, what should the district attorney do?

IN RE A.C.

District of Columbia Court of Appeals, 1990.
573 A.2d 1235.

TERRY, ASSOCIATE JUDGE:

* * *

We are confronted here with two profoundly difficult and complex issues. First, we must determine who has the right to decide the course of medical treatment for a patient who, although near death, is pregnant with a viable fetus. Second, we must establish how that decision should be made if the patient cannot make it for herself—more specifically, how a court should proceed when faced with a pregnant patient, *in extremis,* who is apparently incapable of making an informed decision regarding medical care for herself and her fetus. We hold that in virtually all cases the question of what is to be done is to be decided by the patient—the pregnant woman—on behalf of herself and the fetus. If the patient is incompetent or otherwise unable to give an informed consent to a proposed course of medical treatment, then her decision must be ascertained through the procedure known as substituted judgment. * * *

I

This case came before the trial court when George Washington University Hospital petitioned the emergency judge in chambers for declaratory relief as to how it should treat its patient, A.C., who was close to death from cancer and was twenty-six and one-half weeks pregnant with a viable fetus. After a hearing lasting approximately three hours, which was held at the hospital (though not in A.C.'s room), the court ordered that a caesarean section be performed on A.C. to deliver the fetus. * * * The caesarean was performed, and a baby girl, L.M.C., was delivered. Tragically, the child died within two and one-half hours, and the mother died two days later.

* * *

II

A.C. was first diagnosed as suffering from cancer at the age of thirteen. In the ensuing years she underwent major surgery several times, together with multiple radiation treatments and chemotherapy. A.C. married when she was twenty-seven, during a period of remission, and soon thereafter she became pregnant. She was excited about her pregnancy and very much wanted the child. Because of her medical history, she was referred in her fifteenth week of pregnancy to the high-risk pregnancy clinic at George Washington University Hospital.

On Tuesday, June 9, 1987, when A.C. was approximately twenty-five weeks pregnant, she went to the hospital for a scheduled check-up. Because she was experiencing pain in her back and shortness of breath, an x-ray was taken, revealing an apparently inoperable tumor which nearly filled her right lung. On Thursday, June 11, A.C. was admitted to the hospital as a patient. By Friday her condition had temporarily improved, and when asked if she really wanted to have her baby, she replied that she did.

Over the weekend, A.C.'s condition worsened considerably. Accordingly, on Monday, June 15, members of the medical staff treating A.C. assembled, along with her family, in A.C.'s room. The doctors then informed her that her illness was terminal, and A.C. agreed to palliative treatment designed to extend her life until at least her twenty-eighth week of pregnancy. The "potential outcome [for] the fetus," according to the doctors, would be much better at twenty-eight weeks than at twenty-six weeks if it were necessary to "intervene." A.C. knew that the palliative treatment she had chosen presented some increased risk to the fetus, but she opted for this course both to prolong her life for at least another two weeks and to maintain her own comfort. When asked if she still wanted to have the baby, A.C. was somewhat equivocal, saying "something to the effect of 'I don't know, I think so.' " As the day moved toward evening, A.C.'s condition grew still worse, and at about 7:00 or 8:00 p.m. she consented to intubation to facilitate her breathing.

The next morning, June 16, the trial court convened a hearing at the hospital in response to the hospital's request for a declaratory judgment. The court appointed counsel for both A.C. and the fetus, and the District of Columbia was permitted to intervene for the fetus as *parens patriae.* * * *

* * *

There was no evidence before the court showing that A.C. consented to, or even contemplated, a caesarean section before her twenty-eighth week of pregnancy. There was, in fact, considerable dispute as to whether she would have consented to an immediate caesarean delivery at the time the hearing was held. A.C.'s mother opposed surgical intervention, testifying that A.C. wanted "to live long enough to hold that baby" and that she expected to do so, "even though she knew she was terminal." Dr. Hamner [a treating obstetrician] testified that, given A.C.'s medical problems, he did not think she would have chosen to deliver a child with a substantial degree of impairment. * * *

After hearing this testimony and the arguments of counsel, the trial court made oral findings of fact. It found, first, that A.C. would probably die, according to uncontroverted medical testimony, "within the next twenty-four to forty-eight hours;" second, that A.C. was "pregnant with a twenty-six and a half week viable fetus who, based upon uncontroverted medical testimony, has approximately a fifty to sixty percent chance to survive if a caesarean section is performed as soon as possible;'' third, that because the fetus was viable, ''the state has [an] important and legitimate interest in protecting the potentiality of human life;'' and fourth, that there had been some testimony that the operation ''may very well hasten the death of [A.C.],'' but that there had also been testimony that delay would greatly increase the risk to the fetus and that ''the prognosis is not great for the fetus to be delivered post-mortem * * *.'' Most significantly, the court found:

> The court is of the view that it does not clearly know what [A.C.'s] present views are with respect to the issue of whether or not the child should live or die. She's presently unconscious. As late as Friday of last week, she wanted the baby to live. As late as yesterday, she did not know for sure.

Having made these findings of fact and conclusions of law, * * * the court ordered that a caesarean section be performed to deliver A.C.'s child.

The court's decision was then relayed to A.C., who had regained consciousness. [When the court reconvened later in the day, Dr. Hamner testified that A.C. then consented to the procedure.] When the court suggested moving the hearing to A.C.'s bedside, Dr. Hamner discouraged the court from doing so, but he and Dr. Weingold, together with A.C.'s mother and husband, went to A.C.'s room to confirm her consent to the procedure. What happened then was recounted to the court a few minutes later:

* * *

> Dr. Weingold: She does not make sounds because of the tube in her windpipe. She nods and she mouths words. One can see what she's saying rather readily. She asked whether she would survive the operation. She asked [Dr.] Hamner if he would perform the operation. He told her he would only perform it if she authorized it but it would be done in any case. She understood that. She then seemed to pause for a few moments and then very clearly mouthed words several times, *I don't want it done, I don't want it done.* Quite clear to me.

> I would obviously state the obvious and that is this is an environment in which, from my perspective as a physician, this would not be an informed consent one way or the other. She's under tremendous stress with the family on both sides, but I'm satisfied that I heard clearly what she said. * * *

> Dr. Weingold later qualified his opinion as to A.C.'s ability to give an informed consent, stating that he thought the environment for an informed consent was non-existent because A.C. was in intensive care, flanked by a weeping husband and mother. He added:

> I think she's in contact with reality, clearly understood who Dr. Hamner was. Because of her attachment to him [she] wanted him to perform the surgery. Understood he would not unless she consented and did not consent.

> That is, in my mind, very clear evidence that she is responding, understanding, and is capable of making such decisions. * * *

After hearing this new evidence, the court found that it was ''still not clear what her intent is'' and again ordered that a caesarean section be performed. * * * The operation took place, but the baby lived for only a few hours, and A.C. succumbed to cancer two days later.

* * *

IV

* * *

A. *Informed Consent and Bodily Integrity*

* * *

* * * [O]ur analysis of this case begins with the tenet common to all medical treatment cases: that any person has the right to make an informed choice, if competent to do so, to accept or forgo medical treatment. * * *

In the same vein, courts do not compel one person to permit a significant intrusion upon his or her bodily integrity for the benefit of another person's health. See, e.g., *McFall v. Shimp,* 10 Pa.D. & C.3d 90 (Allegheny County Ct.1978). In *McFall* the court refused to order Shimp to donate bone marrow which was necessary to save the life of his cousin, McFall:

> The common law has consistently held to a rule which provides that one human being is under no legal compulsion to give aid or to take action to save another human being or to rescue. * * *

Even though Shimp's refusal would mean death for McFall, the court would not order Shimp to allow his body to be invaded. It has been suggested that fetal cases are different because a woman who "has chosen to lend her body to bring [a] child into the world" has an enhanced duty to assure the welfare of the fetus, sufficient even to require her to undergo caesarean surgery. [ ] Surely, however, a fetus cannot have rights in this respect superior to those of a person who has already been born.[6]

* * *

There are two additional arguments against overriding A.C.'s objections to caesarean surgery. First, as the American Public Health Association cogently states in its *amicus curiae* brief:

> Rather than protecting the health of women and children, court-ordered caesareans erode the element of trust that permits a pregnant woman to communicate to her physician—without fear of reprisal—all information relevant to her proper diagnosis and treatment. An even more serious consequence of court-ordered intervention is that it drives women at high risk of complications during pregnancy and childbirth out of the health care system to avoid coerced treatment.

Second, and even more compellingly, any judicial proceeding in a case such as this will ordinarily take place—like the one before us here—under time constraints so pressing that it is difficult or impossible for the mother to

---

6. There are also practical consequences to consider. What if A.C. had refused to comply with a court order that she submit to a caesarean? Enforcement could be accomplished only through physical force or its equivalent. A.C. would have to be fastened with restraints to the operating table, or perhaps involuntarily rendered unconscious by forcibly injecting her with an anesthetic, and then subjected to unwanted major surgery. Such actions would surely give one pause in a civilized society, especially when A.C. had done no wrong.

communicate adequately with counsel, or for counsel to organize an effective factual and legal presentation in defense of her liberty and privacy interests and bodily integrity. * * *

* * *

B.   Substituted Judgment

* * * Sometimes, however, as our analysis presupposes here, a once competent patient will be unable to render an informed decision. In such a case, we hold that the court must make a substituted judgment on behalf of the patient, based on all the evidence. This means that the duty of the court, "as surrogate for the incompetent, is to determine as best it can what choice that individual, if competent, would make with respect to medical procedures." [ ]

* * *

We have found no reported opinion applying the substituted judgment procedure to the case of an incompetent pregnant patient whose own life may be shortened by a caesarean section, and whose unborn child's chances of survival may hang on the court's decision. Despite this precedential void, we conclude that substituted judgment is the best procedure to follow in such a case because it most clearly respects the right of the patient to bodily integrity. * * *

* * *

Because it is the patient's decisional rights which the substituted judgment inquiry seeks to protect, courts are in accord that the greatest weight should be given to the previously expressed wishes of the patient. This includes prior statements, either written or oral, even though the treatment alternatives at hand may not have been addressed. * * *

Courts in substituted judgment cases have also acknowledged the importance of probing the patient's value system as an aid in discerning what the patient would choose. We agree with this approach. [The court then discussed the ways in which it could determine the substituted judgment of the patient. For a fuller discussion of this issue, see chapter 5.]

C.   The Trial Court's Ruling

* * * The [trial] court did not * * * make a finding as to what A.C. would have chosen to do if she were competent. Instead, the court undertook to balance the state's and [the fetus's] interests in surgical intervention against A.C.'s perceived interest in not having the caesarean performed.

* * *

What a trial court must do in a case such as this is to determine, if possible, whether the patient is capable of making an informed decision about the course of her medical treatment. If she is, and if she makes such a decision, her wishes will control in virtually all cases. If the court finds that the patient is incapable of making an informed consent (and thus incompetent), then the court must make a substituted judgment. * * *

Having said that, we go no further. We need not decide whether, or in what circumstances, the state's interests can ever prevail over the interests of a pregnant patient. * * * Indeed, some may doubt that there could ever be a situation extraordinary or compelling enough to justify a massive intrusion into a person's body, such as a caesarean section, against that person's will. Whether such a situation may someday present itself is a question that we need not strive to answer here. * * *

* * *

BELSON, ASSOCIATE JUDGE, concurring in part and dissenting in part:

* * *

I think it appropriate * * * to state my disagreement with the very limited view the majority opinion takes of the circumstances in which the interests of a viable unborn child can afford such compelling reasons. The state's interest in preserving human life and the viable unborn child's interest in survival are entitled, I think, to more weight than I find them assigned by the majority when it states that "in virtually all cases the decision of the patient * * * will control." I would hold that in those instances, fortunately rare, in which the viable unborn child's interest in living and the state's parallel interest in protecting human life come into conflict with the mother's decision to forgo a procedure such as a caesarean section, a balancing should be struck in which the unborn child's and the state's interest are entitled to substantial weight.

* * *

The balancing test should be applied in instances in which women become pregnant and carry an unborn child to the point of viability. This is not an unreasonable classification because, I submit, a woman who carries a child to viability is in fact a member of a unique category of persons. Her circumstances differ fundamentally from those of other potential patients for medical procedures that will aid another person, for example, a potential donor of bone marrow for transplant. This is so because she has undertaken to bear another human being, and has carried an unborn child to viability. Another unique feature of the situation we address arises from the singular nature of the dependency of the unborn child upon the mother. A woman carrying a viable unborn child is not in the same category as a relative, friend, or stranger called upon to donate bone marrow or an organ for transplant. Rather, the expectant mother has placed herself in a special class of persons who are bringing another person into existence, and upon whom that other person's life is totally dependent. Also, uniquely, the viable unborn child is literally captive within the mother's body. No other potential beneficiary of a surgical procedure on another is in that position.

* * *

I next address the sensitive question of how to balance the competing rights and interests of the viable unborn child and the state against those of the rare expectant mother who elects not to have a caesarean section necessary to save the life of her child. The indisputable view that a woman carrying a viable child has an extremely strong interest in her own life, health, bodily integrity, privacy, and religious beliefs necessarily requires that her election be given correspondingly great weight in the balancing process. In a case, however, where the court in an exercise of a substituted judgment has concluded that the patient would probably opt against a caesarean section, the court should vary the weight to be given this factor in proportion to the confidence the court has in the accuracy of its conclusion. Thus, in a case where the indicia of the incompetent patient's judgment are equivocal, the court should accord this factor correspondingly less weight. The appropriate weight to be given other factors will have to be worked out by the development of law in this area, and cannot be prescribed in a single court opinion. Some considerations obviously merit special attention in the balancing process. One such consideration is any danger to the mother's life or health, physical or mental, including the relatively small but still significant danger that necessarily inheres in any caesarean delivery, and including especially any danger that exceeds that level. The mother's religious beliefs as they relate to the operation would appear to deserve inclusion in the balancing process.

On the other side of the analysis, it is appropriate to look to the relative likelihood of the unborn child's survival. * * * The child's interest in being born with as little impairment as possible should also be considered. This may weigh in favor of a delivery sooner rather than later. The most important factor on this side of the scale, however, is life itself, because the viable unborn child that dies because of the mother's refusal to have a caesarean delivery is deprived, entirely and irrevocably, of the life on which the child was about to embark.

* * *

Notes and Questions

1. As the opinions in *A.C.* suggest, potential fetal-maternal conflicts force courts to answer two questions. First, should the court balance the interests of the fetus (or the interests of the state in protecting the fetus) with the interests of the mother? If the answer to that question is "no," as it was for the majority in *A.C.*, the issue becomes the comparatively simple one of determining the wishes of the mother. See In re Baby Boy Doe, 260 Ill.App.3d 392, 198 Ill.Dec. 267, 632 N.E.2d 326 (1994), where the court refused to balance the interests of a fetus (or the interests of the state in protecting a fetus) against the interests of a competent pregnant woman who refused a caesarean section, even though her decision put the life of her fetus at stake.

If there is a decision to balance the interests, however, as the dissenting opinion in *A.C.* suggests, the court must also face the question of what standards to apply. Are the interests of the fetus or the state as strong as the interests of the mother? Can the relative strengths of these different interests vary from case to case, depending upon the stage of development of the fetus, the consequences of the decision to be made, or other factors?

2. *In re A.C.* was not the first case in which a court was asked to order a pregnant woman to undergo medical treatment for the benefit of her fetus. In Raleigh Fitkin–Paul Morgan Memorial Hospital v. Anderson, 42 N.J. 421, 201 A.2d 537 (1964), the New Jersey Supreme Court ordered blood transfusions to save an "unborn child" over the objections of the Jehovah's Witness mother. See also In re Application of Jamaica Hospital, 128 Misc.2d 1006, 491 N.Y.S.2d 898

(Sup.Ct.1985) (blood transfusion to save fetus who was not yet viable). In Jefferson v. Griffin Spalding County Hospital Authority, 247 Ga. 86, 274 S.E.2d 457 (1981), the Georgia Supreme Court ordered a caesarean section against the religiously motivated wishes of the mother when physicians argued that failure to do so would result in the death of both the mother and the fetus. The court acted because of the "duty of the state to protect a living, unborn human being from meeting * * * death before being given the opportunity to live." 274 S.E.2d at 460. More recently, the issue arose in Pemberton v. Tallahassee Memorial Regional Medical Center, 66 F.Supp.2d 1247 (N.D.Fl.1999), in which a fully competent pregnant woman was legally (and physically) required to undergo a caesarean section to preserve the life of her full term fetus. The Pemberton court explicitly addressed the A.C. case, and determined that "A.C. left open the possibility that a non-consenting patient's interest would yield to a more compelling countervailing interest in an 'extremely rare and truly exceptional' case.[ ] This is such a case." 66 F.Supp.2d at 1254. The court agreed that "[I]n anything other than an extraordinary and overwhelming case, the right to decide would surely rest with the mother, not with the state. * * * [T]his was an extraordinary and overwhelming case; no reasonable or even unreasonable argument could be made in favor of vaginal delivery at home with the attendant risk of death to the baby (and concomitant grave risk to the mother)." Id.

3. One reason that many commentators have opposed judicial intervention to require pregnant women to undergo medical care for the benefit of their fetuses is the fact that medical diagnosis in this area is often wrong. Doctors seem willing to testify that intervention is necessary to save the fetus even when the prognosis following nonintervention is quite uncertain. There is a series of cases that suggests that when doctors testify that a caesarean is necessary for the health of the fetus, but the mother "escapes" and attempts a normal vaginal birth, there is a good chance the child will be born without complication. J. Fletcher, Drawing Moral Lines in Fetal Therapy, 29 Clin. Obstetrics & Gynecology 595 (1986). Fletcher summarizes his review of six cases:

> First, inaccuracies and possible misdiagnosis appear to be involved in half of the cases * * * since babies were born healthy after vaginal delivery. If precedents flow from examples flawed by faulty assumptions or mistaken evaluations, errors may be replicated. These outcomes also should remind all concerned of the possibility of misdiagnosis before fetal therapy. Forced fetal therapy on the basis of misdiagnosis would constitute an ethical megadisaster.

29 Clin. Obstetrics and Gynecology at 599. See In re Baby Boy Doe, 260 Ill.App.3d 392, 198 Ill.Dec. 267, 270, 632 N.E.2d 326, 329 (1994) (mother delivered a "normal and healthy" baby despite predictions of disaster).

In 2003 a hospital sought an order to gain guardianship of a fetus that, the hospital argued, could not safely be delivered vaginally. The court issued an order that would have required the mother to have a caesarean birth if the medical authorities at the hospital thought it necessary. The mother went to another hospital, where she delivered a healthy child, and she is considering a civil rights action against the first hospital. Would she have a good claim? What facts would you need to know to make that determination? See Terrie Morgan–Besecker, Hospital Faces Fight in Birth Dispute, Times Leader, January 18, 2004.

4. Not all moral obligations are enforceable through the use of the legal process. First, we must ask if a pregnant woman has a *moral* obligation to act to preserve the health of her fetus. Only if we find such a moral obligation must we address the second question: Should this obligation be enforceable in law? Some (including the majority in *A.C.*) argue that the wishes of the mother (who is

unquestionably a person) always trump the presumed interests of the fetus (whose "personhood" status is uncertain). Some argue that the interests of the fetus (who has yet to experience life) always trump the wishes of the mother.

If you adopt neither absolute, you must address the balancing issue raised above in note 1. How do you weigh the wishes of the pregnant woman against the interests of the fetus (or the interest of the state in protecting fetal life)? What are the relevant factors? Is the viability status of the fetus relevant? Is the likely outcome of the proposed medical procedure relevant? Is the burden this procedure places on the mother relevant? Is the determination by the mother that she will bear the child—that she definitely will not have an abortion, even if that is legally permitted—relevant? Some have argued that this last factor is especially important because where the mother has decided to carry her fetus to term and give birth to a child, the mother's interest must be weighed against the greater interest of this yet-to-be-born person, not the lesser interest of a fetus who may yet be aborted. See J. Robertson and J. Schulman, Pregnancy and Prenatal Harm to Offspring: The Case of Mothers with PKU, 17 Hastings Center Rep. (4) 23 (Aug./Sept.1987).

5.   If society were to enforce the moral obligation of a mother to care for the health of her fetus by law, it could do so in many ways.

a.   Civil Remedies

Civil remedies could include mandatory injunctions (or their equivalents) like those sought in *A.C.* and granted in *Jefferson* or findings of abuse, neglect or dependency. Some states define children born dependent on drugs or alcohol as deprived or abused. See, e.g., Okl. Stat. Ann. Tit. 10 § 1101(4)(c) ("deprived child" includes one born dependent on a controlled substance); Ind. Code Ann. § 31–6–4–3.1(a)(1) ("children in need of services" includes fetal alcohol syndrome babies and those born with any amount of a controlled substance in their bodies). Compare In re Noah M., 212 Cal.App.3d 30, 260 Cal.Rptr. 309 (1989) (infant a deprived child because of prenatal amphetamine exposure) and In re Baby Boy Blackshear, 90 Ohio St.3d 197, 736 N.E.2d 462 (2000) (newborn with positive toxicology screen an "abused child" per se) with In re Fletcher, 141 Misc.2d 333, 533 N.Y.S.2d 241 (Fam.Ct.1988) (prenatal cocaine use alone insufficient basis for a finding of neglect). Can a court permit a state child protective services agency to take custody of a *fetus* under civil abuse and neglect law? Can taking custody of a fetus be distinguished from taking custody of the pregnant woman whose body contains the fetus? Do you think that the fact that a pregnant woman exposed her baby to illegal drugs prenatally is sufficient to show neglect?

In a large number of high risk pregnancies the pregnant woman is herself a child, and there seems to be some relationship between drug and alcohol use and teenage pregnancy. If the pregnant woman is herself a minor, is *her* parents' inability to control her conduct to assure the safety of the fetus itself evidence that the pregnant woman is a neglected child who can be taken into custody to protect her (and, indirectly, her fetus)?

Should civil damages be available to a child born alive who is injured by the pre-birth conduct of her mother? Compare Grodin v. Grodin, 102 Mich.App. 396, 301 N.W.2d 869 (1980) (suit by child against mother who took tetracycline during pregnancy, resulting in discoloration of child's teeth; potential liability in insurance company that issued mother a homeowner's policy) with Chenault v. Huie, 989 S.W.2d 474 (Tex. App. 1999)(no tort action permitted against mother by child allegedly injured by mother's illegal drug use during pregnancy). If we allow children born alive to seek tort damages against others who injure them prenatally, is there a reason to treat their tortfeasing parents differently and more favorably?

b. Criminal Remedies

The law could also apply criminal penalties to those who put their fetuses at risk. States could apply the criminal law of child abuse and neglect to a mother's care for her fetus. Since these criminal statutes generally make failing to provide adequate medical care to a child a form of neglect, they could be interpreted to mean that failing to provide adequate medical care to a fetus would constitute neglect. If the baby were to die as a result, could the mother be guilty of murder? In early 2004 a 28 year old Utah woman was arrested and charged with murder showing a "depraved indifference to human life" when she allegedly refused to have the caesarean section recommended by her physician to deliver twins. The district attorney alleged that she rejected the proposed c-section because of the scar it would leave on her body. One of her two fetuses was born alive, but the other died in utero two days before it was ultimately delivered. See S. Goldenberg, Caesarean Refusal Leads to Murder Charge, The Guardian (London), March 13, 2004, at 2. Might such a charge deter other pregnant women from putting the lives of their babies at risk? On the other hand, might such an interpretation of the law, which could turn any pregnant woman who fails to follow her doctor's advice into a criminal, discourage women at risk from seeking prenatal care?

Other criminal laws also could be used to protect fetuses. Some lifestyle choices that put a fetus at risk (like use of cocaine or heroin) are illegal and can result independently in criminal sanctions against the pregnant woman. There have been several prosecutions for prenatal delivery of illegal drugs by a pregnant woman to her fetus. Should the fact that a subsequently born child is neither addicted nor disabled in any other way be relevant to such a prosecution against that child's mother? Should the fact that the mother is an addict be relevant? To the extent that some criminal sanctions (such as imprisonment) might protect the fetus, are they particularly appropriate for pregnant women who would continue their risky behavior unless they were confined? If a mother is imprisoned for the term of her pregnancy *in order to protect her fetus,* is she being punished for the crime she committed, or for her pregnancy? Is there any deterrence value in imprisoning a pregnant woman who violates the criminal law in a way that adversely affects her fetus?

Might the criminal law be available as a lever to encourage women to get treatment for their addiction during the "teachable moment" provided by a pregnancy? In 1989 the Medical University of South Carolina, along with other state and local law enforcement and social service agencies, hatched a plan to deal with what they saw as the pernicious effects of drug use by pregnant women. Women who met certain guidelines (e.g. those with little or incomplete prenatal care) were tested for cocaine use when they arrived at the hospital to deliver their babies. Those who tested positive were given a choice between enrolling in a substance abuse program and being arrested for their drug use. Those who chose the treatment option were not prosecuted unless they failed to adhere to the treatment plan or failed a subsequent drug test; the others were reported to, and subsequently arrested by, the police. No other hospital in Charleston chose to participate in the program. The majority of the women covered by the program were poor, and most were African American. The generally wealthier White mothers who delivered their babies at other hospitals were not given an opportunity (or forced, against their will, depending on your perspective) to participate in this program.

Ten of the arrested mothers brought suit against the hospital and others. In 2001 the Supreme Court, 6–3, determined that the Charleston process constituted an illegal warrantless search and seizure prohibited by the Fourth Amendment. Ferguson v. City of Charleston, 532 U.S. 67, 121 S.Ct. 1281, 149 L.Ed.2d 205 (2001). Justice Stevens, for the Court, pointed out that the "direct and primary purpose" of the test was to aid the police in enforcing a criminal law, and that the Fourth Amendment was implicated even if the ultimate goal of the hospital was to encourage women to get treatment. Justice Kennedy, concurring, pointed out that the case did not prohibit a state from punishing women who put their fetuses at risk, and Justice Scalia, dissenting, said that the majority "proves once again that no good deed goes unpunished."

Public health groups had filed amicus briefs opposing the policy, employing the A.C. argument that such a policy would have the effect of deterring women from seeking prenatal care. Is that a good argument? Was this policy an appropriate way of encouraging pregnant women to act in a way that did not compromise their babies? For the Fourth Circuit opinion upholding the hospital's policy, see Ferguson v. City of Charleston, 186 F.3d 469 (4th Cir.1999).

Generally, criminal prosecution for maternal drug use has been ultimately unsuccessful. See Reinesto v. Superior Court, 182 Ariz. 190, 894 P.2d 733 (App.1995); Johnson v. State, 602 So.2d 1288 (Fla.1992) (reversing a conviction for delivery of a controlled substance from a mother to her child after birth, but before the umbilical cord was severed); State v. Gray, 62 Ohio St.3d 514, 584 N.E.2d 710 (1992); Commonwealth v. Welch, 864 S.W.2d 280 (Ky.1993); People v. Morabito, 151 Misc.2d 259, 580 N.Y.S.2d 843 (City Ct.1992). In December of 2002 a Kansas judge dismissed child endangerment charges that had been filed against a woman who took drugs before giving birth to her child on the side of Interstate 35. The prosecutor argued that earlier Kansas cases holding that a fetus could not be the victim of a crime should not govern this case because in this case the perpetrator of the crime—the mother—knew that her fetus would be born alive. The mother's motion to dismiss another charge, causing a child to be a child in need of care, was denied. See T. Rizzo, Judge Dismisses One Charge Against Woman Who Gave Birth Along I–35, Kansas City Star, December 11, 2002, at 1.

Some prosecutions have been successful. In State v. McKnight, 352 S.C. 635, 576 S.E.2d 168 (2003), a woman was convicted of homicide by child abuse when her cocaine use during pregnancy resulted in a stillbirth; she was sentenced to 20 years imprisonment. Compare Louise M. Chan, S.O.S. From the Womb: A Call For New York Legislation Criminalizing Drug Use During Pregnancy, 21 Fordham Urban L.J. 199 (1993) (advocating use of the criminal law) with Patricia Sexton, Imposing Criminal Sanctions on Pregnant Drug Users: Throwing the Baby Out with the Bath Water, 32 Washburn L.J. 410 (1993) (opposing the use of the criminal law).

c.   Civil Commitment and Court Ordered Protective Custody

Finally, the remedy of civil commitment or court ordered protective custody may be available to protect fetuses from abuse by mentally ill, drug abusing, or alcoholic mothers under some state laws that permit commitment to treat these conditions, or that provide for custody of the mother to protect the fetus under some circumstances. Some states have promulgated statutes that provide explicitly that women who put their fetuses at risk may be restrained from doing so by the court. In 1998, for example, following a judicial decision that suggested that there was no legal authority for confining a pregnant woman, State ex rel. Angela M.W.

v. Kruzicki, 209 Wis.2d 112, 561 N.W.2d 729 (1997), the Wisconsin legislature provided that a pregnant woman could be held in custody to protect the fetus:

> An adult expectant mother of an unborn child may be held under [this statute] if the intake worker determines that there is probable cause to believe that the adult expectant mother is within the jurisdiction of the court, to believe that if the adult expectant mother is not held, there is a substantial risk that the physical health of the unborn child, and of the child when born, will be seriously affected or endangered by the adult expectant mothers habitual lack of self-control in the use of alcohol beverages, controlled substances or controlled substance analogs, exhibited to a severe degree, and to believe that the adult expectant mother is refusing or has refused to accept any alcohol or other drug abuse services offered to her or is not making or has not made a good faith effort to participate in any alcohol or other drug abuse services offered to her.

Wis. Stat. Section 48.205. Where do you think pregnant women are held under this statute? Where should they be held—a jail? A hospital? A mental health clinic? At home? South Dakota has promulgated a statute allowing for the brief (2–day) commitment of pregnant women by family members, and court ordered commitment of those same women for up to nine months. S.D. Codified Laws section 34–20A–63 to 70.

In 2002 an Arkansas state judge ordered the state to take custody of a neglected fetus when he sent the mother to jail for criminal contempt of an order not to use drugs. The trial judge, whose order was opposed by the state Human Services Department, added a suggestion that the pregnant woman undergo a tubal ligation after the baby is born. See T. Shurley, Custody Ruling on Fetus Irks Officials; State Lacks Authority to Assume Fetal Care, Arkansas Democrat–Gazette, December 17, 2002, at 11. For an interesting account of the Corneau case, a Massachusetts case in which a pregnant woman who was allegedly a member of a religious cult that opposed all medical care was locked up to assure that her fetus got adequate medical attention at delivery, see Robin Power Morris, The Corneau Case: Furthering Trends of Fetal Rights and Religious Freedom, 28 N.Eng. J. on Crim. & Conf. 89 (2002).

Are fetuses (and mothers) better protected because of the existence of the possibility of civil commitment? What would make these processes more effective? What problems are the most likely to render these processes ineffective? Is the use of the civil commitment or protective custody remedy any less troublesome than the use of the criminal sanction against the mother to protect the fetus?

6. What should be done if the generally appropriate commitment and treatment of a drug abusing pregnant woman is inconsistent with the best interest of the fetus? For example, heroin addicts are often "treated" by replacing their heroin addiction with a methadone addiction. Methadone is a safer addiction because its use does not result in the ups and downs brought on by heroin, and its supply and purity can be regulated by medical authorities. On the other hand, it is harder to withdraw from methadone than from heroin, and a fetus may be put at great risk if the pregnant woman switches addictions during the pregnancy. A fetus may also be put at great risk if the pregnant woman withdraws from heroin "cold turkey" during pregnancy.

Should a pregnant heroin addict who wishes to start methadone (or stop taking drugs altogether) be allowed to do so? Should she be encouraged to do so? How should a doctor legally and ethically treat a pregnant heroin addict? May she tell her patient that she should continue using heroin throughout her pregnancy? Must she tell her that?

Some have suggested that a substantial number of places in drug rehabilitation programs be put aside for pregnant women. With the very long waiting lines for admission to these programs, would this be a good idea? Might it encourage women who are desperate for treatment to get pregnant so they will qualify for expedited assistance?

7.   Of course, not all behavior that is unhealthy for the fetus is also illegal for the mother. Consumption of any amount of alcohol during pregnancy may result in fetal alcohol syndrome, which is now the most common known cause of mental retardation at birth in the United States. Is there any reason to distinguish a woman who puts her child at risk of fetal alcohol syndrome from a woman who puts her child at risk through the use of another proscribed drug? For an informative and moving account of fetal alcohol syndrome and its consequences on families and communities, see M. Dorris, The Broken Cord (1989). Author Michael Dorris raised an adopted fetal alcohol syndrome child, and it made him sensitive to the need to protect children who face a lifetime of deprivation due to the addiction of their alcoholic mothers. See In re Smith, 128 Misc.2d 976, 492 N.Y.S.2d 331 (Fam.Ct.1985) (prenatal alcohol use contributed to the birth of a neglected child). See also Claire Dineen, Fetal Alcohol Syndrome: The Legal and Social Responses to its Impact on Native Americans, 70 N. Dak. L.Rev. 1 (1994).

8.   There is another area in which a pregnant woman's decisions have the potential to put the health of her fetus at risk, and that is the workplace. Some employment environments that are safe for workers may not be safe for workers' fetuses. Employers may seek to exclude pregnant women (or even women who may become pregnant) from jobs that could put the fetuses at risk—either because the employers wish to protect the fetuses, or because the employers wish to protect themselves from adverse publicity, increased health insurance costs and potential tort liability. The employee and her fetus may have interests in conflict: the financial advantage and emotional fulfillment of the employee may come at an increased risk of damage to her yet-to-be-born (or even yet-to-be-conceived) child. Should an employer be able to force women in the workplace to choose between ineligibility to work in certain jobs and ineligibility (through sterilization, for example) to conceive children? This issue has received attention almost exclusively where the employee is a woman (i.e., a potential mother) rather than a man (i.e., a potential father) even though occupational hazards to men may affect the health of the fetus as well. Why do you think this is the case?

The United States Supreme Court considered this issue under Title VII of the Civil Rights Act of 1964 in International Union, United Automobile Workers v. Johnson Controls, 499 U.S. 187, 111 S.Ct. 1196, 113 L.Ed.2d 158 (1991). Johnson Controls had excluded women of child bearing age from its battery manufacturing operation unless they had been sterilized because workers in that process sometimes developed very high levels of lead in their blood. The United States Supreme Court determined that this policy constituted disparate treatment by sex, which could be justified under Title VII only if sex was a bona fide occupational qualification (BFOQ). The court's conclusion was supported by the Pregnancy Discrimination Act of 1978, which defined discrimination "because of or on the basis of pregnancy, childbirth or related medical conditions" as discrimination on the basis of sex. The Court concluded:

It is no more appropriate for the courts than it is for individual employers to decide whether a woman's reproductive role is more important to herself and her family than her economic role. Congress has left this choice to the woman as hers to make.

9. If a pregnant woman and her fetus may have different and conflicting interests, should they each be separately and independently represented in court? Consider the next case.

GUARDIANSHIP OF J.D.S.

Court of Appeal of Florida, 2004.
864 So.2d 534

THOMPSON, J.

INTRODUCTION

Jennifer Wixtrom appeals an order denying her petition to be appointed guardian of the fetus of J.D.S., an incapacitated female. We conclude that the trial court correctly denied the petition and affirm.

FACTS AND PROCEDURAL HISTORY

[T]he Department of Children and Family Services ("Department") filed a petition seeking an order authorizing emergency adult protective services for J.D.S. In its petition, the Department alleged that J.D.S. was in need of temporary emergency protective services because it had received a report that J.D.S. was pregnant as a result of a sexual battery, which occurred while she was residing in a group home. The petition stated that J.D.S. was a 22–year old woman suffering from severe mental retardation, cerebral palsy, autism, and seizure disorder and that she was unable to adequately provide for her own care and protection. The petition also stated that J.D.S. was nonverbal, unable to make decisions, and unable to comprehend her own mental, physical, or environmental limitations. The petition alleged that J.D.S. was taking numerous medications, which could be detrimental to the fetus. [T]he Department filed an amended petition seeking appointment of a guardian for J.D.S. and a separate guardian for the fetus. The Department alleged that J.D.S.'s interests and needs were potentially adverse to those of the fetus. The Department stated that J.D.S.'s guardian was required to avoid conflicts of interest, but that a conflict of interest was likely because J.D.S.'s medications could be detrimental to the fetus.

* * *

Jennifer Wixtrom filed a petition to be appointed guardian of J.D.S.'s fetus. Wixtrom alleged that the appointment was essential because J.D.S. lacked the mental capacity to provide proper prenatal care and to make necessary decisions for the protection and enhancement of the fetus during its formative months. * * * [T]he trial court ruled that it is error to appoint a guardian ad litem for a fetus. The trial court also cited several cases which held that a fetus is not a "person" within the meaning of certain statutes.

* * * After Wixtrom's motion for rehearing was denied, Wixtrom filed a notice of appeal. Thereafter, the trial court entered an order stating that J.D.S.'s guardian had created a plan for J.D.S. which stated that an abortion would not be performed on J.D.S.

* * *

ANALYSIS

On its face [the Florida statute] which governs guardianships, does not provide for the appointment of a guardian for a fetus. * * * [T]he definitions section * * * defines the terms, "guardian," "ward," and other terms used within the chapter, but it does not define or use the term, "fetus." Furthermore, the term, "fetus" is not used in [the statute], and no section * * * entitles a fetus or unborn child to a guardian. "When the language of the statute is clear and unambiguous and conveys a clear and definite meaning, there is no occasion for resorting to the rules of statutory interpretation and construction; the statute must be given its plain and obvious meaning. [ ] The legislature has, in other contexts, explicitly provided protection for fetuses. [ ] ("'vehicular homicide' is the killing of a human being, or the killing of a viable fetus" by operation of a motor vehicle); [ ] (willful killing of an unborn child by injury to mother shall be deemed manslaughter). Had the legislature decided that a fetus was entitled to the protection of the guardianship statutes, it would have so legislated. * * *

Furthermore, [the] section defines a "guardian" as "a person who has been appointed by the court to act on behalf of a ward's person or property or both." A " 'ward' means a person for whom a guardian has been appointed." [ ] It follows that a fetus must be considered a "person" to be appointed a guardian. We find no Florida statute or case law that has determined a fetus to be a person. Rather, the opposite is true. For instance, the Florida Supreme Court declined to rule that a fetus is a "person" within the meaning of the Florida Wrongful Death Act, [ ] and the Fourth District declined to apply a child abuse statute in a case involving a fetus[ ]. See also *Roe v. Wade* [ ] ("the word 'person,' as used in the Fourteenth Amendment, does not include the unborn"). Also persuasive are holdings from other jurisdictions which have concluded that a fetus is not a "person" and not subject to guardianship * * *

Wixtrom is concerned that J.D.S.'s guardian could have authorized an abortion of the fetus. Florida law provides safeguards to insure that a guardian does not act capriciously or cavalierly when considering the health of the incapacitated mother and fetus. * * *

CONCLUSION

Having concluded that [the statute] does not provide for the appointment of a guardian for a fetus, explicitly or implicitly, we find that the trial court correctly denied Wixtrom's petition to be appointed guardian of J.D.S.'s fetus.

ORFINGER, J., concurring and concurring specially.

The unfortunate facts of this case compel us to confront a difficult question: is a fetus a "person" under Florida law? "One can find no consensus on the issue among physicians, politicians, theologians, academics or judges." Few topics in American law have generated as much impassioned debate as the status and rights, if any, of the unborn. "When there is a 'potential life' at stake, the relationship between the right to decide and the right of government to intrude becomes far more emotional and complex. . . . Depending on one's religious or philosophic views, life may begin anywhere from conception to . . . birth."

The fetal rights debate began in earnest when the United States Supreme Court declared in *Roe v. Wade*, [ ] that a fetus is not a person for the purposes of the Fourteenth Amendment of the United States Constitution. Florida, like most states, has followed the common law "born alive" rule when determining the rights, if any, of the unborn. Under that rule, the unborn generally have no legally recognized rights until, and unless, a live birth occurs.

As the majority opinion correctly observes, through the enactment of numerous statutes, the Florida Legislature has distinguished between the unborn and persons born alive. Consequently, although the State has a legitimate interest in protecting the "potentiality of human life," an interest that becomes compelling once the unborn achieves viability, if the Legislature intends to depart from the traditional interpretation of the words "minor," "person," or "human being," as those terms are used in the guardianship or other Florida Statutes, it must do so expressly, as such words generally apply to human life only postnatally. [ ]

The Legislature is the appropriate forum to debate the proper balance between the State's compelling interest in protecting the unborn and the mother's constitutional right to privacy and personal bodily integrity, assuming that such a balance can be achieved. While the debate is typically framed in the context of the State's right to interfere with a woman's decision regarding an abortion, taking control of a woman's body and supervising her conduct or lifestyle during pregnancy or forcing her to undergo medical treatment in order to protect the health of the fetus creates its own universe of troubling questions. Should the State have the authority to prohibit a pregnant woman from smoking cigarettes or drinking alcohol, both legal activities with recognized health risks to the unborn? Could the Legislature do so constitutionally given our supreme court's broad interpretation of Florida's constitutional right of privacy and the limitations placed on the State's ability to act by Roe?

While Wixtrom and the amici curae supporting her position would limit this court's ruling to situations involving a legally incompetent mother pregnant with a viable fetus, viewing the problem through that narrow a lens distorts the real issue of the scope, if any, of fetal rights. If a fetus has rights, then all fetuses have rights. And, if a fetus is a person, then all fetuses are people, not just those residing in the womb of an incompetent mother. If we recognize a fetus as a person, we must accept that the unborn would have the rights guaranteed persons under the Constitutions of the United States and the State of Florida. While it is inviting to view this case as narrowly as Wixtrom suggests, it would be dangerous to do so when the potential for state intrusion into the lives of women is so significant. The Legislature, as the people's elected representatives, must consider and weigh that delicate balance, consistent with constitutional limitations on the State's ability to interfere with a pregnant woman's right of privacy and bodily integrity.

Consistent with the holding in Roe v. Wade, the State has the authority to protect potential human life in the absence of a countervailing fundamental right or a more compelling state interest. At the same time, Roe recognized that the State's compelling interest may be sacrificed to protect the life or health of the mother. [ ] State regulation of fundamental rights is justified only by a compelling state interest. [ ] Balancing the interests of the mother and the unborn is problematic, and, at least in the context of Florida guardianship law, has not yet been addressed by the Legislature. Whether the State can confer previously unrecognized rights on the unborn under Florida law is a question that we must leave to another day. Our conclusion here is simply that the Legislature has not yet done so, at least in the context of Florida guardianship law.

Our opinion should not be read to suggest that we believe that the Legislature can constitutionally grant rights to the unborn that might be in conflict with the mother's right of privacy. Nor do we conclude that a viable fetus is not alive; rather, we hold that in the context of Florida guardianship law, the Legislature has not yet addressed the rights, if any, of the unborn, and when, if at all, a fetus acquires personhood, entitling it to the full protections of the law. Whether the Legislature can confer rights on the unborn will be decided by the courts only if, and when, the Legislature enacts such legislation. But in doing so, the Legislature must consider the mother's paramount right to privacy and bodily integrity.

"Protecting the health and welfare of potential life is both an important and altruistic enterprise; one that states can and, for the sake of humanitarianism, should undertake. However, in creating laws that advance fetal protections, states should take caution to ensure preservation of our society's most sacred and fundamental interests: privacy, personal liberty, and bodily integrity." Amy Kay Boatright, *State Control Over the Bodies of Pregnant Women,* 11 J. Contemp. Legal Issues 903, 903 (2001).

PLEUS, J., dissenting.

* * *

The order under appeal unrealistically reasoned that the guardian for J.D.S. could resolve any "dilemma" between the interests of J.D.S. and the unborn child. On the other hand, it was silent as to who would be charged with representing the best interests of the unborn baby.

Wixtrom's petition was for her appointment as a plenary guardian * * *, and not a guardian *ad litem.* It is important to note the difference between a guardian *ad litem* and a plenary guardian appointed pursuant [to the Florida statute]. [A]ny person interested in the welfare of a minor may be appointed guardian of the minor without the necessity to adjudicate the minor incompetent * * *. A guardian appointed for a minor, whether of the person or property, has the authority of a plenary guardian. On the other hand, * * * a guardian *ad litem* is a person appointed to represent an incompetent party in civil litigation. A guardian *ad litem* has none of the powers of a plenary guardian and totally different responsibilities. A guardian *ad litem* is simply an advocate for the best interest of the child.

* * *

This case is not about the choice of a mother to terminate a pregnancy, but it well could have been. J.D.S. is incapable of exercising the choice of life or death for her unborn baby. Because the baby is viable, the only question in the context of abortion would be whether the termination of the pregnancy is medically necessary to protect the life or health of J.D.S. On the other hand, as explained later, future cases may involve the termination of human life. The majority opinion would allow no voice for the unborn child in such cases.

* * *

THE MAIN ISSUE

At the outset it should be emphasized that the issue in this case is not about the right of a mother to choose to kill her unborn baby. J.D.S. is incapable of exercising this "choice." In the context of abortion, the only issue would be whether the termination of life for the baby is medically necessary, and that is not an issue in this case. It well could have been.

According to the majority, the issue in this case is whether Florida law allows the appointment of a plenary "fetal" guardian in cases such as this one. I would define the issue in terms of an unborn child. In other words, does the court have the power to appoint a plenary guardian for an unborn child? The majority feels the main issue is whether a "fetus" is a "person" under Florida law.

I believe that under [the statute], a trial court has full authority to appoint a plenary guardian for an unborn child because the child is a "minor" as the term is used in the statute.

* * *

All sides to this case concede that the State has a compelling interest in the health, welfare and life of the unborn child. Appointment of a guardian for the unborn baby is not an undue burden and is the only means to ensure that the State's compelling interest in the health, welfare and life of an unborn child is protected. The United States Supreme Court has ruled that a state has a legitimate interest at the outset of a pregnancy in protecting the health of a woman and the life of a fetus that may become a child. *Planned Parenthood of Southeastern Pa. v. Casey* [ ]. This legitimate interest becomes a compelling interest after the unborn child is a viable life. *Roe v. Wade* [ ]. At all times material to the decision of the trial court, Baby S was viable.

The *Casey* court reaffirmed *Roe's* definition of "viability" to be "the time at which there is a realistic possibility of maintaining and nourishing a life outside the womb so that independent existence of second life can in reason and in all fairness be the object of State protection that now overrides the rights of women." [ ]. In other words, upon viability, the State has a compelling interest in "promoting the life or potential life of the unborn." To protect the health and welfare of the unborn child, states may take action to restrict a woman's liberties by any means that does not create an "undue burden." In defining what is not an undue burden, the United States Supreme Court has ruled that regulations which do no more than create a structural mechanism by which the state, or the parent or guardian of a minor, may express profound respect for the life of the unborn are permitted.

Because the State has a compelling interest in a preservation of life upon viability, the trial court was obligated to determine if the appointment of a guardian over the unborn child constituted "an undue burden." In fact, there is no indication that the trial court even considered or applied the undue burden test.

* * *

The appointment of a guardian for an unborn baby of a woman in her third trimester is consistent with *Roe* and *Casey*. The appointment of a guardian on behalf of the unborn child advances the State's interest in the life of the unborn by (a) insuring compliance with all statutory requirements and (b) appointing a zealous advocate to cross-examine witnesses offering medical testimony thereby representing the State's interest in preserving the life of the unborn child. In this case, the only interests at stake are the State's interest in preserving the life of the unborn child and the guardian's interest in determining whether it is medically necessary to terminate the pregnancy in order to preserve the life or health of the mother. Absent clear and convincing evidence that the mother's life or health is at risk due to the continued pregnancy, the scale tips in favor of the State and the life of the unborn baby must be preserved. A guardian on behalf of the unborn baby would act as an advocate for the State's interest in that unborn life.

Because the majority concludes that an unborn, viable child is not a "person" or a "minor" unless the Legislature says so, I would urge the Legislature to overturn this decision and affirm the fact that an unborn child is a person. Such action would be a clear and unambiguous acknowledgment of human life.

I would submit further that defining "person" by using terms such as "embryo" or "fetus" is confusing, outdated and meaningless. Such terms cloud the issue of when human life begins. The better view would be for the Legislature to adopt a bright line point in time, and that point in time must be the moment of conception.

Sooner or later, as happened when *Brown v. Board of Education* [ ] overturned *Plessy v. Ferguson* [ ], *Roe's* unrestricted abortions will be overturned, and the rights of the unborn will be extended to the moment of conception.

My concern with the ramifications of the majority opinion compels me to write the following. I have a new grandson. His name is Nicholas. His heart started beating a short time after conception and during the first trimester. At the end of the first trimester, or early in the second trimester, we were able to view a sonogram and determine that Nicholas was a boy. We have pictures of sonograms taken when Nicholas was only fourteen weeks old. You can see his head, his eyes, his hands and feet. You could tell he was alive because he moved his arms and legs. He was so strong you could watch him move his mother's pregnant belly. Before he was born, his parents placed a sign over his future crib. It read simply: "NICHOLAS." Nicholas now lives outside his mother's womb, but from the moment of his conception, Nicholas was a human life.

If all the judges in the world and all justices on the supreme court decided that Nicholas was not a person and merely a "fetus" until his birth, I would know them blind to reality. Before his birth, Nicholas was alive. Nicholas had identity. Nicholas was a person. Nicholas has been a person since conception. Our rule of law can no longer remain blind to the realities of human life.

We now know the baby of J.D.S. is a girl. She is called Baby S. She was born through Caesarean section. Ironically, within a short time after her birth, a guardian was appointed for Baby S. It makes no sense to me that Baby S could have a guardian after the Caesarean but not before. Was Baby S any less human before the surgery?

* * *

Notes and Questions

1.   This case garnered a great deal of national attention; what could be more symbolic of a fetus as a person than to appoint a lawyer on his or her behalf? Among the amici that filed briefs in the case were the ACLU, Center for Reproductive Rights, NOW, Right to Life, the Advocacy Center for People with Disabilities and the Women's Law project. Should courts appoint guardians or guardians ad litem in cases that implicate the interests of a fetus? Is there any disadvantage in appointing a guardian for the fetus under such circumstances? Does the appointment of such a guardian (or the failure to appoint one) effectively prejudge the issue of the fetus's standing to participate in the litigation, and, thus, the outcome of the case? Are you surprised that the majority spoke of the "fetus" while the dissenting judge spoke of the "unborn child"?

2.   In *A.C.* the court appointed a guardian ad litem to represent the fetus. In J.D.S. the petitioner sought to be appointed guardian—not guardian ad litem. What is the difference? What would be the task of a plenary guardian? A guardian ad litem? Might it be appropriate to appoint both?

3.   What, exactly, is the role of the guardian or guardian ad litem in these cases. Presumably, the guardian will not be able to act on the wishes of her client, and, instead, she will be required to serve the best interest of the fetus. But what is in the best interest of the fetus? How could the guardian make this determination? Is the guardian for a fetus always required to advocate that her client be born alive, even if that means that the client will be born with serious anomalies? Could the guardian act altruistically on behalf of the fetus, and seek to preserve the health of the mother? Under *Roe*, would the guardian be obliged to do so?

4.   The petitioner in J.D.S. argued that the rule allowing for the appointment of a guardian for the fetus could apply only to those cases where the pregnant woman is incompetent, and thus cannot make the decisions that a mother normally would make. In such cases, the petitioner argued, it is unfair to give one incompetent (the mother) a guardian, while the other (the fetus) is denied one; the chance for a conflict between the two interested parties is just too great. At the oral argument, though, Judge Thompson asked the petitioner's lawyer, "But isn't that conflict apparent in a woman who is healthy and bright, but drinks a lot? Couldn't a guardian be important because the fetus is in danger of being abused by fetal alcohol syndrome, or if the mother is a heavy smoker or overweight?"

Where would you draw the line? Should no fetus ever be appointed a guardian? Should all fetuses have guardians to protect them against prospective maternal (and other) depredations? If you would choose a line between those, where would it be?

5.   Could the Florida legislature change the law and allow for the appointment of guardians for fetuses? Could it require such appointments under some circumstances? Could the legislature require the appointment of guardians who are required to support the live birth of the child under every circumstance?

6.   The question of whether a guardian should be appointed for a fetus has not been litigated often. Sometimes—as in A.C.—it is unchallenged, or the appointment of the guardian is not a part of the substantive appeal. It has been considered in other states, too, though. See In re Brown, 294 Ill.App.3d 159, 228 Ill.Dec. 525, 689 N.E.2d 397 (1997).

Bibliographical Note

For a good short summary of the legal issues implicated in cases of fetal-maternal decisionmaking, see J. Robertson, Legal Issues in Prenatal Therapy, 29 Clin. Obstetrics & Gynecology 603 (1986). For particularly clear descriptions of the underlying issues, see Kristen Burgess, Protective Custody: Will it Eradicate Fetal Abuse and Lead to the Perfect Womb?, 35 Houston L. Rev. 227 (1998), and Alice Noble–Allgire, Court–Ordered Caesarean Sections, 10 J. Legal Med. 211 (1989); Also see Alicia Ouellette, New Medical Technology: A Chance to Reexamine Court–Ordered Medical Procedures During Pregnancy, 57 Alb. L. Rev. 927 (1994), Dawn Johnsen, Shared Interests: Promoting Healthy Births Without Sacrificing Women's Liberty, 43 Hastings L. J. 569 (1992), Lisa Ikemoto, The Code of Perfect Pregnancy: At the Intersection of the Ideology of Motherhood, the Practice of Defaulting to Science and the Interventionist Mindset of the Law, 53 Ohio State L. J. 1205 (1992), Dawn Johnsen, The Creation of Fetal Rights: Conflicts with Women's Constitutional Rights to Liberty, Privacy, and Equal Protection, 95 Yale L.J. 599 (1986), April Cherry, The Free Exercise Rights of Pregnant Women Who Refuse Medical Treatment, 69 Tenn. L. Rev. 563 (2002), and Cheryl Plambeck, Divided Loyalties: Legal and Bioethical Considerations of Physician–Patient Confidentiality and Prenatal Drug Abuse, 23 J. Legal Med. 1 (2002). For a Canadian perspective on this issue, see Sheilah Martin and Murray Coleman, Judicial Intervention in Pregnancy, 40 McGill L. J. 947 (1995). For a particularly helpful more general perspective, see Bonnie Steinbock, Life Before Birth: The Moral and Legal Status of Embryos and Fetuses (1992) and Nancy Rhoden, The Judge in the Delivery Room: The Emergence of Court–Ordered Cesareans, 74 Calif.L.Rev. 1951 (1986).

For a discussion on the limits of requiring fetal therapy, see Krista Newkirk, State–Compelled Fetal Surgery: The Viability Test is not so Viable, 4 Wm. & Mary J. Women & L. 467 (1998), David Blickenstaff, Defining the Boundaries of Personal Privacy: Is There a Paternal Interest in Compelling Therapeutic Fetal Surgery?, 88 Nw. U. L.Rev. 1157 (1994) and Bonnie Steinbock, Maternal–Fetal Conflict and In Utero Fetal Therapy, 57 Alb.L.Rev. 781 (1994).

Chapter 3

LEGAL, SOCIAL AND ETHICAL ISSUES IN HUMAN GENETICS

I. INTRODUCTION

It appears that each week's news events have included the discovery of a "new gene" which promises an explanation for any one of a seemingly limitless range of human characteristics. Genes for cystic fibrosis, breast cancer, colon cancer, obesity, homosexuality, and many other conditions, characteristics, behaviors, and personal identities were identified in the 1990s. One magazine seemed to capture it all with a headline on its front cover: "Infidelity—Is It In Your Genes?"

The basic foundations of genetic research arose centuries ago as farmers bred domestic animals and crops to achieve the desired characteristics for productivity and durability. Observation of this manipulation around phenotype (physical characteristic) led to the work of Gregor Mendel, an Austrian monk, who came to be known as the "Father of Genetics" for his work in the nineteenth century. The first half of the twentieth century carried forward this work by linking genetics to DNA. James Watson and Francis Crick revolutionized genetics when they determined the double helix structure of DNA, with its repeated four bases (adenine, guanine, cytosine and thymine, *aka* A, G, C, and T) in 1953.

Within the past two decades, the field of genetics has "gone molecular." No longer are genes detected and identifiable only through their shadows— the phenotypes or physical expressions of the gene. Scientists have sequenced or mapped the genome and are able to manipulate this basic material.

The more recent explosion of knowledge in genetics is the result of the Human Genome Project (HGP). The HGP is a multi-national project involving sixteen nations. The United States worked most closely with Great Britain, France and Japan. In the U.S., the project was funded primarily by the National Institutes of Health (through the National Center for Human Genome Research) and the Department of Energy (through the Human Genome Project). The primary goal of the project was to discover and map all 30,000 to 40,000 genes, which together make up the human genome, and to make the genome itself accessible for biological study. The effort was expected to cost approximately $3 billion and to take about 15 years, but on April 14,

2003, the project was completed over two years ahead of schedule at the cost of $2.7 billion. The genome map contains 99 percent of the gene-containing sequence and is 99.9 percent accurate. Scientists expect that working with this data will produce advancements in the diagnosis of disease, detection of genetic predispositions, and improved drug design. To learn more about the Human Genome Project, see http://www.genome.gov/.

From the beginning, the "new genetics" has created hopes and fears. Despite the promise, there is a fear that history will repeat itself, for eugenics does not have a happy history. In Buck v. Bell, 274 U.S. 200, 47 S.Ct. 584, 71 L.Ed. 1000 (1927), for example, the Supreme Court tragically misused (and misunderstood) genetics and decided that the forced sterilization of a mentally retarded woman, whose mother and grandmother were also believed to be mentally retarded, was not a violation of her Constitutional rights. Justice Holmes, in a now infamous declaration, stated that it is desirable "to prevent those who are manifestly unfit from continuing their kind.... Three generations of imbeciles are enough." Paul Lombardo, Three Generations, No Imbeciles: New Light on Buck v. Bell, 60 N.Y.U.L.R. 30 (1985). In 2002, the Governor of the State of Virginia issued a formal apology for the state's program of forced sterilization that was conducted as part of the eugenics movement of the early part of the twentieth century. About 8,000 low-income, uneducated and mentally retarded Virginians were sterilized as part of a eugenics program in that state between 1924 and 1979. Thirty states engaged in such programs, and 65,000 individuals nationwide were involuntarily sterilized. Calling the program a "shameful effort," the Governor stated that "the state government never should have been involved." American Political Network–Health Line, 5/3/2002.

For a ten-year perspective on shifting emphases in public policy relating to genetics, see Frances H. Miller, Foreword: Phase II of the Genetics Revolution: Sophisticated Issues for Home and Abroad, 28 Am.J.L. & Med. 145 (2002), introducing a symposium issue. Public health issues in genetics are highlighted in a symposium published in 30 J.L., Med. & Ethics (Summer 2002).

In light of our often moralistic attitudes toward sickness and the continuing human history of exclusion and discrimination against minorities and the disabled, there is concern that "imperfect humans" will be devalued and penalized. See, Eric Rakowski, Who Should Pay for Bad Genes, 90 Cal. L.Rev. 1345 (2002), arguing that parents who choose to bear such a "genetically disadvantaged" child would incur a greater liability for the costs of the child's care. On the other hand, others are concerned about the drive toward "genetic enhancement." Maxwell Mehlman, The Law of Above Averages: Leveling the New Genetic Enhancement Playing Field, 85 Iowa L.Rev. 517 (2000); Michael Malinowski, Choosing the Genetic Makeup of Our Children: Our Eugenics Past–Present, and Future, 36 Conn. L. Rev. 125 (2003).

What Does It Mean to Have the Gene for ...?

Assume that you have been told that you, or your spouse or your child or your siblings or parents, have the gene for Huntington's Disease or for breast cancer or for colon cancer or for obesity or for homosexuality or for sickle-cell anemia. What does it mean to have the gene for any of these conditions? Does it predict the future?

Some genetically-related diseases are monogenic; that is they are associated with a single gene. But even with monogenic conditions, which would appear to present the most simple connection between gene and disease, the presence of the gene may not provide a clue as to whether the individual will be severely or moderately affected or will experience no symptoms of the disease at all.

Most of the genes "for" cancer are not monogenic or polygenic (requiring the interaction of more than one gene), but rather are multifactorial. Multifactorial conditions are those in which there is a genetic predisposition, but in which environmental or nongenetic factors are also essential or determinative. Nor are genes necessarily single-effect. Rather, the same gene that is associated with a particular disease may also increase resistance to another. Many diseases involve mutation in genes, but not all mutated genes are associated with or cause disease. A mutated gene may not have any health consequences at all. Also, mutations do not occur only prior to birth. Gene mutation may be caused at any time of life, for example, from radiation or virus or by age.

Furthermore, it has been known for decades that someone (a carrier) may have the gene for a particular condition, such as cystic fibrosis or sickle-cell anemia, but not have the disease itself. Carriers bear the burden of the risk of having children affected by the disease itself, often depending on the genetic traits of his or her mate.

The method used to identify a genetic connection to particular conditions may also affect the meaning of a genetic "association" with a disease or condition. Most of the genetic connections established prior to the advances of the latter part of the last century were based on epidemiological studies of the occurrence of particular characteristics or conditions, rather than by direct identification of the gene itself. An association between genetic trait and disease established by epidemiological studies alone typically cannot predict the presence of the trait in any single individual.

Discoveries of genetic associations with what might be termed nonmedical or nondisease characteristics, including homosexuality or brilliance for example, have been particularly unstable. Such associations are regularly announced and just as regularly disclaimed.

Because knowledge concerning the nature of the genetic basis for particular human traits evolves so rapidly, often producing conflicting information within a period of months, it is not wise to provide particular examples here. You might find it useful to do some research on your own. What is the most recent information available concerning the genetic basis for one of the following: Alzheimer's disease; breast cancer (BRCA1 and BRCA2); cystic fibrosis; homosexuality; obesity; colon cancer, for example? By what method was the association established? Is the condition monogenic, polygenic, or multifactorial? Is there a genetic test available? Does detection require testing the family as well as the individual himself or herself? Is the condition more often associated with a particular ethnic group? Does it affect both genders in the same way? Is there a therapy available? The HGP website at http://www.genome.gov has a very good section on "genetic disorders" as well as sections on policy and ethics.

What Is . . . "Illness"?

We still operate with inadequate linguistics for genetics. Does it make a difference if something is called a genetic "trait" as compared to a genetic "condition" or a genetic "disease," "defect," or "anomaly"? Are these medical terms? What judgments enter the decision to view a characteristic as any of these and what impact might the chosen categorization have? Recall the material on sickness and health in Chapter 1, especially the case of Katskee v. Blue Cross/Blue Shield of Nebraska, 245 Neb. 808, 515 N.W.2d 645 (1994). In that case, Sindie Katskee was diagnosed with breast-ovarian carcinoma syndrome, a genetically-based condition. Her health insurance refused to pay for prophylactic surgery on the sole ground that Ms. Katskee was not being treated for an "illness." The court held that Ms. Katskee was ill, even though she experienced no symptoms or limitations and did not have cancer.

What implications might the definition of illness have? If Katskee were merely a carrier of a genetically-related disorder, would that qualify her as ill? What is the "normal" human genotype? Which genetic traits should be fixed, or cured, or removed, if possible? Who decides whether a genetic trait should be remedied? Is a variable definition of illness, depending on the reason for the label, useful in genetics or public policy? See, e.g., Donald Ramsey, The Trigger of Coverage for Cancer: When Does Genetic Mutation Become "Bodily Injury, Sickness, Or Disease?" 41 Santa Clara L.Rev. 293 (2001).

Population Genomics

Because of the Mendelian character of genetics, genetic information is likely to have implications for groups. See, e.g., Eric Racine, Discourse Ethics as an Ethics of Responsibility: Comparison and Evaluation of Citizen Involvement in Population Genomics, 31 J. L. Med. & Ethics 390 (2003). Genetic traits are not evenly distributed by race or ethnicity: the sickle cell trait is more common in African Americans; Tay Sachs, more common in Jews of Eastern European extraction; and spina bifida more common among those whose ancestors came from the British Isles.

A recent example of this dynamic is the case of mutations of BRCA1, a tumor-suppressor gene in which particular mutations appear to create a susceptibility to breast and ovarian cancer. When the association between BRCA1 and breast cancer was first identified in 1994, popular reports of the discovery made it appear that the BRCA1 gene itself was the "culprit" and that it was "bad" to have this cancer gene, when actually it is a mutation of that gene that is associated with cancer. These reports also created the impression that the presence of the cancer gene accounted for most breast cancer. In fact, most breast cancer is not hereditary—only 5% to 10% of breast cancer is due to a genetic factor although a recent estimate goes as high as 27%. In addition, most women (and men) with mutations of BRCA 1 (or BRCA 2) never develop cancer. Finally, even now, the actual cancer risks for people with mutations of BRCA1 are not yet established, although it appears that women with certain mutations who are in high risk families carry a 36% to 85% lifetime risk of breast cancer and a 15% to 60% lifetime risk of ovarian cancer. (Lifetime risks for breast cancer decrease rather than increase with age. In the general population, a female at birth has a 12% lifetime risk for breast cancer, and a woman at age 70 who has not had breast cancer has a lifetime risk of 7%) Katrina Armstrong, et al., Assessing the Risk of Breast Cancer (Review Article), 342 NEJM 564 (Feb. 24, 2000).

For one group, however, the association between particular mutations of BRCA1 and 2 and cancer is very powerful. For individuals of Ashkenazi (Eastern European) Jewish descent, the incidence of the identified mutations is approximately 2.65% (perhaps ten times higher than the general population). Ashkenazi Jewish women with certain mutations of the BRCA1 and 2 genes may have an increased lifetime breast cancer risk regardless of family history, although only 7% of breast cancer in this group is associated with genetic mutation and the group as a whole may have a lower risk of breast cancer than the general population. Mary–Claire King, et al., Breast and Ovarian Cancer Risks Due to Inherited Mutations in BRCA1 and BRCA2, 302 Science 643 (Dec. 24, 2003). HGP website at http://www.genome.gov/10000507. See also, Karen H. Rothenberg, Breast Cancer, The Genetic "Quick Fix," and the Jewish Community, 7 Health Matrix 97 (1997).

Gene Therapy

Much of the driving force for the mapping of the human genome and the enormous investment in genetic research is the promise of the development of drugs genetically tailored to individual persons ("pharmacogenetics" or "pharmacogenomics") and the development of "gene therapy," in which a vector delivers corrected genetic material. This promise is often viewed as a counterweight to the potential negative effects of the genetic revolution.

Success in gene therapy on a clinical level suffered two serious setbacks at the turn of this century. In 1999, Jesse Gelsinger died as a result of an experimental genetic intervention in which an adenovirus was used as a vector to deliver a gene to correct a liver disorder. The virus injected directly into his liver unexpectedly infiltrated several other organs and caused widespread inflammation which ultimately was fatal. After the death of the patient, the scientists injected the vector into mice and found the same reaction. A Valuable Lesson in Gene Therapy, Gene Therapy Weekly, Feb. 8, 2001. The case is discussed in more detail in Chapter 6.

In October 2002, it was discovered that one of five boys treated with experimental gene therapy for SCID (severe combined immunodeficiency, the "bubble boy" disease) had developed leukemia as a result of the therapy. Later, another boy developed the same disease. This occurred only six months after the researchers had reported in the New England Journal of Medicine that the replacement of a defective gene with a functional one had produced apparently healthy immune systems 30 months after the intervention. The authors at that time had stated that the therapy should be tested in a larger cohort of patients. Hacein–Bey–Abina et al., Sustained Correction of X–Linked Severe Combined Immunodeficiency by ex Vivo Gene Therapy, 346 NEJM 1185 (April 18, 2002). This episode with SCID, combined with Jesse Gelsinger's case, raised significant fundamental issues in the science of gene therapy relating to the vectors that are used to deliver the genetic material.

Few doubt, however, that gene therapy will eventually succeed and that pharmacogenomics is even closer. Of course, these developments also raise issues. For example, who will have access to these likely expensive therapies? What genetic traits require "fixing?" May individuals use genetic therapy to improve their physical or mental condition? Who would stop them?

II. LEGAL RESPONSES

"Coded Future Diary?" Or, "Genetic Exceptionalism?"

At least one question appears repeatedly in this chapter: Is there anything special about genetic information, as compared to other health information, which requires special treatment in law? Opinions on this question differ.

George Annas refers to human DNA as a "coded future diary" and argues that "the information contained in an individual's genome ... [provides] a basis not only for counseling, but also for stigmatization and discrimination." He argues that genetic information has "unique privacy implications" because the "genetic information is immutable ... and will also provide information about the individual's parents, siblings and children." In regard to DNA databases in particular, Annas cites the power of computer technology and the threat of "large, bureaucratic record-keeping systems." George J. Annas, Privacy Rules for DNA Databanks Protecting Coded Future Diaries, 270 JAMA 2346 (1993). In contrast, Larry Gostin and James Hodge take exception to "genetic exceptionalism" and argue that special rules for genetic information "are often unfair because they treat people facing the same social risks differently based on the biological cause of their otherwise identical health conditions." Lawrence O. Gostin and James G. Hodge, Jr., Genetic Privacy and the Law: An End to Genetic Exceptionalism, 40 Jurimetrics 21 (1999), part of a Symposium issue on Respecting Genetic Privacy. Mark Rothstein observes that, even if genetic information were unique, it is simply impossible to develop a "working definition" for genetic information as any definition is either too narrow or too broad. Mark A. Rothstein, Why Treating Genetic Information Separately is a Bad Idea, 4 Tex. Rev. of L. and Politics 33 (1999). Still, Dr. Francis Collins, director of the National Human Genome Research Institute at the National Institutes of Health, asked Congress to take action to prevent discrimination based on the information that genomics will produce. Genetic Discrimination: Leaders in Genetic Code Discoveries Underscore Need for Anti–Discrimination Law, BNA Health Law Reporter, July 13, 2000. See also, Lori Andrews, A Conceptual Framework for Genetic Policy: Comparing the Medical, Public Health, and Fundamental Rights Models, 79 Wash. U.L.Q. 221 (2001).

The legal and policy issues generated by the potential of the Human Genome Project range from privacy and discrimination through criminal justice through patents and so on. This chapter focuses on three issues that have been the subject of substantial legal activity:

* Privacy and Confidentiality of Genetic Information

* Discrimination Based on Genetic Traits

* Ownership of Genetic Information and Resultant Products

The state statutes below will be used as reference materials for several of the subsections that follow.

CODE OF GEORGIA: GENETIC TESTING

33–54–2 Definitions.

As used in this chapter, the term:

(1) "Genetic testing" means laboratory tests of human DNA or chromosomes for the purpose of identifying the presence or absence of inherited alterations in genetic material or genes which are associated with a disease or illness that is asymptomatic at the time of testing and that arises solely as a result of such abnormality in genes or genetic material. For purposes of this chapter, genetic testing shall not include routine physical measurements; chemical, blood, and urine analysis; tests for abuse of drugs; and tests for the presence of the human immunodeficiency virus.

(2) "Insurer" means an insurer, a fraternal benefit society, a nonprofit medical service corporation, a health care corporation, a health maintenance corporation, or a self-insured health plan not subject to the exclusive jurisdiction of the Employee Retirement Income Security Act of 1974, 29 U.S.C. Section 1001, et seq.

33–54–3 Purpose of testing; consent required; confidential and privileged information.

(a) Except as otherwise provided in this chapter, genetic testing may only be conducted to obtain information for therapeutic or diagnostic purposes. Genetic testing may not be conducted without the prior written consent of the person to be tested.

(b) Information derived from genetic testing shall be confidential and privileged and may be released only to the individual tested and to persons specifically authorized by such individual to receive the information. Any insurer that possesses information derived from genetic testing may not release the information to any third party without the explicit written consent of the individual tested. Information derived from genetic testing may not be sought by any insurer.

33–54–4 Prohibited use of information.

Any insurer that receives information derived from genetic testing may not use the information for any nontherapeutic purpose.

33–54–6 Use of information for scientific research purposes authorized.

Notwithstanding the provisions of Code Sections 33–54–3 and 33–54–4, any research facility may conduct genetic testing and may use the information derived from genetic testing for scientific research purposes so long as the identity of any individual tested is not disclosed to any third party, except that the individual's identity may be disclosed to the individual's physician with the consent of the individual.

33–54–7 Applicability of chapters.

This chapter shall not apply to a life insurance policy, disability income policy, accidental death or dismemberment policy, medicare supplement policy, long-term care insurance policy, credit insurance policy, specified disease policy, hospital indemnity policy, blanket accident and sickness policy, franchise policy issued on an individual basis to members of an association, limited accident policy, health insurance policy written as a part of workers' compensation equivalent coverage, or other similar limited accident and sickness policy.

CALIFORNIA CIVIL CODE: CONFIDENTIALITY OF MEDICAL INFORMATION

56.17. Genetic test results; unlawful disclosure; written authorization; penalties.

(a) This section shall apply to the disclosure of genetic test results contained in an applicant or enrollee's medical records by a health care service plan.

[Sections (b), (c), and (d) provide for civil fines and payment of damages for the disclosure of "results of a test for a genetic characteristic to any third party, in a manner that identifies or provides identifying characteristics, of the person to whom the test results apply, except pursuant to a written authorization, as described in subdivision (g)."]

(e) In addition to the penalties listed [above], any person who commits any act described [above] shall be liable to the subject for any actual damages, including damages for economic, bodily or emotional harm which is proximately caused by the act.

* * *

(i) For purposes of this section, "genetic characteristic" has the same meaning as that set forth in subdivision (d) of Section 1374.7 of the Health and Safety Code.

CALIFORNIA HEALTH AND SAFETY CODE: INSURANCE

1374.7. Genetic disability characteristics; discrimination in enrollment terms, conditions, benefits, rates or commissions.

(a) No [health care service or self-insured employee welfare] plan shall refuse to enroll any person or accept any person as a subscriber after appropriate application on the basis of a person's genetic characteristics that may, under some circumstances, be associated with disability in that person or that person's offspring. No plan shall require a higher rate or charge, or offer or provide different terms, conditions, or benefits, on the basis of a person's genetic characteristics that may, under some circumstances, be associated with disability in that person or that person's offspring.

(b) No plan shall seek information about a person's genetic characteristics for any nontherapeutic purpose.

* * *

(d) "Genetic characteristics" as used in this section means any of the following:

(1) Any scientifically or medically identifiable gene or chromosome, or combination or alteration thereof, that is known to be a cause of a disease or disorder in a person or his or her offspring, or that is determined to be associated with a statistically increased risk of development of a disease or disorder, and that is presently not associated with any symptoms of any disease or disorder.

(2) Inherited characteristics that may derive from the individual or family member, that are known to be a cause of a disease or disorder in a person or his or her offspring, or that are determined to be associated with a

statistically increased risk of development of a disease or disorder, and that are presently not associated with any symptoms of any disease or disorder.

CALIFORNIA INSURANCE CODE

10148. Test for presence of genetic characteristic for determination of insurability.

No [life or disability insurance plan] shall require a test for the presence of a genetic characteristic for the purpose of determining insurability other than for those policies that are contingent on review or testing for other diseases or medical conditions. In those cases, the test shall be done in accordance with the informed consent and privacy protection provisions [of California law].

A. PRIVACY AND CONFIDENTIALITY OF GENETIC INFORMA- TION

SAFER v. PACK

Superior Court of New Jersey, Appellate Division, 1996.
291 N.J.Super. 619, 677 A.2d 1188.

KESTIN, J.A.D.

Plaintiffs appeal from the trial court's order dismissing their complaint and denying their cross-motion for partial summary judgment as to liability only. We reverse that portion of the order dismissing the complaint and affirm the denial of plaintiffs' motion.

Donna Safer's claim arises from the patient-physician relationship in the 1950s and 1960s between her father, Robert Batkin, a resident of New Jersey, and Dr. George T. Pack, also a resident of New Jersey, who practiced medicine and surgery in New York City and treated Mr. Batkin there. It is alleged that Dr. Pack specialized in the treatment and removal of cancerous tumors and growths.

In November 1956, Mr. Batkin was admitted to the hospital with a pre-operative diagnosis of retroperitoneal cancer. A week later, Dr. Pack performed a total colectomy and an ileosigmoidectomy for multiple polyposis of the colon with malignant degeneration in one area. The discharge summary noted the finding in a pathology report of the existence of adenocarcinoma developing in an intestinal polyp, and diffuse intestinal polyposis "from one end of the colon to the other." Dr. Pack continued to treat Mr. Batkin postoperatively.

In October 1961, Mr. Batkin was again hospitalized. Dr. Pack performed an ileoabdominal perineal resection with an ileostomy. The discharge summary reported pathology findings of "ulcerative adenocarcinoma of colon Grade II with metastases to Levels II and III" and "adenomatous polyps." Dr. Pack again continued to treat Mr. Batkin postoperatively. He also developed a physician-patient relationship with Mrs. Batkin relative to the diagnosis and treatment of a vaginal ulcer.

In December 1963, Mr. Batkin was hospitalized once again at Dr. Pack's direction. The carcinoma of the colon had metastasized to the liver with secondary jaundice and probable retroperitoneal disease causing pressure on the sciatic nerve plexus. After some treatment, Mr. Batkin died on January 3,

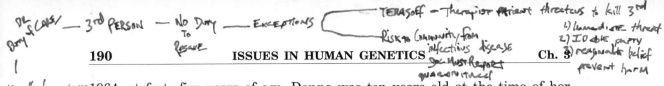

1964, at forty-five years of age. Donna was ten years old at the time of her father's death. Her sister was seventeen.

In February 1990, Donna Safer, then thirty-six years of age and newly married, residing in Connecticut, began to experience lower abdominal pain. Examinations and tests revealed a cancerous blockage of the colon and multiple polyposis. In March, Ms. Safer underwent a total abdominal colectomy with ileorectal anastomosis. A primary carcinoma in the sigmoid colon was found to extend through the serosa of the bowel and multiple polyps were seen throughout the entire bowel. Because of the detection of additional metastatic adenocarcinoma and carcinoma, plaintiff's left ovary was also removed. Between April 1990 and mid–1991, Ms. Safer underwent chemotherapy treatment.

In September 1991, plaintiffs obtained Robert Batkin's medical records, from which they learned that he had suffered from polyposis. Their complaint was filed in March 1992, alleging a violation of duty (professional negligence) on the part of Dr. Pack in his failure to warn of the risk to Donna Safer's health.

Plaintiffs contend that multiple polyposis is a hereditary condition that, if undiscovered and untreated, invariably leads to metastatic colorectal cancer. They contend, further, that the hereditary nature of the disease was known at the time Dr. Pack was treating Mr. Batkin and that the physician was required, by medical standards then prevailing, to warn those at risk so that they might have the benefits of early examination, monitoring, detection and treatment, that would provide opportunity to avoid the most baneful consequences of the condition.

The summary judgment proceeding in the trial court was based upon a scanty record, largely comprised of hospital records. Dr. Pack himself had died in 1969; none of his individual records were before the court. The reports of the parties' medical experts and a deposition of plaintiffs' expert were submitted. Ida Batkin, Donna Safer's mother, had also given a deposition in which she testified, among other details, that neither her husband nor Dr. Pack had ever told her that Mr. Batkin suffered from cancer; and that, throughout the courses of surgery and treatment, Dr. Pack advised her that he was treating a "blockage" or an unspecified "infection". On the one or two occasions when Mrs. Batkin inquired of Dr. Pack whether the "infection" would affect her children, she was told not to worry.

In dismissing, the trial court held that a physician had no "legal duty to warn a child of a patient of a genetic risk.[ ]" In the absence of any evidence whether Dr. Pack had warned Mr. Batkin to provide information concerning his disease for the benefit of his children, the motion judge "assume[d] that Dr. Pack did not tell Robert Batkin of the genetic disease."

The motion judge's reasoning proceeded from the following legal premise: "[i]n order for a doctor to have a duty to warn, there must be a patient/physician relationship or circumstances requiring the protection of the public health or the community [at] large." Finding no physician-patient relationship between Dr. Pack and his patient's daughter Donna, the court then held genetically transmissible diseases to differ from contagious or infectious diseases or threats of harm in respect of the duty to warn, because "the harm is already present within the non-patient child, as opposed to being introduced, by a patient who was not warned to stay away. The patient is taking no action in which to cause the child harm."

* * *

The Florida Supreme Court has since dealt with the issue [in] Pate v. Threlkel, 661 So.2d 278 (1995). Because the case had initially been decided on defendants' motions to dismiss the complaint for failure to state a cause of action, the Supreme Court was required to accept as true the [plaintiffs'] allegations that pursuant to the prevailing standard of care, the health care providers were under a duty to warn [the patient] of the importance of testing her children for [the genetically transmissible] carcinoma.

The court held:

> * * * Our holding should not be read to require the physician to warn the patient's children of the disease. In most instances the physician is prohibited from disclosing the patient's medical condition to others except with the patient's permission. See § 455.241(2), Fla.Stat. (1989). Moreover, the patient ordinarily can be expected to pass on the warning. To require the physician to seek out and warn various members of the patient's family would often be difficult or impractical and would place too heavy a burden upon the physician. Thus, we emphasize that in any circumstances in which the physician has a duty to warn of a genetically transferable disease, that duty will be satisfied by warning the patient. [Pate v. Threlkel, supra, 661 So.2d at 282.]

Because the issue before us arose on a motion for summary judgment, we, too, are obliged to accept plaintiffs' proffer through their medical expert that the prevailing standard of care at the time Dr. Pack treated Mr. Batkin required the physician to warn of the known genetic threat. The legal standard of care, knowledge and skill is that which is "ordinarily possessed and exercised in similar situations by the average member of the profession practicing in the field." [ ] Whether the conduct of a practitioner in established circumstances at a particular time comported with prevailing standards of care is preeminently a question to be determined by the finder of fact, not an issue of law to be resolved by the court. [ ] Where, as here, a genuine issue of fact in this regard is presented, the matter is not amenable to resolution on summary judgment. [ ]

Whether a legal duty exists is, however, a matter of law. [ ] We see no impediment, legal or otherwise, to recognizing a physician's duty to warn those known to be at risk of avoidable harm from a genetically transmissible condition. In terms of foreseeability especially, there is no essential difference between the type of genetic threat at issue here and the menace of infection, contagion or a threat of physical harm. [ ] The individual or group at risk is easily identified, and substantial future harm may be averted or minimized by a timely and effective warning.

The motion judge's view of this case as one involving an unavoidable genetic condition gave too little significance to the proffered expert view that early monitoring of those at risk can effectively avert some of the more serious consequences a person with multiple polyposis might otherwise experience. We cannot conclude either, as the trial court did, that Dr. Pack breached no duty because avoidable harm to Donna was not foreseeable, i.e., "that Dr. Pack's conduct did not create a 'foreseeable zone of risk.'" Such a determination would ignore the presumed state of medical knowledge at the time. * * *

Although an overly broad and general application of the physician's duty to warn might lead to confusion, conflict or unfairness in many types of circumstances, we are confident that the duty to warn of avertible risk from genetic causes, by definition a matter of familial concern, is sufficiently narrow to serve the interests of justice. Further, it is appropriate, for reasons already expressed by our Supreme Court, [ ] that the duty be seen as owed not only to the patient himself but that it also "extend[s] beyond the interests of a patient to members of the immediate family of the patient who may be adversely affected by a breach of that duty." [ ] We need not decide, in the present posture of this case, how, precisely, that duty is to be discharged, especially with respect to young children who may be at risk, except to require that reasonable steps be taken to assure that the information reaches those likely to be affected or is made available for their benefit. We are aware of no direct evidence that has been developed concerning the nature of the communications between physician and patient regarding Mr. Batkin's disease: what Dr. Pack did or did not disclose; the advice he gave to Mr. Batkin, if any, concerning genetic factors and what ought to have been done in respect of those at risk; and the conduct or expressed preferences of Mr. Batkin in response thereto. There may be enough from Mrs. Batkin's testimony and other evidence for inferences to be drawn, however.

We decline to hold as the Florida Supreme Court did in Pate v. Threlkel, [ ] that, in all circumstances, the duty to warn will be satisfied by informing the patient. It may be necessary, at some stage, to resolve a conflict between the physician's broader duty to warn and his fidelity to an expressed preference of the patient that nothing be said to family members about the details of the disease. We cannot know presently, however, whether there is any likelihood that such a conflict may be shown to have existed in this matter or, if it did, what its qualities might have been. As the matter is currently constituted, it is as likely as not that no such conflict will be shown to have existed and that the only evidence on the issue will be Mrs. Batkin's testimony, including that she received no information, despite specific inquiry, that her children were at risk. We note, in addition, the possible existence of some offsetting evidence that Donna was rectally examined as a young child, suggesting that the risk to her had been disclosed.

This case implicates serious and conflicting medical, social and legal policies, many aptly identified in Sonia M. Suter, Whose Genes Are These Anyway? Familial Conflicts Over Access to Genetic Information, 91 Mich. L.Rev. 1854 (1993) and in other sources. * * * Some such policy considerations may need to be addressed in ultimately resolving this case. For example, if evidence is produced that will permit the jury to find that Dr. Pack received instructions from his patient not to disclose details of the illness or the fact of genetic risk, the court will be required to determine whether, as a matter of law, there are or ought to be any limits on physician-patient confidentiality, especially after the patient's death where a risk of harm survives the patient, as in the case of genetic consequences. See generally Janet A. Kobrin, Confidentiality of Genetic Information, 30 UCLA L.Rev. 1283 (1983).

Issues of fact remain to be resolved, as well. What was the extent of Donna's risk, for instance? We are led to understand from the experts' reports that the risk of multiple polyposis was significant and that, upon detection, an early full colectomy, i.e., an excision of her entire colon, may well have been the treatment of choice to avoid resultant cancer—including metastasis, the loss of other organs and the rigors of chemotherapy. Full factual development may, however, cast a different light on these issues of fact and others.

* * *

Because of the necessarily limited scope of our consideration, we have highlighted only a few of the potentially troublesome issues presented by this case. Such questions are best conceived and considered in the light of a fully developed record rather than in the abstract.

* * *

Notes and Questions

1. The Health Insurance Portability and Accountability Act (HIPAA) provides for federal protection of the privacy of medical records. These provisions are discussed extensively in Chapter 5. HIPAA privacy regulations, at 45 CFR § 160.203, establish minimum standards for protection of medical records and preempt any contrary state law unless that law fits within one or more exceptions which include:

(a) A determination is made by the Secretary . . . that the provision of State law: (1) Is necessary: (i) To prevent fraud and abuse related to the provision of or payment for health care; (ii) To ensure appropriate State regulation of insurance and health plans to the extent expressly authorized by statute or regulation; (iii) For State reporting on health care delivery or costs; or (iv) For purposes of serving a compelling need related to public health, safety, or welfare and, if a standard, requirement, or implementation specification under part 164 of this subchapter is at issue, if the Secretary determines that the intrusion into privacy is warranted when balanced against the need to be served. . . .

(b) The provision of State law relates to the privacy of individually identifiable health information and is more stringent than [the requirements of these regulations].

(c) The provision of State law . . . provides for the reporting of disease or injury, child abuse, birth, or death, or for the conduct of public health surveillance, investigation, or intervention.

At CFR § 164.512(j), the regulations provide:

Standard: Uses and disclosures to avert a serious threat to health or safety.

(1) Permitted disclosures. A covered entity may, consistent with applicable law and standards of ethical conduct, use or disclose protected health information, if the covered entity, in good faith, believes the use or disclosure:

(i)(A) Is necessary to prevent or lessen a serious and imminent threat to the health or safety of a person or the public; and

(B) Is to a person or persons reasonably able to prevent or lessen the threat, including the target of the threat. . . .

How would you advise a physician in New Jersey who is confronted with the duty created in *Safer* and the restrictions under HIPAA?

2. HIPAA does not provide any special protection for genetic information. What would justify treating all medical information the same? Treating genetic information differently? Does it depend on the degree of protection afforded medical information generally? See, Mark A. Rothstein (ed.), Genetic Secrets: Protecting Privacy and Confidentiality in the Genetic Era (1997); Jennifer Kulynych, Use and Disclosure of Health Information in Genetic Research: Weighing the Impact of The New Federal Medical Privacy Rule, 28 Am. J.L. Med. 309 (2002).

3. What is the scope of the duty in *Safer* as compared to *Pate*? Should physicians be prohibited from informing family members? Should they be required to do so? See, Ellen Wright Clayton, What Should the Law Say About Disclosure of Genetic Information to Relatives?, 1 J. of Health Care L. and Pol. 373 (1998), part of a Symposium on Testing and Telling?: Implications for Genetic Privacy, Family Disclosure and the Law.

4. Ms. Safer was a young child at the time of her father's death. Is it appropriate to inform a child of his or her genetic characteristics, especially those that might predict disease or an increased susceptibility to disease or developmental limitations or capacities? See Janet L. Dolgin, Choice, Tradition, and the New Genetics: The Fragmentation of the Ideology of Family, 32 Conn.L.Rev. 523 (2000); Diane E. Hoffmann and Eric A. Wufsberg, Testing Children for Genetic Predispositions: Is It in Their Best Interest?, 23 J. of L., Med. & Ethics 331 (1995).

5. Would the duty established in New Jersey extend to other situations or is it limited to situations in which there is avoidable physical harm? If a physician, in the course of testing parents and child for a genetically-based medical condition, discovers that the one who believes he is the father cannot possibly be so, should he or she tell the man? Must the doctor tell him? Should the doctor tell the mother? If the "child" is an adult who is making reproductive decisions himself or herself, does that child have a right to know?

Problem: All in the Family

Ibrahim Abdul Salaam decided to seek genetic testing to determine whether he was a carrier of the sickle cell trait when he and his wife, Sarai, who are both African–American, decided to have children. Several of his and Mrs. Salaam's relatives have been afflicted with sickle-cell disease. Mr. Salaam was assured by the testing physician that the testing was simple and painless, and that the results would be confidential. The genetic screen for sickle-cell trait came back positive—i.e., Mr. Salaam is a carrier of the recessive trait for sickle cell anemia.

While Mr. Salaam was discussing the results of the test with his physician, he mentioned that his sister was recently married, and that her husband knows that he is a carrier for sickle-cell trait. The physician suggested that she be told of her brother's test result because of the increased chance that she, too, could be a carrier. Mr. Salaam decided against telling his sister because he did not want others in his family to know about his carrier status. As he pointed out to his physician, he did not intend to tell even his wife because his family is Islamic and neither his wife nor his sister would ever consider amniocentesis or abortion; he was merely seeking some personal reassurance (which he did not get, of course) through his own test.

May the doctor inform Mr. Salaam's wife? Must he? May he inform Mr. Salaam's sister? Must he? If Mr. Salaam's sister were to give birth to a child with severe sickle cell disease two years from now, might the doctor be liable in damages?

B. DISCRIMINATION BASED ON GENETIC TRAITS

Just as we have language difficulties in describing genetic traits, conditions, anomalies, defects, we do not have an agreed upon term for decisions based on genetic information. Is it "genetic discrimination?" "Geneticism?" See, Susan Wolf, Beyond "Genetic Discrimination:" Toward the Broader Harm of Geneticism, 23 J.L. Med. & Ethics 345 (1995), coining the phrase. Or, is it "genetic exceptionalism?" See Sonia Suter, The Allure and Peril of Genetics Exceptionalism: Do We Need Special Genetics Legislation? 79 Wash. U.L.Q. 669 (2001); Lainie Friedman Ross, Genetic Exceptionalism v. Paradigm Shift: Lessons From HIV, 29 J.L. Med. & Ethics 141 (2001). Finally, from a legal perspective in particular, an important threshold question is what counts as "genetic information," as illustrated in the following section.

1. *Insurance*

Problem: Insurance Decisions

In each of the following cases, evaluate the insurer's decision under the Georgia and California statutes above. In each of the scenarios, consider whether the insurer could charge higher rates to the applicant compared to other enrollees.

a. Arlo has applied for health insurance. His father Woody died in his mid–50s from Huntington's Disease, a genetically-based disease which usually becomes symptomatic in the individual's 40's or 50's and which is invariably fatal. Based only on his father having had Huntington's, Arlo has a 50% chance of developing the disease, although a genetic test is available which would confirm whether Arlo will in fact develop the disease. Arlo is 39 and has not been tested for the gene because he does not want to know. The insurer knows of Arlo's family history from insurance claims filed by Arlo's father for care during his illness. The claims had been placed in the Medical Information Bureau by Woody's insurer, and as a member of the MIB, Arlo's insurer has access to these claims. May the insurer legally deny Arlo coverage due to his risk of Huntington's?

b. May the insurer deny coverage, but inform Arlo that it will reconsider if Arlo can produce evidence that he does not have the gene for Huntington's?

c. Assume that Arlo has decided to be tested, and that the test has revealed that he does not have the gene for Huntington's and so will not develop that disease. May Arlo have the advantage of that result, and may the insurer reverse an earlier decision to deny coverage?

d. If Arlo has been tested and the test has revealed that he does have the gene for Huntington's, how should he answer insurance application questions concerning whether he has any "known illness or disease" at the time of the application? How should he answer questions related to "known family history of diabetes, cancer, hyptertension, obesity, multiple sclerosis or other chronic illness?"

e. Judith's grandmother, mother and sister all died of breast cancer at an early age. At the time of their deaths, Judith was only a young teenager, but her aunt told her that she should make sure that she had very frequent physical examinations to catch the condition earlier than did her relatives. Although she followed her aunt's advice, Judith now has breast cancer herself, and her treatment for the cancer has disabled her. She has applied for payments under the partial and total disability insurance policy she purchased some years ago. The insurer has denied her claim relying on the following clause: "The policy does not cover disabilities caused by medical conditions for which medical advice, diagnosis, care, or treatment had been recommended or received prior to the purchase of the policy." Is the insurer's denial illegal under either state's statute?

Notes and Questions

1. Insurance practices in the United States generally base the price and availability of coverage on the health status of the insured individual or group. Why would genetics raise special issues? Or does it? Is a prohibition against denial of coverage based on genetic information unfair to persons with other medical conditions? Does the scope of the definition of genetic information matter?

2. The federal Health Insurance Portability and Accountability Act, discussed above, prohibits group health plans, narrowly defined, from basing eligibility on an individual's health status, including genetic information, and does not treat genetic conditions differently from other medical conditions. The Americans with Disabilities Act, discussed in Chapters 8, 9, and 12, also prohibits discrimination in insurance. There have been many projects looking specifically at the issue of genetics and insurance. One of the most prominent groups recommended that the entire structure of the health insurance system in the U.S. be changed rather than providing for special treatment for genetically related conditions. See, NIH–DOE Working Group on Ethical, Legal, and Social Implications of Human Genome Research, Genetic Information and Health Insurance: Report of the Task Force on Genetic Information and Insurance (NIH Pub. No. 93–3686, May 10, 1993). See also, John Jacobi, Genetic Discrimination in a Time of False Hopes, 30 Fla. St. U.L. Rev. 363 (2003).

3. Although fears of uninsurability have driven much of the concern over genetic discrimination, there is some evidence that insurers do not yet, and perhaps will not, use genetic information in health insurance decisions. See Mark A. Hall, Legal Rules and Industry Norms: The Impact of Laws Restricting Health Insurers' Use of Genetic Information, 40 Jurimetrics 93 (1999). But see, Governor Signs Legislation Barring Insurers From Using Genetic Tests, BNA Health Law Reporter, May 8, 1997, describing insurers' statements that they would refuse to issue long-term care and disability coverage in the state because of the new statute. Should health insurers be restricted on the use of genetic information while disability and long-term care insurers are not similarly restricted?

2. Employment

The Equal Employment Opportunity Commission, the federal agency charged with enforcement of the Americans with Disabilities Act as it applies to employment, considers asymptomatic genetic conditions as disabilities because persons with such traits may be "regarded as" having a disability. EEOC Compliance Manual § 902.8. The Manual uses the illustration of a genetic trait associated with susceptibility to colon cancer as an illustration. The EEOC's position may be questioned in light of the Supreme Court's series of cases narrowing the definition of disability under the ADA. See also, Laura F. Rothstein, Genetic Discrimination: Why Bragdon Does Not Ensure Protection, 3 J. Health Care L. and Pol. 330 (2000).

In 2002, Burlington Northern Santa Fe Railroad (BNSF) agreed to pay 36 workers up to $2.2 million in settlement of a claim brought by the EEOC on behalf of the employees under the ADA. This was the first action ever brought by the EEOC concerning employment-based genetic testing.

The company also agreed it will no longer use genetic tests in required medical examinations of current employees, will provide additional ADA training to its medical and claims staff, and will require senior management review of all significant medical policies and practices. In an earlier court order granting a preliminary injunction against the company, BNSF "admit[ed] that it requested certain employees who claimed that they had developed work-related carpal tunnel syndrome to submit to an evaluative 34–item medical examination conducted by outside health-care providers and that one item of that examination was a blood test for a genetic marker." The company denied that the testing violated the ADA, although the EEOC found that it did.

According to the EEOC's brief submitted in support of the preliminary injunction, employees were tested without their knowledge and had not been informed that blood tests would include genetic testing. The employees had received notification that the company required the employee to undergo medical examination, including laboratory testing, to prove whether the carpal tunnel syndrome was a work-related injury, but they had not been told that the genetic testing would be included. Presumably, the testing was done as a defense to potential employee claims that the syndrome was a compensable work-place injury.

The genetic testing came to light when an employee's spouse (who was a nurse) asked why blood tests were being performed to ascertain whether the carpal tunnel syndrome experienced by her husband was work-related. The EEOC's brief claims that the employee was told he would be terminated if he did not submit to the genetic test. In response to the EEOC's petition, BNSF agreed to the entry of the District Court's order that the company cease testing immediately and protect the medical information and physical samples already in its possession.

BNSF was testing for the presence of a rare genetic condition called Hereditary Neuropathy with liability to Pressure Palsies (HNPP). The company that performed the testing states in its testing protocol that carpal tunnel syndrome may be a manifestation of HNPP. (See website http://www.athena-diagnositcs.com) One estimate is that HNPP occurs in 2 to 5 of 100,000 individuals. Nelis E, et al., Estimation of the mutation frequencies in Charcot–Marie–Tooth disease type 1 and hereditary neuropathy with liability to pressure palsies: a European collaborative study. *Eur J. Hum. Genet.* 4:25–33 (1996), cited in http://geneclinics.org.

The claim that the testing itself violated the ADA relied on the Act's restrictions on testing current employees. An employer may test current employees only where the testing is job-related or a matter of business necessity. The EEOC has issued guidance that the standard requires that the employer have a reasonable belief that the employee's ability to perform the job will be impaired or that the employee poses a direct threat in the workplace. At least some of the BNSF employees had been evaluated as "work ready" and were working at the time of the testing.

In statements concerning the settlement, BNSF maintained that the testing did not violate the ADA. The president-CEO of BNSF said, "at no time did the company use, or intend to use, any genetic test to screen out asymptomatic employees. We are pleased with the commission's acknowledgment, that BNSF did not engage in genetic screening of asymptomatic employees for any employment action, which should correct any public misimpression about this matter."

For a sophisticated analysis of the Burlington Northern settlement, genetic testing and employment, see Anita Silvers and Michael Ashley Stein, An Equality Paradigm for Preventing Genetic Discrimination, 55 Vand. L. Rev. 1341 (2002). On employment issues generally, see Mark A. Rothstein, Genetic Discrimination in Employment, 29 Hous. L. Rev. 23 (1992). For an interesting and accessible discussion of the issues raised in workplace genetic testing, see Cynthia Nance, Paul Miller, and Mark Rothstein, Discrimination in Employment on the Basis of Genetics: Proceedings of the 2002 Annual Meeting, Association of American Law Schools, 6 Emp.Rights and Emp.Pol. J. 57 (2002). In that discussion, Mark Rothstein asks:

> "Is it that the genetic information is really not very accurate, that it's not predictive at all, and that employers will be unfairly making mistakes by excluding certain people from employment? ... The other possibility is that we're concerned about genetic discrimination because genetic information is, in fact, predictive, but nevertheless we still shouldn't allow employers to use genetic information because it violates some public policy."

Does framing the issue in this way make a difference in your analysis of the following? See also Condon McGlothlen, Genetic testing: the solution to ergonomics claims?, CTD News, Aug. 1, 2002 (2002 WL 16418453). See also, Colin Diver and Jane Cohen, Genophobia: What Is Wrong With Genetic Discrimination? 149 U. Pa. L. Rev. 1439 (2001); Henry Greely, Genotype Discrimination: The Complex Case for Some Legislative Protection, 149 U. Pa. L. Rev. 1483 (2001).

Problem: Preventing Harms?

Assume that an employer-client of yours has asked for your advice on whether they should contract with MediTest, Inc., which offers genetic screening services to employers. MediTest's portfolio offers the following services:

DNA testing to show that heart attack is associated with a particular genetic trait, which the employer would want to use to contest worker's compensation claims or to assign susceptible employees to less strenuous and less risky work.

Analysis of medical history of employees who are filing for worker's compensation claims to ascertain whether the medical condition is one that has occurred before or one for which the employee has a family history.

If you were a state legislator, would you support legislation to make either one of these services illegal? Would the employer's use of these services be illegal under the Missouri statute below?

MISSOURI STATUTES TITLE XXIV.
BUSINESS AND FINANCIAL INSTITUTIONS

375.1306. Genetic information or test results, discrimination—penalty

1. An employer shall not use any genetic information or genetic test results of an employee or prospective employee to distinguish between, discriminate

against, or restrict any right or benefit otherwise due or available to such employee or prospective employee. The requirements of this section shall not prohibit:

(1) Underwriting in connection with individual or group life, disability income or long-term care insurance;

(2) Any action required or permissible by law or regulation;

(3) Action taken with the written permission of an employee or prospective employee or such person's authorized representative; or

(4) The use of genetic information when such information is directly related to a person's ability to perform assigned job responsibilities.

2. Any person who violates the provisions of this section shall be fined not more than five hundred dollars for each violation of this section.

"Genetic information" is defined as "the results of a genetic test [not including] family history, the results of routine physical measurements, or the results of chemical, blood, urine analysis, or the results of tests for drugs or the presence of [HIV], or from the results of any other tests commonly accepted in clinical practice at the time." VAMS 375.1300(3).

C. OWNERSHIP OF GENETIC INFORMATION AND RESULTANT PRODUCTS

The potential for gaining new knowledge and developing new products, such as diagnostic tests and drugs, using techniques developed by the Human Genome Project has increased the value of stored human tissue and blood dramatically. This has drawn attention to the use of stored tissue in medical research. One typical scenario is that the tissue was collected and stored some years ago for a purpose other than the specific research project now contemplated and that the original source/donor of the tissue may or may not be identifiable. The other common situation is that the tissue is collected specifically for research purposes that may or may not be known at the time of the collection.

One thing is certain: DNA depositories or DNA databases are commercial gold mines. Tissue once thought to be a storage or disposal problem now is viewed as a rich vein of raw material. As with all such finds, ownership of genetic material and the resultant products is at issue.

GREENBERG v. MIAMI CHILDREN'S HOSPITAL RESEARCH INSTITUTE

United States District Court, S.D. Florida, 2003.
264 F.Supp.2d 1064.

MORENO, District Judge.

[Ed. Note: "Canavan disease is a relatively rare, but always fatal, inherited, degenerative brain disorder that primarily affects children of eastern and central European Jewish (Ashkenazi) descent.... [T]here is no cure for the disease, which usually becomes apparent when the infant is three to nine months old.... Most children do not live past age 10." http://www.canavan-foundation.org.]

* * *

The Complaint alleges a tale of a successful research collaboration gone sour. In 1987, Canavan disease still remained a mystery—there was no way to identify who was a carrier of the disease, nor was there a way to identify a fetus with Canavan disease. Plaintiff Greenberg approached Dr. Matalon, a research physician who was then affiliated with the University of Illinois at Chicago for assistance. Greenberg requested Matalon's involvement in discovering the genes that were ostensibly responsible for this fatal disease, so that tests could be administered to determine carriers and allow for prenatal testing for the disease.

At the outset of the collaboration, Greenberg and the Chicago Chapter of the National Tay–Sachs and Allied Disease Association, Inc. ("NTSAD") located other Canavan families and convinced them to provide tissue (such as blood, urine, and autopsy samples), financial support, and aid in identifying the location of Canavan families internationally. The other individual Plaintiffs began supplying Matalon with the same types of information and samples beginning in the late 1980s. Greenberg and NTSAD also created a confidential database and compilation—the Canavan registry—with epidemiological, medical and other information about the families.

Defendant Matalon became associated in 1990 with Defendants Miami Children's Hospital Research Institute, Inc. and Variety Children's Hospital d/b/a Miami Children's Hospital. Defendant Matalon continued his relationship with the Plaintiffs after his move, accepting more tissue and blood samples as well as financial support.

The individual Plaintiffs allege that they provided Matalon with these samples and confidential information "with the understanding and expectations that such samples and information would be used for the specific purpose of researching Canavan disease and identifying mutations in the Canavan disease which could lead to carrier detection within their families and benefit the population at large." Plaintiffs further allege that it was their "understanding that any carrier and prenatal testing developed in connection with the research for which they were providing essential support would be provided on an affordable and accessible basis, and that Matalon's research would remain in the public domain to promote the discovery of more effective prevention techniques and treatments and, eventually, to effectuate a cure for Canavan disease." This understanding stemmed from their "experience in community testing for Tay–Sachs disease, another deadly genetic disease that occurs most frequently in families of Ashkenazi Jewish descent."

There was a breakthrough in the research in 1993. Using Plaintiffs' blood and tissue samples, familial pedigree information, contacts, and financial support, Matalon and his research team successfully isolated the gene responsible for Canavan disease. After this key advancement, Plaintiffs allege that they continued to provide Matalon with more tissue and blood in order to learn more about the disease and its precursor gene.

In September 1994, unbeknownst to Plaintiffs, a patent application was submitted for the genetic sequence that Defendants had identified. This application was granted in October 1997, and Dr. Matalon was listed as an inventor on the gene patent and related applications for the Canavan disease. Through patenting, Defendants acquired the ability to restrict any activity related to the Canavan disease gene, including without limitation: carrier and prenatal testing, gene therapy and other treatments for Canavan disease and research involving the gene and its mutations.

Although the Patent was issued in October 1997, Plaintiffs allege that they did not learn of it until November 1998, when MCH revealed their intention to limit Canavan disease testing through a campaign of restrictive licensing of the Patent. Specifically, on November 12, 1998, Plaintiffs allege that Defendants MCH and MCHRI began to "threaten" the centers that offered Canavan testing with possible enforcement actions regarding the recently-issued patent. Defendant MCH also began restricting public accessibility through negotiating exclusive licensing agreements and charging royalty fees.

Plaintiffs allege that at no time were they informed that Defendants intended to seek a patent on the research. Nor were they told of Defendants' intentions to commercialize the fruits of the research and to restrict access to Canavan disease testing.

Based on these facts, Plaintiffs filed a six-count complaint on October 30, 2000, against Defendants asserting the following causes of action: (1) lack of informed consent; (2) breach of fiduciary duty; (3) unjust enrichment; (4) fraudulent concealment; (5) conversion; and (6) misappropriation of trade secrets. Plaintiffs generally seek a permanent injunction restraining Defendants from enforcing their patent rights, damages in the form of all royalties Defendants have received on the Patent as well as all financial contributions Plaintiffs made to benefit Defendants' research. Plaintiffs allege that Defendants have earned significant royalties from Canavan disease testing in excess of $75,000 through enforcement of their gene patent, and that Dr. Matalon has personally profited by receiving a recent substantial federal grant to undertake further research on the gene patent.

[The court rejects plaintiffs' claims of lack of informed consent, breach of fiduciary duty, fraudulent concealment, and misappropriation of trade secrets.]

* * *

Unjust Enrichment

* * * Plaintiffs allege that MCH is being unjustly enriched by collecting license fees under the Patent. Under Florida law, the elements of a claim for unjust enrichment are (1) the plaintiff conferred a benefit on the defendant, who had knowledge of the benefit; (2) the defendant voluntarily accepted and retained the benefit; and (3) under the circumstances it would be inequitable for the defendant to retain the benefit without paying for it. [ ] The Court finds that Plaintiffs have sufficiently alleged the elements of a claim for unjust enrichment to survive Defendants' motion to dismiss.

While the parties do not contest that Plaintiffs have conferred a benefit to Defendants, including, among other things, blood and tissue samples and soliciting financial contributions, Defendants contend that Plaintiffs have not suffered any detriment, and note that no Plaintiff has been denied access to Canavan testing. Furthermore, the Plaintiffs received what they sought—the successful isolation of the Canavan gene and the development of a screening test. Plaintiffs argue, however, that when Defendants applied the benefits for unauthorized purposes, they suffered a detriment. Had Plaintiffs known that

Defendants intended to commercialize their genetic material through patenting and restrictive licensing, Plaintiffs would not have provided these benefits to Defendants under those terms.

Naturally, Plaintiffs allege that the retention of benefits violates the fundamental principles of justice, equity, and good conscience. While Defendants claim that they have invested significant amounts of time and money in research, with no guarantee of success and are thus entitled to seek reimbursement, the same can be said of Plaintiffs. Moreover, Defendants' attempt to seek refuge in the endorsement of the U.S. Patent system, which gives an inventor rights to prosecute patents and negotiate licenses for their intellectual property fails, as obtaining a patent does not preclude the Defendants from being unjustly enriched. [ ] The Complaint has alleged more than just a donor-donee relationship for the purposes of an unjust enrichment claim. Rather, the facts paint a picture of a continuing research collaboration that involved Plaintiffs also investing time and significant resources in the race to isolate the Canavan gene. Therefore, given the facts as alleged, the Court finds that Plaintiffs have sufficiently pled the requisite elements of an unjust enrichment claim and the motion to dismiss for failure to state a claim is DENIED as to this count.

* * *

Conversion

The Plaintiffs allege * * * that they had a property interest in their body tissue and genetic information, and that they owned the Canavan registry in Illinois which contained contact information, pedigree information and family information for Canavan families worldwide. They claim that MCH and Matalon converted the names on the registry and the genetic information by utilizing them for the hospitals' "exclusive economic benefit." The Court disagrees and declines to find a property interest for the body tissue and genetic information voluntarily given to Defendants. These were donations to research without any contemporaneous expectations of return of the body tissue and genetic samples, and thus conversion does not lie as a cause of action.

* * *

First, Plaintiffs have no cognizable property interest in body tissue and genetic matter donated for research under a theory of conversion. This case is similar to *Moore v. Regents of the University of California,* where the Court declined to extend liability under a theory of conversion to misuse of a person's excised biological materials. [ ] The plaintiff in *Moore* alleged that he had retained a property right in excised bodily material used in research, and therefore retained some control over the results of that research. The California Supreme Court, however, disagreed and held that the use of the results of medical research inconsistent with the wishes of the donor was not conversion, because the donor had no property interest at stake after the donation was made. [ ] * * * The Court also recognized that the patented result of research is "both factually and legally distinct" from excised material used in the research. [ ]

Second, limits to the property rights that attach to body tissue have been recognized in Florida state courts. * * * The property right in blood and tissue samples also evaporates once the sample is voluntarily given to a third party.

Plaintiffs rely on *Pioneer Hi–Bred v. Holden Foundation,* 1987 WL 341211 (S.D.Iowa, Oct.30, 1987), *aff'd,* 35 F.3d 1226 (8th Cir.1994), for their assertion that genetic information itself can constitute property for the purposes of the tort of conversion. [ ] In that case, the Court held that a [corn seed seller's] property interest in the genetic message contained in a corn seed variety is property protected by the laws of conversion. [ ] Plaintiffs argue that giving permission for one purpose (gene discovery) does not mean they agreed to other uses (gene patenting and commercialization). Yet, the *Pioneer* court recognized that, "where information is gathered and arranged at some cost and sold as a commodity on the market, it is properly protected as property." [ ] This seemingly provides more support for property rights inherent in Defendants' research rather than the donations of Plaintiffs' DNA. Finally, Plaintiffs cite a litany of cases in other jurisdictions that have recognized that body tissue can be property in some circumstances. [ ] These cases, however, do not involve voluntary donations to medical research.

Additionally, the Florida statute on genetic testing is cited by Plaintiffs in support of their contention that persons who contribute body tissue for researchers to use in genetic analysis do not relinquish ownership of the results of the analysis. Fla. Stat. § 760.40 (2002). This statute, however, is inapplicable under a common law theory of conversion, because by its plain meaning, it only provides penalties for disclosure or lack of informed consent if a person is being genetically analyzed. [ ] Plaintiffs have not cited any case that interprets the statute as applying to an analogous factual situation, and this Court's investigation did not find any relevant case either. Moreover, even assuming, *arguendo,* that the statute does create a property right in genetic material donated for medical research purposes, it is unclear whether this confers a property right for conversion, a common law cause of action.

Finally, although the Complaint sets out that Plaintiff Greenberg owned the Canavan Registry, the facts alleged do not sufficiently allege the elements of a *prima facie* case of conversion, as the Plaintiffs have not alleged how the Defendants' use of the Registry in their research was an expressly unauthorized act. * * *

The Court finds that Florida statutory and common law do not provide a remedy for Plaintiffs' donations of body tissue and blood samples under a theory of conversion liability. Indeed, the Complaint does not allege that the Defendants used the genetic material for any purpose *but* medical research. Plaintiffs claim that the *fruits* of the research, namely the patented material, was commercialized. This is an important distinction and another step in the chain of attenuation that renders conversion liability inapplicable to the facts as alleged. If adopted, the expansive theory championed by Plaintiffs would cripple medical research as it would bestow a continuing right for donors to possess the results of any research conducted by the hospital. At the core, these were donations to research without any contemporaneous expectations of return. Consequently, the Plaintiffs have failed to state a claim upon which relief may be granted on this issue. Accordingly, this claim is DISMISSED.

* * *

Notes and Questions

1. The Florida statute on genetic testing cited by the court provides:

DNA analysis may be performed only with the informed consent of the person to be tested, and the results of such DNA analysis, whether held by a public or private entity, are the exclusive property of the person tested, are confidential, and may not be disclosed without the consent of the person tested.

The statute defines "DNA analysis" as "the medical and biological examination and analysis of a person to identify the presence and composition of genes in that person's body." Do you agree with the court that this statute is "inapplicable"? Would § 33–54–6 of the Georgia statute, *supra*, resolve the property claim in *Greenberg*? The court also held, in a portion not included here, that the statute did not require that the researcher secure the consent of the participants because "none of the individual plaintiffs alleged that they were personally tested, just that they donated their genetic material."

2. The primary purpose of patent law is to promote progress in science while encouraging inventors to disclose their inventions by securing their property rights in the invention through the award of a patent. A patent is issued by the U.S. Patent and Trademark Office (PTO) and grants its owner the right to exclude all others from making or practicing the invention for twenty years from the time of filing. The three statutory criteria for the award of a patent are: novelty, known utility, and non-obviousness.

The commercial development of large-scale applications of gene sequencing, function and diagnosis has presented a challenge in the application of the patent standards. Can a DNA sequence be novel? What utility does a sequence have? When is a gene not obvious?

In Diamond v. Chakrabarty, 447 U.S. 303, 100 S.Ct. 2204, 65 L.Ed.2d 144 (1980), the U.S. Supreme Court held that a "human-made, genetically engineered bacterium" was entitled to a patent, ushering in the age of biotechnology. The issue in *Chakrabarty* was whether an oil-eating bacterium was a "manufacture" or "composition of matter" (a combination of two or more substances), or was simply a natural object. Because the Court viewed the bacteria as having "markedly different characteristics from any found in nature and ... potential for significant utility," it concluded that a patent should issue. Since 1980, the scope of patentability for genetic material has steadily expanded to include gene sequences, and at one point even gene fragments. While establishing the patentability of the products of early stages in genetic research was important in stimulating investment in such research, it has been criticized as thwarting research as well by excluding competing researchers from developing the full potential of the patented genetic material.

Novelty can be established for partial and complete gene sequences because isolation and purification of DNA allows for uses that are not possible when the DNA is in its natural state. In order to meet the standard for utility, the patent application must prove that the invention has immediate and practical utility or real-world value. This is a highly individualized inquiry, decided on a case-by-case basis. This requirement raised an issue in genomics especially in the early stages, when applicants applied for patents on gene sequences before a specific use was known. The PTO has become more conservative in applying the utility standard. The final standard of non-obviousness raises issues where the patent applicant claims DNA sequences that have already been identified and disclosed.

3. The owner of a patent on genetic material may exploit the commercial value of that material in a number of ways. For example, in *Greenberg*, the defendants licensed the use of the isolated gene to entities that developed a genetic test for Canavan Disease. The licensees pay the patent holder royalty fees. Alternatively, Dr. Matalon and Miami Children's could have established their own company to develop and produce the genetic test. Michelle Henry, et al., A Pilot Survey on The Licensing of DNA Inventions, 31 J. L. Med. & Ethics 442 (2003). The plaintiffs in *Greenberg* stated that they believed that the research would "remain in the public domain to promote the discovery of more effective prevention techniques and treatments." Does a patent awarded to the researcher who isolated the gene discourage or encourage research and product development? Do property rights in genetic material encourage development or discourage new learning? Does your answer depend on who holds the property right—the researcher or the individual who is the "source" of the raw material?

4. *Greenberg* involves a genetic disorder that disproportionately affects a certain population. Does the fact that genetics tends to be population-based raise issues regarding the use of genetic screens? One of the earliest public health genetic screening programs was for sickle cell, a genetic condition that occurs most frequently in African–Americans. One scholar has noted:

> In the 1970s, large scale screening [for sickle cell] was undertaken with the goal of changing African American mating behavior. Unfortunately, the initiative promoted confusion regarding the difference between carriers and those with the disease. This confusion resulted in widespread discrimination against African Americans. Some states passed legislation requiring all African American children entering school to be screened for the sickle-cell trait, even though there was no treatment or cure for the sickle-cell disease. Some states required prisoners to be tested, even though there would be no opportunity for them to pass on the trait. Job and insurance discrimination were both real and attempted. The military considered banning all African Americans from the armed services. African American airline stewardesses were fired. Insurance rates went up for carriers. Some companies refused to insure carriers. During that period, many African Americans came to believe that the sickle-cell screening initiative was merely a disguised genocide attempt, since often the only advice given to African Americans with the trait was, "Don't have kids." Vernellia R. Randall, Trusting the Health Care System Ain't Always Easy! An African American Perspective on Bioethics, 15 St. Louis U. Public L. Rev. 191 (1996).

What criteria should a state use in deciding whether or not to test newborns for genetic traits? Should consent always be required, or are there circumstances where the state should presume consent or forgo consent entirely?

5. *Greenberg* involved several questions relating to the conduct of research. These are treated in Chapter 6.

Note on Government–Owned Biobanks and Joint Ventures for Commercial Development

Iceland has established a national database covering the entire population of the country and linking genetic material to medical records available within its health care system. The goals of the database include medical research and improvement of the health care system. The government has contracted with deCode, a private corporation, to organize existing data and has given the corporation rights to develop commercial products using the database. A central purpose of the project is to diversify Iceland's "cod economy," and the agreement explicitly anticipated commercial development of the country's DNA database.

Jamaica Potts describes the building blocks of the database: the homogeneity of Iceland's population as a result of a series of natural disasters that decimated and isolated the population for the past millennium; the nation's cultural commitment to excellent genealogy, which provides accurate family trees; and the presence of comprehensive health records on individuals. In 1998, the Icelandic parliament enacted legislation providing that health records are not owned by patients, health care providers, or companies. This provided the legal basis for the consolidation of these health records into a national database.

The project uses "presumed consent" with an opt-out option rather than individual consent for access to medical records and tissue samples. The use of presumed consent was approved by legislation and supported by a poll indicating that 75% of Icelanders supported the statute, and of those who had an opinion on the act, 90% supported it. Jeffrey R. Gulcher and Kari Stefansson, The Icelandic Healthcare Database and Informed Consent, 342 N.E.J.M. 1827 (June 15, 2000).

Nevertheless, the development of the national health database has been controversial. Potts reports that ethicists in that country threatened litigation, and approximately one-third of Icelandic physicians are withholding medical records on patients. The Icelandic Medical Association has been opposed to the creation of the national health database, but finally reached a compromise with deCode by establishing a set of principles and mechanisms to govern the project. As part of this compromise, the "opt out" process was strengthened, and 7% of Iceland's population of just over 750,000 have opted out of the project. In part because of the degree of opposition, the health records database is not complete.

Professor Potts provides a detailed analysis of the agreement between the Icelandic government and deCode, the private joint venturer. The company pays an annual fee of approximately $700,000 for the license, which expires after 12 years; bears all of the expenses of developing and maintaining the health records database; pays for the expenses of the government oversight mechanism; and pays the government 6% of pretax profits of any product developed as a result of the Icelandic information, although the total of fees is capped at $1.4 million. All of the database work must be done in Iceland itself, and the database is "tethered" to Iceland for purposes of control, oversight, and development. Finally, the database reverts to the government when the lease expires. Roche, the pharmaceutical firm, has entered into a joint venture with deCode, under which medications developed through the project will be provided to Iceland without charge. Jamaica Potts, At Least Give the Natives Glass Beads: An Examination of the Bargain Made Between Iceland and deCode Genetics with Implications for Global Prospecting, 7 Va. J. Law & Tech. 8 (2002). See also, Ashok Pinto, (Note) Corporate Genomics: DeCode's Efforts at Disease Mapping in Iceland for Advancement of Science and Profits, 2002 U. Ill. J. L. Tech. & Pol'y. 467 (2002); David Winickoff, Governing Population Genomics: Law, Bioethics, and Biopolitics in Three Case Studies, 43 Jurimetrics J. 187 (2003). A particular concern arises when the DNA material is collected from marginalized communities or developing nations, which is sometimes called "bioprospecting" or "bioimperialism." See, e.g., Symposium on Legal and Ethical Issues in Genetic Research on Indigenous Populations, 42 Jurimetrics J. (2002).

A similar DNA/medical history databank is being developed in Britain. Security Plan for U.K. Medical Database Fails to Satisfy Genetic Privacy Watchdog, 12 Health Law Reporter 1510 (Oct. 2, 2003). Howard University also has established the Genomic Research in the African Diaspora Biobank, in a joint venture with First Genetic Trust, to study genetically-related diseases affecting African Americans. Healy, The Race Factor, L.A. Time, 9/8/2003.

Not all DNA depositories or databases are established for commercial development. Some are maintained for forensic purposes. See, e.g., Mayfield v. Dalton, 109 F.3d 1423 (9th Cir. 1997), concerning the development of a DNA database of all military personnel. The Department of Defense claimed that its database would be used only for identification of remains. Should the Department of Defense be prohibited from using the stored DNA samples to identify genetic sensitivities to particular environmental factors among those veterans who have complained of the post-Gulf War syndrome as compared to veterans who have reported no symptoms? Should a court order the military to undergo the expense and effort to collect DNA samples or secure consent for this purpose when they already have samples in storage, or should a court allow the research on susceptibility to chemical agents because it will benefit soldiers in the future? Once a biobank is established, is one use just the same as any other?

Almost all of the states have mandated newborn screening for genetic or other medical conditions. The states usually have stored these blood samples for many years. A specially appointed state panel in Michigan considered what the state should do with the 2 million blood (DNA) samples in its possession. The panel recommended that the state retain the samples indefinitely because of their value to future public health screenings, medical research, and forensic identification. State Should Keep Blood Samples as Research, Police Resource, Panel Suggests, 8 Health Law Reporter 244 (Feb. 11, 1999). For commentary on use of DNA databases by law enforcement, see Paul E. Tracy and Vincent Morgan, Big Brother and His Science Kit: DNA Databases for 21st Century Crime Control?, 90 J. of Crim. L. and Criminology 635 (2000); Michelle Hibbert, DNA Databanks: Law Enforcement's Greatest Surveillance Tool?, 34 Wake Forest L. Rev. 767 (1999); Davins Bressler, Criminal DNA Databank Statutes and Medical Research, 43 Jurimetrics J. 51 (2002); Mark A. Rothstein, The Role of IRBs in Research Involving Commercial Biobanks, 30 J.L. Med. & Ethics 105 (2002).

Problem: Creating the Treasure Trove

The Icelandic experience has direct application in the United States. On January 21, 2003, the Governor of Utah announced a new joint venture called GenData—a not-for-profit corporation formed by the state, the University of Utah and the Huntsman Cancer Foundation.

The project combines databases now held by the three partners and creates a database that will form the foundation for medical research. The joint public-private project also will allow researchers to link to state databases such as the state's cancer registry. The Governor said that the project is enriched in Utah because of the wealth of genealogical information maintained in that state.

The database at the University was begun approximately 20 years ago with the support and cooperation of members of the Church of Jesus Christ of Latter-day Saints, who provided family medical histories for the good of research. One news article reported that "few DNA codes" are currently included in the database, and instead it consists primarily of family medical histories, genealogy records, the state's vital statistics records, driver's licenses and so on. The executive director of the Huntsman Cancer Foundation said that "knowing the genetic cause of disease is important, but also knowing the interaction of environment and other population factors could play a huge role in improved science."

The leaders of the project said the information is entirely confidential. In his State of the State address, the Governor asked the legislature to "build into law an impenetrable wall of privacy protection."

The Governor also stated that the project will attract venture capital and pharmaceutical and medical research organizations "from all over the world" to the state of Utah. The Governor declared that the project would create a "scientific treasure." Joe Bauman and Amy Joi Bryson, "Leavitt Announces Utah Genetics Project," Deseret News B03 (1/22/03); Troy Goodman, "State Invests in Database for Biotech," Salt Lake Trib. A1 (1/22/03).

Assume that you are a member of the Utah legislature, would you do anything during the next legislative session to respond to this development? Would you attach nondiscrimination provisions and privacy provisions, and, if so, what would be the scope of these prohibitions? Will you require consent from Utah citizens for inclusion in the database? Will you instead use presumed consent and allow individuals to opt out? How do you make sure that the state and its citizens reap the profits of the results of this effort? Who owns the information in the database? Any medical tissue that is used in the project? Any products that are developed as a result? If the government licensed access to the database, including samples of genetic material, to a commercial partner, would the government be taking property without due process?

Chapter 4

DEFINING DEATH

Problem: When Does Death Occur?

Alberto Arcturus was face down by the side of the road, apparently after being run down by a hit-and-run driver, when a passing motorist saw him and called the local emergency medical services. An ambulance with two paramedics arrived on the scene about fifteen minutes after the call, and they found that Mr. Arcturus was not breathing and that he had no pulse. They also discovered that a substantial portion of his head (including his forehead and forebrain) was crushed. One paramedic looked at the other and said, "He's dead; let's call the morgue." The second, less experienced paramedic insisted on trying to resuscitate Mr. Arcturus, as was required by the emergency medical services manual for paramedics. They placed him in the ambulance and administered cardiopulmonary resuscitation throughout the fifteen minute ride to the nearest hospital emergency room.

At the emergency room physicians confirmed that Mr. Arcturus did not breathe spontaneously and had no spontaneous cardiac activity. One doctor told the charge nurse that he was dead, and that "dead on arrival" should be marked on his chart. A young intern balked at this, however, because the hospital emergency room protocol required more before a brain injured patient could be declared dead. The physicians then administered drugs and used paddles that sent an electric current through Mr. Arcturus's chest in an effort to start his heart. After some time they managed to get a weak pulse, and they placed Mr. Arcturus on a ventilator and moved him to the intensive care unit. A neurology consult revealed that Mr. Arcturus's neocortex was completely and irreversibly destroyed—most of it was literally gone, left on the highway—although his brain stem remained intact. Another consult revealed that Mr. Arcturus had two healthy kidneys and a healthy liver, heart and pancreas, each of which could be transplanted to save the life of another patient in the hospital. With the help of a ventilator (necessary because of the head and chest injuries to the patient), Mr. Arcturus's body could continue functioning indefinitely. If the ventilator were to be removed, Mr. Arcturus's heart and lung function would cease in the next few minutes.

After considerable investigation, police have captured a person who, they believe, was the hit-and-run driver who ran into Mr. Arcturus. They wish to know whether to charge him with vehicular homicide (a felony), or something else (all other potential offenses would be misdemeanors). The doctors and Mr. Arcturus's family want to know whether he is dead or alive. Further, if he is dead, they want to know when he died—at the roadside, in the hospital emergency room, in the intensive care unit, or somewhere else. Mr. Arcturus's health insurer is denying coverage because, they say, "we only pay for necessary medical services, and no services are necessary when the patient is dead." Finally, the transplant team at the hospital wants to know if Mr. Arcturus's organs are available for transplantation, or, at the least, if they could be easily made so.

Would your answers to any of these questions be different if Mr. Arcturus himself had said, just two months before the accident, while delivering a sermon at his Unitarian church, that "for religious reasons and other reasons of conscience, I wish to be considered dead when my cognitive abilities are gone?"

I. INTRODUCTION

As we saw in Chapter 2, defining "personhood" has vexed commentators for centuries. Determining when a "person" died, however, was simple until the last few decades. Death occurred when several simultaneous physical changes occurred. These changes included the cessation of all cardiopulmonary (heart and lung) function, the cessation of all cognitive activity, the cessation of all responsive activity, and with only slight delay, the onset of rigormortis, livormortis, and, eventually, putrefaction. There could be no question about whether death would occur if all cognitive and responsive activity ceased but cardiopulmonary function continued because those functions were so closely related that the existence of one without the other would be impossible for more than a few hours. Because the cessation of cardiopulmonary functions was so much easier to observe than the cessation of cognitive ability, responsive activity, and other delayed attributes of death, the cessation of cardiopulmonary functions became, informally and practically, the definition of death. This test was never really anything more significant than the most convenient *evidence* of death; there is no suggestion that there was any basis for making cardiopulmonary functions definitional.

The development of mechanical substitutes for hearts and lungs forced reconsideration of the definition of death. It is now possible for a person to be without cognitive or responsive activity (i.e., without any brain activity), and yet maintain cardiopulmonary functions with the assistance of technological devices. Logically, this temporal division of these formerly contemporaneous attributes requires a determination of what death is. Is it the cessation of cardiopulmonary functions or is it the cessation of some, or all, brain functions?

The definition of death, like any other definition in law, ought to be functional. It is impossible to determine what ought to constitute death before the purpose of the definition is articulated. It should not be surprising that the legal function of defining death might be very different from the psychological function, which might be very different from the historical, sociological, anthropological, and medical functions. For example, the law must establish a time to distribute property from the estate, to require the payment of death contracts (i.e., life insurance), and to purge voting lists. Psychologists, however, may determine that death is a period of settling relationships, mourning, and healing. Physicians may view it as a time when their obligation to act in the interest of the patient ceases. There are many definitions of death, and, ultimately, attempts to develop an interdisciplinary consensus on the definition of death may be futile.

This chapter will review the distinction between the cardiopulmonary death and brain death models, and evaluate whether they are inconsistent. Next, this chapter will review the development of a legal definition of death over the last several years and consider the legal consequences of the general acceptance of brain death or a combined brain death-cardiopulmonary death definition. This chapter will then review the arguably unique case of the anencephalic infant and ask whether our current definitions of death work in that case. Finally, it will ask whether each of us ought to be able to choose our own definition of death.

Note: Religious Perspective on Death

There are a variety of social conceptions of death; many of the most pervasive of those considerations are theological. For many people, death is significant not just because it ends life, but because it begins something else.

> For Christians, death is not seen as the destruction or annihilation of the person. Although dissolution of the spirit-body bond that exists during our life is painful, death, viewed as transformation of the person to a new state of existence, is not. Furthermore, the Christian belief is that he will be resurrected, that the body in some way will share in the new life promised by Jesus Christ. Thus, the Christian is able to view the determination of death from a wider perspective than purely medical. This understanding provides the proper perspective for approaching the legal aspects of the determination of death.

J. Stuart Showalter, Determining Death: The Legal and Theological Aspects of Brain–Related Criteria, 27 Catholic Lawyer 112, 116 (1982). Many commentators have noted the importance of religious beliefs in establishing the legal definition of death. See, e.g., Michael Grodin, Religious Exemptions: Brain Death and Jewish Law, 36 J. Church & St. 357 (1994) and Scott Idleman, The Role of Religious Values in Judicial Decision Making, 68 Ind. L.J. 433 (1993). For a discussion of laws accommodating religious preferences for particular definitions of death, see Section IV, below.

II. THE DEVELOPMENT OF THE "BRAIN DEATH" DEFINITION

A. HISTORY

The first well-accepted definition of death to include brain death came from the Harvard Medical School and was published in the Journal of the American Medical Association. The Ad Hoc Committee of the Harvard Medical School used the term "irreversible coma" to define what is now generally called brain death and suggested that "no statutory change in the law should be necessary since the law treats this question essentially as one of fact to be determined by physicians."

The Ad Hoc Committee was explicit in describing its purpose in promulgating its new definition of death:

> Our primary purpose is to define irreversible coma as a new criterion for death. There are two reasons why there is need for a definition: (1) Improvements in resuscitative and supportive measures have led to increased efforts to save those who are desperately injured. Sometimes these efforts have only partial success so that the result is an individual

whose heart continues to beat but whose brain is irreversibly damaged. The burden is great on patients who suffer permanent loss of intellect, on their families, on the hospitals, and on those in need of hospital beds already occupied by these comatose patients. (2) Obsolete criteria for the definition of death can lead to controversy in obtaining organs for transplantation.

Report of the Ad Hoc Committee of the Harvard Medical School to Examine the Definition of Brain Death, 205 J.A.M.A. 85 (Aug.1968). In addition to listing the characteristics of irreversible coma—unreceptivity and unresponsitivity, no movements or breathing, no reflexes, and flat electro-encephalogram—the Ad Hoc Committee recommended that death be declared before the respirator is turned off ("in our judgment it will provide a greater degree of legal protection to those involved"), that the physician in charge consult with others before the declaration of death is made, that the physician (rather than the family) make the decision, and that the decision to declare death be made by physicians who are not involved "in any later effort to transplant organs or tissue from the deceased individual." Id.

The Ad Hoc Committee's determination that brain death ought to constitute death met surprisingly little medical opposition. There has been debate over the precise nature of the characteristics of "irreversible coma" that can give rise to brain death and over whether the issue should be left to physicians or be brought into the domain of public debate and converted into a formal legal standard. The Ad Hoc Committee contributed substantially to this debate by the publication of its report. They also contributed to the confusion that subsequently has surrounded the issue by using such terms as "irreversible coma," which is now generally used to refer to something less than brain death, and "hopelessly damaged," as synonyms for brain death. The Ad Hoc Committee Report (through the language it used) may have perpetuated the misunderstanding that "brain death" is a medical diagnosis that constitutes something very close to death, but that it does not constitute "real" death. Brain death, of course, is just as "real" a death as heart-lung death. The consensus that brain death is, in fact, death of the human being confirms that the cessation of heart-lung activity may never have been more than evidence of death. The real defining characteristic is that there be, in the words of the Ad Hoc Committee, "no discernible central nervous system activity."

The Ad Hoc Committee concluded:

From ancient times down to the recent past it was clear that, when the respiration and heart stopped, the brain would die in a few minutes; so the obvious criterion of no heart beat as synonymous with death was sufficiently accurate. In those times the heart was considered to be the central organ of the body; it is not surprising that its failure marked the onset of death. This is no longer valid when modern resuscitative and supportive measures are used. These improved activities can now restore "life" as judged by the ancient standards of persistent respiration and continuing heart beat. This can be the case even when there is not the remotest possibility of an individual recovering consciousness following massive brain damage. In other situations "life" can be maintained only by means of artificial respiration and electrical stimulation of the heart beat, or in temporarily by-passing the heart, or, in conjunction with these things, reducing with cold the body's oxygen requirement.

Id. As the leading legal and medical experts point out, the Ad Hoc Committee marked the beginning of the public debate over brain death; closure was not to come until some time later.

> Not surprisingly, disquiet over the change in medical attitude and practice arose in lay as well as medical circles. The prospect of physicians agreeing amongst themselves to change the rules by which life is measured in order to salvage a larger number of transplantable organs met with something short of universal approval. Especially with increasing disenchantment over heart transplantation (the procedure in which the traditional criteria for determining death posed the most difficulties), some doubt arose whether it was wise to adopt measures which encouraged a medical "advance" that seemed to have gotten ahead of its own basic technology. Furthermore, many people—doctors included—found themselves with nagging if often unarticulated doubts about how to proceed in the situation, far more common than transplantation, in which a long-comatose patient shows every prospect of "living" indefinitely with artificial means of support. As a result of this growing public and professional concern, elected officials, with the encouragement of the medical community, have urged public discussion and action to dispel the apprehension created by the new medical knowledge and to clarify and reformulate the law. Some commentators, however, have argued that public bodies and laymen in general have no role to play in this process of change. Issue is therefore joined on at least two points: (1) ought the public to be involved in "defining" death? and (2) if so, how ought it to be involved—specifically, ought governmental action, in the form of legislation, be taken?

A. Capron and L. Kass, A Statutory Definition of the Standards for Determining Human Death: An Appraisal and a Proposal, 121 U.Pa.L.Rev. 87, 91–92 (1972).

The first state to promulgate a statute adopting brain death was Kansas. The 1970 Kansas statute provided alternatively for both brain death and traditional cardiopulmonary death:

> A person will be considered medically and legally dead if, in the opinion of a physician, based on ordinary standards of medical practice, there is the absence of spontaneous respiratory and cardiac function and, because of the disease or condition which caused, directly or indirectly, these functions to cease, or because of the passage of time since these functions ceased, attempts at resuscitation are considered hopeless; and, in this event, death will have occurred at the time these functions ceased; or

> A person will be considered medically and legally dead if, in the opinion of a physician, based on ordinary standards of medical practice, there is the absence of spontaneous brain function; and if based on ordinary standards of medical practice, during reasonable attempts to either maintain or restore spontaneous circulatory or respiratory function in the absence of aforesaid brain function, it appears that further attempts at resuscitation or supportive maintenance will not succeed, death

will have occurred at the time when these conditions first coincide. Death is to be pronounced before artificial means of supporting respiratory and circulatory function are terminated and before any vital organ is removed for purposes of transplantation.

These alternative definitions of death are to be utilized for all purposes in this state, including the trials of civil and criminal cases, any laws to the contrary notwithstanding.

Kan.Stat.Ann. § 77–202.

The statute was quickly copied and just as quickly criticized. The primary criticism was directed to the alternative definitions of death, which some believed might lead to the conclusion that a person could be either dead or alive depending on which paragraph of the definition the determining physician invoked. It is hard to believe, however, that these alternative definitions would result in any confusion in fact, and there has been no case that has engendered such confusion in Kansas or any other state with a similar statute. Professor Capron and Dr. Kass proposed an alternative to the Kansas statute. Their proposal grew out of the Research Group on Death and Dying at the Hastings Center and sought to eliminate the notion that there were two independent definitions of death, and that physicians (and others) thus had discretion to determine whether a patient was truly dead. The 1980 Uniform Act, which superseded a 1978 Uniform Act, and which gives explicit credit to Capron and Kass in its prefatory note, returns to the alternative definitions of death. This is not because the Commissioners determined that there were two independent definitions of death. Rather, it treated death as a phenomenon that could be *tested* by two alternative criteria.

B. UNIFORM DETERMINATION OF DEATH ACT (1980)

§ 1. [Determination of Death]

An individual who has sustained either (1) irreversible cessation of circulatory and respiratory functions, or (2) irreversible cessation of all functions of the entire brain, including the brain stem, is dead. A determination of death must be made in accordance with accepted medical standards.

———————

Since 1980 there have been some suggested modifications to the Uniform Determination of Death Act. In 1982 three Dartmouth Medical School professors argued:

The UDDA statute is not desirable, we believe, because it too is ambiguous and it elevates the irreversible cessation of cardiopulmonary functioning to the level of a standard of death, when it is really only a test, although a test that may be used in most circumstances. Permanent cessation of spontaneous cardiopulmonary functioning works as a test of death only in the absence of artificial cardiopulmonary support because only there does it produce the true standard of death-the irreversible cessation of all brain functions. A conceptually satisfactory statute would not need to mention cessation of cardiopulmonary function at all. It would be sufficient to include only irreversible cessation of whole brain functioning and allow physicians to select validated and agreed-upon tests (prolonged absence of spontaneous cardiopulmonary function would be one) to measure irreversible cessation of whole brain function.

J. Bernat, C. Culver and B. Gert, Defining Death in Theory and Practice, 12 Hastings Center Report 5 (Feb. 1982). They proposed their own statute, which begins, "An individual who has sustained irreversible cessation of all functions of the entire brain, including the brain stem, is dead." Id. The proposed statute then lists two ways to determine whether there has been irreversible cessation of all functions of the entire brain—the prolonged absence of spontaneous circulatory and respiratory functions, or, as an alternative in the presence of artificial means of cardiopulmonary support, direct tests of brain function. Id. In part because the difference between the Uniform Determination of Death Act and the Dartmouth professors' alternative amounts to little more than a legal quibble with insubstantial practical, legal or medical consequences, there has been little interest in formally changing the language of the Uniform Act, even among those who find the unitary brain death definition (with alternative *criteria* for determining whether the entire brain is dead) intellectually preferable to the alternative-definitions form employed by the Uniform Act.

The Uniform Determination of Death Act has now been adopted, more or less as proposed by the Commission, in most states. For an excellent judicial history of the adoption of the brain death standard, see People v. Mitchell, 132 Cal.App.3d 389, 183 Cal.Rptr. 166 (1982). Bernat and his colleagues were not completely unsuccessful; there is now nearly a consensus among philosophers that it is really the irreversible cessation of all brain function that constitutes death, whether it be measured through tests of the brain function itself or tests for cardiopulmonary activity. Even those few dissenters who would return to the heart-lung criteria as the sole legal criteria agree that those who meet the whole brain death definition should be allowed to die (or even be candidates for euthanasia). See James Humber, Statutory Criteria for Determining Human Death, 42 Mercer L. Rev. 1069 (1991).

Note: Brain Death and Homicide Statutes

Brain death has not been adopted into the law wholly through statutes. In some states courts have been willing to adopt the brain death definition. This issue necessarily comes before the court in criminal cases where the defendant argues that he cannot be charged with homicide because the victim, although without any brain activity because of the criminal conduct, could have been kept "alive" with mechanically assisted heart and lungs indefinitely (or at least for a year and a day, which is all that is usually required for the defendant to avoid the homicide charge). Some homicide defendants have argued that the victims were not dead until brain death was declared by the physicians, and that the physicians really made the declaration so that organs could be removed for transplantation. They have argued that the harvesting of the organs, not their underlying criminal acts, was the proximate cause of death. Several states which have faced various manifestations of this very clever and obviously desperate argument have denied this defense; in no case has it been successful.

A representative set of facts comes from People v. Eulo, 63 N.Y.2d 341, 482 N.Y.S.2d 436, 472 N.E.2d 286 (1984), were the New York Court of Appeals dealt explicitly with the New York Legislature's failure to define death. The facts of that case provide a useful background:

On the evening of July 19, 1981, defendant and his girlfriend attended a volunteer firemen's fair in Kings Park, Suffolk County. Not long after they arrived, the two began to argue, reportedly because defendant was jealous over one of her former suitors, whom they had seen at the fair. The argument continued through the evening; it became particularly heated as the two sat in defendant's pick-up truck, parked in front of the home of the girlfriend's parents. Around midnight, defendant shot her in the head with his unregistered handgun.

The victim was rushed by ambulance to the emergency room of St. John's Hospital. A gunshot wound to the left temple causing extreme hemorrhaging was apparent. A tube was placed in her windpipe to enable artificial respiration and intravenous medication was applied to stabilize her blood pressure.

Shortly before 2:00 a.m., the victim was examined by a neurosurgeon, who undertook various tests to evaluate damage done to the brain. Painful stimuli were applied and yielded no reaction. Various reflexes were tested and, again, there was no response. A further test determined that the victim was incapable of spontaneously maintaining respiration. An electroencephalogram (EEG) resulted in "flat," or "isoelectric", readings indicating no activity in the part of the brain tested.

Over the next two days, the victim's breathing was maintained solely be a mechanical respirator. Her heartbeat was sustained and regulated through medication. Faced with what was believed to be an imminent cessation of these two bodily functions notwithstanding the artificial maintenance, the victim's parents consented to the use of certain of her organs for transplantation.

On the afternoon of July 23, a second neurosurgeon was called in to evaluate whether the victim's brain continued to function in any manner. A repetition of all of the previously conducted tests led to the same diagnosis: the victim's entire brain had irreversibly ceased to function. This diagnosis was reviewed and confirmed by the Deputy Medical Examiner for Suffolk County and another physician.

The victim was pronounced dead at 2:20 p.m. on July 23, although at that time she was still attached to a respirator and her heart was still beating. Her body was taken to a surgical room where her kidneys, spleen, and lymph nodes were removed. The mechanical respirator was then disconnected, and her breathing immediately stopped, followed shortly be a cessation of the heartbeat.

Defendant was indicted for second degree murder. After a jury trial, he was convicted of manslaughter. * * *

482 N.Y.S.2d at 439, 472 N.E.2d at 289.

The court held that "a recognition of brain-based criteria for determining death is not unfaithful to prior judicial definitions of 'death', as presumptively adopted in the many statutes using that term. Close examination of the common-law conception of death and the traditional criteria used to determine when death has occurred leads inexorably to this conclusion." Id. at 444, 472 N.E.2d at 294. The court determined that "[d]eath remains the single phenomenon identified at common law," and that the courts could appropriately adapt criteria "to account for the 'changed conditions' that a dead body may be attached to a machine so as to exhibit demonstrably false indicia of life." Id. The Eulo court went on:

> This court searches in vain for evidence that, apart from the concept of death, the legislature intended to render immutable the criteria used to determine death. By extension, to hold to the contrary would be to say that the law could not recognize diagnostic equipment such as the stethoscope or more sensitive equipment even when it became clear that these instruments more accurately measured the presence of signs of life.

Id. Thus, the court concluded,

> when a determination has been made according to accepted medical standards that person has suffered an irreversible cessation of heartbeat and respiration, or, when these functions are maintained solely by extraordinary mechanical means, an irreversible cessation of all functions of the entire brain, including the brain stem, no life traditionally recognized by the law is present in that body.

Id. The Court of Appeals described with some precision just when medical intervention could constitute a superseding cause that would relieve a defendant from criminal homicide liability:

> If the victims were properly diagnosed as dead, of course, no subsequent medical procedure such as organ removal would be deemed a cause of death. If victims' deaths were prematurely announced due to a doctor's negligence, the subsequent procedures may have been a cause of death, but that negligence would not constitute a superseding cause of death relieving defendants of liability []. If, however, the pronouncements of death were premature due to the gross negligence or the intentional wrongdoing of doctors, as determined by a grave deviation from accepted medical practices or disregard for legally cognizable criteria for determining death, the intervening medical procedure would interrupt the chain of causation and become the legal cause of death [].

Id. at 447, 472 N.E.2d at 297. Surprisingly, the *Eulo* defense has come up in more subtle ways since 1984. In People v. Hall, 134 Misc.2d 515, 511 N.Y.S.2d 532 (1987), the court held that a defendant could be convicted of the murder of a viable fetus which had to be delivered prematurely after the shooting of its mother. The court concluded that the fact that the infant was maintained on a ventilator after the C-section birth did not alter its status as one who was "born alive," and thus a "person" under the murder statute. In People v. Lai, 131 A.D.2d 592, 516 N.Y.S.2d 300 (1987), the court announced that *Eulo* would allow the jury to determine whether the brain death standard or the heart-lung standard ought to be applied in a homicide case to determine the time of death. Does this seem like an issue of fact properly within the province of the jury?

Should the judicially created definition of death in *Eulo* extend to criminal actions only, or should it also apply in civil actions (in tort actions, for example)? See Strachan v. John F. Kennedy Memorial Hosp., 109 N.J. 523, 538 A.2d 346 (1988).

C. HIGHER BRAIN DEATH

Why is there such a consensus that it is brain death, not cardiopulmonary death, that is the true defining characteristic of the death of a person? The President's Commission reached that conclusion from its premise that death was "the permanent cessation of functioning of the organism as a whole." How should we deal with a person with no cerebral function, but with continued brain stem function? Such a person would be incapable of any cognitive activity—incapable of any communication, self concept, pleasure or pain—yet still be capable of breathing, maintaining heart activity and responding reflexively. Can that person be said to be functioning as a whole organism? Is the absence of higher brain function, rather than merely *any* brain function, the real evidence of the disintegration of any functioning of the organism as a whole, and thus the real definition of death? There are two primary objections to "higher brain death" proposal. As they point out:

> An important weakness of the higher brain formulation of death is the "slippery slope" problem. Just how much neocortical damage is necessary for death? By this definition, would not severely demented patients also be considered dead? Then what about those somewhat less severely brain damaged? Because personhood is inherently a vague concept, strict criteria for its loss are difficult to identify.

J. Bernat, C. Culver and B. Gert, Defining Death in Theory and Practice, Hastings Center Report (Feb. 1982) at 6.

Robert Veatch, a leading proponent of the "higher brain death" definition, disagrees:

> It does not follow that advocates of higher-brain formulations are more vulnerable to the slippery-slope problem than defenders of whole brain grounds for pronouncing a person dead. Advocates of what brain pronouncement of death must, as Harry Beecher quickly discovered, rule out spinal cord reflexes. They must rule out isolated cellular activity that continues to produce micro-volt electron potentials on an electroencephalogram. Their own question could be forced back on them: "Just how much brain tissue damage is necessary for death?" Would they consider someone alive who had a few brain stem cells functioning? What about one or two intact brain stem reflexes? The advocates of higher-brain concepts of death are in no better, but no worse a position. They think it is as easy to draw a hard and fast line between higher-brain (cortical) functions and other brain functions as between the brain stem and the high spinal cord. They can say *any cortical* function signals protectable life, just as the whole-brainers can say *any brain* function does. One is not on any slipperier slope than the other. If there is a slippery slope, anyone who leaves the comfortable confines of the pericardium and begins ascending the spinal cord toward the cerebral cortex is already on it.
>
> Those of us who favor some version of the higher-brain formulations do so precisely because we believe that a person does not function as a whole unless some higher brain function is present. The argument goes back to old Judeo–Christian notions of what it means to be whole. While the Greeks gave priority to the soul, the Judeo–Christian tradition consistently affirms that the human is a necessarily integrated unity of body and mind. Yet [some] hold that a person can function as a whole even when all mental function is totally and irreversibly gone. What a vitalistic, animalistic, biological view of the nature of the human! It confuses the person with the body as badly as the old heart/lung formulations did.
>
> It is all right if some people want to hold that view. If we cannot accurately measure the irreversible loss of all mental capacity today anyway, it may be better to have a conceptually inadequate formulation of what it means to be dead in order to prevent some muddled clinician from pronouncing someone dead prematurely. The problem of false

positive diagnoses of life is worth thinking about, however. It protects us from confusing the person as a whole from his or her flesh and blood. If we were not worried about false positive diagnoses of life, we might as well retreat to the safe and sure heart/lung based formulations and be done with it.

Robert Veatch, Correspondence, 12 Hastings Center Report (5) at 45 (Oct. 1982). See also Francis Bennion, Legal Death of Brain–Damaged Persons, 44 N. Ireland Legal. Q. 269 (1993), advocating a definition of death that would encompass the permanently unconscious.

The primary objection to the "higher brain death" proposal is a practical one. Remember, any legal definition of death ought to serve the function of such a definition. While the "higher brain function" definition may allow for the distribution of a decedent's property and his purge from voting lists, many people would feel uncomfortable burying a person who is still breathing. Is this discomfort simply irrational and anachronistic or is it supported by some principle that ought to be recognized in law?

For a complete account of the argument supporting cardiopulmonary definition of death, whole brain death, and neocortical death, see President's Commission for the Study of Ethical Problems in Medicine and Biomedical and Behavioral Research, Defining Death: A Report on the Medical, Legal, and Ethical Issues In the Determination of Death (1981).

The best account of arguments in support of (and in opposition to) neocortical death are found in David Randall Smith, Legal Recognition of Neocortical Death, 71 Cornell L.Rev. 850 (1986) which includes a proposed neocortical death statute. See also Robert Veatch, The Definition of Death: Ethical, Philosophical and Policy Confusion, 315 Annals N.Y.Acad. of Sci. 307 (1978); R. Dworkin, Death in Context, 48 Ind.L.J. 623 (1973).

III.   THE "DEAD DONOR" RULE AND EXPANDING CLASSES OF ORGAN DONORS— ANENCEPHALIC INFANTS AND "NON–HEART BEATING" DONORS

A.   ANENCEPHALIC INFANTS

The whole brain death standard was adopted, in part, to facilitate removal of organs for transplantation. There is still a close connection between proffered standards for determining death and the desire to have access to organs for transplant. Consider the following case:

IN RE T.A.C.P.

Supreme Court of Florida, 1992.
609 So.2d 588.

KOGAN, JUSTICE.

We have for review an order of the trial court certified by the Fourth District Court of Appeal as touching on a matter of great public importance requiring immediate resolution by this Court. We frame the issue as follows:

Is an anencephalic newborn considered "dead" for purposes of organ donation solely by reason of its congenital deformity?

* * *

I. FACTS

At or about the eight month of pregnancy, the parents of the child T.A.C.P. were informed that she would be born with anencephaly. * * *

In this case, T.A.C.P. actually survived only a few days after birth. The medical evidence in the record shows that the child T.A.C.P. was incapable of developing any sort of cognitive process, may have been unable to feel pain or experience sensation due to the absence of the upper brain, and at least for part of the time was placed on a mechanical ventilator to assist her breathing. * * *

On the advice of physicians, the parents continued the pregnancy to term and agreed that the mother would undergo caesarean section during birth. The parents agreed to the caesarean procedure with the express hope that the infant's organs would be less damaged and could be used for transplant in other sick children. Although T.A.C.P. had no hope of life herself, the parents both testified in court that they wanted to use this opportunity to give life to others. However, when the parents requested that T.A.C.P. be declared legally dead for this purpose, her health care providers refused out of concern that they thereby might incur civil or criminal liability. * * *

II. THE MEDICAL NATURE OF ANENCEPHALY

Although appellate courts appear never to have confronted the issue, there already is an impressive body of published medical scholarship on anencephaly. From our review of this material, we find that anencephaly is a variable but fairly well defined medical condition. Experts in the field have written that anencephaly is the most common severe birth defect of the central nervous system seen in the United States, although it apparently has existed throughout human history.

A statement by the Medical Task Force on Anencephaly ("Task Force") printed in the New England Journal of Medicine generally described "anencephaly" as "a congenital absence of major portions of the brain, skull, and scalp, with its genesis in the first month of gestation." David A. Stumpf et al., *The Infant with Anencephaly*, 322 New Eng.J.Med. 669, 669 (1990). The large opening in the skull accompanied by the absence or severe congenital disruption of the cerebral hemispheres is the characteristic feature of the condition. *Id.*

The Task Force defined anencephaly as diagnosable only when all of the following four criteria are present:

(1) A large portion of the skull is absent. (2) The scalp, which extends to the margin of the bone, is absent over the skull defect. (3) Hemorrhagic, fibrotic tissue is exposed because of defects in the skull and scalp. (4) Recognizable cerebral hemispheres are absent.

* * *

Thus, it is clear that anencephaly is distinguishable from some other congenital conditions because its extremity renders it uniformly lethal. * * *

The Task Force stated that most reported anencephalic children die within the first few days after birth, with survival any longer being rare. * * * The Task Force reported, however, that these survival rates are confounded somewhat by the variable degrees of medical care afforded to anencephalics. Some such infants may be given considerable life support while others may be given much less care.

The Task Force reported that the medical consequences of anencephaly can be established with some certainty. All anencephalics by definition are permanently unconscious because they lack the cerebral cortex necessary for conscious thought. Their condition thus is quite similar to that of persons in a persistent vegetative state. Where the brain stem is functioning, as it was here, spontaneous breathing and heartbeat can occur. In addition, such infants may show spontaneous movements of the extremities, "startle" reflexes, and pupils that respond to light. Some may show feeding reflexes, may cough, hiccup, or exhibit eye movements, and may produce facial expressions.

* * *

After the advent of new transplant methods in the past few decades, anencephalic infants have successfully been used as a source of organs for donation. * * *

There appears to be general agreement that anencephalics usually have ceased to be suitable organ donors by the time they meet all the criteria for "whole brain death," i.e., the complete absence of brainstem function. * * * There also is no doubt that a need exists for infant organs for transplantation. Nationally, between thirty and fifty percent of children under two years of age who need transplants die while waiting for organs to become available. * * *

III. LEGAL DEFINITIONS OF "DEATH" & "LIFE"

[The Florida Court described the legal developments that lead to the Uniform Determination of Death Act, but pointed out that Florida "struck out on its own," adopting no comprehensive statutory definition of death. Instead, the Florida statute merely permits the use of "irreversible cessation of the functioning of the entire brain" as the standard for determining death when a person's respiratory and circulatory systems are maintained "artificially;" the Florida statute does not expressly recognize cardiopulmonary death. Under this Florida definition, an anencephalic infant would be considered alive until there were irreversible cessation of the functioning of the entire brainstem.]

IV. COMMON LAW & POLICY

* * *

The question remaining is whether there is good reason in public policy for this Court to create an additional common law standard applicable [only] to anencephalics. Alterations of the common law, while rarely entertained or allowed, are within this Court's prerogative. * * * We believe, for example, that our adoption of the cardiopulmonary definition of death today is required by public necessity and, in any event, merely formalizes what has been the common practice in this state for well over a century.

Such is not the case with petitioners' request. Our review of the medical, ethical, and legal literature on anencephaly discloses absolutely no consensus that public necessity or fundamental rights will be better served by granting this request.

We are not persuaded that a public necessity exists to justify this action, in light of the other factors in this case—although we acknowledge much ambivalence about this particular question. We have been deeply touched by the altruism and unquestioned motives of the parents of T.A.C.P. The parents have shown great humanity, compassion, and concern for others. The problem we as a Court must face, however, is that the medical literature shows unresolved controversy over the extent to which anencephalic organs can or should be used in transplants.

* * *

We express no opinion today about who is right and who is wrong on these issues—if any "right" or "wrong" can be found here. The salient point is that no consensus exists as to: (a) the utility of organ transplants of the type at issue here; (b) the ethical issues involved; or (c) the legal and constitutional problems implicated.

V. CONCLUSIONS

Accordingly, we find no basis to expand the common law to equate anencephaly with death. We acknowledge the possibility that some infants' lives might be saved by using organs from anencephalics who do not meet the traditional definition of "death" we reaffirm today. But weighed against this is the utter lack of consensus, and the questions about the overall utility of such organ donations. The scales clearly tip in favor of not extending the common law in this instance.

To summarize: We hold that Florida common law recognizes the cardiopulmonary definition of death as stated above; and Florida statutes create a "whole-brain death" exception applicable whenever cardiopulmonary function is being maintained artificially. There are no other legal standards for determining death under present Florida law.

Because no Florida statute applies to the present case, the determination of death in this instance must be judged against the common law cardiopulmonary standard. The evidence shows that T.A.C.P.'s heart was beating and she was breathing at the times in question. Accordingly, she was not dead under Florida law, and no donation of her organs would have been legal.

COUNCIL ON ETHICAL AND JUDICIAL AFFAIRS, AMERICAN MEDICAL ASSOCIATION, THE USE OF ANENCEPHALIC NEONATES AS ORGAN DONORS
273 JAMA 1614 (1995) [withdrawn 1996].

Hundreds of children die each year of cardiac, hepatic, or renal failure because there are not enough hearts, livers, or kidneys available for transplantation from other children. Consequently, various measures have been considered over the years to increase the organ supply for pediatric transplantation. One approach that has received particular attention is the possibility of using organs from anencephalic neonates.

* * *

In 1988, this Council examined the ethical issues surrounding the use of organs from anencephalic neonates and concluded that it is ethically acceptable to remove organs from anencephalic neonates only after they have died, whether the death occurs by cessation of cardiac function or brain function. * * * The new opinion states that it is ethically acceptable to transplant the organs of anencephalic neonates even before the neonates die, as long as there is parental consent and certain other safeguards are followed.

* * *

ANENCEPHALY

Anencephaly is a developmental abnormality of the central nervous system that results in the "congenital absence of major portion of the brain, skull, and scalp." Because anencephalic neonates lack functioning cerebral hemispheres, they never experience any degree of consciousness. They never have thoughts, feelings, sensations, desires, or emotions. There is no purposeful action, social interaction, memory, pain, or suffering. Anencephalic neonates have fully or partially functioning brain stem tissue. Accordingly, they are able to maintain at least some of the body's autonomic function (ie, unconscious activity), including the functions of the heart, lungs, kidneys, and intestinal tract, as well as certain reflex actions. They may be able to breathe, suck, engage in spontaneous movements of their eyes, arms, and legs, respond to noxious stimuli with crying or avoidance maneuvers, and exhibit facial expressions typical of healthy infants. While all of this activity gives the appearance that the anencephalic neonate has some degree of consciousness, there is none. Anencephalic neonates are totally unaware of their existence and the environment in which they live.

* * *

BENEFITS OF PERMITTING PARENTAL DONATION OF ORGANS FROM ANENCEPHALIC NEONATES

The argument in favor of parental donation of organs from anencephalic neonates is compelling: many children will be saved from death, and many other children will realize a substantial improvement in their quality of life. * * *

Organ transplantation from anencephalic neonates can bring profound benefit not only to the recipients of the organs but also to the parents of the anencephalic neonate. When confronted with the tragedy of bearing a child who can never experience consciousness and who will die in a matter of days, parents may find much of their psychological distress alleviated by the good that results from donating their child's organs and thereby providing lifesaving benefits to other children. * * *

OBJECTIONS TO PARENTAL DONATION OF ORGANS FROM ANENCEPHALIC NEONATES

Several objections are commonly raised against proposals for parental donation of organs from anencephalic neonates: (1) donation violates the prohibition against removal of life-necessary organs from living persons, (2) false diagnosis of anencephaly may result in the death of neonates who could achieve consciousness, (3) permitting donation from anencephalic neonates may open the door to organ removal from patients who are in a persistent vegetative state or in other severely disabling conditions, (4) anencephalic neonates would rarely be a source of organs for transplantation, and (5) allowing donation of organs from anencephalic neonates will undermine public confidence in the organ transplantation system. As discussed herein, however, these concerns do not justify a prohibition on parental donation of organs from anencephalic infants.

1. Prohibition Against Remove from Living Persons

Both law and ethics require that persons be dead before their life-necessary, nonrenewable organs are taken (the "dead donor" rule). This critical principle ensures that one person's life will not be sacrificed for the benefit of another person, even to preserve the life of that other person. While this principle must be vigorously maintained, it must not be applied without regard to whether its application serves its purposes. After consideration of the purposes of the general prohibition against removal of life-necessary organs before death, it is clear that those purposes would not be compromised by permitting parental donation of organs from anencephalic neonates.

Protecting the Interests of Persons From Whom Organs are Taken. Ordinarily, the dead donor rule protects the fundamental interest in life of persons from whom organs are taken. However, it does not make sense to speak of an interest of anencephalic neonates in staying alive. Because they have never experienced consciousness and will never experience consciousness, anencephalic neonates cannot have interests of any kind. * * *

Providing Reassurance to Other Individuals. By protecting the interests of persons from whom organs are taken, the dead donor rule provides reassurance to other individuals that, if they choose to become organ donors, their lives will not be shortened by the removal of their organs for the benefit of someone in need of an organ transplant. While this is a critical purpose of the dead donor rule, parental donation of organs from anencephalic neonates will not undermine the rule's reassuring role. * * *

Preserving the Value of Respect for Life. * * * First it is important to emphasize that respect for the essential worth of life is an absolute value in the sense that it exists irrespective of a person's quality of life. However, it is not an absolute value in the sense of overriding all other values. Rather, it must be balanced with other important social values, including, as in this case, the fundamental social value of saving lives. * * *

Indeed, the primary argument in favor of permitting parental donation is an argument based on the value of respect for life. The whole point of allowing such donation is to ensure that many lives that would otherwise be lost are saved.

2. Accuracy of Diagnosis

There has been concern that allowing parental donation of organs from anencephalic neonates could lead to parental donation of organs from infants with similar, severe conditions but who are not anencephalic. Indeed, when researchers at Loma Linda University Medical Center conducted a protocol involving anencephalic neonates, some physicians referred infants to the protocol who were not in fact anencephalic. * * *

Nevertheless, while the possibility of misdiagnoses cannot be entirely eliminated, it can readily be reduced to an insignificant level with the adoption of appropriate safeguards. * * * To ensure that the diagnosis of anencephaly is as accurate as possible, the diagnosis should be confirmed by two physicians with special expertise in diagnosing anencephaly who are not part of the organ transplant team. * * *

3. Slippery Slope Concerns

* * *

There is an important reason why the slippery slope risk is not a serious one if society decides to permit parental donation of organs from anencephalic neonates. Anencephalic neonates are unique among persons because they have no history of consciousness and no possibility of ever being conscious. * * *

4. Number of Children Who Would Benefit

* * * The number of children who could benefit from the organs of anencephalic neonates may be considerably smaller than 1000; indeed, according to one estimate, no more than about 20 infants a year would gain a longterm survival from a heart or liver transplant, and no more than another 25 infants would receive a long-term benefit from kidney transplantation.

This concern about the number of children who would benefit should not be a barrier to parental donation of organs from anencephalic neonates. First, the estimates are probably much too low. * * * More importantly, even assuming that there would be only 20 long-term survivals gained each year and that only long-term survivals matter, it is not clear why that should be an objection to parental donation of organs from anencephalic neonates. Among the different goals that health care can achieve, saving lives is of fundamental importance; indeed, it is never insignificant to save 20 lives.

* * *

5. Public Trust in the Organ Procurement System

Some commentators suggest that creating an exception to the dead donor rule may undermine society's confidence in the organ procurement system and cause a chilling effect on overall organ donations. * * * Inasmuch as the change in the definition of death has not compromised the effectiveness of the organ procurement system but has led to greater numbers of lives saved by organ transplantation, it is likely that permitting parental donation of organs from anencephalic neonates will also lead to greater numbers of lives saved rather than to compromise of the organ procurement system. In addition, while it is true that existing organ procurement practices should not be changed without due deliberation, change should be possible in response to important, unmet social needs and evolving understanding of the ethical and scientific issues surrounding anencephaly.

Accordingly, rather than prohibit parental donation of organs from anencephalic neonates, certain safeguards should be used to preserve public trust in the organ procurement system. First, parental donation of organs from anencephalic neonates should occur only if the discussion of donation is initiated by the parents of the neonates, not if it is initiated by members of the health care team. Second, parental donation should not occur without the fully informed consent of the parents of the anencephalic neonate. Third, a pilot program for parental donation of organs from anencephalic neonates should be undertaken to assess its impact before the practice becomes widespread. * * *

CONCLUSION

For the reasons described herein, the Council has developed the following opinion,

2.162 Anencephalic Neonates as Organ Donors.

* * *

It is ethically permissible to consider the anencephalic neonate as a potential organ donor, although still alive under the current definition of death, only if: (1) the diagnosis of anencephaly is certain and is confirmed by two physicians *with special expertise* who are not part of the organ transplant team; (2) the parents of the neonate *initiate any discussions about organ retrieval and* indicate their desire for retrieval in writing, and (3) there is compliance with the Council's Guidelines for the Transplantation of Organs [ ].

In the alternative, a family wishing to donate the organs of their anencephalic neonate may choose to provide the neonate with ventilator assistance and other medical therapies that might sustain organ perfusion and viability until such time as a determination of death can be made in accordance with current medical standards and relevant law. In this situation, the family should be informed of the possibility that the organs might deteriorate in the process, rendering them unsuitable for transplantation.

It is normally required that a person be legally dead before removal of their life-necessary organs (the "dead donor rule"). The use of the anencephalic neonate as a live donor is a limited exception to the general standard because of the fact that the infant has never experienced, and will never experience, consciousness.

Notes on the Use of Anencephalic Infants as Organ Donors

1. The Council's opinion proved far more controversial among AMA members than was expected, and it was withdrawn shortly after it was released. The issue is now under study—as it is expected to be for several years, until a social consensus is reached on this issue.

2. If you were representing the parents of an anencephalic infant seeking to have the court allow the child to be an organ donor, what arguments would you make? Would you argue that the child is dead, and thus can provide organs consistently with the "dead donor" rule, or would you argue that the child should be permitted to be a donor even though he is alive? What jurisprudential concerns are likely to motivate the court when it considers either of these arguments? Do you think that it would be easier for a court to change the state law's definition of death to encompass anencephalics, or to change the state law's acceptance of the "dead donor" rule to encompass this class of living donors?

3. Did the Florida court properly decide the issue in *In re T.A.C.P.*? Would the court have been influenced by the 1995 statement of the Council? The Council

was moved to adopt this position, in part, because of *T.A.C.P.* case, which it discusses in the introduction to its report.

4. The AMA Council would require several procedures to safeguard the integrity of any anencephalic who is to become an organ donor before death. First, it would require that two physicians with special expertise who are not members of the transplant team confirm the diagnosis of anencephaly. Given the fact that few states require a second physician to confirm even a diagnosis of brain death, and given the fact that anencephaly is more obvious and easier to diagnose than brain death, is it appropriate to have this confirmation requirement?

Second, it would permit donation of live anencephalic organs only if the discussion were initiated by the family of the anencephalic, not if it were initiated by members of the health care team. If the choice of organ donation is a reasonable and ethically sound one, though, shouldn't the family be informed of possibility of donation in any case? If organ donation is psychologically important to many parents of anencephalic infants, shouldn't the medically ignorant have the same opportunity to donate their children's organs as the medically sophisticated who know that anencephalic neonates' organs can be made available for transplant under some circumstances? Does the doctrine of informed consent require that the parents be told of this option?

Third, the AMA Council would begin with a pilot program for anencephalic organ donation at a "major medical center." Is there value in running such a pilot? Given the few organs likely to be transplanted from anencephalic donors, would a single-center pilot be likely to generate much generalizable knowledge on how successful this program would be? In any case, what criteria would you use to determine if such a pilot were successful?

Are there other safeguards you would add to assure the integrity of anencephalic infants who are potential donors?

5. The American Academy of Pediatrics recommends that the brain death standard not be applied to children under seven days old. Because most anencephalics do not live those seven days, the brain death analysis is unlikely ever to be applied to anencephalic infants who are potential donors. Does this help explain why the AMA Council recommended that anencephalics be treated as potential donors *even though they are alive* rather than that they be treated as dead, and, for that reason, eligible to be organ donors? Others, too, have suggested that anencephalics be treated as "brain absent" rather than "brain dead." For some purposes, the "brain absent" could be treated like dead people (e.g., they could be allowed to donate organs), while for other purposes they could be treated as living children (e.g., in a hospital they could be accorded all appropriate treatment).

6. There is some debate about whether anencephalics can feel pain or suffer. How would the resolution of that question affect your analysis of this issue?

7. One reason there has been relatively little interest in the use of anencephalic infants as organ donors over the past several years is that there appear to be a relatively small (and decreasing) number of such potential donors. This is, in part, a consequence of physicians' expertise in diagnosing this condition in utero, and the subsequent availability of abortion. The legal protection of the decision to have an abortion to avoid the birth of an anencephalic child was recognized in Britell v. United States, 204 F.Supp.2d 182 (D. Mass. 2002), where the District Court ordered CHAMPUS (the now renamed source of health insurance for those in the military) to pay for an abortion for a woman carrying an anencephalic fetus.

The court determined that the prohibition on such a payment failed even the weak "rational basis" standard, and that it was thus unconstitutional. As the court pointed out that, "There is no rational justification for CHAMPUS' refusal to fund Britell's abortion of her anencephalic fetus. Through the funding power the government seeks to encourage Britell and women similarly situated to suffer by carrying their anencephalic fetuses until they are born to a certain death. This rationale is no rationale at all. It is irrational, and worse yet, it is cruel." 204 F.Supp.2d at 198.

8. While most studies show that anencephalic infants live for only a very short period of time—a few days—these studies do not suggest just how long anencephalics can live. Without aggressive treatment, anencephalic infants will die very quickly, and they rarely are provided any life-prolonging treatment. With very aggressive treatment, however, they may live much longer. The *Baby K* case, which follows, is a good example of a case in which an anencephalic was provided the extremely aggressive treatment her mother demanded; she lived more than two years.

9. An excellent brief bibliography on the use of anencephalic infants as organ donors is found in the "references" section of the AMA Council report, at 273 JAMA 1618 (1995). For a discussion of some of the medical issues, see Medical Task Force on Anencephaly, The Infant with Anencephaly, 322 N.Eng.J.Med. 669 (1990). See also D. Shewmon, Anencephaly: Selected Medical Aspects, 18(5) Hastings Cen. Rep. 11 (1988). For a good general account of the area, see J. Botkin, Anencephalic Infants as Organ Donors, 82 Pediatrics 250 (1988). The first medical center to attempt a transplant from an anencephalic in the United States is Loma Linda Medical Center. An account of its most famous case—the "Baby Gabrielle" case—is found in George Annas, From Canada with Love: Anencephalic Newborns as Organ Donors, 17 Hastings Cen. Rep. 36 (December 1987). For a comment on *In re T.A.C.P.*, see J.S. Justice, Personhood and Death—The Proper Treatment of Anencephalic Organ Donors Under the Law, 62 U. Cin. L. Rev. 1227 (1994). For a detailed account of the disadvantages of using anencephalics as organ donors, see David McDowell, Death of an Idea: The Anencephalic as an Organ Donor, 72 Tex. L. Rev. 893 (1994) and Paul Byrne et al., Anencephaly—Organ Transplantation?, 9 Issues L. & Med. 23 (1993).

10. The question of whether anencephalic infants should be maintained or "allowed to die" arises in contexts other than the availability of transplantation of organs. If the Florida court in In Re T.A.C.P. had extended the legal standard for death to include anencephalic infants, could it have crafted an exception for Baby K, an infant whose mother demanded that she receive all available care? If you can draft such an exception, should the law make such a distinction? Should the law provide that an anencephalic is dead only for the purpose of organ harvesting? Should the appropriate treatment of anencephalic babies be determined primarily through the application of the law on determination of death?

IN RE BABY K
United States Court of Appeals, Fourth Circuit, 1994.
16 F.3d 590.

WILKINS, J.:

The Hospital instituted this action against Ms. H, Mr. K, and Baby K, seeking a declaratory judgment that it is not required under the Emergency Medical Treatment and Active Labor Act (EMTALA), [ ], to provide treatment other than warmth, nutrition, and hydration to Baby K, an anencephalic infant. Because we agree with the district court that EMTALA gives rise to a duty on the part of the Hospital to provide respiratory support to Baby K when she is presented at the Hospital in respiratory distress and treatment is requested for her, we affirm.

Baby K was born at the Hospital in October of 1992 with Anencephaly. * * *

When Baby K had difficulty breathing on her own at birth, Hospital physicians placed her on a mechanical ventilator. This respiratory support allowed the doctors to confirm the diagnosis and gave Ms. H, the mother, an opportunity to fully understand the diagnosis and prognosis of Baby K's condition. The physicians explained to Ms. H that most anencephalic infants die within a few days of birth due to breathing difficulties and other complications. Because aggressive treatment would serve no therapeutic or palliative purpose, they recommended that Baby K only be provided with supportive care in the form of nutrition, hydration, and warmth. Physicians at the Hospital also discussed with Ms. H the possibility of a "Do Not Resuscitate Order" that would provide for the withholding of lifesaving measures in the future.

The treating physicians and Ms. H failed to reach an agreement as to the appropriate care. Ms. H insisted that Baby K be provided with mechanical breathing assistance whenever the infant developed difficulty breathing on her own, while the physicians maintained that such care was inappropriate. As a result of this impasse, the Hospital sought to transfer Baby K to another hospital. This attempt failed when all of the hospitals in the area with pediatric intensive care units declined to accept the infant. In November of 1992, when Baby K no longer needed the services of an acute-care hospital, she was transferred to a nearby nursing home.

Since being transferred to the nursing home, Baby K has been readmitted to the Hospital three times due to breathing difficulties. Each time she has been provided with breathing assistance and, after stabilization, has been discharged to the nursing home. Following Baby K's second admission, the Hospital filed this action to resolve the issue of whether it is obligated to provide emergency medical treatment to Baby K that it deems medically and ethically inappropriate. Baby K's guardian ad litem and her father, Mr. K, joined in the Hospital's request for a declaration that the Hospital is not required to provide respiratory support or other aggressive treatments. Ms. H contested the Hospital's request for declaratory relief. * * * [The district court denied the hospital the requested relief and the petitioners appealed to the Court of Appeals.]

* * *

In the application of these provisions to Baby K, the Hospital concedes that when Baby K is presented in respiratory distress a failure to provide "immediate medical attention" would reasonably be expected to cause serious impairment of her bodily functions. [ ] Thus, her breathing difficulty qualifies as an emergency medical condition, and the diagnosis of this emergency medical condition triggers the duty of the hospital to provide Baby K with stabilizing treatment or to transfer her in accordance with the provisions of

EMTALA. Since transfer is not an option available to the Hospital at this juncture, the Hospital must stabilize Baby K's condition.

The Hospital acknowledged in its complaint that aggressive treatment, including mechanical ventilation, is necessary to "assure within a reasonable medical probability, that no material deterioration of Baby K's condition is likely to occur." Thus, stabilization of her condition requires the Hospital to provide respiratory support through the use of a respirator or other means necessary to ensure adequate ventilation. In sum, a straightforward application of the statute obligates the Hospital to provide respiratory support to Baby K when she arrives at the emergency department of the Hospital in respiratory distress and treatment is requested on her behalf.

In an effort to avoid the result that follows from the plain language of EMTALA, the Hospital offers four arguments. The Hospital claims: (1) that this court has previously interpreted EMTALA as only requiring uniform treatment of all patients exhibiting the same condition; (2) that in prohibiting disparate emergency medical treatment Congress did not intend to require physicians to provide treatment outside the prevailing standard of medical care; (3) that an interpretation of EMTALA that requires a hospital or physician to provide respiratory support to an anencephalic infant fails to recognize a physician's ability, under Virginia law, to refuse to provide medical treatment that the physician considers medically or ethically inappropriate; and (4) that EMTALA only applies to patients who are transferred from a hospital in an unstable condition. We find these arguments unavailing.

* * *

If, as the Hospital suggests, it were only required to provide uniform treatment, it could provide any level of treatment to Baby K, including a level of treatment that would allow her condition to materially deteriorate, so long as the care she was provided was consistent with the care provided to other individuals. [ ] The definition of stabilizing treatment advocated by the Hospital directly conflicts with the plain language of EMTALA.

* * * The terms of EMTALA as written do not allow the Hospital to fulfill its duty to provide stabilizing treatment by simply dispensing uniform treatment. Rather, the Hospital must provide that treatment necessary to prevent the material deterioration of each patient's emergency medical condition. In the case of Baby K, the treatment necessary to prevent the material deterioration of her condition when she is in respiratory distress includes respiratory support.

* * *

The second argument of the Hospital is that, in redressing the problem of disparate emergency medical treatment, Congress did not intend to require physicians to provide medical treatment outside the prevailing standard of medical care. The Hospital asserts that, because of their extremely limited life expectancy and because any treatment of their condition is futile, the prevailing standard of medical care for infants with anencephaly is to provide only warmth, nutrition, and hydration. Thus, it maintains that a requirement to provide respiratory assistance would exceed the prevailing standard of medical care. However, the plain language of EMTALA requires stabilizing treatment for any individual who comes to a participating hospital, is diagnosed as having an emergency medical condition, and cannot be transferred ... We recognize the dilemma facing physicians who are requested to provide treatment they consider morally and ethically inappropriate, but we cannot ignore the plain language of the statute ...

The Hospital further argues that EMTALA cannot be construed to require it to provide respiratory support to anencephalics when its physicians deem such care inappropriate, because Virginia law permits physicians to refuse to provide such care.

* * *

It is well settled that state action must give way to federal legislation where a valid "act of Congress, fairly interpreted, is in actual conflict with the law of the state," [ ] and EMTALA provides that state and local laws that directly conflict with the requirements of EMTALA are preempted.

* * *

It is beyond the limits of our judicial function to address the moral or ethical propriety of providing emergency stabilizing medical treatment to anencephalic infants. We are bound to interpret federal statutes in accordance with their plain language and any expressed congressional intent. EMTALA does not carve out an exception for anencephalic infants in respiratory distress any more than it carves out an exception for comatose patients, those with lung cancer, or those with muscular dystrophy-all of whom may repeatedly seek emergency stabilizing treatment for respiratory distress and also possess an underlying medical condition that severely affects their quality of life and ultimately may result in their death ...

SPROUSE, J., dissenting:

* * * I simply do not believe, that Congress, in enacting EMTALA, meant for the judiciary to superintend the sensitive decision-making process between family and physicians at the bedside of a helpless and terminally ill patient under the circumstances of this case. Tragic end-of-life hospital dramas such as this one do not represent phenomena susceptible of uniform legal control. In my view, Congress, even in its weakest moments, would not have attempted to impose federal control in this sensitive, private area.

I also submit that EMTALA's language concerning the type and extent of emergency treatment to be extended to all patients was not intended to cover the continued emergencies that typically attend patients like Baby K ... The hospital argues that anencephaly, not the subsidiary respiratory failure, is the condition that should be reviewed in order to judge the applicability vel non of EMTALA. I agree. I would consider anencephaly as the relevant condition and the respiratory difficulty as one of many subsidiary conditions found in a patient with the disease. EMTALA was not designed to reach such circumstances.

The tragic phenomenon Baby K represents exemplifies the need to take a case-by-case approach to determine if an emergency episode is governed by EMTALA. Baby K's condition presents her parents and doctors with decision-making choices that are different even from the difficult choices presented by other terminal diseases * * *. Given this unique medical condition, whatever treatment is appropriate for her unspeakably tragic illness should be regarded as a continuum, not as a series of discrete emergency medical conditions to be considered in isolation. Humanitarian concerns dictate appropriate care. However, if resort must be had to our courts to test the appropriateness of the care, the legal vehicle should be state malpractice law.

Notes and Questions

1. For a full discussion of the Emergency Medical Treatment and Active Labor Act ("EMTALA"), see Chapter 11 of Furrow et al., Health Law (5th ed., 2004).

2. Was *Baby K* properly decided? Is it compelled by the "plain meaning" rule? Is its application to an anencephalic newborn an anomaly? Is there any reason that EMTALA should not be applied to an anencephalic newborn if it is applied to everyone else?

3. The health care providers who wanted to stop providing emergency care to Baby K and their supporters (including the American Academy of Pediatrics) decided not to seek review of this case in the Supreme Court. Can you imagine why they would make this decision? What are the risks and benefits of seeking such review?

4. Of course, if Judge Wilkins misinterpreted the will of Congress, Congress could amend EMTALA and make it clear that it did not apply to anencephalic infants. Should Congress amend EMTALA to avoid the result in *Baby K*? How would you draft an amendment that would serve this purpose without otherwise weakening that statute? Why do you think the American Academy of Pediatrics decided against seeking relief from Congress also?

5. If Baby K had never left the hospital, would resuscitation have been required under EMTALA? In Bryan v. Rectors and Visitors of the University of Virginia, 95 F.3d 349 (4th Cir.1996), the Court of Appeals held that the plaintiff did not have an EMTALA claim where the patient had been admitted to the hospital in an emergency condition but where the hospital had entered a "do not resuscitate" (DNR) order some twelve days after admission. The order was entered over the protests of the patient's family. A week after the order was entered, the patient died, according to the plaintiff due to the DNR order. Is this case distinguishable from the Circuit's earlier decision in *Baby K*? Should the duty under EMTALA dissipate over time? Is the duty "renewed" when someone is discharged from an institution and then reappears at the institution's emergency room? Do we need a similar statute that would require continuing treatment?

6. The claims by the hospital and physicians in *Baby K* that physicians ought to be able to refuse treatment that they consider futile are considered in the discussion of "medical futility" in Chapter 5.

7. Baby K was shuffled back and forth between the nursing home and the hospital six times until she died, shortly after her second birthday, on April 15, 1995. Upon her death her mother, who had fought so hard to keep her alive, said, "She's in heaven. She's in peace. Knowing that she's with God is a comfort." See M. Tousignant, Death of Baby K Leaves a Legacy of Legal Precedents, Washington Post, April 7, 1985, p.8. Baby K, who was known by her real name, Stephanie, when she died, amassed medical bills of $500,000 during her short life. The hospital bill, which itself ran $250,000, was fully paid by Stephanie's mother's insurance and by Medicaid. Is the cost of her care relevant in determining what care is proper? How would you use that information in making a general policy

decision about the treatment that ought to be afforded anencephalic infants? About the treatment that ought to be afforded Stephanie herself?

8. Is the motivation of the one seeking care for the anencephalic child relevant? What if a parent seeks that treatment of her newborn because she believes her religion requires it? Because she believes that some miracle will save her baby? Because she doesn't believe the prognosis made by the physician because she doesn't trust any doctors? Because she qualifies for some form of state aid only as long as she has a dependent child? Baby K's mother visited her every day. Would you view the case differently if Baby K's mother provided no care for her, never visited her, and depended entirely on Medicaid funds to pay for the care? Are these factors relevant to the court's legal analysis in *Baby K*.

B. NON–HEART–BEATING DONORS

Problem: Holy Central Hospital's Organ Harvesting Proposal

Holy Central Hospital (HCH) is a large teaching hospital associated with a medical school, and it faces a rather bleak economic future. In an effort to develop those programs that produce a substantial net revenue stream, the hospital decided to increase the size and activity of its transplant program. It hired a new transplant medical director, Dr. Joshua Niblet, who had been directing a financially very successful program at a competing hospital, and it authorized him to do "whatever is necessary" to develop HCH's transplant program. As a newly minted health lawyer and newly appointed assistant hospital counsel, you have been assigned to work with Dr. Niblet to help him institute the new program.

Dr. Niblet has reminded you that there is a substantial waiting list for all transplantable organs at HCH, and that the only real limit on the growth of transplant services is the availability of transplantable organs. To increase the supply of available organs, Dr. Niblet has already assured that an appropriate inquiry will be made of patients and their families whenever a potential donor may be available. Until now, all organs donated at HCH have come from patients who have been declared brain dead while they are on mechanical heart or lung support. The organs from these bodies tend to be the healthiest (and thus make the most successful transplants) because they remain well oxygenated until the moment of removal.

Dr. Niblet would now like to obtain organs from those whose death has been declared as a result of the cessation of their heart and lung functions as well as those who are brain dead. These non-heart-beating donors (also called "donors without a heartbeat" or "asystolic donors") include those who are dead on arrival at the hospital, those who do not respond to resuscitation, and those from whom life sustaining medical treatment (e.g., a ventilator) have been withdrawn. See Ethics Committee, American College of Critical Care Medicine, Society of Critical Care medicine, Recommendations for Nonheartbeating Organ Donation, 29 Crit. Care Med. 1826 (2001)("Critical Care Ethics Committee"). See also Y.W. Cho et al., Transplantation of Kidneys From Donors Whose Hearts Have Stopped Beating, 338 N. Eng. L. Med. 221 (1998). While the use of such organs accounts for only a small percentage of all transplant surgery today–191 cases, or 2% of all transplant cases in 2002—the number is increasing, and one report suggests that "as many as 20% of donors are in this class in certain procurement regions." Id at 1826. See also Institute of Medicine, Non–Heart–Beating Organ Transplantation: Medical and Ethical Issues in Procurement, 1997.

There may be some practical problems with the use of organs from non-heart-beating donors. Some transplant physicians believe that they do not work quite as well as organs from the traditional class of brain dead donors. There seems to be a delay in graft function in organs drawn from these sources, although the evidence is inconsistent and, Dr. Niblet insists, inconclusive. The best recent study shows that the long term (ten year) survival rate for is about the same for each kind of organ source. See Markus Weber et al., Kidney Transplantation from Donors Without a Heartbeat, 347 N.E.J.Med. 248 (2002). Second, very few hospitals are set up to identify potential non-heart-beating donors, even if they have developed procedures (mainly directed at the emergency room and the intensive care units) that assure that the traditional classes of potential organ donors will be identified. Dr. Niblet has assured you that these minor problems, as he describes them, will be overcome by the medical staff.

More significantly, though, there are four potential legal and ethical impediments to the development of such a plan. First, HCH must confront the unspoken uncertainty inherent in the declaration of death based on heart-lung criteria. Death is marked by the irreversible cessation of heart and lung functions, but does that refer to a cessation that will be irreversible in the absence of any intervention designed to restore these functions, or cessation that will be reversible even if there are attempts at resuscitation? The Critical Care Ethics Committee prefers the first, "weaker," definition, but are they right? In any case, how long must a physician wait to be certain that the cessation of those functions is truly irreversible? The longer that doctors wait after heart and lung functions have ceased before declaring the patient dead, the more the potentially transplantable organs will deteriorate. Transplant physicians (and potential recipients) generally hope that there will be little lag between the cessation of these functions and the declaration of death; others are concerned about this rush to judgment about death when a patient who could be revived might be declared dead prematurely. A number of time-lag standards have been adopted, and they differ from place to place. For example, European medical institutions seem to have settled on a ten minute delay between cessation of function and the declaration of death, while the Institute of Medicine in the United States recommends five minutes, and one of the nation's most active transplant centers, the University of Pittsburgh Medical Center, recommended only a two minute delay. The Critical Care Ethics Committee proposes that the wait be at least two minutes, and it views any wait of longer than five minutes as inappropriate.

Second, a non-heart-beating donor's body is often treated to preserve organs for transplant before the donor is declared dead. The donor may be given heparin and phentolamine (or other medications) in an effort to thin the blood, expand the blood vessels, cool down the body and thus preserve the organs. While a potential donor's death is always imminent when these medications are administered, these medications themselves may hasten the death of some patients—primarily, those with bleeding in the brain. Further, it is very rarely appropriate to impose a medical treatment on one person for the benefit of another; that would constitute the ethically unacceptable use of the first person for the benefit of the second. When the law does permit it (in the cases of blood donation and, rarely, live organ donation), the law is particularly skeptical of surrogate consent on behalf of incompetent donors. In the cases of non-heart-beating organ donors, however, any consent that would be obtained would, as a general matter, come from the patient's family, because the patient is likely to be incompetent. In fact, Dr. Niblet would like to be able to begin administering the medications while the HCH staff seeks out the family to obtain consent for the organ donations.

Third, and derivative of the first two, the local district attorney has declared that an attempt to obtain organs from non-heart-beating donors would appear to constitute murder. Further, the district attorney has announced that she would consider a prosecution for aggravated murder "in an appropriate case" where the murder was committed by those who would benefit financially as a result of the death, i.e., the transplant team. For an example of such a threat (and its result), see Joan Mazzolini, Guidelines Sought for Taking Organs from Patients Not Declared Brain–Dead, Cleveland Plain Dealer, December 20, 1997, pg. 1A.

Fourth, the largely religious Board of Directors of the Wholly Holy Health System, which operates HCH, has expressed its concern over the non-heart-beating donor protocols at some of its hospitals in other cities. Their concern was sparked by the decision of the Archdiocese of St. Louis to oppose such organ retrievals in 2003. The Archdiocesan newspaper called the practice "cruel and dangerous" and said that it failed to "meet standards of respect for human life," and it pointed out that "[t]he donation of an organ to save another's life does not make killing the donor morally admissible." See Deborah Shelton, Archdiocese Criticizes Some Organ Retrievals, St. Louis Post Dispatch, June 11, 2003, at A1.

What advice would you give to Dr. Niblet? Would you encourage him to begin seeking organ donations from non-heart-beating donors at the hospital? Would you discourage him? What advice would you give to him with regard to how he should operate any program he decides to undertake? What would you tell him with regard to (1) what "cessation of heart and lung functions" means, (2) how long a delay there should be between the cessation of heart and lung functions and and the declaration of death, (3) who should make the declaration of death (i.e., can Dr. Niblet make that declaration just before he removes the organs for transplant?), (4) how consent should be obtained from the donor or the donor's surrogate, (5) whether medications can be administered to the donor (and other "treatment" provided) to preserve the organs for transplant before the donor is declared dead, (6) the position of the Wholly Holy Hospital Board, (7) the potential interest of the district attorney, and (8) the public relations consequences of the decision? Would you seek out the district attorney and talk with her about this issue? What would you tell her? Could you work out an understanding with her that would define those cases when the use of non-heart-beating donors would not subject your medical team to prosecution? With all of these factors in mind, draft the "HCH Policy on Non–Heart–Beating Donors."

Note

The use of non-heart beating donors has remained controversial in the United States and elsewhere around the world. Although the prosecutor who threatened the transplant team that obtained organs from non-heart-beating donors has been replaced, the new district attorney has taken the same position. Has this issue been ensnared by the debate on abortion, so that almost no room for logical debate remains on either side? Those who support the practice are more likely to be utilitarian defenders of patient autonomy. Those who oppose the practice often come from the ranks of pro-life advocates. See Harlan Spector, Misgivings Again About Organ Donations; How Do We Decide When Life Really Ends?, Cleveland Plain Dealer, November 27, 2002, at A1. See also Wesley Smith, The Ethics of Organ Donation; Mere Boosterism Won't be Enough to Encourage This Ultimate Charitable Act, Weekly Standard, May 28, 2001, at 24.

Is there any factual issue that you would need resolved before you could take a position on the propriety of non-heart-beating donors? What issue? Are the questions around whether we should encourage or permit non-heart-beating organ donation really questions of fundamental principle, not fact, like so many other issues that serve as surrogates for the national divide over abortion?

IV. RELIGIOUS AND OTHER OBJECTIONS TO DEFINITIONS OF DEATH: LETTING THE PATIENT DECIDE WHICH DEFINITION TO USE

For a host of religious or moral reasons, or because one mistrusts those charged with determining death, or for some other reason, one may wish to choose a definition of death that is different from the one that has been adopted by law. Some religious groups—Orthodox Jews, some sects of Muslims and some Buddhists, for example—do not accept the notion of brain death. Should states impose their "brain death" statutes on those who oppose them on such religious grounds? To what extent, if any, should states recognize or accommodate differing religious notions of death? At least two states have promulgated laws that take into account the fact that people with some religious beliefs may not accept the state's definition of death, and in those states those people are permitted to opt out of the general state definition of death under some circumstances. The New Jersey "exemption to accommodate personal religious beliefs" provides:

> The death of an individual shall not be declared upon the basis of neurological criteria pursuant to [other] sections of this act when the licensed physician authorized to declare death, has reason to believe, on the basis of information in the individual's available medical records, or information provided by a member of the individual's family or any other person knowledgeable about the individual's personal religious beliefs that such a declaration would violate the personal religious beliefs of the individual. In these cases, death shall be declared, and the time of death fixed, solely upon the basis of cardio-respiratory criteria * * *.

N.J. Stat. Ann. Sec. 26:6A–5. For a review of this statute, see Paul Armstrong and Robert Olick, Innovative Legislature Initiatives: The New Jersey Declaration of Death and Advance Directives for Health Care Acts, 16 Seton Hall Legis. J. 177 (1992). New York has done much the same thing by regulation. See N.Y. Codes, Rules and Regs., Title 10, Sec. 400–16.

How should the New Jersey statute be applied? Should physicians understand the basic principles of all religious faiths concerning brain death, and also seek to know all of their patients' religious beliefs? Should physicians presume that Orthodox Jews, for example, do not want to be pronounced dead based on neurological criteria? Should they presume that Presbyterians all accept brain death (or, at least, do not reject it on religious grounds)? Is a brain dead (but not heart-lung dead) patient at the mercy of the religious whims of his family? What if some family members disagree with others over whether the patient would accept the application of brain death criteria? What if a family member disagrees with an "other person knowledgeable about the individual's personal religious beliefs?" On the other hand, doesn't it make sense for the state to honor its citizens religious beliefs over such an important and fundamental, literally life and death, matter, even if there might be an occasional uncertainty?

The "brain death" criteria may not be the only criteria for death that creates problems for individuals. Is there any reason to allow a patient to opt out of the brain death criteria but not the heart-lung criteria? What if a New Age religionist argues that his deeply held religious views require that he be treated as dead when he loses higher brain function? Must the state honor his request if it honors the Orthodox Jew's request to apply the heart-lung criteria? What if a patient claims that his personal religious beliefs require that he be treated as dead as soon as he is diagnosed as being terminally ill? Whenever he loses more than $200 at the slots? For a discussion of these issues (except for the issue of casino gambling), see Kathleen Boozang, Deciding the Fate of Religious Hospitals in the Emerging Health Care Market, 31 Hous. L. Rev. 1429 (1995).

Not all deeply held beliefs are religious, of course. Would it be a violation of the establishment clause to allow individuals or families to opt out of the state mandated definition of death for religious reasons, but not for other moral, political or personal reasons? Law aside, is there any policy reason to treat decisions in this area based on religious views in a different way than the identical decisions based on other views? Is the solution to allow all individuals to choose their own definition of death? Perhaps the state could adopt a default position on the definition of death—perhaps the Uniform Determination of Death Act—and then maintain a central registry of all of those who would prefer to have some other standard applied. Are there any practical problems with this approach? Could they be overcome?

Chapter 5

LIFE AND DEATH DECISIONS

I. INTRODUCTION

Over the last several years the law has been invoked regularly by physicians and other health care providers concerned about the ethical, legal, and medical propriety of discontinuing what is now generally referred to as "life sustaining treatment." A number of questions taken to the courts and legislatures arguably are outside the competence of the law. For example, consider what might constitute a "terminal illness," a concept that some have considered relevant in bioethical decision making. While there surely is a medical element to a determination that a patient is "terminally ill," reflection upon the suggestion that there could be a lab test for this condition indicates that it is more than that. Classifying a patient as "terminally ill" depends on a combination of the patient's medical condition and the social, ethical, and legal consequences of the classification. If such a classification triggers a provision in a living will or a durable power of attorney, or if it allows a physician to participate in an assisted suicide, for example, it might be treated differently than if it triggers the patient's relocation from one room to another within a hospital.

If a determination of terminal illness is not solely a medical decision, but rather a hybrid medical, ethical, social, political, and legal determination, where is the locus of appropriate decision making? Should the decision be made by health care professionals alone? By a patient and his family? By a hospital committee? By some external committee? By a court appointed guardian? By the court itself? By the state legislature? By Congress? Should the decision be based upon principles and rules that emerge from medicine, ethics, religion, litigation, or legislative social policy making? Finally, what substantive principles ought to govern the decision-maker?

The difficulties in allocating decision-making authority and developing appropriate substantive principles are not limited to the "terminal illness" classification. They extend to such defining terms as "irreversible coma," "life-sustaining treatment," "death prolonging," "maintenance medical care," "extraordinary means," "heroic efforts," "intractable pain," "suffering," "persistent vegetative state," and even breathing and feeding. For almost every question that arises within the bioethics sphere, we must make two determinations: (1) where should the problem be resolved, and (2) what substantive principles should apply. Thus, the questions become ones of process (who will decide and how) and substance (what principles must form the basis of a recognized decision). As one might expect, the substantive questions are often hidden in apparently procedural inquiries.

Substantive Principles. Three substantive principles form the basis of many bioethics debates: autonomy, beneficence, and social justice. Autonomy and beneficence are the principles most directly implicated in the questions considered in this chapter, although questions of cost allocation and rationing generally implicate social justice.

The principle of autonomy declares that each person is in control of his own person, including his body and mind. This principle, in its purest form, presumes that no other person or social institution ought to intervene to overcome a person's desires, whether or not those desires are "right" from any external perspective. If Mr. Smith wants to die, then Mr. Smith is entitled to die as he sees fit, at least as long as he chooses a method that does not substantially affect anyone else.

The principle of beneficence declares that what is best for each person should be accomplished. The principle incorporates both the negative obligation of nonmaleficence ("primum non nocere"—"first of all, do no harm"— the foundation of the Hippocratic oath) and the positive obligation to do that which is good. Thus, a physician is obliged, under the principle of beneficence, to provide the highest quality medical care for each of his patients. Similarly, a physician ought to treat a seriously ill newborn in a way that is most medically beneficial for that infant, whatever he may think the infant "wants" and whatever the baby's parents may desire.

When a person does not desire what others determine to be in his interest, the principles of autonomy and beneficence conflict. For example, if we treat the continued life of a healthy person to be in that person's interest, the values of autonomy and beneficence become inconsistent when a healthy competent adult decides to take his own life. As a general matter, most courts now appear to recognize the principle of autonomy as the first principle of medical ethics. The principle of beneficence is generally applied by courts and bioethics scholars when autonomy is impossible to apply, as where the patient is a newborn infant who has not developed any values, wishes or desires. As we will soon see, though, the primacy of the principles can be changed by legislative enactments, and they may also change in accord with prevailing judicial philosophies.

Because issues of bioethics have started to come before the courts only over the past few decades, the courts have looked elsewhere to find principles upon which to base their judgments. Courts have regularly looked both to the traditions of the common law and the traditions of ethics and medicine. Analogously, judicial decisions have often formed the basis for new ethical and medical approaches. In fact, the debate over appropriate ethical policy in determining when life support systems should be initiated or discontinued, and over whether physicians should be permitted to aid in the death of a patient, now involve lawyers as much as bioethics scholars, and the public debates on these issues have centered on the judicial resolution of cases as much as on any other source of formal principles. The law is not merely looking to ethics for potential methods of analysis, it is usurping ethics in debate on these issues.

The law is not developed only through rationally justified and formally articulated judicial opinions. The law also comes out of political compromises, consequent legislative action, and public perceptions of well-publicized bioethical cases. Congress's decision to fund kidney dialysis through an expansion of the Medicare program for all those who need it, for example, has had a substantial effect on determining who shall live and who shall die. Although it is hard to find a scholar of bioethics who supports Dr. Kevorkian's euthanasia procedures, he is largely responsible for starting the current active public debate on physician assisted death. Infants have names, and cry, and can be cuddled, while fetuses do none of these things; not surprisingly, we are willing to spend a great deal more to treat seriously ill newborns than we are to provide prenatal care.

Finally, the increasingly overtly political nature of some questions—such as whether physicians may assist in their patients' deaths—has brought formerly nonpolitical, personal questions into the political sphere. As a matter of social policy, is this society spending too much to extend the life of the very ill? In 1985, Governor Lamm of Colorado was considered outrageous when he suggested that the elderly may have an obligation to die; today the social consequences of health care decisions have become a matter of real concern to those who realize that all of their family assets easily could be consumed by a final illness. Additionally, there is real controversy over whether there is any truth to the public perception that medical resources are being used (much less, wasted) to prolong the dying process.

While courts formally look to general rules of health care decision making to determine when a patient or a patient's family may terminate life sustaining medical treatment, those general rules are not often defined with precision. Of course, the starting point is generally the law of informed consent. The law of informed consent is bolstered by state administrative regulations (often from the state health department or its equivalent), state statutes (for example, patients' rights provisions in some states), state constitutional provisions (including the sometimes state-protected right of privacy), federal regulations (like those governing research involving human subjects), federal statutes, and the United States Constitution. Because of the significance of medical decisions that will result in death, those decisions are more likely than other medical decisions to be litigated. As a result, general health care decision making principles frequently have been developed in these end-of-life cases, and then generalized to other, arguably easier, cases. Thus, this chapter will address "life and death decisions," but the principles that arise out of it are principles that apply to other health care decisions, too. In the *Cruzan* and *Glucksberg* cases, which you are about to read, the United States Supreme Court was called upon to apply the Constitution to end-of-life care, but the principles it established in those cases have ramifications throughout the health care system.

In reading this chapter, consider what role individuals, families, hospitals, health care professionals, courts, legislatures, and others ought to play in dealing with the ethical, medical, legal, social and political questions that often arise out of our new found technical ability to maintain life. As you review the way courts and others have considered individual cases, attempt to distill reasoned principles from their judgments and apply them to the following problem. What issues arise at each point in the course of the problem? Do the issues change? Is your analysis a procedural or substantive one? Who ought to be involved in the decision making at each point? What principles are relevant to your analysis at each point?

Problem: Right to Die

Mr. Karl, an otherwise healthy 62 year–old man, arrived at the Pleasant City General Hospital emergency room by ambulance. He had serious stab wounds to his chest and back, and he was losing blood quickly. The emergency technician on the ambulance explained to the emergency room physicians that he was called to the Howdy Podner Bar by its owner, who telephoned to report a fight and request an ambulance. He said that Mr. Karl complained that he had been knifed by his son and that Mr. Karl was generally uncooperative, but was too weak to success-fully oppose the ambulance attendants on the four block drive to the hospital. Mr. Karl's wife, who was called by another patron at the bar, arrived at the emergency room at the same time as Mr. Karl.

When an emergency room physician explained to Mr. Karl that he required several units of blood, Mr. Karl absolutely refused to accept that form of treatment. He said that he understood the consequences of not receiving blood under the circumstances—that death would be likely, if not inevitable. However, he explained that his Jehovah's Witness faith did not allow him to consent to a blood transfusion. In any case, he explained, religion or not, he "had his own reasons" for not wanting to survive this stabbing, and he did not want any blood. His wife, who is also a Jehovah's Witness, begged the doctor to provide the blood and save her husband's life. She explained that her husband was misinterpreting Jehovah's Witness doctrine, which permitted a blood transfusion in certain circumstances. In fact, she argued, their faith does not require that he not be given blood, it merely requires that he not actively give his consent to receiving blood. She pointed out that they had been married for 35 years and that she knew he wanted the transfusion, but that he felt obliged by his religion to appear to oppose it. Physicians treated his wounds but did not provide any blood. They did begin intravenous fluid support, which ameliorated the effect of lost blood.

Mr. Karl was maintained in the emergency room. He continued to object to any form of blood transfusion, but after several hours of blood loss he became less coherent. He began to cry about the guilt he suffered from stabbing his son, and he began talking about the Lord's revenge upon evil men. When he was ap-proached by physicians, he demanded that they kill him—or allow him to kill himself—or, at least, allow him to die. At one point he screamed "can't you morphine me to death like the other patients? Please, help me die; I want to die but I cannot face the pain."

About 10 hours after he arrived at the emergency room, he was afflicted with an apparent stroke and slipped into unconsciousness. He then was moved to the intensive care unit. He lost breathing capacity and the intensive care physician placed him on a ventilator. Shortly after his move, his three daughters arrived, confirmed what their mother had said earlier, and begged that their father be given all available treatment, including blood. His only son, with whom he had been fighting earlier in the evening, was arrested and remained in jail.

Within the next several hours all bleeding ceased, and Mr. Karl remained in stable condition. Given the consequences of the stroke, his physicians concluded that there was virtually no hope that Mr. Karl would regain any cognitive abilities. Although a special surgical procedure for dealing with cases like Mr. Karl's was undergoing clinical trials at a major medical center a thousand miles away, that technique (the "Watson Shunt") had never been successful, and Mr. Karl's family was not told about it. Intravenous nutritional supplementation was commenced, then replaced by a nasogastric tube (i.e., a tube inserted through the nose into the stomach) through which nutrition was passed directly to his stomach.

After her father had spent two weeks in intensive care, one of the daughters requested that her father's ventilator be removed. The doctors explained that they had several options. The ventilator could be removed at once, which would surely lead to her father's death. He could be "weaned" from the ventilator, with ventilator support slowly removed (and reinstated when necessary), a process which would not result in his immediate death but would be likely to shorten his life substantially. He could be "terminally weaned," which would be the same as the weaning process except that the support would not be reinstated, even if it were necessary; in this case he would be given enough medication to assure that he would suffer no distress although the medication would likely depress his ability to breath on his own, if he had that capacity. Finally, he could be maintained on the ventilator.

Mr. Karl's wife and daughters determined that he should be removed from the ventilator in whatever manner the physician thought proper, and he was successfully "weaned" from it. A week later Mr. Karl's wife asked that his feeding tube be removed. She said, "He always said that the worst thing that could ever happen to him was to be a vegetable like that Cruzan girl. He wouldn't want to live if he could not go hunting and watch football." In addition, his family physician reported that he had once talked to Mr. Karl about advance directives and that Mr. Karl had asked for a form, although he had not filled it out. Two of the three daughters agreed with their mother that the feeding tube should be removed, but one strongly objected, saying that she believed it would be wrong, from a moral and religious point of view, to do so. In fact, she had thoroughly researched the issue and learned about the "Watson shunt" trials. She insisted that her father be given the Watson shunt, or transferred to a hospital where he could receive it, because, "who knows, there is a 1 in a million chance it will work, and it is his best hope." Mr. Karl's son's criminal defense lawyer, speaking for his client, also objects to any action that will result in Mr. Karl's death.

Mr. Karl's wife and children are his only heirs. He has always been particularly close to the daughter who does not want his feeding tube removed. His family physician reports that during a previous hospitalization for an ulcer, Mr. Karl depended heavily upon his wife, and left every treatment decision to her. The current medical and hospital charges of about $5500 per day are paid by Mr. Karl's insurance, which is provided through his employer (80%), and by his family (through their 20% coinsurance obligation). Mr. & Mrs. Karl's savings will be exhausted in another few weeks when the maximum lifetime payout on the health insurance policy will also have been met. Mrs. Karl has not been able to work at her full time hourly-wage job since her husband's hospitalization; although she has not been fired, she is paid only for the hours she works. Mrs. Karl is considering a second mortgage for their modest home. Eventually, Mr. Karl's care will be covered by Medicaid, through which the State will pay medical and hospital expenses of about $3000 per day to provide for his treatment. He will have no copay obligation when Medicaid begins paying for his care.

What treatment would have been appropriate at each point in Mr. Karl's hospitalization? How should that have been decided? What judicial consequences could (and should) each medical decision have? Would your answer be different if you were Mr. Karl? A member of Mr. Karl's family? One of his creditors? His lawyer? A member of the hospital board of directors? The hospital administrator? The doctor? A nurse? The hospital ethics committee? The hospital lawyer? The doctor's (or hospital's) insurance company? A judge? Is there other information you would need to answer these questions? What information? How, exactly, would it affect your answers?

II.   THE UNITED STATES CONSTITUTION AND THE "RIGHT TO DIE"

CRUZAN v. DIRECTOR, MISSOURI DEPARTMENT OF HEALTH

Supreme Court of the United States, 1990.
497 U.S. 261, 110 S.Ct. 2841, 111 L.Ed.2d 224.

CHIEF JUSTICE REHNQUIST delivered the opinion of the Court.

Petitioner Nancy Beth Cruzan was rendered incompetent as a result of severe injuries sustained during an automobile accident. Co-petitioners Lester and Joyce Cruzan, Nancy's parents and co-guardians, sought a court order directing the withdrawal of their daughter's artificial feeding and hydration equipment after it became apparent that she had virtually no chance of recovering her cognitive faculties. The Supreme Court of Missouri held that because there was no clear and convincing evidence of Nancy's desire to have life-sustaining treatment withdrawn under such circumstances, her parents lacked authority to effectuate such a request. We granted certiorari and now affirm.

On the night of January 11, 1983, Nancy Cruzan lost control of her car as she traveled down Elm Road in Jasper County, Missouri. The vehicle overturned, and Cruzan was discovered lying face down in a ditch without detectable respiratory or cardiac function. Paramedics were able to restore her breathing and heartbeat at the accident site, and she was transported to a hospital in an unconscious state. An attending neurosurgeon diagnosed her as having sustained probable cerebral contusions compounded by significant anoxia (lack of oxygen). The Missouri trial court in this case found that permanent brain damage generally results after 6 minutes in an anoxic state; it was estimated that Cruzan was deprived of oxygen from 12 to 14 minutes. She remained in a coma for approximately three weeks and then progressed to an unconscious state in which she was able to orally ingest some nutrition. In order to ease feeding and further the recovery, surgeons implanted a gastrostomy feeding and hydration tube in Cruzan with the consent of her then husband. Subsequent rehabilitative efforts proved unavailing. She now lies in a Missouri state hospital in what is commonly referred to as a persistent vegetative state: generally, a condition in which a person exhibits motor reflexes but evinces no indications of significant cognitive function. The State of Missouri is bearing the cost of her care.

After it had become apparent that Nancy Cruzan had virtually no chance of regaining her mental faculties her parents asked hospital employees to terminate the artificial nutrition and hydration procedures. All agree that such a removal would cause her death. The employees refused to honor the request without court approval. The parents then sought and received authorization from the state trial court for termination. The court found that a person in Nancy's condition had a fundamental right under the State and Federal Constitutions to refuse or direct the withdrawal of "death prolonging procedures." The court also found that Nancy's "expressed thoughts at age twenty-five in somewhat serious conversation with a housemate friend that if sick or injured she would not wish to continue her life unless she could live at least halfway normally suggests that given her present condition she would not wish to continue on with her nutrition and hydration."

The Supreme Court of Missouri reversed by a divided vote. * * *

We granted certiorari to consider the question of whether Cruzan has a right under the United States Constitution which would require the hospital to withdraw life-sustaining treatment from her under these circumstances.

* * *

State courts have available to them for decision a number of sources—state constitutions, statutes, and common law—which are not available to us. In this Court, the question is simply and starkly whether the United States Constitution prohibits Missouri from choosing the rule of decision which it did. This is the first case in which we have been squarely presented with the issue of whether the United States Constitution grants what is in common parlance referred to as a "right to die."

* * *

The Fourteenth Amendment provides that no State shall "deprive any person of life, liberty, or property, without due process of law." The principle that a competent person has a constitutionally protected liberty interest in refusing unwanted medical treatment may be inferred from our prior decisions. * * *

But determining that a person has a "liberty interest" under the Due Process Clause does not end the inquiry;[7] "whether respondent's constitutional rights have been violated must be determined by balancing his liberty interests against the relevant state interests." [ ]

Petitioners insist that under the general holdings of our cases, the forced administration of life-sustaining medical treatment, and even of artificially-delivered food and water essential to life, would implicate a competent person's liberty interest. Although we think the logic of the cases discussed above would embrace such a liberty interest, the dramatic consequences involved in refusal of such treatment would inform the inquiry as to whether the deprivation of that interest is constitutionally permissible. But for purposes of this case, we assume that the United States Constitution would grant a competent person a constitutionally protected right to refuse lifesaving hydration and nutrition.

Petitioners go on to assert that an incompetent person should possess the same right in this respect as is possessed by a competent person. * * *

The difficulty with petitioners' claim is that in a sense it begs the question: an incompetent person is not able to make an informed and

---

7. Although many state courts have held that a right to refuse treatment is encompassed by a generalized constitutional right of privacy, we have never so held. We believe this issue is more properly analyzed in terms of a Fourteenth Amendment liberty interest. See *Bowers v. Hardwick,* 478 U.S. 186, 194–195 (1986).

voluntary choice to exercise a hypothetical right to refuse treatment or any other right. Such a "right" must be exercised for her, if at all, by some sort of surrogate. Here, Missouri has in effect recognized that under certain circumstances a surrogate may act for the patient in electing to have hydration and nutrition withdrawn in such a way as to cause death, but it has established a procedural safeguard to assure that the action of the surrogate conforms as best it may to the wishes expressed by the patient while competent. Missouri requires that evidence of the incompetent's wishes as to the withdrawal of treatment be proved by clear and convincing evidence. The question, then, is whether the United States Constitution forbids the establishment of this procedural requirement by the State. We hold that it does not.

Whether or not Missouri's clear and convincing evidence requirement comports with the United States Constitution depends in part on what interests the State may properly seek to protect in this situation. Missouri relies on its interest in the protection and preservation of human life, and there can be no gainsaying this interest. As a general matter, the States—indeed, all civilized nations—demonstrate their commitment to life by treating homicide as serious crime. Moreover, the majority of States in this country have laws imposing criminal penalties on one who assists another to commit suicide. We do not think a State is required to remain neutral in the face of an informed and voluntary decision by a physically-able adult to starve to death.

But in the context presented here, a State has more particular interests at stake. The choice between life and death is a deeply personal decision of obvious and overwhelming finality. We believe Missouri may legitimately seek to safeguard the personal element of this choice through the imposition of heightened evidentiary requirements. It cannot be disputed that the Due Process Clause protects an interest in life as well as an interest in refusing life-sustaining medical treatment. Not all incompetent patients will have loved ones available to serve as surrogate decisionmakers. * * * A State is entitled to guard against potential abuses in such situations. Similarly, a State is entitled to consider that a judicial proceeding to make a determination regarding an incompetent's wishes may very well not be an adversarial one, with the added guarantee of accurate factfinding that the adversary process brings with it. [ ] Finally, we think a State may properly decline to make judgments about the "quality" of life that a particular individual may enjoy, and simply assert an unqualified interest in the preservation of human life to be weighed against the constitutionally protected interests of the individual.

In our view, Missouri has permissibly sought to advance these interests through the adoption of a "clear and convincing" standard of proof to govern such proceedings.

* * *

We think it self-evident that the interests at stake in the instant proceedings are more substantial, both on an individual and societal level, than those involved in a run-of-the-mine civil dispute. But not only does the standard of proof reflect the importance of a particular adjudication, it also serves as "a societal judgment about how the risk of error should be distributed between the litigants." [ ] The more stringent the burden of proof a party must bear, the more that party bears the risk of an erroneous decision. We believe that Missouri may permissibly place an increased risk of an erroneous decision on those seeking to terminate an incompetent individual's life-sustaining treatment. An erroneous decision not to terminate results in a maintenance of the status quo; the possibility of subsequent developments such as advancements in medical science, the discovery of new evidence regarding the patient's intent, changes in the law, or simply the unexpected death of the patient despite the administration of life-sustaining treatment, at least create the potential that a wrong decision will eventually be corrected or its impact mitigated. An erroneous decision to withdraw life-sustaining treatment, however, is not susceptible of correction.

* * *

In sum, we conclude that a State may apply a clear and convincing evidence standard in proceedings where a guardian seeks to discontinue nutrition and hydration of a person diagnosed to be in a persistent vegetative state. * * *

The Supreme Court of Missouri held that in this case the testimony adduced at trial did not amount to clear and convincing proof of the patient's desire to have hydration and nutrition withdrawn. * * * The testimony adduced at trial consisted primarily of Nancy Cruzan's statements made to a housemate about a year before her accident that she would not want to live should she face life as a "vegetable," and other observations to the same effect. The observations did not deal in terms with withdrawal of medical treatment or of hydration and nutrition. We cannot say that the Supreme Court of Missouri committed constitutional error in reaching the conclusion that it did.

* * *

JUSTICE O'CONNOR, concurring.

I agree that a protected liberty interest in refusing unwanted medical treatment may be inferred from our prior decisions, and that the refusal of artificially delivered food and water is encompassed within that liberty interest. I write separately to clarify why I believe this to be so.

As the Court notes, the liberty interest in refusing medical treatment flows from decisions involving the State's invasions into the body. Because our notions of liberty are inextricably entwined with our idea of physical freedom and self-determination, the Court has often deemed state incursions into the body repugnant to the interests protected by the Due Process Clause. [ ] The State's imposition of medical treatment on an unwilling competent adult necessarily involves some form of restraint and intrusion. A seriously ill or dying patient whose wishes are not honored may feel a captive of the machinery required for life-sustaining measures or other medical interventions. Such forced treatment may burden that individual's liberty interests as much as any state coercion. [ ]

The State's artificial provision of nutrition and hydration implicates identical concerns. Artificial feeding cannot readily be distinguished from other forms of medical treatment. * * * Whether or not the techniques used to pass food and water into the patient's alimentary tract are termed "medical treatment," it is clear they all involve some degree of intrusion and restraint. Feeding a patient by means of a nasogastric tube requires a physician to pass a long flexible tube through the patient's nose, throat and esophagus and into the stomach. Because of the discomfort such a tube causes, "[m]any patients need to be restrained forcibly and their hands put into large mittens to prevent them from removing the tube." * * * A gastrostomy tube (as was used to provide food and water to Nancy Cruzan), or jejunostomy tube must be surgically implanted into the stomach or small intestine. * * * Requiring a competent adult to endure such procedures against her will burdens the patient's liberty, dignity, and freedom to determine the course of her own treatment. Accordingly, the liberty guaranteed by the Due Process Clause must protect, if it protects anything, an individual's deeply personal decision to reject medical treatment, including the artificial delivery of food and water.

I also write separately to emphasize that the Court does not today decide the issue whether a State must also give effect to the decisions of a surrogate decisionmaker. In my view, such a duty may well be constitutionally required to protect the patient's liberty interest in refusing medical treatment. Few individuals provide explicit oral or written instructions regarding their intent to refuse medical treatment should they become incompetent. States which decline to consider any evidence other than such instructions may frequently fail to honor a patient's intent. Such failures might be avoided if the State considered an equally probative source of evidence: the patient's appointment of a proxy to make health care decisions on her behalf.

* * *

Today's decision, holding only that the Constitution permits a State to require clear and convincing evidence of Nancy Cruzan's desire to have artificial hydration and nutrition withdrawn, does not preclude a future determination that the Constitution requires the States to implement the decisions of a patient's duly appointed surrogate. Nor does it prevent States from developing other approaches for protecting an incompetent individual's liberty interest in refusing medical treatment. * * * Today we decide only that one State's practice does not violate the Constitution; the more challenging task of crafting appropriate procedures for safeguarding incompetents' liberty interests is entrusted to the "laboratory" of the States, in the first instance.

JUSTICE SCALIA, concurring.

* * *

While I agree with the Court's analysis today, and therefore join in its opinion, I would have preferred that we announce, clearly and promptly, that the federal courts have no business in this field; that American law has always accorded the State the power to prevent, by force if necessary, suicide—including suicide by refusing to take appropriate measures necessary to preserve one's life; that the point at which life becomes "worthless," and the point at which the means necessary to preserve it become "extraordinary" or "inappropriate," are neither set forth in the Constitution nor known to the nine Justices of this Court any better than they are known to nine people picked at random from the Kansas City telephone directory; and hence, that even when it *is* demonstrated by clear and convincing evidence that a patient no longer wishes certain measures to be taken to preserve her life, it is up to the citizens of Missouri to decide, through their elected representatives, whether that wish will be honored. It is quite impossible (because the Constitution says nothing about the matter) that those citizens will decide upon a line less lawful than the one we would choose; and it is unlikely (because we know no more about "life-and-death" than they do) that they will decide upon a line less reasonable.

The text of the Due Process Clause does not protect individuals against deprivations of liberty *simpliciter*. It protects them against deprivations of liberty "without due process of law." To determine that such a deprivation would not occur if Nancy Cruzan were forced to take nourishment against her will, it is unnecessary to reopen the historically recurrent debate over whether "due process" includes substantive restrictions. [ ] It is at least true that no "substantive due process" claim can be maintained unless the claimant demonstrates that the State has deprived him of a right historically and traditionally protected against State interference. [ ] That cannot possibly be established here.

* * * "[T]here is no significant support for the claim that a right to suicide is so rooted in our tradition that it may be deemed 'fundamental' or 'implicit in the concept of ordered liberty.' "[ ]

Petitioners rely on three distinctions to separate Nancy Cruzan's case from ordinary suicide: (1) that she is permanently incapacitated and in pain; (2) that she would bring on her death not by any affirmative act but by merely declining treatment that provides nourishment; and (3) that preventing her from effectuating her presumed wish to die requires violation of her bodily integrity. None of these suffices.

[Scalia points out (1) that pain and incapacity have never constituted legal defenses to a charge of suicide, (2) that the distinction between "action" and "inaction" is logically and legally meaningless, and (3) that preventing suicide often (or always) requires the violation of bodily integrity, and it begs the question of whether the refusal of treatment is itself suicide.]

* * *

To raise up a constitutional right here we would have to create out of nothing (for it exists neither in text nor tradition) some constitutional principle whereby, although the State may insist that an individual come in out of the cold and eat food, it may not insist that he take medicine; and although it may pump his stomach empty of poison he has ingested, it may not fill his stomach with food he has failed to ingest. Are there, then, no reasonable and humane limits that ought not to be exceeded in requiring an individual to preserve his own life? There obviously are, but they are not set forth in the Due Process Clause. What assures us that those limits will not be exceeded is the same constitutional guarantee that is the source of most of our protection—what protects us, for example, from being assessed a tax of 100% of our income above the subsistence level, from being forbidden to drive cars, or from being required to send our children to school for 10 hours a day, none of which horribles is categorically prohibited by the Constitution. Our salvation is the Equal Protection Clause, which requires the democratic majority to accept for themselves and their loved ones what they impose on you and me. This Court need not, and has no authority to, inject itself into every field of human activity where irrationality and oppression may theoretically occur, and if it tries to do so it will destroy itself.

JUSTICE BRENNAN, with whom JUSTICE MARSHALL and JUSTICE BLACKMUN join, dissenting.

* * *

Today the Court, while tentatively accepting that there is some degree of constitutionally protected liberty interest in avoiding unwanted medical treatment, including life-sustaining medical treatment such as artificial nutrition and hydration, affirms the decision of the Missouri Supreme Court. The majority opinion, as I read it, would affirm that decision on the ground that a State may require "clear and convincing" evidence of Nancy Cruzan's prior decision to forgo life-sustaining treatment under circumstances such as hers in order to ensure that her actual wishes are honored. Because I believe that Nancy Cruzan has a fundamental right to be free of unwanted artificial nutrition and hydration, which right is not outweighed by any interests of the State, and because I find that the improperly biased procedural obstacles imposed by the Missouri Supreme Court impermissibly burden that right, I respectfully dissent. Nancy Cruzan is entitled to choose to die with dignity.

* * *

The right to be free from unwanted medical attention is a right to evaluate the potential benefit of treatment and its possible consequences according to one's own values and to make a personal decision whether to subject oneself to the intrusion. For a patient like Nancy Cruzan, the sole benefit of medical treatment is being kept metabolically alive. Neither artificial nutrition nor any other form of medical treatment available today can cure or in any way ameliorate her condition. Irreversibly vegetative patients are devoid of thought, emotion and sensation; they are permanently and completely unconscious. As the President's Commission concluded in approving the withdrawal of life support equipment from irreversibly vegetative patients:

> "[T]reatment ordinarily aims to benefit a patient through preserving life, relieving pain and suffering, protecting against disability, and returning maximally effective functioning. If a prognosis of permanent unconsciousness is correct, however, continued treatment cannot confer such benefits. Pain and suffering are absent, as are joy, satisfaction, and pleasure. Disability is total and no return to an even minimal level of social or human functioning is possible." [ ]

There are also affirmative reasons why someone like Nancy might choose to forgo artificial nutrition and hydration under these circumstances. Dying is personal. And it is profound. For many, the thought of an ignoble end, steeped in decay, is abhorrent. A quiet, proud death, bodily integrity intact, is a matter of extreme consequence. "In certain, thankfully rare, circumstances the burden of maintaining the corporeal existence degrades the very humanity it was meant to serve." * * *

Such conditions are, for many, humiliating to contemplate, as is visiting a prolonged and anguished vigil on one's parents, spouse, and children. A long, drawn-out death can have a debilitating effect on family members. [ ] For some, the idea of being remembered in their persistent vegetative states rather than as they were before their illness or accident may be very disturbing.

* * *

The only state interest asserted here is a general interest in the preservation of life. But the State has no legitimate general interest in someone's life, completely abstracted from the interest of the person living that life, that could outweigh the person's choice to avoid medical treatment. * * * [T]he State's general interest in life must accede to Nancy Cruzan's particularized and intense interest in self-determination in her choice of medical treatment. There is simply nothing legitimately within the State's purview to be gained by superseding her decision.

* * *

This is not to say that the State has no legitimate interests to assert here. As the majority recognizes Missouri has a *parens patriae* interest in providing Nancy Cruzan, now incompetent, with as accurate as possible a determination of how she would exercise her rights under these circumstances. Second, if and when it is determined that Nancy Cruzan would want to continue treatment, the State may legitimately assert an interest in providing that treatment. But *until* Nancy's wishes have been determined, the only state interest that may be asserted is an interest in safeguarding the accuracy of that determination.

Accuracy, therefore, must be our touchstone. Missouri may constitutionally impose only those procedural requirements that serve to enhance the accuracy of a determination of Nancy Cruzan's wishes or are at least consistent with an accurate determination. The Missouri "safeguard" that the Court upholds today does not meet that standard. The determination needed in this context is whether the incompetent person would choose to live in a persistent vegetative state on life-support or to avoid this medical treatment. Missouri's rule of decision imposes a markedly asymmetrical evidentiary burden. Only evidence of specific statements of treatment choice made by the patient when competent is admissible to support a finding that the patient, now in a persistent vegetative state, would wish to avoid further medical treatment. Moreover, this evidence must be clear and convincing. No proof is required to support a finding that the incompetent person would wish to continue treatment.

Even more than its heightened evidentiary standard, the Missouri court's categorical exclusion of relevant evidence dispenses with any semblance of accurate factfinding. The court adverted to no evidence supporting its decision, but held that no clear and convincing, inherently reliable evidence had been presented to show that Nancy would want to avoid further treatment. * * * The court did not specifically define what kind of evidence it would consider clear and convincing, but its general discussion suggests that only a living will or equivalently formal directive from the patient when competent would meet this standard.

* * *

Finally, I cannot agree with the majority that where it is not possible to determine what choice an incompetent patient would make, a State's role as *parens patriae* permits the State automatically to make that choice itself. [ ] Under fair rules of evidence, it is improbable that a court could not determine what the patient's choice would be. Under the rule of decision adopted by Missouri and upheld today by this Court, such occasions might be numerous. But in neither case does it follow that it is constitutionally acceptable for the State invariably to assume the role of deciding for the patient. A State's legitimate interest in safeguarding a patient's choice cannot be furthered by simply appropriating it.

* * *

JUSTICE STEVENS, dissenting.

* * *

Choices about death touch the core of liberty. Our duty, and the concomitant freedom, to come to terms with the conditions of our own mortality are undoubtedly "so rooted in the traditions and conscience of our people as to be ranked as fundamental," [ ] and indeed are essential incidents of the unalienable rights to life and liberty endowed us by our Creator. [ ]

The more precise constitutional significance of death is difficult to describe; not much may be said with confidence about death unless it is said from faith, and that alone is reason enough to protect the freedom to conform choices about death to individual conscience. We may also, however, justly assume that death is not life's simple opposite, or its necessary terminus, but rather its completion. Our ethical tradition has long regarded an appreciation of mortality as essential to understanding life's significance. It may, in fact, be impossible to live for anything without being prepared to die for something. * * *

These considerations cast into stark relief the injustice, and unconstitutionality, of Missouri's treatment of Nancy Beth Cruzan. Nancy Cruzan's death, when it comes, cannot be an historic act of heroism; it will inevitably be the consequence of her tragic accident. But Nancy Cruzan's interest in life, no less than that of any other person, includes an interest in how she will be thought of after her death by those whose opinions mattered to her. There can be no doubt that her life made her dear to her family, and to others. How she dies will affect how that life is remembered. The trial court's order authorizing Nancy's parents to cease their daughter's treatment would have permitted the family that cares for Nancy to bring to a close her tragedy and her death. Missouri's objection to that order subordinates Nancy's body, her family, and the lasting significance of her life to the State's own interests. The decision we review thereby interferes with constitutional interests of the highest order.

To be constitutionally permissible, Missouri's intrusion upon these fundamental liberties must, at a minimum, bear a reasonable relationship to a legitimate state end. [ ] Missouri asserts that its policy is related to a state interest in the protection of life. In my view, however, it is an effort to define life, rather than to protect it, that is the heart of Missouri's policy.

* * *

Life, particularly human life, is not commonly thought of as a merely physiological condition or function. Its sanctity is often thought to derive from the impossibility of any such reduction. When people speak of life, they often mean to describe the experiences that comprise a person's history, as when it is said that somebody "led a good life."[20] They may also mean to refer to the practical manifestation of the human spirit, a meaning captured by the familiar observation that somebody "added life" to an assembly. If there is a shared thread among the various opinions on this subject, it may be that life is an activity which is at once the matrix for and an integration of a person's interests. In any event, absent some theological abstraction, the idea of life is not conceived separately from the idea of a living person. Yet, it is by precisely such a separation that Missouri asserts an interest in Nancy Cruzan's life in opposition to Nancy Cruzan's own interests.

* * *

Only because Missouri has arrogated to itself the power to define life, and only because the Court permits this usurpation, are Nancy Cruzan's life and liberty put into disquieting conflict. If Nancy Cruzan's life were defined by reference to her own interests, so that her life expired when her biological existence ceased serving *any* of her own interests, then her constitutionally protected interest in freedom from unwanted treatment would not come into conflict with her constitutionally protected interest in life. Conversely, if there were *any* evidence that Nancy Cruzan herself defined life to encompass every form of biological persistence by a human being, so that the continuation of treatment would serve Nancy's own liberty, then once again there would be no conflict between life and liberty. The opposition of life and liberty in this case are thus not the result of Nancy Cruzan's tragic accident, but are instead the artificial consequence of Missouri's effort, and this Court's willingness, to abstract Nancy Cruzan's life from Nancy Cruzan's person.

* * *

The Cruzan family's continuing concern provides a concrete reminder that Nancy Cruzan's interests did not disappear with her vitality or her consciousness. However commendable may be the State's interest in human life, it cannot pursue that interest by appropriating Nancy Cruzan's life as a symbol for its own purposes. Lives do not exist in abstraction from persons, and to pretend otherwise is not to honor but to desecrate the State's responsibility for protecting life. A State that seeks to demonstrate its commitment to life may do so by aiding those who are actively struggling for life and health. In this endeavor, unfortunately, no State can lack for opportunities: there can be no need to make an example of tragic cases like that of Nancy Cruzan.

Notes and Questions

1. Subsequent to this judgment the Missouri trial court heard additional evidence, provided by Nancy Cruzan's friends and colleagues, that she had made explicit and unambiguous statements that demonstrated, clearly and convincingly,

20. It is this sense of the word that explains its use to describe a biography: for example, Boswell's Life of Johnson or Beveridge's The Life of John Marshall. The reader of a book so titled would be surprised to find that it contained a compilation of biological data.

that she would not want continued the treatment that she was receiving. Without opposition from the Attorney General of Missouri, the trial court authorized Ms. Cruzan's guardians to terminate her nutrition and hydration.

2.   Does the Opinion of the Court recognize a constitutional right to die? Many authoritative sources presumed that the opinion did recognize a constitutionally protected liberty interest in a competent person to refuse unwanted medical treatment. Indeed, the syllabus prepared for the Court says just that, and the case was hailed by the New York Times as the first to recognize a right to die. On the other hand, the Chief Justice's language does not support such a conclusion. While the majority agrees that "[t]he principle that a competent person has a constitutionally protected liberty interest in refusing unwanted medical treatment *may* be inferred from our prior decisions," (emphasis added) the Court never makes the inference itself. In fact, the opinion says explicitly that *"for purposes of this case,* we assume that the United States Constitution would grant a competent person a constitutionally protected right to refuse life saving nutrition and hydration." (emphasis added)

Why is this assumption limited to the "purposes of this case"? Does the Court question (1) whether there is a constitutionally protected liberty interest in refusing unwanted medical treatment, (2) whether the right extends to life sustaining treatment, or (3) whether it covers hydration and nutrition?

It must have been difficult for the Chief Justice to craft an opinion that would be joined by a majority of the court. Justice Scalia clearly does not believe that there is any constitutional right implicated. If the Chief Justice were to formally recognize a constitutional right, he might have lost Justice Scalia's signature—and thus lost an opportunity for there to be any majority opinion.

The dissents filed in this case are long and obviously heartfelt. Do the dissenters, all of whom would recognize a constitutionally protected right to die, and Justice O'Connor, who would also do so, create a majority in support of this constitutional position?

3.   The majority opinion permits a state to limit its consideration to those wishes previously expressed by the patient and to ignore the decisions of another person acting on behalf of the patient. In fact, the Court explicitly does not address the question of whether a state must defer to an appropriately nominated surrogate acting on behalf of the patient. On the other hand, the dissenting justices would recognize the decisions of a surrogate under appropriate circumstances, and Justice O'Connor suggests that the duty to give effect to those decisions "may well be constitutionally required." What is the constitutional status of surrogate decision-making after *Cruzan*?

4.   Note that none of the opinions refers to the "right of privacy," a term which has caused the Court such tremendous grief in the abortion context. The Chief Justice analyzes this issue in the more general terms of a fourteenth amendment liberty interest, and none of the counsel argued the case in terms of the right to privacy. Apparently the Court just did not wish to entangle itself any further with the "P" word.

5.   Seven years after *Cruzan* was decided, the Supreme Court again considered end-of-life medical decision making in *Washington v. Glucksberg*, below in Section VI, which addressed the Constitutional status of physician assisted death. Chief Justice Rehnquist, writing for the Court, announced that "We have * * * assumed, and strongly suggested, that the Due Process Clause protects the

traditional right to refuse unwanted lifesaving medical treatment." Is that an accurate description of the holding in *Cruzan*? A few pages later, in the same opinion, Chief Justice Rehnquist describes the *Cruzan* case slightly differently: "[A]lthough Cruzan is often described as a 'right to die' case [ ], we were, in fact, more precise: we assumed that the Constitution granted competent persons a 'constitutionally protected right to refuse lifesaving hydration and nutrition.' " Is that a more accurate account of what the Court decided in *Cruzan*?

Justice O'Connor, concurring in *Glucksberg*, says that "there is no need to address the question whether suffering patients have a constitutionally cognizable interest in obtaining relief from the suffering that they may experience in the last days of their lives." This issue, according to Justice O'Connor, was decided by *Cruzan*. Is she right? Justice Stevens also commented on the *Cruzan* case in the course of his concurring opinion in *Glucksberg*. He explained that "Cruzan did give recognition * * * to the more specific interest in making decisions about how to confront an imminent death. * * * Cruzan makes it clear that some individuals who no longer have the option of deciding whether to live or to die because they are already on the threshold of death have a constitutionally protected interest [in deciding how they will die] that may outweigh the State's interest in preserving life at all costs." Is this an accurate description of *Cruzan*? If the Justices who participated in both the *Cruzan* and *Glucksberg* cases cannot agree on just what the case really means, how can your health law teacher expect you to do so?

6. Except for a glancing reference by Justice Stevens in his dissent, the opinions do not consider the cost of providing care to Nancy Cruzan. Should the cost be relevant? Should the constitutional right (to liberty or to life) vary depending on who bears the cost? See Harris v. McRae, 448 U.S. 297, 100 S.Ct. 2671, 65 L.Ed.2d 784 (1980). Would your analysis of this case be any different if the costs were being paid by an insurance company, by the health maintenance organization to which you belong, by Ms. Cruzan's parents, or by community fund raising in Nancy Cruzan's neighborhood, rather than by the state of Missouri? Should the one who pays the bills get to participate in the health care decision making?

At the oral argument of this case one Justice asked the counsel for Missouri several questions about the cost. If the cost were borne by the Cruzan family, and if the state could require the continued treatment of Nancy Cruzan, could the state also impose a duty on the family to pay for that treatment? Counsel for Missouri never argued that the state could require the family to pay for treatment that members of the family believed the patient would not want. Instead, he simply argued that the cost question was not before the Court because the entire cost was being borne by the state of Missouri. But what if the family were paying? Would it seem especially cruel to require a family to spend all its resources on treatment it believes is terribly burdensome to the patient and that it is certain the patient would not want? Should this be a matter of constitutional law?

Judge Blackmar's dissent to the Missouri Supreme Court's opinion in *Cruzan* addresses the disutility of requiring some patients to be kept alive, at great expense, while the state is unable (or unwilling) to provide adequate care to others. He points out:

> The absolutist position is also infirm because the state does not stand prepared to finance the preservation of life, without regard to the cost, in very many cases. In this particular case the state has Nancy in its possession, and is litigating its right to keep her. Yet, several years ago, a respected judge needed extraordinary treatment which the hospital in which he was a patient

was not willing to furnish without a huge advance deposit and the state apparently had no desire to help out. Many people die because of the unavailability of heroic medical treatment. It simply cannot be said that the state's interest in preserving and prolonging life is absolute.

760 S.W.2d at 429. Judge Blackmar also points out, in a footnote, that "an absolutist would undoubtedly be offended by an inquiry as to whether the state, by prolonging Nancy's life at its own expense, is disabling itself from [providing] needed treatment to others who do not have such dire prognosis." 760 S.W.2d at 429 n. 4.

7. The result of the *Cruzan* case is that most law regarding health care decision making has continued to be established on a state by state basis; there seems to be very little, if any, United States constitutional limit on what states may do. The *Cruzan* case thus may have deflected the "right to die" debate to the political decision making process in the way that several recent ambivalent abortion decisions have done the same with the abortion question. See Chapter 16, above.

8. The decision of the United States Supreme Court to opt out of providing much constitutional guidance to the states may allow a crazy quilt of state laws to persist such that a patient who would have a "right to die" that could be exercised by his family in California or New Jersey would not have that right (or would not have a right that could be exercised by his family) in Missouri, Michigan or New York. Indeed, the conditions and extent of, and the restrictions and exceptions to, any "right to die" might be different in each state. State policies will thus require different results in factually identical cases. Is there anything wrong with this?

What would happen if Nancy Cruzan's family had decided to move her to the Yale Medical Center "because of the more favorable medical facilities" there? Could they have moved her from Missouri to Connecticut, where removal of the gastrostomy clearly would be legally permitted, just for the purpose of removing the gastrostomy? If they could not, then Nancy Cruzan could have become a prisoner of a state that rejects her family's values—values that have been incorporated into official state policies in other jurisdictions. If they could move her, however, Missouri would have allowed the family to undercut the important policy objectives of the state law and imperil the very life the law was designed to protect. Would it violate any criminal statute to move someone across state lines for the purpose of avoiding the laws governing termination of life support in the first state? Could a state make such an action a crime?

In early 1991 the father and guardian of Christine Busalacchi sought to have his daughter moved from Missouri to Minnesota for medical consultation with a nationally known neurologist. Ms. Busalacchi, who had been living in the same nursing home that had housed Nancy Cruzan, was arguably in a persistent vegetative state. The state of Missouri sought (and obtained) an order forbidding the move because of the fear that her father wanted only to find some place where his daughter could die. A divided Missouri Court of Appeals determined that the trial court was required to commence a new hearing on whether the move could be justified by other medical objectives. In deciding the case, the majority made it clear that " * * * we will not permit [the] guardian to forum shop in an effort to control whether Christine lives or dies." The dissent argued that " * * * Minnesota is not a medical or ethical wasteland * * *. There is a parochial arrogance in suggesting, as the state does, that only in Missouri can Christine's medical, physical, and legal well being be protected and only here will her best interests be considered." Matter of Busalacchi, 1991 WL 26851 (Mo.App.1991), transferred to Mo. Sup. Ct. Ultimately, the State decided not to pursue the case and Busalacchi died at the nursing home in Missouri. See also Mack v. Mack, 329 Md. 188, 618 A.2d 744 (App.1993) (Maryland Court denies full faith and credit to Florida judgment appointing the Florida-resident wife of a Maryland patient in persistent vegetative state as guardian so that patient could be removed to Florida, where life sustaining treatment could be withdrawn.)

Might the *Cruzan* and *Busalacchi* cases give rise to medic alert bracelets that say, "If I am in a persistent vegetative state, keep me out of Missouri?"

9. Missouri is not the only state to adopt the strict standard approved by the majority and decried by the dissenters. At the least, that standard has also been adopted in New York and Michigan. See In re Westchester County Medical Center on Behalf of O'Connor, 72 N.Y.2d 517, 534 N.Y.S.2d 886, 531 N.E.2d 607 (1988) and In re Martin, 450 Mich. 204, 538 N.W.2d 399 (1995). Arguably, the same standard has also been adopted in California, Conservatorship of Wendland, 26 Cal.4th 519, 28 P.3d 151, 110 Cal.Rptr.2d 412 (2001).

10. There is much to discuss about the health care decisionmaking issues in *Cruzan*, and the rest of this chapter is devoted to that inquiry. The September/October 1990 Hastings Center Report includes an excellent symposium on all aspects of the *Cruzan* case. The symposium includes an article written by counsel for the Cruzans, one by Christine Busalacchi's father, and several by leading bioethics scholars.

III. THE "RIGHT TO DIE"—PATIENTS WITH DECISIONAL CAPACITY

Problem: The Christian Scientist in the Emergency Room

Shortly after Ms. Elizabeth Boroff was hit by a drunk driver who went through a red light and directly into her Volkswagen bus, she found herself being attended by paramedics and loaded into an ambulance for a trip to the Big County General Hospital emergency room. Although she was briefly unconscious at the scene of the accident, and although she suffered a very substantial blood loss, several broken bones and a partially crushed skull, she had regained consciousness by her arrival at the hospital. The doctors explained to her that her life was at risk and that she needed a blood transfusion and brain surgery immediately. She explained that she was a Christian Scientist, that she believed in the healing power of prayer, that she rejected medical care, and that she wished to be discharged immediately so that she could consult a Christian Science healer.

A quick conference of emergency room staff revealed a consensus that failure to relieve the pressure caused by her intracranial bleed would result in loss of consciousness within a few hours, and, possibly, her death. When this information was provided to her she remained unmoved. The hospital staff asked her to identify her next of kin, and she explained that she was a widow with no living relatives except for her seven minor children, ages 1 through 9. Further inquiries revealed that she was the sole support for these children, that she had no life insurance, that she had an elementary school education and that she had been employed as a clerk since her husband, a self employed maintenance man, was himself killed in an automobile accident a year ago. Uncertain of what to do, the emergency room staff called you, the hospital legal counsel, for advice. What advice should you give? Should they discharge Ms. Boroff, as she requests? Should you commence a legal action to keep her in the hospital and institute treatment?

If you were to file a legal action, what relief would you seek, and what would be the substantive basis of your claim?

A. THE GENERAL RULE

For years, commentators have concluded that competent adult patients (i.e. patients with the decisional capacity to make life and death decisions—a concept discussed below) have the right to refuse any form of medical treatment, even if the refusal is certain to cause death. It was not until 1984, however, that an appellate court directly confronted a situation in which a clearly competent patient refused treatment without which he would surely die. Bartling v. Superior Court, 163 Cal.App.3d 186, 209 Cal.Rptr. 220 (1984). Any tentativeness in the *Bartling* opinion was overcome by the case of Elizabeth Bouvia, in which the California Court of Appeal went so far as to require the hospital to provide adequate support to Ms. Bouvia during her dying process. The court confirmed that hospitals are obliged to serve the autonomous interests of patients, as defined by those patients. The California hospital was not only required to refrain from providing life-sustaining treatment for Ms. Bouvia, the hospital was required to provide the medical assistance that would allow her to die without avoidable pain, i.e., that would allow her to die the way she wanted to die.

BOUVIA v. SUPERIOR COURT

California Court of Appeal, Second District, 1986.
179 Cal.App.3d 1127, 225 Cal.Rptr. 297.

BEACH, ASSOCIATE JUSTICE.

Petitioner, Elizabeth Bouvia, a patient in a public hospital, seeks the removal from her body of a nasogastric tube inserted and maintained against her will and without her consent by physicians who so placed it for the purpose of keeping her alive through involuntary forced feeding.

* * *

Petitioner is a 28–year–old woman. Since birth she has been afflicted with and suffered from severe cerebral palsy. She is quadriplegic. She is now a patient at a public hospital maintained by one of the real parties in interest, the County of Los Angeles. Other parties are physicians, nurses and the medical and support staff employed by the County of Los Angeles. Petitioner's physical handicaps of palsy and quadriplegia have progressed to the point where she is completely bedridden. Except for a few fingers of one hand and some slight head and facial movements, she is immobile. She is physically helpless and wholly unable to care for herself. * * * She suffers also from degenerative and severely crippling arthritis. She is in continual pain. * * *

She is intelligent, very mentally competent. She earned a college degree. She was married but her husband has left her. She suffered a miscarriage. She lived with her parents until her father told her that they could no longer care for her. She has stayed intermittently with friends and at public facilities. A search for a permanent place to live where she might receive the constant care which she needs has been unsuccessful. She is without financial means to support herself and, therefore, must accept public assistance for medical and other care.

She has on several occasions expressed the desire to die. In 1983 she sought the right to be cared for in a public hospital in Riverside County while she intentionally "starved herself to death." A court in that county denied her judicial assistance to accomplish that goal. * * * Thereafter, friends took her to several different facilities, both public and private, arriving finally at her present location. Efforts by * * * social workers to find her an apartment of her own with publicly paid live-in help or regular visiting nurses to care for her, or some other suitable facility have proved fruitless.

Petitioner must be spoon fed in order to eat. Her present medical and dietary staff have determined that she is not consuming a sufficient amount of nutrients. Petitioner stops eating when she feels she cannot orally swallow more, without nausea and vomiting. As she cannot now retain solids, she is fed soft liquid-like food. Because of her previously announced resolve to starve herself, the medical staff feared her weight loss might reach a life-threatening level. Her weight since admission to real parties' facility seems to hover between 65 and 70 pounds. Accordingly, they inserted the subject tube against her will and contrary to her express written instructions.[2]

Petitioner's counsel argue that her weight loss was not such as to be life threatening and therefore the tube is unnecessary. However, the trial court found to the contrary as a matter of fact, a finding which we must accept. Nonetheless, the point is immaterial, for, as we will explain, a patient has the right to refuse any medical treatment or medical service, even when such treatment is labeled "furnishing nourishment and hydration." This right exists even if its exercise creates a "life threatening condition."

THE RIGHT TO REFUSE MEDICAL TREATMENT

"[A] person of adult years and in sound mind has the right, in the exercise of control over his own body, to determine whether or not to submit to lawful medical treatment." [ ] It follows that such a patient has the right to refuse *any* medical treatment, even that which may save or prolong her life. [ ]

* * *

A recent Presidential Commission for the Study of Ethical Problems in Medicine and Biomedical and Behavioral Research concluded in part: "The voluntary choice of a competent and informed patient should determine whether or not life-sustaining therapy will be undertaken, just as such choices provide the basis for other decisions about medical treatment. Health care institutions and professionals should try to enhance patients' abilities to make decisions on their own behalf and to promote understanding of the available treatment options * * *. Health care professionals serve patients best by maintaining a presumption in favor of sustaining life, while recognizing that competent patients are entitled to choose to forgo any treatments, including those that sustain life."

* * *

2. Her instructions were dictated to her lawyers, written by them and signed by her by means of her making a feeble "x" on the paper with a pen which she held in her mouth.

The American Hospital Association Policy and Statement of Patients' Choices of Treatment Options, approved by the American Hospital Association in February of 1985 discusses the value of a collaborative relationship between the patient and the physician and states in pertinent part: "Whenever possible, however, the authority to determine the course of treatment, if any, should rest with the patient" and "the right to choose treatment includes the right to refuse a specific treatment *or all treatment * * *.*"

* * *

Significant also is the statement adopted on March 15, 1986, by the Council on Ethical and Judicial Affairs of the American Medical Association. It is entitled "Withholding or Withdrawing Life Prolonging Medical Treatment." In pertinent part, it declares: "The social commitment of the physician is to sustain life and relieve suffering. Where the performance of one duty conflicts with the other, the choice of the patient, or his family or legal representative if the patient is incompetent to act in his own behalf, should prevail."

* * *

It is indisputable that petitioner is mentally competent. She is not comatose. She is quite intelligent, alert and understands the risks involved.

THE CLAIMED EXCEPTIONS TO THE PATIENT'S RIGHT TO CHOOSE ARE INAPPLICABLE

* * * The real parties in interest, a county hospital, its physicians and administrators, urge that the interests of the State should prevail over the rights of Elizabeth Bouvia to refuse treatment. Advanced by real parties under this argument are the State's interests in (1) preserving life, (2) preventing suicide, (3) protecting innocent third parties, and (4) maintaining the ethical standards of the medical profession, including the right of physicians to effectively render necessary and appropriate medical service and to refuse treatment to an uncooperative and disruptive patient. Included, whether as part of the above or as separate and additional arguments, are what real parties assert as distinctive facts not present in other cases, i.e., (1) petitioner is a patient in a public facility, thereby making the State a party to the result of her conduct, (2) she is not comatose, nor incurably, nor terminally ill, nor in a vegetative state, all conditions which have justified the termination of life-support system in other instances, (3) she has asked for medical treatment, therefore, she cannot accept a part of it while cutting off the part that would be effective, and (4) she is, in truth, trying to starve herself to death and the State will not be a party to a suicide.

* * *

At bench the trial court concluded that with sufficient feeding petitioner could live an additional 15 to 20 years; therefore, the preservation of petitioner's life for that period outweighed her right to decide. In so holding the trial court mistakenly attached undue importance to the *amount of time* possibly available to petitioner, and failed to give equal weight and consideration for the *quality* of that life; an equal, if not more significant, consideration.

All decisions permitting cessation of medical treatment or life-support procedures to some degree hastened the arrival of death. In part, at least, this was permitted because the quality of life during the time remaining in those cases had been terribly diminished. In Elizabeth Bouvia's view, the quality of her life has been diminished to the point of hopelessness, uselessness, unenjoyability and frustration. She, as the patient, lying helplessly in bed, unable to care for herself, may consider her existence meaningless. She cannot be faulted for so concluding. If her right to choose may not be exercised because there remains to her, in the opinion of a court, a physician or some committee, a certain arbitrary number of years, months, or days, her right will have lost its value and meaning.

Who shall say what the minimum amount of available life must be? Does it matter if it be 15 to 20 years, 15 to 20 months, or 15 to 20 days, if such life has been physically destroyed and its quality, dignity and purpose gone? As in all matters lines must be drawn at some point, somewhere, but that decision must ultimately belong to the one whose life is in issue.

Here Elizabeth Bouvia's decision to forgo medical treatment or life-support through a mechanical means belongs to her. It is not a medical decision for her physicians to make. Neither is it a legal question whose soundness is to be resolved by lawyers or judges. It is not a conditional right subject to approval by ethics committees or courts of law. It is a moral and philosophical decision that, being a competent adult, is hers alone.

* * *

Here, if force fed, petitioner faces 15 to 20 years of a painful existence, endurable only by the constant administrations of morphine. Her condition is irreversible. There is no cure for her palsy or arthritis. Petitioner would have to be fed, cleaned, turned, bedded, toileted by others for 15 to 20 years! Although alert, bright, sensitive, perhaps even brave and feisty, she must lie immobile, unable to exist except through physical acts of others. Her mind and spirit may be free to take great flights but she herself is imprisoned and must lie physically helpless subject to the ignominy, embarrassment, humiliation and dehumanizing aspects created by her helplessness. We do not believe it is the policy of this State that all and every life must be preserved against the will of the sufferer. It is incongruous, if not monstrous, for medical practitioners to assert their right to preserve a life that someone else must live, or, more accurately, endure, for "15 to 20 years." We cannot conceive it to be the policy of this State to inflict such an ordeal upon anyone.

* * * Being competent she has the right to live out the remainder of her natural life in dignity and peace. It is precisely the aim and purpose of the many decisions upholding the withdrawal of life-support systems to accord and provide as large a measure of dignity, respect and comfort as possible to every patient for the remainder of his days, whatever be their number. This goal is not to hasten death, though its earlier arrival may be an expected and understood likelihood.

* * *

Moreover, the trial court seriously erred by basing its decision on the "motives" behind Elizabeth Bouvia's decision to exercise her rights. If a right exists, it matters not what "motivates" its exercise. We find nothing in the law to suggest the right to refuse medical treatment may be exercised only if the patient's *motives* meet someone else's approval. It certainly is not illegal or immoral to prefer a natural, albeit sooner, death than a drugged life attached to a mechanical device.

* * *

We do not purport to establish what will constitute proper medical practice in all other cases or even other aspects of the care to be provided petitioner. We hold only that her right to refuse medical treatment even of the life-sustaining variety, entitles her to the immediate removal of the nasogastric tube that has been involuntarily inserted into her body. The hospital and medical staff are still free to perform a substantial, if not the greater part of their duty, i.e., that of trying to alleviate Bouvia's pain and suffering.

Petitioner is without means to go to a private hospital and, apparently, real parties' hospital as a public facility was required to accept her. Having done so it may not deny her relief from pain and suffering merely because she has chosen to exercise her fundamental right to protect what little privacy remains to her.

Personal dignity is a part of one's right of privacy. * * *

Notes and Questions

1. The *Bouvia* court depended, in large part, upon Bartling v. Superior Court, 163 Cal.App.3d 186, 209 Cal.Rptr. 220 (1984), the first case to confirm a competent patient's right to make decisions to forgo life sustaining treatment. Mr. Bartling was a competent adult suffering from depression (the original reason for his hospitalization), a tumor on his lung, and emphysema. He had a living will, a separate declaration asking that treatment be discontinued, and a durable power of attorney appointing his wife to make his health care decisions. He and his wife continuously asked that the ventilator that was preserving his life be removed, and he, his wife and his daughter all executed documents releasing the hospital from any liability claims arising out of honoring Mr. Bartling's request. Still, the hospital, which was a Christian hospital established and operated on pro-life principles, opposed allowing Mr. Bartling to die on ethical grounds. The California Court of Appeal found that the trial court should have granted Mr. Bartling's request for an injunction against the hospital, concluding that, "if the right to patient self-determination as to his own medical treatment means anything at all, it must be paramount to the interests of the patient's hospital and doctors. The right of a competent adult to refuse medical treatment is a constitutionally guaranteed right which must not be abridged."

2. Do you agree that the hospital had an obligation to accept Ms. Bouvia and provide her with medical relief from her pain and suffering, even though the physicians and hospital found her conduct immoral and her request an abuse of the medical profession? Is the obligation anything more than to provide adequate end-of-life care, even when the patient refuses a particular course of treatment? Cf. Brophy v. New England Sinai Hospital, Inc., 398 Mass. 417, 497 N.E.2d 626 (1986), where the Massachusetts Supreme Judicial Court found that a patient in a persistent vegetative state could, through his family, deny consent to feeding through a gastric tube, but that the hospital need not remove or clamp the tube if it found it to be contrary to the ethical dictates of the medical profession. The *Brophy* decision required that the family move the patient to another medical institution more receptive to his apparent desires for his feeding tube to be removed. The New Jersey Supreme Court took a middle ground In re Jobes, 108 N.J. 394, 529 A.2d 434, 450 (1987):

The trial court held that the nursing home could refuse to participate in the withdrawal of the j-tube by keeping Mrs. Jobes connected to it until she is transferred out of that facility. Under the circumstances of this case, we disagree, and we reverse that portion of the trial court's order.

Mrs. Jobes' family had no reason to believe that they were surrendering the right to choose among medical alternatives when they placed her in the nursing home. [ ] The nursing home apparently did not inform Mrs. Jobes' family about its policy toward artificial feeding until May of 1985 when they requested that the j-tube be withdrawn. In fact there is no indication that this policy has ever been formalized. Under these circumstances Mrs. Jobes and her family were entitled to rely on the nursing home's willingness to defer to their choice among courses of medical treatment. * * *

We do not decide the case in which a nursing home gave notice of its policy not to participate in the withdrawal or withholding of artificial feeding at the time of a patient's admission. Thus, we do not hold that such a policy is never enforceable. But we are confident in this case that it would be wrong to allow the nursing home to discharge Mrs. Jobes. The evidence indicates that at this point it would be extremely difficult, perhaps impossible, to find another facility that would accept Mrs. Jobes as a patient. Therefore, to allow the nursing home to discharge Mrs. Jobes if her family does not consent to continued artificial feeding would essentially frustrate Mrs. Jobes' right of self-determination. See generally George Annas, "Transferring the Ethical Hot Potato," 17 Hastings Center Report 20–21 (Feb.1987) (explaining how patients' rights are threatened by legal decisions that allow medical institutions to discharge "patients who do not accept everything they offer").

Is the fact that Bouvia could not afford any other hospital care relevant? Do only private, not public, hospitals have the luxury of living up to what they view to be ethical mandates?

3.   If we take seriously the *Bouvia* suggestion that hospitals have an obligation to provide comfort to patients who choose to forgo treatment and thus die, do physicians have an obligation to inform patients of the various ways of dying that are available to them, and the consequences of choosing any one of them? Consider M. Pabst Battin, The Least Worst Death, 13 Hastings Center Rep. 13–16 (April 1983):

In the face of irreversible, terminal illness, a patient may wish to die sooner but "naturally," without artificial prolongation of any kind. By doing so, the patient may believe he is choosing a death that is, as a contributor to the *New England Journal of Medicine* has put it, "comfortable, decent, and peaceful". "[N]atural death," the patient may assume, means a death that is easier than a medically prolonged one.

[H]e may assume that it will allow time for reviewing life and saying farewell to family and loved ones, for last rites or final words, for passing on hopes, wisdom, confessions, and blessings to the next generation. These ideas are of course heavily stereotyped * * * : Even the very term "natural" may have stereotyped connotations for the patient: something close to nature, uncontrived, and appropriate. As a result of these notions, the patient often takes "natural death" to be a painless, conscious, dignified, culminative slipping-away.

Now consider what sorts of death actually occur under the rubric of "natural death." A patient suffers a cardiac arrest and is not resuscitated. Result: sudden unconsciousness, without pain, and death within a number of seconds. Or a patient has an infection that is not treated. Result: * * * fever, delirium, rigor or shaking, and lightheadedness; death usually takes one or two days, depending on the organism involved.

* * *

But active killing aside, the physician can do much to grant the dying patient the humane death he has chosen by using the sole legally protected mechanism that safeguards the right to die: refusal of treatment. This mechanism need not always backfire. For in almost any terminal condition, death can occur in various ways, and there are many possible outcomes of the patient's present condition. * * * What the patient who rejects active euthanasia or assisted suicide may realistically hope for is this: the least worst death among those that could naturally occur. Not all unavoidable surrenders need involve rout: in the face of inevitable death, the physician becomes strategist, the deviser of plans for how to meet death most favorably.

* * *

To recognize the patient's right to autonomous choice in matters concerning the treatment of his own body, the physician must provide information about all the legal options open to him, not just information sufficient to choose between accepting or rejecting a single proposed procedure.

* * *

In the current enthusiasm for "natural death" it is not patient autonomy that dismays physicians. What does dismay them is the way in which respect for patient autonomy can lead to cruel results. The cure for that dismay lies in the realization that the physician can contribute to the *genuine* honoring of the patient's autonomy and rights, assuring him of "natural death" in the way in which the patient understands it, and still remain within the confines of good medical practice and the law.

4. After the California Supreme Court confirmed Ms. Bouvia's right to choose to die, she changed her mind and decided to accept the medical care necessary to keep her alive. As of January, 2004 she was still alive. Why would someone seek judicial confirmation of a "right to die" and then not act upon it? Does it indicate that people waver on this issue? Does it suggest that knowing that one has the choice—when it becomes necessary—contributes to that person's well being? Are those who seek a judicially confirmed "right to die" really seeking control over their destiny, not their death? Ironically, the existence of a right to die may be the reason that some people choose to live. For a discussion of related issues, see L.M. Cohen, M.J. Germain and D.M. Poppel, Practical Considerations in Dialysis Withdrawal: "To Have That Option is a Blessing," 289 JAMA 2113 (2003).

5. Is it surprising that the fundamental principle that competent adults can make all of their own health care decisions has made it into the statutes of only a very few states? For an exception to this general rule, see N.M. Stat. Ann. Section 24–7A–2. Especially after the concern shown for this issue in *Bouvia*, one might expect more legislatures to have confirmed this right. Have they failed to do so because the law is so clear that legislative confirmation is unnecessary, or because there is a real dispute about the substance of the principle?

6. It is not always easy to determine the wishes of a competent patient. In order to express a wish, the patient must be fully informed, but the very information that is most useful to a patient in deciding whether to forgo life-sustaining medical treatment may not be available, or the health care providers

may not realize that it is relevant to the patient making the decision. One recent study set out to determine what kind of information is significant to patients making decisions about the removal of life-sustaining medical care:

> The provision of care at the end of life should honor patients' preferences. If these preferences are to be honored, they must first be understood. Our results suggest than an understanding of patients' preferences depends on an assessment of [1] how they view the burden of treatment [2] in relation to their possible outcomes and [3] their likelihood. The possibility of functional or cognitive impairment has a particularly important role in patients' preferences and thus merits explicit consideration in advance care planning.

Terri R. Fried et al., Understanding the Treatment Preferences of Seriously Ill Patients, 346 N. Eng. J. Med. 1061 (2002). What information would be relevant to you in making decisions about end-of-life care? Do you think that this study was correct in determining the significance of possible functional or cognitive impairments? For an interesting approach to this issue, see D.E. Meier and R.S. Morrison, Autonomy Reconsidered, 346 N. Eng. J. Med. 1087 (2002). For evaluations of these issues within particular medical specialties, A.K. Simonds, Ethics and Decision Making in End Stage Lung Disease, 58 Thorax 272 (2003) and C.O. Granai, What Matters Matter?, 102 Obstetrics & Gynecology 393 (2003).

Note: Countervailing State Interests

The right to choose to forgo life-sustaining treatment is not absolute, even for competent adults. In Superintendent of Belchertown State School v. Saikewicz, 373 Mass. 728, 370 N.E.2d 417 (1977), the Massachusetts Supreme Judicial Court first identified the four "countervailing State interests" that could overcome a patient's choice:

(1) preservation of life;

(2) protection of the interests of innocent third parties;

(3) prevention of suicide; and

(4) maintenance of the ethical integrity of the medical profession.

Saikewicz involved an incompetent, mentally retarded patient. Those four interests have also been reiterated in subsequent cases involving competent patients—including *Bouvia*—but they have never been found to be sufficient to overcome the choice of a *competent* patient. You will see states' interests discussed in almost every case in this chapter.

In *Saikewicz* the Massachusetts Supreme Judicial Court explored the significance of these four state interests and their limitations:

> It is clear that the most significant of the asserted State interests is that of the preservation of human life. Recognition of such an interest, however, does not necessarily resolve the problem where the affliction or disease clearly indicates that life will end soon, and inevitably be extinguished. The interest of the State in prolonging a life must be reconciled with the interest of an individual to reject the traumatic cost of that prolongation. There is a substantial distinction in the State's insistence that human life be saved where the affliction is curable, as opposed to the State interest where, as here, the issue is not whether but when, for how long, and at what cost to the individual that life may be briefly extended. Even if we assume that the State has an additional interest in seeing to it that individual decisions on the prolongation of life do not in any way tend to "cheapen" the value which is placed on the concept of living, we believe it is not inconsistent to recognize a right to decline medical treatment in a situation of incurable illness. The

constitutional right to privacy, as we conceive it, is an expression of the sanctity of individual free choice and self-determination as fundamental constituents of life. The value of life as so perceived is lessened not by a decision to refuse treatment, but by the failure to allow a competent human being the right of a choice.

A second interest of considerable magnitude, which the State may have some interest in asserting, is that of protecting third parties, particularly minor children, from the emotional and financial damage which may occur as a result of the decision of a competent adult to refuse life-saving or life-prolonging treatment. Thus, even when the State's interest in preserving an individual's life was not sufficient, by itself, to outweigh the individual's interest in the exercise of free choice, the possible impact on minor children would be a factor which might have a critical effect on the outcome of the balancing process.

* * *

The last State interest requiring discussion[11] is that of the maintenance of the ethical integrity of the medical profession as well as allowing hospitals the full opportunity to care for people under their control. The force and impact of this interest is lessened by the prevailing medical ethical standards. Prevailing medical ethical practice does not, without exception, demand that all efforts toward life prolongation be made in all circumstances. Rather, the prevailing ethical practice seems to be to recognize that the dying are more often in need of comfort than treatment. Recognition of the right to refuse necessary treatment in appropriate circumstances is consistent with existing medical mores; such a doctrine does not threaten either the integrity of the medical profession, the proper role of hospitals in caring for such patients or the State's interest in protecting the same. It is not necessary to deny a right of self-determination to a patient in order to recognize the interest of doctors, hospitals, and medical personnel in attendance on the patient. Also, if the doctrines of informed consent and right of privacy have as their foundations in the right to bodily integrity, and control of one's own fate, then those rights are superior to the institutional considerations. 370 N.E.2d at 425–427.

In fact, the recitation of these four interests raises issues beyond those discussed in Saikewicz:

(1) If the value of the preservation of life is the very question faced by the court in right-to-die cases, does it make sense to define it, *a priori,* as a value that is countervailing to the patient's desire to discontinue treatment?

The nature of the state's interest in the preservation of life was discussed in the *Cruzan* case, in which it was the only interest advanced by the state of Missouri. The Chief Justice said that "a state may properly decline to make judgments about the 'quality' of life that a particular individual may enjoy, and simply assert an unqualified interest in the preservation of human life to be

---

11. The interest in protecting against suicide seems to require little if any discussion. In the case of the competent adult's refusing medical treatment such an act does not necessarily constitute suicide since (1) in refusing treatment the patient may not have the specific intent to die, and (2) even if he did, to the extent that the cause of death was from natural causes, the patient did not set the death producing agent in motion with the intent of causing his own death. Furthermore, the underlying State interest in this area lies in the prevention of irrational self-destruction. What we consider here is a competent, rational decision to refuse treatment when death is inevitable, and the treatment offers no hope of cure or preservation of life. There is no connection between the conduct here in issue and any State concern to prevent suicide.

weighed against the constitutionally protected interests of the individual." Not surprisingly, the dissenters viewed the state's interest in the preservation of life very differently. Justice Stevens objected to Missouri's policy of "equating [Cruzan's] life with the biological persistence of her bodily functions." He pointed out that, "[l]ife, particularly human life, is not commonly thought of as a merely physiological condition or function. Its sanctity is often thought to derive from the impossibility of any such reduction. When people speak of life, they often mean to describe the experiences that comprise a person's history. * * * " Justice Brennan was especially offended by the notion that the generalized state interest in life could overcome the liberty interest to forgo life-sustaining treatment. One's rights, he argued, may not be sacrificed just to make society feel good:

> If Missouri were correct that its interests outweigh Nancy's interests in avoiding medical procedures as long as she is free of pain and physical discomfort, [ ] it is not apparent why a state could not choose to remove one of her kidneys without consent on the ground that society would be better off if the recipient of that kidney were saved from renal poisoning * * *, patches of her skin could also be removed to provide grafts for burn victims, and scrapings of bone marrow to provide grafts for someone with leukemia. * * * Indeed, why could the state not perform medical experiments on her body, experiments that might save countless lives, and would cause her no greater burden than she already bears by being fed through her gastrostomy tube? This would be too brave a new world for me and, I submit, for our constitution.

497 U.S. 261, 312–14 n. 13, 110 S.Ct. 2841, 2869–70 n. 13, 111 L.Ed.2d 224. Of course, Chief Justice Rehnquist reminded us in *Glucksberg* that *Cruzan* had decided that states may choose to act to protect the sanctity of all life, independent of any inquiry into quality of life, and independent of the value of that life to the one living it.

(2) Does the protection of the interests of innocent third parties have any meaning if courts are not willing to force people to stop pursuing their own interests and to serve some undefined communal goal? Is it merely a make-weight argument in a society as individualistic as ours? On the other hand, might children, for example, have a claim on the lives of their parents? Under what circumstances would such a claim be strongest?

(3) Although *Glucksberg* confirmed that a state could make assisting suicide a crime, committing suicide is no longer a crime in any state. Is there still a consensus behind Justice Nolan's position, dissenting in *Brophy*, 398 Mass. 417, 497 N.E.2d 626, 640 (1986), that "suicide is direct self-destruction and is intrinsically evil. No set of circumstances can make it moral * * *."

(4) Finally, there is no longer any reason to believe that the ethics of the medical profession do not permit discontinuation of medical treatment to a competent patient who refuses it. See AMA Ethical Opinion 2.20, Withholding or Withdrawing Life–Sustaining Medical Treatment. Even if there were, though, should the protection of the "ethical integrity of the medical profession" overcome an otherwise proper decision to forgo some form of treatment? Why would the judiciary to uphold the ethical integrity of the medical profession where it is inconsistent with good social policy? If all other analyses point to allowing a patient to deny consent to some form of treatment, in what cases, if any, should the medical profession be able to require the treatment in the interest of its own self-defined integrity?

Are there special circumstances in which the interest of the patient ought not to be recognized or the interest of the state is especially important? Does the national interest allow the military to require its soldiers to undergo life saving (or other) medical care so that they can be returned to the front? Can a prisoner refuse kidney dialysis that is necessary to save his life unless the prison administration moves him from a medium to minimum security prison? See Commissioner of Correction v. Myers, 379 Mass. 255, 399 N.E.2d 452 (1979) (interest in "orderly prison administration" outweighs any privacy right of the prisoner). Can a prison administration force feed a prisoner who is on a hunger strike to protest that prisoner's assignment? See *People ex rel. Illinois Department of Corrections v. Millard*, 335 Ill.App.3d 1066, 270 Ill.Dec. 407, 782 N.E.2d 966 (2003) For a general discussion of several court's approaches to balancing a patient's right to refuse treatment with these countervailing state interests, see Alan Meisel, The Right to Die §§ 8.14–8.19 (2d ed. 1995).

Note: State Law Bases for a "Right to Die"

The strength of any of these countervailing interests depends upon the strength of the patient's right to choose to forgo treatment. That, in turn, may depend upon the source of that right. Although some courts have found that right in the United States Constitution, *Cruzan*'s interpretation of the Fourteenth Amendment has encouraged state courts to look for other bases for this right, too. Some courts find this right in state common law, state statutes, or state constitutions.

The vast majority of state courts that have found a right to refuse life-sustaining treatment have found that right in state common law, usually in the law of informed consent. As the Chief Justice recognized in *Cruzan,* "the informed consent doctrine has become firmly entrenched in American tort law * * * the logical corollary of the doctrine of informed consent is that the patient generally possesses the right not to consent, that is, to refuse treatment. * * * " Once a court finds a common law right, it is not necessary to determine whether the right is also conferred by statute or by the constitution. See, e.g., In re Storar, 52 N.Y.2d 363, 438 N.Y.S.2d 266, 420 N.E.2d 64 (1981). Some courts, on the other hand, find that their common law basis for a "right to die" can be bolstered by references to the state and federal constitutions. See In the Matter of Tavel, 661 A.2d 1061 (Del.1995). While the New Jersey court initially recognized a constitutional "right to die" in In re Quinlan, 70 N.J. 10, 355 A.2d 647, 664 (1976), it later recognized that the constitutional determination was unnecessary and retrenched: "While the right of privacy might apply in a case such as this, we need not decide that since the right to decline medical treatment is, in any event, embraced within the common law right to self determination." In re Conroy, 98 N.J. 321, 486 A.2d 1209, 1223 (1985).

Some courts have found the right to refuse life-sustaining treatment in state statutes. Generally, courts that find a statutory "right to die" also find a consistent common law right. See, e.g., McConnell v. Beverly Enterprises–Connecticut, Inc., 209 Conn. 692, 553 A.2d 596, 601–602 (1989). The Illinois Supreme Court, for example, explicitly rejected state and federal constitutional justifications for a "right to die" because of the existence of both state common law and state statutory remedies. In re Estate of Longeway, 133 Ill.2d 33, 139 Ill.Dec. 780, 785, 549 N.E.2d 292, 297 (1989).

In addition, several state courts have found the "right to die" in their state constitutions. A decision based on the state constitution may be the strongest kind of support such a right can ever find, because it is not subject to review by the

United States Supreme Court (absent an improbable argument that a state created right would itself violate the United States Constitution) and it is not subject to review by the state legislature (except through the generally cumbersome state constitutional amendment process). Relevant state constitutional provisions take different forms. For example, the Florida Constitution provides that "[e]very natural person has the right to be let alone and free from governmental intrusion into his private life except as otherwise provided herein. * * * " Fla. Const., art. 1, section 23. The Arizona Constitution provides that "[n]o person shall be disturbed in his private affairs or his home invaded, without authority of law." Arizona Const., art. 2, section 8. Both of these constitutional provisions have given rise to state court recognized rights to forgo life-sustaining treatment. See In re Guardianship of Barry, 445 So.2d 365 (Fla.App.1984) and Rasmussen v. Fleming, 154 Ariz. 207, 741 P.2d 674 (1987). See also DeGrella v. Elston, 858 S.W.2d 698 (Ky.1993) and Lenz v. L.E. Phillips Career Dev. Ctr., 167 Wis.2d 53, 482 N.W.2d 60 (1992). The California Court of Appeal also found that such a right for competent patients could be found in the California Constitution. See *Bouvia,* supra.

B. THE RIGHT TO REFUSE MEDICAL TREATMENT FOR RELIGIOUS REASONS

The right to choose to die is usually based upon the premise that a person rationally may decide that death is preferable to the pain, expense, and inconvenience of life. Given that the process of weighing the value of life and death is necessarily based in personal history, religious and moral values, and individual sensitivity to a number of different factors, and given that it finds its philosophical basis in the principle of autonomy, is there any justification for independent second-party evaluation of whether the balancing was properly, or even rationally, performed by the patient? In fact, the most difficult cases have arisen over decisions based upon the dictates of religious principles. For example, Christian Scientists generally accept the healing power of prayer to the exclusion of medical assistance—most Christian Scientists refuse almost all traditional medical care. Jehovah's Witnesses, on the other hand, accept most medical care, but they do not accept blood transfusions, which they perceive to be a violation of the biblical prohibition on the ingestion of blood. Should a court treat a Christian Scientist or Jehovah's Witness who chooses for religious reasons to forgo necessary care any differently than it treats Elizabeth Bouvia? Is it relevant that others consider the religious ban on the ingestion of blood or the rejection of all medical treatment to be irrational?

Because courts were less able to empathize with patients who had unusual religious beliefs than with others, for many years courts were less willing to entertain the right to forgo life-sustaining treatment on religious grounds than on other grounds. Are the arguments used to justify judicial intervention to require blood transfusions for Jehovah's Witnesses when such transfusions are necessary to preserve life persuasive examples of the social value of law and medicine, or are they unconvincing examples of the paternalistic heritage of both professions? Consider a venerable old case ordering a transfusion for a Jehovah's Witness adult:

APPLICATION OF THE PRESIDENT AND DIRECTORS OF GEORGETOWN COLLEGE, INC.

United States Court of Appeals, District of Columbia Circuit, 1964.
331 F.2d 1000, 9 A.L.R.3d 1367.

J. Skelly Wright, Circuit Judge.

Mrs. Jones was brought to the hospital by her husband for emergency care, having lost two thirds of her body's blood supply from a ruptured ulcer. She had no personal physician, and relied solely on the hospital staff. She was a total hospital responsibility. It appeared that the patient, age 25, mother of a seven-month-old child, and her husband were both Jehovah's Witnesses, the teachings of which sect, according to their interpretation, prohibited the injection of blood into the body. When death without blood became imminent, the hospital sought the advice of counsel, who applied to the District Court in the name of the hospital for permission to administer blood. Judge Tamm of the District Court denied the application, and counsel immediately applied to me, as a member of the Court of Appeals, for an appropriate writ.

* * *

Mr. Jones, the husband of the patient * * * [s]aid, that if the court ordered the transfusion, the responsibility was not his.

* * *

I tried to communicate with her, advising her again as to what the doctors had said. The only audible reply I could hear was "Against my will." It was obvious that the woman was not in a mental condition to make a decision. I was reluctant [t]o press her because of the seriousness of her condition and because I felt that to suggest repeatedly the imminence of death without blood might place a strain on her religious convictions. I asked her whether she would oppose the blood transfusion if the court allowed it. She indicated, as best I could make out, that it would not then be her responsibility.

* * *

I thereupon signed the order allowing the hospital to administer such transfusions as the doctors should determine were necessary to save her life.

It has been firmly established that the courts can order compulsory medical treatment of children for any serious illness or injury, and that adults, sick or well, can be required to submit to compulsory treatment or prophylaxis, at least for contagious diseases, *e.g.*, Jacobson v. Massachusetts. [ ] And there are no religious exemptions from these orders * * *.

The right to practice religion freely does not include liberty to expose the community or the child to communicable disease or the latter to ill health or death. [ ]

Of course, there is here no sick child or contagious disease. However, the sick child cases may provide persuasive analogies because she was as little able competently to decide for herself as any child would be. Under the circumstances, it may well be the duty of a court of general jurisdiction, such as the United States District Court for the District of Columbia, to assume the responsibility of guardianship for her, as for a child, at least to the extent of authorizing treatment to save her life. And if, as shown above, a parent has no power to forbid the saving of his child's life, *a fortiori* the husband of the patient here had no right to order the doctors to treat his wife in a way so that she would die. * * *

[Another] set of considerations involved the position of the doctors and the hospital. Mrs. Jones was their responsibility to treat. The hospital doctors had the choice of administering the proper treatment or letting Mrs. Jones die in the hospital bed, thus exposing themselves, and the hospital, to the risk of civil and criminal liability in either case. * * *

[N]either the principle that life and liberty are inalienable rights, nor the principle of liberty of religion, provides an easy answer to the question whether the state can prevent martyrdom. Moreover, Mrs. Jones had no wish to be a martyr. And her religion merely prevented her consent to a transfusion. If the law undertook the responsibility of authorizing the transfusion without her consent, no problem would be raised with respect to her religious practice. Thus, the effect of the order was to preserve for Mrs. Jones the life she wanted without sacrifice of her religious beliefs.

The final, and compelling, reason for granting the emergency writ was that a life hung in the balance. There was no time for research and reflection. Death could have mooted the cause in a matter of minutes, if action were not taken to preserve the *status quo*. To refuse to act, only to find later that the law required action, was a risk I was unwilling to accept. I determined to act on the side of life.

Notes

1. The Jehovah's Witness belief that the ingestion of blood is prohibited finds its source in a number of Biblical passages. See Leviticus 17:10 ("As for any man * * * who eats any sort of blood, I shall certainly set my face against the soul that is eating the blood * * * "), Leviticus 17:14 ("You must not eat the blood of any sort of flesh * * * "), Acts 15:10 and Genesis 9:4. These passages cause Witnesses to believe that receiving blood products will render them unable to obtain resurrection and eternal life. Is the fact that Biblical and religious scholars of other faiths reject the Witness reading of these passages significant? Should the courts ever engage in Biblical exegesis? Should the courts ever attempt to decide whether an interpretation of the Bible is reasonable?

Christian Scientists may be less likely than Jehovah's Witnesses to find themselves in litigation over their refusal of medical treatment because they are less likely to be at the hospital seeking medical care. Jehovah's Witnesses do believe in medicine, remember—outside of the use of blood; many Christian Scientists reject it outright. For an account of the Christian Science position, see Mary Baker Eddy, Manual of the Mother Church, 17–19 (1935). Given the ability of eighteenth century medicine, it was likely that in its early days the Christian Science faith saved more lives than it cost by discouraging its adherents from seeing doctors. More recent literature suggests that Christian Scientists do not live quite as long as others. See W. Simpson, Comparative Longevity in a College Cohort of Christian Scientists, 262 JAMA 1657 (1989).

Many other sects also believe that God will provide any cure that is appropriate for each sick person, and their actions pose the same legal and ethical problems as do those of the Christian Scientists and the Jehovah's Witnesses. In

England the "Peculiar People" presented the British courts with this issue long before the first case arose on this side of the Atlantic. See R v. Senior, All ER 511 (1895–9).

2.   In *Georgetown College* Judge Wright concluded that Jehovah's Witnesses were not required by their religious code to forgo blood transfusions; they were merely required to refuse consent to those transfusions. Thus, a weak denial was taken as a plea for medical intervention against the patient's stated, but misleading, request to be left without adequate care. Would the decision, based on this reasoning, vindicate the principle of autonomy? Is it appropriate for Judge Wright, in his role as a federal judge, to determine that the Jehovah's Witness faith requires only that an adherent deny consent to a transfusion, not that she avoid actually having one? Is it relevant that Jehovah's Witness religious authorities generally reject this position?

The other reasons for the court's decision in *Georgetown College* seem equally fragile. The hospital could hardly claim that the risk of civil or criminal liability would require the transfusion after the hospital went to court to determine its legal responsibility. Finally, the presumption that anyone so ill as to need a blood transfusion to save her life is likely to be incompetent is simply unsupported by fact. These bases for the decision demonstrate why this opinion by one of the great Federal judges of the last century has come to be seen as one of the most painful examples of judicial rationalization.

3.   Most of the more recent cases that have considered this issue have concluded that competent adult Jehovah's Witnesses may choose to forgo medical treatment, whatever the results of those decisions may be, because the patient bears the consequences of choosing to forgo life-sustaining treatment. See, for example, Norwood Hospital v. Munoz, 409 Mass. 116, 564 N.E.2d 1017 (1991), In re Brooks' Estate, 32 Ill.2d 361, 205 N.E.2d 435 (1965), In re Osborne, 294 A.2d 372 (D.C.App.1972), Mercy Hospital, Inc. v. Jackson, 62 Md.App. 409, 489 A.2d 1130 (1985), vacated on other grounds, 306 Md. 556, 510 A.2d 562 (1986) (affirming denial of petition to appoint a guardian to consent to Jehovah's witness blood transfusion during C–Section). Compare Fosmire v. Nicoleau, 75 N.Y.2d 218, 551 N.Y.S.2d 876, 551 N.E.2d 77 (1990) (Jehovah's witness mother permitted to forgo a blood transfusion during child birth even though her life was thus put at risk) and Raleigh Fitkin–Paul Morgan Memorial Hospital v. Anderson, 42 N.J. 421, 201 A.2d 537 (1964), cert. denied, 377 U.S. 985, 84 S.Ct. 1894, 12 L.Ed.2d 1032 (1964) (pregnant Jehovah's Witness not permitted to refuse a necessary transfusion).

Even when others (such as children) are indirectly affected, the courts now tend to recognize the competent adult's right to forgo treatment:

PUBLIC HEALTH TRUST OF DADE COUNTY v. WONS

Supreme Court of Florida, 1989.
541 So.2d 96.

* * *

The Court of Appeal has certified the following question as one of great public importance:

WHETHER A COMPETENT ADULT HAS A LAWFUL RIGHT TO REFUSE A BLOOD TRANSFUSION WITHOUT WHICH SHE MAY WELL DIE.

* * *

The issues presented by this difficult case challenge us to balance the right of an individual to practice her religion and protect her right of privacy against the state's interest in maintaining life and protecting innocent third parties.

Norma Wons entered * * * a medical facility operated by the Public Health Trust of Dade County, with a condition known as dysfunctional uterine bleeding. Doctors informed Mrs. Wons that she would require treatment in the form of a blood transfusion or she would, in all probability, die. Mrs. Wons, a practicing Jehovah's Witness and mother of two minor children, declined the treatment on ground that it violated her religious principles to receive blood from outside her own body. At the time she refused consent Mrs. Wons was conscious and able to reach an informed decision concerning her treatment.

The Health Trust petitioned the Circuit Court to force Mrs. Wons to undergo a blood transfusion. * * * [T]he court granted the petition, ordering the hospital doctors to administer the blood transfusion, which was done while Mrs. Wons was unconscious. The trial judge reasoned that minor children have a right to be reared by two loving parents, a right which overrides the mother's rights of free religious exercise and privacy. Upon regaining consciousness, Mrs. Wons appealed to the Third District which reversed the order. After holding that the case was not moot due to the recurring nature of Mrs. Wons condition * * *, the district court held that Mrs. Wons' constitutional rights of religion and privacy could not be overridden by the state's purported interests.

* * *

The Health Trust asserts that the children's right to be reared by two loving parents is sufficient to trigger the compelling state interest [in protection of innocent third parties]. While we agree that the nurturing and support by two parents is important in the development of any child, it is not sufficient to override fundamental constitutional rights. * * * As the district court noted in its highly articulate opinion below:

Surely nothing, in the last analysis, is more private or more sacred than one's religion or view of life, and here the courts, quite properly, have given great deference to the individual's right to make decisions vitally affecting his private life according to his own conscience. It is difficult to overstate this right because it is, without exaggeration, the very bedrock upon which this country was founded.

Notes

1. A concurring opinion in *Wons* depends in part upon the fact that the children would be cared for by relatives even if Mrs. Wons were to die. In that opinion the Chief Justice points out:

The medical profession may consider a blood transfusion a rather ordinary or routine procedure, but, given Mrs. Wons' religious beliefs, that procedure for her is extraordinary. * * * [W]e must not assume from her choice that Mrs. Wons was not considering the best interests of her children. She knows they will be well cared for by her family. As a parent, however, she also must consider the example she sets for her children, how to teach them to follow what she believes is God's law if she herself does not. The choice for her can not be an easy one, but it is hers to make. It is not for this court to judge the reasonableness or validity of her beliefs. Absent a truly compelling state interest to the contrary, the law must protect her right to make that choice.

2. The dissent in *Wons* depended in part upon another portion of *Application of the President and Directors of Georgetown College, Inc.,* supra, where Judge Wright concluded that "[t]he state, as parens patriae, will not allow a parent to abandon a child, and so it should not allow this most ultimate of voluntary abandonments. The patient had a responsibility to the community to care for her infant. Thus the people had an interest in preserving the life of this mother." Would this rationale support state intervention and an injunction to stop a mother who had decided to take up hang-gliding, bronco-riding, working as a firefighter, or some other dangerous occupation? Why do you think it is applied in the case of a Jehovah's Witness, and not in any of these other cases? For a thorough discussion of the issue of potential fetal-maternal conflict, see Chapter 16, section III, *supra*.

3. The rule allowing patients to adhere to their religious faiths, even if that means that they choose to forgo life-sustaining treatment, is different for children. The Supreme Court has always held that children are not permitted to become martyrs to their parents' (or their own) religious beliefs. Where the refused treatment is not highly invasive, and where it is likely to return the child to full health—as in the case of a blood transfusion for a Jehovah's witnesses child— courts universally will order the treatment. On the other hand, where the chance of success is lower—as in the case of certain kinds of chemotherapy for some childhood cancers—the courts are less likely to overrule the parents and the child. See section V, below. For a general discussion of this issue, see Alan Meisel, The Right to Die § 15.6 (2d ed. 1995). For an interesting account of the values at stake in balancing the scientifically based medical interests of the child with the religious interests of the child and the family, see Janna Merrick, Spiritual Healing, Sick Kids and the Law: Inequities in the American Healthcare System, 29 Am. J. L. & Med. 269 (2003).

IV. THE "RIGHT TO DIE"—PATIENTS WITHOUT DECISIONAL CAPACITY

A. DETERMINING DECISIONAL CAPACITY

Problem: Determining the Decisional Capacity of a Dying Patient

Theodore Flores is a 27 year old who has suffered from quadriplegia since a serious auto accident (in which he was driving while intoxicated) about a year ago. His spinal injury was so high and so substantial that he requires intermittent ventilator support, and he is fed through a gastrostomy tube that has been inserted directly into his stomach. Although he has not worked since his accident, he was employed as a pharmacist until the accident. He now communicates with others by winking his eyes or blowing through a straw connected to an alphabet board. The accident appears to have had no affect on his intellectual abilities, although he is now unable to concentrate for more than a few minutes at a time, and he sometimes refuses to communicate to outsiders for days at a time.

Mr. Flores has now informed his physician that he wishes to have the ventilator disconnected and the feeding tube removed. His physician has informed him of the certainty that death will follow from either of these acts. Mr. Flores refuses to respond to such information, except to repeat his request. Mr. Flores has read most of the important recent medical journal articles about his condition, and his physician believes that Mr. Flores understands the risks, benefits, and alternatives more thoroughly than most similarly situated patients. Despite this, though, the physician is concerned about whether Mr. Flores has the capacity to decide to forgo ventilator support and nutrition and hydration. His concern grows out of several circumstances, including Mr. Flores's limited concentration span, his occasional unwillingness to communicate with anyone, and the following three factors:

(1) A psychiatrist who has been seeing Mr. Flores regularly has informed his physician that Mr. Flores became seriously depressed about three weeks ago, when he began to realize that there would never be any improvement in his physical conditions. As the psychiatrist pointed out, of course, most reasonable people would become depressed upon such a realization. The psychiatrist has recommended antidepressants for Mr. Flores, but he refuses to take them.

(2) Since the accident, Mr. Flores has become a devoted follower of August Marsh, a religious leader who preaches that self-abnegation (and, particularly, self abnegation leading to death) is the only way to gain salvation. In particular, Rev. Marsh believes that the self discipline of starvation (he usually recommends a period of a week) can bring eternal joy.

(3) Mr. Flores desperately wants to father a child—an event not precluded by his current condition. While the doctors have explained to Mr. Flores that his reproductive system is intact and unaffected by the accident, he simply refuses to believe that and he insists that he will not be able to have children. No matter what the medical staff does, and despite Mr. Flores's generally sophisticated understanding of his medical condition, he simply refuses to understand this fact.

Does Mr. Flores possess sufficient decisional capacity to make the choice to forgo nutrition and hydration and ventilator support? What other information would you want to have before you make this determination? Remember, you are looking only for information relevant to a determination of decisional capacity, you are not looking for information that is relevant to the substantive decision. What process should be employed to make this determination? Is a court order required to confirm Mr. Flores's capacity? Incapacity? What kind of evidence should be introduced in the hearing that would lead to an appropriate court order?

———————

To determine whether a patient can choose to undergo (or forgo) medical care, someone must determine whether the patient has the capacity to make that choice. Because the theory behind decisional capacity is thus employed to serve the social principle of autonomy, capacity determinations should not be entirely medical; social, philosophical, and political factors should also be considered.

Until recently, most courts that addressed this issue referred to the "competency" of the patient. In other areas of law, such as those concerned with guardianships and conservatorships, "competency" was often employed as a term with all-or-nothing consequences. A person was either competent for all purposes and at all times, or incompetent for all purposes and at all times. When we evaluate the ability of a patient to make a health care decision, though, we are dealing with something far more subtle. A patient may have the capacity to make some, simple health care decisions, and not to make other, more complex, decisions. Similarly, a patient may be able to make certain decisions at some times but not at others. To recognize these potential variabilities in competency, some courts (and many legislatures) have begun to use the term "decisional capacity"—a term which focuses on the actual decision to be made—rather than "competency"—a term which focuses on the status of the patient. In this text, the terms are used interchangeably.

Courts have been reluctant to articulate a standard for capacity. There are few reported opinions in which courts state and apply any formal principle. Courts have been much more likely to finesse the issue out of the law and back into medicine by inviting physicians, especially psychiatrists, to testify about the mental state and, thus, capacity of a patient.

For many years, physicians were likely to find that a patient had decisional capacity to make a serious medical decision whenever that patient agreed with the physician. When the patient disagreed with the physician—especially if that disagreement would lead to the death of the patient—the physician, and subsequently the court, would be likely to find that the patient lacked capacity and then seek out some surrogate decision-maker more likely to agree with the physician. In reaction to this, and as a consequence of the frustration of attempting to develop any consistent and practical definition of competence, consumerist attorneys and physicians in the 1970s suggested that any patient who could indicate an affirmative or negative ought to be considered to have decisional capacity. Of course, this reactionary view is no more satisfactory than the previously prevailing view. Neither serves the purpose of protecting the individual personality of the patient and the authority of the patient to control his own life in a way that is consistent with his own values.

Despite the extremes described above, some scholars have attempted to categorize the possible tests for decisional capacity (or competency) that could be applied to patients of questionable capacity. Five different kinds of tests are outlined in the following article prepared by a psychiatrist, a lawyer, and a sociologist with extensive expertise in psychiatry. Compare these approaches with the President's Commission suggestion, which follows it.

LOREN H. ROTH, ALAN MEISEL, AND CHARLES W. LIDZ, TESTS OF COMPETENCY TO CONSENT TO TREATMENT

134 Am.J.Psychiatry 279 (1977).

* * *

TESTS FOR COMPETENCY

Several tests for competency have been proposed in the literature; others are readily inferable from judicial commentary. Although there is some overlap, they basically fall into five categories: 1) evidencing a choice, 2) "reasonable" outcome of choice, 3) choice based on "rational" reasons, 4) ability to understand, and 5) actual understanding.

Evidencing a Choice

This test for competency is set at a very low level and is the most respectful of the autonomy of patient decision making. Under this test the competent patient is one who evidences a preference for or against treatment. This test focuses not on the quality of the patient's decision but on the presence or absence of a decision. * * * This test of competency encompasses at a minimum the unconscious patient: in psychiatry it encompasses the mute patient who cannot or will not express an opinion.

* * *

"Reasonable" Outcome of Choice

This test of competency entails evaluating the patient's capacity to reach the "reasonable," the "right," or the "responsible" decision. The emphasis in this test is on outcome rather than on the mere fact of decision or how it has been reached. The patient who fails to make a decision that is roughly congruent with the decision that a "reasonable" person in like circumstances would make is viewed as incompetent.

This test is probably used more often than might be admitted by both physicians and courts. Judicial decisions to override the desire of patients with certain religious beliefs not to receive blood transfusions may rest in part on the court's view that the patient's decision is not reasonable. When life is at stake and a court believes that the patient's decision is unreasonable, the court may focus on even the smallest ambiguity in the patient's thinking to cast doubt on the patient's competency so that it may issue an order that will preserve life or health. * * *

Mental health laws that allow for involuntary treatment on the basis of "need for care and treatment" without requiring a formal adjudication of incompetency in effect use an unstated reasonable outcome test in abridging the patient's common-law right not to be treated without giving his or her consent. These laws are premised on the following syllogism: the patient needs treatment; the patient has not obtained treatment on his or her own initiative; therefore, the patient's decision is incorrect, which means that he or she is incompetent, thus justifying the involuntary imposition of treatment.

* * * Ultimately, because the test rests on the congruence between the patient's decision and that of a reasonable person or that of the physician, it is biased in favor of decisions to accept treatment, even when such decisions are made by people who are incapable of weighing the risks and benefits of treatment. In other words, if patients do not decide the "wrong" way, the issue of competency will probably not arise.

Choice Based on "Rational" Reasons

Another test is whether the reasons for the patient's decision are "rational," that is, whether the patient's decision is due to or is a product of mental illness. As in the reasonable outcome test, if the patient decides in favor of treatment the issue of the patient's competency (in this case, whether the decision is the product of mental illness) seldom if ever arises because of the medical profession's bias toward consent to treatment and against refusal of treatment.

* * *

The test of rational reasons, although it has clinical appeal and is probably much in clinical use, poses considerable conceptual problems; as a legal test it is probably defective. The problems include the difficulty of distinguishing rational from irrational reasons and drawing inferences of causation between any irrationality believed present and the valence (yes or no) of the patient's decision. Even if the patient's reasons seem irrational, it is not possible to prove that the patient's actual decision making has been the product of such irrationality. * * * The emphasis on rational reasons can too easily become a global indictment of the competency of mentally disordered individuals, justifying widespread substitute decision making for this group.

The Ability to Understand

This test—the ability of the patient to understand the risks, benefits, and alternatives to treatment (including no treatment)—is probably the most consistent with the law of informed consent. Decision making need not be rational in either process or outcome; unwise choices are permitted. Nevertheless, at a minimum the patient must manifest sufficient ability to understand information about treatment, even if in fact he or she weighs this information differently from the attending physician. What matters in this test is that the patient is able to comprehend the elements that are presumed by law to be a part of treatment decision making. How the patient weighs these elements, values them, or puts them together to reach a decision is not important.

The patient's capacity for understanding may be tested by asking the patient a series of questions concerning risks, benefits, and alternatives to treatment. By providing further information or explanation to the patient, the physician may find deficiencies in understanding to be remediable or not.

* * *

Furthermore, how potentially sophisticated must understanding be in order that the patient be viewed as competent? There are considerable barriers, conscious and unconscious and intellectual and emotional, to understanding proposed treatments. Presumably the potential understanding required is only that which would be manifested by a reasonable person provided a similar amount of information. A few attempts to rank degrees of understanding have been made. However, this matter is highly complex and beyond the scope of the present inquiry. Certainly, at least with respect to nonexperimental treatment, the patient's potential understanding does not have to be perfect or near perfect for him or her to be considered competent, although one court seemed to imply this with respect to experimental psychosurgery. A final problem with this test is that its application depends on unobservable and inferential mental processes rather than on concrete and observable elements of behavior.

Actual Understanding

Rather than focusing on competency as a construct or intervening variable in the decision-making process, the test of actual understanding reduces competency to an epiphenomenon of this process. The competent patient is by definition one who has provided a knowledgeable consent to treatment. Under this test the physician has an obligation to educate the patient and directly ascertain whether he or she has in fact understood. If not, according to this test the patient may not have provided informed consent. Depending on how sophisticated a level of understanding is to be required, this test delineates a potentially high level of competency, one that may be difficult to achieve.

* * *

The practical and conceptual limitations of this test are similar to those of the ability-to-understand test. What constitutes adequate understanding is vague, and deficient understanding may be attributable in whole or in part to physician behavior as well as to the patient's behavior or character. An advantage that this test has over the ability-to-understand test, assuming the necessary level of understanding can be specified *a priori,* is its greater reliability. Unlike the ability-to-understand test, in which the patient's comprehension of material of a certain complexity is used as the basis for an assumption of comprehension of other material of equivalent complexity (even if this other material is not actually tested), the actual understanding test makes no such assumption. It tests the very issues central to patient decision making about treatment.

* * *

PRESIDENT'S COMMISSION FOR THE STUDY OF ETHICAL PROBLEMS IN MEDICINE AND BIOMEDICAL AND BEHAVIORAL RESEARCH, DECISIONMAKING CAPACITY

1 Making Health Care Decisions 57–60 (1980).

Elements of Capacity. In the view of the Commission, any determination of the capacity to decide on a course of treatment must relate to the individual abilities of a patient, the requirements of the task at hand, and the consequences likely to flow from the decision. Decision-making capacity requires, to greater or lesser degree: (1) possession of a set of values and goals; (2) the ability to communicate and to understand information; and (3) the ability to reason and to deliberate about one's choices.

The first, a framework for comparing options, is needed if the person is to evaluate possible outcomes as good or bad. * * * The patient must be able to make reasonably consistent choices. Reliance on a patient's decision would be difficult or impossible if the patient's values were so unstable that the patient could not reach or adhere to a choice at least long enough for a course of therapy to be initiated with some prospect of being completed.

The second element includes the ability to give and receive information, as well as the possession of various linguistic and conceptual skills needed for at least a basic understanding of the relevant information. These abilities can be evaluated only as they relate to the task at hand and are not solely cognitive, as they ordinarily include emotive elements. To use them, a person also needs sufficient life experience to appreciate the meaning of potential alternatives: what it would probably be like to undergo various medical procedures, for example, or to live in a new way required by a medical condition or intervention.

Some critics of the doctrine of informed consent have argued that patients simply lack the ability to understand medical information relevant to decisions about their care. Indeed, some empirical studies purport to have demonstrated this by showing that the lay public often does not know the meaning of common medical terms, or by showing that, following an encounter with a physician, patients are unable to report what the physician said about their illness and treatment. Neither type of study establishes the fact that patients cannot understand. The first merely finds that they do not currently know the right definitions of some terms; the second, which usually fails to discover what the physician actually did say, rests its conclusions on an assumption that information was provided that was subsequently not understood.

* * *

The third element of decisionmaking capacity—reasoning and deliberation—includes the ability to compare the impact of alternative outcomes on personal goals and life plans. Some ability to employ probabilistic reasoning about uncertain outcomes is usually necessary, as well as the ability to give appropriate weight in a present decision to various future outcomes.

Notes and Questions

1. Roth, Meisel, and Lidz suggest that each of their tests is biased by the evaluator's analysis of whether the treatment would succeed—that is, whether the evaluator would consent or not. The authors conclude that where the benefit of treatment is likely to far outweigh the risk (i.e., the evaluator would choose to undergo it), there is likely to be a low standard for competency when the patient consents and a high standard for competency when the patient refuses. Analogously, where the risk greatly outweighs the benefit (again, of course, in the evaluator's mind), a low standard for competency will be applied if the patient refuses treatment, but a high standard will be applied when the patient consents. The authors point out:

> Of course, some grossly impaired patients cannot be determined to be competent under any conceivable test, nor can most normally functioning people be found incompetent merely by selective application of the test of competency. However, within limits and when the patient's competency is not absolutely clear cut, a test of competency that will achieve the desired medical or social end despite the actual condition of the patient may be selected. We do not imply that this is done maliciously either by physicians or by the court; rather we believe that it occurs as a consequence of the strong societal bias in favor of treating treatable patients so long as it does not expose them to serious risks.

134 Am.J.Psych. at 283. The authors do not hold out much hope for the development of a clear test for competence that can be easily applied because no such test could be consistent with the different reasons that we seek to determine competence:

> The search for a single test of competency is a search for a Holy Grail. Unless it is recognized that there is no magical definition of competency to make decisions about treatment, the search for an acceptable test will never end. "Getting the words just right" is only part of the problem. In practice, judgments of competency go beyond semantics or straightforward applications of legal rules; such judgments reflect social considerations and societal biases as much as they reflect matters of law and medicine.

Id.

2.   The issue of whether a patient of questionable capacity is competent to forgo life-sustaining treatment has arisen on many occasions. One case that squarely faced the question involved Robert Quakenbush, a seventy-two-year-old recluse whose gangrenous leg would have to be amputated to avoid a certain, quick death. He was rambunctious, belligerent, and "a conscientious objector to medical therapy" who had shunned medical care for 40 years. In deciding that the patient was competent, the court depended on the testimony of two psychiatrists, both of whom treated the issue of competency as entirely medical, and the judge's own visit with Mr. Quackenbush.

The testimony concerning Quackenbush's mental condition was elicited from two psychiatrists. The first, appearing for the hospital, was Dr. Michael Giuliano. Dr. Giuliano * * * saw Quackenbush once on January 6. The doctor's conclusions are that Quackenbush is suffering from an organic brain syndrome with psychotic elements. He asserts that the organic brain syndrome is acute—i.e., subject to change—and could be induced by the septicemia * * *. [Dr. Giuliano] concluded that Quackenbush's mental condition was not sufficient to make an informed decision concerning the operation.

Dr. Abraham S. Lenzner, a Board-certified psychiatrist for 25 years and specialist in geriatric psychiatry, testified as an independent witness at the request of the court. Dr. Lenzner is Chief of Psychiatry at the Memorial Hospital and a professor at the New Jersey College of Medicine and Dentistry.

Dr. Lenzner is of the opinion, based upon reasonable medical certainty, that Quackenbush has the mental capacity to make decisions, to understand the nature and extent of his physical condition, to understand the nature and extent of the operations, to understand the risks involved if he consents to the operation, and to understand the risks involved if he refuses the operation * * *.

I visited with Quackenbush for about ten minutes on January 12. During that period he did not hallucinate, his answers to my questions were responsive and he seemed reasonably alert. His conversation did wander occasionally but to no greater extent than would be expected of a 72-year-old man in his circumstances. He spoke somewhat philosophically about his circumstances and desires. He hopes for a miracle but realizes there is no great likelihood of its occurrence. He indicates a desire—plebeian, as he described it—to return to his trailer and live out his life. He is not experiencing any pain and indicates that if he does, he could change his mind about having the operation.

* * *

The matter may be tried before a judge without a jury. My findings pursuant to this authority are that Robert Quackenbush is competent and capable of exercising informed consent on whether or not to have the operation. I do not question the events and conditions described by Dr. Giuliano but find they were of a temporary, curative, fluctuating nature, and whatever their cause the patient's lucidity is sufficient for him to make an informed choice.

* * *

In re Quackenbush, 156 N.J.Super. 282, 383 A.2d 785, 788 (1978).

Ultimately, it is difficult to determine whether the court merely chose the more credible of the two psychiatrists, or whether the court depended upon some intuitive conclusions that followed the judge's ten minute visit with the patient.

Which would be the more satisfying basis for the court's determination of competency?

Whatever one may think of the process the court employed for determining competency in *Quackenbush,* the case stands for two principles that have been repeated constantly since. The first is that a patient who fluctuates between capacity and incapacity cannot be denied an opportunity to make decisions concerning medical care, even life-sustaining medical care, just because of the temporary absence of capacity. The desires of that patient, articulated during a period of competence, must be respected by the physician, the hospital, and the courts. See Lane v. Candura, 6 Mass.App.Ct. 377, 376 N.E.2d 1232 (1978). The second principle assumed in *Quackenbush* is that a patient may have capacity for some purposes and not for others. Some state statutes explicitly recognize and protect the variably competent person.

3.   To what extent do value judgments and prejudices enter into decisions regarding competency? Would the Quackenbush case have been a simpler one if Mr. Quackenbush were a retired lawyer leading a middle class life rather than a belligerent hermit? One fascinating review of "right to die" cases suggests that gender may be an important factor, and that the legal system takes the expressed wishes of men more seriously than those of women. Steven Miles and Allison August, Courts, Gender, and "The Right to Die," 18 Law, Med. & Health Care 85 (1990).

4.   How significant is it that terminally ill patients who seek a right to die are often perceived as depressed? Isn't it natural for someone dying of an incurable disease to be depressed? Does it make any sense to extend our social perception of suicide among the medically well to the decision of the terminally ill to forgo life sustaining treatment? Two psychiatrists have recently suggested that physicians should attempt to treat depression in the seriously ill, but that psychiatrists also should recognize that some depression in terminally ill patients is not treatable, and that "[g]ravely ill medical patients should not lose their right to refuse medical treatment simply because they have been transferred to a medical-psychiatric unit. Just as internists must at some point decide 'enough is enough,' so might psychiatrists at some point appropriately stop trying to intervene and let the dying process proceed." Mark Sullivan and Stuart Youngner, Depression, Competence, and the Right to Refuse Lifesaving Medical Treatment, 151 Am.J. Psychiatry 971, 977 (1994). The authors conclude that "[p]sychiatrists need to recognize that some treatment refusals that result in death are legitimate, even if they are accompanied by suicidal intent. * * * It is often valuable to diagnose and treat depression in the seriously ill patient, but sometimes it is valuable to accept the patient's decision to die." Id. Do any of the suggested tests help you decide when depression renders a person incapable of making a health care decision?

5.   For a more comprehensive account of judicial attempts to determine competency, see Kevin R. Wolff, Determining Patient Competency in Treatment Refusal Cases, 24 Ga.L.Rev. 733 (1990). For a useful attempt at reconciling the theory and practice of judicial determinations of incapacity, see Wendy Margolis, The Doctor Knows Best?: Patient Capacity for Health Care Decisionmaking, 71 Or.L.Rev. 909 (1992).

B.   DETERMINING THE PATIENT'S CHOICE

It is very difficult to serve the underlying goal of autonomy, if that goal is defined as personal choice, in patients without decisional capacity. One way to serve this principle is through the application of the doctrine of substituted judgment. Under this doctrine, a person, committee, or institution attempts to determine what the patient would do if the patient had decisional capacity. It may be possible to review the values of a formerly competent patient to determine whether that patient would choose to undergo or forgo proposed medical care. This can be done through a thoughtful analysis of the patient's values during life or, more precisely, through review of formal statements made by the patient when the patient had capacity. The most relevant considerations may be statements made by the patient about the proposed treatment itself. Indeed, such statements may provide the only *constitutionally* relevant information about an incompetent patient's wishes after *Cruzan*.

Of course, there is no way to know with certainty what the patient would do under those circumstances. Some have argued that the doctrine of substituted judgment is too speculative to be applied reliably and that there is simply no way to protect the autonomy of a patient without decisional capacity. Where there is no possible method for establishing what the autonomous patient would do, bioethicists (and increasingly, courts) move to the second principle of bioethical decision-making, beneficence. In these circumstances, the alternative to serving autonomy is serving beneficence, and the alternative to the doctrine of substituted judgment is the doctrine of the "best interest" of the patient. As we shall see, the more difficult it becomes to decide what the patient would do if that patient had decisional capacity, the more likely it is that the court will apply the principle of beneficence rather than the principle of autonomy.

1. A Statutory Framework for Health Care Decision Making: Advance Directives and Surrogate Decisionmakers

UNIFORM HEALTH–CARE DECISIONS ACT

1994.

SECTION 1. DEFINITIONS. In this [Act]:

(1) "Advance health-care directive" means an individual instruction or a power of attorney for health care.

(2) "Agent" means an individual designated in a power of attorney for health care to make a health-care decision for the individual granting the power.

(3) "Capacity" means an individual's ability to understand the significant benefits, risks, and alternatives to proposed health care and to make and communicate a health-care decision.

(4) "Guardian" means a judicially appointed guardian or conservator having authority to make a health-care decision for an individual.

(5) "Health care" means any care, treatment, service, or procedure to maintain, diagnose, or otherwise affect an individual's physical or mental condition.

(6) "Health-care decision" means a decision made by an individual or the individual's agent, guardian, or surrogate, regarding the individual's health care, including:

(i) selection and discharge of health-care providers and institutions;

(ii) approval or disapproval of diagnostic tests, surgical procedures, programs of medication, and orders not to resuscitate; and

(iii) directions to provide, withhold, or withdraw artificial nutrition and hydration and all other forms of health care.

* * *

(9) "Individual instruction" means an individual's direction concerning a health-care decision for the individual.

* * *

(12) "Power of attorney for health care" means the designation of an agent to make health-care decisions for the individual granting the power.

* * *

(16) "Supervising health-care provider" means the primary physician or, if there is no primary physician or the primary physician is not reasonably available, the health-care provider who has undertaken primary responsibility for an individual's health care.

(17) "Surrogate" means an individual, other than a patient's agent or guardian, authorized under this [Act] to make a health-care decision for the patient.

SECTION 2. ADVANCE HEALTH–CARE DIRECTIVES.

(a) An adult or emancipated minor may give an individual instruction. The instruction may be oral or written. The instruction may be limited to take effect only if a specified condition arises.

(b) An adult or emancipated minor may execute a power of attorney for health care, which may authorize the agent to make any health-care decision the principal could have made while having capacity. The power must be in writing and signed by the principal. The power remains in effect notwithstanding the principal's later incapacity and may include individual instructions. * * *

(c) Unless otherwise specified in a power of attorney for health care, the authority of an agent becomes effective only upon a determination that the principal lacks capacity, and ceases to be effective upon a determination that the principal has recovered capacity.

(d) Unless otherwise specified in a written advance health-care directive, a determination that an individual lacks or has recovered capacity, or that another condition exists that affects an individual instruction or the authority of an agent, must be made by the primary physician.

(e) An agent shall make a health-care decision in accordance with the principal's individual instructions, if any, and other wishes to the extent known to the agent. Otherwise, the agent shall make the decision in accordance with the agent's determination of the principal's best interest. In determining the principal's best interest, the agent shall consider the principal's personal values to the extent known to the agent.

(f) A health-care decision made by an agent for a principal is effective without judicial approval.

(g) A written advance health-care directive may include the individual's nomination of a guardian of the person.

(h) An advance health-care directive is valid for purposes of this [Act] if it complies with this [Act], regardless of when or where executed or communicated.

SECTION 3. REVOCATION OF ADVANCE HEALTH–CARE DIRECTIVE.

(a) An individual may revoke the designation of an agent only by a signed writing or by personally informing the supervising health-care provider.

(b) An individual may revoke all or part of an advance health-care directive, other than the designation of an agent, at any time and in any manner that communicates an intent to revoke.

(c) A health-care provider, agent, guardian, or surrogate who is informed of a revocation shall promptly communicate the fact of the revocation to the supervising health-care provider and to any health-care institution at which the patient is receiving care.

(d) A decree of annulment, divorce, dissolution of marriage, or legal separation revokes a previous designation of a spouse as agent unless otherwise specified in the decree or in a power of attorney for health care.

(e) An advance health-care directive that conflicts with an earlier advance health-care directive revokes the earlier directive to the extent of the conflict.

SECTION 4. OPTIONAL FORM. The following form may, but need not, be used to create an advance health-care directive. The other sections of this [Act] govern the effect of this or any other writing used to create an advance health-care directive. An individual may complete or modify all or any part of the following form:

ADVANCE HEALTH–CARE DIRECTIVE

Explanation

You have the right to give instructions about your own health care. You also have the right to name someone else to make health-care decisions for you. This form lets you do either or both of these things. It also lets you express your wishes regarding donation of organs and the designation of your primary physician. If you use this form, you may complete or modify all or any part of it. You are free to use a different form.

Part 1 of this form is a power of attorney for health care. Part 1 lets you name another individual as agent to make health-care decisions for you if you become incapable of making your own decisions or if you want someone else to make those decisions for you now even though you are still capable. You may also name an alternate agent to act for you if your first choice is not willing, able, or reasonably available to make decisions for you. Unless related to you, your agent may not be an owner, operator, or employee of [a residential long-term health-care institution] at which you are receiving care.

Unless the form you sign limits the authority of your agent, your agent may make all health-care decisions for you. This form has a place for you to limit the authority of your agent. You need not limit the authority of your agent if you wish to rely on your agent for all health-care decisions that may have to be made. If you choose not to limit the authority of your agent, your agent will have the right to:

(a) consent or refuse consent to any care, treatment, service, or procedure to maintain, diagnose, or otherwise affect a physical or mental condition;

(b) select or discharge health-care providers and institutions;

(c) approve or disapprove diagnostic tests, surgical procedures, programs of medication, and orders not to resuscitate; and

(d) direct the provision, withholding, or withdrawal of artificial nutrition and hydration and all other forms of health care.

Part 2 of this form lets you give specific instructions about any aspect of your health care. Choices are provided for you to express your wishes regarding the provision, withholding, or withdrawal of treatment to keep you alive, including the provision of artificial nutrition and hydration, as well as the provision of pain relief. Space is also provided for you to add to the choices you have made or for you to write out any additional wishes.

* * *

After completing this form, sign and date the form at the end. It is recommended but not required that you request two other individuals to sign as witnesses. Give a copy of the signed and completed form to your physician, to any other health-care providers you may have, to any health-care institution at which you are receiving care, and to any health-care agents you have named. You should talk to the person you have named as agent to make sure that he or she understands your wishes and is willing to take the responsibility.

You have the right to revoke this advance health-care directive or replace this form at any time.

PART 1

POWER OF ATTORNEY FOR HEALTH CARE

(1) DESIGNATION OF AGENT: I designate the following individual as my agent to make health-care decisions for me:

* * *

OPTIONAL: If I revoke my agent's authority or if my agent is not willing, able, or reasonably available to make a health-care decision for me, I designate as my first alternate agent:

* * *

(2) AGENT'S AUTHORITY: My agent is authorized to make all health-care decisions for me, including decisions to provide, withhold, or withdraw artificial nutrition and hydration and all other forms of health care to keep me alive, except as I state here:

(Add additional sheets if needed.)

(3) WHEN AGENT'S AUTHORITY BECOMES EFFECTIVE: My agent's authority becomes effective when my primary physician determines that I am unable to make my own health-care decisions unless I mark the following box.

If I mark this box [___], my agent's authority to make health-care decisions for me takes effect immediately.

(4) AGENT'S OBLIGATION: My agent shall make health-care decisions for me in accordance with this power of attorney for health care, any instructions I give in Part 2 of this form, and my other wishes to the extent known to my agent. To the extent my wishes are unknown, my agent shall make health-care decisions for me in accordance with what my agent determines to be in my best interest. In determining my best interest, my agent shall consider my personal values to the extent known to my agent.

(5) NOMINATION OF GUARDIAN: If a guardian of my person needs to be appointed for me by a court, I nominate the agent designated in this form. If that agent is not willing, able, or reasonably available to act as guardian, I nominate the alternate agents whom I have named, in the order designated.

PART 2

INSTRUCTIONS FOR HEALTH CARE

If you are satisfied to allow your agent to determine what is best for you in making end-of-life decisions, you need not fill out this part of the form. If you do fill out this part of the form, you may strike any wording you do not want.

(6) END–OF–LIFE DECISIONS: I direct that my health-care providers and others involved in my care provide, withhold, or withdraw treatment in accordance with the choice I have marked below:

[___] (a) Choice Not To Prolong Life

I do not want my life to be prolonged if (i) I have an incurable and irreversible condition that will result in my death within a relatively short time, (ii) I become unconscious and, to a reasonable degree of medical certainty, I will not regain consciousness, or (iii) the likely risks and burdens of treatment would outweigh the expected benefits, OR

[___] (b) Choice To Prolong Life

I want my life to be prolonged as long as possible within the limits of generally accepted health-care standards.

(7) ARTIFICIAL NUTRITION AND HYDRATION: Artificial nutrition and hydration must be provided, withheld, or withdrawn in accordance with the choice I have made in paragraph (6) unless I mark the following box. If I mark this box [___], artificial nutrition and hydration must be provided regardless of my condition and regardless of the choice I have made in paragraph (6).

(8) RELIEF FROM PAIN: Except as I state in the following space, I direct that treatment for alleviation of pain or discomfort be provided at all times, even if it hastens my death:

* * *

(9) OTHER WISHES: (If you do not agree with any of the optional choices above and wish to write your own, or if you wish to add to the instructions you have given above, you may do so here.) I direct that:

* * *

[Part III, dealing with organ donation, and Part IV, dealing with the appointment of a primary physician, is omitted]

(12) EFFECT OF COPY: A copy of this form has the same effect as the original.

(13) SIGNATURES: Sign and date the form here:

* * *

(Optional) SIGNATURES OF WITNESSES:

* * *

SECTION 5. DECISIONS BY SURROGATE.

(a) A surrogate may make a health-care decision for a patient who is an adult or emancipated minor if the patient has been determined by the primary physician to lack capacity and no agent or guardian has been appointed or the agent or guardian is not reasonably available.

(b) An adult or emancipated minor may designate any individual to act as surrogate by personally informing the supervising health-care provider. In the absence of a designation, or if the designee is not reasonably available, any member of the following classes of the patient's family who is reasonably available, in descending order of priority, may act as surrogate:

> (1) the spouse, unless legally separated;

> (2) an adult child;

> (3) a parent; or

> (4) an adult brother or sister.

(c) If none of the individuals eligible to act as surrogate under subsection (b) is reasonably available, an adult who has exhibited special care and concern for the patient, who is familiar with the patient's personal values, and who is reasonably available may act as surrogate.

(d) A surrogate shall communicate his or her assumption of authority as promptly as practicable to the members of the patient's family specified in subsection (b) who can be readily contacted.

(e) If more than one member of a class assumes authority to act as surrogate, and they do not agree on a health-care decision and the supervising health-care provider is so informed, the supervising health-care provider shall comply with the decision of a majority of the members of that class who have communicated their views to the provider. If the class is evenly divided concerning the health-care decision and the supervising health-care provider is so informed, that class and all individuals having lower priority are disqualified from making the decision.

(f) A surrogate shall make a health-care decision in accordance with the patient's individual instructions, if any, and other wishes to the extent known to the surrogate. Otherwise, the surrogate shall make the decision in accordance with the surrogate's determination of the patient's best interest. In determining the patient's best interest, the surrogate shall consider the patient's personal values to the extent known to the surrogate.

(g) A health-care decision made by a surrogate for a patient is effective without judicial approval.

(h) An individual at any time may disqualify another, including a member of the individual's family, from acting as the individual's surrogate by a signed writing or by personally informing the supervising health-care provider of the disqualification.

* * *

SECTION 6. DECISIONS BY GUARDIAN.

(a) A guardian shall comply with the ward's individual instructions and may not revoke the ward's advance health-care directive unless the appointing court expressly so authorizes.

(b) Absent a court order to the contrary, a health-care decision of an agent takes precedence over that of a guardian.

(c) A health-care decision made by a guardian for the ward is effective without judicial approval.

SECTION 7. OBLIGATIONS OF HEALTH–CARE PROVIDER.

(a) Before implementing a health-care decision made for a patient, a supervising health-care provider, if possible, shall promptly communicate to the patient the decision made and the identity of the person making the decision.

(b) A supervising health-care provider who knows of the existence of an advance health-care directive, a revocation of an advance health-care directive, or a designation or disqualification of a surrogate, shall promptly record its existence in the patient's health-care record and, if it is in writing, shall request a copy and if one is furnished shall arrange for its maintenance in the health-care record.

(c) A primary physician who makes or is informed of a determination that a patient lacks or has recovered capacity, or that another condition exists which affects an individual instruction or the authority of an agent, guardian, or surrogate, shall promptly record the determination in the patient's health-care record and communicate the determination to the patient, if possible, and to any person then authorized to make health-care decisions for the patient.

(d) Except as provided in subsections (e) and (f), a health-care provider or institution providing care to a patient shall:

(1) comply with an individual instruction of the patient and with a reasonable interpretation of that instruction made by a person then authorized to make health-care decisions for the patient; and

(2) comply with a health-care decision for the patient made by a person then authorized to make health-care decisions for the patient to the same extent as if the decision had been made by the patient while having capacity.

(e) A health-care provider may decline to comply with an individual instruction or health-care decision for reasons of conscience. A health-care institution may decline to comply with an individual instruction or health-care decision if the instruction or decision is contrary to a policy of the institution which is expressly based on reasons of conscience and if the policy was timely communicated to the patient or to a person then authorized to make health-care decisions for the patient.

(f) A health-care provider or institution may decline to comply with an individual instruction or health-care decision that requires medically ineffective health care or health care contrary to generally accepted health-care standards applicable to the health-care provider or institution.

(g) A health-care provider or institution that declines to comply with an individual instruction or health-care decision shall:

(1) promptly so inform the patient, if possible, and any person then authorized to make health-care decisions for the patient;

(2) provide continuing care to the patient until a transfer can be effected; and

(3) unless the patient or person then authorized to make health-care decisions for the patient refuses assistance, immediately make all reasonable efforts to assist in the transfer of the patient to another health-care provider or institution that is willing to comply with the instruction or decision.

(h) A health-care provider or institution may not require or prohibit the execution or revocation of an advance health-care directive as a condition for providing health care.

SECTION 8. HEALTH–CARE INFORMATION. Unless otherwise specified in an advance health-care directive, a person then authorized to make health-care decisions for a patient has the same rights as the patient to request, receive, examine, copy, and consent to the disclosure of medical or any other health-care information.

SECTION 9. IMMUNITIES.

(a) A health-care provider or institution acting in good faith and in accordance with generally accepted health-care standards applicable to the health-care provider or institution is not subject to civil or criminal liability or to discipline for unprofessional conduct for:

(1) complying with a health-care decision of a person apparently having authority to make a health-care decision for a patient, including a decision to withhold or withdraw health care;

(2) declining to comply with a health-care decision of a person based on a belief that the person then lacked authority; or

(3) complying with an advance health-care directive and assuming that the directive was valid when made and has not been revoked or terminated.

(b) An individual acting as agent or surrogate under this [Act] is not subject to civil or criminal liability or to discipline for unprofessional conduct for health-care decisions made in good faith.

* * *

SECTION 11. CAPACITY.

(a) This [Act] does not affect the right of an individual to make health-care decisions while having capacity to do so.

(b) An individual is presumed to have capacity to make a health-care decision, to give or revoke an advance health-care directive, and to designate or disqualify a surrogate.

* * *

SECTION 13. EFFECT OF [ACT].

(a) This [Act] does not create a presumption concerning the intention of an individual who has not made or who has revoked an advance health-care directive.

(b) Death resulting from the withholding or withdrawal of health care in accordance with this [Act] does not for any purpose constitute a suicide or homicide or legally impair or invalidate a policy of insurance or an annuity providing a death benefit, notwithstanding any term of the policy or annuity to the contrary.

(c) This [Act] does not authorize mercy killing, assisted suicide, euthanasia, or the provision, withholding, or withdrawal of health care, to the extent prohibited by other statutes of this State.

(d) This [Act] does not authorize or require a health-care provider or institution to provide health care contrary to generally accepted health-care standards applicable to the health-care provider or institution.

* * *

SECTION 14. JUDICIAL RELIEF. On petition of a patient, the patient's agent, guardian, or surrogate, a health-care provider or institution involved with the patient's care, or an individual described in Section 5(b) or (c), the [appropriate] court may enjoin or direct a health-care decision or order other equitable relief. A proceeding under this section is governed by [here insert appropriate reference to the rules of procedure or statutory provisions governing expedited proceedings and proceedings affecting incapacitated persons].

* * *

Notes on Advance Directives

1. *The History of Advance Directives: The Rise of Living Wills.* Nearly two decades before the Uniform Health Care Decisions Act was proposed, many people first became concerned about the potential abuses of powerful new forms of life-sustaining medical treatment. Frightened by the "treatment" provided to Karen Quinlan, they began to search for a way to avoid a similar fate. Within two years of the first press reports of the *Quinlan* case several states had adopted statutes that formally recognized certain forms of written statements requesting that some kinds of medical care be discontinued. These statutes, generally referred to as "living will" statutes, "right to die" legislation, or "natural death" acts, provided a political outlet for the frustration that accompanied the empathy for Ms. Quinlan.

The statutes, which still provide the governing law in most jurisdictions, differ in several respects. In some states living wills may be executed by any person, at any time (and in some states they may be executed on behalf of minors), while in other states they require a waiting period, and may not be executed during a terminal illness. In most states they are of indefinite duration, although in some states they expire after a determined number of years. Some statutes address only the terminally ill, others include those in "irreversible coma" or persistent vegetative state, and still others provide for different conditions to trigger the substantive provisions of the document. Some states require the formalities of a will for the living will to be recognized by statute, while other states require different formalities. The statutes generally relieve physicians and other health care providers of any civil or criminal liability if they properly follow the requirements of the statute and implement the desires expressed in a legally executed living will. Some of the statutes also require that any physician who cannot, in good conscience, carry out those provisions, transfer the patient to a physician who can. The statutes also provide that carrying out the provisions of a properly executed living will does not constitute suicide for insurance purposes. It is hard to know whether the absence of litigation over the terms of living wills means that these documents are working well or not at all.

Many living will statutes do not apply to those in persistent vegetative state, irreversible coma, or any other medical condition that may not be considered "terminal". Thus, these statutes would be of no assistance to people in the position of Nancy Cruzan. Is there a reason to limit legislation to terminal conditions, or should such statutes be extended to other conditions, like persistent vegetative state, where there is broad social consensus that patients should have the right to forgo life-sustaining treatment?

Many living will statutes specifically exclude "the performance of any procedure to provide nutrition or hydration" from the definition of death-prolonging procedures, and thus do not extend any statutory protection to those who remove nutrition or hydration from a patient. For the most famous example, see Vernon's Ann.Mo.Stat. § 459.010(3). After the United States Supreme Court decision in *Cruzan,* are such exceptions legally meaningful? Are they constitutional? In *Cruzan,* the Chief Justice reviewed those state cases that have treated nutrition and hydration just like any other form of medical care, apparently with approval. In her concurring opinion, Justice O'Connor cited AMA Ethical Opinion 2.20, Withholding or Withdrawing a Life–Prolonging Medical Treatment, to support her proposition that "artificial feeding cannot readily be distinguished from other forms of medical treatment." In his dissent, Justice Brennan states without reservation: "No material distinction can be drawn between the treatment to which Nancy Cruzan continues to be subject—artificial nutrition and hydration—and any other medical treatment." For a fuller discussion on the legal position of the withdrawal of nutrition and hydration, see pages 306-308, below. For an example of judicial avoidance of the apparent consequences of a nutrition and hydration exception to a living will statute, see McConnell v. Beverly Enterprises–Connecticut, Inc., 209 Conn. 692, 553 A.2d 596 (1989). See also In re Guardianship of Browning, 568 So.2d 4 (Fla.1990).

2. *The Next Step: Durable Powers of Attorney for Health Care.* Another means of identifying who should speak for the patient when the patient is incompetent is to allow the patient to designate a spokesperson during the patient's period of competence. This may be accomplished through the patient's execution of a durable power of attorney.

Powers of attorney have been available over the past several centuries to allow for financial transactions to be consummated by agents of a principal. A power of attorney may be executed, under oath, by any competent person. It provides that the agent designated shall have the right to act on behalf of the principal for purposes that are described and limited in the document itself. Thus, a principal may give an agent a power of attorney to enter into a particular contract, a particular kind of contract, or all contracts. The power may be limited by time, by geographic area, or in any other way. It may be granted to any person, who, upon appointment, becomes the agent and "attorney-in-fact" for the principal. At common law, a power of attorney expired upon the "incapacity" of the principal. This was necessary to assure that the principal could maintain adequate authority over his agent. As long as a power of attorney expired upon the incapacity of the principal, the power of attorney had no value in making medical decisions. After all, a competent patient could decide for himself; there was no reason for him to delegate authority to an agent.

In the mid 1970s it became clear that the value of the power of attorney could be increased if it could extend beyond the incapacity of the principal. For example, as an increasing number of very elderly people depended upon their children and others to handle their financial affairs, it became important that there be some device by which they could delegate their authority to these agents. For such principals it was most important that the authority remain with their agents when they did become incapacitated. The Uniform Probate Code was amended to provide for a durable power of attorney; that is, a power of attorney that would remain in effect (or even become effective) upon the incapacity of the principal. That statute explicitly provides:

> A durable power of attorney is a power of attorney by which a principal designates another his attorney in fact in writing and the writing contains the words "this power of attorney shall not be affected by subsequent disability or incapacity of the principal, or lapse of time," or "this power of attorney shall become effective upon the disability or incapacity of the principal," or similar words showing the intent of the principal that the authority conferred shall be exercisable notwithstanding the principal's subsequent disability or incapacity, and, unless it states a time of determination, notwithstanding the lapse of time since the execution of the instrument.

Uniform Probate Code § 35–501.

The question of whether general durable powers of attorney may be used for nonfinancial determinations, such as health care decisionmaking, was never conclusively answered by the courts. There is no reported opinion formally holding that the authority of a durable power of attorney executed under the Uniform Probate Code extends to health care decision-making. For two suggesting that there would be such authority, see In re Peter, 108 N.J. 365, 378–379, 529 A.2d 419, 426 (1987) ("Although the statute does not specifically authorize conveyance of durable authority to make medical decisions, it should be interpreted that way.") and In re Westchester County Medical Center (O'Connor), 72 N.Y.2d 517, 534 N.Y.S.2d 886, 531 N.E.2d 607, 612 fn. 2 (1988). The President's Commission assumed, without any discussion, that it could be used for this purpose. See President's Commission, Deciding to Forego Life–Sustaining Treatment, 145–149 (1983). On the other hand, two statutory sources of these acts—the Uniform Probate Code and the Model Special Power of Attorney for Small Interests Act— were conceived originally as ways of controlling property, not health care decisions. Is there any intellectual problem in extending this simple statute to health care decision-making?

The vast majority of states have now adopted statutes that formally authorize the execution of durable powers of attorney for health care decisions. There is an extremely wide variety among these statutes. One of the first, in California, turned into a nightmare of political compromise. As originally promulgated, it was long, complex, and highly technical. For example, in its original form it prescribed that a "warning to person executing this document" be included in 10–point boldface type, and the warning itself was longer than the entire durable power prescribed by statutes of other states. The Illinois statute, which is far more permissive, contains a non-mandatory "Illinois statutory short form power of attorney for health care" which is several typed pages long. See 755 ILCS 45/4–1. While the Illinois statute at least provides that "the form of health care agency in this article is not intended to be exclusive * * *", the Rhode Island statute explicitly provides:

> "[t]he statutory form of durable power of attorney as set forth in [this act] shall be used and shall be the only form by which a person may execute a durable power of attorney for health care. * * * It shall not be altered in any

manner and shall preclude the use of any other form to exercise the durable power of attorney for health care.''

R.I.Gen.Laws §§ 23–410–1.

The New Mexico legislature originally dealt with the issue very simply by listing health care decisions among other kinds of decisions that principals may wish to delegate to attorneys-in-fact in more general durable powers of attorney. Among the boxes that could be checked off on the New Mexico statutory durable power form are real estate transactions, bond, share and commodity transactions, chattel and goods transactions, a host of other business transactions—and ''decisions regarding life-saving and life-prolonging medical treatment,'' ''decisions relating to medical treatment, surgical treatment, nursing care, medication, hospitalization, institutionalization in a nursing home or other facility and home health care,'' and, most remarkably, ''transfer of property or income as a gift to the principal spouse for the purpose of qualifying the principal for governmental medical assistance.''

Some state laws now permit durable powers of attorney to arrange not only for decisionmaking after the principal's incapacity, but also for decisionmaking after the principal's death. These statutes allow the principal to provide for the disposition of his body through a durable power. See, e.g., 755 ILCS 45/4–10 and Kan.Stat.Ann. § 58–632.

Further, some state allows an agent authorized by a durable power of attorney to make health care decisions for a principal even if the principal has capacity—as long as that is the explicit desire of the principal. Does the grant of such authority make any sense? Why should an agent make a decision for a principal *with* capacity? Doesn't that undermine the principle of autonomy? The drafters of that statute argue that it is convenient for health care providers to have a surrogate decisionmaker to turn to in the case of a patient with capacity that is highly variable. That is, some argue, in such cases health care providers ought to be able to depend upon the articulated consent of some surrogate without doing a full competency analysis each time a health care decision is to be made. Of course, the decision of the surrogate can always be overruled by the patient herself if she has capacity.

The legal significance of a durable power of attorney for health care is defined by each state's durable power statute. In her concurring opinion in the *Cruzan* case, Justice O'Connor suggests that there may also be constitutional significance to a properly executed durable power of attorney:

> I also write separately to emphasize that the Court does not today decide the issue whether a state must also give effect to the decisions of a surrogate decision-maker. In my view, such a duty may well be Constitutionally required to protect the patient's liberty interest in refusing medical treatment.

497 U.S. at 289, 110 S.Ct. at 2857. She commends those several states that have recognized ''the practical wisdom of such a procedure by enacting durable power of attorney statutes'' and she suggests that a written appointment of a proxy ''may be a valuable additional safeguard of the patient's interest in directing his medical care.'' In the final paragraph of her opinion she points out that ''[t]oday's decision * * * does not preclude a future determination that the Constitution requires the states to implement the decisions of a patient's duly appointed surrogate.''

3. *The Development of The Uniform Health Care Decisions Act.* The Uniform Health Care Decisions Act (UHCDA), which you have just read, was designed to replace the Uniform Rights of the Terminally Ill Act, state durable powers acts

and parts of the Uniform Anatomical Gifts Act. It was approved by the National Conference of Commissioners on Uniform State Laws in 1993 and by the American Bar Association House of Delegates in 1994. As you can see, the UHCDA substantially alters the form and utility of living wills and durable powers, and it provides a method of making health care decisions for incompetent patients who do not have advance directives. As of early 2004, some version of the uniform act was adopted in Alabama, Delaware, Hawaii, Maine, Mississippi and New Mexico. The California statute governing health care decisions is also largely based on the UHCDA and the Alaska legislature was considering the Act as this book went to press.

The proposed act takes a comprehensive approach by placing the living will (which is retitled the "individual instruction"), the durable power of attorney (now called the "power of attorney for health care"), a family consent law, and some provisions concerning organ donation together in one statute. Further, the statute integrates the current living will and durable power (and statement of desire to donate organs) into a single document. The UHCDA provides a statutory form, but it also explicitly declares that the form is not a mandatory one, and that individuals may draft their own form that includes only some of the kinds of instructions permitted in the unified form.

Can you see how the UHCDA very substantially broadens the role of the living will? The new "individual instruction" can apply to virtually any health care decision, not just the end of life decisions to which living wills are typically applicable. Further, "health care decision" is defined very broadly.

The uniform act also makes the execution of the unified document very easy. It has no witness requirement, and it does not require that the document be notarized. The drafters of the proposed act concluded that the formalities often associated with living wills and durable powers served to discourage their execution more than to deter fraud.

The residual decisionmaking portion of the act is very much like the family consent statutes that have now been adopted in a majority of states, and which are discussed in note 4, below, and this section of the act applies only if there is no applicable individual instruction or appointed agent. While it provides for a common family hierarchy of decisionmakers for decisionally incapacitated patients, it also provides that the family can be trumped by an "orally designated surrogate," who may be appointed by a patient informing her "supervising physician" that the surrogate is entitled to make health care decisions on her behalf. Thus, patients can effectively orally appoint decisionmaking agents who previously could only be appointed in a writing signed pursuant to a rigorous process. In the same manner a patient may orally *disqualify* someone who otherwise would be entitled to make decisions on her behalf. If you do not want your brother making health care decisions for you, you need only tell your supervising physician. Thus, in essence, any health care decision will be made by the first available in this hierarchy:

(1) the patient, if competent,

(2) the patient, through an individual instruction,

(3) an agent appointed by the patient in a written power of attorney for health care, unless a court has given this authority explicitly to a guardian,

(4) a guardian appointed by the court,

(5) a surrogate appointed orally by the patient,

(6) a surrogate selected from the list of family members and others who can make health care decisions on behalf of the patient.

The drafters of the UHCDA make it clear in their comments that one purpose of the statute is to assure that these intimate health care decisions remain within the realm of the patient, the patient's family and close friends, and the health care providers, and that others not be permitted to disrupt that process. The court would very rarely have a role in any decision making under this statute, and outsiders (including outside organizations) who do not think a patient is adequately protected have no standing to seek judicial intervention. See Protection and Advocacy System, Inc. v. Presbyterian Healthcare Services, 128 N.M. 73, 989 P.2d 890 (App. 1999).

The UHCDA has explicitly determined that the decisionmaker (whether an agent, guardian or surrogate) should make a decision based on the principle of substituted judgment (i.e., on the basis of what the patient would choose, if that patient were competent) rather than the best interest principle. If it is impossible to apply the substituted judgment principle, the statute would apply the best interests principle.

The UHCDA includes the normal raft of recordkeeping provisions, limitations on the reach of the criminal law, assurances regarding the insurance rights of those who execute the documents, and restrictions on the liability of those who act under the statute in good faith. A provision for $500 in liquidated damages in actions for breach of the act may not encourage litigation when the statute is ignored, but the provision for attorney's fees in those cases might provide an incentive for lawyers to bring those cases. The act applies only to adults.

While there does not appear to be any strong opposition to the general intent or structure of the UHCDA, some advocates for the elderly and the disabled are worried by some parts of this proposed statute. They are worried that the streamlined procedures for execution of a document allow a greater opportunity for fraud to be perpetrated against those who wish to sign, and they are concerned about the virtually unrestrained authority the proposed act gives to physicians to make determinations that a patient lacks decisional capacity. In addition, there is some concern that any change in the law will undercut the significant amount of community education that has been directed to the current law over the past few years. Are these concerns justified? Is there a way to address these concerns that would be consistent with the values expressed in the rest of the statute?

Should your state adopt the UHCDA? If you were advising your state legislature on this issue, what portions of the uniform act would you suggest be changed? How would you change those portions?

4. *Family Consent Laws.* Over the past century it became standard medical practice to seek consent to any medical procedure from close family members of an incompetent patient. There is no common law authority for this practice; it is an example of medical practice (and good common sense) being subtly absorbed by the law. The President's Commission suggests five reasons for this deference to family members:

(1) The family is generally most concerned about the good of the patient.

(2) The family will also usually be most knowledgeable about the patient's goals, preferences, and values.

(3) The family deserves recognition as an important social unit that ought to be treated, within limits, as a responsible decisionmaker in matters that intimately affect its members.

(4) Especially in a society in which many other traditional forms of community have eroded, participation in a family is often an important dimension of personal fulfillment.

(5) Since a protected sphere of privacy and autonomy is required for the flourishing of this interpersonal union, institutions and the state should be reluctant to intrude, particularly regarding matters that are personal and on which there is a wide range of opinion in society.

President's Commission, Deciding to Forego Life–Sustaining Treatment, 127 (1983). It is difficult to determine whether the resort to close relatives to give consent is merely a procedural device to discover what the patient, if competent, would choose, or whether it is based in an independent substantive doctrine. Although it seems essentially procedural—the family is most likely to know what the patient would choose—many courts are willing to accept the decisions of family members even when there is little support for the position that these family members are actually choosing what the patient would choose. Of course, consulting with family members also neutralizes potential malpractice plaintiffs; this factor probably accounts for part of the current popularity of this decision-making process.

Over the past decade most states have enacted "family consent laws" that authorize statutorily designated family members to make health care decisions for their relatives in circumscribed situations. These statutes often apply to a wide range of health care decisions (including, in most cases, decisions to forgo life sustaining treatment), although sometimes they apply only when there has been a physician's certification of the patient's inability to make the health care decision and sometimes they are limited to particular kinds of treatment (e.g., cardiopulmonary resuscitation). In addition, "family consent laws" often provide immunity from liability for family members and physicians acting in good faith, and judicial authority to resolve disputes about the authority of the family members under the statutes. The definition of "family member" and the position of each family member in the hierarchy varies from state to state. In some states those in a long term spouse-like relationship with the patient are included in the list of family members who can make decisions for the incompetent patient; in some states they are not. Some lists include a residuary class of anyone who knows the values, interest and wishes of the patient; some states list the physician as the residuary decisionmaker; some provide for no residuary decisionmaker. Some states give a general guardian top priority; some states do not. Some states allow the statutory surrogate to make any health care decisions, some states put some kinds of decisions (like discontinuing nutrition and hydration) off limits. Section 5 of the UHCDA provides a good example of a family consent law. Are there other classes of decisionmakers you would add to that hierarchy?

5.   Why do you think that no two state health care decisionmaking statutes are identical? What relevant political groups are likely to be stronger in some states and weaker in others? In some states the political nature of the right to die has driven the legislature to enact virtually meaningless statutes to avoid political fallout from all sides. Of course, the existence of these impotent statutes might do more harm than good. Justice Welliver, dissenting from the Missouri Supreme Court decision in *Cruzan,* points this out with regard to that state's living will statute:

> We Missourians can sign an instrument directing the withholding or withdrawing of death-prolonging procedures, but, after the Missouri amendments, "death-prolonging procedure" does not include: (1) "the administration of medication," * * * (3) "the performance of any procedure to provide nutrition," [or] (4) "the performance of any procedure to provide * * *

hydration." If we cannot authorize withdrawing or withholding "medication," "nutrition" or "hydration," then what can we authorize to be withheld in Missouri? The Missouri Living Will Act is a fraud on Missourians who believe we have been given a right to execute a living will, and to die naturally, respectably, and in peace.

Cruzan v. Harmon, 760 S.W.2d 408, 422 (Mo.1988).

6. *The Patient Self–Determination Act and Advance Directives.* The Patient Self–Determination Act became law as a part of the Federal Omnibus Budget Reconciliation Act of 1990, and it was designed to increase the role that advance directives—both living wills and durable powers of attorney—play in medical decisionmaking. The statute applies to hospitals, skilled nursing facilities, home health agencies, hospice programs, and HMOs that receive Medicaid or Medicare funding. It requires each of those covered by the Act to provide each patient with written information concerning:

> (i) an individual's rights under State law (whether statutory or as recognized by the courts of the State) to make decisions concerning * * * medical care, including the right to accept or refuse medical or surgical treatment and the right to formulate advance directives * * * and

> (ii) the written policies of the provider or organization respecting the implementation of such rights.

42 U.S.C.A. § 1395cc(a)(1)(f)(1)(A). In addition, those covered must document in each patient's record whether that patient has signed an advance directive, assure that the state law is followed in the institution, and provide for education of both the staff and the public concerning living wills and durable powers of attorney.

Although the Patient Self Determination Act showed great promise, and while it has changed the practice of some health care institutions, "[a]necdotal evidence suggests that the statute has not had the effect of encouraging physicians to initiate end-of-life discussions with patients." Alan Meisel, The Right to Die § 10.21 (2d ed. 1995) (citing Diane M. Gianelli, Many Say Doctors Aren't Living Up to Expectations of Living Will Law, Am.Med. News, May 17, 1993, at 1).

7. A few states have also taken action to increase the utility of advance directives. For example, a couple of states have central registries of advance directives, and a handful of states provide for drivers' licenses to show if a patient has an advance directive. Hawaii is implementing a new statute that requires managed health care providers to discuss advance directives with their patients/enrollees.

2. Decisionmaking for Incompetent Patients in the Absence of a Governing Statute

a. Discovering the Patient's Wishes

IN RE EICHNER

New York Court of Appeals, 1981.
52 N.Y.2d 363, 438 N.Y.S.2d 266, 420 N.E.2d 64.

WACHTLER, JUDGE.

For over 66 years Brother Joseph Fox was a member of the Society of Mary, a Catholic religious order which, among other things, operates Chaminade High School in Mineola. * * *

While [an] operation was being performed * * * he suffered cardiac arrest, with resulting loss of oxygen to the brain and substantial brain damage. He lost the ability to breathe spontaneously and was placed on a respirator which maintained him in a vegetative state. The attending physicians informed Father Philip Eichner, who was the president of Chaminade and the director of the society at the school, that there was no reasonable chance of recovery and that Brother Fox would die in that state.

After retaining two neurosurgeons who confirmed the diagnosis, Father Eichner requested the hospital to remove the respirator. The hospital, however, refused to do so without court authorization. Father Eichner then applied * * * to be appointed committee of the person and property of Brother Fox, with authority to direct removal of the respirator. The application was supported by the patient's 10 nieces and nephews, his only surviving relatives. The court appointed a guardian ad litem and directed that notice be served on various parties, including the District Attorney.

At the hearing the District Attorney opposed the application and called medical experts to show that there might be some improvement in the patient's condition. All the experts agreed, however, that there was no reasonable likelihood that Brother Fox would ever emerge from the vegetative coma or recover his cognitive powers.

There was also evidence, submitted by the petitioner, that before the operation rendered him incompetent the patient had made it known that under these circumstances he would want a respirator removed. Brother Fox had first expressed this view in 1976 when the Chaminade community discussed the moral implications of the celebrated *Karen Ann Quinlan* case, in which the parents of a 19–year–old New Jersey girl who was in a vegetative coma requested the hospital to remove the respirator [ ]. These were formal discussions prompted by Chaminade's mission to teach and promulgate Catholic moral principles. At that time it was noted that the Pope had stated that Catholic principles permitted the termination of extraordinary life support systems when there is no reasonable hope for the patient's recovery and that church officials in New Jersey had concluded that use of the respirator in the *Quinlan* case constituted an extraordinary measure under the circumstances. Brother Fox expressed agreement with those views and stated that he would not want any of this "extraordinary business" done for him under those circumstances. Several years later, and only a couple of months before his final hospitalization, Brother Fox again stated that he would not want his life prolonged by such measures if his condition were hopeless.

* * *

In this case the proof was compelling. There was no suggestion that the witnesses who testified for the petitioner had any motive other than to see that Brother Fox' stated wishes were respected. The finding that he carefully reflected on the subject, expressed his views and concluded not to have his life prolonged by medical means if there were no hope of recovery is supported by his religious beliefs and is not inconsistent with his life of unselfish religious devotion. These were obviously solemn pronouncements and not casual remarks made at some social gathering, nor can it be said that he was too young to realize or feel the consequences of his statements [ ]. That this was a persistent commitment is evidenced by the fact that he reiterated the decision but two months before his final hospitalization. There was, of course, no need to speculate as to whether he would want this particular medical procedure to be discontinued under these circumstances. What occurred to him was identical to what happened in the *Karen Ann Quinlan* case, which had originally prompted his decision. In sum, the evidence clearly and convincingly shows that Brother Fox did not want to be maintained in a vegetative coma by use of a respirator.

* * *

Note: Applying the Principle of Substituted Judgment

Three states, Michigan, Missouri and New York, have, at one time or another, rejected substituted judgment except where it is based on the formally articulated desires of the patient. See *Cruzan*, above at 243, In re Westchester Medical Center (O'Connor), discussed below in Note 1, page 302, In re Martin, 450 Mich. 204, 538 N.W.2d 399 (1995). In these states it would appear to be almost impossible to remove life sustaining treatment from incompetent patients because it is rare indeed to have a patient foresee and describe his condition and the treatment he would wish with the specificity with which Brother Fox spoke. More often, patients have not addressed the questions and others must decide on their behalf exercising substituted judgment for the patient. Of course, the impracticality of applying the "formally articulated desires" standard may cause it to be ignored, *de facto*, in some courts. This appears to be the case in Missouri, where courts are willing to stretch the principle. In New York, on the other hand, the standard appears to be more strictly applied. See Blouin v. Spitzer, 356 F.3d 348 (2d Cir. 2004).

The Illinois court described the principle of substituted judgment clearly and simply:

> Under substituted judgment, a surrogate decisionmaker attempts to establish, with as much accuracy as possible, what decision the patient would make if he were competent to do so. Employing this theory, the surrogate first tries to determine if the patient had expressed explicit intent regarding this type of medical treatment prior to becoming incompetent. [ ] Where no clear intent exists, the patient's personal value system must guide the surrogate. * * *

In re Estate of Longeway, 133 Ill.2d 33, 139 Ill.Dec. 780, 787, 549 N.E.2d 292, 299 (1989).

In such cases, courts (except in Michigan, Missouri and New York, as noted) look wherever they can to determine the patient's wishes. In Brophy v. New England Sinai Hospital, Inc., 398 Mass. 417, 497 N.E.2d 626 (1986), the Massachusetts Supreme Court based its conclusion that food and hydration could be withheld from a comatose adult on the substituted judgment analysis done by the lower court.

> [After full hearing] the judge found on the basis of ample evidence which no one disputes, that Brophy's judgment would be to decline the provision of food and water and to terminate his life. In reaching that conclusion, the judge considered various factors including the following: (1) Brophy's expressed preferences; (2) his religious convictions and their relation to refusal of treatment; (3) the impact on his family; (4) the probability of adverse side effects; and (5) the prognosis, both with and without treatment. The judge also considered present and future incompetency as an element which Brophy would consider in his decision-making process. The judge relied on several statements made by Brophy prior to the onset of his illness. Although he never had discussed specifically whether a G-tube or feeding tube should be withdrawn in the event that he was diagnosed as being in a persistent

vegetative state following his surgery, the judge inferred that, if presently competent, Brophy would choose to forgo artificial nutrition and hydration by means of a G-tube. The judge found that Brophy would not likely view his own religion as a barrier to that choice.

Other factors that have been considered include the patient's diagnosis, life history, ability to knowingly participate in treatment, potential quality of life, and, more generally, the patient's values and attitude toward health care. See, e.g., Mack v. Mack, 329 Md. 188, 618 A.2d 744 (1993) (focusing on the "moral views, life goals, and values" of the patient, and her "attitudes toward sickness, medical procedures, suffering and death"), and DeGrella v. Elston, 858 S.W.2d 698 (Ky.1993). For a thorough and well annotated list of twenty-two relevant factors that have been considered by the courts see Alan Meisel, The Right to Die § 7.9 (2d ed. 1995).

How difficult is it for a surrogate decisionmaker to distinguish what the patient would really want from what that decisionmaker would want if she were in the position of that patient? Is it really possible to clearly distinguish the subjective "substituted judgment" standard from an objective standard that asks what a reasonable person would do under the circumstances? Courts do struggle to distinguish the "substituted judgment" and "best interest" principles, and even those who appear to adopt the "best interest" approach may qualify it by requiring that the best interest of the patient be defined in terms of the wishes, values and desires of the patient. Some state courts appear to adopt the best interest test while they actually take the "substituted judgment" approach. See Conservatorship of Drabick, 200 Cal.App.3d 185, 245 Cal.Rptr. 840 (1988) (discussed in *Wendland*, below) and In re Gordy, 658 A.2d 613 (Del.Ch.1994).

The *Conroy* court also addressed the question of whether life-support systems could be removed from patients who have never clearly expressed their desires about such treatment. The court developed three tests, depending upon the existence (vel non) of any trustworthy evidence that the patient would forgo the life-sustaining treatment.

IN RE CONROY

Supreme Court of New Jersey, 1985.
98 N.J. 321, 486 A.2d 1209.

SCHREIBER, JUSTICE.

* * * [W]e hold that life-sustaining treatment may be withheld or withdrawn from an incompetent patient when it is clear that the particular patient would have refused the treatment under the circumstances involved. The standard we are enunciating is a subjective one, consistent with the notion that the right that we are seeking to effectuate is a very personal right to control one's own life. The question is not what a reasonable or average person would have chosen to do under the circumstances but what the particular patient would have done if able to choose for himself.

* * *

We * * * hold that life-sustaining treatment may also be withheld or withdrawn from a patient in Claire Conroy's situation [i.e., a patient who was competent but is now incompetent] if either of two "best interests" tests—a limited-objective or a pure-objective test—is satisfied.

Under the limited-objective test, life-sustaining treatment may be withheld or withdrawn from a patient in Claire Conroy's situation when there is some trustworthy evidence that the patient would have refused the treatment, and the decision-maker is satisfied that it is clear that the burdens of the patient's continued life with the treatment outweigh the benefits of that life for him. By this we mean that the patient is suffering, and will continue to suffer throughout the expected duration of his life, unavoidable pain, and that the net burdens of his prolonged life (the pain and suffering of his life with the treatment less the amount and duration of pain that the patient would likely experience if the treatment were withdrawn) markedly outweigh any physical pleasure, emotional enjoyment, or intellectual satisfaction that the patient may still be able to derive from life. This limited-objective standard permits the termination of treatment for a patient who had not unequivocally expressed his desires before becoming incompetent, when it is clear that the treatment in question would merely prolong the patient's suffering.

* * *

This limited-objective test also requires some trustworthy evidence that the patient would have wanted the treatment terminated. This evidence could take any one or more of the various forms appropriate to prove the patient's intent under the subjective test. Evidence that, taken as a whole, would be too vague, casual, or remote to constitute the clear proof of the patient's subjective intent that is necessary to satisfy the subjective test—for example, informally expressed reactions to other people's medical conditions and treatment—might be sufficient to satisfy this prong of the limited-objective test.

In the absence of trustworthy evidence, or indeed any evidence at all, that the patient would have declined the treatment, life-sustaining treatment may still be withheld or withdrawn from a formerly competent person like Claire Conroy if a third, pure-objective test is satisfied. Under that test, as under the limited-objective test, the net burdens of the patient's life with the treatment should clearly and markedly outweigh the benefits that the patient derives from life. Further, the recurring, unavoidable and severe pain of the patient's life with the treatment should be such that the effect of administering life-sustaining treatment would be inhumane. Subjective evidence that the patient would not have wanted the treatment is not necessary under this pure-objective standard. Nevertheless, even in the context of severe pain, life-sustaining treatment should not be withdrawn from an incompetent patient who had previously expressed a wish to be kept alive in spite of any pain that he might experience.

* * * [W]e expressly decline to authorize decision-making based on assessments of the personal worth or social utility of another's life, or the value of that life to others.

* * *

We are aware that it will frequently be difficult to conclude that the evidence is sufficient to justify termination of treatment under either of the "best interests" tests that we have described. Often, it is unclear whether and to what extent a patient such as Claire Conroy is capable of, or is in fact, experiencing pain. Similarly, medical experts are often unable to determine with any degree of certainty the extent of a nonverbal person's intellectual functioning or the depth of his emotional life. When the evidence is insufficient to satisfy either the limited-objective or pure-objective standard, however, we cannot justify the termination of life-sustaining treatment as clearly furthering the best interests of a patient like Ms. Conroy.

* * * When evidence of a person's wishes or physical or mental condition is equivocal, it is best to err, if at all, in favor of preserving life. * * *

Notes and Questions

1. *The Martin Case, the Conroy Classifications, and the Principle of Autonomy.* The most substantial criticism of the "subjective", "limited-objective" and "pure objective" classifications is provided in In re Martin, 450 Mich. 204, 538 N.W.2d 399 (1995):

> Rather than choose between the best interest standard and the substituted judgment standard, the New Jersey Supreme Court attempted to synthesize these two standards by creating an hierarchical decision-making continuum. [ ]. The starting point on the continuum is anchored by a purely subjective analysis, an approach that requires more definitive evidence of what the patient would choose than the substituted judgment standard. The other end of the continuum is anchored by a purely objective analysis, which is, in essence, a best interest standard.

> We find that a purely subjective analysis is the most appropriate standard to apply under the circumstances of this case. The pure subjective standard allows the surrogate to withhold life-sustaining treatment from an incompetent patient "when it is clear that the particular patient would have refused the treatment under the circumstances involved." [ ]. Given that the right the surrogate is seeking to effectuate is the incompetent patient's right to control his own life, "the question is not what a reasonable or average person would have chosen to do under the circumstances but what the particular patient would have done if able to chose for himself."

> The subjective and objective standards involve conceptually different bases for allowing he surrogate to make treatment decisions. The subjective standard is based on a patient's right to self-determination, while the objective standard is grounded in the state's parens patriae power. [ ]. An objective, best interest, standard cannot be grounded in the common-law right of informed consent because the right and the decision-making standard inherently conflict.

* * *

> Any move from a purely subjective standard to an analysis that encompasses objective criteria is grounded in the state's parens patriae power, not in the common-law right of informed consent or self-determination. Thus, while the clearly expressed wishes of a patient, while competent, should be honored regardless of the patient's condition, we find nothing that prevents the state from grounding any objective analysis on a threshold requirement of pain, terminal illness, foreseeable death, a persistent vegetative state, or affliction of a similar genre.

Martin, 538 N.W.2d at 407–408. Do you agree that only the decision to apply the subjective standard (and not the decision to apply the two objective standards) can be justified by the principles behind the doctrine of informed consent? Is the application of any form of objective test (whether it be termed "substituted judgment" or "best interest") a *per se* violation of the principle of autonomy, as *Martin* suggests? If this is true, what is the justification for the application of the theory of substituted judgment? See Rebecca Dresser and John Robertson, Quality of Life and Non–Treatment Decisions for Incompetent Patients, a Critique of the

Orthodox Approach, 17 L.Med. & Health Care 234 (1989). See also Rebecca Dresser, Life, Death and Incompetent Patients: Conceptual Infirmities and Hidden Values in the Law, 28 Ariz.L.Rev. 378 (1986).

Is the Michigan Court correct that a pure subjective analysis does not constitute a true "substituted judgment" because when we make such an analysis we are not, in fact, substituting any person's judgment for a patient's judgment; we are, instead, simply implementing the patient's decision, which we (subjectively) know? Can we ever truly know with certainty just what another person wants? Are we certain that even a competent patient truly wants what she is requesting? Do we know for sure whether the patient is accurately communicating what she wants? Is it really possible for a second (or third) party to carry out the subjective analysis, or does any decision by one person on behalf of another inevitably involve at least some element of substituted judgment?

2.   *The Conroy Standard and Patients in Persistent Vegetative State.* Despite its rejection in the *Martin* case, the *Conroy* case has been extremely influential; it is cited by most courts that have dealt with decisionmaking for incompetent patients since 1985 and its three-tiered set of tests—the subjective, limited-objective, and pure-objective tests—are generally well regarded. In 1987 the New Jersey Supreme Court decided a trilogy of cases that called into question whether every case of the discontinuation of life-sustaining treatment in an incompetent patient could be resolved by reference to one of these three Conroy tests. In re Farrell, 108 N.J. 335, 529 A.2d 404 (1987); In re Jobes, 108 N.J. 394, 529 A.2d 434 (1987); In re Peter, 108 N.J. 365, 529 A.2d 419 (1987).

In *Farrell* the court affirmed the right of a competent patient to discontinue life-sustaining treatment and, in dicta, approved the "subjective" test that had been adopted in *Conroy.* In *Jobes* and *Peter,* however, the court side-stepped the *Conroy* test because of the condition of the patients. Each of those cases involved a patient in persistent vegetative state. In an explanation subsequently adopted by the United States Supreme Court in *Cruzan,* 497 U.S. 261 n. 1, 110 S.Ct. 2841 n. 1, 111 L.Ed.2d 224 (1990), the *Jobes* court defined "persistent vegetative state" by quoting the trial testimony of Dr. Fred Plum, who created the term:

> [Persistent] vegetative state describes a body which is functioning entirely in terms of its internal controls. It maintains temperature. It maintains heartbeat and pulmonary ventilation. It maintains digestive activity. It maintains reflex activity of muscles and nerves for low level conditioned responses. But there is no behavioral evidence of either self-awareness or awareness of the surroundings in a learned manner.

529 A.2d at 438.

The New Jersey Supreme Court held in *Peter* that "the balancing tests set forth in *Conroy* are [not] appropriate in the case of a persistently vegetative patient." As the court pointed out,

> Even in the case of a patient like Claire Conroy—the type of patient for whom the balancing tests were created—it can be difficult or impossible to measure the burdens of embarrassment, frustration, helplessness, rage and other emotional pain, or the benefits of enjoyable feelings like contentment, joy, satisfaction, gratitude, and well being that the patient experiences as a result of life-sustaining treatment. "[M]edical experts are often unable to determine with any degree of medical certainty the extent of a nonverbal person's intellectual functioning or the depth of his emotional life." [citing *Conroy*]

> While a benefits-burdens analysis is difficult with marginally cognitive patients like Claire Conroy, it is essentially impossible with patients in a

persistent vegetative state. By definition such patients, like Ms. Peter, do not experience any of the benefits or burdens that the *Conroy* balancing tests are intended or able to appraise. Therefore, we hold that these tests should not be applied to patients in the persistent vegetative state.

In re Peter, 529 A.2d at 424–425.

In *Peter* the court was able to depend upon the subjective prong of the *Conroy* test, and thus it did not have to address the alternative test to be applied when an incompetent patient did not leave clear and convincing evidence of that patient's desires. In *Jobes,* however, the court was required to look for an alternative test. The court determined that the appropriate test in the case of a patient in persistent vegetative state who had not left clear and convincing evidence of the patient's desires was the test that had been applied in *Quinlan* almost a decade before. Although there was some ambiguity in the early *Quinlan* decision, the *Jobes* court made it clear that "the right of a patient in an irreversibly vegetative state to determine whether to refuse life-sustaining medical treatment may be exercised by the patient's family or close friend. If there are close and caring family members who are willing to make this decision there is no need to have a guardian appointed." 529 A.2d at 447. In effect, in *Peter* and *Jobes* the New Jersey Supreme Court said that the limited-objective and pure-objective tests of Conroy make it too difficult to terminate the treatment of patients in persistent vegetative states, even if those standards could reasonably be applied to other incompetent patients.

Does it make any sense to treat a patient in a persistent vegetative state any differently from another incompetent patient? Is there any reason to permit the termination of life-sustaining treatment in a patient in persistent vegetative state when it would not be permitted in an otherwise identically situated patient with a scintilla of higher brain function? Is the New Jersey retreat from *Conroy* in the case of patients in persistent vegetative state a narrowing or a broadening of the *Conroy* rule? What position does the Uniform Health Care Decisions Act take with respect to patients in a persistent vegetative state? Are they treated any differently from patients who are not in that condition?

For a description of every case in which state and federal courts have permitted the discontinuation of life support treatments in patients in persistent vegetative state prior to 1990, see Justice Stevens's dissent in Cruzan, 497 U.S. 261, 349 n. 21, 110 S.Ct. 2841, 2888 n. 21, 111 L.Ed.2d 224. Justice Stevens points out that the *Cruzan* case itself is unique in not permitting the termination of treatment in a patient in persistent vegetative state.

3. *Distinguishing Active and Passive Conduct.* Courts have been called upon to determine the legal significance of the difference between active and passive conduct, and ordinary and extraordinary forms of medical intervention. These anachronistic distinctions have not found a safe harbor in the law, just as they have been increasingly recognized as meaningless in ethics. The Conroy opinion specifically and carefully considered each of these distinctions, and summarized the ethical and legal literature and the reasons for rejecting the distinctions. As to the distinction between active and passive conduct, the *Conroy* court announced:

We emphasize that in making decisions whether to administer life-sustaining treatment to patients such as Claire Conroy, the primary focus should be the patient's desires and experience of pain and enjoyment—not the type of treatment involved. Thus, we reject the distinction that some have made between actively hastening death by terminating treatment and passively allowing a person to die of a disease as one of limited use in a legal analysis of such a decision-making situation.

Characterizing conduct as active or passive is often an elusive notion, even outside the context of medical decision-making * * *. The distinction is particularly nebulous, however, in the context of decisions whether to withhold or withdraw life-sustaining treatment. In a case like that of Claire Conroy, for example, would a physician who discontinued nasogastric feeding be actively causing her death by removing her primary source of nutrients; or would he merely be omitting to continue the artificial form of treatment, thus passively allowing her medical condition, which includes her inability to swallow, to take its natural course? [ ] The ambiguity inherent in this distinction is further heightened when one performs an act within an over-all plan of non-intervention, such as when a doctor writes an order not to resuscitate a patient. * * *

For a similar reason, we also reject any distinction between withholding and withdrawing life-sustaining treatment. Some commentators have suggested that discontinuing life-sustaining treatment once it has been commenced is morally more problematic than merely failing to begin the treatment. Discontinuing life-sustaining treatment, to some, is an "active" taking of life, as opposed to the more "passive" act of omitting the treatment in the first instance.

This distinction is more psychologically compelling than logically sound. As mentioned above, the line between active and passive conduct in the context of medical decisions is far too nebulous to constitute a principled basis for decisionmaking. Whether necessary treatment is withheld at the outset or withdrawn later on, the consequence—the patient's death—is the same. Moreover, from a policy standpoint, it might well be unwise to forbid persons from discontinuing a treatment under circumstances in which the treatment could permissibly be withheld. Such a rule could discourage families and doctors from even attempting certain types of care and could thereby force them into hasty and premature decisions to allow a patient to die. [ ]

486 A.2d at 1233–1234.

This policy interest was recognized by Justice Brennan in his *Cruzan* dissent:

Moreover, there may be considerable danger that Missouri's rule of decision would impair rather than serve any interest the state does have in sustaining life. Current medical practice recommends use of heroic measures if there is a scintilla of a chance that the patient will recover, on the assumption that the measures will be discontinued should the patient improve. When the President's Commission in 1982 approved the withdrawal of life support equipment from irreversibly vegetative patients, it explained that "[a]n even more troubling wrong occurs when a treatment that might save life or improve health is not started because the health care personnel are afraid that they will find it very difficult to stop the treatment if, as is fairly likely, it proves to be of little benefit and greatly burdens the patient."

497 U.S. at 314, 110 S.Ct. at 2870.

4. *Distinguishing Ordinary and Extraordinary Treatment.* As to the distinction between ordinary and extraordinary treatment, *Conroy* pointed out:

We also find unpersuasive the distinction relied upon by some courts, commentators, and theologians between "ordinary" treatment, which they would always require, and "extraordinary" treatment, which they deem optional. * * * The terms "ordinary" and "extraordinary" have assumed too many conflicting meanings to remain useful. To draw a line on this basis for determining whether treatment should be given leads to a semantical milieu that does not advance the analysis.

The distinction between ordinary and extraordinary treatment is frequently phrased as one between common and unusual, or simple and complex, treatment [ ]; "extraordinary" treatment also has been equated with elaborate, artificial, heroic, aggressive, expensive, or highly involved or invasive forms of medical intervention [ ]. Depending on the definitions applied, a particular treatment for a given patient may be considered both ordinary and extraordinary. [ ] Further, since the common/unusual and simple/complex distinctions among medical treatments "exist on continuums with no precise dividing line," [ ] and the continuum is constantly shifting due to progress in medical care, disagreement will often exist about whether a particular treatment is ordinary or extraordinary. In addition, the competent patient generally could refuse even ordinary treatment; therefore, an incompetent patient theoretically should also be able to make such a choice when the surrogate decision-making is effectuating the patient's subjective intent. In such cases, the ordinary/extraordinary distinction is irrelevant except insofar as the particular patient would have made the distinction.

The ordinary/extraordinary distinction has also been discussed in terms of the benefits and burdens of treatment for the patient. If the benefits of the treatment outweigh the burdens it imposes on the patient, it is characterized as ordinary and therefore ethically required; if not, it is characterized as extraordinary and therefore optional. [ ] This formulation is extremely fact-sensitive and would lead to different classifications of the same treatment in different situations.

* * * Moreover, while the analysis may be useful in weighing the implications of the specific treatment for the patient, essentially it merely restates the question: whether the burdens of a treatment so clearly outweigh its benefits to the patient that continued treatment would be inhumane.

468 A.2d at 1234–1235. See also Brophy v. New England Sinai Hospital, Inc., 398 Mass. 417, 497 N.E.2d 626 (1986) ("while we believe that the distinction between extraordinary and ordinary care is a factor to be considered, the use of such a distinction as the sole, or major, factor of decision tends * * * to create a distinction without meaning.")

5. *The Special Status of Nutrition and Hydration.* The issue of withdrawing nutrition and hydration has become an especially contentious one. Generally, courts have concluded that the termination of nutrition and hydration is no different from the termination of other forms of mechanical support. For example, *Conroy* suggested:

Some commentators, * * * have made yet [another] distinction, between the termination of artificial feedings and the termination of other forms of life-sustaining medical treatment. * * * According to the Appellate Division:

If, as here, the patient is not comatose and does not face imminent and inevitable death, nourishment accomplishes the substantial benefit of sustaining life until the illness takes its natural course. Under such circumstances nourishment always will be an essential element of ordinary care which physicians are ethically obligated to provide. [ ]

Certainly, feeding has an emotional significance. As infants we could breathe without assistance, but we were dependent on others for our lifeline of nourishment. Even more, feeding is an expression of nurturing and caring, certainly for infants and children, and in many cases for adults as well.

Once one enters the realm of complex, high-technology medical care, it is hard to shed the "emotional symbolism" of food. * * * Analytically, artificial feeding by means of a nasogastric tube or intravenous infusion can be seen as equivalent to artificial breathing by means of a respirator. Both prolong life through mechanical means when the body is no longer able to perform a vital bodily function on its own.

Furthermore, while nasogastric feeding and other medical procedures to ensure nutrition and hydration are usually well tolerated, they are not free from risks or burdens; they have complications that are sometimes serious and distressing to the patient.

* * *

Finally, dehydration may well not be distressing or painful to a dying patient. For patients who are unable to sense hunger and thirst, withholding of feeding devices such as nasogastric tubes may not result in more pain than the termination of any other medical treatment. * * * Thus, it cannot be assumed that it will always be beneficial for an incompetent patient to receive artificial feeding or harmful for him not to receive it. * * *

Under the analysis articulated above, withdrawal or withholding of artificial feeding, like any other medical treatment, would be permissible if there is sufficient proof to satisfy the subjective, limited-objective, or pure-objective test. A competent patient has the right to decline any medical treatment, including artificial feeding, and should retain that right when and if he becomes incompetent. In addition, in the case of an incompetent patient who has given little or no trustworthy indication of an intent to decline treatment and for whom it becomes necessary to engage in balancing under the limited-objective or pure-objective test, the pain and invasiveness of an artificial feeding device, and the pain of withdrawing that device, should be treated just like the results of administering or withholding any other medical treatment.

98 N.J. 321, 486 A.2d 1209, 1235–1237.

See also, In re Jobes, 108 N.J. 394, 529 A.2d 434 (1987); In re Peter, 108 N.J. 365, 529 A.2d 419 (1987); Gray v. Romeo, 697 F.Supp. 580 (D.R.I.1988) ("Although an emotional symbolism attaches itself to artificial feeding, there is no legal difference between a mechanical device that allows a person to breathe artificially and a mechanical device that allows a person nourishment. If a person has right to decline a respirator, then a person has the equal right to decline a gastrostomy tube."); Brophy v. New England Sinai Hospital, Inc., 398 Mass. 417, 497 N.E.2d 626 (1986); Corbett v. D'Alessandro, 487 So.2d 368 (Fla.App.1986) ("we see no reason to differentiate between the multitude of artificial devices that may be available to prolong the moment of death."); Bouvia v. Superior Court, 179 Cal.App.3d 1127, 225 Cal.Rptr. 297 (1986).

In McConnell v. Beverly Enterprises–Connecticut, Inc., 209 Conn. 692, 553 A.2d 596 (1989), the court authorized the withdrawal of feeding by a gastrostomy tube despite a statute that appeared to say that under such circumstances "nutrition and hydration must be provided." The court reasoned that the nutrition and hydration that was implicated in the statute was that provided by "a spoon or a straw," and that feeding by gastrostomy tube was no different than any other mechanical or electronic medical intervention.

In 1990, at least, a majority of the Supreme Court (the four dissenters and concurring Justice O'Connor in *Cruzan*) viewed nutrition and hydration as another form of medical care. As Justice O'Connor pointed out, "artificial feeding cannot readily be distinguished from other forms of medical treatment. Whether or not the techniques used to pass food and water into the patient's alimentary tract are termed 'medical treatment,' it is clear they all involve some degree of intrusion and restraint." She concluded that "the liberty guaranteed by the due process clause must protect, if it protects anything, an individual's deeply personal decision to reject medical treatment, including the artificial delivery of food and water."

In his dissent, Justice Brennan reached the same conclusion, vividly describing the medical processes involved:

> The artificial delivery of nutrition and hydration is undoubtedly medical treatment. The technique to which Nancy Cruzan is subject—artificial feeding through a gastrostomy tube—involves a tube implanted surgically into her stomach through incisions in her abdominal wall. It may obstruct the intestinal tract, erode and pierce the stomach wall, or cause leakage of the stomach's contents into the abdominal cavity. [ ] The tube can cause pneumonia from reflux of the stomach's contents into the lung. [ ] Typically, and in this case, commercially prepared formulas are used, rather than fresh food. [ ] The type of formula and method of administration must be experimented with to avoid gastrointestinal problems. [ ] The patient must be monitored daily by medical personnel as to weight, fluid intake and fluid output; blood tests must be done weekly.

> Artificial delivery of food and water is regarded as medical treatment by the medical profession and the federal government. * * * The federal government permits the cost of the medical devices and formulas used in enteral feeding to be reimbursed under Medicare. [ ] The formulas are regulated by the Federal Drug Administration as "medical foods," [ ] and the feeding tubes are regulated as medical devices [ ].

497 U.S. at 306–308, 110 S.Ct. at 2866–67.

To many, nutrition and hydration remain symbols of the bonds between human beings; the care we provide to the ones we love includes, at the very least, food and water. On the other hand, medical sources generally recognize the irrelevancy of distinguishing between nutrition and hydration and other forms of medical treatment. The Council on Ethical and Judicial Affairs of the American Medical Association has determined that "life-sustaining medical treatment may include but is not limited to artificial nutrition or hydration." Opinion 2.20 (1996). Today only the Missouri courts appear to be sticking to the conclusion that nutrition and hydration are not medical treatments. In re Warren, 858 S.W.2d 263 (Mo.App.1993).

Note: Choosing Futile Medical Care

The Wanglie Case

In December 1989, Helen Wanglie, an 87–year-old retired school teacher in Minneapolis, tripped on a rug in her home and fractured her hip. One month later, after surgery in one hospital, she was transferred to Hennepin County Medical Center, where her doctors determined she needed assistance in breathing and placed her on a ventilator. Three months later, in May 1990, she was transferred to yet another hospital to see if she could be weaned from her ventilator. While there, she suffered cardiac arrest and was resuscitated, but only after she suffered severe and irreversible brain damage that put her in a persistent vegetative state. She was moved back to Hennepin County Medical Center, where she was maintained on a ventilator and fed through a gastrostomy tube. Mrs. Wanglie remained in a persistent vegetative state for several months before her physicians determined that the continuation of high-tech medical intervention was inappropriate. In essence, the doctors determined that the care Mrs. Wanglie was receiving was no longer among the reasonable medical alternatives for a person in her condition.

Mrs. Wanglie's husband and her two children disagreed. As Mrs. Wanglie's husband pointed out, "Only He who gave life has the right to take life." He also pointed out, "I am a prolifer. I take the position that human life is sacred." He and the children agreed that Mrs. Wanglie would want treatment continued, even if the doctors believed that there were no chance of recovery. This was, as the family pointed out, a determination based on the patient's values, and there was no reason to defer to the doctors' collective ethical judgment.

The physicians and the hospital searched in vain for some healthcare facility in Minnesota that would be willing to take Mrs. Wanglie and continue to provide her care. None came forward. Frustrated by what they considered the continued inappropriate use of medicine, the hospital sought a court order appointing a conservator to replace Mr. Wanglie to make healthcare decisions for Mrs. Wanglie so that her treatment could be discontinued.

The July–August 1991 issue of the Hastings Center Report contains several good articles on the *Wanglie* case, including a summary of the medical facts prepared by her neurologist. This description of the Wanglie case is reprinted from R. Schwartz, Autonomy, Futility and the Limits of Medicine, 2 Camb. Q. Healthcare Ethics 159, 160–61 (1992). The case, *Conservatorship of Wanglie*, No. PX–91–283 (Minn., Hennepin County Dist.Ct., 1993), was never appealed and is unreported.

Futility

How should a physician (or a court) deal with a request for futile medical care? When is requested care truly "futile"? Was the request for treatment of Ms. Wanglie a request for futile care? Treatment is *scientifically futile* when it cannot achieve the medical result that is expected by the patient (or by the family) making the request. Scientifically futile treatment need not be offered or provided to a patient. A seriously ill cancer patient need not be provided with laetrile, a useless drug that has been popularized by those who would prey upon desperate patients and their families, even if that treatment is requested. A child with a viral illness need not be prescribed an antibiotic, even if the child's parents request one, because, as a matter of science, the antibiotic will not be effective in treating that illness. Doctors need not do a CAT scan on a patient with a cold, even if that is what the patient wants, because there is no reason to believe that there will be any connection between what can be discovered on the scan and the appropriate treatment of the cold. As a general matter healthcare providers, who are trained in the science of medicine, are entitled to determine which treatments are scientifically futile.

A harder question arises when a patient requests treatment that is not scientifically futile, but that is, in the opinion of the health care provider, *ethically futile*. Treatment is ethically futile if it will not serve the underlying interests of the patient. For example, some providers believe that it is ethically futile to keep a patient's body aerated and nourished when that patient is in persistent vegetative state. These healthcare providers believe that it is beyond the scope of medicine to sustain mere corporeal existence if there can never be anything beyond that. Some healthcare providers believe that it would be ethically futile to engage in CPR under circumstances in which the most that can be accomplished through that intervention would be to prolong the patient's life by a few hours. Of course, families may disagree with physicians over what constitutes ethically futile treatment, and there is no reason to adopt the provider's perspective, rather than the family's, as the ethically "correct" one. In the *Wanglie* case, for example, the family viewed the continued treatment as effective (in keeping the patient alive) while the healthcare providers viewed the treatment as ineffective (in serving any of the real goals of medicine). The Council on Ethical and Judicial Affairs of the American Medical Association has determined that:

> [p]hysicians are not ethically obliged to deliver care that, in their best professional judgment, will not have a reasonable chance of benefiting their patients. Patients should not be given treatments simply because they demand them. Denials of treatment should be justified by reliance on openly stated ethical principles and acceptable standards of care, * * * not on the concept of "futility," which cannot be meaningfully defined.

Council on Ethical and Judicial Affairs, American Medical Association, Current Opinion 2.035 ("Futility"), Code of Medical Ethics.

Is the Council's position a convincing one, or is it merely a device to transfer the authority to make ethically charged decisions from patients to physicians? Can futility be meaningfully defined? How *should* the providers deal with the arguably ethically futile treatment provided to Wanglie? Should it be continued if the family wishes it to be? Are health care providers required to tell patients and their families about treatment alternatives which they consider to be ethically futile, but which the family might wish anyway?

How are autonomy and patients' choices honored if they are recognized only when a patient wants to refuse treatment, and not when they want to continue treatment? Were *Conroy* and other cases in which patients were allowed to forgo treatment while in persistent vegetative state really a subterfuge for a standard that says that it is inappropriate to provide medical treatment to extend life in those circumstances?

There is a great deal of good writing on the proper legal approach to arguably futile treatment. For a good account of the fundamental issues at stake, see L. Schneiderman and N. Jecker, Wrong Medicine (1995) and S. Rubin, When Doctors Say No: The Battleground of Medical Futility (1998). See. also Judith Daar, Medical Futility and Implications for Physician Autonomy, 21 Am. J. L. & Med. 221 (1995), Paul Sorum, Limiting Cardiopulmonary Resuscitation, 57 Alb. L. Rev. 617 (1994), Erich Loewy and Richard Carlson, Futility and Its Wider Implications: A Concept in Need of Further Examination, 153 Arch. Internal Md. 429 (1993), Daniel Callahan, Medical Futility, Medical Necessity: The Problem–Without–A–Name, Hastings Center Rep. 30 (July–August 1991).

Problem

Emile Nighthorse is a 77–year–old man who has been hospitalized on and off over the past year. He suffers from serious kidney disease, congestive heart failure, severe headaches and increasingly severe dementia. His current hospitalization, which commenced two weeks ago, has resulted in him being supplied with kidney dialysis, which will, it appears, have to continue indefinitely, and a ventilator, which probably will be removed in a few weeks. He does not really understand his condition (or where he is), and he is cranky and abusive with the nurses, whom he believes to be torturing him. A psychiatrist does not believe there is any way to treat his mental condition without extremely heavy sedation. His prognosis is poor; his dementia will surely get worse, and his multi-system failure makes it likely that he will not live more than a few months. It is unlikely he will ever be discharged from the hospital.

Mr. Nighthorse never talked about his condition with anyone, and he has had a strained relationship with his wife of 50 years, who lives with him but rarely comes to the hospital to see him. He has two children who live in another city, and they both claim to have a relatively distant relationship with their father. Until his dementia became too severe, he spent most of his time at the Order of Eagles Aerie playing whist, and his long time whist partner, Ben Bitts, has been with Emile constantly from the moment he entered the hospital. Whenever Mr. Nighthorse is asked a question about his care, he turns to Ben and asks him what "they" should do.

Ben has asked the physician responsible for Emile's care to discontinue the dialysis and the ventilator, and to begin antibiotics. There is no medical reason to use antibiotics, but Ben argues that he is absolutely sure that Emile would want them anyway—he always wanted antibiotics when he was sick, even when his doctors told him that such drugs would be worthless. Ben says that he never really talked with Emile about what should be done under these circumstances, but that they had played whist together so long (almost 20 years) that he figures that he knows what Emile would want. Mrs. Nighthorse has told the doctor to do whatever Ben wants to do; she doesn't care. The two children have not returned to town. When contacted by phone, they both insist that everything should be done to save their father, but neither is willing to come to the hospital.

Mr. Nighthorse's primary physician has asked you—the hospital legal counsel—what he should do. What should you tell him? Would your answer be different if the Uniform Health Care Decisions Act had been adopted in your jurisdiction? If no statute regarding health care decision making had been adopted? What additional facts would help you render a reliable legal opinion?

b. The Role of the Courts and the Burden of Proof in Cases Involving the Decision to Forego Lifesustaining Treatment

There is a near consensus that where a patient has not left a formal prior directive, the goal of medicine should be to do what that patient, if competent, would want done. When, if ever, is it necessary for a court to be involved in making that decision—and when should the decision be left to the family, health care providers, or others? If the court is involved, what procedures should it employ? The procedural issues which have caused the greatest difficulty for state courts are the nature of evidence that would be relevant in determining a patient's wishes and the burden of proof to be applied to decisions to authorize the removal of life-sustaining treatment. As you read the next case, which formally addresses these issues, ask what kind of evidence should be (1) relevant and (2) sufficient for a determination of this issue.

CONSERVATORSHIP OF WENDLAND

Supreme Court of California, 2001.
26 Cal.4th 519, 28 P.3d 151, 110 Cal.Rptr.2d 412.

WERDEGAR, J.

In this case we consider whether a conservator of the person may withhold artificial nutrition and hydration from a conscious conservatee who is not terminally ill, comatose, or in a persistent vegetative state, and who has not left formal instructions for health care or appointed an agent or surrogate for health care decisions. Interpreting the Probate Code in light of the relevant provisions of the California Constitution, we conclude a conservator may not withhold artificial nutrition and hydration from such a person absent clear and convincing evidence the conservator's decision is in accordance with either the conservatee's own wishes or best interest.

The trial court in the case before us, applying the clear and convincing evidence standard, found the evidence on both points insufficient and, thus, denied the conservator's request for authority to withhold artificial nutrition and hydration. The Court of Appeal, which believed the trial court was required to defer to the conservator's good faith decision, reversed. We reverse the decision of the Court of Appeal.

I. FACTS AND PROCEDURAL HISTORY

On September 29, 1993, Robert Wendland rolled his truck at high speed in a solo accident while driving under the influence of alcohol. The accident injured Robert's brain, leaving him conscious yet severely disabled, both mentally and physically, and dependent on artificial nutrition and hydration. Two years later Rose Wendland, Robert's wife and conservator, proposed to direct his physician to remove his feeding tube and allow him to die ... Robert's mother and sister ... objected to the conservator's decision. This proceeding arose under the provisions of the Probate Code authorizing courts to settle such disputes.

Following the accident, Robert remained in a coma, totally unresponsive, for several months. During this period Rose visited him daily, often with their children, and authorized treatment as necessary to maintain his health.

Robert eventually regained consciousness. His subsequent medical history is described in a comprehensive medical evaluation later submitted to the court. According to the report, Rose "first noticed signs of responsiveness sometime in late 1994 or early 1995 and alerted [Robert's] physicians and nursing staff." ... At his highest level of function between February and July, 1995, Robert was able to do such things as throw and catch a ball, operate an electric wheelchair with assistance, turn pages, draw circles, draw an 'R' and perform two-step commands." For example, "[h]e was able to respond appropriately to the command 'close your eyes and open them when I say the number 3.' ... He could choose a requested color block out of four color blocks. He could set the right peg in a pegboard. He remained unable to vocalize. Eye blinking was successfully used as a communication mode for a while, however no consistent method of communication was developed."

Despite improvements made in therapy, Robert remained severely disabled, both mentally and physically. The same medical report summarized his continuing impairments as follows: "severe cognitive impairment that is not possible to fully appreciate due to the concurrent motor and communication impairments ..."; "maladaptive behavior characterized by agitation, aggressiveness and non-compliance"; "severe paralysis on the right and moderate paralysis on the left"; "severely impaired communication, without compensatory augmentative communication system"; "severe swallowing dysfunction, dependent upon non-oral enteric tube feeding for nutrition and hydration";

"incontinence of bowel and bladder"; "moderate spasticity"; "mild to moderate contractures"; "general dysphoria"; "recurrent medical illnesses, including pneumonia, bladder infections, sinusitis"; and "dental issues."

After Robert regained consciousness and while he was undergoing therapy, Rose authorized surgery three times to replace dislodged feeding tubes. When physicians sought her permission a fourth time, she declined. She discussed the decision with her daughters and with Robert's brother Michael, all of whom believed that Robert would not have approved the procedure even if necessary to sustain his life. Rose also discussed the decision with Robert's treating physician, Dr. Kass, other physicians, and the hospital's ombudsman, all of whom apparently supported her decision. Dr. Kass, however, inserted a nasogastric feeding tube to keep Robert alive pending input from the hospital's ethics committee.

Eventually, the 20–member ethics committee unanimously approved Rose's decision. In the course of their deliberations, however, the committee did not speak with Robert's mother or sister. [They] learned, apparently through an anonymous telephone call, that Dr. Kass planned to remove Robert's feeding tube [and] applied for a temporary restraining order to bar him from so doing, and the court granted the motion ex parte.

Rose immediately thereafter petitioned for appointment as Robert's conservator. In the petition, she asked the court to determine that Robert lacked the capacity to give informed consent for medical treatment and to confirm her authority "to withdraw and/or withhold medical treatment and/or life-sustaining treatment, including, but not limited to, withholding nutrition and hydration." [Robert's mother and sister] (hereafter sometimes objectors) opposed the petition. After a hearing, the court appointed Rose as conservator but reserved judgment on her request for authority to remove Robert's feeding tube. * * *

After [a 60 day observation period] elapsed without significant improvement in Robert's condition, the conservator renewed her request for authority to remove his feeding tube. The objectors asked the trial court to appoint independent counsel for the conservatee. The trial court declined, and the Court of Appeal summarily denied the objectors' petition for writ of mandate. We granted review and transferred the case to the Court of Appeal, which then directed the trial court to appoint counsel. [ ] Appointed counsel, exercising his independent judgment [ ], decided to support the conservator's decision. * * *

* * *

The [consequent] trial generated the evidence set out above. The testifying physicians agreed that Robert would not likely experience further cognitive recovery. Dr. Kass, Robert's treating physician, testified that, to the highest degree of medical certainty, Robert would never be able to make medical treatment decisions, walk, talk, feed himself, eat, drink, or control his bowel and bladder functions.

* * *

Robert's wife, brother and daughter recounted preaccident statements Robert had made about his attitude towards life-sustaining health care.

Robert's wife recounted specific statements on two occasions. The first occasion was Rose's decision whether to turn off a respirator sustaining the life of her father, who was near death from gangrene. Rose recalls Robert saying: "I would never want to live like that, and I wouldn't want my children to see me like that and look at the hurt you're going through as an adult seeing your father like that." On cross-examination, Rose acknowledged Robert said on this occasion that Rose's father "wouldn't want to live like a vegetable" and "wouldn't want to live in a comatose state."

After his father-in-law's death, Robert developed a serious drinking problem. After a particular incident, Rose asked Michael, Robert's brother, to talk to him. When Robert arrived home the next day he was angry to see Michael there, interfering in what he considered a private family matter. Rose remembers Michael telling Robert: "I'm going to get a call from Rosie one day, and you're going to be in a terrible accident." Robert replied: "If that ever happened to me, you know what my feelings are. Don't let that happen to me. Just let me go. Leave me alone." ... Robert's daughter Katie remembers him saying on this occasion that "if he could not be a provider for his family, if he could not do all the things that he enjoyed doing, just enjoying the outdoors, just basic things, feeding himself, talking, communicating, if he could not do those things, he would not want to live."

* * * Specifically, the court found the conservator "ha[d] not met her duty and burden to show by clear and convincing evidence that conservatee Robert Wendland, who is not in a persistent vegetative state nor suffering from a terminal illness would, under the circumstances, want to die. Conservator has likewise not met her burden of establishing that the withdrawal of artificially delivered nutrition and hydration is commensurate with conservatee's best interests. * * * Based on these findings, the court granted the objectors' motion for judgment [ ], thus denying the conservator's request for confirmation of her proposal to withdraw treatment. The court also found the conservator had acted in good faith and would be permitted to remain in that office. Nevertheless, the court limited her powers by ordering that she would "have no authority to direct ... [any] health care provider to remove the conservatee's life sustaining medical treatment in the form of withholding nutrition and hydration." [ ]

The conservator appealed this decision. The Court of Appeal reversed. In the Court of Appeal's view, "[t]he trial court properly placed the burden of producing evidence on [the conservator] and properly applied a clear and convincing evidence standard. However, the court erred in requiring [the conservator] to prove that [the conservatee], while competent, expressed a desire to die in the circumstances and in substituting its own judgment concerning [the conservatee's] best interests * * * ." Instead, the trial court's role was "merely to satisfy itself that the conservator had considered the conservatee's best interests in good faith * * * ." * * * We granted review of this decision.

II. DISCUSSION

A. *The Relevant Legal Principles*

* * *

1. Constitutional and common law principles

One relatively certain principle is that a competent adult has the right to refuse medical treatment, even treatment necessary to sustain life. The Legislature has cited this principle to justify legislation governing medical care decisions [ ], and courts have invoked it as a starting point for analysis, even in cases examining the rights of incompetent persons and the duties of surrogate decision makers [ ]. This case requires us to look beyond the rights of a competent person to the rights of incompetent conservatees and the duties of conservators, but the principle just mentioned is a logical place to begin.

That a competent person has the right to refuse treatment is a statement both of common law and of state constitutional law. [The court then discussed the development of this right in common law, depending on informed consent and other cases.]

The Courts of Appeal have found another source for the same right in the California Constitution's privacy clause. * * *

Federal law has little to say about the competent person's right to refuse treatment, but what it does say is not to the contrary. The United States Supreme Court spoke provisionally to the point in *Cruzan* [where the Court] acknowledged that "a competent person['s] * * * constitutionally protected liberty interest in refusing unwanted medical treatment may be inferred" [ ] from prior decisions holding that state laws requiring persons to submit to involuntary medical procedures must be justified by countervailing state interests. The "logic" of such cases would, the court thought, implicate a competent person's liberty interest in refusing artificially delivered food and water essential to life. [ ] Whether any given state law infringed such a liberty interest, however, would have to be determined by balancing the liberty interest against the relevant state interests, in particular the state's interest in preserving life. [ ]

In view of these authorities, the competent adult's right to refuse medical treatment may be safely considered established, at least in California.

The same right survives incapacity, in a practical sense, if exercised while competent pursuant to a law giving that act lasting validity. For some time, California law has given competent adults the power to leave formal directions for health care in the event they later become incompetent; over time, the Legislature has afforded ever greater scope to that power. * * *

Effective July 1, 2000, the Health Care Decisions Law [ ] gives competent adults extremely broad power to direct all aspects of their health care in the event they become incompetent. . . . Briefly, and as relevant here, the new law permits a competent person to execute an advance directive about "any aspect" of health care. Among other things, a person may direct that life-sustaining treatment be withheld or withdrawn under conditions specified by the person and not limited to terminal illness, permanent coma, or persistent vegetative state. A competent person may still use a power of attorney for health care to give an agent the power to make health care decisions [ ], but a patient may also orally designate a surrogate to make such decisions by personally informing the patient's supervising health care provider. [ ] Under the new law, agents and surrogates are required to make health care decisions "in accordance with the principal's individual health care instructions, if any, and other wishes to the extent known to the agent." [ ]

All of the laws just mentioned merely give effect to the decision of a competent person, in the form either of instructions for health care or the designation of an agent or surrogate for health care decisions. Such laws may accurately be described, as the Legislature has described them, as a means to respect personal autonomy by giving effect to competent decisions: * * *

In contrast, decisions made by conservators typically derive their authority from a different basis—the *parens patriae* power of the state to protect incompetent persons. Unlike an agent or a surrogate for health care, who is voluntarily appointed by a competent person, a conservator is appointed by the court because the conservatee "has been adjudicated to lack the capacity to make health care decisions."

* * *

2.   *[The Probate Code]*

[The court then analyzed the history of the relevant Probate Code provision.]

B.   *The Present Case*

This background illuminates the parties' arguments, which reduce in essence to this: The conservator has claimed the power under [the Probate Code] to direct the conservatee's health care providers to cease providing artificial nutrition and hydration. In opposition, the objectors have contended the statute violates the conservatee's rights to privacy and life under the facts of this case if the conservator's interpretation of the statute is correct.[10]

* * *

1.   *The primary standard: a decision in accordance with the conservatee's wishes*

The conservator asserts she offered sufficient evidence at trial to satisfy the primary statutory standard, which contemplates a decision "in accordance with the conservatee's * * * wishes * * * ." [ ] The trial court, however, determined the evidence on this point was insufficient. The conservator did "not [meet] her duty and burden," the court expressly found, "to show by clear and convincing evidence that [the] conservatee ... , who is not in a persistent vegetative state nor suffering from a terminal illness would, under the circumstances, want to die." * * *

The conservator argues the Legislature understood and intended that the low preponderance of the evidence standard would apply. Certainly this was the Law Revision Commission's understanding [in drafting the statute]. * * *

10. The conservator argues that a conservator's decision to withdraw life support does not entail state action and, thus, cannot implicate the conservatee's constitutional rights. State action, however, is of no concern because the state constitutional right to privacy (Cal. Const., art. I, § 1), one of the traditional sources of a patient's right to autonomy and bodily integrity, protects against private conduct and is sufficiently broad to justify our conclusion. [ ] A conservatee's right to life (Cal. Const., art. I, § 1), which coincides here with the state's interest in protecting life, also supports the conclusion and enjoys some protection against private conduct, as illustrated by the laws prohibiting homicide and expressing legislative disapproval of mercy killing, assisted suicide, and euthanasia [ ].

The objectors, in opposition, argue that [the relevant section] would be unconstitutional if construed to permit a conservator to end the life of a conscious conservatee based on a finding by the low preponderance of the evidence standard that the latter would not want to live. We see no basis for holding the statute unconstitutional on its face. We do, however, find merit in the objectors' argument. We therefore construe the statute to minimize the possibility of its unconstitutional application by requiring clear and convincing evidence of a conscious conservatee's wish to refuse life-sustaining treatment when the conservator relies on that asserted wish to justify withholding life-sustaining treatment* * *. [W]e see no constitutional reason to apply the higher evidentiary standard to the majority of health care decisions made by conservators not contemplating a conscious conservatee's death.

* * *

Notwithstanding the foregoing, one must acknowledge that the primary standard for decisionmaking set out in [the Probate Code] does articulate what will in some cases form a constitutional basis for a conservator's decision to end the life of a conscious patient: deference to the patient's own wishes. This standard also appears in the new provisions governing decisions by agents and surrogates designated by competent adults. [ ] As applied in that context, the requirement that decisions be made "in accordance with the principal's individual health care instructions * * * and other wishes" [ ] merely respects the principal-agent relationship and gives effect to the properly expressed wishes of a competent adult. Because a competent adult may refuse life-sustaining treatment [ ], it follows that an agent properly and voluntarily designated by the principal may refuse treatment on the principal's behalf unless, of course, such authority is revoked. [ ]

The only apparent purpose of requiring conservators to make decisions in accordance with the conservatee's wishes, when those wishes are known, is to enforce the fundamental principle of personal autonomy. The same requirement, as applied to agents and surrogates freely designated by competent persons, enforces the principles of agency. A reasonable person presumably will designate for such purposes only a person in whom the former reposes the highest degree of confidence. A conservator, in contrast, is *not* an agent of the conservatee, and unlike a freely designated agent cannot be presumed to have special knowledge of the conservatee's health care wishes.* * * While it may be constitutionally permissible to assume that an agent freely designated by a formerly competent person to make all health care decisions, including life-ending ones, will resolve such questions "in accordance with the principal's ... wishes" [ ] one cannot apply the same assumption to conservators and conservatees. [ ] For this reason, when the legal premise of a conservator's decision to end a conservatee's life by withholding medical care is that the conservatee would refuse such care, to apply a high standard of proof will help to ensure the reliability of the decision.

The function of a standard of proof is to instruct the fact finder concerning the degree of confidence our society deems necessary in the correctness of factual conclusions for a particular type of adjudication, to allocate the risk of error between the litigants, and to indicate the relative importance attached to the ultimate decision. [ ] Thus, "the standard of proof may depend upon the 'gravity of the consequences that would result from an erroneous determination of the issue involved.' " [ ] The default standard of proof in civil cases is the preponderance of the evidence. [ ] Nevertheless, courts have applied the clear and convincing evidence standard when necessary to protect important rights.

We applied the clear and convincing evidence standard, for example * * * to ensure that a conservator's decision to authorize sterilization of a developmentally disabled conservatee was truly in the latter's best interests. We have also applied the clear and convincing evidence standard to findings necessary to terminate parental rights [ ] and to findings supporting the discipline of judges [ ] The Courts of Appeal have required clear and convincing evidence of a person's inability to provide for his or her personal needs as a prerequisite to the appointment of a conservator [ ] and of a conservatee's incompetence to accept or reject treatment as a prerequisite to permitting involuntary electroconvulsive therapy [ ]. Similarly, the United States Supreme Court has applied the clear and convincing evidence standard in cases implicating fundamental liberty interests protected by the Fourteenth Amendment, such as proceedings to terminate parental rights [ ], to commit to a mental hospital [ ], and to deport [ ].

In this case, the importance of the ultimate decision and the risk of error are manifest. So too should be the degree of confidence required in the necessary findings of fact. The ultimate decision is whether a conservatee lives or dies, and the risk is that a conservator, claiming statutory authority to end a conscious conservatee's life "in accordance with the conservatee's ... wishes" [ ] by withdrawing artificial nutrition and hydration, will make a decision with which the conservatee subjectively disagrees and which subjects the conservatee to starvation, dehydration and death. This would represent the gravest possible affront to a conservatee's state constitutional right to privacy, in the sense of freedom from unwanted bodily intrusions, and to life. * * * Certainly it is possible, as the conservator here urges, that an incompetent and uncommunicative but conscious conservatee might perceive the efforts to keep him alive as unwanted intrusion and the withdrawal of those efforts as welcome release. But the decision to treat is reversible. The decision to withdraw treatment is not. The role of a high evidentiary standard in such a case is to adjust the risk of error to favor the less perilous result. * * *

In conclusion, to interpret [the Probate Code] to permit a conservator to withdraw artificial nutrition and hydration from a conscious conservatee based on a finding, by a mere preponderance of the evidence, that the conservatee would refuse treatment creates a serious risk that the law will be unconstitutionally applied in some cases, with grave injury to fundamental rights. Under these circumstances, we may properly ask whether the statute may be construed in a way that mitigates the risk. * * * Here, where the risk to conservatees' rights is grave and the proposed construction is consistent with the language of the statute, to construe the statute to avoid the constitutional risk is an appropriate exercise of judicial power.

* * *

One amicus curiae argues that "[i]mposing so high an evidentiary burden [i.e., clear and convincing evidence] would ... frustrate many genuine treatment desires—particularly the choices of young people, who are less likely than older people to envision the need for advanced directives, or poor people, who are less likely than affluent people to have the resources to obtain formal legal documents." But the Legislature has already accommodated this concern in large part by permitting patients to nominate surrogate decision makers by orally informing a supervising physician [ ] and by giving effect to specific oral health care instructions [ ]. To go still farther, by giving conclusive effect to wishes inferred from informal, oral statements proved only by a preponderance of the evidence, may serve the interests of incompetent persons whose wishes are correctly determined, but to do so also poses an unacceptable risk of violating other incompetent patients' rights to privacy and life, as already explained. To the argument that applying a high standard of proof in such cases impermissibly burdens the right to determine one's own medical treatment, one need only repeat the United States Supreme Court's response to the same assertion: "The differences between the choice made *by* a competent person to refuse medical treatment, and the choice made *for* an incompetent person by someone else to refuse medical treatment, are so obviously different that the State is warranted in establishing rigorous procedures for the latter class of cases which do not apply to the former class." *Cruzan [ ]*

* * *

In the case before us, the trial court found that the conservator failed to show "by clear and convincing evidence that conservatee Robert Wendland, who is not in a persistent vegetative state nor suffering from a terminal illness would, under the circumstances, want to die." The conservator does not appear to challenge the trial court's finding on this point; her challenge, rather, is to the trial court's understanding of the law. For these reasons, we need not review the sufficiency of the evidence to support the finding. Nevertheless, given the exceptional circumstances of this case, we note that the finding appears to be correct.

* * *

2. The best interest standard

Having rejected the conservator's argument that withdrawing artificial hydration and nutrition would have been "in accordance with the conservatee's * * * wishes" [ ], we must next consider her contention that the same action would have been proper under the fallback best interest standard. Under that standard, "the conservator shall make the decision in accordance with the conservator's determination of the conservatee's best interest. In determining the conservatee's best interest, the conservator shall consider the conservatee's personal values to the extent known to the conservator." [ ] The trial court, as noted, ruled the conservator had the burden of establishing that the withdrawal of artificially delivered nutrition and hydration was in the conservatee's best interest, and had not met that burden.

Here, as before, the conservator argues that the trial court applied too high a standard of proof. This follows, she contends, from [the Probate Code], which gives her as conservator "the *exclusive* authority" to give consent for such medical treatment as she "in good faith based on medical advice determines to be necessary" * * *. Based on these statements, the conservator argues the trial court has no power other than to verify that she has made the decision for which the Probate Code expressly calls: a "good faith" decision "based on medical advice" and "consider[ing] the conservatee's personal values" whether treatment is "necessary" in the conservatee's "best interest."[ ] The trial court, as noted, rejected the conservator's assessment of the conservatee's best interest but nevertheless found by clear and convincing evidence that she had acted "in good faith, based on medical evidence and after consideration of the conservatee's best interests, including his likely wishes, based on his previous statements." This finding, the conservator concludes, should end the litigation as a matter of law in her favor.

* * *. To be sure, the statute provides that "the conservator shall make the decision in accordance with *the conservator's determination* of the conservatee's best interest." [ ] But the conservator herself concedes the court must be able to review her decision for abuse of discretion. This much, at least, follows from the conservator's status as an officer of the court subject to judicial supervision. While the assessment of a conservatee's best interest belongs in the first instance to the conservator, this does not mean the court must invariably defer to the conservator regardless of the evidence.

In the exceptional case where a conservator proposes to end the life of a conscious but incompetent conservatee, we believe the same factor that principally justifies applying the clear and convincing evidence standard to a determination of the conservatee's wishes also justifies applying that standard to a determination of the conservatee's best interest: The decision threatens the conservatee's fundamental rights to privacy and life. * * *

We need not in this case attempt to define the extreme factual predicates that, if proved by clear and convincing evidence, might support a conservator's decision that withdrawing life support would be in the best interest of a conscious conservatee. Here, the conservator offered no basis for such a finding other than her own subjective judgment that the conservatee did not enjoy a satisfactory quality of life and legally insufficient evidence to the effect that he would have wished to die. On this record, the trial court's decision was correct.

III. CONCLUSION

For the reasons set out above, we conclude the superior court correctly required the conservator to prove, by clear and convincing evidence, either that the conservatee wished to refuse life-sustaining treatment or that to withhold such treatment would have been in his best interest; lacking such evidence, the superior court correctly denied the conservator's request for permission to withdraw artificial hydration and nutrition. We emphasize, however, that the clear and convincing evidence standard does not apply to the vast majority of health care decisions made by conservators under [the Probate Code]. Only the decision to withdraw life-sustaining treatment, because of its effect on a conscious conservatee's fundamental rights, justifies imposing that high standard of proof. Therefore, our decision today affects only a narrow class of persons: conscious conservatees who have not left formal directions for health care and whose conservators propose to withhold life-sustaining treatment for the purpose of causing their conservatees' deaths. Our conclusion does not affect permanently unconscious patients, including those who are comatose or in a persistent vegetative state [ ], persons who have left legally cognizable instructions for health care [ ], persons who have designated agents or other surrogates for health care [ ], or conservatees for whom conservators have made medical decisions other than those intended to bring about the death of a conscious conservatee.

The decision of the Court of Appeal is reversed.

Notes and Questions

1.   The Wendland court applies the "clear and convincing evidence" standard to two separate substantive issues—to the determination of Robert's wishes (when the court applies a substituted judgment standard) and, separately, to the determination of what is in Robert's best interest (when the court decides that it cannot make a determination based on substituted judgment). More than ten years before, in a seminal New York case, In re Westchester County Medical Center (O'Connor), 72 N.Y.2d 517, 534 N.Y.S.2d 886, 531 N.E.2d 607 (1988), the Court of Appeals applied the "clear and convincing evidence" standard to determine if a family member could make a substituted judgment to remove life sustaining medical treatment. Chief Judge Wachtler, for the Court, articulated the standard it was applying in deciding that this high level of proof was absent in the case before the court:

Neither of the doctors had known Mrs. O'Connor before she became incompetent and thus knew nothing of her attitudes toward the use of life-sustaining measures. The respondents' first witness on this point was * * * a former co-worker and longtime friend of Mrs. O'Connor. * * * He testified that his first discussion with Mrs. O'Connor concerning artificial means of prolonging life occurred about 1969. At that time his father, who was dying of cancer, informed him that he would not want to continue life by any artificial method if he had lost his dignity because he could no longer control his normal bodily functions. The witness said that when he told Mrs. O'Connor of this she agreed wholeheartedly and said: "I would never want to be a burden on anyone and I would never want to lose my dignity before I passed away." He noted that she was a "very religious woman" who "felt that nature should take its course and not use further artificial means." They had similar conversations on two or three occasions between 1969 and 1973. During these discussions Mrs. O'Connor variously stated that it is "monstrous" to keep someone alive by using "machinery, things like that" when they are "not going to get better"; that she would never want to be in the same situation as her husband * * * and that people who are "suffering very badly" should be allowed to die.

Mrs. O'Connor's daughter Helen testified that her mother informed her on several occasions that if she became ill and was unable to care for herself she would not want her life to be sustained artificially. * * * Mrs. O'Connor's other daughter, Joan, essentially adopted her sister's testimony. She described her mother's statements on this subject as less solemn pronouncements: "it was brought up when we were together, at times when in conversations you start something, you know, maybe the news was on and maybe that was the topic that was brought up and that's how it came about."

However, all three of these witnesses also agreed that Mrs. O'Connor had never discussed providing food or water with medical assistance, nor had she ever said that she would adhere to her view and decline medical treatment "by artificial means" if that would produce a painful death. When Helen was asked what choice her mother would make under those circumstances she admitted that she did not know. Her sister Joan agreed, noting that this had never been discussed, "unfortunately, no."

* * *

It has long been the common-law rule in this State that a person has the right to decline medical treatment, even life-saving treatment, absent an overriding State interest [ ]. In 1981, we held, in two companion cases, that a hospital or medical facility must respect this right even when a patient becomes incompetent, if while competent, the patient stated that he or she did not want certain procedures to be employed under specified circumstances. [*Eichner*]

* * * *Eichner* had been competent and capable of expressing his will before he was silenced by illness. In those circumstances, we concluded that it would be appropriate for the court to intervene and direct the termination of artificial life supports, in accordance with the patient's wishes, because it was established by "clear and convincing evidence" that the patient would have so directed if he were competent and able to communicate. We selected the "clear and convincing evidence" standard in *Eichner* because it " 'impress[es] the factfinder with the importance of the decision' * * * and it 'forbids relief whenever the evidence is loose, equivocal or contradictory.' "[ ] Nothing less than unequivocal proof will suffice when the decision to terminate life supports is at issue.

Dissenting Judge Simons responded:

The majority refuses to recognize Mrs. O'Connor's expressed wishes because they were not solemn pronouncements made after reflection and because they were too indefinite.

Respondents have established the reliability of the statements under any standard. * * * These were not "casual remarks," but rather expressions evidencing the long-held beliefs of a mature woman who had been exposed to sickness and death in her employment and her personal life. Mrs. O'Connor had spent 20 years working in the emergency room and pathology laboratory of Jacobi Hospital, confronting the problems of life and death daily. She suffered through long illnesses of her husband, stepmother, father and two brothers who had died before her. She herself has been hospitalized for congestive heart failure and she understood the consequences of serious illnesses.

Because of these experiences, Mrs. O'Connor expressed her wishes in conversations with her daughters, both trained nurses, and a coemployee from the hospital who shared her hospital experience. There can be no doubt she was aware of the gravity of the problem she was addressing and the significance of her statements, or that those hearing her understood her intentions. She clearly stated the values important to her, a life that does not burden others and its termination with dignity, and what she believed her best interests required in the case of severe, debilitating illness. * * *

Notwithstanding this, the majority finds the statements entitled to little weight because Mrs. O'Connor's exposure was mostly to terminally ill cancer patients, or because her desire to remain independent and avoid burdening her children constituted little more than statements of self-pity by an elderly woman. There is no evidence to support those inferences and no justification for trivializing Mrs. O'Connor's statements. She is entitled to have them accepted without reservation. * * *

* * *

The [majority's] rule is unworkable because it requires humans to exercise foresight they do not possess. It requires that before life-sustaining treatment may be withdrawn, there must be proof that the patient anticipated his or her present condition, the means available to sustain life under the circumstances, and then decided that the alternative of death without mechanical assistance, by starvation in this case, is preferable to continued life [ ].

* * *

Even if a patient possessed the remarkable foresight to anticipate some future illness or condition, however, it is unrealistic to expect or require a lay person to be familiar with the support systems available for treatment—to say nothing of requiring a determination of which is preferable or the consequences that may result from using or foregoing them. Indeed, the conditions and consequences may change from day to day. * * *

In short, Mary O'Connor expressed her wishes in the only terms familiar to her, and she expressed them as clearly as a lay person should be asked to express them. To require more is unrealistic, and for all practical purposes, it precludes the right of patients to forego life-sustaining treatment.

Would the *Wendland* court agree with the majority in *O'Connor*, or with Judge Simons? Who do you think has the better argument about the propriety of applying the "clear and convincing evidence" standard?

2.   The propriety of the "clear and convincing evidence" standard applied by the Missouri Supreme Court in the *Cruzan* case was the primary issue before the United States Supreme Court in that case. The Court concluded that "a state may apply a clear and convincing evidence standard in proceedings where a guardian seeks to discontinue nutrition and hydration of a person diagnosed to be in a persistent vegetative state." This holding, which, the Chief Justice assures us, describes only the outer limit of what the Constitution permits, is supported by a lengthy description of civil cases in which the "clear and convincing evidence" standard is applied. See *Cruzan,* supra at 243.

While New York, California and Missouri are the only states where appellate courts have written opinions supporting the denial of requests to terminate treatment based on the "clear and convincing evidence" standard, most states have adopted a "clear and convincing evidence" standard in "right to die" cases. What that evidentiary standard means, and whether it is a substantive standard or a true evidentiary standard, varies from state to state—and, as the *O'Connor* case suggests, from judge to judge within a state. See, e.g., McConnell v. Beverly Enterprises–Connecticut, Inc., 209 Conn. 692, 553 A.2d 596 (1989); In re Conroy, 98 N.J. 321, 486 A.2d 1209 (1985); In re Jobes, 108 N.J. 394, 529 A.2d 434 (1987) (In New Jersey "evidence is 'clear and convincing' when it produce[s] in the mind of the trier of fact a firm belief or conviction as to the truth of the allegations sought to be established, evidence so clear, direct and weighty and convincing as to enable [the fact finder] to come to a clear conviction, without hesitancy, of the truth of the precise facts at issue.") While disputed evidence may still be "clear and convincing," it is also true that uncontroverted evidence may not rise to that level. In re Jobes, 529 A.2d at 441, citing In re Welfare of Colyer, 99 Wash.2d 114, 143–45, 660 P.2d 738, 754–55 (1983) (Dore, J., dissenting).

The choice of the appropriate burden of proof is not always between "clear and convincing evidence" and the normal civil "preponderance" standard. In *Eichner,* in which this issue was first raised before the New York Court of Appeals, the district attorney seeking the continuation of treatment for Brother Fox argued that "proof beyond a reasonable doubt" was the appropriate burden. The Court of Appeals explained why it chose the clear and convincing evidence standard:

The Supreme Court and the Appellate Division found that the evidence on [Brother Fox's decision] as well as proof of the patient's subsequent incompetency and chances of recovery was "clear and convincing." We agree that this is the appropriate burden of proof and that the evidence in the record satisfies this standard.

Although this is a civil case in which a preponderance of the evidence is generally deemed sufficient, the District Attorney urges that the highest burden of proof beyond a reasonable doubt should be required when granting the relief may result in the patient's death. But that burden, traditionally reserved for criminal cases where involuntary loss of liberty and possible stigmatization are at issue [ ] is inappropriate in cases where the purpose of granting the relief is to give effect to an individual's right by carrying out his stated intentions. However, we agree with the courts below that the highest standard applicable to civil cases should be required. There is more involved here than a typical dispute between private litigants over a sum of money. Where particularly important personal interests are at stake, clear and convincing evidence should be required. It is constitutionally required in cases of involuntary civil commitments and we have recognized the need for the higher standard in exceptional civil matters. Clear and convincing proof should also be required in cases where it is claimed that a person, now incompetent, left instructions to terminate life sustaining procedures when there is no hope of recovery. This standard serves to "impress the factfinder with the importance of the decision" and it " 'forbids relief whenever the evidence is loose, equivocal or contradictory' "[ ].

In re Eichner, 420 N.E.2d at 72.

3. Of course, the "clear and convincing evidence" standard is not a symmetrical one; it applies to one seeking to *terminate* life sustaining treatment, but not to one seeking to *maintain* it. Really, the application of the "clear and convincing evidence" standard to these cases serves only to recognize a policy that it is better to err on the side of maintaining life than on the side of terminating it. Many courts have repeated this principle of direction-of-error almost as a mantra, but does it make sense to establish the maintenance of life sustaining treatment as the default position in all cases? As the *Martin* court points out,

To err either way has incalculable ramifications. To end the life of a patient who still derives meaning and enjoyment from life or to condemn persons to lives from which they cry out for release is nothing short of barbaric.

Martin at 401. Despite this, the Court goes on to say that "[i]f we are to err, however, we must err in preserving life." Id. But should the default position—the presumed desire of the patient—be the *continuation* of treatment for every subgroup of cases? Should it be the default position where the patient is in excruciating and intractable pain, or where the patient is in persistent vegetative state? How many people do you know who wish to be kept alive under those circumstances? Why should the default position be one shared by so few?

4. The question of what burden of proof is appropriate is different from the issue of what kinds of evidence ought to be admissible to meet the burden. While most courts agree on the appropriate burden of proof in these cases, there is little agreement about the admissibility or weight to be given to different kinds of potential evidence.

Of course, what evidence is relevant will depend upon what facts are material to the resolution of the case under state substantive law. Assume that the wishes of the patient are material to the outcome of the case. How should the court consider previous statements of a currently incompetent patient? Should it make any difference that the statements were in writing? Made to relatives? In response to news events (like the *Cruzan* case)? In response to a family emergency or a death in the family? Would your prior statements about this issue be considered serious or off-hand by a court if tomorrow you were in a persistent vegetative state? Obviously, the characterization a court puts upon the nature of the evidence will determine the weight it is to be accorded. That, in turn, is likely to determine whether a petitioner can meet the generally accepted "clear and convincing evidence" standard.

The *Martin* majority provides one assessment of what kinds of evidence can meet the clear and convincing standard:

> Among the factors identified as important in defining clear and convincing evidence, [ ] the predominant factor is "a prior directive in which the patient addresses the situations in which the patient would prefer that medical intervention cease." Optimally, the prior directive would be expressed in a living will, patient advocate designation, or durable power of attorney. While a written directive would provide the most accurate evidence of the patient's decisions, and we strongly urge all persons to create such a directive, we do not preclude consideration of oral statements, made under the proper circumstances.

> The amount of weight accorded prior oral statements depends on the remoteness, consistency, specificity, and solemnity of the prior statement. The decisionmaker should examine the statement to determine whether it was a well thought out, deliberate pronouncement or a casual remark made in reaction to the plight of another. Statements made in response to seeing or hearing about another's prolonged death do not fulfill the clear and convincing standard.

> If such statements were routinely held to be clear and convincing proof of a general intent to decline all medical treatment once incompetency sets in, few nursing home patients would ever receive life-sustaining medical treatment in the future. The aged and infirm would be placed at grave risk if the law uniformly but unrealistically treated the expression of such sentiments as a calm and deliberative resolve to decline all life-sustaining medical assistance once the speaker is silenced by mental disability.

> While the degree of similarity between the physical conditions contemplated in the patient's prior statement and the patient's current physical situation also partakes of the fiction of substituted judgment, we do not exclude it as a factor to be considered in assessing the probative value of the prior statement. Only when the patient's prior statements clearly illustrate a serious, well thought out, consistent decision to refuse treatment under these exact circumstances, or circumstances highly similar to the current situation, should treatment be refused or withdrawn.

Martin, *supra* at 410–411.

Do you agree that "[s]tatements made in response to seeing or hearing about another's prolonged death do not fulfill the clear and convincing standard?" The dissenting judge in Martin argued that "[t]his bright line rule ignores that many persons only consider their own mortality seriously upon hearing about the end of other people's lives. Admittedly the emotional content of such statements must be carefully considered in weighing their probative value. But the majority's categorical exclusion of [this] relevant evidence dispenses with any semblance of accurate factfinding." Martin, at 399 (Levin, J., dissenting).

5. The *Wendland* case explicitly provides that the "clear and convincing evidence" standard applies only to cases where the proposed termination of treatment would result in the death of the patient; the court would not apply it in other judicial actions reviewing health care decision making. The Uniform Health Care Decision Act, on the other hand, applies the same standard to all health care decisions. Does it make sense to have one standard for decision that will result in death, and one standard for other cases? What are the advantages (and disadvantages) of a uniform standard, consistent across all kinds of health care decisions?

6. In *Wendland*, the California Supreme Court would have supported the decision of the conservator, and allowed for the termination of life sustaining medical care, if Robert had been unconscious. Of course, Robert Wendland *was* unconscious for some time before he emerged from the coma. Could Rose have decided to terminate life-sustaining medical treatment if she had acted quickly, before he regained consciousness? Might the *Wendland* case encourage families to act quickly to discontinue life-sustaining treatment to protect the patient from the harsh rule—virtually forbidding termination of treatment—that would apply if the patient should regain the tiniest amount of consciousness? The California Supreme Court say it means to exempt only the "permanently unconscious" from the *Wendland* rule, not any "unconscious" patient. Can we ever be sure that a patient is "permanently unconscious"? What tests should physicians apply to make this diagnosis?

7. Because it is almost impossible to predict exactly what kinds of medical care one might need and what kind of medical condition one will suffer, some courts and scholars have suggested that the most helpful kind of advance directive would be one that deals generally with the medical interests and values of the patient. One form of such an advance directive would have patients anticipate the nature and extent of intervention they would want in a host of clearly described alternative medical scenarios. See Linda L. Emmanuel and Ezekiel J. Emmanuel, The Medical Directive: A New Comprehensive Advance Care Document, 261, 3288 (1989). Another possibility would be to encourage every competent person to articulate values that are likely to be significant in subsequent decisionmaking.

One particularly good device for encouraging such discussion (and for recording the results) is the "Values History Form," which asks prospective patients about their general values, their medical values, their relationships with family members, friends, and health care providers, their wishes in particular cases and a host of other issues likely to become relevant if they become incompetent and health care decisions must be made on their behalf. While such a values history has no formal legal significance, and while some may be put off by such questions as "What makes you laugh?" and "What makes you cry?," there is no doubt that the existence of such a document would be of great value to a substitute decisionmaker, and to any court called upon to confirm that substitute's decision. See Joan McIver Gibson, Reflecting on Values, 51 Ohio St.L.J. 451 (1990).

In addition, over the past few years the "Five Wishes" document, a simple and easy to use advance directive that is (arguably) legally effective under the laws of 35 different states, has become popular. The Five Wishes document "lets your family and doctors know:

1. Which person you want to make health care decisions for you when you can't make them,

2. The kind of medical treatment you want or don't want,

3. How comfortable you want to be,

4.   How you want people to treat you,

5.   What you want your loved ones to know."

It was developed by Aging with Dignity, and the form is available at www.agingwithdignity,org (visited January 21, 2004).

8.   For a discussion of the judicial process that ought to be available to address health care decision making issues, see the Notes following the *Schiavo* case, below.

c.   *Disputes Among Family Members Acting as Decision Makers*

In 2004 the public began discussing many of the issues raised in this section as a result of the uproar surrounding the case of Terri Schiavo. Although that case has been heard by several state and federal courts (and the Florida legislature), the first substantive appeal was decided, and the facts were carefully laid out in 2001:

GUARDIANSHIP OF SCHIAVO

Court of Appeal of Florida, Second District, 2001.
780 So.2d 176.

weight of evidence
given to outside Expert
Religing

ALTENBERND, Judge.

Robert and Mary Schindler, the parents of Theresa Marie Schiavo, appeal the trial court's order authorizing the discontinuance of artificial life support to their adult daughter. Michael Schiavo, Theresa's husband and guardian, petitioned the trial court in May 1998 for entry of this order. We have carefully reviewed the record. The trial court made a difficult decision after considering all of the evidence and the applicable law. We conclude that the trial court's decision is supported by competent, substantial evidence and that it correctly applies the law. Accordingly, we affirm the decision.

Theresa Marie Schindler was born on December 3, 1963, and lived with or near her parents in Pennsylvania until she married Michael Schiavo on November 10, 1984. Michael and Theresa moved to Florida in 1986. They were happily married and both were employed. They had no children.

On February 25, 1990, their lives changed. Theresa, age 27, suffered a cardiac arrest as a result of a potassium imbalance. Michael called 911, and Theresa was rushed to the hospital. She never regained consciousness.

Since 1990, Theresa has lived in nursing homes with constant care. She is fed and hydrated by tubes. The staff changes her diapers regularly. She has had numerous health problems, but none have been life threatening.

The evidence is overwhelming that Theresa is in a permanent or persistent vegetative state. It is important to understand that a persistent vegetative state is not simply a coma. She is not asleep. She has cycles of apparent wakefulness and apparent sleep without any cognition or awareness. As she breathes, she often makes moaning sounds. Theresa has severe contractures of her hands, elbows, knees, and feet.

Over the span of this last decade, Theresa's brain has deteriorated because of the lack of oxygen it suffered at the time of the heart attack. By mid–1996, the CAT scans of her brain showed a severely abnormal structure. At this point, much of her cerebral cortex is simply gone and has been replaced by cerebral spinal fluid. Medicine cannot cure this condition. Unless an act of God, a true miracle, were to recreate her brain, Theresa will always remain in an unconscious, reflexive state, totally dependent upon others to feed her and care for her most private needs. She could remain in this state for many years.

Theresa has been blessed with loving parents and a loving husband. Many patients in this condition would have been abandoned by friends and family within the first year. Michael has continued to care for her and to visit her all these years. He has never divorced her. He has become a professional respiratory therapist and works in a nearby hospital. As a guardian, he has always attempted to provide optimum treatment for his wife. He has been a diligent watch guard of Theresa's care, never hesitating to annoy the nursing staff in order to assure that she receives the proper treatment.

Theresa's parents have continued to love her and visit her often. No one questions the sincerity of their prayers for the divine miracle that now is Theresa's only hope to regain any level of normal existence. No one questions that they have filed this appeal out of love for their daughter.

This lawsuit is affected by an earlier lawsuit. In the early 1990's, Michael Schiavo, as Theresa's guardian, filed a medical malpractice lawsuit. That case resulted in a sizable award of money for Theresa. This fund remains sufficient to care for Theresa for many years. If she were to die today, her husband would inherit the money under the laws of intestacy. If Michael eventually divorced Theresa in order to have a more normal family life, the fund remaining at the end of Theresa's life would presumably go to her parents.

Since the resolution of the malpractice lawsuit, both Michael and the Schindlers have become suspicious that the other party is assessing Theresa's wishes based upon their own monetary self-interest. The trial court discounted this concern, and we see no evidence in this record that either Michael or the Schindlers seek monetary gain from their actions. Michael and the Schindlers simply cannot agree on what decision Theresa would make today if she were able to assess her own condition and make her own decision.

There has been discussion among the parties that the money remaining when Theresa dies should be given to a suitable charity as a lasting memorial. If anything is undeniable in this case, it is that Theresa would never wish for this money to drive a wedge between the people she loves. We have no jurisdiction over the disposition of this money, but hopefully these parties will consider Theresa's desires and her memory when a decision about the money is ultimately required.

This is a case to authorize the termination of life-prolonging procedures * * *.

First, the Schindlers maintain that the trial court was required to appoint a guardian ad litem for this proceeding because Michael stands to inherit under the laws of intestacy. When a living will or other advance directive does not exist, it stands to reason that the surrogate decision-maker will be a person who is close to the patient and thereby likely to inherit from the patient. [ ] Thus, the fact that a surrogate decision-maker may ultimately inherit from the patient should not automatically compel the appointment of a guardian. On the other hand, there may be occasions when an inheritance could be a reason to question a surrogate's ability to make an objective decision.

In this case, however, Michael Schiavo has not been allowed to make a decision to disconnect life-support. The Schindlers have not been allowed to make a decision to maintain life-support. Each party in this case, absent their disagreement, might have been a suitable surrogate decision-maker for Theresa. Because Michael Schiavo and the Schindlers could not agree on the proper decision and the inheritance issue created the appearance of conflict, Michael Schiavo, as the guardian of Theresa, invoked the trial court's jurisdiction to allow the trial court to serve as the surrogate decision-maker.

[As this court said some years ago,]

We emphasize, * * * that courts are always open to adjudicate legitimate questions pertaining to the written or oral instructions. First, the surrogate or proxy may choose to present the question to the court for resolution. Second, interested parties may challenge the decision of the proxy or surrogate. [ ]

In this case, Michael Schiavo used the first approach. Under these circumstances, the two parties, as adversaries, present their evidence to the trial court. The trial court determines whether the evidence is sufficient to allow it to make the decision for the ward to discontinue life support. In this context, the trial court essentially serves as the ward's guardian. Although we do not rule out the occasional need for a guardian in this type of proceeding, a guardian ad litem would tend to duplicate the function of the judge, would add little of value to this process, and might cause the process to be influenced by hearsay or matters outside the record. Accordingly, we affirm the trial court's discretionary decision in this case to proceed without a guardian ad litem.

Second, the Schindlers argue that the trial court should not have heard evidence from Beverly Tyler, the executive director of Georgia Health Decisions. Although it is doubtful that this issue is preserved for appeal, we have reviewed the issue as if it were. Ms. Tyler has studied American values, opinions, and attitudes about the decision to discontinue life-support systems. As a result, she has some special expertise concerning the words and expressions that Americans often use in discussing these difficult issues. She also has knowledge about trends within American attitudes on this subject.

We have considerable doubt that Ms. Tyler's testimony provided much in the way of relevant evidence. She testified about some social science surveys. Apparently most people, even those who favor initial life-supporting medical treatment, indicate that they would not wish this treatment to continue indefinitely once their medical condition presented no reasonable basis for a cure. There is some risk that a trial judge could rely upon this type of survey evidence to make a "best interests" decision for the ward. In this case, however, we are convinced that the trial judge did not give undue weight to this evidence and that the court made a proper surrogate decision rather than a best interests decision.

Finally, the Schindlers argue that the testimony, which was conflicting, was insufficient to support the trial court's decision by clear and convincing evidence. We have reviewed that testimony and conclude that the trial court had sufficient evidence to make this decision. The clear and convincing standard of proof, while very high, permits a decision in the face of inconsistent or conflicting evidence. [ ]

[As we have] stated:

> In making this difficult decision, a surrogate decisionmaker should err on the side of life.... In cases of doubt, we must assume that a patient would choose to defend life in exercising his or her right of privacy. [ ]

We reconfirm today that a court's default position must favor life.

The testimony in this case establishes that Theresa was very young and very healthy when this tragedy struck. Like many young people without children, she had not prepared a will, much less a living will. She had been raised in the Catholic faith, but did not regularly attend mass or have a religious advisor who could assist the court in weighing her religious attitudes about life-support methods. Her statements to her friends and family about the dying process were few and they were oral. Nevertheless, those statements, along with other evidence about Theresa, gave the trial court a sufficient basis to make this decision for her.

In the final analysis, the difficult question that faced the trial court was whether Theresa Marie Schindler Schiavo, not after a few weeks in a coma, but after ten years in a persistent vegetative state that has robbed her of most of her cerebrum and all but the most instinctive of neurological functions, with no hope of a medical cure but with sufficient money and strength of body to live indefinitely, would choose to continue the constant nursing care and the supporting tubes in hopes that a miracle would somehow recreate her missing brain tissue, or whether she would wish to permit a natural death process to take its course and for her family members and loved ones to be free to continue their lives. After due consideration, we conclude that the trial judge had clear and convincing evidence to answer this question as he did.

Affirmed.

Note on the Legal and Political History of the Schiavo Case

The story of the Schiavo case runs through thirteen years and all three branches of government in Florida. As Chief Judge Altenbernd points out, it is a sad story of uncertainty, mistrust, hope, understanding (and misunderstanding) and politics. It is difficult to disentangle Schiavo the person (a shy animal lover and a quiet, kind young woman) from Schiavo the cause (on both sides of the issue).

The case returned to the Court of Appeals twice in 2001, and in the second of those the court determined that the trial court was required to have an evidentiary hearing on the Schindlers' motion seeking relief from the original judgment on the grounds that there were new treatments available for Terri. The remand included an instruction that each party be allowed to present two physician expert witnesses to support their position, and that the trial court appoint a fifth. These physicians were to be given access to all of Terri's medical records, including "high-quality brain scans." On remand, all of the experts agreed that there was "extensive permanent damage to her brain," and the only debate was "whether she has a small amount of living tissue in her cerebral cortex, or whether she has no living tissue in her cerebral cortex." Guardianship of Schiavo (Schiavo IV), 851 So.2d 182 (Fla.App.2003). The court's appointed expert agreed with Michael's experts, and the trial court denied the Schindler's motion to reopen. The Court of Appeals affirmed in Schiavo IV, in an opinion again written by Judge Altenbernd. The difficulty of the decision—and the propriety of having the substantive decision made by the judge, applying the principle of substituted judgment—were again clearly articulated:

> The judges on this panel are called upon to make a collective, objective decision concerning a question of law. Each of us, however, has our own family, our own loved ones, our own children. From our review of the videotapes of Mrs. Schiavo, despite the irrefutable evidence that her cerebral cortex has sustained the most severe of irreparable injuries, we understand why a parent who had raised and nurtured a child from conception would hold out hope that some level of cognitive function remained. If Mrs. Schiavo were our own daughter, we could not but hold to such a faith.

> But in the end, this case is not about the aspirations that loving parents have for their children. It is about Theresa Schiavo's right to make her own decision, independent of her parents and independent of her husband. In circumstances such as these, when families cannot agree, the law has opened the doors of the circuit courts to permit trial judges to serve as surrogates or proxies to make decisions about life-prolonging procedures. It is the trial judge's duty not to make the decision that the judge would make for himself or herself or for a loved one. Instead, the trial judge must make a decision that the clear and convincing evidence shows the ward would have made for herself. It is a thankless task, and one to be undertaken with care, objectivity, and a cautious legal standard designed to promote the value of life. But it is also a necessary function if all people are to be entitled to a personalized decision about life-prolonging procedures independent of the subjective and conflicting assessments of their friends and relatives. It may be unfortunate that when families cannot agree, the best forum we can offer for this private, personal decision is a public courtroom and the best decision-maker we can provide is a judge with no prior knowledge of the ward, but the law currently provides no better solution that adequately protects the interests of promoting the value of life. We have previously affirmed the guardianship court's decision in this regard, and we now affirm the denial of a motion for relief from that judgment.

851 So.2d at 187. The court remanded to the trial court "solely for the purpose of entering a new order scheduling the removal of the nutrition and hydration tube." On remand, the trial court set October 15, 2003, for the removal of the tube. By this time, several Right to Life and disability advocacy groups had enlisted Governor Jeb Bush to help them find some way to save Terri's life, and Right to Die groups were organizing to oppose them. On October 15 the feeding tube was removed, and Terri was expected to die within the next two weeks.

An advocacy group also sought relief in the federal court, where it filed a petition for a temporary restraining order requiring the continuation of Terri's feeding until it could do a full investigation of alleged abuse and neglect against Terri. The federal court refused to be drawn into the controversy, and, after denying the order, the judge declared:

> This case offers a vivid opportunity for the public, whose collective will ultimately decides such matters, to contemplate the confounding issues associated with degenerative illness and catastrophic disability and thereafter, by a means consistent with government in a republic, to direct their representatives to legislate in accord with their concerted desires, if in a conflict with the present state of the law.

Advocacy Center for Persons With Disabilities v. Schiavo, 8:03–CV–2167–T–23EAJ, 2003 WL 23305833 (M.D.Fla. 2003). Wasting no time, those advocating for continued feeding took the case to the floor of the state legislature on the very afternoon that the federal court decision was rendered, and the legislature was urged by the Governor to overturn the decision of the Florida Court of Appeals. Almost immediately (but with more than the normal wailing and gnashing of teeth) the Florida legislature passed, and the Governor signed, what has become known as "Terri's Law." While the accuracy of titles of legislative acts named for individuals is often open to question, this was truly Terri's law; her case is the only one to which it can ever apply. The statute provides that:

> The Governor shall have the authority to issue a one-time stay to prevent the withholding of nutrition and hydration from a patient if, as of October 15, 2003:
>
> (a) That patient has no written advance directive;
>
> (b) The court has found that the patient is in persistent vegetative state;
>
> (c) That patient has had nutrition and hydration withheld; and
>
> (d) A member of that patient's family has challenged the withholding of nutrition and hydration.

2003 Fl. Laws ch. 418. The statute provided that the Governor's authority would expire 15 days after the passage of the Act, and that upon the granting of such a stay the court would appoint a guardian ad litem for the patient "to make a recommendation to the Governor and the court."

The Governor issued the "one-time stay" immediately, and the court appointed Professor Jay Wolfson to be the guardian ad litem. Almost as quickly, Michael began challenging the constitutionality of Terri's law on the grounds that it violated the privacy provisions of the Florida constitution and the principles of separation of powers (because it amounted to a legislative reversal of a particular judicial decision). Professor Wolfson submitted his report in December of 2003, and he supported Michael's position that the tube be removed. In a separate action, the trial court also determined that Terri's Law was presumptively unconstitutional. Governor Bush's attempt to disqualify the judge because of that ruling resulted in a Court of Appeals opinion that supported the trial judge. Bush v. Schiavo, 861 So.2d 506 (Fla. App. 2003).

As this book goes to press, Terri Schiavo is still being kept alive on a feeding tube and a court is considering the Governor's request that he be allowed to do a further investigation as a part of the case challenging the constitutionality of Terri's law. The Governor wants to ask Michael why he did not inform the court of Terri's wish to avoid extraordinary care when it awarded her $700,000 for her future medical care in her original malpractice case. Governor Bush also expressed concern that Michael, who is now living with a woman with whom he has had two children, might not have Terri's best interest in mind. See Bush v. Schiavo, 866 So.2d 136 (Fla.App.2004). The Governor believes that he is entitled to a jury trial on the issue of what choice Terri would make. The Schindlers' mistrust of Michael is demonstrated by a pleading they filed in the federal court action, in which they called him an "egomaniacal visionary who views Terri's hoped-for death as a fulfillment of his personal messianic mission." David Sommer, Court Urged to Move Schiavo Case, Tampa Tribune, September 10, 2003, at 4. This is not a case likely to be resolved by mediation.

Note: Wendland, Schiavo and the Role of the Court in Making Health Care Decisions for Those Without Capacity

1.   How should this case have been handled? What could Michael have done to avoid this nightmare? What could the Schindlers have done? Is there anything the courts (or the legislature) could have done?

2.   Whether the courts have any role at all in these matters has been the subject of some debate. On the one hand, there is a fear that the absence of judicial oversight will lead to arbitrary decisions and, thus, arbitrary deaths. On the other hand, any attempt to bring all of these cases to the courts would yield an intolerable caseload and delay the deaths of many patients who desperately seek that relief. In addition, as the *Wendland* case suggested, there is little reason to believe that courts have any wisdom that will make them better than a patient's family at making these decisions. The Massachusetts Supreme Judicial Court changed its view of the necessity of judicial confirmation of a guardian's decision that a patient should forgo life-sustaining treatment. See In re Spring, 380 Mass. 629, 405 N.E.2d 115 (1980) (no review required in most circumstances; reversing prior position). Should judicial review of all decisions to terminate life-sustaining treatment be required? Should such judicial review be required in some cases? In cases in which there is no written advance directive? In which there is no agreement among family members? In which the patients disagree with the health care providers? In which the health care providers disagree among themselves? In which the decisionmaker is self interested? In which there is an ambiguity in the previous statements of the patient? Is there any way to adequately categorize those cases in which judicial review ought to be required? If judicial review is not required, should some other form of review—by an ethics committee, for example—be required in its stead? Is the choice of the Uniform Health Care Decisions Act, which would rarely countenance judicial involvement in any health care decision, the best choice? Why?

3.   When resort to a court is required, what procedure ought to be employed by the court? Should the court's involvement be limited to the appointment of a decisionmaker, should the court make the decision itself, or should the court review every decision (or some decisions) made by an appointed decisionmaker? Should the action be a special statutory action, an injunction action, a guardianship, or does the form of the action really make much difference? Should the court always appoint a guardian *ad litem* for the patient? What would the role of such a guardian be in the *Schiavo* case? If so, is the role of the guardian ad litem to represent what that person believes the patient would want, or what that person believes is in the best interest of the patient? Alternatively, should the guardian ad litem always oppose the petitioner (who is usually seeking the termination of the treatment)? Every state has a nursing home ombudsman. Should the ombudsman be notified whenever discontinuation of treatment of a nursing home patient is requested? Should the ombudsman participate in every such case? See In re Conroy, 486 A.2d at 1237–1242.

In In re Guardianship of Hamlin, 102 Wash.2d 810, 689 P.2d 1372 (1984), the Washington Supreme Court announced two entirely separate processes—one to be followed where there is "total agreement among the patient's family, treating physicians and prognosis committee as to the course of medical treatment," and one to be followed where there is "an incompetent with no known family, who has never made his wishes known." No judicial process and no formal guardianship is required in the first case where "the incompetent patient is in * * * a persistent vegetative state with no reasonable chance of recovery and * * * the patient's life is being maintained by life support systems." In the second situation a guardian must be appointed by the court, but that guardian need not obtain judicial confirmation of any particular decision "if the treating physicians and prognosis committee are unanimous that life-sustaining efforts should be withheld or withdrawn and the guardian concurs." Of course, most cases fall between the two extremes discussed in *Hamlin*.

4. Should Robert Wendland's mother and sister have had standing to challenge the decision of his conservator? Should the Schindlers have had standing to challenge the decision made by their son in law? Who else should have standing to commence a judicial action seeking to review a decision to terminate life-sustaining medical treatment? All relatives? Health care providers? Health care institutions? Patient advocacy groups? Right-to-Life or Right-to-Die or disability advocacy groups? Who should be able to join such litigation as a party? Is the Uniform Health Care Decisions Act approach to this issue—that there will be no judicial hearing unless a relative or health care provider is willing to file an action—the best way of dealing with this? See Protection and Advocacy System, Inc. v. Presbyterian Healthcare Services, 128 N.M. 73, 989 P.2d 890 (App.1999) (no standing in advocacy group to challenge unanimous decision of family members and health care providers).

5. If there is to be a judicial process, should it be an adversary process? While the Chief Justice appears to think that the adversary process is helpful in these cases, Cruzan, 497 U.S. 261 n. 9, 110 S.Ct. 2841, 2853 n. 9, 111 L.Ed.2d 224, that part of the opinion gave Justice Stevens pause:

> The Court recognizes that "the state has been involved as an adversary from the beginning" in this case only because Nancy Cruzan "was a patient at a state hospital when this litigation commenced." * * * It seems to me, however, that the Court draws precisely the wrong conclusion from this insight. The Court apparently believes that the absence of the state from the litigation would have created a problem, because agreement among the family and the independent guardian *ad litem* as to Nancy Cruzan's best interests might have prevented her treatment from becoming the focus of a "truly adversarial" proceeding. [ ] It may reasonably be debated whether some judicial process should be required before life-sustaining treatment is discontinued; this issue has divided the state courts. Compare *In re Estate of Longeway,* (requiring judicial approval of guardian's decision) with *In re Hamlin* (discussing circumstances in which judicial approval is unnecessary). * * * I tend, however, to agree * * * that the intervention of the state in these proceedings as an *adversary* is not so much a cure as it is part of the disease.

Cruzan, 497 U.S. 261, 341, n. 13, 110 S.Ct. 2841, 2884, n. 13, 111 L.Ed.2d 224 (Stevens, J., dissenting). A decade earlier the Florida Supreme Court had expressed the same reservations: "Because the issue with its ramifications is fraught with complexity and encompasses the interests of the law, both civil and criminal, medical ethics and social morality, it is not one which is well suited for a solution in an adversary judicial proceeding." Satz v. Perlmutter, 379 So.2d 359, 360 (Fla.1980); Protection and Advocacy System, Inc. v. Presbyterian Healthcare Services, 128 N.M. 73, 989 P.2d 890 (App. 1999). Are the "advantages" of an adversary proceeding truly advantageous in these agonizing cases?

6. "Right to die" cases seeking damages to vindicate the federal privacy rights of patients against state entities (like state hospitals) may be based on 42 U.S.C.A. § 1983. When one successfully raises a federal civil rights claim under

that statute, the prevailing party is entitled to attorney's fees under 42 U.S.C.A. § 1988. While most such attempts to collect attorneys fees have failed, some have been successful. In Gray v. Romeo, 697 F.Supp. 580 (D.R.I.1988), the successful attorney was awarded $38,495.95. Gray v. Romeo, Order of March 8, 1989. In addition, the petitioner's legal counsel in the *Bouvia* case was awarded attorneys' fees under the state's statutory "private attorney general" provision because the case vindicated important public rights. Bouvia v. County of L.A., 195 Cal.App.3d 1075, 241 Cal.Rptr. 239 (1987). But see Blouin v. Spitzer, 356 F.3d 348 (2d Cir. 2004)(state attorney general was immune from damages for advice that removal of life sustaining medical treatment would be illegal under state law). See also M. Rose Gasner, Financial Penalties for Failing to Honor Patient Wishes to Refuse Treatment, 11 St. Louis U.Pub.L.Rev. 499 (1992). The Uniform Health Care Decisions Act explicitly provides for attorneys fees in cases where there has been an "intentional" violation of the Act. Is this an appropriate standard?

Problem: Not Quite Persistent Vegetative State

When unhelmeted 57 year old Tad Gonzales ran his motorcycle into a bridge support post on an interstate highway, he was revived at the scene and rushed to Big Central Hospital. There he underwent several hours of emergency surgery designed to preserve his life and repair the very substantial head injuries he sustained. A few days after the surgery he began to regain consciousness, and a week later he was able to be removed from the ventilator which was supporting his breathing, although he still needs ventilator assistance from time to time. During his first two weeks in the hospital, Tad showed little improvement. He was not in a coma, but he was only occasionally responsive, and he demonstrated no awareness of Ralph Ressner, his partner of twenty-two years, or his two brothers and his parents, even though Tad had always shared a close relationship with all of them.

After two weeks, Big City Hospital transferred Tad to Commercial Affiliated Nursing Home, where he began receiving physical and occupational therapy. After a year of care there, he has shown little improvement. He still does not seem to recognize Ralph, who visits daily, or anyone else. He is able to sit up and his eyes sometimes seem to be following images on a screen. He grunts when he is hungry or uncomfortable. He cannot eat or drink, and he is fed through a feeding tube in his abdomen. He cannot control his bowels or bladder. He has regularly suffered from urinary tract infections and asthma during his nursing home stay, although his need for the ventilator is becoming rarer. On a few, increasingly rare, occasions, his heart stopped beating, but he was resuscitated immediately. Doctors believe that there is little chance of substantial improvement in his condition (although, in the words of one doctor, "Who knows? Anything can happen"). Tad's doctors estimate that his life expectancy could be another twenty years or more.

Tad's doctor and Ralph have developed a good working relationship, and the doctor has called upon Ralph to approve any change in Tad's treatment regimen; Tad never signed any kind of advance directive. Ralph has now informed the doctor that he believes that Tad would want the use of the feeding tube (and the occasional use of the ventilator) discontinued, and that he would want to be DNR. When the doctor challenged him on this, Ralph respectfully ordered the doctor to terminate feeding, and to note that Tad was not to be mechanically ventilated or resuscitated. Ralph explained that he had spoken with Tad often about "this kind of thing," and that Tad had said that the indignity of being fed, or wearing diapers, or being bed-bound, was not worth the value of life to him. In particular, Ralph remembers Tad describing one of their friends, another motorcyclist who became a quadriplegic and suffered some intellectual impairment after an accident, as "better off dead." Tad and Ralph promised each other that neither would ever let that happen to the other. Tad's parents and one of his brothers agree that there is no doubt that Tad would want all treatment terminated under these circumstances. Tad's other brother disagrees. As he has articulated it, "How can we know what he would want? He could never have imagined himself in this situation, and we shouldn't read anything in to what he said about other people. Maybe he thought those other people could feel more pain than he can."

Tad's doctor has approached you, the hospital counsel, to ask you what she should do. Should she discontinue feeding? The use of the ventilator? Should the hospital pursue an action in court? What position should the hospital take if Ralph, or Tad's dissenting brother, pursue an action in court? How should that action be resolved?

3.   Making Health Care Decisions for Patients Who Have Never Been Competent

Where the patient has never been competent—where the patient has been severely retarded from birth, for example—the courts still make an attempt to determine what the patient's choice would be. Of course, it is exceptionally difficult to imagine what an incompetent person, who has never been competent, would want to do if that person were suddenly competent. Compare the next two cases, one of which confirms the principle of substituted judgment and one of which abandons that approach to apply the principle of beneficence and seeks to do what is in the best interest of such a patient. *Superintendent of Belchertown State School v. Saikewicz,* involves a 67–year–old profoundly retarded adult suffering from leukemia without any family willing to aid in decisionmaking. The court addresses the question of whether the chemotherapy that would be likely to be provided to others in his condition should be withheld. *Matter of Storar,* the companion case to *Matter of Eichner,* concerns a profoundly retarded 52–year–old cancer patient and the propriety of blood transfusions.

SUPERINTENDENT OF BELCHERTOWN STATE SCHOOL v. SAIKEWICZ

Supreme Judicial Court of Massachusetts, 1977.
373 Mass. 728, 370 N.E.2d 417.

LIACOS, JUSTICE.

* * *

The question what legal standards govern the decision whether to administer potentially life-prolonging treatment to an incompetent person encompasses two distinct and important subissues. First, does a choice exist? That is, is it the unvarying responsibility of the State to order medical treatment in all circumstances involving the care of an incompetent person? Second, if a choice does exist under certain conditions, what considerations enter into the decision-making process?

We think that principles of equality and respect for all individuals require the conclusion that a choice exists * * *. We recognize a general right in all persons to refuse medical treatment in appropriate circumstances. The recognition of that right must extend to the case of an incompetent, as well as a competent, patient because the value of human dignity extends to both.

This is not to deny that the State has a traditional power and responsibility, under the doctrine of *parens patriae,* to care for and protect the *"best interests"* of the incompetent person.

The "best interests" of an incompetent person are not necessarily served by imposing on such persons results not mandated as to competent persons similarly situated. It does not advance the interest of the State or the ward to treat the ward as a person of lesser status or dignity than others. To protect the incompetent person within its power, the State must recognize the dignity and worth of such a person and afford to that person the same panoply of rights and choices it recognizes in competent persons. If a competent person faced with death may choose to decline treatment which not only will not cure the person but which substantially may increase suffering in exchange for a possible yet brief prolongation of life, then it cannot be said that it is always in the "best interests" of the ward to require submission to such treatment. Nor do statistical factors indicating that a majority of competent persons similarly situated choose treatment resolve the issue. The significant decisions of life are more complex than statistical determinations. Individual choice is determined not by the vote of the majority but by the complexities of the singular situation viewed from the unique perspective of the person called on to make the decision. To presume that the incompetent person must always be subjected to what many rational and intelligent persons may decline is to downgrade the status of the incompetent person by placing a lesser value on his intrinsic human worth and vitality.

* * * This leads us to the question of how the right of an incompetent person to decline treatment might best be exercised so as to give the fullest possible expression to the character and circumstances of that individual.

* * *

To put the above discussion in proper perspective, we realize that an inquiry into what a majority of people would do in circumstances that truly were similar assumes an objective viewpoint not far removed from a "reasonable person" inquiry. While we recognize the value of this kind of indirect evidence, we should make it plain that the primary test is subjective in nature—that is, the goal is to determine with as much accuracy as possible the wants and needs of the individual involved. This may or may not conform to what is thought wise or prudent by most people. The problems of arriving at an accurate substituted judgment in matters of life and death vary greatly in degree, if not in kind, in different circumstances. * * * Joseph Saikewicz was profoundly retarded and noncommunicative his entire life, which was spent largely in the highly restrictive atmosphere of an institution. While it may thus be necessary to rely to a greater degree on objective criteria, such as the supposed inability of profoundly retarded persons to conceptualize or fear death, the effort to bring the substituted judgment into step with the values and desires of the affected individual must not, and need not, be abandoned.

The "substituted judgment" standard which we have described commends itself simply because of its straightforward respect for the integrity and autonomy of the individual. * * *

* * * [W]e now reiterate the substituted judgment doctrine as we apply it in the instant case. We believe that both the guardian *ad litem* in his recommendation and the judge in his decision should have attempted (as they did) to ascertain the incompetent person's actual interests and preferences. In short, the decision in cases such as this should be that which would be made by the incompetent person, if that person were competent, but taking into account the present and future incompetency of the individual as one of the factors which would necessarily enter into the decision-making process of the competent person. Having recognized the right of a competent person to make for himself the same decision as the court made in this case, the question is, do the facts on the record support the proposition that Saikewicz himself would have [declined treatment]. We believe they do.

* * *

IN RE STORAR

New York Court of Appeals, 1981.
52 N.Y.2d 363, 438 N.Y.S.2d 266, 420 N.E.2d 64.

WACHTLER, JUDGE.

* * *

John Storar was profoundly retarded with a mental age of about 18 months. At the time of this proceeding he was 52 years old and a resident of the Newark Development Center, a State facility, which had been his home since the age of 5. His closest relative was his mother * * *.

In 1979 physicians at the center noticed blood in his urine and asked his mother for permission to conduct diagnostic tests. She * * * gave her consent. The tests, completed in July, 1979, revealed that he had cancer of the bladder. It was recommended that he receive radiation therapy at a hospital in Rochester. When the hospital refused to administer the treatment without the consent of a legal guardian, Mrs. Storar applied to the court and was appointed guardian of her son's person and property in August, 1979. With her consent he received radiation therapy for six weeks after which the disease was found to be in remission.

However in March, 1980, blood was again observed in his urine. The lesions in his bladder were cauterized in an unsuccessful effort to stop the bleeding. At that point his physician diagnosed the cancer as terminal, concluding that after using all medical and surgical means then available, the patient would nevertheless die from the disease.

In May the physicians at the center asked his mother for permission to administer blood transfusions. She initially refused but the following day withdrew her objection. For several weeks John Storar received blood transfusions when needed. However, on June 19 his mother requested that the transfusions be discontinued.

The director of the center then brought this proceeding, pursuant to [ ] the Mental Hygiene Law, seeking authorization to continue the transfusions, claiming that without them "death would occur within weeks." Mrs. Storar cross-petitioned for an order prohibiting the transfusions, and named the District Attorney as a party. The court appointed a guardian ad litem and signed an order temporarily permitting the transfusions to continue, pending the determination of the proceeding.

At the hearing in September the court heard testimony from various witnesses including Mrs. Storar, several employees at the center, and seven medical experts. All the experts concurred that John Storar had irreversible cancer of the bladder, * * * with a very limited life span, generally estimated to be between 3 and 6 months. They also agreed that he had an infant's mentality and was unable to comprehend his predicament or to make a reasoned choice of treatment. In addition, there was no dispute over the fact that he was continuously losing blood.

* * *

It was conceded that John Storar found the transfusions disagreeable. He was also distressed by the blood and blood clots in his urine which apparently increased immediately after a transfusion. He could not comprehend the purpose of the transfusions and on one or two occasions had displayed some initial resistance. To eliminate his apprehension he was given a sedative approximately one hour before a transfusion. He also received regular doses of narcotics to alleviate the pain associated with the disease.

On the other hand several experts testified that there was support in the medical community for the view that, at this stage, transfusions may only prolong suffering and that treatment could properly be limited to administering pain killers. Mrs. Storar testified that she wanted the transfusions discontinued because she only wanted her son to be comfortable. She admitted that no one had ever explained to her what might happen to him if the transfusions were stopped. She also stated that she was not "sure" whether he might die sooner if the blood was not replaced and was unable to determine whether he wanted to live. However, in view of the fact that he obviously disliked the transfusions and tried to avoid them, she believed that he would want them discontinued.

* * *

John Storar was never competent at any time in his life. * * * Thus it is unrealistic to attempt to determine whether he would want to continue potentially life prolonging treatment if he were competent. * * * Mentally, John Storar was an infant and that is the only realistic way to assess his rights in this litigation. Thus this case bears only superficial similarities to *Eichner* and the determination must proceed from different principles.

A parent or guardian has a right to consent to medical treatment on behalf of an infant. [ ] The parent, however, may not deprive a child of life saving treatment, however well intentioned. * * *

In the *Storar* case there is the additional complication of two threats to his life. There was cancer of the bladder which was incurable and would in all probability claim his life. There was also the related loss of blood which posed the risk of an earlier death, but which, at least at the time of the hearing, could be replaced by transfusions. Thus, as one of the experts noted, the transfusions were analogous to food—they would not cure the cancer, but they could eliminate the risk of death from another treatable cause. Of course, John Storar did not like them, as might be expected of one with an infant's mentality. But the evidence convincingly shows that the transfusions did not involve excessive pain and that without them his mental and physical abilities would not be maintained at the usual level. With the transfusions on the other hand, he was essentially the same as he was before except of course he had a fatal illness which would ultimately claim his life. Thus, on the record, we have concluded that the application for permission to continue the transfusions should have been granted. Although we understand and respect his mother's despair, as we respect the beliefs of those who oppose transfusions on religious grounds, a court should not in the circumstances of this case allow an incompetent patient to bleed to death because someone, even someone as close as a parent or sibling, feels that this is best for one with an incurable disease.

* * *

Notes and Questions

1. How would the Supreme Judicial Court of Massachusetts have decided *Storar?* How would the New York Court of Appeals have decided *Saikewicz?* Might there be cases for which the principles of *Storar* and the principles of *Saikewicz* would lead to different results? Which principle is preferable? Why?

2. The approach of the Massachusetts court in Saikewicz has been criticized on the grounds that it makes no sense to apply the doctrine of substituted judgment to the case of a patient who has never been competent. Do you agree with this criticism? Despite it, Massachusetts has retained the *Saikewicz* rule. See Guardianship of Doe, 411 Mass. 512, 583 N.E.2d 1263 (1992) and In re R.H., 35 Mass.App.Ct. 478, 622 N.E.2d 1071 (1993). Not all justices on the Massachusetts court agree with the approach of the court, however. One justice strongly disagrees for reasons he expressed briefly in dissent from an opinion in which the court applied the doctrine of substituted judgment to allow for the removal of life sustaining treatment for an infant who had been in an irreversible comma since an auto accident in her first year of life:

> [T]he court again has approved application of the doctrine of substituted judgment where there is not a soupcon of evidence to support it. The trial judge did not have a smidgen of evidence on which to conclude that if this child who is now about five and one half years old were competent to decide, she would elect certain death to a life with no cognitive ability. The route by which the court arrived at its conclusion is a cruel charade which is being perpetuated whenever we are faced with a life and death decision of an incompetent person.

Care and Protection of Beth, 412 Mass. 188, 587 N.E.2d 1377, 1383 (1992) (Nolan, J., dissenting.)

3. How would the Uniform Health Care Decisions Act address the issue of a patient who had never been competent to make health care decisions? Many people believe that our society undervalues the lives of the disabled. Does this suggest that the courts should review decisions to remove life sustaining medical treatment from patients in this class, even if the courts need not be involved in similar cases with previously-competent patients? See Protection and Advocacy System, Inc. v. Presbyterian Healthcare Services, 128 N.M. 73, 989 P.2d 890 (App.1999).

V. THE "RIGHT TO DIE"—CHILDREN AND NEWBORNS

A. CHILDREN

Problem: Choosing to Forgo Cancer Treatment

Bob Anderson was a healthy, socially well adjusted intelligent fourteen-year-old when he discovered that he had testicular cancer which had also produced a mass in his liver. The prognosis was not terribly optimistic: with intensive intervention he would have about a 50% chance of surviving for 2 years, and a 25% chance of a "cure" (i.e., of surviving five years). "Intensive intervention" would include six to eight months of extremely unpleasant chemotherapy, surgery to remove part of his liver and his testes, and a substantial amount of radiation therapy. Without treatment, Bob would probably die within six months.

Bob has informed his oncologist that he has decided to forgo the proposed surgery, even though he recognizes that this will result in his death. He explained that he reached this conclusion after reading everything accessible to him about his cancer and the proposed treatment, after praying with his religious advisor and mentor (a Presbyterian minister), and after discussing the issue with his family, friends, and two patients (names provided by the oncologist) who had previously undergone the same surgery and chemotherapy. He also admits that the playground razzing he has taken over the primary location of his disease, and his consequent extreme embarrassment, were not irrelevant factors in his decision.

Bob's parents, who are divorced and have joint legal and physical custody, are split on this issue. His father believes that it is Bob's decision to make, and he supports Bob's decision. His mother insists that the oncologist and the hospital provide the proposed treatment. In addition, a social worker in the local child protective services office (which was informed about the case by one of Bob's teachers) has informed all of the parties that, in her opinion, Bob would be a neglected child if the treatment were not administered.

Bob's parents have now filed cross petitions seeking to vindicate their positions. Bob has filed a petition as well. The oncologist and the hospital have filed a declaratory judgment action seeking an order of the court before taking any action, and the child protective services agency has file a neglect petition against the father. How should the judge proceed? What kind of hearing, if any, should the judge hold? How should she rule?

NEWMARK v. WILLIAMS

Supreme Court of Delaware, 1991.
588 A.2d 1108.

MOORE, JUSTICE.

Colin Newmark, a three year old child, faced death from a deadly aggressive and advanced form of pediatric cancer known as Burkitt's Lymphoma. We were presented with a clash of interests between medical science, Colin's tragic plight, the unquestioned sincerity of his parents' religious beliefs as Christian Scientists, and the legal right of the State to protect dependent children from perceived neglect when medical treatment is withheld on religious grounds. The Delaware Division of Child Protective Services

("DCPS") petitioned the Family Court for temporary custody of Colin to authorize the Alfred I. DuPont Institute ("DuPont Institute"), a nationally recognized children's hospital, to treat Colin's condition with chemotherapy. His parents, Morris and Kara Newmark, are well educated and economically prosperous. As members of the First Church of Christ, Scientist ("Christian Science") they rejected medical treatment proposed for Colin, preferring instead a course of spiritual aid and prayer. The parents rely upon provisions of Delaware law, which exempt those who treat their children's illnesses "solely by spiritual means" from the abuse and neglect statutes. Thus, they opposed the State's petition. [ ] The Newmarks also claimed that removing Colin from their custody would violate their First Amendment right, guaranteed under the United States Constitution, to freely exercise their religion.

* * *

[The Court explained how the Newmarks discovered that Colin suffered from Burkitt's Lymphoma, an extremely fast growing and dangerous form of pediatric cancer, when they took him to the doctor "out of concern for their potential criminal liability. . . ."]

We have concluded that Colin was not an abused or neglected child under Delaware law. Parents enjoy a well established legal right to make important decisions for their children. Although this right is not absolute, the State has the burden of proving by clear and convincing evidence that intervening in the parent-child relationship is necessary to ensure the safety or health of the child, or to protect the public at large. DCPS did not meet this heavy burden. This is especially true where the purpose of the custody petition was to administer, over the objections of Colin's parents, an extremely risky, toxic and dangerously life threatening medical treatment offering less than a 40% chance for "success".

* * *

Dr. Meek [an attending physician and board certified pediatric hematologist—oncologist] opined that chemotherapy offered a 40% chance of "curing" Colin's illness. She concluded that he would die within six to eight months without treatment. The Newmarks * * * advised Dr. Meek that they would place him under the care of a Christian Science practitioner and reject all medical treatment for their son. Accordingly, they refused to authorize the chemotherapy. There was no doubt that the Newmarks sincerely believed, as part of their religious beliefs, that the tenets of their faith provided an effective treatment.

II.

We start with an overview of the relevant Delaware statutory provisions. Delaware law defines a neglected child as:

[A] child whose physical, mental or emotional health and well-being is threatened or impaired because of inadequate care and protection by the child's custodian, who has the ability and financial means to provide for the care but does not or will not provide adequate care; or a child who has been abused or neglected * * *

[The statute] further defines abuse and neglect as:

Physical injury by other than accidental means, injury resulting in a mental or emotional condition which is a result of abuse or neglect, negligent treatment, sexual abuse, maltreatment, mistreatment, nontreatment, exploitation or abandonment, of a child under the age of 18. (Emphasis added).

Sections of the Delaware Code, however, contain spiritual treatment exemptions which directly affect Christian Scientists. Specifically, the exemptions state:

No child who in good faith is under treatment solely by spiritual means through prayer in accordance with the tenets and practices of a recognized church or religious denomination by a duly accredited practitioner thereof shall for that reason alone be considered a neglected child for purposes of this chapter.

[ ] These exceptions reflect the intention of the Delaware General Assembly to provide a "safe harbor" for parents, like the Newmarks, to pursue their own religious beliefs. [We recognize] that the spiritual treatment exemptions reflect, in part, "the policy of this State with respect to the quality of life" a desperately ill child might have in the caring and loving atmosphere of his or her family, versus the sterile hospital environment demanded by physicians seeking to prescribe excruciating, and life threatening, treatments of doubtful efficacy.

* * * [W]e recognize the possibility that the spiritual treatment exemptions may violate the ban against the establishment of an official State religion guaranteed under both the Federal and Delaware Constitutions. Clearly, in both reality and practical effect, the language providing an exemption only to those individuals practicing "in accordance" with the "practices of a recognized church or religious denomination by a duly accredited practitioner thereof" is intended for the principal benefit of Christian Scientists. Our concern is that it possibly forces us to impermissibly determine the validity of an individual's own religious beliefs.

Neither party challenged the constitutionality of the spiritual treatment exemptions in either the Family Court or on appeal. Thus, except to recognize that the issue is far more complicated than was originally presented to us, we must leave such questions for another day.

III.

Addressing the facts of this case, we turn to the novel legal question whether, under any circumstances, Colin was a neglected child when his parents refused to accede to medical demands that he receive a radical form of chemotherapy having only a forty percent chance of success. [The court then explained that it would apply a balancing test to answer this question.]

* * *

A.

Any balancing test must begin with the parental interest. The primacy of the familial unit is a bedrock principle of law. [ ]. We have repeatedly emphasized that the parental right is sacred which can be invaded for only the most compelling reasons.

* * *

Courts have also recognized that the essential element of preserving the integrity of the family is maintaining the autonomy of the parent-child relationship. [ ] In Prince v. Commonwealth of Massachusetts, [ ] the United States Supreme Court announced:

> It is cardinal with us that the custody, care and nurture of the child reside first in the parents, whose primary function and freedom include preparation for obligations the state can neither supply nor hinder. [ ]

Parental autonomy to care for children free from government interference therefore satisfies a child's need for continuity and thus ensures his or her psychological and physical well-being. [ ]

Parental authority to make fundamental decisions for minor children is also a recognized common law principle. A doctor commits the tort of battery if he or she performs an operation under normal circumstances without the informed consent of the patient. [ ] Tort law also assumes that a child does not have the capacity to consent to an operation in most situations. [ ] Thus, the common law recognizes that the only party capable of authorizing medical treatment for a minor in "normal" circumstances is usually his parent or guardian. [ ]

Courts, therefore, give great deference to parental decisions involving minor children. In many circumstances the State simply is not an adequate surrogate for the judgment of a loving, nurturing parent. [ ] As one commentator aptly recognized, the "law does not have the capacity to supervise the delicately complex interpersonal bonds between parent and child." [ ]

B.

We also recognize that parental autonomy over minor children is not an absolute right. Clearly, the State can intervene in the parent-child relationship where the health and safety of the child and the public at large are in jeopardy. [ ] Accordingly, the State, under the doctrine of parens patriae, has a special duty to protect its youngest and most helpless citizens.

The parens patriae doctrine is a derivation of the common law giving the State the right to act on behalf of minor children in certain property and marital disputes. [ ] More recently, courts have accepted the doctrine of parens patriae to justify State intervention in cases of parental religious objections to medical treatment of minor children's life threatening conditions. [ ] The Supreme Court of the United States [pointed out] that parental autonomy, under the guise of the parents' religious freedom, was not unlimited. [ ] Rather, the Court held:

> Parents may be free to become martyrs themselves. But it does not follow they are free, in identical circumstances, to make martyrs of their children before they have reached the age of full and legal discretion when they can make that choice for themselves. [ ]

The basic principle underlying the parens patriae doctrine is the State's interest in preserving human life. [ ] Yet this interest and the parens patriae doctrine are not unlimited. In its recent Cruzan opinion, the Supreme Court of the United States announced that the state's interest in preserving life must "be weighed against the constitutionally protected interests of the individual." [ ]

The individual interests at stake here include both the Newmarks' right to decide what is best for Colin and Colin's own right to life. We have already considered the Newmarks' stake in this case and its relationship to the parens patriae doctrine. The resolution of the issues here, however, is incomplete without a discussion of Colin's interests.

C.

All children indisputably have the right to enjoy a full and healthy life. Colin, a three year old boy, unfortunately lacked the ability to reach a detached, informed decision regarding his own medical care. This Court must therefore substitute its own objective judgment to determine what is in Colin's "best interests." [ ]

There are two basic inquiries when a dispute involves chemotherapy treatment over parents' religious objections. The court must first consider the effectiveness of the treatment and determine the child's chances of survival with and without medical care. [ ] The court must then consider the nature of the treatments and their effect on the child. [ ]

The "best interests" analysis is hardly unique or novel. Federal and State courts have unhesitatingly authorized medical treatment over a parent's religious objection when the treatment is relatively innocuous in comparison to the dangers of withholding medical care. [ ] Accordingly, courts are reluctant to authorize medical care over parental objection when the child is not suffering a life threatening or potential life threatening illness. [ ]

The linchpin in all cases discussing the "best interests of a child," when a parent refuses to authorize medical care, is an evaluation of the risk of the procedure compared to its potential success. This analysis is consistent with the principle that State intervention in the parent-child relationship is only justifiable under compelling conditions. [ ] The State's interest in forcing a minor to undergo medical care diminishes as the risks of treatment increase and its benefits decrease.

* * *

Applying the foregoing considerations to the "best interests standard" here, the State's petition must be denied. The egregious facts of this case indicate that Colin's proposed medical treatment was highly invasive, painful, involved terrible temporary and potentially permanent side effects, posed an unacceptably low chance of success, and a high risk that the treatment itself would cause his death. The State's authority to intervene in this case, therefore, cannot outweigh the Newmarks' parental prerogative and Colin's inherent right to enjoy at least a modicum of human dignity in the short time that was left to him.

IV.

Dr. Meek originally diagnosed Colin's condition as Burkitt's Lymphoma. She testified that the cancer was "a very bad tumor" in an advanced disseminated state and not localized to only one section of the body. She accordingly recommended that the hospital begin an "extremely intensive" chemotherapy program scheduled to extend for at least six months.

[The court then explained how intensive such a chemotherapy program would be, and how such a treatment program would itself threaten Colin's life.]

Dr. Meek prescribed "maximum" doses of at least six different types of cancer-fighting drugs during Colin's chemotherapy. This proposed "maximum" treatment represented the most aggressive form of cancer therapy short of a bone marrow transplant. The side effects would include hair loss, reduced immunological function creating a high risk of infection in the patient, and certain neurological problems. The drugs also are toxic to bone marrow.

The record demonstrates that this form of chemotherapy also would adversely affect other parts of Colin's body.

* * *

The physicians planned to administer the chemotherapy in cycles, each of which would bring Colin near death. Then they would wait until Colin's body recovered sufficiently before introducing more drugs.

* * *

Dr. Meek also wanted the State to place Colin in a foster home after the initial phases of hospital treatment. Children require intensive home monitoring during chemotherapy. For example, Dr. Meek testified that a usually low grade fever for a healthy child could indicate the presence of a potentially deadly infection in a child cancer patient. She believed that the Newmarks, although well educated and financially responsible, were incapable of providing this intensive care because of their firm religious objections to medical treatment.

Dr. Meek ultimately admitted that there was a real possibility that the chemotherapy could kill Colin. In fact, assuming the treatment did not itself prove fatal, she offered Colin at "best" a 40% chance that he would "survive."[3] Dr. Meek additionally could not accurately predict whether, if Colin completed the therapy, he would subsequently suffer additional tumors.

A.

No American court, even in the most egregious case, has ever authorized the State to remove a child from the loving, nurturing care of his parents and subject him, over parental objection, to an invasive regimen of treatment which offered, as Dr. Meek defined the term, only a forty percent chance of "survival."

* * *

3. Dr. Meek testified that there was no available medical data to conclude that Colin could survive to adulthood. Rather, she stated that the term "survival", as applied to victims of leukemia or lymphoma, refers only to the probability that the patient will live two years after chemotherapy without a recurrence of cancer.

B.

The aggressive form of chemotherapy that Dr. Meek prescribed for Colin was more likely to fail than succeed. The proposed treatment was also highly invasive and could have independently caused Colin's death. Dr. Meek also wanted to take Colin away from his parents and family during the treatment phase and place the boy in a foster home. This certainly would have caused Colin severe emotional difficulties given his medical condition, tender age, and the unquestioned close bond between Colin and his family.

In sum, Colin's best interests were served by permitting the Newmarks to retain custody of their child. Parents must have the right at some point to reject medical treatment for their child. Under all of the circumstances here, this clearly is such a case. The State's important and legitimate role in safeguarding the interests of minor children diminishes in the face of this egregious record.

Parents undertake an awesome responsibility in raising and caring for their children. No doubt a parent's decision to withhold medical care is both deeply personal and soul wrenching. It need not be made worse by the invasions which both the State and medical profession sought on this record. Colin's ultimate fate therefore rested with his parents and their faith.

Notes and Questions

1. Most judicial encounters with parents' rights to refuse medical treatment for their children follow the pattern established in *Newmark*. The court first announces the legal presumption that parents can make important decisions, including health care decisions, for their children. This is a common law right in every state, and it is protected by the United States Constitution as well. See Parham v. J.R., 442 U.S. 584, 99 S.Ct. 2493, 61 L.Ed.2d 101 (1979). However, this presumption can be overcome if the conditions of the state's child protective services statute are met. Most state child abuse and neglect statutes are similar to the Delaware statute discussed in *Newmark*, and they provide—with greater or lesser specificity—that the parents' failure to provide adequate health care for their children constitutes neglect. If parents neglect their children, the state may commence a legal process (as the state did in *Newmark*) to obtain legal custody of the child to assure that the child is no longer medically neglected. The state need not take physical custody of the child, and the child can (as a technical legal matter) remain in the physical custody of the parents even while receiving the medical care to which the parents object.

2. Ultimately, what is the legal test that the court applied to determine that Colin Newmark should not be ordered to undergo the proposed chemotherapy? Did the court apply a straight "best interests" test and determine that it was in Colin's best interests not to undergo this treatment, or did the court apply a balancing test and determine that the parents' interest in maintaining custody of their child (and in making health care decisions for their child) outweighed the state's interest in providing Colin with potentially life saving treatment? The choice between these two alternative forms of analysis may make no difference in this particular case, but can you think of a case in which the choice between these two legal positions would be dispositive?

3. As a general matter, courts reviewing young children's decisions to forgo life sustaining treatment apply the "best interests" test (with a substantial bow to the articulated desires of the parents, who are deemed to have the best interests of

their children in mind when they act). While the application of the "substituted judgment" standard seems appropriate as the children approach majority, a few states attempt to apply the "substituted judgment" theory to very young children, too. Compare, e.g., Care and Protection of Beth, 412 Mass. 188, 587 N.E.2d 1377 (1992), Custody of a Minor, 385 Mass. 697, 434 N.E.2d 601 (1982) and In re L.H.R., 253 Ga. 439, 321 S.E.2d 716 (1984) (applying the substituted judgment test) with In re K.I., B.I. and D.M., 735 A.2d 448 (D.C.1999) (applying the best interests test). See Matter of AB, 196 Misc.2d 940, 768 N.Y.S.2d 256 (Sup. Ct. 2003)(applying a combination of these tests; see below) and In re Christopher I., 106 Cal.App.4th 533, 131 Cal.Rptr.2d 122 (2003) (applying the best interest test to a child in the custody of the state). Does the "substituted judgment" standard make any sense when it is applied to infants or very young children? Although it may be absurd to search for the values, interests, desires, and expectancies of a newborn or a 3–month old, or even a four year old, might not a seven or eight year old child's parents be able to talk about all of those attributes? Of course, it is hard to imagine anyone other than the parents (or their legal substitutes) being able to evaluate such factors. Does that mean that a court's decision to apply a substituted judgment standard to small children amounts to a *de facto* decision to defer to the parent's wishes?

In Matter of AB, supra, the New York Supreme Court confirmed the right of a mother of a child in persistent vegetative state to discontinue life-sustaining medical treatment—but only because the best interest test had been met:

> Thus, this Court holds that it is [the mother's] right, as a parent and natural guardian of AB, to exercise her responsibility and prerogative to make this decision to withhold extraordinary life-prolonging measures, with the assistance of treating physicians. CD's parental choice, made in the best interest of her child, to allow her daughter to pass away peacefully and with dignity are to be honored. This decision respects the values of family privacy without compromising a patient's rights or overstepping the State's legitimate interests.

> Having sought judicial intervention, CD has proven by clear and convincing evidence that it is in the best interest of her child to remove the mechanical ventilator. As CD sought intervention, this Court has employed the best interest standard, weighing whether the burdens of prolonged life outweigh any physical pleasure, emotional enjoyment, or intellectual satisfaction that the child may still be able to derive from life.

768 N.Y.S.2d at 271–272. In that case, AB's mother had sought a court order only because the hospital refused to permit the removal of the care unless a court order supported that decision. Is the mother free to make health care decisions for her child—but only if the court agrees that the decisions are in the best interest of the child? Who is the real decision maker in this case?

4. How is a court to determine what is in the best interest of a child? Does the court look to its own values, to values derived from community sources, to values held by the child's family, or elsewhere? For example, in the case of a neurologically devastated child with no cognitive facilities and no hope of regaining any—a child who is entirely insensate and can not feel pleasure or pain—is the terminal removal of a feeding tube or a ventilator *always* in the child's best interest, *never* in the child's best interest, or *sometimes* in the child's best interest? If you chose "sometimes," what other factors are relevant? In *Matter of AB*, the court depended on standards provided by the New York Surrogate Court Procedures Act (SCPA) and American Medical Association guidelines. The SCPA, which was designed to apply to a guardian's decision making process for a developmentally disabled person, provides:

the assessment of "best interest" must include the following considerations: "(i) the dignity and uniqueness of every person; (ii) the preservation, improvement or restoration of the mentally retarded person's health; (iii) the relief of the mentally retarded person's suffering by means of palliative care and pain management; (iv) the unique nature of artificially provided nutrition or hydration, and the effect it may have on the mentally retarded person; and (v) the entire medical condition of the person." SCPA section 1750–b (2)(b).

768 N.Y.S.2d 256, 266. The American Medical Association best interest guidelines, which are designed to address decisionmaking for newborns, provide:

> Factors that should be considered when making decisions about life-sustaining or life-saving treatment for a seriously ill newborn include: 1) the chance the therapy will succeed, 2) the risks involved with treatment and nontreatment, 3) the degree to which the therapy if successful will extend life, 4) the pain and discomfort associated with the therapy and 5) the anticipated quality of life for the newborn with and without treatment.

American Medical Association, Council on Ethical and Judicial Affairs, Opinion 2:215, *Treatment Decisions for Seriously Ill Newborns*, June 1992. In *In re Christopher I*, the court announced a more exhaustive list of factors, drawn from local and national state court guidelines:

> We conclude that a court making the decision of whether to withhold or withdraw life-sustaining medical treatment from a dependent child should consider the following factors: (1) the child's present levels of physical, sensory, emotional and cognitive functioning; (2) the quality of life, life expectancy and prognosis for recovery with and without treatment, including the futility of continued treatment; (3) the various treatment options, and the risks, side effects, and benefits of each; (4) the nature and degree of physical pain or suffering resulting from the medical condition; (5) whether the medical treatment being provided is causing or may cause pain, suffering, or serious complications; (6) the pain or suffering to the child if the medical treatment is withdrawn; (7) whether any particular treatment would be proportionate or disproportionate in terms of the benefits to be gained by the child versus the burdens caused to the child; (8) the likelihood that pain or suffering resulting from withholding or withdrawal of treatment could be avoided or minimized; (9) the degree of humiliation, dependence and loss of dignity resulting from the condition and treatment; (10) the opinions of the family, the reasons behind those opinions, and the reasons why the family either has no opinion or cannot agree on a course of treatment; (11) the motivations of the family in advocating a particular course of treatment; and (12) the child's preference, if it can be ascertained, for treatment.

131 Cal.Rptr. at 551, 552. How helpful are these lists of factors? What factors do you believe a court should employ in determining if the removal of life sustaining medical care is in the best interest of a child?

5. Parental rights to make health care decisions for their children are terminated when the child reaches majority. Those rights may be terminated earlier if the child is a "mature minor," a condition governed by statute (in some states) or the common law (in other states) or both. At the very least, a child is a mature minor when he can "present clear and convincing evidence that he [is] mature enough to exercise an adult's judgment and [understand] the consequences of his decision." *Newmark*, at 1116 n. 9. See In re E.G., 133 Ill.2d 98, 139 Ill.Dec. 810, 549 N.E.2d 322 (1989), where a Jehovah's Witness child "just months shy of her eighteenth birthday" was found to be sufficiently mature to choose to forgo a blood transfusion in a case with a rather dim chance of long term survival. See also Belcher v. Charleston Area Medical Center, 188 W.Va. 105, 422 S.E.2d

827 (1992) (17 year old should have had the right to demand a DNR order). But see In re Application of Long Island Jewish Med. Ctr., 147 Misc.2d 724, 557 N.Y.S.2d 239 (Sup.Ct.1990). In Commonwealth v. Nixon, 563 Pa. 425, 761 A.2d 1151 (2000), this issue arose in the context of a defense in a criminal action. The Pennsylvania Supreme Court unanimously rejected the parents' appeal of their involuntary manslaughter and child endangerment convictions (and their consequent 2 1/2 to 5 year sentences) after their sixteen year old daughter died at home as a result of the religiously-based decision not to seek diabetes treatment. The parents had argued that their daughter had decided, on her own, against seeking treatment, and that she was a "mature minor" under Pennsylvania law and thus entitled to make that decision, but the court concluded that she didn't meet the narrow definition of a "mature minor" under Pennsylvania law.

Courts may give some weight to the statements of older children, even if those courts are reluctant to declare those children "emancipated" or "mature minors." Although children under 16 are not found sufficiently mature to independently choose to forgo life sustaining treatment, many courts have given considerable weight to the statements made by children considerably younger than that. See, e.g., In re Guardianship of Crum, 61 Ohio Misc.2d 596, 580 N.E.2d 876 (Prob.Ct., Franklin Co.1991). For a discussion of the ways in which children could be included in advance directive legislation, see Lisa Hawkins, Living Will Statutes: A Minor Oversight, 78 Va. L. Rev. 1581 (1992).

6. As the *Newmark* court explained, courts have "unhesitatingly authorized medical treatment over a parent's religious objection when the treatment is relatively innocuous in comparison with the dangers of withholding medical care." Of course, what constitutes an innocuous treatment for most of us might constitute a very serious intrusion for others. Most people are not terribly concerned by the prospect of a blood transfusion; for others, it may eliminate a possibility of eternal salvation. Despite this, courts have not flinched when they have been presented with requests for treatment that is "medically necessary"—i.e., when the child will surely die if the treatment is not provided, and just as surely will live if the treatment is provided. Courts routinely and consistently order blood transfusions for children of objecting Jehovah's Witness parents, at least when they meet this requirement of medical necessity; in this sense the courts treat Jehovah's Witness children very differently from Jehovah's Witness adults. On the other hand, courts generally do not order treatment for children who do not face life threatening conditions. The hardest cases, like the *Newmark* case, are those cases in which the proposed treatment is highly invasive, but the child faces a life threatening condition. The *Newmark* case reviews five other such cases—all involving childhood cancer. See *Newmark*, at 1119–1120. As the chance of temporary remission and long term cure increases, the courts are more likely to order the treatment. Is this consistent with evaluation under the factors listed in note 4, above?

7. While courts regularly face parental decisions that their children not receive treatment, they are sometimes confronted with the reverse situation, too. In In re K.I., B.I. and D.M., 735 A.2d 448 (D.C.1999) the District of Columbia Court of Appeals approved a DNR order for a neglected, comatose two year old child who was born "neurologically devastated." The child was taken from his drunken mother after he had been left alone for days without his necessary heart and lung medication. The mother opposed the hospital's request that the child be given DNR status. Applying the best interest (rather than the substituted judgment) standard, the court recognized that the mother might be criminally liable for homicide if the child were to die, and it thus disregarded her request that

there be aggressive attempts at resuscitation. Can you imagine other circumstances in which a parent might inappropriately demand treatment for her child? Should these cases be treated any differently from those in which the parent denies consent for (rather than demands) the recommended care? See also *In re Christopher I*, above, in which the father, whose abuse had resulted in the child's serious neurological injury, argued that the child's life should be maintained.

8. Like Delaware, most states have promulgated statutes that provide that "spiritual healing" *per se* cannot constitute child abuse or neglect for purposes of the state's criminal or child protective services statutes. In fact, for some time the existence of such protections were required as a condition of receiving some forms of federal funding. These spiritual healing statutes were the consequence of lobbying by the Christian Science church, and they were written using terms (e.g., "accredited practitioner") that have well defined meanings within that church. Are such statutes Constitutional? Might they violate the establishment clause of the first amendment because they give a preference to Christian Scientists, and protect them in ways that they do not protect others? Is it relevant that the statute only protects members of "recognized" religions, and that the state is called upon to determine which religions it will "recognize"? Might they violate the establishment clause because they disfavor children within certain religious communities? After all, Presbyterian children are protected from death at the hands of their irrational parents by the state's abuse and neglect process, while Christian Science children are not. Most commentators who have considered the issue have determined that these statutes are not Constitutional (at least as they are applied to civil abuse and neglect proceedings) because they violate either the establishment clause or the equal protection clause of the fourteenth amendment. For a good account of the best arguments on this issue, see Ann MacLean Massie, The Religion Clauses and Parental Health Care Decisionmaking for Children: Suggestions for a New Approach, 21 Hastings Const. L. Q. 725 (1994). Also see State v. Miskimens, 22 Ohio Misc.2d 43, 490 N.E.2d 931 (Com.Pl.1984) and Walker v. Superior Court, 222 Cal.Rptr. 87 (App.1986) aff'd 47 Cal.3d 112, 253 Cal.Rptr. 1, 763 P.2d 852 (1988) (especially the concurring opinion of Justice Mosk).

B. NEWBORNS

Problem: Newborn With Spina Bifida

Baby Roe's parents decided their child would be born at Pleasant City Birthing Center despite medical advice that the advanced age of the mother made a hospital delivery advisable. At birth, the baby appeared to have spina bifida and hydrocephalus, serious congenital heart problems, and several other less serious medical problems.

Spina bifida is a midline defect of the osseous spine. In this case there is an external saccular protrusion high on the spine, and the protruding sac, which is filled with spinal fluid, includes a portion of the spinal cord. This medical condition is known as myelomeningocele. Hydrocephalus, which is often associated with spina bifida, consists of a cranial capacity engorged by fluids. The pressure of this fluid on the brain can have substantial adverse consequences. None of those problems are related to advanced maternal age.

The physician on call for the birthing center was telephoned immediately, and he ordered the baby to be moved to the Pleasant City General Hospital Neonatal Intensive Care Unit (NICU), which he called to inform of the baby's imminent arrival. Physicians at the NICU concluded that the child would die of infection within a few months if the opening in the spine were not closed. To give Baby Roe any chance of long term survival, dozens of operations and virtually full time hospitalization would be required over a two year period. With maximum intervention, he might live 60 or 70 years. During this existence, he might be able to feel pain and experience pleasure; the physicians simply could not be sure. If he had any cognitive ability whatsoever, he would be likely to be severely mentally and physically disabled.

The parents, who are extremely distraught, are very angry that their child was moved to the NICU. They believe that he should not have been removed without their consent, which they would have denied. The parents have also denied consent for the placement of a shunt necessary to minimize the effect of the hydrocephalus by relieving pressure on the brain. In addition, they refuse consent to the heart wall repair which is necessary to keep their son alive. The family physician and all other physicians working in the NICU agree that it would be medically appropriate either to provide all treatment or not to provide any treatment in this case.

One of the nurses, however, disagrees. She explains that she recognizes the awful dilemma faced by the parents, but she believes that their needs can be attained in ways that do not result in the death of their child. As she points out, the state child protective services agency has a list of members of the local Citizens for Life organization who are willing to adopt immediately any child born with any serious birth defect. People on the list are willing to provide the full cost of any treatment required by such children. The nurse believes the case should be referred to the state child protective service agency, which can then arrange for the termination of current parental rights and the adoption of the child by someone who will provide adequate medical care.

What actions ought the parents, physicians, nurses, and others take? What judicial consequences could (and should) each medical decision have?

Note: *Treating Seriously Ill Newborns*

If it is difficult to apply the principle of autonomy to an incompetent adult who has been competent, and nearly impossible to apply that principle to serve an incompetent adult who has never been competent (but who has expressed likes and dislikes), it is simply impossible to apply that principle to a seriously ill newborn. The principle of beneficence, then, must become primary. The obligation of health care professionals and institutions is to do what is in the best interest of the child. As a matter of general course, because parents are presumed to be acting in the best interest of their children, parents of seriously ill newborns traditionally have been permitted to determine whether their infants would receive treatment, and what kind of treatment that should be. Thus, if a parent of a newborn with some severe anomaly determined that it would be best for that child not to receive life-sustaining treatment, that determination traditionally was honored even though it would result in the certain death of a child whose life otherwise might be saved.

The question of what treatment must be provided to a seriously ill newborn, however, has proved to be not quite so simple. Philosophically, the difficulties arise out of the fact that parents of newborn infants with serious defects may not always act entirely in the best interest of those infants. While parents undoubtedly feel responsibility for all of their children, a seriously ill newborn is likely to be a particularly great financial and emotional drain on the parents and the rest of the family. With some, however minor, risk that the parents' interest will be in conflict with the newborn's best interest, should we still allow the parents to make health care decisions for their newborn child? In addition, questions surrounding seriously ill newborns often require a determination of whether life-sustaining treatment should be forgone. Is it philosophically sensible to declare that death is in the "best interest" of a newborn who may be capable of so little brain activity that he will be without pain? What can "best interest" mean under such circumstances? Is it any easier to apply the principle of beneficence than the principle of autonomy under these conditions?

These are precisely the kinds of questions that are generally answered at the local institutional level within our health care system. Indeed, that is exactly what had been happening throughout the country; the ultimate determination generally was left to the parents, who were heavily influenced by the hospital medical staff. Without much public attention, and with discussion limited primarily to medical and ethical professional organizations, somewhat different standards were applied in somewhat different institutions. Then came Baby Doe.

THE BABY DOE CASES

Baby Doe was born on April 9, 1982, in Bloomington, Indiana. He was born with Down's Syndrome and a tracheoesophageal fistula which would require repair to allow the baby to consume nutrition orally. The parents decided not to authorize the necessary surgery, and the baby was given phenobarbital and morphine until he died, six days after birth. During Baby Doe's short life he was the subject of a suit commenced by the hospital in the local children's court, which refused to order that the surgery be done. The Indiana Supreme Court denied an extraordinary writ that would have had the same effect, and the attorneys for the hospital were on their way to Washington to seek a stay from the United States Supreme Court when the issue was rendered moot by Baby Doe's death. Baby Doe presents a very clean case for philosophical and jurisprudential analysis. The physicians refused to do the operation because the parents refused to consent. The parents refused to consent because their child had Down's Syndrome. If the child had not been born with Down's Syndrome, he would have been provided the surgery.

Several political groups, including right to life groups and advocacy groups for the developmentally disabled, were outraged by the circumstances of Baby Doe's death. Looking for some way to redress this issue, the Health and Human Services Department hit upon Section 504 of the Rehabilitation Act of 1974, 29 U.S.C.A. § 794, which forbids any agency receiving federal funds from discriminating on the basis of handicap. In March of 1983 the Secretary of Health and Human Services issued emergency regulations to assure that no hospital would avoid providing necessary treatment for seriously ill newborns. These regulations, purportedly authorized by Section 504 of the Rehabilitation Act, provided for federal "Baby Doe squads" to swoop down upon any hospital that put at risk the life or health of a handicapped infant by denying that infant life-sustaining treatment. The regulations also required large signs describing federal policy in all maternity and pediatric wards and newborn nurseries, and they established a toll free number to report violations of the regulation.

The regulations were challenged by the American Academy of Pediatrics, which successfully argued that they were defective because they had not been issued after the notice and comment period required by the Administrative Procedures Act. American Academy of Pediatrics v. Heckler, 561 F.Supp. 395

(D.D.C.1983). The Department of Health and Human Services then proposed slightly revised regulations ("Baby Doe II") and invited comments. In early 1984 the new final regulations ("Baby Doe III") were issued. These regulations were based on the articulated substantive principle that "nourishment and medically beneficial treatment (as determined with respect to reasonable medical judgments) should not be withheld from handicapped infants solely on the basis of their present or anticipated mental or physical impairments."

Under the final regulations the federal government maintained its investigatory and enforcement roles, state child protective services agencies were required to develop processes to investigate cases of non-treatment of seriously ill newborns, and individual institutions were encouraged to establish "Infant Care Review Committees" to review appropriate cases. The American Medical Association and the American Hospital Association challenged "Baby Doe III" and the Supreme Court, without any majority opinion, ultimately determined that the regulation had been improperly promulgated. Bowen v. American Hospital Association, 476 U.S. 610, 106 S.Ct. 2101, 90 L.Ed.2d 584 (1986).

While the challenge to Baby Doe III was wending its way through the courts, principals on both sides of the issue agreed to a compromise that was turned into the Child Abuse Amendments of 1984, 42 U.S.C.A. § 5102 (1986). This statute is considerably weaker than the regulation that preceded it, but it does condition each state's receipt of some federal child abuse prevention funding on the maintenance of procedures for dealing with reports of the medical neglect of newborns. Regulations issued under the Child Abuse Amendments interpret "medical neglect" to include "the withholding of medically indicated treatment from a disabled infant with a life threatening condition." 45 C.F.R. § 1340.15(b)(1). Further, the regulations provide that the

> "withholding of medically indicated treatment" means the failure to respond to the infant's life threatening conditions by providing treatment (including appropriate nutrition, hydration, and medication) which in the treating physicians' * * * reasonable medical judgment will be most likely to be effective in ameliorating or correcting all such conditions.

45 C.F.R. § 1340.15(b)(2). There is no obligation to provide care to an infant who is "chronically and irreversibly comatose," when the treatment would "merely prolong the dying process" of the infant and not ameliorate or correct the underlying medical problem (and thus be futile), or when the treatment would be "virtually futile" and "inhumane." *Id.* Are these substantively appropriate standards? How could you redraft them, if you could? Is the process for enforcing them (through the potential cut-off of federal funding for state child abuse programs) appropriate? What kind of enforcement mechanism do you think would be better?

Although the issue increasingly rarely arises in the judicial setting, courts are loathe to allow infants who can be "saved" to die. Compare, e.g., Iafelice v. Zarafu, 221 N.J.Super. 278, 534 A.2d 417 (App.Div.1987) (parents may not withhold consent to a shunt to be placed in a spina bifida infant, even when substantial mental retardation is extremely likely) with In re K.I, B.I. and D.M., 735 A.2d 448 (D.C.1999), discussed above. In the United Kingdom, on the other hand, there is far more toleration of a family decision to discontinue treatment of an infant with a "brain incapable of even limited intellectual function. * * * " The British courts are willing to explicitly consider the quality of life of a seriously ill newborn, as was demonstrated in one case in which treatment was not required for a newborn because "[c]oupled with her total physical handicap, the quality of her life will be demonstrably awful and intolerable." In re C (Minor) [1989] 2 All E.R. 782 (C.A.). See also In re J (Minor), [1990] 3 All E.R. 930 (C.A.) (court applies principle of substituted judgment to determine that a severely mentally and physically handicapped baby would not choose to live, and thus certain treatments could be withheld from him). Treatment decisions made for seriously ill newborns depend heavily on the values of the physicians involved in the decision making, and upon the country in which the decision is made. One recent study of attitudes in European neonatal intensive care units showed that newborns were more likely to be kept alive under all circumstances in Hungary, Estonia, Latvia and Italy than they were in the United Kingdom, the Netherlands and Sweden. See M. Rebagliato, Physicians' Attitudes and Relationships With Self-reported Practices in Ten European Countries, 284 JAMA 2451 (2000).

National attention was drawn to the issue of the appropriate treatment of seriously ill newborns in 2003 as a consequence of a high profile Texas lawsuit in which, a jury returned a verdict for over $60,000,000 (including thirteen million in punitive damages) against a health care institution for failing to follow parents' instructions to withhold life-sustaining treatment from their infant. Ultimately, the Supreme Court of Texas reviewed the case:

MILLER v. HCA

Supreme Court of Texas, 2003.
118 S.W.3d 758.

JUSTICE ENOCH delivered the opinion of the Court.

The narrow question we must decide is whether Texas law recognizes a claim by parents for either battery or negligence because their premature infant, born alive but in distress at only twenty-three weeks of gestation, was provided resuscitative medical treatment by physicians at a hospital without parental consent. The court of appeals, with one justice dissenting, held that neither claim could be maintained as a matter of law because parents have no right to refuse urgently-needed life-sustaining medical treatment for their child unless the child's condition is "certifiably terminal" under the Natural Death Act [ ]. And here it is undisputed that the Millers' new-born infant was not "certifiably terminal."

Although we agree with the court of appeals' judgment, our reasoning differs somewhat. First, there is no dispute in the evidence that the Millers' premature infant could not be fully evaluated for medical treatment until birth. As a result, any decisions concerning treatment for the Millers' child would not be fully informed decisions until birth. Second, the evidence further established that once the infant was born, the physician attending the birth was faced with emergent circumstances—*i.e.*, the child might survive with treatment but would likely die if treatment was not provided before either parental consent or a court order overriding the withholding of such consent could be obtained.

We hold that circumstances like these provide an exception to the general rule imposing liability on a physician for treating a child without consent. That exception eliminates the Millers' claim for battery. We further conclude that the Millers' negligence claim—premised not on any physician's negligence in treating the infant but on the hospital's policies, or lack thereof, permitting a physician to treat their infant without parental consent—fails as a matter of law for the same reasons. We accordingly affirm the court of appeals' judgment.

I. FACTS

The unfortunate circumstances of this case began in August 1990, when approximately four months before her due date, Karla Miller was admitted to Woman's Hospital of Texas (the "Hospital") in premature labor. An ultrasound revealed that Karla's fetus weighed about 629 grams or 1 1/4 pounds and had a gestational age of approximately twenty-three weeks. Because of the fetus's prematurity, Karla's physicians began administering a drug designed to stop labor.

Karla's physicians subsequently discovered that Karla had an infection that could endanger her life and require them to induce delivery. Dr. Mark Jacobs, Karla's obstetrician, and Dr. Donald Kelley, a neonatologist at the Hospital, informed Karla and her husband, Mark Miller, that if they had to induce delivery, the infant had little chance of being born alive. The physicians also informed the Millers that if the infant was born alive, it would most probably suffer severe impairments, including cerebral palsy, brain hemorrhaging, blindness, lung disease, pulmonary infections, and mental retardation. Mark testified at trial that the physicians told him they had never had such a premature infant live and that anything they did to sustain the infant's life would be guesswork.

After their discussion, Drs. Jacobs and Kelley asked the Millers to decide whether physicians should treat the infant upon birth if they were forced to induce delivery. At approximately noon that day, the Millers informed Drs. Jacob and Kelley that they wanted no heroic measures performed on the infant and they wanted nature to take its course. Mark testified that he understood heroic measures to mean performing resuscitation, chest massage, and using life support machines. Dr. Kelley recorded the Millers' request in Karla's medical notes, and Dr. Jacobs informed the medical staff at the Hospital that no neonatologist would be needed at delivery. Mark then left the Hospital to make funeral arrangements for the infant.

In the meantime, the nursing staff informed other Hospital personnel of Dr. Jacobs' instruction that no neonatologist would be present in the delivery room when the Millers' infant was born. An afternoon of meetings involving Hospital administrators and physicians followed. Between approximately 4:00 p.m. and 4:30 p.m that day, Anna Summerfield, the director of the Hospital's neonatal intensive care unit, and several physicians, including Dr. Jacobs, met with Mark upon his return to the Hospital to further discuss the situation. Mark testified that Ms. Summerfield announced at the meeting that the Hospital had a policy requiring resuscitation of any baby who was born weighing over 500 grams. * * *

Moreover, the physicians at the meeting testified that they and Hospital administrators agreed only that a neonatologist would be present to evaluate the Millers' infant at birth and decide whether to resuscitate based on the infant's condition at that time.

* * *

Although Dr. Eduardo Otero, the neonatologist present in the delivery room when Sidney was born, did not attend that meeting, he confirmed that he needed to actually see Sidney before deciding what treatment, if any, would be appropriate * * *.

Mark testified that, after the meeting, Hospital administrators asked him to sign a consent form allowing resuscitation according to the Hospital's plan, but he refused. Mark further testified that when he asked how he could prevent resuscitation, Hospital administrators told him that he could do so by removing Karla from the Hospital, which was not a viable option given her condition. Dr. Jacobs then noted in Karla's medical charts that a plan for evaluating the infant upon her birth was discussed at that afternoon meeting.

That evening, Karla's condition worsened and her amniotic sac broke. Dr. Jacobs determined that he would have to augment labor so that the infant would be delivered before further complications to Karla's health developed. Dr. Jacobs accordingly stopped administering the drug to Karla that was designed to stop labor, substituting instead a drug designed to augment labor. At 11:30 p.m. that night, Karla delivered a premature female infant weighing 615 grams, which the Millers named Sidney. Sidney's actual gestational age was twenty-three and one-seventh weeks. And she was born alive.

* * *

Sidney initially responded well to the treatment, as reflected by her Apgar scores. An Apgar score records five different components of a new-born infant: respiratory effort, heart rate, reflex activity, color, and muscle tone. Each component gets a score of zero, one, or two, with a score of two representing the best condition. Sidney's total Apgar score improved from a three at one minute after birth to a six at five minutes after birth. But at some point during the first few days after birth, Sidney suffered a brain hemorrhage—a complication not uncommon in infants born so prematurely.

There was conflicting testimony about whether Sidney's hemorrhage occurred because of the treatment provided or in spite of it. Regardless of the cause, as predicted by Karla's physicians, the hemorrhage caused Sidney to suffer severe physical and mental impairments. At the time of trial, Sidney was seven years old and could not walk, talk, feed herself, or sit up on her own. The evidence demonstrated that Sidney was legally blind, suffered from severe mental retardation, cerebral palsy, seizures, and spastic quadriparesis in her limbs. She could not be toilet-trained and required a shunt in her brain to drain fluids that accumulate there and needed care twenty-four hours a day. The evidence further demonstrated that her circumstances will not change.

The Millers sued HCA, Inc., HCA–Hospital Corporation of America, Hospital Corporation of America, and Columbia/HCA Healthcare Corporation (collectively, "HCA"), and the Hospital, a subsidiary of HCA. They did not sue any physicians, including Dr. Otero, the physician who actually treated Sidney. Instead, the Millers asserted battery and negligence claims only against HCA and the Hospital.

The Millers' claims stemmed from their allegations that despite their instructions to the contrary, the Hospital not only resuscitated Sidney but performed experimental procedures and administered experimental drugs, without which, in all reasonable medical probability, Sidney would not have survived.

* * *

Though the Hospital was not a party at the trial against HCA, the trial court submitted questions to the jury about the Hospital's conduct. The jury found that the Hospital, without the consent of Karla or Mark Miller, performed resuscitative treatment on Sidney. The jury also found that the Hospital's and HCA's negligence "proximately caused the occurrence in question." The jury concluded that HCA and the Hospital were grossly negligent and that the Hospital acted with malice. * * * The trial court rendered judgment jointly and severally against the HCA defendants on the jury's verdict of $29,400,000 in actual damages for medical expenses, $17,503,066 in prejudgment interest, and $13,500,000 in exemplary damages.

HCA appealed. The court of appeals, with one justice dissenting, reversed * * *.

* * *

II. ANALYSIS

This case requires us to determine the respective roles that parents and healthcare providers play in deciding whether to treat an infant who is born alive but in distress and is so premature that, despite advancements in neonatal intensive care, has a largely uncertain prognosis. Although the parties have cited numerous constitutional provisions, statutes, and cases, we conclude that neither the Texas Legislature nor our case law has addressed this specific situation. We accordingly begin our analysis by focusing on what the existing case law and statutes do address.

Generally speaking, the custody, care, and nurture of an infant resides in the first instance with the parents. As the United States Supreme Court has acknowledged, parents are presumed to be the appropriate decision-makers for their infants [quoting Parham v. J.R., 442 U.S. 584 (1979)].

The Texas Legislature has likewise recognized that parents are presumed to be appropriate decision-makers, giving parents the right to consent to their infant's medical care and surgical treatment. A logical corollary of that right, as the court of appeals here recognized, is that parents have the right not to consent to certain medical care for their infant, i.e., parents have the right to refuse certain medical care.

Of course, this broad grant of parental decision-making authority is not without limits. The State's role as *parens patriae* permits it to intercede in parental decision-making under certain circumstances.

* * *

The Texas Legislature has acknowledged the limitations on parental decision-making. For example, the Legislature has provided in the Family Code that the rights and duties of parents are subject to modification by court order. And Texas courts have recognized their authority to enter orders, under appropriate circumstances, appointing a temporary managing conservator who may consent to medical treatment refused by a child's parents.

With respect to consent, the requirement that permission be obtained before providing medical treatment is based on the patient's right to receive information adequate for him or her to exercise an informed decision to accept or refuse the treatment. Thus, the general rule in Texas is that a physician who provides treatment without consent commits a battery. But there are exceptions. * * *

[Texas precedent] acknowledges that a physician does not commit a legal wrong by operating on a minor without consent when the operation is performed under emergent circumstances—*i.e.*, when death is likely to result immediately upon the failure to perform it.

* * *

We recognize that the *Restatement (Second) of Torts § 892D* provides that an individual is not liable for providing emergency treatment without consent if that individual has no reason to believe that the other, if he or she had the opportunity to consent, would decline. But that requirement is inapplicable here because * * * the emergent circumstances exception does not imply consent.

Further, the emergent circumstances exception acknowledges that the harm from failing to treat outweighs any harm threatened by the proposed treatment, because the harm from failing to provide life-sustaining treatment under emergent circumstances is death. And as we acknowledged * * *, albeit in the different context of a wrongful life claim, it is impossible for the courts to calculate the relative benefits of an impaired life versus no life at all.

Following these guiding principles, we now determine whether the Millers can maintain their battery and negligence claims against HCA. The jury found that the Hospital, through Dr. Otero, treated Sidney without the Millers' consent. The parties do not challenge that finding. Thus, we only address whether the Hospital was required to seek court intervention to overturn the lack of parental consent—which it undisputedly did not do— before Dr. Otero could treat Sidney without committing a battery.

The Millers acknowledge that numerous physicians at trial agreed that, absent an emergency situation, the proper course of action is court intervention when health care providers disagree with parents' refusal to consent to a child's treatment. And the Millers contend that, as a matter of law, no emergency existed that would excuse the Hospital's treatment of Sidney without their consent or a court order overriding their refusal to consent. The Millers point out that before Sidney's birth, Drs. Jacobs and Kelley discussed with them the possibility that Sidney might suffer from the numerous physical and mental infirmities that did, in fact, afflict her. And some eleven hours before Sidney's birth, the Millers indicated that they did not want any heroic measures performed on Sidney. The Millers note that these factors prompted the dissenting justice in the court of appeals to conclude that "anytime a group of doctors and a hospital administration have the luxury of multiple meetings to change the original doctors' medical opinions, without taking a more obvious course of action, there is no medical emergency."

We agree that a physician cannot create emergent circumstances from his or her own delay or inaction and escape liability for proceeding without consent. But the Millers' reasoning fails to recognize that, in this case, the evidence established that Sidney could only be properly evaluated when she was born. Any decision the Millers made before Sidney's birth concerning her treatment at or after her birth would necessarily be based on speculation. Therefore, we reject the Millers' argument that a decision could adequately be made pre-birth that denying all post-birth resuscitative treatment would be in Sidney's best interest. Such a decision could not control whether the circumstances facing Dr. Otero were emergent because it would not have been a fully informed one according to the evidence in this case.

The Millers point out that physicians routinely ask parents to make pre-birth treatment choices for their infants including whether to accept or refuse in utero medical treatment and to continue or terminate a pregnancy. While that may be entirely true, the evidence here established that the time for evaluating Sidney was when she was born. The evidence further reflected that Sidney was born alive but in distress. At that time, Dr. Otero had to make a spilt-second decision on whether to provide life-sustaining treatment. While the Millers were both present in the delivery room, there was simply no time to obtain their consent to treatment or to institute legal proceedings to challenge their withholding of consent, had the Millers done so, without jeopardizing Sidney's life. Thus, although HCA never requested a jury instruction, nor challenged the absence of a jury instruction, on whether Dr. Otero treated Sidney under emergent circumstances, the evidence conclusively established that Dr. Otero was faced with emergent circumstances when he treated Sidney. Those circumstances resulted from not being able to evaluate Sidney until she was born* * *.

We acknowledge that certain physicians in this case initially asked the Millers to decide whether Sidney should be resuscitated some eleven hours before her birth. And certain physicians and Hospital administrators asked the Millers to consent to the subsequent plan developed to have a neonatologist present at Sidney's delivery to evaluate and possibly treat her. We agree that, whenever possible, obtaining consent in writing to evaluate a premature infant at birth and to render any warranted medical treatment is the best course of action. And physicians and hospitals should always strive to do so. But if such consent is not forthcoming, or is affirmatively denied, we decline to impose liability on a physician solely for providing life-sustaining treatment under emergent circumstances to a new-born infant without that consent.

* * *

There was testimony that Dr. Otero's resuscitative treatment caused Sidney's mental and physical infirmities. But there was also testimony that it did not and, in fact, the oxygen provided during the first days of Sidney's life prevented her from suffering even further brain damage. Although the jury found that the HCA's and the Hospital's negligence caused the "occurrence in question," it is unclear what was meant by the "occurrence in question."

If that phrase refers to Sidney's mental and physical infirmities, the Millers never sued Dr. Otero or any other physician. And there was no allegation that they negligently treated Sidney, which caused her infirmities. Instead, the Millers' only negligence claim was that HCA and the Hospital had policies, or lacked policies, and took actions that allowed Sidney to be treated without their consent. Thus, their negligence claim is based on the lack of consent before treatment, just like their battery claim.

If the phrase refers to Dr. Otero resuscitating Sidney against the Millers' wishes, it was not HCA's or the Hospital's policies, or lack thereof, that permitted Dr. Otero to treat Sidney without consent. Rather, it was the emergent circumstances that caused that to happen. Because Dr. Otero treated Sidney under emergent circumstances, he did not commit a battery. And because Dr. Otero did not commit a battery, HCA is not liable derivatively. Nor was the Hospital negligent for allowing Dr. Otero to treat Sidney under the circumstances without the Millers' consent.

The Millers raise additional arguments that we need not address, given our holding on the emergent circumstances exception. Similarly, HCA raises several arguments about why it cannot be held liable for the Millers' battery and negligence claims. Although we do not need to address those arguments to resolve this case, we do address two matters that the court of appeals discussed.

HCA argues that the federal "Baby Doe" regulations are part of Texas law and forbid any denial of medical care based on quality-of-life considerations. While we do not disagree with HCA's assertion as a general proposition, HCA cites [the Federal Child Abuse Amendments] as support for its contention that the Baby Doe regulations were "scrupulously followed in this case" and "faithful adherence to the public policy established by the regulations should not be thwarted through civil liability in damages...." But [that statute] provides that a federally-funded state must implement "procedures for responding to the reporting of medical neglect" which include authority, under State law, for the State child protective services system to pursue any legal remedies, including the authority to initiate legal proceedings in a court of competent jurisdiction, as may be necessary to prevent the withholding of medically indicated treatment from disabled infants with life-threatening conditions.

Assuming that this provision applies here, it states that Texas must provide a mechanism by which the child protective services system can initiate legal proceedings to prevent the withholding of medical treatment from infants. And the Family Code and Texas Administrative Code contain such provisions.

But it is undisputed that neither the Hospital nor HCA initiated or requested child protective services to initiate legal proceedings to override the Millers' "withholding of medical treatment" by refusing to consent to Sidney's treatment. Thus, the federal funding regulations appear to contemplate legal proceedings to override the lack of parental consent, and they do not answer the question of whether Dr. Otero committed a battery by providing treatment without doing so. Further, we agree with the court of appeals' conclusion that the disposition of that issue is governed by state law rather than federal funding authorities.

HCA also argues, and the court of appeals agreed, that parents can withhold "urgently-needed life-sustaining medical treatment" for their child only when the requirements of the Natural Death Act are satisfied—*i.e.*, only when the child is certifiably terminal. But the Act expressly states that it does not impair or supersede any legal right a person may have to withhold or withdraw life-sustaining treatment in a lawful manner. In any event, we need not decide this issue. The Millers asserted battery and negligence claims based on Dr. Otero treating Sidney without their consent. As we have discussed, when emergent circumstances exist, a physician cannot be held liable under either battery or negligence theories solely for providing life-sustaining medical treatment to a minor child without parental consent.

III. Conclusion

Dr. Otero provided life-sustaining treatment to Sidney under emergent circumstances as a matter of law. Those circumstances provide an exception to the general rule imposing liability on a physician for providing treatment to a minor child without first obtaining parental consent. Therefore, Dr. Otero did not commit a battery. And HCA cannot be held liable for the Millers' battery and negligence claims. We are not presented with and do not decide the question of whether the rule we have announced applies to adults. We affirm the court of appeals' judgment.

Notes and Questions

1. While a few babies born at Sidney's level of development and with Sidney's weight live normal lives, others die very quickly. For a description of the dilemma faced by Sidney's parents at her birth, see D. W. Linden and M. W. Doron, Eyes of Texas Fasten on Life, Death and the Premature Infant, New York Times, April 30, 2002, p. F5.

2. Dissenting Judge Amidei on the Court of Appeals formally considered and rejected the application of the emergency exception to this case:

The majority repeatedly refers to "urgently needed life sustaining treatment" and to the "emergency exception" without explaining how we can hold the "emergency exception" applies without a jury finding on the issue. I would hold as a matter of law there was no emergency. * * *

[The defendant hospitals] had alternative courses available to them early on. Particularly, the course of withholding life support (no resuscitation), as first suggested by the Millers' doctors, and with which the Millers agreed, could have been accomplished by a simple change of doctors. Another doctor holding a different opinion could have delivered the baby and not applied resuscitation. The [defendants] did not suggest to the Millers they could change doctors. There was ample time during which the [defendants] met and decided their chosen course of action without obtaining the Millers' consent. The urgency, if any, was due to the [defendant's] indecision and delay. Eleven hours elapsed after the Millers informed their doctors they wanted to take their original advice and not resuscitate the baby, if born alive. The [defendants] decided there was going to be resuscitation and performed it knowing the Millers were there and available to consult regarding the consent. This was not a medical emergency which excuses not having a consent. A true medical emergency is where a doctor must operate and no one is available to give the proper consent. The Millers were present in the hospital at all times leading up to the birth and resuscitation, but [defendants] chose not to try to change the Miller minds, change doctors, or try to obtain a court order. Anytime a group of doctors and a hospital administration has the luxury of multiple meetings to change the original doctors' medical opinions, without taking a more obvious course of action, there is no medical emergency.

In the event there was no emergency as a matter of law, it was still the appellant's burden to plead and prove as a defense an emergency or circumstances requiring the immediate resuscitative procedure without consent of the Millers. [ ] No defense questions were submitted to the jury. Specifically no question as to an emergency which would excuse having no consent was requested. [ ] Appellant's have not raised any issue regarding an emergency jury question on appeal. Therefore, we cannot consider whether an emergency existed which would imply consent and, in effect, deem the issue in favor [defendants]. * * *

The resulting conflict could have and should have been avoided by the [defendants]. [Defendants] were not entitled to immunity or a deemed finding that an emergency existed to excuse obtaining a consent. I would * * * affirm the trial court.

HCA v. Miller, 36 S.W.3d 187 (Tx. App. 2000). Who has the better of this argument? Should the "emergency exception" apply in this case, as the Texas Supreme Court decided, or is it improper to apply that doctrine when appropriate decision makers (in this case, the parents) are available?

3. Should there be a cut-off below which premature babies are not provided intensive treatment? Even if the parents want that treatment? How would you establish that line? Gestational age? Weight? Medical prognosis, considering both of those factors? Should the fact that a newborn *can* be kept alive be enough to assure that the newborn *will* be kept alive, whatever the parents might want? Instead, should we require that there be a chance that the newborn will lead a "normal life" before the parents' decision to forgo life-sustaining treatment at birth is overruled? What is a "normal life"? What if there is only a 10% chance of a "normal life"? A one percent chance? A one-tenth of one percent chance? What if the child will lead a "normal life" except for severe mental retardation? Except for severe heart disease?

4. What does it mean to describe a newborn infant as "terminal"? This term can be confusing when it is used to describe someone reaching the end of a long life; it is more difficult to apply it to a newborn. If a newborn is likely to die from birth anomalies—but not for years—is that newborn "terminal"? What if the newborn is likely to die in months? Weeks? If a newborn would die in the absence of highly invasive life-sustaining treatment, but could be kept alive for a year through the use of that machinery, is the newborn "terminal"? Might you want to define "terminal" differently for newborns than you do for others?

5. If you were consulted as counsel by someone in the position of the Miller family, what would you say? If the parents were committed to making sure that their baby did not go through the decade of medical intervention that Sidney received, what advice would you give them? Should you report them to the state child protective services office as parents about to medically neglect their child? On the other hand, could you seek a declaratory judgment that the hospital is not permitted to keep the infant alive against the wishes of the parents? How would you draft the complaint? The proposed order? Would it be appropriate for you to advise the parents that they should leave the country if they do not want all available medical resources used to keep their newborn alive?

6. How much of the Miller case is a result of the court's analysis of the underlying health care decision-making issue, and how much is driven by the fact that the case is a medical malpractice damages action? Would the analysis be the same if the issue came up in an action for injunctive relief or declaratory judgment? Should it be? Compare the analysis in HCA with the analysis in Matter of AB, 196 Misc.2d 940, 768 N.Y.S.2d 256 (Sup.Ct. 2003). See Vincent Gibbons et al., Legal and Institutional Responses to Medical Futility, 8 J. Health & Hosp. L. 1 (1997) (comparing results in futility cases pursued through malpractice litigation with results in those cases litigated in advance of the medical decision to be made).

7. The structure of the legal analysis regularly applied to these issues was first described in John A. Robertson, Involuntary Euthanasia of Defective Newborns: A Legal Analysis, 27 Stan.L.Rev. 213 (1975). See also Carl E. Schneider, Rights Discourse and Neonatal Euthanasia, 76 Cal. L. Rev. 151 (1988) and Robert F. Weir, Selective Nontreatment of Handicapped Newborns (1984). For an argument for not treating some impaired newborns, see Robert F. Weir and J.F. Bale, Selective Treatment of Neurologically Impaired Neonates, 7 Neurol. Clinics 807 (1989).

Problem: Conjoined Twins

In 2000, after a woman was diagnosed as carrying conjoined (i.e., "Siamese") twins, she left her home village of Xaghra on the Mediterranean island of Gozo to seek medical care at a hospital in the United Kingdom well known for its care of such birth anomalies. At the birth it was clear that one baby's heart and lungs were providing for the circulation in both babies. That baby, Jodie, was generally healthy, while her conjoined sibling, Mary, suffered from severe brain damage as well as other substantial disabilities. The doctors concluded that Jodie could lead a fairly normal life if she were separated from her sister and provided a series of other reconstructive surgeries. Of course, the separation would result in Mary's immediate death. Alternatively, the failure to separate the twins would result in both of their deaths within the next several months.

The devout Catholic parents denied consent for the surgery, saying "[w]e cannot begin to accept or contemplate that one of our children should die to enable the other one to survive." Others also pointed out that the decision to allow Mary to die during the separation surgery could be met with horror in Xaghra, and make it very difficult for the family to return home. The physicians, however, were distressed that both children would be allowed to die when one could be saved, and they sought an order from the court to authorize the separation surgery.

Would it be homicide to do the surgery with the certain knowledge that it would result in Mary's death? Is it medical neglect to deny consent to surgery which will save one child but result in the death of the second? Should the decision be left to the parents, or should the state intervene and exercise its *parens patriae* authority? What would you do if you were (1) a parent of these children? (2) the primary care physician for these children? (3) the judge before whom the case was presented? The court was well briefed in this case. In addition to counsel retained by the parents and the public health service, a guardian ad litem was appointed for each child. What position should each of those GALs take? If the same issue were to arise in the United States, would the Baby Doe regulations apply? Would the surgery be required, permitted (but not required), or forbidden by those regulations?

For a description of this case (and how it came out), see Marjorie Miller, Agonizing Over Who Lives, Dies, Los Angeles Times, September 11, 2000, page A–1, and Alexander MacLeod, Medical, Religious Values Clash Over Conjoined Twins, Christian Science Monitor, September 29, 2000, page 7.

VI. PHYSICIAN ASSISTED DEATH

A. THE CONSTITUTIONAL FRAMEWORK

WASHINGTON v. GLUCKSBERG

Supreme Court of the United States, 1997.
521 U.S. 702, 117 S.Ct. 2258, 138 L.Ed.2d 772.

REHNQUIST, C. J., delivered the opinion of the Court, in which O'CONNOR, SCALIA, KENNEDY, and THOMAS, JJ., joined. O'CONNOR, J., filed a concurring opinion, in which GINSBURG and BREYER, JJ., joined in part. STEVENS, J., SOUTER, J., GINSBURG, J., and BREYER, J., filed opinions concurring in the judgment.

CHIEF JUSTICE REHNQUIST delivered the opinion of the Court.

The question presented in this case is whether Washington's prohibition against "causing" or "aiding" a suicide offends the Fourteenth Amendment to the United States Constitution. We hold that it does not.

* * *

The plaintiffs assert [ ] "the existence of a liberty interest protected by the Fourteenth Amendment which extends to a personal choice by a mentally competent, terminally ill adult to commit physician-assisted suicide." [ ] Relying primarily on Planned Parenthood v. Casey, [ ] and Cruzan v. Director, Missouri Dept. of Health, [ ] the District Court agreed, [ ] and concluded that Washington's assisted-suicide ban is unconstitutional because it "places an undue burden on the exercise of [that] constitutionally protected liberty interest." [ ] The District Court also decided that the Washington statute violated the Equal Protection Clause's requirement that " 'all persons similarly situated . . . be treated alike.' "[ ]

A panel of the Court of Appeals for the Ninth Circuit reversed, emphasizing that "in the two hundred and five years of our existence no constitutional right to aid in killing oneself has ever been asserted and upheld by a court of final jurisdiction." [ ] The Ninth Circuit reheard the case en banc, reversed the panel's decision, and affirmed the District Court. [ ] Like the District Court, the en banc Court of Appeals emphasized our Casey and Cruzan decisions. [ ] The court also discussed what it described as "historical" and "current societal attitudes" toward suicide and assisted suicide, [ ] and concluded that "the Constitution encompasses a due process liberty interest in controlling the time and manner of one's death—that there is, in short, a constitutionally-recognized 'right to die.' "[ ] After "weighing and then balancing" this interest against Washington's various interests, the court held that the State's assisted-suicide ban was unconstitutional "as applied to terminally ill competent [ ] adults who wish to hasten their deaths with medication prescribed by their physicians." [ ] We granted certiorari [ ] and now reverse.

I

We begin, as we do in all due-process cases, by examining our Nation's history, legal traditions, and practices. [ ] In almost every State—indeed, in almost every western democracy—it is a crime to assist a suicide. The States' assisted-suicide bans are not innovations. Rather, they are longstanding expressions of the States' commitment to the protection and preservation of all human life. [ ] Indeed, opposition to and condemnation of suicide—and, therefore, of assisting suicide—are consistent and enduring themes of our philosophical, legal, and cultural heritages. [ ]

More specifically, for over 700 years, the Anglo—American common-law tradition has punished or otherwise disapproved of both suicide and assisting suicide. * * * [The Chief Justice then reviews the common law of England and the American colonies and states with regards to suicide, from the 13th century to the present.]

* * *

Attitudes toward suicide itself have changed since [the 13th Century prohibitions on suicide] * * * but our laws have consistently condemned, and continue to prohibit, assisting suicide. Despite changes in medical technology and notwithstanding an increased emphasis on the importance of end-of-life decisionmaking, we have not retreated from this prohibition. Against this backdrop of history, tradition, and practice, we now turn to respondents' constitutional claim.

II

The Due Process Clause guarantees more than fair process, and the "liberty" it protects includes more than the absence of physical restraint. [ ] The Clause also provides heightened protection against government interference with certain fundamental rights and liberty interests. [ ] In a long line of cases, we have held that, in addition to the specific freedoms protected by the Bill of Rights, the "liberty" specially protected by the Due Process Clause includes the rights to marry, [ ]; to have children, [ ]; to direct the education and upbringing of one's children, [ ]; to marital privacy, [ ]; to use contraception, [ ]; to bodily integrity, [ ] and to abortion, [ ]. We have also assumed, and strongly suggested, that the Due Process Clause protects the traditional right to refuse unwanted lifesaving medical treatment. [ ]

But we "have always been reluctant to expand the concept of substantive due process because guideposts for responsible decisionmaking in this unchartered area are scarce and open-ended." [ ] By extending constitutional protection to an asserted right or liberty interest, we, to a great extent, place the matter outside the arena of public debate and legislative action. We must therefore "exercise the utmost care whenever we are asked to break new ground in this field" [ ] lest the liberty protected by the Due Process Clause be subtly transformed into the policy preferences of the members of this Court [ ].

Our established method of substantive-due-process analysis has two primary features: First, we have regularly observed that the Due Process Clause specially protects those fundamental rights and liberties which are, objectively, "deeply rooted in this Nation's history and tradition" [ ] and "implicit in the concept of ordered liberty," such that "neither liberty nor justice would exist if they were sacrificed" [ ]. Second, we have required in substantive-due-process cases a "careful description" of the asserted fundamental liberty interest. [ ] Cruzan, supra, at 277–278. Our Nation's history, legal traditions, and practices thus provide the crucial "guideposts for responsible decision-making" [ ] that direct and restrain our exposition of the Due Process Clause. As we stated recently in Flores, the Fourteenth Amendment "forbids the government to infringe ... 'fundamental' liberty interests at all, no matter what process is provided, unless the infringement is narrowly tailored to serve a compelling state interest." [ ]

* * *

Turning to the claim at issue here, the Court of Appeals stated that "properly analyzed, the first issue to be resolved is whether there is a liberty interest in determining the time and manner of one's death" [ ] or, in other words, "is there a right to die?" [ ]. Similarly, respondents assert a "liberty to choose how to die" and a right to "control of one's final days," [ ] and describe the asserted liberty as "the right to choose a humane, dignified death" [ ] and "the liberty to shape death" [ ]. As noted above, we have a tradition of carefully formulating the interest at stake in substantive-due-process cases. For example, although Cruzan is often described as a "right to die" case [ ] we were, in fact, more precise: we assumed that the Constitution granted competent persons a "constitutionally protected right to refuse life-saving hydration and nutrition." [ ] The Washington statute at issue in this case prohibits "aiding another person to attempt suicide," [ ] and, thus, the question before us is whether the "liberty" specially protected by the Due Process Clause includes a right to commit suicide which itself includes a right to assistance in doing so.

* * * With this "careful description" of respondents' claim in mind, we turn to Casey and Cruzan.

[The Chief Justice next discusses the Cruzan case, where, he says,] "we assumed that the United States Constitution would grant a competent person a constitutionally protected right to refuse lifesaving hydration and nutrition."

* * *

The right assumed in Cruzan, however, was not simply deduced from abstract concepts of personal autonomy. Given the common-law rule that forced medication was a battery, and the long legal tradition protecting the decision to refuse unwanted medical treatment, our assumption was entirely consistent with this Nation's history and constitutional traditions. The decision to commit suicide with the assistance of another may be just as personal and profound as the decision to refuse unwanted medical treatment, but it has never enjoyed similar legal protection. Indeed, the two acts are widely and reasonably regarded as quite distinct. [ ] In Cruzan itself, we recognized that most States outlawed assisted suicide—and even more do today—and we certainly gave no intimation that the right to refuse unwanted medical treatment could be somehow transmuted into a right to assistance in committing suicide. [ ]

Respondents also rely on Casey. There, the Court's opinion concluded that "the essential holding of Roe v. Wade should be retained and once again reaffirmed." [ ] We held, first, that a woman has a right, before her fetus is viable, to an abortion "without undue interference from the State"; second, that States may restrict post-viability abortions, so long as exceptions are made to protect a woman's life and health; and third, that the State has legitimate interests throughout a pregnancy in protecting the health of the woman and the life of the unborn child. [ ] In reaching this conclusion, the opinion discussed in some detail this Court's substantive-due-process tradition of interpreting the Due Process Clause to protect certain fundamental rights and "personal decisions relating to marriage, procreation, contraception, family relationships, child rearing, and education," and noted that many of those rights and liberties "involve the most intimate and personal choices a person may make in a lifetime." [ ]

* * *

That many of the rights and liberties protected by the Due Process Clause sound in personal autonomy does not warrant the sweeping conclusion that any and all important, intimate, and personal decisions are so protected, [ ] and Casey did not suggest otherwise.

The history of the law's treatment of assisted suicide in this country has been and continues to be one of the rejection of nearly all efforts to permit it. That being the case, our decisions lead us to conclude that the asserted "right" to assistance in committing suicide is not a fundamental liberty interest protected by the Due Process Clause. The Constitution also requires, however, that Washington's assisted-suicide ban be rationally related to legitimate government interests. [ ] This requirement is unquestionably met here. As the court below recognized, [ ] Washington's assisted-suicide ban implicates a number of state interests. [ ]

First, Washington has an "unqualified interest in the preservation of human life."

* * *

Relatedly, all admit that suicide is a serious public-health problem, especially among persons in otherwise vulnerable groups. [ ] The State has an interest in preventing suicide, and in studying, identifying, and treating its causes. [ ]

* * *

The State also has an interest in protecting the integrity and ethics of the medical profession. * * * [T]he American Medical Association, like many other medical and physicians' groups, has concluded that "physician-assisted suicide is fundamentally incompatible with the physician's role as healer." [ ] And physician-assisted suicide could, it is argued, undermine the trust that is essential to the doctor-patient relationship by blurring the time-honored line between healing and harming. [ ]

Next, the State has an interest in protecting vulnerable groups—including the poor, the elderly, and disabled persons—from abuse, neglect, and mistakes. * * * [One respected state task force] warned that "legalizing physician-assisted suicide would pose profound risks to many individuals who are ill and vulnerable.... The risk of harm is greatest for the many individuals in our society whose autonomy and well-being are already compromised by poverty, lack of access to good medical care, advanced age, or membership in a stigmatized social group." [ ] If physician-assisted suicide were permitted, many might resort to it to spare their families the substantial financial burden of end-of-life health-care costs.

* * * The State's assisted-suicide ban reflects and reinforces its policy that the lives of terminally ill, disabled, and elderly people must be no less valued than the lives of the young and healthy, and that a seriously disabled person's suicidal impulses should be interpreted and treated the same way as anyone else's. [ ]

Finally, the State may fear that permitting assisted suicide will start it down the path to voluntary and perhaps even involuntary euthanasia. * * * [Justice Rehnquist then discussed how this fear could arise out of the practice in the Nertherlands.]

We need not weigh exactingly the relative strengths of these various interests. They are unquestionably important and legitimate, and Washington's ban on assisted suicide is at least reasonably related to their promotion and protection. We therefore hold that [ ] [the Washington ban on assisting suicide] does not violate the Fourteenth Amendment, either on its face or "as applied to competent, terminally ill adults who wish to hasten their deaths by obtaining medication prescribed by their doctors."[24] [ ]

* * *

Throughout the Nation, Americans are engaged in an earnest and profound debate about the morality, legality, and practicality of physician-assisted suicide. Our holding permits this debate to continue, as it should in a democratic society. The decision of the en banc Court of Appeals is reversed, and the case is remanded for further proceedings consistent with this opinion.

It is so ordered.

JUSTICE O'CONNOR, concurring [in both Glucksberg and Vacco].*

Death will be different for each of us. For many, the last days will be spent in physical pain and perhaps the despair that accompanies physical deterioration and a loss of control of basic bodily and mental functions. Some will seek medication to alleviate that pain and other symptoms.

---

24. Justice Stevens states that "the Court does conceive of respondents' claim as a facial challenge—addressing not the application of the statute to a particular set of plaintiffs before it, but the constitutionality of the statute's categorical prohibition...." [ ] We emphasize that we today reject the Court of Appeals' specific holding that the statute is unconstitutional "as applied" to a particular class. [ ] Justice Stevens agrees with this holding, [ ] but would not "foreclose the possibility that an individual plaintiff seeking to hasten her death, or a doctor whose assistance was sought, could prevail in a more particularized challenge," ibid. Our opinion does not absolutely foreclose such a claim. However, given our holding that the Due Process Clause of the Fourteenth Amendment does not provide heightened protection to the asserted liberty interest in ending one's life with a physician's assistance, such a claim would have to be quite different from the ones advanced by respondents here.

* Justice Ginsburg concurs in the Court's judgments substantially for the reasons stated in this opinion. Justice Breyer joins this opinion except insofar as it joins the opinions of the Court.

The Court frames the issue in this case as whether the Due Process Clause of the Constitution protects a "right to commit suicide which itself includes a right to assistance in doing so," [ ] and concludes that our Nation's history, legal traditions, and practices do not support the existence of such a right. I join the Court's opinions because I agree that there is no generalized right to "commit suicide." But respondents urge us to address the narrower question whether a mentally competent person who is experiencing great suffering has a constitutionally cognizable interest in controlling the circumstances of his or her imminent death. I see no need to reach that question in the context of the facial challenges to the New York and Washington laws at issue here. [ ] The parties and amici agree that in these States a patient who is suffering from a terminal illness and who is experiencing great pain has no legal barriers to obtaining medication, from qualified physicians, to alleviate that suffering, even to the point of causing unconsciousness and hastening death. [ ] In this light, even assuming that we would recognize such an interest, I agree that the State's interests in protecting those who are not truly competent or facing imminent death, or those whose decisions to hasten death would not truly be voluntary, are sufficiently weighty to justify a prohibition against physician-assisted suicide. [ ]

Every one of us at some point may be affected by our own or a family member's terminal illness. There is no reason to think the democratic process will not strike the proper balance between the interests of terminally ill, mentally competent individuals who would seek to end their suffering and the State's interests in protecting those who might seek to end life mistakenly or under pressure. As the Court recognizes, States are presently undertaking extensive and serious evaluation of physician-assisted suicide and other related issues. [ ] In such circumstances, "the ... challenging task of crafting appropriate procedures for safeguarding ... liberty interests is entrusted to the 'laboratory' of the States ... in the first instance." [ ]

In sum, there is no need to address the question whether suffering patients have a constitutionally cognizable interest in obtaining relief from the suffering that they may experience in the last days of their lives. There is no dispute that dying patients in Washington and New York can obtain palliative care, even when doing so would hasten their deaths. The difficulty in defining terminal illness and the risk that a dying patient's request for assistance in ending his or her life might not be truly voluntary justifies the prohibitions on assisted suicide we uphold here.

JUSTICE STEVENS, concurring in the judgments [in both Glucksberg and Vacco].

The Court ends its opinion with the important observation that our holding today is fully consistent with a continuation of the vigorous debate about the "morality, legality, and practicality of physician-assisted suicide" in a democratic society. [ ] I write separately to make it clear that there is also room for further debate about the limits that the Constitution places on the power of the States to punish the practice.

I

The morality, legality, and practicality of capital punishment have been the subject of debate for many years. In 1976, this Court upheld the constitutionality of the practice in cases coming to us from Georgia, Florida, and Texas. In those cases we concluded that a State does have the power to place a lesser value on some lives than on others; there is no absolute requirement that a State treat all human life as having an equal right to preservation. Because the state legislatures had sufficiently narrowed the category of lives that the State could terminate, and had enacted special procedures to ensure that the defendant belonged in that limited category, we concluded that the statutes were not unconstitutional on their face. In later cases coming to us from each of those States, however, we found that some applications of the statutes were unconstitutional.

Today, the Court decides that Washington's statute prohibiting assisted suicide is not invalid "on its face," that is to say, in all or most cases in which it might be applied. That holding, however, does not foreclose the possibility that some applications of the statute might well be invalid.

* * *

History and tradition provide ample support for refusing to recognize an open-ended constitutional right to commit suicide. Much more than the State's paternalistic interest in protecting the individual from the irrevocable consequences of an ill-advised decision motivated by temporary concerns is at stake. There is truth in John Donne's observation that "No man is an island." The State has an interest in preserving and fostering the benefits that every human being may provide to the community—a community that thrives on the exchange of ideas, expressions of affection, shared memories and humorous incidents as well as on the material contributions that its members create and support. The value to others of a person's life is far too precious to allow the individual to claim a constitutional entitlement to complete autonomy in making a decision to end that life. Thus, I fully agree with the Court that the "liberty" protected by the Due Process Clause does not include a categorical "right to commit suicide which itself includes a right to assistance in doing so." [ ]

But just as our conclusion that capital punishment is not always unconstitutional did not preclude later decisions holding that it is sometimes impermissibly cruel, so is it equally clear that a decision upholding a general statutory prohibition of assisted suicide does not mean that every possible application of the statute would be valid. A State, like Washington, that has authorized the death penalty and thereby has concluded that the sanctity of human life does not require that it always be preserved, must acknowledge that there are situations in which an interest in hastening death is legitimate. Indeed, not only is that interest sometimes legitimate, I am also convinced that there are times when it is entitled to constitutional protection.

II

In Cruzan [ ] the Court assumed that the interest in liberty protected by the Fourteenth Amendment encompassed the right of a terminally ill patient to direct the withdrawal of life-sustaining treatment. As the Court correctly observes today, that assumption "was not simply deduced from abstract concepts of personal autonomy." [ ] Instead, it was supported by the common-law tradition protecting the individual's general right to refuse unwanted medical treatment. [ ] We have recognized, however, that this common-law right to refuse treatment is neither absolute nor always sufficiently weighty to overcome valid countervailing state interests. * * *

Cruzan, however, was not the normal case. Given the irreversible nature of her illness and the progressive character of her suffering, Nancy Cruzan's interest in refusing medical care was incidental to her more basic interest in controlling the manner and timing of her death. In finding that her best interests would be served by cutting off the nourishment that kept her alive, the trial court did more than simply vindicate Cruzan's interest in refusing medical treatment; the court, in essence, authorized affirmative conduct that would hasten her death. When this Court reviewed the case and upheld Missouri's requirement that there be clear and convincing evidence establishing Nancy Cruzan's intent to have life-sustaining nourishment withdrawn, it made two important assumptions: (1) that there was a "liberty interest" in refusing unwanted treatment protected by the Due Process Clause; and (2) that this liberty interest did not "end the inquiry" because it might be outweighed by relevant state interests. [ ] I agree with both of those assumptions, but I insist that the source of Nancy Cruzan's right to refuse treatment was not just a common-law rule. Rather, this right is an aspect of a far broader and more basic concept of freedom that is even older than the common law. This freedom embraces, not merely a person's right to refuse a particular kind of unwanted treatment, but also her interest in dignity, and in determining the character of the memories that will survive long after her death. In recognizing that the State's interests did not outweigh Nancy Cruzan's liberty interest in refusing medical treatment, Cruzan rested not simply on the common-law right to refuse medical treatment, but—at least implicitly—on the even more fundamental right to make this "deeply personal decision," [ ].

* * *

While I agree with the Court that Cruzan does not decide the issue presented by these cases, Cruzan did give recognition, not just to vague, unbridled notions of autonomy, but to the more specific interest in making decisions about how to confront an imminent death. Although there is no absolute right to physician-assisted suicide, Cruzan makes it clear that some individuals who no longer have the option of deciding whether to live or to die because they are already on the threshold of death have a constitutionally protected interest that may outweigh the State's interest in preserving life at all costs. The liberty interest at stake in a case like this differs from, and is stronger than, both the common-law right to refuse medical treatment and the unbridled interest in deciding whether to live or die. It is an interest in deciding how, rather than whether, a critical threshold shall be crossed.

III

The state interests supporting a general rule banning the practice of physician-assisted suicide do not have the same force in all cases. First and foremost of these interests is the " 'unqualified interest in the preservation of human life' "[ ].

* * *. Although as a general matter the State's interest in the contributions each person may make to society outweighs the person's interest in

ending her life, this interest does not have the same force for a terminally ill patient faced not with the choice of whether to live, only of how to die. * * *

Similarly, the State's legitimate interests in preventing suicide, protecting the vulnerable from coercion and abuse, and preventing euthanasia are less significant in this context. I agree that the State has a compelling interest in preventing persons from committing suicide because of depression, or coercion by third parties. But the State's legitimate interest in preventing abuse does not apply to an individual who is not victimized by abuse, who is not suffering from depression, and who makes a rational and voluntary decision to seek assistance in dying.

* * *

The final major interest asserted by the State is its interest in preserving the traditional integrity of the medical profession. The fear is that a rule permitting physicians to assist in suicide is inconsistent with the perception that they serve their patients solely as healers. But for some patients, it would be a physician's refusal to dispense medication to ease their suffering and make their death tolerable and dignified that would be inconsistent with the healing role * * * .

* * * I do not * * * foreclose the possibility that an individual plaintiff seeking to hasten her death, or a doctor whose assistance was sought, could prevail in a more particularized challenge. Future cases will determine whether such a challenge may succeed.

IV

* * *

There may be little distinction between the intent of a terminally-ill patient who decides to remove her life-support and one who seeks the assistance of a doctor in ending her life; in both situations, the patient is seeking to hasten a certain, impending death. The doctor's intent might also be the same in prescribing lethal medication as it is in terminating life support. * * *

Thus, although the differences the majority notes in causation and intent between terminating life-support and assisting in suicide support the Court's rejection of the respondents' facial challenge, these distinctions may be inapplicable to particular terminally ill patients and their doctors. Our holding today in Vacco v. Quill that the Equal Protection Clause is not violated by New York's classification, just like our holding in Washington v. Glucksberg that the Washington statute is not invalid on its face, does not foreclose the possibility that some applications of the New York statute may impose an intolerable intrusion on the patient's freedom.

There remains room for vigorous debate about the outcome of particular cases that are not necessarily resolved by the opinions announced today. How such cases may be decided will depend on their specific facts. In my judgment, however, it is clear that the so-called "unqualified interest in the preservation of human life," [ ] is not itself sufficient to outweigh the interest in liberty that may justify the only possible means of preserving a dying patient's dignity and alleviating her intolerable suffering.

JUSTICE SOUTER, concurring in the judgment.

* * *

When the physicians claim that the Washington law deprives them of a right falling within the scope of liberty that the Fourteenth Amendment guarantees against denial without due process of law, they are not claiming some sort of procedural defect in the process through which the statute has been enacted or is administered. Their claim, rather, is that the State has no substantively adequate justification for barring the assistance sought by the patient and sought to be offered by the physician. Thus, we are dealing with a claim to one of those rights sometimes described as rights of substantive due process and sometimes as unenumerated rights, in view of the breadth and indeterminacy of the "due process" serving as the claim's textual basis. The doctors accordingly arouse the skepticism of those who find the Due Process Clause an unduly vague or oxymoronic warrant for judicial review of substantive state law, just as they also invoke two centuries of American constitutional practice in recognizing unenumerated, substantive limits on governmental action. * * *

* * *

[Justice Souter explained that he was adopting Justice Harlan's approach to the Constitutional evaluation and protection of unenumerated rights under the Due Process Clause, as articulated in his dissent in Poe v. Ullman.] My understanding of unenumerated rights in the wake of the Poe dissent and subsequent cases avoids the absolutist failing of many older cases without embracing the opposite pole of equating reasonableness with past practice described at a very specific level. [ ] That understanding begins with a concept of "ordered liberty," [ ] comprising a continuum of rights to be free from "arbitrary impositions and purposeless restraints" [ ].

* * *

This approach calls for a court to assess the relative "weights" or dignities of the contending interests, and to this extent the judicial method is familiar to the common law. Common law method is subject, however, to two important constraints in the hands of a court engaged in substantive due process review. First, such a court is bound to confine the values that it recognizes to those truly deserving constitutional stature, either to those expressed in constitutional text, or those exemplified by "the traditions from which [the Nation] developed," or revealed by contrast with "the traditions from which it broke." [ ]

The second constraint, again, simply reflects the fact that constitutional review, not judicial lawmaking, is a court's business here. The weighing or valuing of contending interests in this sphere is only the first step, forming the basis for determining whether the statute in question falls inside or outside the zone of what is reasonable in the way it resolves the conflict between the interests of state and individual.

* * *

The State has put forward several interests to justify the Washington law as applied to physicians treating terminally ill patients, even those competent to make responsible choices: protecting life generally [ ], discouraging suicide even if knowing and voluntary [ ], and protecting terminally ill patients from involuntary suicide and euthanasia, both voluntary and nonvoluntary [ ].

It is not necessary to discuss the exact strengths of the first two claims of justification in the present circumstances, for the third is dispositive for me. * * * [Justice Souter then explained why the Washington state legislature, on the basis of information now available, could have reasonably decided that a statute forbidding assisting suicide might protect terminally ill patients.]

* * *

The Court should accordingly stay its hand to allow reasonable legislative consideration. While I do not decide for all time that respondents' claim should not be recognized, I acknowledge the legislative institutional competence as the better one to deal with that claim at this time.

JUSTICE BREYER, concurring in the judgments [in both Glucksberg and Vacco].

I believe that Justice O'Connor's views, which I share, have greater legal significance than the Court's opinion suggests. I join her separate opinion, except insofar as it joins the majority. * * *

I agree with the Court in Vacco v. Quill [ ] that the articulated state interests justify the distinction drawn between physician assisted suicide and withdrawal of life-support. I also agree with the Court that the critical question in both of the cases before us is whether "the 'liberty' specially protected by the Due Process Clause includes a right" of the sort that the respondents assert. [ ] I do not agree, however, with the Court's formulation of that claimed "liberty" interest. The Court describes it as a "right to commit suicide with another's assistance." [ ] But I would not reject the respondents' claim without considering a different formulation, for which our legal tradition may provide greater support. That formulation would use words roughly like a "right to die with dignity." But irrespective of the exact words used, at its core would lie personal control over the manner of death, professional medical assistance, and the avoidance of unnecessary and severe physical suffering—combined.

* * *

I do not believe, however, that this Court need or now should decide whether or a not * * * [a right to die with dignity] is "fundamental." That is because, in my view, the avoidance of severe physical pain (connected with death) would have to comprise an essential part of any successful claim and because * * * the laws before us do not force a dying person to undergo that kind of pain. [ ] Rather, the laws of New York and of Washington do not prohibit doctors from providing patients with drugs sufficient to control pain despite the risk that those drugs themselves will kill. [ ] And under these circumstances the laws of New York and Washington would overcome any remaining significant interests and would be justified, regardless.

* * *

Were the legal circumstances different—for example, were state law to prevent the provision of palliative care, including the administration of drugs as needed to avoid pain at the end of life—then the law's impact upon serious and otherwise unavoidable physical pain (and accompanying death) would be more directly at issue. And as JUSTICE O'CONNOR suggests, the Court might have to revisit its conclusions in these cases.

* * *

VACCO v. QUILL

Supreme Court of the United States, 1997.
521 U.S. 793, 117 S.Ct. 2293, 138 L.Ed.2d 834.

CHIEF JUSTICE REHNQUIST delivered the opinion of the Court.

In New York, as in most States, it is a crime to aid another to commit or attempt suicide, but patients may refuse even lifesaving medical treatment. The question presented by this case is whether New York's prohibition on assisting suicide therefore violates the Equal Protection Clause of the Fourteenth Amendment. We hold that it does not.

* * * Respondents, and three gravely ill patients who have since died, sued the State's Attorney General in the United States District Court. They urged that because New York permits a competent person to refuse life-sustaining medical treatment, and because the refusal of such treatment is "essentially the same thing" as physician-assisted suicide, New York's assisted-suicide ban violates the Equal Protection Clause. [ ]

The District Court disagreed * * *.

The Court of Appeals for the Second Circuit reversed. [ ] The court determined that, despite the assisted-suicide ban's apparent general applicability, "New York law does not treat equally all competent persons who are in the final stages of fatal illness and wish to hasten their deaths," because "those in the final stages of terminal illness who are on life-support systems are allowed to hasten their deaths by directing the removal of such systems; but those who are similarly situated, except for the previous attachment of life-sustaining equipment, are not allowed to hasten death by self-administering prescribed drugs." [ ] The Court of Appeals then examined whether this supposed unequal treatment was rationally related to any legitimate state interests, and concluded that "to the extent that [New York's statutes] prohibit a physician from prescribing medications to be self-administered by a mentally competent, terminally-ill person in the final stages of his terminal illness, they are not rationally related to any legitimate state interest." [ ] We granted certiorari [ ] and now reverse.

The Equal Protection Clause commands that no State shall "deny to any person within its jurisdiction the equal protection of the laws." This provision creates no substantive rights. [ ] Instead, it embodies a general rule that States must treat like cases alike but may treat unlike cases accordingly. [ ] If a legislative classification or distinction "neither burdens a fundamental right nor targets a suspect class, we will uphold [it] so long as it bears a rational relation to some legitimate end." [ ]

New York's statutes outlawing assisting suicide affect and address matters of profound significance to all New Yorkers alike. They neither infringe fundamental rights nor involve suspect classifications. [ ] These laws are therefore entitled to a "strong presumption of validity." [ ]

On their faces, neither New York's ban on assisting suicide nor its statutes permitting patients to refuse medical treatment treat anyone differently than anyone else or draw any distinctions between persons. Everyone, regardless of physical condition, is entitled, if competent, to refuse unwanted lifesaving medical treatment; no one is permitted to assist a suicide. Generally speaking, laws that apply evenhandedly to all "unquestionably comply" with the Equal Protection Clause. [ ]

The Court of Appeals, however, concluded that some terminally ill people—those who are on life-support systems—are treated differently than those who are not, in that the former may "hasten death" by ending treatment, but the latter may not "hasten death" through physician-assisted suicide. [ ] This conclusion depends on the submission that ending or refusing lifesaving medical treatment "is nothing more nor less than assisted suicide." [ ] Unlike the Court of Appeals, we think the distinction between assisting suicide and withdrawing life-sustaining treatment, a distinction widely recognized and endorsed in the medical profession and in our legal traditions, is both important and logical; it is certainly rational. [ ]

The distinction comports with fundamental legal principles of causation and intent. First, when a patient refuses life-sustaining medical treatment, he dies from an underlying fatal disease or pathology; but if a patient ingests lethal medication prescribed by a physician, he is killed by that medication. [ ]

Furthermore, a physician who withdraws, or honors a patient's refusal to begin, life-sustaining medical treatment purposefully intends, or may so intend, only to respect his patient's wishes and "to cease doing useless and futile or degrading things to the patient when [the patient] no longer stands to benefit from them." [ ] The same is true when a doctor provides aggressive palliative care; in some cases, painkilling drugs may hasten a patient's death, but the physician's purpose and intent is, or may be, only to ease his patient's pain. A doctor who assists a suicide, however, "must, necessarily and indubitably, intend primarily that the patient be made dead." [ ] Similarly, a patient who commits suicide with a doctor's aid necessarily has the specific intent to end his or her own life, while a patient who refuses or discontinues treatment might not. [ ]

The law has long used actors' intent or purpose to distinguish between two acts that may have the same result. [ ] Put differently, the law distinguishes actions taken "because of" a given end from actions taken "in spite of" their unintended but foreseen consequences. [ ]

Given these general principles, it is not surprising that many courts, including New York courts, have carefully distinguished refusing life-sustaining treatment from suicide. * * *

Similarly, the overwhelming majority of state legislatures have drawn a clear line between assisting suicide and withdrawing or permitting the refusal of unwanted lifesaving medical treatment by prohibiting the former and permitting the latter. [ ] And "nearly all states expressly disapprove of suicide and assisted suicide either in statutes dealing with durable powers of attorney in health-care situations, or in 'living will' statutes." [ ] Thus, even as the

States move to protect and promote patients' dignity at the end of life, they remain opposed to physician-assisted suicide.

* * *

This Court has also recognized, at least implicitly, the distinction between letting a patient die and making that patient die. In Cruzan [ ] we concluded that "the principle that a competent person has a constitutionally protected liberty interest in refusing unwanted medical treatment may be inferred from our prior decisions," and we assumed the existence of such a right for purposes of that case [ ]. But our assumption of a right to refuse treatment was grounded not, as the Court of Appeals supposed, on the proposition that patients have a general and abstract "right to hasten death," [ ] but on well established, traditional rights to bodily integrity and freedom from unwanted touching [ ]. In fact, we observed that "the majority of States in this country have laws imposing criminal penalties on one who assists another to commit suicide." [ ] Cruzan therefore provides no support for the notion that refusing life-sustaining medical treatment is "nothing more nor less than suicide."

For all these reasons, we disagree with respondents' claim that the distinction between refusing lifesaving medical treatment and assisted suicide is "arbitrary" and "irrational."[11] Granted, in some cases, the line between the two may not be clear, but certainty is not required, even were it possible. Logic and contemporary practice support New York's judgment that the two acts are different, and New York may therefore, consistent with the Constitution, treat them differently. By permitting everyone to refuse unwanted medical treatment while prohibiting anyone from assisting a suicide, New York law follows a longstanding and rational distinction.

New York's reasons for recognizing and acting on this distinction—including prohibiting intentional killing and preserving life; preventing suicide; maintaining physicians' role as their patients' healers; protecting vulnerable people from indifference, prejudice, and psychological and financial pressure to end their lives; and avoiding a possible slide towards euthanasia—are discussed in greater detail in our opinion in Glucksberg, ante. These valid and important public interests easily satisfy the constitutional requirement that a legislative classification bear a rational relation to some legitimate end.

The judgment of the Court of Appeals is reversed.

* * *

Justice Souter, concurring in the judgment.

Even though I do not conclude that assisted suicide is a fundamental right entitled to recognition at this time, I accord the claims raised by the patients and physicians in this case and Washington v. Glucksberg a high degree of importance, requiring a commensurate justification. [ ] The reasons

---

11. Respondents also argue that the State irrationally distinguishes between physician-assisted suicide and "terminal sedation," a process respondents characterize as "inducing barbiturate coma and then starving the person to death." [ ] Petitioners insist, however, that "'although proponents of physician-assisted suicide and euthanasia contend that terminal sedation is covert physician-assisted suicide or euthanasia, the concept of sedating pharmacotherapy is based on informed consent and the principle of double effect.'"[ ] Just as a State may prohibit assisting suicide while permitting patients to refuse unwanted lifesaving treatment, it may permit palliative care related to that refusal, which may have the foreseen but unintended "double effect" of hastening the patient's death. [ ]

that lead me to conclude in Glucksberg that the prohibition on assisted suicide is not arbitrary under the due process standard also support the distinction between assistance to suicide, which is banned, and practices such as termination of artificial life support and death-hastening pain medication, which are permitted. I accordingly concur in the judgment of the Court.

* * *

Notes and Questions

1. The Ninth Circuit's *en banc* decision and an extraordinarily diverse and thoughtful set of opinions in Glucksberg can be found at Compassion in Dying v. Washington, 79 F.3d 790 (9th Cir.1996). The en banc court reversed a 2–1 decision of the original panel, which also included an impassioned opinion on each side of the issue. See 49 F.3d 586 (9th Cir.1995). The meticulously organized district court opinion in the Compassion in Dying case is reported at 850 F.Supp. 1454 (W.D.Wash.1994). The Second Circuit's opinion in Quill v. Vacco can be found at 80 F.3d 716 (2nd Cir.1996).

2. These cases generated many highly emotional responses. Although the Supreme Court's unanimous decision brought a semblance of propriety back to the discussion of these issues, supporters and opponents of physician assisted death continue to attack the arguments of their opponents—and, as in the case of the abortion debate—they continue to attack their opponents, too. Some of the commentary on the Ninth Circuit opinions was especially personal. Judge Reinhardt (who wrote the primary decision finding the Washington law to be unconstitutional) was roundly criticized for his ACLU connections, which, some said, made it impossible for him to fairly decide the case. On the other hand, Judge Noonan (who would have upheld the statute for the first panel) had been criticized for his right-to-life connections which, others argued, made it impossible for *him* to be impartial. Should judges recuse themselves from cases involving these difficult and controversial bioethics issues if they have deeply held personal beliefs about the underlying practice—here physician assisted suicide? Does it make a difference if they were members (or officers, or high ranking employees) of organizations which have taken explicit positions on the underlying issues? On the particular case in litigation? Should they recuse themselves if the issue is one on which the religion to which they subscribe has taken a formal position? Should Catholic judges recuse themselves from abortion and physician assisted death cases? Should judges who belong to the United Church of Christ (which has been strongly pro-choice for over 25 years) recuse themselves from abortion cases? Should the member of a congregation whose rabbi helped organize a voting rights march recuse himself from all voting rights cases? Is their obligation any different from the obligation of a judge who is a dedicated ACLU (or American Family Association, or Republican Party) member and who confronts a case upon which the ACLU (or the American Family Association, or the Republican Party) has taken a firm position? The issue of whether a judge should recuse himself because of his religious affiliation is raised almost exclusively with regard to Catholic judges. Why do you think that is the case?

3. Judge Calabresi concurred in the Second Circuit decision in the Quill case, but on entirely different grounds. Depending on the theory of statutory construction that he had explained fifteen years earlier in his text, A Common Law for the Age of Statutes (1982), he concluded that the history of the New York manslaughter statute suggested that there was no reason to believe that its framers ever intended it to apply to cases of competent terminally ill patients seeking aid in dying from physicians. Still, as he pointed out, "neither Cruzan, nor

Casey, nor the language of our Constitution, nor our constitutional tradition clearly makes these laws invalid."

So, what should the court do with a "highly suspect" but "not clearly invalid" statute that may no longer serve the purposes for which it was originally promulgated? The answer, according to Judge Calabresi, is the "constitutional remand."

> I contend that when a law is neither plainly unconstitutional * * * nor plainly constitutional, the courts ought not to decide the ultimate validity of that law without current and clearly expressed statements by the people or their elected officials of the state involved. It is my further contention, that, absent such statements, the courts have frequently struck down such laws, while leaving open the possibility of reconsideration if appropriate statements were subsequently made.

Thus, Judge Calabresi finds the New York statute unconstitutional, but he "takes no position" on whether verbatim identical statutes would be constitutional "were New York to reenact them while articulating the reasons for the distinctions it makes* * *." Is this a reasonable way to deal with ancient statutes effectively criminalizing physician assisted death? Is this argument still available to those challenging state statutes that forbid assisting suicide?

4. Why has physician assisted death become such a subject of interest over the last two decades? Daniel Callahan has a suggestion:

> The power of medicine to extend life under poor circumstances is now widely and increasingly feared. The combined powers of a quasi-religious tradition of respect for individual life and a secular tradition of relentless medical progress creates a bias toward aggressive, often unremitting treatment that appears unstoppable.
>
> How is control to be gained? For many the answer seems obvious and unavoidable: active euthanasia and assisted suicide.

19 Hastings Center Rep., Special Supplement, 4 (Jan./Feb. 1989). Dr. Callahan goes on to suggest that those who strongly oppose active euthanasia, as he does, ought to focus on "dampening * * * the push for medical progress, a return to older traditions of caring as an alternative to curing, and a willingness to accept decline and death as part of the human conditions (not a notable feature of American medicine)." Id. Is he right? It used to be that people were afraid that if they went to the hospital they would die there. Now people are afraid that if they go to the hospital they will be kept alive there. Is it this fear that gives rise to our current interest in euthanasia?

5. Nothing has done more to keep the spotlight on physician assisted death issues than the actions of Dr. Jack Kevorkian. Dr. Kevorkian employed a "suicide machine" that allowed patients—sometimes young and still relatively healthy patients—to end their lives. Dr. Kevorkian chose Michigan for his practice because assisted suicide *per se* was not a crime in Michigan. On the other hand, an early Michigan case, People v. Roberts, 211 Mich. 187, 178 N.W. 690 (1920), had determined that assisting suicide could constitute murder. In that case a husband pleaded guilty to murder after he placed a poisonous mixture next to his wife, who was suffering from multiple sclerosis, was in excruciating pain, and had begged her husband to help her end her misery. The Michigan court determined that murder by poison, a form of first degree murder, was the proper charge.

In 1990 prosecutors in Michigan indicted Dr. Kevorkian on homicide charges, which were subsequently dismissed. As a direct result of Kevorkian's activities, in

1992 the Michigan legislature created the crime of assistance to suicide, which rendered one criminally liable if one "provide[d] the physical means by which the other person attempt[ed] or commit[ted] suicide" or participated in the physical act of the suicide. Mich. Comp. Laws Ann. section 752–1027. The legislature created this crime with an expiration date to give the state the opportunity to work out this issue without the sense of thoughtless urgency that prevailed in 1992. The statute has since expired.

Just before Michigan's new assisted suicide statute became law, Dr. Kevorkian was again indicted—this time for murder and for the delivery of drugs for an unauthorized purpose. Dr. Kevorkian was bound over for trial on the murder charge, which was subsequently dismissed by the circuit court. As soon as the new assisted suicide statute was passed several terminally ill patients and some health care providers brought a declaratory judgment action seeking to have the new statute declared void because it violated due process, because it passed the legislature in a bill that did not have "a single object," because the purpose of the bill changed during the course of its consideration in the Michigan legislature, and because it was inadequately titled, all in violation of the Michigan constitution. Ultimately the circuit court found the statute unconstitutional in the declaratory judgment action. It was not long before Dr. Kevorkian was charged under the new assisted suicide statute—twice, in fact, once in Wayne County and once in Oakland County. In each case the circuit court dismissed the action because the court found the new assisted suicide statute to be unconstitutional.

All four cases (the second murder case, the two assisted suicide cases and the declaratory judgment case) were appealed to the Michigan Supreme Court, which consolidated them. In December of 1994 a divided Michigan Supreme Court issued a brief *per curiam* memorandum opinion and a series of separate opinions dealing with the various issues raised by the four appeals. The court decided that (1) there was no technical problem in the form of the bill passed by the legislature (by unanimous vote), (2) a criminal statute penalizing assisted suicide does not violate the United States Constitution (5–2 vote), (3) *People v. Roberts* should be over-ruled; merely intentionally providing the means for another to commit suicide does not, as a general matter, constitute murder (5–2 vote) and (4) whether there was sufficient evidence to prosecute Dr. Kevorkian for murder should be reconsidered by the circuit court (4–3 vote). See People v. Kevorkian, 447 Mich. 436, 527 N.W.2d 714 (1994) for the lengthy, thoughtful and heartfelt opinions on all sides of all of these issues.

Another prosecution for murder ended in a jury verdict of acquittal for Dr. Kevorkian, as did a 1996 prosecution for violation of the Michigan common law crime of assisting suicide (by 1996 he had to be charged under the common law because the Michigan statute had expired).

Finally, on March 26, 1999 Dr. Kevorkian was convicted of second-degree murder after a very short trial in which he represented himself. While past cases had involved Dr. Kevorkian's use of a suicide machine which was actually operated by his client (patient? victim?), in this case he injected a lethal drug directly into Thomas Youk, a 52 year old man suffering from amyotrophic lateral sclerosis (Lou Gehrig's disease). What is more, he filmed the entire process, which was then shown to a national audience on "60 Minutes," the CBS news show, in November, 1998.

Dr. Kevorkian was originally charged with first-degree murder and assisted suicide. The trial judge ruled that evidence of Mr. Youk's suffering, which would be provided by the testimony of his family members, would be relevant and admissible on the assisted suicide charge, but not on the murder charge. The prosecutor decided to drop the assisted suicide charge to keep out that kind of evidence, which had played so well in Dr. Kevorkian's earlier trials. The jury apparently found no premeditation, making the second degree murder conviction the most serious available. Dr. Kevorkian was also found guilty of delivery of a controlled substance.

Leading supporters of euthanasia were concerned by the conviction. The executive director of the Hemlock Society said, "To call it murder is barbaric. It highlights the necessity to change the law over the country * * * so that a compassionate physician can help a suffering patient die." One leader of a disability group expressed satisfaction that this "serial killer" of the disabled had finally been brought to justice. For an account of the trial, see Pam Belluck, Dr. Kevorkian is a Murderer, The Jury Finds, New York Times, March 27, 1999, at A–1.

6. Physician assisted death may constitute murder, manslaughter, some other form of homicide, or no crime at all, depending on the state statute and the nature of the physician's act. While most states criminalize assisting suicide, it is not always easy to determine which acts are prohibited by those statutes. Consider one representative statute, the California statute criminalizing aiding, advising or encouraging suicide.

> Every person who deliberately aids, or advises, or encourages another to commit suicide, is guilty of a felony.

Cal. Pen. Code § 401.

Would this statute apply to a physician who clamps a feeding tube? To a physician who withholds antibiotics? To a physician who prescribes morphine to a patient in persistent pain, and provides enough tablets to take a lethal dose? To a physician who prescribes that same morphine and tells the patient what would constitute a lethal dose? To those who publish instructions on how to commit suicide for the use of those who are terminally ill or in excruciating pain? To those who make generally available information about how to commit suicide at home? For an interesting application of the statute to those who play rock music with lyrics that suggest that suicide is acceptable, see McCollum v. CBS, Inc., 202 Cal.App.3d 989, 249 Cal.Rptr. 187 (1988).

7. Much of the American discussion on the propriety of allowing physician assisted death focuses upon the Netherlands, where euthanasia is now legal under some circumstances. The Dutch experience is often unfairly distilled into the polemics of those who approve—or disapprove—of the process, and who thus believe that the United States should follow the successful Dutch example—or be dissuaded by its failure. An honest account of the state of euthanasia in the Netherlands is provided by a long time scholar of that issue:

Margaret Pabst Battin, A Dozen Caveats Concerning The Discussion
of Euthanasia in the Netherlands*
in M.P. Battin, the Least Worst Death 130 (1994).

*The Institutional Circumstances of Euthanasia in
the Netherlands are Easily Misunderstood*

Although many American observers of Dutch euthanasia risk misinterpreting many features of this practice, a particularly frequent error arises from failing to

---

* Professor Battin's thoughtful account of the Dutch process was written in 1994, when the country was engaged in debate over whether the practice of physician assisted death

appreciate differences between health-care delivery systems and other social institutions in the Netherlands and those in the United States. In the United States virtually all physician care is provided in a professional or institutional setting: an office, clinic, care facility, or hospital. By contrast, most primary care in the Netherlands is provided in the patient's home or in the physician's home office by the *huisarts*, the general practitioner or family physician. The family physician, who typically serves a practice of about 2,300 people and is salaried on a capitation basis rather than paid on a fee-for-service basis, typically lives in the neighborhood and makes frequent house calls when a patient is ill. This provides not only closer, more personal contact between physician and patient but also an unparalleled opportunity for the physician to observe features of the patient's domestic circumstances, including any family support or pressures that might be relevant in a request for euthanasia.

Furthermore, all Dutch have a personal physician: this is a basic feature of how primary care is provided within the Netherlands' national health system. While euthanasia is sometimes performed in hospitals (about 700 of the 2,300 cases), usually when the family physician has been unable to control the patient's pain and it has been necessary to readmit the patient to the hospital, or when the patient has had extensive hospital care and feels most "at home" there, and while most hospitals now have protocols for doing so, the large majority of cases take place in the patient's home, typically after hospitalization and treatment have proved ineffective in arresting a terminal condition and the patient has come home to die. In these settings, euthanasia is most often performed by the physician who has been the long-term primary care provider for the family, and it is performed in the presence of the patient's family and others whom the patient may request, such as the visiting nurse or the pastor, but outside public view. Yet the (non) institutional circumstances of euthanasia in the Netherlands (about 40 percent of Dutch deaths occur at home, and 48 percent of cancer deaths), in the United States as many as 85 percent of deaths occur in a hospital or other health-care institution, where attendance by a long-term family physician is far less frequently the case.

* * *

The Dutch Don't Want to Defend Everything

The Dutch are sometimes accused of being self-serving or, alternatively, of being self-deceived in their efforts to defend the practice of euthanasia. To be sure, not all Dutch accept the practice. There is a vocal group of about a thousand physicians adamantly opposed to it, and there is some opposition among the public and within specific political parties (in particular, the Christian Democratic Party, which has for years controlled the Netherlands coalition government) and religious groups (especially the Catholic church). Yet the practice is supported by a majority of the Dutch populace * * * as well as a majority of Dutch physicians. Of

should be decriminalized rather than simply legally tolerated (but, still, technically criminal). In 1998 the Dutch law was changed to provide for reporting of assisted deaths to a public registrar rather than to a prosecutor in order to separate the medical process from the formal criminal process. In 2001, the practice became legal. The law essentially adopts the Royal Dutch Medical Association's standards, and it provides that an election of physician assisted death be made voluntarily, by a fully informed patient, without suggestion by the physician, when that patient is confronting

unbearable suffering, and after physician consultation with one other physician. The new law does not require that the patient be terminally ill. A provision in an earlier draft that would have permitted children as young as 12 to elect a physician assisted death was omitted in the final version; the unencumbered choice is available only to those over 16.

You should read Professor Battin's description of this process as an historical one, describing the law and practice during the debate that gave rise to the new legislation.

physicians interviewed for the Remmelink study [the leading neutral report on the practice in the Netherlands], 54 percent said they had practiced euthanasia at the explicit and persistent request of the patient or had assisted in suicide at least once (62 percent of the general practitioners, 44 percent of specialists, and 12 percent of nursing home physicians), and only 4 percent said they would neither perform euthanasia nor refer a patient to a physician who would. In the words of the Remmelink Commission's comment on the report, "a large majority of physicians in the Netherlands see euthanasia as an accepted element of medical practice under certain circumstances."

But this is not to say that the Dutch seek to whitewash the practice. They are disturbed by reports of cases that do not fit the guidelines and are not explained by other moral considerations although these may be quite infrequent. Of the approximately 1,000 cases of active termination in which there was no explicit, current request * * * 36 percent of patients were competent, the physician knew the patient for an extended period (on average, 2.4 years for a specialist physician, or 7.2 years for a *huisarts* or general practitioner), and in 84 percent life was shortened somewhere between a few hours and a week. Because there was no current, explicit request, these cases are sometimes described in the United States as coldblooded murder, yet most are explained by other moral considerations. Of these 1,000 cases, * * *, about 600 did involve some form of antecedent discussion of euthanasia with the patient. These ranged from a rather vague earlier expression of a wish for euthanasia, as in comments like "If I cannot be saved anymore, you must give me something," or "Doctor, please don't let me suffer for too long," to much more extensive discussions, yet still short of an explicit request. (Thus, these cases are best understood in a way that approximates them to advance-directive cases in other situations.) In all other cases, discussion with the patient was no longer possible. In almost all of the remaining 400 cases, there was neither an antecedent nor current request from the patient, but at the time of euthanasia—possibly with a few exceptions—the patient was very close to death, incapable of communication, and suffering grievously. For the most part, this occurred when the patient underwent unexpectedly rapid deterioration in the final stages of a terminal illness. (These cases are best understood as cases of mercy killing, with emphasis on the motivation of mercy.) In these cases, * * *, "the decision to hasten death was then nearly always taken after consultation with the family, nurses, or one or more colleagues." Most Dutch also defend these cases, though as critics point out, the danger here is that the determination of what counts as intolerable suffering in these cases is essentially up to the doctor.

Direct termination of life is also performed in a handful of pediatric cases, about ten a year, usually involving newborns with extremely severe deficits who are not in the ICU and from whom, therefore, life-prolonging treatment cannot be withdrawn. These cases are regarded as difficult and controversial. Equally controversial—and as rare or rarer—are cases concerning patients in permanent coma or persistent vegetative state; patients whose suffering, though intolerable and incurable, is mental rather than physical; and patients who have made explicit requests for euthanasia by means of advance directives, but after becoming incompetent no longer appear to be suffering.

[There is also some] suggestion, though no clear evidence, that there may be a small fraction of cases in which there is no apparent choice by the patient and in which a merciful end of suffering for a patient *in extremis* is not the issue. These cases do disturb the Dutch: they are regarded as highly problematic, and it is clearly intended that if they occur, they should be stopped. * * *, [I]nterviews with physicians revealed only two instances, both from the early 1980s, in which a fully competent patient was suffering severely. * * * [T]he physician in one of these cases indicated that under present-day circumstances, with increased openness about these issues, he probably would have initiated more extensive consultations. There is no evidence of any patient being put to death *against* his or her expressed or implied wish.

* * *

The Dutch See the Role of Law Rather Differently

Not only is Dutch law a civil law system rather than a common law one; not only does it contain the distinctive Dutch doctrine involving practices that are statutorily illegal but *gedogen*, or tolerated, by the public prosecutor, the courts, or both; and not only does it involve very little medical malpractice activity, but the Dutch also tend to see law as appropriately formulated at a different point in the evolution of a social practice. Americans, it is sometimes said, *begin* to address a social issue by first making laws and then challenging them in court to fine-tune and adjust them; the Dutch, on the other hand, allow a practice to evolve by "tolerating" but not legalizing it, and only when the practice is adequately controlled—when they've got it right, so to speak—is a law made to regulate the practice as it has evolved. That the Dutch do not yet have a law fully shaped to accommodate their open practice of euthanasia may not show, as some have claimed, that they are ambivalent about the practice, but perhaps rather that they are waiting for the practice to evolve to a point where it is under adequate, acceptable control, at which time it will be appropriate to finally revise the law.

* * *

The Economic Circumstances of Euthanasia in the Netherlands are also Easily Misunderstood

The Netherlands' national system of mixed public and private health insurance provides extensive care to all patients—including all hospitalization, nursing home care, home care, and the services of physicians, nurses, physical therapists, nutritionists, counselors, and other care providers, both in institutional settings and in the home. Virtually all residents of the Netherlands, 99.4 percent, are comprehensively insured for all medical expenses (those who are not are those who, with incomes above a stipulated level, are wealthy enough to self-insure), and 100 percent are insured for the costs of long-term illness. All insurance, both public and private, has a mandated minimum level that is very ample. Americans who raise the issue of whether some patients' requests for euthanasia are motivated by financial pressures or by fear of the effect of immense medical costs to their families are committing perhaps the most frequent mistake made by American observers: to assume that the choices of patients in the Netherlands are subject to the same pressures that the choices of patients in the United States would be. While there may be some administrative changes to the national health insurance system in the Netherlands in the near future, cost pressures on the system as a whole are met by rationing and queuing (neither currently severe), not by exclusion of individuals from coverage or by increased costs to patients. The costs to oneself or one's family of an extended illness, something that might make euthanasia attractive to a patient in the United States, are something the Dutch patient need not consider.

Differences in Social Circumstances Often Go Unnoticed

In American discussions of euthanasia, considerable emphasis is placed on slippery slope arguments, pointing out risks of abuse, particularly with reference to the handicapped, the poor, racial minorities, and other who might seem to be ready targets for involuntary euthanasia. The Netherlands, however, exhibits much less disparity between rich and poor, has much less racial prejudice, virtually no uninsured people, and very little homelessness. These differences underscore the difficulty both of treating the Netherlands as a model for the United States in advocating the legalization of euthanasia and also of assessing the plausibility of slippery slope arguments opposing legalization in the United States.

8. Might women, specifically, be put at risk in a society that permits physician assisted death? That is the argument that is made by Susan Wolf, who regularly has argued that women's requests should be respected by the health care system and that requests to remove life sustaining treatment should be heeded.

> As I have argued, there is a strong right to be free of unwanted bodily invasion. Indeed, for women, a long history of being harmed specifically through unwanted bodily invasion such as rape presents particularly compelling reasons for honoring a woman's refusal of invasion and effort to maintain bodily intactness. When it comes to the question of whether women's suicides should be aided, however, or whether women should be actively killed, there is no right to command physician assistance, the dangers of permitting assistance are immense, and the history of women's subordination cuts the other way. Women have historically been seen as fit objects for bodily invasion, self-sacrifice, and death at the hands of others. The task before us is to challenge all three.

> Certainly some women, including some feminists, will see this problem differently. That may be especially true of women who feel in control of their lives, are less subject to subordination by age or race or wealth, and seek yet another option to add to their many. I am not arguing that women should lose control of their lives and selves. Instead, I am arguing that when women request to be put to death or ask help in taking their own lives, they become part of a broader social dynamic of which we have properly learned to be extremely wary. These are fatal practices. We can no longer ignore questions of gender or the insights of feminist argument.

Susan M. Wolf, Gender, Feminism and Death: Physician Assisted Suicide and Euthanasia, in S.M. Wolf, Feminism & Bioethics: Beyond Reproduction 282, 308 (1996).

9. Organized medical groups generally oppose any medical participation in euthanasia or assisted death. See AMA Council on Ethical and Judicial Affairs, Code of Medical Ethics, Current Opinion 2.21, Euthanasia, and Opinion 2.211, Physician–Assisted Death (1998–99 ed.). Is this because it is morally reprehensible, or because it is too morally complicated? Drs. Cassel and Meier suggest that it could be, at least in part, the second:

> A strict proscription against aiding in death may betray a limited conceptual framework that seeks the safety of ironclad rules and principles to protect the physician from the true complexity of individual cases. Patients seeking comfort in their dying should not be held hostage to our inability or unwillingness to be responsible for knowing right from wrong in each specific situation.

C. Cassel and D. Meier, Morals and Moralism in the Debate Over Euthanasia and Assisted Suicide, 323 N.Eng.J.Med. 750, 751 (1990).

10. Litigation seeking a right to physician assisted death need not be based only on the United States Constitution, it may have a basis in state law as well, especially in states with particularly strong constitutional privacy provisions. In Krischer v. McIver, 697 So.2d 97 (Fla.1997), a terminally ill AIDS patient and his physician sought an injunction against the prosecution of the physician for assisting in his patient's suicide. The Florida Supreme Court rejected a claim that the privacy provision of Article I, section 23 of the Florida Constitution included the right to have a physician assist in one's suicide. The Court announced that a properly drawn statute authorizing physician-assisted suicide would be constitutionally permissible, but that principles of separation of powers left the decision about whether it should be made legal to the legislature. The Chief Justice filed a vigorous dissent, arguing that, " * * *the right of privacy attaches with unusual force at the death bed. * * * What possible interest does society have in saving life when there is nothing of life to save but a final convulsion of agony? The state has no business in this arena." 697 So.2d at 111.

B. LEGISLATION TO SUPPORT PHYSICIAN ASSISTED DEATH— "DEATH WITH DIGNITY" INITIATIVES

The debate over the proper role of physicians in assisting their patients in death has been carried on through the legislative and citizen initiative processes also. "Death with Dignity" initiatives were narrowly defeated in California in 1991 and in Washington in 1992. However, Measure 16, the Oregon "Death with Dignity" initiative, was approved by voters in the November 1994 election, and it thus became part of the statute law of Oregon.

THE OREGON DEATH WITH DIGNITY ACT

Or.Rev.Stat. §§ 127.800–.897.

127.800. Definitions.

The following words and phrases, whenever used in ORS 127.800 to 127.897, have the following meanings:

(1) "Adult" means an individual who is 18 years of age or older.

(2) "Attending physician" means the physician who has primary responsibility for the care of the patient and treatment of the patient's terminal disease.

(3) "Capable" means that in the opinion of a court or in the opinion of the patient's attending physician or consulting physician, psychiatrist or psychologist, a patient has the ability to make and communicate health care decisions to health care providers, including communication through persons familiar with the patient's manner of communicating if those persons are available.

(4) "Consulting physician" means a physician who is qualified by specialty or experience to make a professional diagnosis and prognosis regarding the patient's disease.

(5) "Counseling" means one or more consultations as necessary between a state licensed psychiatrist or psychologist and a patient for the purpose of determining that the patient is capable and not suffering from a psychiatric or psychological disorder or depression causing impaired judgment.

(6) "Health care provider" means a person licensed, certified or otherwise authorized or permitted by the law of this state to administer health care

or dispense medication in the ordinary course of business or practice of a profession, and includes a health care facility.

(7) "Informed decision" means a decision by a qualified patient, to request and obtain a prescription to end his or her life in a humane and dignified manner, that is based on an appreciation of the relevant facts and after being fully informed by the attending physician of:

(a) His or her medical diagnosis;

(b) His or her prognosis;

(c) The potential risks associated with taking the medication to be prescribed;

(d) The probable result of taking the medication to be prescribed; and

(e) The feasible alternatives, including, but not limited to, comfort care, hospice care and pain control.

(8) "Medically confirmed" means the medical opinion of the attending physician has been confirmed by a consulting physician who has examined the patient and the patient's relevant medical records.

(9) "Patient" means a person who is under the care of a physician.

(10) "Physician" means a doctor of medicine or osteopathy licensed to practice medicine by the Board of Medical Examiners for the State of Oregon.

(11) "Qualified patient" means a capable adult who is a resident of Oregon and has satisfied the requirements of ORS 127.800 to 127.897 in order to obtain a prescription for medication to end his or her life in a humane and dignified manner.

(12) "Terminal disease" means an incurable and irreversible disease that has been medically confirmed and will, within reasonable medical judgment, produce death within six months.

127.805. Who may initiate a written request for medication.

(1) An adult who is capable, is a resident of Oregon, and has been determined by the attending physician and consulting physician to be suffering from a terminal disease, and who has voluntarily expressed his or her wish to die, may make a written request for medication for the purpose of ending his or her life in a humane and dignified manner in accordance with ORS 127.800 to 127.897.

(2) No person shall qualify under the provisions of ORS 127.800 to 127.897 solely because of age or disability.

127.810. Form of the written request.

(1) A valid request for medication under ORS 127.800 to 127.897 shall be in substantially the form described in ORS 127.897, signed and dated by the patient and witnessed by at least two individuals who, in the presence of the patient, attest that to the best of their knowledge and belief the patient is capable, acting voluntarily, and is not being coerced to sign the request.

(2) One of the witnesses shall be a person who is not:

(a) A relative of the patient by blood, marriage or adoption;

(b) A person who at the time the request is signed would be entitled to any portion of the estate of the qualified patient upon death under any will or by operation of law; or

(c) An owner, operator or employee of a health care facility where the qualified patient is receiving medical treatment or is a resident.

(3) The patient's attending physician at the time the request is signed shall not be a witness.

(4) If the patient is a patient in a long term care facility at the time the written request is made, one of the witnesses shall be an individual designated by the facility and having the qualifications specified by the Department of Human Services by rule.

127.815. Attending physician responsibilities.

(1) The attending physician shall:

(a) Make the initial determination of whether a patient has a terminal disease, is capable, and has made the request voluntarily;

(b) Request that the patient demonstrate Oregon residency pursuant to ORS 127.860;

(c) To ensure that the patient is making an informed decision, inform the patient of:

(A) His or her medical diagnosis;

(B) His or her prognosis;

(C) The potential risks associated with taking the medication to be prescribed;

(D) The probable result of taking the medication to be prescribed; and

(E) The feasible alternatives, including, but not limited to, comfort care, hospice care and pain control;

(d) Refer the patient to a consulting physician for medical confirmation of the diagnosis, and for a determination that the patient is capable and acting voluntarily;

(e) Refer the patient for counseling if appropriate pursuant to ORS 127.825;

(f) Recommend that the patient notify next of kin;

(g) Counsel the patient about the importance of having another person present when the patient takes the medication prescribed pursuant to ORS 127.800 to 127.897 and of not taking the medication in a public place;

(h) Inform the patient that he or she has an opportunity to rescind the request at any time and in any manner, and offer the patient an opportunity to rescind at the end of the 15 day waiting period pursuant to ORS 127.840;

(i) Verify, immediately prior to writing the prescription for medication under ORS 127.800 to 127.897, that the patient is making an informed decision;

(j) Fulfill the medical record documentation requirements of ORS 127.855;

(k) Ensure that all appropriate steps are carried out in accordance with ORS 127.800 to 127.897 prior to writing a prescription for medication to enable a qualified patient to end his or her life in a humane and dignified manner; and

    (A) Dispense medications directly* * *or [(B) through a pharmacist].

(2) Notwithstanding any other provision of law, the attending physician may sign the patient's death certificate.

127.820. Consulting physician confirmation.

Before a patient is qualified under ORS 127.800 to 127.897, a consulting physician shall examine the patient and his or her relevant medical records and confirm, in writing, the attending physician's diagnosis that the patient is suffering from a terminal disease, and verify that the patient is capable, is acting voluntarily and has made an informed decision.

127.825. Counseling referral.

If in the opinion of the attending physician or the consulting physician a patient may be suffering from a psychiatric or psychological disorder or depression causing impaired judgment, either physician shall refer the patient for counseling. No medication to end a patient's life in a humane and dignified manner shall be prescribed until the person performing the counseling determines that the patient is not suffering from a psychiatric or psychological disorder or depression causing impaired judgment.

127.830. Informed decision.

No person shall receive a prescription for medication to end his or her life in a humane and dignified manner unless he or she has made an informed decision as defined in ORS 127.800 (7). Immediately prior to writing a prescription for medication under ORS 127.800 to 127.897, the attending physician shall verify that the patient is making an informed decision.

127.835. Family notification.

The attending physician shall recommend that the patient notify the next of kin of his or her request for medication pursuant to ORS 127.800 to 127.897. A patient who declines or is unable to notify next of kin shall not have his or her request denied for that reason.

127.840. Written and oral requests.

In order to receive a prescription for medication to end his or her life in a humane and dignified manner, a qualified patient shall have made an oral request and a written request, and reiterate the oral request to his or her attending physician no less than fifteen (15) days after making the initial oral request. At the time the qualified patient makes his or her second oral request, the attending physician shall offer the patient an opportunity to rescind the request.

127.845. Right to rescind request.

A patient may rescind his or her request at any time and in any manner without regard to his or her mental state. No prescription for medication under ORS 127.800 to 127.897 may be written without the attending physician offering the qualified patient an opportunity to rescind the request.

127.850. Waiting periods.

No less than fifteen (15) days shall elapse between the patient's initial oral request and the writing of a prescription under ORS 127.800 to 127.897. No less than 48 hours shall elapse between the patient's written request and the writing of a prescription under ORS 127.800 to 127.897.

* * *

127.860. Residency requirement.

Only requests made by Oregon residents under ORS 127.800 to 127.897 shall be granted. Factors demonstrating Oregon residency include but are not limited to [being licensed to drive, registering to vote, owning property, and paying taxes in Oregon.]

* * *

127.880. Construction of Act.

Nothing in ORS 127.800 to 127.897 shall be construed to authorize a physician or any other person to end a patient's life by lethal injection, mercy killing or active euthanasia. Actions taken in accordance with ORS 127.800 to 127.897 shall not, for any purpose, constitute suicide, assisted suicide, mercy killing or homicide, under the law.

* * *

127.897. Form of the request.

A request for a medication as authorized by ORS 127.800 to 127.897 shall be in substantially the following form:

REQUEST FOR MEDICATION TO END MY LIFE
IN A HUMANE AND DIGNIFIED MANNER

I, _____, am an adult of sound mind.

I am suffering from _____, which my attending physician has determined is a terminal disease and which has been medically confirmed by a consulting physician.

I have been fully informed of my diagnosis, prognosis, the nature of medication to be prescribed and potential associated risks, the expected result, and the feasible alternatives, including comfort care, hospice care and pain control.

I request that my attending physician prescribe medication that will end my life in a humane and dignified manner.

INITIAL ONE:

_____ I have informed my family of my decision and taken their opinions into consideration.

_____ I have decided not to inform my family of my decision.

_____ I have no family to inform of my decision.

I understand that I have the right to rescind this request at any time.

I understand the full import of this request and I expect to die when I take the medication to be prescribed. I further understand that although most deaths occur within three hours, my death may take longer and my physician has counseled me about this possibility.

I make this request voluntarily and without reservation, and I accept full moral responsibility for my actions.

[Signature line; witness lines]

* * *

Early in 1999 the Oregon Department of Health issued its first annual report, which collected data on those who received lethal prescriptions under the Act during its first year of operation. The Fifth Annual Report on the operation of the Death with Dignity Act was released in March of 2003. The full text of that report is available at the new state Death with Dignity Act web site, http://www.ohd.hr.state.or.us/chs/pas.htm. The "Results" section of this report summarizes the way in which the Act was applied during its first five years in effect. In this report, "PAS" refers to physician assisted suicide.

OREGON DEPARTMENT OF HUMAN SERVICES, OFFICE OF DISEASE PREVENTION AND EPIDEMIOLOGY, FIFTH ANNUAL REPORT ON OREGON'S DEATH WITH DIGNITY ACT.

March 6, 2003.

* * *

Results

* * *

Both the number of prescriptions written and the number of Oregonians using PAS have increased over the five years that PAS has been legal in Oregon. In 2002, 58 prescriptions for lethal doses of medication were written by 33 physicians. This compares to 44 prescriptions written in 2001, 39 in 2000, 33 in 1999 and 24 in 1998. Thirty-six of the patients who received prescriptions during 2002 died after ingesting the lethal medication and 6 were alive on December 31, 2002. In addition, two patients who received their prescriptions during 2001 died in 2002 after ingesting lethal medications for a total of 38 PAS deaths during 2002. This compares to 21 deaths in 2001, 27 deaths in 2000, 27 deaths in 1999, and 16 deaths in 1998.

Patients participating in 2002 were similar to those in previous years except that more males and persons without a college degree used PAS [ ]. Similar to previous years, most patients (84%) choosing PAS had cancer.

During 2001, a total of 30,128 Oregonians died. Thus, patients ingesting lethal medications in 2002 represented an estimated 13/10,000 total Oregon deaths. By comparison, 2001 patients represented 7/10,000 deaths, 2000 and 1999 PAS patients, 9/10,000 deaths, and 1998 PAS patients represented 6/10,000 deaths.

Patient Characteristics

The characteristics of the 129 PAS patients who died in 1998–2002 differed in several ways from the 42,274 Oregonians who died from the same underlying causes. An inverse relationship exists between age and participation with younger patients more likely to use PAS than older patients [ ]. Although based on relatively few deaths (four), Asian residents were three times more likely to use PAS than were non-hispanic whites. Divorced Oregonians were almost twice as likely to use PAS than their married counterparts. As educational attainment increases, so too does the likelihood of a terminally ill Oregonian choosing to use PAS; compared to those without a high school diploma, college graduates were 6.5 times more likely to use PAS. Finally, the type of terminal illness was related to use of PAS; residents with cancer and amyotrophic lateral sclerosis (ALS) were more likely to use PAS.

During 2002, all patients died at home and all but one had some form of health insurance [ ]. As in previous years, most (92%) of the patients who used PAS in 2002 were enrolled in hospice care. The median length of the patient-physician relationship was 11 weeks.

Physician Characteristics

The prescribing physicians of patients who used PAS during 2002 had been in practice a median of 18.5 years. Their medical specialties included: internal medicine (29%), oncology (45%), family medicine (24%), and other (5%). [Note: the sum of the percentages do not equal 100 because some physicians had two specialities.]

Prescribing physicians were present while 13 (34%) of the 38 patients ingested the lethal medications. Among the remaining 25 patients, attendant status was known for 23. Of these individuals, 78% ingested the medication in the presence of another health care provider/volunteer.

No physicians were reported to the Oregon Board of Medical Examiners in 2002.

* * *

Complications

During 2002, after ingesting the prescribed medication, one patient coughed and gagged for 10–15 seconds, expectorating some clear mucoid material and another patient vomited; the first patient died 13 minutes after ingesting the opiate while the other died two hours later. Three patients lived more than six hours after drinking the lethal medication: one participant, who had impaired digestion, lived 14 hours; another, with a complete bowel obstruction, lived nine hours; and a third lived 12 hours for unknown reasons. * * * No patient regained consciousness after taking the medications.

End of Life Concerns

The most frequently reported concerns included losing autonomy (84%), a decreasing ability to participate in activities that make life enjoyable (84%), and losing control of bodily functions (47%).

Comments:

During the five years since legalization, the number of prescriptions written for physician-assisted suicide and the number of terminally-ill patients taking lethal medication has increased. However, even with this increase the number has remained small compared to the total number of deaths in Oregon, with fewer than 1/8 of one percent of Oregonians dying by PAS. This proportion is consistent with numbers from a survey of Oregon physicians. Overall, smaller numbers of patients appear to use PAS in Oregon compared to the Netherlands. However, as detailed in previous reports, our numbers are based on a reporting system for terminally-ill patients who legally receive prescriptions for lethal medications, and do not include patients and physicians who may act outside the law.

That educated patients are more likely to choose PAS is consistent with findings that Oregon patients with at least a college degree are more likely to be knowledgeable about end-of-life choices.

Over the last five years the rate of PAS among patients with ALS in Oregon has been substantially higher than among patients with other illnesses. This finding is consistent with other studies. In the Netherlands, where both PAS and euthanasia are openly practiced, one in five ALS patients died as a result of PAS or euthanasia. A study of Oregon and Washington ALS patients found that one-third of these patients discussed wanting PAS in the last month of life . It is not known with certainty why ALS patients appear to be more likely to be interested in choosing PAS than other terminally ill patients.

Over the five years, physicians have consistently reported that concern about loss of autonomy and participation in activities that make life enjoyable have been important motivating factors in patient requests for lethal medication across all five years. Interviews with family members during 1999 corroborated physician reports. These findings were supported by a recent study of hospice nurses and social workers caring for PAS patients in Oregon .

The availability of PAS may have led to efforts to improve end-of-life care through other modalities. While it may be common for patients with a terminal illness to consider PAS, a request for PAS can be an opportunity for a medical provider to explore with patients their fears and wishes around end-of-life care, and to make patients aware of other options. Often once the provider has addressed patients' concerns, they may choose not to pursue PAS. The availability of PAS as an option in Oregon also may have spurred Oregon doctors to address other end-of life care options more effectively. In one study Oregon physicians reported that, since the passage of the Death with Dignity Act in 1994, they had made efforts to improve their knowledge of the use of pain medications in the terminally ill, to improve their recognition of psychiatric disorders such as depression, and to refer patients more frequently to hospice.

Notes and Questions

1. The Oregon Death with Dignity Act also provides that no contract or statute can affect a person's request for physician assisted suicide, and that no insurance policy can be conditioned upon, or affected by, a patient's decision to choose (or reject) physician assisted suicide. The measure includes a section providing immunity for those who follow the requirements of the statute, and imposing liability on those who violate it.

2. As the Fifth Annual Report suggests, most Oregonians who have sought physician assisted death have done so because of their fear of losing control of

their lives (and the concomitant suffering that would follow), not because of physical pain. An excerpt from Oregon's Second Annual Report, published in 2000, explains this:

> Responses from both physician and family interviews indicate that patient's decisions to request PAS were motivated by multiple interrelated concerns. Physical suffering was discussed by several families as a cause of loss of autonomy, inability to participate in activities that made life enjoyable, or a "non-existent" quality of life. For example, "She would have stuck it out through the pain if she thought she'd get better ... [but she believed that] when quality of life has no meaning, it's no use hanging around." For another participant, a feeling of being trapped because of ALS contributed to concern about loss of autonomy. Family members frequently commented on loss of control of bodily functions when discussing loss of autonomy. Those reporting patient concern about being a burden on friends and family also reported concern about loss of autonomy and control of bodily functions. Reasons for requesting a prescription were sometimes so interrelated they were difficult to categorize. According to one family member being asked to distinguish reasons for the patient's decision, "It was everything; it was nothing; [he was suffering terribly]."

> Difficulty categorizing and differences in interpreting the nature of the concerns made physician and family member responses hard to compare quantitatively. Nonetheless, family interviews corroborate physician reports from both years that patients are greatly concerned about issues of autonomy and control. In addition, responses of both physicians and family consistently pointed to patient concerns about quality of life and the wish to have a means of controlling the end of life should it become unbearable. As one family member said, "She always thought that if something was terminal, she would [want to] control the end ... It was not the dying that she dreaded, it was getting to that death."

* * *

> Oregonians choosing physician-assisted suicide appeared to want control over how they died. One woman had purchased poison over a decade before her participation, when her cancer was first diagnosed, so that she would never be without the means of controlling the end of her life should it become unbearable. Like many others who participated, she was described as "determined" to have this control. Another woman was described as a "gutsy woman" who was "... determined in her lifetime, and determined about [physician-assisted suicide]." Family members expressed profound grief at losing a loved one. However, mixed with this grief was great respect for the patient's determination and choice to use physician-assisted suicide. As one husband said about his wife of almost 50 years, "She was my only girl; I didn't want to lose her ... but she wanted to do this."

Are those who do take advantage of the statute brave? Cowardly?

3. The United States District Court in Oregon issued a preliminary injunction against enforcing the initiative shortly after the initiative passed. The court permanently enjoined enforcement of the statute several months later. Ultimately the Ninth Circuit reversed the District Court, finding that those challenging the Oregon initiative had no standing to raise the issue in federal court. Lee v. Oregon, 107 F.3d 1382 (9th Cir.1997).

4. The Act has been amended, but the changes that have been made are not substantial. The legislature added the definition of "capable," added some new language designed to encourage patients to discuss the matter with their families,

and provided some factors to be considered in determining residency. The amendments also made clear the broad extent of the institutional conscience exception to the statute, which permits health care institutions to limit physicians from engaging in assisted death on their premises or in their organizations, and it changed the written consent form to assure that patients recognize that death will probably, but not always, take place about three hours after taking the medication.

5. Emboldened by the success in Oregon, many "Death With Dignity" groups have sought state statutes that would accomplish what Oregon's Measure 16 sought to do. A measure similar to the Oregon statute was very narrowly defeated at the polls in Maine in 2000. In part as a result of the narrow defeat of the Maine measure, during the next legislative session both supporters and opponents of physician assisted death joined to support a number of bills improving the quality of end-of-life care in that State. The question of physician assisted death itself has not moved off the legislative radar screen, though. In 2002 the Hawai'i House of Representatives passed an Oregon-like bill that came within a couple of votes of passing the Senate. More legislative action—on Oregon-like bills and compromise end-of-life care bills—is expected in other states in 2004. Not all state actions have been supportive of physician assisted death, though. Several states have passed new statutes that outlaw (or increase the penalty for) assisting suicide. On balance, since 1997 more states have acted to outlaw or limit assisted suicide than to permit it.

6. Is there some common ground available to those, on the one hand, who believe that permitting physician assisted death is necessary for patients to be properly treated at the end of life, and those, on the other hand, who believe that physician assisted death must be outlawed for patients to be properly treated? Both groups agree that pain is often inadequately treated at the end of life, in part because physicians fear legal action for homicide (if pain relief results in the death of the patient) or distribution of drugs (if the condition of a patient requires a larger dose of narcotic medication than is standard). In some states advocates on both sides of the physician assisted death issue have joined together to support intractable pain relief statutes, which are designed to protect health care providers who deliver adequate pain relief from adverse licensing and criminal actions. These statutes generally provide that a health care provider will not be liable in a state disciplinary proceeding or a criminal action for the aggressive prescription of pain medication as long as the use of that medication is in accord with accepted guidelines for pain management. Several states have promulgated intractable pain relief acts, and several more are considering them. For a model "Pain Relief Act," see 24 J.L., Med. & Ethics 317(1996).

Federal and state policy may conflict on one kind of palliative care—the use of marijuana. Some cancer patients, patients with glaucoma, AIDS patients, patients with multiple sclerosis, those with migraine headaches and others find that they can obtain relief from some of the symptoms of the diseases—or from some of the side effects of the treatments for the diseases—through the use of marijuana. In particular, some cancer patients find that marijuana helps them overcome the nausea that follows the use of many chemotherapeutic agents. While several states have now legalized the use of marijuana under such circumstances, the manufacture and distribution of marijuana, a schedule I drug, is still a felony under the Federal Controlled Substances Act. Whether the Federal law outlawing such manufacture and distribution effectively trump the new state laws that permit its use under controlled circumstances, and under medical prescription, was resolved by the Supreme Court in 2001. For a full discussion of this issue, see section VII of this chapter, below.

7. The federal government has not ignored physician assisted death itself, either. Even before the Oregon statute became effective, Congress passed the Assisted Suicide Prevention Restriction Act of 1997, which outlaws the use of federal money to aid physician assisted death, directly or indirectly.

Shortly after the Oregon Death with Dignity Act became effective, some suggested that any physician who prescribed a lethal drug under that statute would be prescribing that drug without a "legitimate medical purpose," and thus would be acting inconsistently with the Federal Controlled Substances Act. A physician's violation of the Act could lead to both the loss of prescribing authority and criminal indictment. In June of 1998, after the matter had been pending for some time, the United States Department of Justice published its report concluding that use of controlled substances under the Oregon statute would satisfy the "legitimate medical purpose" requirement of the Federal Act.

Immediately, members of the House and Senate introduced the Lethal Drug Abuse Prevention Act of 1998, which would have expanded the authority of the Drug Enforcement Agency to investigate lethal use of controlled substances, which could not be used with the *intent* of causing death. Supporters of physician assisted death joined many of their staunchest opponents and mainstream medical organizations (including the AMA) to oppose the bill because, they said, it would be likely to chill physicians from providing adequate pain relief at the end of life. Although the bill failed, it was resurrected in slightly milder form in 2000 as the Pain Relief Promotion Act ("PRPA"), which included a well publicized section announcing that the provision of medication with the intent to manage pain (and not the intent to cause death) was protected. The 2000 version of the bill also provided for the education of health care professionals on issues related to pain management, and it was supported by the AMA (but opposed by the ABA and the American Cancer Society). Although the stated purpose of PRPA was to promote adequate pain relief practices, its effect would be (and, some say, its real purpose was) to render it impossible for physicians in Oregon to carry out the provisions of the Death With Dignity Act. PRPA died when Congress adjourned in late 2000.

The new Attorney General, John Ashcroft, reversed the Department of Justice position on the issue of the application of the Controlled Substances Act in late 2001. He set federal government machinery in motion to prosecute anyone who prescribed or dispensed medications under the Death with Dignity Act. Within a day of the announcement of the change in the federal position, Oregon sought relief from the Attorney General's decision in the United States District Court. A private action also seeking an injunction against the Ashcroft position was filed shortly thereafter on behalf of an Oregon oncologist. The District Court restrained the United States from enforcing the new interpretation of the Controlled Substances Act, and in 2002 permanently enjoined its enforcement, in part because no federal agency is authorized "to establish a national medical practice or act as a national medical board." Oregon v. Ashcroft, 192 F.Supp.2d 1077 (D. Or. 2002). The district court was affirmed by a divided panel of the Court of Appeals. Oregon v. Ashcroft, 368 F.3d 1118 (9th Cir. 2004).

8. Despite the high level of publicity given to the Oregon statute, Oregonians (like the rest of us) remain confused about what options are actually available at the end of life. M. Silveira et al., Patient's Knowledge of Options at the End of Life: Ignorance in the Face of Death, 284 JAMA 2483 (2000). What is more, terminally ill patients and their families remain highly ambivalent about physi-

cian assisted death. One recent study showed that while 60% of terminally ill patients would support the use of physician assisted death under some circumstances, only 10% had seriously considered it in their own cases. E. Emanuel et al, Attitudes and Desires Related to Euthanasia and Physician–Assisted Suicide Among Terminally Ill Patients and Their Caregivers, 284 JAMA 2460 (2000).

9. The public interest in this issue is not limited to the United States. For a discussion of the law in the Netherlands, see pages 382-386, above. Belgium recently joined the Netherlands in legalizing physician assisted death under some circumstances, and the practice has been officially tolerated in Switzerland, too. The French have been debating the issue since Mireille Jospin, the mother of a former Prime Minister, committed suicide just before Christmas in 2002. The 92 year old was still active, but she wanted to make sure that she did not deteriorate and lose control of her own destiny. Australia's Northern Territory's parliament passed The Rights of the Terminally Ill Act (1995), which permitted what some have called "voluntary euthanasia" under some limited circumstances; however, the national parliament effectively overturned that territorial statute.

Problem: Drafting Legislation

You are the nonpolitical legislative counsel to a state legislature. Currently that state has a statute prohibiting assisting suicide. You have been asked by several members of the legislature to draft bills designed to regulate physician assisted death for introduction at a legislative session that will soon be convened. One member has asked you to draft a bill that would outlaw all physician assisted death, under all circumstances. A second member wants you to draft a bill that would put as few limitations on physician assisted death as is possible; this libertarian member believes that the decision should be left to individual doctors and patients. Another member has asked you to draft a statute that would protect health care providers from potential liability for participating in physician assisted deaths, and would give providers an option to avoid participating in physician assisted deaths if they chose not to do so. Yet another member has asked you to draft a statute that would prohibit managed care organizations from directly or indirectly giving any incentives to their members to choose physician assisted deaths. Finally, one long time incumbent has asked you to draft a consensus statute—one with enough political support across the spectrum that it has a reasonable chance of passing.

How would you go about drafting these statutes? How would they be different? What facts (about the legal landscape in this state, about the politics of the current officeholders, about the religious backgrounds of those within the state, about other issues) would you want to have before you started drafting these statutes?

VII. REGULATION OF END–OF–LIFE CARE: THE CASE OF MEDICAL MARIJUANA

UNITED STATES v. OAKLAND CANNABIS BUYERS' COOPERATIVE

Supreme Court of the United States, 2001.
532 U.S. 483, 121 S.Ct. 1711, 149 L.Ed.2d 722.

JUSTICE THOMAS delivered the opinion of the Court.

The Controlled Substances Act, [ ] prohibits the manufacture and distribution of various drugs, including marijuana. In this case, we must decide whether there is a medical necessity exception to these prohibitions. We hold that there is not.

I

In November 1996, California voters enacted an initiative measure entitled the Compassionate Use Act of 1996. Attempting "to ensure that seriously ill Californians have the right to obtain and use marijuana for medical purposes," [ ] the statute creates an exception to California laws prohibiting the possession and cultivation of marijuana. These prohibitions no longer apply to a patient or his primary caregiver who possesses or cultivates marijuana for the patient's medical purposes upon the recommendation or approval of a physician. [ ] In the wake of this voter initiative, several groups organized "medical cannabis dispensaries" to meet the needs of qualified patients. [ ] Respondent Oakland Cannabis Buyers' Cooperative is one of these groups.

The Cooperative is a not-for-profit organization that operates in downtown Oakland. A physician serves as medical director, and registered nurses staff the Cooperative during business hours. To become a member, a patient must provide a written statement from a treating physician assenting to marijuana therapy and must submit to a screening interview. If accepted as a member, the patient receives an identification card entitling him to obtain marijuana from the Cooperative.

In January 1998, the United States sued the Cooperative * * * in the United States District Court for the Northern District of California. Seeking to enjoin the Cooperative from distributing and manufacturing marijuana, the United States argued that, whether or not the Cooperative's activities are legal under California law, they violate federal law. Specifically, the Government argued that the Cooperative violated the Controlled Substances Act's prohibitions on distributing, manufacturing, and possessing with the intent to distribute or manufacture a controlled substance. [ ] Concluding that the Government had established a probability of success on the merits, the District Court granted a preliminary injunction. [ ]

The Cooperative did not appeal the injunction but instead openly violated it by distributing marijuana to numerous persons [ ]. To terminate these violations, the Government initiated contempt proceedings. In defense, the Cooperative contended that any distributions were medically necessary. Marijuana is the only drug, according to the Cooperative, that can alleviate the severe pain and other debilitating symptoms of the Cooperative's patients. [ ] The District Court rejected this defense, however, after determining there was insufficient evidence that each recipient of marijuana was in actual danger of imminent harm without the drug. [ ] The District Court found the Cooperative in contempt and, at the Government's request, modified the preliminary injunction to empower the United States Marshal to seize the Cooperative's premises. Although recognizing that "human suffering" could result, the District Court reasoned that a court's "equitable powers [do] not permit it to ignore federal law." [ ] Three days later, the District Court summarily rejected a motion by the Cooperative to modify the injunction to permit distributions that are medically necessary.

The Cooperative appealed both the contempt order and the denial of the Cooperative's motion to modify. Before the Court of Appeals for the Ninth Circuit decided the case, however, the Cooperative voluntarily purged its contempt by promising the District Court that it would comply with the initial preliminary injunction. Consequently, the Court of Appeals determined that the appeal of the contempt order was moot. [ ]

The denial of the Cooperative's motion to modify the injunction, however, presented a live controversy * * *. Reaching the merits of this issue, the Court of Appeals reversed and remanded. According to the Court of Appeals, the medical necessity defense was a "legally cognizable defense" that likely would apply in the circumstances. [ ] Moreover, the Court of Appeals reasoned, the District Court erroneously "believed that it had no discretion to issue an injunction that was more limited in scope than the Controlled Substances Act itself." [ ] Because, according to the Court of Appeals, district courts retain "broad equitable discretion" to fashion injunctive relief, the District Court could have, and should have, weighed the "public interest" and considered factors such as the serious harm in depriving patients of marijuana. [ ] Remanding the case, the Court of Appeals instructed the District Court to consider "the criteria for a medical necessity exemption, and, should it modify the injunction, to set forth those criteria in the modification order."[ ] Following these instructions, the District Court granted the Cooperative's motion to modify the injunction to incorporate a medical necessity defense.[2]

The United States petitioned for certiorari to review the Court of Appeals' decision that medical necessity is a legally cognizable defense to violations of the Controlled Substances Act. Because the decision raises significant questions as to the ability of the United States to enforce the Nation's drug laws, we granted certiorari. [ ]

II

The Controlled Substances Act provides that, "except as authorized by this subchapter, it shall be unlawful for any person knowingly or intentionally ... to manufacture, distribute, or dispense, or possess with intent to manufacture, distribute, or dispense, a controlled substance." [ ] The subchapter, in turn, establishes exceptions. For marijuana (and other drugs that have been classified as "schedule I" controlled substances), there is but one express exception, and it is available only for Government-approved research projects [ ]. Not conducting such a project, the Cooperative cannot, and indeed does not, claim this statutory exemption.

2. The amended preliminary injunction reaffirmed that the Cooperative is generally enjoined from manufacturing, distributing, and possessing with the intent to manufacture or distribute marijuana, but it carved out an exception for cases of medical necessity. Specifically, the District Court ordered that "the foregoing injunction does not apply to the distribution of cannabis by [the Cooperative] to patient-members who (1) suffer from a serious medical condition, (2) will suffer imminent harm if the patient-member does not have access to cannabis, (3) need cannabis for the treatment of the patient-member's medical condition, or need cannabis to alleviate the medical condition or symptoms associated with the medical condition, and (4) have no reasonable legal alternative to cannabis for the effective treatment or alleviation of the patient-member's medical condition or symptoms associated with the medical condition because the patient-member has tried all other legal alternatives to cannabis and the alternatives have been ineffective in treating or alleviating the patient-member's medical condition or symptoms associated with the medical condition, or the alternatives result in side effects which the patient-member cannot reasonably tolerate." [ ]

The Cooperative contends, however, that notwithstanding the apparently absolute language * * *, the statute is subject to additional, implied exceptions, one of which is medical necessity. According to the Cooperative, because necessity was a defense at common law, medical necessity should be read into the Controlled Substances Act. We disagree.

As an initial matter, we note that it is an open question whether federal courts ever have authority to recognize a necessity defense not provided by statute. * * *

We need not decide, however, whether necessity can ever be a defense when the federal statute does not expressly provide for it. In this case, to resolve the question presented, we need only recognize that a medical necessity exception for marijuana is at odds with the terms of the Controlled Substances Act. The statute, to be sure, does not explicitly abrogate the defense. But its provisions leave no doubt that the defense is unavailable.

Under any conception of legal necessity, one principle is clear: The defense cannot succeed when the legislature itself has made a "determination of values." [ ] In the case of the Controlled Substances Act, the statute reflects a determination that marijuana has no medical benefits worthy of an exception (outside the confines of a Government-approved research project). Whereas some other drugs can be dispensed and prescribed for medical use, [ ] the same is not true for marijuana. Indeed, for purposes of the Controlled Substances Act, marijuana has "no currently accepted medical use" at all. [ ]

[The Court then describes the structure of the Controlled Substances Act and points out that the fact that Congress, not the Attorney General, classified marijuana as a schedule I drug, is legally irrelevant. A schedule I drug "has no currently acceptable medical use in treatment in the United States" and "has a high potential for abuse."]

* * *

The Cooperative further argues that use of schedule I drugs generally—whether placed in schedule I by Congress or the Attorney General—can be medically necessary, notwithstanding that they have "no currently accepted medical use." According to the Cooperative, a drug may not yet have achieved general acceptance as a medical treatment but may nonetheless have medical benefits to a particular patient or class of patients. We decline to parse the statute in this manner. It is clear from the text of the Act that Congress has made a determination that marijuana has no medical benefits worthy of an exception.

Finally, the Cooperative contends that we should construe the Controlled Substances Act to include a medical necessity defense in order to avoid what it considers to be difficult constitutional questions. In particular, the Cooperative asserts that, shorn of a medical necessity defense, the statute exceeds Congress' Commerce Clause powers, violates the substantive due process rights of patients, and offends the fundamental liberties of the people under the Fifth, Ninth, and Tenth Amendments. As the Cooperative acknowledges, however, the canon of constitutional avoidance has no application in the absence of statutory ambiguity. Because we have no doubt that the Controlled Substances Act cannot bear a medical necessity defense to distributions of marijuana, we do not find guidance in this avoidance principle. Nor do we consider the underlying constitutional issues today. Because the Court of Appeals did not address these claims, we decline to do so in the first instance.

For these reasons, we hold that medical necessity is not a defense to manufacturing and distributing marijuana.[7] The Court of Appeals erred when it held that medical necessity is a "legally cognizable defense." [ ]. It further erred when it instructed the District Court on remand to consider "the criteria for a medical necessity exemption, and, should it modify the injunction, to set forth those criteria in the modification order." [ ]

III

* * *

In this case, the Court of Appeals erred by considering relevant the evidence that some people have "serious medical conditions for whom the use of cannabis is necessary in order to treat or alleviate those conditions or their symptoms," that these people "will suffer serious harm if they are denied cannabis," and that "there is no legal alternative to cannabis for the effective treatment of their medical conditions." [ ] [T]he balance already has been struck [by Congress] against a medical necessity exception. Because the statutory prohibitions cover even those who have what could be termed a medical necessity, the Act precludes consideration of this evidence. It was thus error for the Court of Appeals to instruct the District Court on remand to consider "the criteria for a medical necessity exemption, and, should it modify the injunction, to set forth those criteria in the modification order."

* * *

JUSTICE BREYER took no part in the consideration or decision of this case.

JUSTICE STEVENS, with whom JUSTICE SOUTER and JUSTICE GINSBURG join, concurring in the judgment.

Lest the Court's narrow holding be lost in its broad dicta, let me restate it here: "We hold that medical necessity is not a defense to *manufacturing* and *distributing* marijuana." * * *

* * *

Apart from its limited holding, the Court takes two unwarranted and unfortunate excursions that prevent me from joining its opinion. First, the Court reaches beyond its holding, and beyond the facts of the case, by suggesting that the defense of necessity is unavailable for anyone under the

---

7. Lest there be any confusion, we clarify that nothing in our analysis, or the statute, suggests that a distinction should be drawn between the prohibitions on manufacturing and distributing and the other prohibitions in the Controlled Substances Act. Furthermore, the very point of our holding is that there is no medical necessity exception to the prohibitions at issue, even when the patient is "seriously ill" and lacks alternative avenues for relief. Indeed, it is the Cooperative's argument that its patients are "seriously ill," [ ], and lacking "alternatives," [ ]. We reject the argument that these factors warrant a medical necessity exception. If we did not, we would be affirming instead of reversing the Court of Appeals.

Finally, we share Justice Stevens' concern for "showing respect for the sovereign States that comprise our Federal Union." [ ]. However, we are "construing an Act of Congress, not drafting it." [ ] Because federal courts interpret, rather than author, the federal criminal code, we are not at liberty to rewrite it. Nor are we passing today on a constitutional question, such as whether the Controlled Substances Act exceeds Congress' power under the Commerce Clause.

Controlled Substances Act. [ ] Because necessity was raised in this case as a defense to distribution, the Court need not venture an opinion on whether the defense is available to anyone other than distributors. Most notably, whether the defense might be available to a seriously ill patient for whom there is no alternative means of avoiding starvation or extraordinary suffering is a difficult issue that is not presented here.

[Justice Stevens also questioned the majority's suggestion that whether necessity is a defense to any federal statute is an "open question".]

The overbroad language of the Court's opinion is especially unfortunate given the importance of showing respect for the sovereign States that comprise our Federal Union. That respect imposes a duty on federal courts, whenever possible, to avoid or minimize conflict between federal and state law, particularly in situations in which the citizens of a State have chosen to "serve as a laboratory" in the trial of "novel social and economic experiments without risk to the rest of the country." [ ] In my view, this is such a case.[3] By passing Proposition 215, California voters have decided that seriously ill patients and their primary caregivers should be exempt from prosecution under state laws for cultivating and possessing marijuana if the patient's physician recommends using the drug for treatment. This case does not call upon the Court to deprive *all* such patients of the benefit of the necessity defense to federal prosecution, when the case itself does not involve *any* such patients.

An additional point deserves emphasis. This case does not require us to rule on the scope of the District Court's discretion to enjoin, or to refuse to enjoin, the possession of marijuana or other potential violations of the Controlled Substances Act by a seriously ill patient for whom the drug may be a necessity. * * *

I join the Court's judgment of reversal because I agree that a distributor of marijuana does not have a medical necessity defense under the Controlled Substances Act. I do not, however, join the dicta in the Court's opinion.

Notes and Questions

1. Marijuana has long been at the center of both medical and cultural battles. It was not illegal anyplace in the United States until 1915 when it was outlawed—ironically, given the site of current legal concerns—in California. It became subject to the federal law in the Marijuana Tax Act of 1937, which effectively outlawed the drug in the United States. There was further federal action in 1951 and 1956, and it is now regulated under the 1970 Controlled Substances Act. This Act divides drugs into five schedules. While the classification of most drugs is an administrative action, marijuana has been placed in schedule I, the most restricted list, by Congress itself. Under the Controlled Substances Act, a schedule I drug (1) has no currently accepted medical use, (2) is not safe for medical use, and (3) has a high potential for abuse. 21 U.S.C.A. section 812. Under Federal law, its use is permitted only for research (not therapeutic) purposes approved by the United States. See J. R. Conboy, Smoke Screen: America's Drug Policy and Medical Marijuana, 55 Food and Drug L.J. 601 (2000).

2. Eight states have approved statutes permitting the use of medical marijuana through the voter initiative process, and one state has promulgated such a

3. Cf. Feeney, Bush Backs States' Rights on Marijuana: He Opposes Medical Use But Favors Local Control, Dallas Morning News, Oct. 20, 1999, p. 6 A. 1999 WL 28018944 (then-Governor Bush supporting state self-determination on medical marijuana use).

statute through the normal legislative process. Thus, the medical use of marijuana is now legal, under some circumstances, in nine states—Alaska, Arizona, California, Colorado, Hawaii, Maine, Nevada, Oregon and Washington. Voters approved of medical marijuana in the District of Columbia, but Congress stopped that provision from becoming effective. Given that all but two of the states that have legalized the medical use of marijuana are in the Ninth Circuit, it is not really a surprise that the Ninth Circuit has been the first federal appellate court to see these issues. While there is some variation in these statutes, an early typical statute—and the one to give rise to the most litigation—is the California Compassionate Use Act of 1996:

Use of Marijuana for Medical Purposes
Cal Health & Saf. Code § 11362.5 (2003)

(a) This section shall be known and may be cited as the Compassionate Use Act of 1996.

(b)(1) The people of the State of California hereby find and declare that the purposes of the Compassionate Use Act of 1996 are as follows:

(A) To ensure that seriously ill Californians have the right to obtain and use marijuana for medical purposes where that medical use is deemed appropriate and has been recommended by a physician who has determined that the person's health would benefit from the use of marijuana in the treatment of cancer, anorexia, AIDS, chronic pain, spasticity, glaucoma, arthritis, migraine, or any other illness for which marijuana provides relief.

(B) To ensure that patients and their primary caregivers who obtain and use marijuana for medical purposes upon the recommendation of a physician are not subject to criminal prosecution or sanction.

(C) To encourage the federal and state governments to implement a plan to provide for the safe and affordable distribution of marijuana to all patients in medical need of marijuana.

(2) Nothing in this section shall be construed to supersede legislation prohibiting persons from engaging in conduct that endangers others, nor to condone the diversion of marijuana for nonmedical purposes.

(c) Notwithstanding any other provision of law, no physician in this state shall be punished, or denied any right or privilege, for having recommended marijuana to a patient for medical purposes.

(d) Section 11357, relating to the possession of marijuana, and Section 11358, relating to the cultivation of marijuana, shall not apply to a patient, or to a patient's primary caregiver, who possesses or cultivates marijuana for the personal medical purposes of the patient upon the written or oral recommendation or approval of a physician.

(e) For the purposes of this section, "primary caregiver" means the individual designated by the person exempted under this section who has consistently assumed responsibility for the housing, health, or safety of that person.

3. There is a great deal of evidence that marijuana is useful as a therapeutic agent in some cases, but there is also some evidence that marijuana is a regularly abused drug that is also a "gateway" drug for other drug use. For a summary of the medicinal value of marijuana see L. Grinspoon and J. Bakalar, Marihuana as Medicine, A Plea for Reconsideration, 273 JAMA 1875 (1995), and Conboy, supra note 1. In 1999 the Institute of Medicine of the National Academy of Sciences published the report of their year-long investigation of the therapeutic value of marijuana, concluding that "cannabinoid drugs" had potential value for pain

relief, control of nausea and vomiting and appetite stimulation, especially for patients with some forms of cancer, AIDS, multiple sclerosis, and other identified conditions. It also found the drugs to be potentially valuable as a palliative care agent for those treated with various forms of chemotherapy. See Institute of Med., Marijuana and Medicine (J. Joy et al, eds., 1999). Who should balance the potential medical need for marijuana with the potential social costs of the increased availability of this drug? Does Congress have that power? Do the state legislatures? The courts? Individual doctors?

4. As the *Cannabis Buyers' Cooperative* case suggests, the United States has interpreted federal policy to discourage all use of marijuana, whatever state law may say about this subject. In 1996, after Arizona and California became the first two states to formally legalize the use of medical marijuana, the Office of the National Drug Control Policy consulted with the Drug Enforcement Agency, the Department of Justice and other federal agencies. It then issued a policy aimed at discouraging physicians from mentioning the potential use of marijuana to their patients. Specifically, the policy provided that any physician who recommended or prescribed any schedule I controlled substance would put his DEA registration (and, thus, his authority to prescribe any controlled substance) at risk. The federal policy was challenged by patients and physicians who sought an injunction against its enforcement. The plaintiffs based their arguments on the free speech clause of the First Amendment, while the government argued that the physicians' recommendation of marijuana use would constitute aiding or abetting the violation of the Controlled Substances Act, or the participation in a conspiracy to violate that federal law. The trial court granted an injunction and ordered the government (1) not to threaten to remove the DEA license from physicians who recommended medical marijuana to their patients and (2) not to threaten to investigate physicians solely on the grounds that they recommended medical marijuana. *Conant v. Walters*, 309 F.3d 629 (9th Cir.2002).

This issue eventually made its way to the Ninth Circuit which based its conclusion on the First Amendment rights of the physicians to openly discuss all medical options with their patients. As the court pointed out,

> The government's policy in this case seeks to punish physicians on the basis of the content of doctor-patient communications. Only doctor patient conversations that include discussions of the medical use of marijuana trigger the policy. Moreover, the policy does not merely prohibit the discussion of marijuana; it condemns expression of a particular viewpoint, i.e., that medical marijuana would likely help a specific patient. Such condemnation of particular views is especially troubling in the First Amendment context.

309 F.3d at 637. In his concurring opinion, Judge Kozinski depended upon the patients' First Amendment right to hear that medical advice. As he pointed out, "Those immediately and directly affected * * * are the patients, who will be denied information crucial to their well-being, and the State of California, whose policy of exempting certain patients from the sweep of its drug laws will be thwarted." 309 F.3d at 640 (Kozinksi, J., concurring).

5. In the *Cannabis Buyer's Cooperative* case, the majority explicitly leaves open the question of "whether the Controlled Substances Act exceeds Congress' power under the Commerce clause." In late 2003, the Ninth Circuit reversed a determination of the United States District Court, which had denied a preliminary injunction against the DEA sought by patients "who use marijuana for medical purposes on the recommendation of their doctors." The District Court had denied the preliminary injunction because it found that the plaintiffs could not show that they were likely to succeed on the merits. The Ninth Circuit, with one judge

dissenting, concluded "that the appellants have demonstrated a strong likelihood of success on their claim that, as applied to them, the [Controlled Substances Act] is an unconstitutional exercise of Congress' Commerce Clause authority." Raich v. Ashcroft, 352 F.3d 1222 (9th Cir. 2003). Dissenting Judge Beam questioned whether the issue was ripe for adjudication and whether the plaintiffs (who had not been charged with drug crimes) had standing to challenge the law. Judge Beam ultimately concluded that the Controlled Substances Act did not violate the Constitutional rights of the plaintiffs because, for commerce clause purposes, the Controlled Substances Act was indistinguishable from the Agricultural Adjustment Act (which regulated wheat production, even when the wheat was to be used by the farmer or his family), which the Supreme Court upheld in Wickard v. Filburn, 317 U.S. 111, 63 S.Ct. 82, 87 L.Ed. 122 (1942). Now don't you wish that you had studied those old Constitutional Law cases more closely? Was the majority right, or is Judge Beam?

6. Are there other Constitutional issues that might be raised against the federal government's policy of enforcing the Controlled Substances Act in the manner in which it has chosen? For example, is the federal government "commandeering" the resources of the states to serve a federal purpose with which those states may disagree, in a way that is inconsistent with the rule announced in New York v. United States, 505 U.S. 144, 112 S.Ct. 2408, 120 L.Ed.2d 120 (1992) and Printz v. United States, 521 U.S. 898, 117 S.Ct. 2365, 138 L.Ed.2d 914 (1997)? In the Conant case, issued after *Cannabis Buyers' Cooperative* was decided by the Supreme Court, concurring Judge Kozinski thought that it was. See Conant, 309 F.3d at 645–46. Because the *Raich* court resolved the issue presented through the application of the commerce clause, that court declined "to reach the appellants' other arguments, which are based on the principles of federalism embodied in the Tenth Amendment, the appellants' alleged fundamental rights under the Fifth and Ninth Amendments, and the doctrine of medical necessity."

7. The part of the federal law that was vindicated in *Cannabis Buyers' Cooperative* addresses only the manufacture and distribution of marijuana. Could a state license the use of marijuana without authorizing its manufacture or distribution? Did California do so in the statute reprinted above? Might a state statute avoid the application of the Controlled Substances Act if it provided for physicians to recommend (but not prescribe) marijuana for patients who would then be licensed to cultivate a sufficient supply for their own medical use?

8. Over the past decade the use of medical marijuana has become an issue outside of the United States, too. The concurring opinion in the *Conant* case also provided insight into the development of the law in the United Kingdom and in Canada:

> At about the time the IOM study got underway, the British House of Lords—a body not known for its wild and crazy views—opened public hearings on the medical benefits and drawbacks of cannabis. Like the IOM, the Lords concluded that "cannabis almost certainly does have genuine medical applications, especially in treating the painful muscular spasms and other symptoms of MS and in the control of other forms of pain." Select Comm. on Sci. & Tech., House of Lords, Sess. 1997–98, Ninth Report, *Cannabis: The Scientific and Medical Evidence: Report* § 8.2 (Nov. 4, 1998)[ ]. The Lords recommended that the British government act immediately "to allow doctors to prescribe an appropriate preparation of cannabis, albeit as an unlicensed medicine." *Id.* § 8.6.

> In June 2001, Canada promulgated its Marihuana Medical Access Regulations after an extensive study of the available evidence. *See* Marihuana

Medical Access Regulations, SOR 2001–227 (June 14, 2001)[ ]. The new regulations allow certain persons to cultivate and possess marijuana for medical use, and authorize doctors to recommend and prescribe marijuana to patients who are suffering from severe pain, muscle spasms, anorexia, weight loss or nausea, and who have not found relief from conventional therapies. *See* Office of Cannabis Med. Access, Health Canada, *Medical Access to Marijuana—How the Regulations Work* [ ].

309 F.3d at 641–42. In December of 2003 the Canadian Immigration and Refugee Board refused to grant refugee protection to Steve Kubby, a Californian who claimed refugee status because he was denied access to necessary medical care—medical marijuana—in his home country. Should Canada treat him as a refugee from the harsh American laws that make it impossible for him to get access to the marijuana that his doctor testified he needs?

9. To what extent is the battle over medical marijuana just a reprise of the American culture war of the 1960s? To what extent is this a confrontation between those who approve of the values of those who used marijuana forty years ago, and those who detest those values and thought that every indicia of them had been destroyed?

10. Apply the various theories of ethics and bioethics to the question of the legalization of medical marijuana. What would a utilitarian do? A Kantian? A person attempting to follow the requirements of natural law? A law and economics believer? A critical legal studies advocate? A feminist legal scholar?

Problem: Drafting Medical Marijuana Legislation

Draft a bill for your state legislature that would permit the medical use of marijuana but would not increase the abuse of marijuana. If your state already has such legislation, draft a bill to amend it to make it most effective in light of the *Cannabis Buyers' Cooperative* case. Write your bill so that it is consistent with the requirements of the Federal law, including the Controlled Substances Act, but would still permit the use of medical marijuana when that is recommended (or would you say prescribed?) by a physician. What legal problems do you face? How do you overcome them?

How would you draft the bill to assure yourself of the most political support? Remember—while voters seem to like medical marijuana initiatives, only one state legislature has passed such a bill. Why are state legislatures so reluctant to act? How will medical interest groups react? Patient advocacy groups? Religious groups? Public health advocates? Who will oppose your bill? Is there a way to increase the chance that it will be supported by state prosecutors, police, and other public safety groups? Is there a way to make such legislation consistent with the "war on drugs"?

Who would be able to possess medical marijuana under your bill? How much would they be able to possess? Where would they be able to get a supply? For what symptoms would it be available?

Chapter 6

REGULATION OF RESEARCH INVOLVING HUMAN SUBJECTS

I. THE NUREMBERG CODE

It is unusual that a specific area of law, other than constitutional law, has a foundational document that is the fount of the legal *and* moral principles that govern. Research with human subjects is one of those areas; and the foundational document, the "constitution," for the conduct and regulation of research is the Nuremberg Code.

This Code was borne of tragedy on an enormous scale. The shocking horrors that could be perpetrated by medical experimentation performed by superbly qualified scientists became apparent to the world through the Nazi war crimes trials prosecuting several leading German physicians. These trials unveiled conduct ignominious under any circumstances. For example, they brought to light medical research in which "volunteers," usually concentration camp inmates, were exposed to extremely low atmospheric pressure until they died in order to help the German Air Force prepare for high altitude military operations. They revealed subjects who were forced to drink seawater or breathe mustard gas; were exposed to such epidemics as malaria, jaundice, and typhus; or were placed in ice water until they froze. Several of the experiments were "open" to a wide range of concentration camp inmates, while others were limited to Jews, Gypsies, Polish priests, or other "special" groups.

This experimentation was not perceived as an abuse of medicine by its perpetrators. Rather, it was justified as appropriate conduct, done in the name of healing, and consistent with the Hippocratic Oath. For an account of the professional role of physicians in the Nazi policy of extermination, see R.J. Lifton, The Nazi Doctors (1986). Most of the twenty physicians accused of participating in or directing this experimentation were convicted, and some were hanged. A few were acquitted and one (Dr. Mengele) escaped. In one of the tribunal's most significant and ultimately most important judgments, the court sitting in Nuremberg promulgated a set of principles to be applied to determine when medical experimentation is appropriate.

NUREMBERG CODE: PERMISSIBLE MEDICAL EXPERIMENTS

The great weight of the evidence before us is to the effect that certain types of medical experiments on human beings, when kept within reasonably well-defined bounds, conform to the ethics of the medical profession generally. The protagonists of the practice of human experimentation justify their views on the basis that such experiments yield results for the good of society that are unprocurable by other methods or means of study. All agree, however, that certain basic principles must be observed in order to satisfy moral, ethical and legal concepts:

1.   The voluntary consent of the human subject is absolutely essential.

This means that the person involved should have legal capacity to give consent; should be so situated as to be able to exercise free power of choice, without the intervention of any element of force, fraud, deceit, duress, over-reaching, or other ulterior form of constraint or coercion; and should have sufficient knowledge and comprehension of the elements of the subject matter involved as to enable him to make an understanding and enlightened decision. This latter element requires that before the acceptance of an affirmative decision by the experimental subject there should be made known to him the nature, duration, and purpose of the experiment; the method and means by which it is to be conducted; all inconveniences and hazards reasonably to be expected; and the effects upon his health or person which may possibly come from his participation in the experiment.

The duty and responsibility for ascertaining the quality of the consent rests upon each individual who initiates, directs or engages in the experiment. It is a personal duty and responsibility which may not be delegated to another with impunity.

2.   The experiment should be such as to yield fruitful results for the good of society, unprocurable by other methods or means of study, and not random and unnecessary in nature.

3.   The experiment should be so designed and based on the results of animal experimentation and a knowledge of the natural history of the disease or other problem under study that the anticipated results will justify the performance of the experiment.

4.   The experiment should be so conducted as to avoid all unnecessary physical and mental suffering and injury.

5.   No experiment should be conducted where there is an *a priori* reason to believe that death or disabling injury will occur; except, perhaps, in those experiments where the experimental physicians also serve as subjects.

6.   The degree of risk to be taken should never exceed that determined by the humanitarian importance of the problem to be solved by the experiment.

7.   Proper preparations should be made and adequate facilities provided to protect the experimental subject against even remote possibilities of injury, disability, or death.

8. The experiment should be conducted only by scientifically qualified persons. The highest degree of skill and care should be required through all stages of the experiment by those who conduct or engage in the experiment.

9. During the course of the experiment the human subject should be at liberty to bring the experiment to an end if he has reached the physical or mental state where continuation of the experiment seems to him to be impossible.

10. During the course of the experiment the scientist in charge must be prepared to terminate the experiment at any stage, if he has probable cause to believe, in the exercise of the good faith, superior skill and careful judgment required of him, that a continuation of the experiment is likely to result in injury, disability, or death to the experimental subject.

* * *

Notes and Questions

1. What are the core values evident in the Code? Could you rewrite the Code to give priority to other goals instead? Do any of the concepts need to be updated to better fit modern research or the American culture?

2. The Code, and the federal regulations reproduced below, refer to "human subjects." In 2003, an IOM committee, described *infra*, advocated changing the language to "human participants." What do these different terms each communicate?

3. The Nuremberg Code did not have an immediate influence in the United States, perhaps because the Nazi doctors were viewed as monsters separate and apart from ordinary human nature and outside the tradition of medical ethics in the United States. See George Annas, Mengele's Birthmark: The Nuremberg Code in United States Courts, 7 J. of Contemp. Health L. and Policy 17 (Spring 1991). Nevertheless, the publication of Beecher's landmark article detailing abuses of human subjects in the U.S. made it clear that abuse was possible, if not common, in the U.S. H.K. Beecher, Ethics and Clinical Research, 274 NEJM 1354 (1966). The history of experimentation with human subjects in the United States, as briefly described below, reveals a cycle of abuse, revelation, and reaction. How is the legal framework influenced by the scandal-reform dynamic?

II. REGULATION OF RESEARCH UPON HUMAN SUBJECTS IN THE UNITED STATES

A. HISTORY

One of the defenses raised at the Nazi war trials was that there was no relevant distinction between what the Nazi physicians did and the contemporaneous American practice of using conscientious objectors, the institutionalized mentally ill, and prisoners (including "political" prisoners, such as those convicted of treason) as subjects in research designed to improve America's military strength. The argument that the United States applied a double standard that condemned only Nazi research is bolstered by the fact that there was no effort to seek retribution against Japanese experimenters who were doing work with serious implications for biological warfare, but who cooperated with the United States after their capture. In addition, recent revelations show that as the United States was prosecuting the Nazi doctors, the U.S. government was conducting research on human radiation by injecting subjects (many of whom were inaccurately described as terminally ill) with plutonium or uranium to see what their reaction would be. These subjects were never informed of the nature of the experiments, and their exploitation was clearly inconsistent with the code promulgated at Nuremberg. See Advisory Committee on Human Radiation Experiments, The Human Radiation Experiments (1996); Ruth Faden, The Advisory Committee on Human Radiation Experiments: Reflections on a Presidential Commission, 26 Hastings Center Rep. 22 (1996); Robert Burt, The Suppressed Legacy of Nuremberg, 26 Hastings Center Rep. 30 (1996).

The most famous twentieth century American breach of research ethics was the Tuskegee Syphilis Study. In this study, hundreds of poor African American men in the South were studied so that the United States Public Health Service, could develop an understanding of the natural history of syphilis. Poor rural African Americans were chosen as subjects partly because of the difficulty they might have in seeking treatment for syphilis and because it was thought that African Americans, subject to a racist stereotype as more sexually active and physically and mentally weaker, would be more likely to benefit from the outcome of the study. The USPHC continued this research for forty years. Even when penicillin, the first truly effective treatment for syphilis, became available, the PHS physicians refused to offer that treatment to most of their subjects; and many were expressly and regularly discouraged from seeking effective treatment. The study came to public light in 1972 and was the topic of federal administrative and Congressional hearings in 1973. While participants in the study successfully sued the Public Health Service for compensation, no criminal actions arose out of the case. For a complete account of this shameful episode in American medical history, see J. Jones, Bad Blood (1981); Larry Palmer, Paying for Suffering: The Problem of Human Experimentation, 56 Md. L.Rev. 604 (1997).

The Tuskegee Syphilis study and the human radiation studies do not stand alone as examples of American medical research failing to respect individual subjects. Other publicized cases include the Jewish Chronic Disease Hospital case, in which live cancer cells were injected into patients without their knowledge, and the Willowbrook State Hospital hepatitis study, in which children admitted to a state hospital rife with hepatitis were given the disease as a condition of admission. In each of these cases, as in the Nazi experiments, the only authorities determining whether the subjects were properly selected were the medical investigators themselves. For an excellent history of experimentation on human subjects in the United States and its influence on the role of law in bioethics, see David Rothman, Strangers at the Bedside (1991).

The first formal federal policy requiring outside review of research involving human subjects was imposed in 1966 by the Public Health Service upon those seeking grants from it. The 1966 policy required consideration of "the risks and potential medical benefits of the investigation" before a protocol could be submitted to the Public Health Service.

In 1974, one year after the public disclosure of the Tuskegee Syphilis Study, Congress enacted the National Research Act establishing the National Commission for Protection of Human Subjects of Biomedical and Behavioral

Research, which was to "conduct a comprehensive investigation and study to identify basic ethical principles" that should underlie the conduct of human subjects research. That Commission was also to develop procedures to assure that the research would be consistent with those ethical principles and to recommend guidelines for human subjects research supported by the Department of Health, Education and Welfare. In recognition of the interdisciplinary nature of the issue, the Act required the establishment of institutional review boards (IRBs) at institutions under contract with the Department. By 1975, when the Department issued its "Policy for the Protection of Human Research Subjects," virtually every university, medical school, and research hospital had established IRBs.

B. FEDERAL REGULATION OF RESEARCH

Problem: Is It Research?

What "counts" as research under the federal regulations? Are the activities described below research as defined in the regulations *infra*? Is IRB review required? What information should the patient be given, and is consent required?

   a. An oncologist treating a patient with colon cancer for whom customary chemotherapy drugs have proven ineffective offers his patient the option of trying other drugs. These drugs are currently used for other cancers and are being tested for colon cancer, but the research is not yet complete. Although the oncologist is not participating in any of the protocols concerning this drug, preliminary unpublished reports and informal discussions with researchers testing the drug show promise. If the doctor gives his patient this drug, is it research? See e.g., Nancy King, The Line Between Clinical Innovation and Human Experimentation, 32 Seton Hall L. Rev. 573 (2002).

   b. A nurse anesthetist observes that it is often difficult to intubate seriously overweight adult patients. Because she previously worked at a children's hospital, she suggested that physicians use a pediatric tube for a particular patient in an urgent situation with great success. Assume that the physicians in the hospital decide to adopt this as a regular practice if a first attempt at intubation in such patients fails. Assume further that the nurse presents the practice at a nursing conference or in-service training at the hospital. Is this research? What result if the nurse makes some alterations to the pediatric tube and decides to seek a patent and license design to a manufacturer? Scenario based on Atul Gawande, "When Doctors Make Mistakes" in Complications: A Surgeon's Notes on an Imperfect Science (2002).

   c. A urologist arranged some ten years ago that the teaching hospital at which he worked would store tissue samples from prostatectomies and developed a cataloging system for the stored tissues. The urologist, in collaboration with the university's genome center, is interested in finding out whether there is a genetic connection for prostate cancer. Is their use of this stored tissue research with human subjects as defined in the regulations? Scenario suggested by University Sues Departed Surgeon Over Ownership of Tissue, 12 Health Law Reporter 1336 (Aug. 28, 2003). See National Bioethics Advisory Commission, Research Involving Human Biological Materials: Issues and Policy Guidance (Aug. 1999); Ellen W. Clayton, *et. al*, Informed Consent for Genetic Research on Stored Tissue Samples, 274 JAMA 1786 (1995); Henry T. Greely, Breaking the Stalemate: A Prospective Regulatory Framework for Unforeseen Research Uses of Human Tissue Samples and Health Information, 34 Wake Forest L. Rev. 737 (1999); *Greenberg*, Chapter 17.

d.   Gargantuan Health Maintenance Organization wishes to research the effect of withholds on the behavior of its primary care physicians. Each of its primary care physicians, who work exclusively for Gargantuan and serve only patients who are members of its HMO, is paid a monthly fee of $30 per patient on that physician's primary care list. The Gargantuan administration wants to involve 20 primary care physicians in the study, and to randomize half of the patients on each of those physicians' lists to "withhold" status and maintain half on pure capitation status. While the physicians would continue to receive $30 per capita for the pure capitation patients, they would receive $55 per capita for the "withhold" patients. However, $40 of this $55 would be withheld in a special suspense account, and any costs borne by the HMO as a result of any order of the primary care physician (i.e., the cost of all lab tests, referrals, prescriptions, hospitalizations, and the like) for those patients in the "withhold" group would be subtracted from the suspense account before the balance is paid to the physician at the end of the year. The payment status of each patient would be clearly identified to the primary care physician. Researchers hypothesize that primary care physicians will order fewer additional services and less additional treatment for their "withhold" patients than for their pure capitation patients. Gargantuan intends to keep the results for their own use alone and consider the design of their payment system to be a trade secret.

45 C.F.R. PART 46—BASIC HHS POLICY FOR PROTECTION OF HUMAN RESEARCH SUBJECTS

§ 46.101   To what does this policy apply?

(a) Except as provided in paragraph (b) of this section, this policy applies to all research involving human subjects conducted, supported or otherwise subject to regulation by any federal department or agency which takes appropriate administrative action to make the policy applicable to such research.... It also includes research conducted, supported, or otherwise subject to regulation by the federal government outside the United States.

* * *

(b) Unless otherwise required by department or agency heads, research activities in which the only involvement of human subjects will be in one or more of the following categories are exempt from this policy:

(1) Research conducted in established or commonly accepted educational settings, involving normal educational practices [concerning teaching methods.]

(2) Research involving the use of educational tests (cognitive, diagnostic, aptitude, achievement), survey procedures, interview procedures or observation of public behavior, unless:

(i) Information obtained is recorded in such a manner that human subjects can be identified, directly or through identifiers linked to the subjects; and (ii) any disclosure of the human subjects' responses outside the research could reasonably place the subjects at risk of criminal or civil liability or be damaging to the subjects' financial standing, employability, or reputation.

(3) Research involving the use of educational tests ..., survey procedures, interview procedures, or observation of public behavior that is not exempt under paragraph (b)(2) of this section, if:

(i) The human subjects are elected or appointed public officials or candidates for public office; or (ii) federal statute(s) require(s) without exception that the confidentiality of the personally identifiable information will be maintained throughout the research and thereafter.

(4) Research, involving the collection or study of existing data, documents, records, pathological specimens, or diagnostic specimens, if these sources are publicly available or if the information is recorded by the investigator in such a manner that subjects cannot be identified, directly or through identifiers linked to the subjects.

(5) Research and demonstration projects which are conducted by or subject to the approval of department or agency heads, and which are designed to study, evaluate, or otherwise examine [eligibility, benefits, payments, or procedures of public benefit or service programs].

* * *

(f) This policy does not affect any state or local laws or regulations which may otherwise be applicable and which provide additional protections for human subjects.

(g) This policy does not affect any foreign laws or regulations which may otherwise be applicable and which provide additional protections to human subjects of research.

(h) When research covered by this policy takes place in foreign countries, procedures normally followed in the foreign countries to protect human subjects may differ from those set forth in this policy.... In these circumstances, if a department or agency head determines that the procedures prescribed by the institution afford protections that are at least equivalent to those provided in this policy, the department or agency head may approve the substitution of the foreign procedures in lieu of the procedural requirements provided in this policy.

* * *

§ 46.102 Definitions.

* * *

(c) Legally authorized representative means an individual or judicial or other body authorized under applicable law to consent on behalf of a prospective subject to the subject's participation in the procedure(s) involved in the research.

(d) Research means a systematic investigation, including research development, testing and evaluation, designed to develop or contribute to generalizable knowledge. Activities which meet this definition constitute research for purposes of this policy, whether or not they are conducted or supported under a program which is considered research for other purposes. For example, some demonstration and service programs may include research activities.

(e) Research subject to regulation and similar terms are intended to encompass those research activities for which a federal department or agency has specific responsibility for regulating as a research activity, (for example, Investigational New Drug requirements administered by the Food and Drug Administration)....

* * *

(f) Human subject means a living individual about whom an investigator (whether professional or student) conducting research obtains

(1) Data through intervention or interaction with the individual, or

(2) Identifiable private information.

Intervention includes both physical procedures by which data are gathered (for example, venipuncture) or manipulations of the subject or the subject's environment that are performed for research purposes. Interaction includes communication or interpersonal contact between investigator and subject. Private information includes information about behavior that occurs in a context in which an individual can reasonably expect that no observation or recording is taking place, and information which has been provided for specific purposes by an individual and which the individual can reasonably expect will not be made public (for example, a medical record). Private information must be individually identifiable (i.e., the identity of the subject is or may readily be ascertained by the investigator or associated with the information) in order for obtaining the information to constitute research involving human subjects.

* * *

(i) Minimal risk means that the probability and magnitude of harm or discomfort anticipated in the research are not greater in and of themselves than those ordinarily encountered in daily life or during the performance of routine physical or psychological examinations or tests.

* * *

§ 46.107　IRB membership.

(a) Each IRB shall have at least five members, with varying backgrounds to promote complete and adequate review of research activities commonly conducted by the institution. The IRB shall be sufficiently qualified through the experience and expertise of its members, and the diversity of the members, including consideration of race, gender, and cultural backgrounds and sensitivity to such issues as community attitudes, to promote respect for its advice and counsel in safeguarding the rights and welfare of human subjects. In addition to possessing the professional competence necessary to review specific research activities, the IRB shall be able to ascertain the acceptability of proposed research in terms of institutional commitments and regulations, applicable law, and standards of professional conduct and practice. The IRB shall therefore include persons knowledgeable in these areas. If an IRB regularly reviews research that involves a vulnerable category of subjects, such as children, prisoners, pregnant women, or handicapped or mentally disabled persons, consideration shall be given to the inclusion of one or more individuals who are knowledgeable about and experienced in working with these subjects.

(b) Every nondiscriminatory effort will be made to ensure that no IRB consists entirely of men or entirely of women, including the institution's consideration of qualified persons of both sexes, so long as no selection is made to the IRB on the basis of gender. No IRB may consist entirely of members of one profession.

(c) Each IRB shall include at least one member whose primary concerns are in scientific areas and at least one member whose primary concerns are in nonscientific areas.

(d) Each IRB shall include at least one member who is not otherwise affiliated with the institution and who is not part of the immediate family of a person who is affiliated with the institution.

(e) No IRB may have a member participate in the IRB's initial or continuing review of any project in which the member has a conflicting interest, except to provide information requested by the IRB.

(f) An IRB may, in its discretion, invite individuals with competence in special areas to assist in the review of issues which require expertise beyond or in addition to that available on the IRB. These individuals may not vote with the IRB.

§ 46.109   IRB review of research.

(a) An IRB shall review and have authority to approve, require modification in (to secure approval), or disapprove all research activities covered by this policy.

* * *

(e) An IRB shall conduct continuing review of research covered by this policy at intervals appropriate to the degree of risk, but not less than one per year, and shall have authority to observe or have a third party observe the consent process and the research.

* * *

§ 46.111   Criteria for IRB approval of research.

(a) In order to approve research covered by this policy the IRB shall determine that all of the following requirements are satisfied:

(1) Risks to subjects are minimized: (i) By using procedures which are consistent with sound research design and which do not unnecessarily expose subjects to risk, and (ii) whenever appropriate, by using procedures already being performed on the subjects for diagnostic or treatment purposes.

(2) Risks to subjects are reasonable in relation to anticipated benefits, if any, to subjects, and the importance of the knowledge that may reasonably be expected to result. In evaluating risks and benefits, the IRB should consider only those risks and benefits that may result from the research (as distinguished from risks and benefits of therapies subjects would receive even if not participating in the research). The IRB should not consider possible long-range effects of applying knowledge gained in the research (for example, the

possible effects of the research on public policy) as among those research risks that fall within the purview of its responsibility.

(3) Selection of subjects is equitable. In making this assessment the IRB should take into account the purposes of the research and the setting in which the research will be conducted and should be particularly cognizant of the special problems or research involving vulnerable populations, such as children, prisoners, pregnant women, mentally disabled persons, or economically or educationally disadvantaged persons.

(4) Informed consent will be sought from each prospective subject or the subject's legally authorized representative, in accordance with, and to the extent required by § 46.116.

(5) Informed consent will be appropriately documented, in accordance with, and to the extent required by § 46.117.

(6) When appropriate, the research plan makes adequate provision for monitoring the data collected to ensure the safety of subjects.

(7) When appropriate, there are adequate provisions to protect the privacy of subjects and to maintain the confidentiality of data.

(b) When some or all of the subjects are likely to be vulnerable to coercion or undue influence, such as children, prisoners, pregnant women, mentally disabled persons, or economically or educationally disadvantaged persons, additional safeguards have been included in the study to protect the rights and welfare of these subjects.

§ 46.112   Review by institution.

Research covered by this policy that has been approved by the IRB may be subject to further appropriate review and approval or disapproval by officials of the institution. However, those officials may not approve the research if it has not been approved by an IRB.

§ 46.113   Suspension or termination of IRB approval of research.

An IRB shall have authority to suspend or terminate approval of research that is not being conducted in accordance with the IRB's requirements or that has been associated with unexpected serious harm to subjects. . . .

* * *

§ 46.116   General requirements for informed consent.

Except as provided elsewhere in this policy, no investigator may involve a human being as a subject in research covered by this policy unless the investigator has obtained the legally effective informed consent of the subject or the subject's legally authorized representative. An investigator shall seek such consent only under circumstances that provide the prospective subject or the representative sufficient opportunity to consider whether or not to participate and that minimize the possibility of coercion or undue influence. The information that is given to the subject or the representative shall be in language understandable to the subject or the representative. No informed consent, whether oral or written, may include any exculpatory language through which the subject or the representative is made to waive or appear to waive any of the subject's legal rights, or releases or appears to release the investigator, the sponsor, the institution or its agents from liability for negligence.

(a) Basic elements of informed consent. Except as provided in paragraph (c) or (d) of this section, in seeking informed consent the following information shall be provided to each subject:

(1) A statement that the study involves research, an explanation of the purposes of the research and the expected duration of the subject's participation, a description of the procedures to be followed, and identification of any procedures which are experimental;

(2) A description of any reasonably foreseeable risks or discomforts to the subject;

(3) A description of any benefits to the subject or to others which may reasonably be expected from the research;

(4) A disclosure of appropriate alternative procedures or courses of treatment, if any, that might be advantageous to the subject;

(5) A statement describing the extent, if any, to which confidentiality of records identifying the subject will be maintained;

(6) For research involving more than minimal risk, an explanation as to whether any compensation and an explanation as to whether any medical treatments are available if injury occurs and, if so, what they consist of, or where further information may be obtained;

(7) An explanation of whom to contact for answers to pertinent questions about the research and research subjects' rights, whom to contact in the event of a research-related injury to the subject; and

(8) A statement that participation is voluntary, refusal to participate will involve no penalty or loss of benefits to which the subject is otherwise entitled, and the subject may discontinue participation at any time without penalty or loss of benefits to which the subject is otherwise entitled.

(b) Additional elements of informed consent. When appropriate, one or more of the following elements of information shall also be provided to each subject:

(1) A statement that the particular treatment or procedure may involve risks to the subject (or to the embryo or fetus, if the subject is or may become pregnant) which are currently unforeseeable;

(2) Anticipated circumstances under which the subject's participation may be terminated by the investigator without regard to the subject's consent;

(3) Any additional costs to the subject that may result from participation in the research;

(4) The consequences of a subject's decision to withdraw from the research and procedures for orderly termination of participation by the subject;

(5) A statement that significant new findings developed during the course of the research which may relate to the subject's willingness to continue participation will be provided to the subject; and

(6) The approximate number of subjects involved in the study.

(c) An IRB may approve a consent procedure which does not include, or which alters, some or all of the elements of informed consent set forth above, or waive the requirements to obtain informed consent provided the IRB finds and documents that:

(1) The research or demonstration project is to be conducted by or subject to the approval of state or local government officials and is designed to study, evaluate, or otherwise examine:

(i) Public benefit service programs; (ii) procedures for obtaining benefits or services under those programs; (iii) possible changes in or alternatives to those programs or procedures; or (iv) possible changes in methods or levels of payment for benefits or services under those programs; and

(2) The research could not practicably be carried out without the waiver or alteration.

(d) An IRB may approve a consent procedure which does not include, or which alters, some or all of the elements of informed consent set forth in this section, or waive the requirements to obtain informed consent provided the IRB finds and documents that:

(1) The research involves no more than minimal risks to the subjects;

(2) The waiver or alteration will not adversely affect the rights and welfare of the subjects;

(3) The research could not practicably be carried out without the waiver or alteration; and

(4) Whenever appropriate, the subjects will be provided with additional pertinent information after participation.

(e) The informed consent requirements in this policy are not intended to preempt any applicable federal, state, or local laws which require additional information to be disclosed in order for informed consent to be legally effective.

* * *

§ 46.117   Documentation of informed consent.

(a) Except as provided in paragraph (c) of this section, informed consent shall be documented by the use of a written consent form approved by the IRB and signed by the subject or the subject's legally authorized representative. A copy shall be given to the person signing the form.

* * *

(c) An IRB may waive the requirement for the investigator to obtain a signed consent form for some or all subjects if it finds either:

(1) That the only record linking the subject and the research would be the consent document and the principal risk would be potential harm resulting from a breach of confidentiality. Each subject will be asked whether the subject wants documentation linking the subject with the research, and the subject's wishes will govern; or

(2) That the research presents no more than minimal risk of harm to subjects and involves no procedures for which consent is normally required outside of the research context.

In cases in which the documentation requirement is waived, the IRB may require the investigator to provide subjects with a written statement regarding the research.

* * *

§ 46.122 Use of Federal funds.

Federal funds administered by a department or agency may not be expended for research involving human subjects unless the requirements of this policy have been satisfied.

* * *

Notes and Questions

1. These regulations form the "common rule," so called because more than a dozen federal agencies have promulgated similar, though not identical, regulations to govern research funded by or conducted by those agencies. See, e.g., 7 C.F.R. § 1c.101 (Agriculture); 10 C.F.R. § 35.6 (Energy); 14 CFR § 1230.101 (NASA); 21 CFR § 50.1 (FDA). The common rule applies only to research performed or funded by the United States government, or subject to "regulation by any federal department or agency," as defined in § 46.102. The regulations do not apply to other research, even when conducted at the same institution. This distinction may not have much practical effect within academic research centers, however, because each institution that receives DHHS funding must provide the Secretary assurances that the institution will protect the rights of human subjects. Most institutions meet this "assurance" requirement by agreeing to apply DHHS regulations to all research, even that not funded by DHHS and thus not technically otherwise governed by those regulations. In addition, the Food and Drug Administration requires that research submitted to the FDA in relation to the approval or regulation of drugs, devices or other substances meet similar legal standards, whether or not the research is government-funded. 21 CFR § 50.1.

2. Do the regulations effectively guarantee that the IRB will represent the values that ought to be considered in approving research? Most IRBs include a lawyer. What role should the lawyer assume in serving on the IRB? Does it matter whether the lawyer is institutional counsel? If you were to rewrite § 46.107, what kind of interdisciplinary mix would you require on the IRB? Would you bar the organization's lawyer from voting membership?

3. What is the rationale for committing review authority to a committee of the research entity itself? Should the federal government instead establish an agency that would itself review all protocols? Should there be a federally appointed representative on each IRB? See if your opinion changes after reading *Kennedy Krieger* below.

4. While § 46.111 establishes seven substantive criteria for approval of a research protocol, most IRB time is spent discussing (1) whether the "risks to subjects are reasonable in relationship to anticipated benefits," and (2) whether the informed consent form is adequate. Should these be the primary substantive bases for review of medical research? In the rare instance that a research protocol is turned down by an IRB the reason is usually that the IRB has determined that the risk-to-benefit ratio is not acceptable.

Why do the federal regulations and IRBs spend so much time examining a protocol's provisions for informed consent? In 1982, Paul Appelbaum coined the term "therapeutic misconception" to describe the observation that patients tend to believe that experimental medical intervention will benefit them directly by providing treatment for their condition despite clear statements to the contrary. The Therapeutic Misconception: Informed Consent to Psychiatric Research, 5 Int'l J.L. & Psychiatry 319, 321 (1982). See also, Jay Katz, Human Experimentation and Human Rights, 38 St. Louis U.L.J. 7, 36 (1993); Sharona Hoffman, Regulating Clinical Research: Informed Consent, Privacy, and IRBs, 31 Cap. U.L.Rev. 71 (2003), detailing studies on the ineffectiveness of informed consent in research; Dana Ziker, Reviving Informed Consent: Using Risk Perception in Clinical Trials, 2003 Duke L. & Tech. Rev. 15; T. Mozes, *et al.*, Informed Consent: Myth or Reality, 21 Med. & L. 473 (2002). See, also, the *Kennedy Krieger* case, below.

5. Although consent is critical, the federal regulations do not permit research, even with the consent of the subject, if the risks to the subject are not reasonable as defined in § 46.111. There are several discrete issues within the notion of impermissible risks to subjects that are covered later in these materials. The soundness of the research design is critical to assessing whether risk to subjects is reasonable. Why is this so?

In addition, the IRB has a duty to monitor all approved protocols to assure that implementation is conforming to the parameters of the original approval, including the actual risk to subjects. Some IRBs have established or contracted with data safety monitoring boards (DSMBs) to audit the progress of protocols by reviewing data produced in the course of research, including adverse events, and by identifying points at which the research should be halted either because of unanticipated levels of risk or unexpectedly early positive results. NIH recently halted an NIH Women's Health Initiative (WHI) protocol studying 11,000 female subjects who were taking estrogen (the "estrogen-alone" study) when the WHI data and safety monitoring board found that data showed an increase in strokes in the study population even though the DSMB split on whether the subjects should be told to stop taking the pills or should simply be informed of the newly discovered risks. NIH Press Release, March 2, 2004. For a description of DSMBs, see Vallery M. Gordon, et al., Toward a More Comprehensive Approach to Protecting Human Subjects: The Interface of Data Safety Monitoring Boards and Institutional Review Boards in Randomized Clinical Trials, 20 IRB 1 (1998). Should non-scientific members of the IRB defer to the scientific members on the question of risk assessment, research design, or continuing review of the results being produced by the research protocol? Can they do otherwise?

6. The federal regulations do not directly address the question that arises when an investigator believes that one arm of a therapeutic investigation is really superior to the other. Can that investigator allow his patients to be randomized to one arm or another? One thoughtful commentator suggests that such randomization is ethical when there is "present or imminent controversy in the clinical community over the preferred treatment," whatever the individual investigator may believe. Benjamin Freedman, Equipoise and the Ethics of Clinical Research, 317 NEJM 141 (1987). Similar issues arise with the case of placebos. Sharona Hoffman, The Use of Placebos in Clinical Trials: Responsible Research or Unethical Practice, 33 Conn. L. Rev. 449, 474–75 (2001). See also, Kathleen Boozang, The Therapeutic Placebo: The Case for Patient Deception, 54 Fla. L. Rev. 687 (2002).

7. The HHS regulations are enforced by the Office of Human Research Protection (OHRP) in HHS. (http://ohrp.osophs.dhhs.gov) OHRP enforces the regulations through investigation of complaints and audits. The FDA enforces its regulations in the same way. From 1999 to 2000, OHRP found twenty universi-

ties, including some of the most prestigious research universities in the country, to be in substantial violation of the federal regulations. The sanction was stunning: OHRP suspended federal funding of research for periods ranging from several days to several weeks. If a university holds $100 million in federally funded research annually, that action amounts to a fine of over a quarter million dollars a day. As this is written, the wave of suspensions seems to have dissipated. On the private side, JCAHO and the NCQA formed a partnership to certify research entities. 12 Health Law Reporter 134 (Jan. 23, 2003). The Association of American Medical Asssociations led the founding of the Association for the Accreditation of Human Research Protection Programs, which has an active program. 10 Health Law Reporter 1169 (Jul. 26, 2001).

8.   The FDA has promulgated regulations that allow for research in emergency medicine without consent. 21 CFR § 50.24. These regulations allow research where the "human subjects are in a life-threatening situation, available treatments are unproven or unsatisfactory, and the collection of valid scientific evidence ... is necessary to determine what particular intervention is most beneficial; obtaining consent is not feasible [because subjects will not be able to give consent due to their medical condition and the intervention has to take place before consent from a legal representative is feasible]; participation in the research holds out the prospect of direct benefit to the subjects; the clinical investigation could not practicably be carried out without the waiver [of the consent requirement]; ... and additional protections of the rights and welfare of the subjects will be provided." Additional protections must include "consultation ... with representatives of the communities in which the investigation will be conducted and from which subjects will be drawn; public disclosure [to the community prior to the initiation of the study]; establishment of an independent data monitoring committee ... and ... [documented effort] to contact ... the subject's family member who is not a legally authorized representative [to ask whether the family objects to the subject's participation]." The regulations allow for a placebo arm in which some subjects will receive a placebo rather than a drug. Can this be justified as "direct benefit" to the patient?

C. RESEARCH REGULATION BY LITIGATION: PROTECTING VULNERABLE SUBJECTS

GRIMES v. KENNEDY KRIEGER INSTITUTE, INC.

Court of Appeals of Maryland, 2001.
366 Md. 29, 782 A.2d 807.

CATHELL, Judge.

* * *

[According to the record before the Court on the motion for summary judgment in] these present cases, [the Kennedy Krieger Institute,] a prestigious research institute associated with Johns Hopkins University * * * created a nontherapeutic research program[1] whereby it required certain

---

1. At least to the extent that commercial profit motives are not implicated, therapeutic research's purpose is to directly help or aid a patient who is suffering from a health condition the objectives of the research are designed to address—hopefully by the alleviation, or potential alleviation, of the health condition. Nontherapeutic research generally utilizes subjects who are not known to have the condition the objectives of the research are designed to address, and/or is not designed to directly benefit the subjects utilized in the research, but, rather, is designed to achieve beneficial results for the public at large (or, under some circumstances, for profit).

fail for that reason. In that regard, we note that there are substantial factual differences [among the] cases. But the actions, themselves, are not defective on the ground that no legal duty can, according to the trial courts, possibly exist. * * *

I. The Cases

* * * [Plaintiffs] allege that KKI [Kennedy Krieger Institute] discovered lead hazards in their respective homes and, having a duty to notify them, failed to warn in a timely manner or otherwise act to prevent the children's exposure to the known presence of lead. Additionally, plaintiffs alleged that they were not fully informed of the risks of the research.

[The trial court granted summary judgment on the basis that KKI had no legal duty to warn the subjects of their exposure to lead.]

The trial court was incorrect. Such research programs normally create special relationships and/or can be of a contractual nature, that create duties. The breaches of such duties may ultimately result in viable negligence actions. Because, at the very least, there are viable and genuine disputes of material fact concerning whether a special relationship, or other relationships arising out of agreements, giving rise to duties existed between KKI and both sets of appellants, we hold that the Circuit Court erred in granting KKI's motions for summary judgment in both cases before this Court. * * *

II. Facts & Procedural Background

In summary, KKI conducted a study of five test groups of twenty-five houses each. The first three groups consisted of houses known to have lead present. The amount of repair and maintenance conducted increased from Group 1 to Group 2 to Group 3. The fourth group consisted of houses, which had at one time lead present but had since allegedly received a complete abatement of lead dust. The fifth group consisted of modern houses, which had never had the presence of lead dust. The twenty-five homes in each of the first three testing levels were then to be compared to the two control groups: the twenty-five homes in Group 4 that had previously been abated and the 25 modern homes in Group 5. The research study was specifically designed to do less than full lead dust abatement in some of the categories of houses in order to study the potential effectiveness, if any, of lesser levels of repair and maintenance.

If the children were to leave the houses upon the first manifestation of lead dust, it would be difficult, if not impossible, to test, over time, the rate of the level of lead accumulation in the blood of the children attributable to the manifestation. * * * Thus, it would benefit the accuracy of the test, and thus KKI, the compensated researcher, if children remained in the houses over the period of the study even after the presence of lead dust in the houses became evident.

* * *

B. Case No. 128 [Ms. Viola Hughes and Daughter Ericka Grimes]

* * *

Nowhere in the consent form was it clearly disclosed to the mother that the researchers contemplated that, as a result of the experiment, the child might accumulate lead in her blood, and that in order for the experiment to succeed it was necessary that the child remain in the house as the lead in the child's blood increased or decreased, so that it could be measured. The Consent Form states in relevant part:

PURPOSE OF STUDY:

As you may know, lead poisoning in children is a problem in Baltimore City and other communities across the country. Lead in paint, house dust and outside soil are major sources of lead exposure for children. Children can also be exposed to lead in drinking water and other sources. We understand that your house is going to have special repairs done in order to reduce exposure to lead in paint and dust. On a random basis, homes will receive one of two levels of repair. We are interested in finding out how well the two levels of repair work. The repairs are not intended, or expected, to completely remove exposure to lead.

We are now doing a study to learn about how well different practices work for reducing exposure to lead in paint and dust. We are asking you and over one hundred other families to allow us to test for lead in and around your homes up to 8 to 9 times over the next two years provided that your house qualifies for the full two years of study. Final eligibility will be determined after the initial testing of your home. We are also doing free blood lead testing of children aged 6 months to 7 years, up to 8 to 9 times over the next two years. We would also like you to respond to a short questionnaire every 6 months. This study is intended to monitor the effects of the repairs and is not intended to replace the regular medical care your family obtains.

. . .

BENEFITS

To compensate you for your time answering questions and allowing us to sketch your home we will mail you a check in the amount of $5.00. In the future we would mail you a check in the amount of $15 each time the full questionnaire is completed. The dust, soil, water, and blood samples would be tested for lead at [KKI] at no charge to you. *We would provide you with specific blood-lead results. We would contact you to discuss a summary of house test results and steps that you could take to reduce any risks of exposure.* [Emphasis added [by the court].]

Pursuant to the plans of the research study, KKI collected dust samples [from the Grimes' house] on March 9, 1993, August 23, 1993, March 9, 1994, September 19, 1994, April 18, 1995, and November 13, 1995.[2] The March 9, 1993 dust testing revealed what the researchers referred to as "hot spots" where the level of lead was "higher than might be found in a completely renovated [abated] house." This information about the "hot spots" was not furnished to Ms. Hughes until December 16, 1993, more than nine months

---

2. For some unexplained reason, processing the dust samples typically took several months. KKI notified Ms. Hughes of the dust sample results via letters dated December 16, 1993, December 17, 1993, May 19, 1994, October 28, 1994, July 19, 1995, and January 18, 1996, respectively.

after the samples had been collected and, as we discuss, *infra,* not until after Ericka Grimes's blood was found to contain elevated levels of lead.

KKI drew blood from Ericka Grimes for lead content analysis on April, 9, 1993, September 15, 1993, and March 25, 1994. Unlike the lead concentration analysis in dust testing, the results of the blood testing were typically available to KKI in a matter of days. KKI notified Ms. Hughes of the results of the blood tests by letters dated April 9, 1993, September 29, 1993, and March 28, 1994, respectively. The results of the April 9, 1993 test found Ericka Grimes blood to be [within normal range]. * * * However, on two subsequent retests, long after KKI had identified "hot spots," but before KKI informed Ms. Hughes of the "hot spots," Ericka Grimes's blood lead level registered [highly elevated] on March 25, 1994. Ms. Hughes and her daughter vacated the Monroe Street property in the Summer of 1994, and, therefore, no further blood samples were obtained by KKI after March 25, 1994.

* * *

III. *Discussion*

* * *

Because of the way the cases *sub judice* have arrived, as appeals from the granting of summary judgments, there is no complete record of the specific compensation of the researchers involved. * * * Neither is there in the record any development of what pressures, if any, were exerted in respect to the researchers obtaining the consents of the parents and conducting the experiment. Nor, for the same reason, is there a sufficient indication as to the extent to which the Institute has joined with commercial interests, if it has, for the purposes of profit, that might potentially impact upon the researcher's motivations and potential conflicts of interest—motivations that generally are assumed, in the cases of prestigious entities such as John Hopkins University, to be for the public good rather than a search for profit.

We do note that the institution involved * * * is a highly respected entity, considered to be a leader in the development of treatments, and treatment itself, for children infected with lead poisoning. With reasonable assurance, we can note that its reputation alone might normally suggest that there was no realization or understanding on the Institute's part that the protocols of the experiment were questionable, except for the letter from the IRB requesting that the researchers mischaracterize the study.

* * *

C. *Negligence*

* * *

The relationship that existed between KKI and both sets of appellants in the case at bar was that of medical researcher and research study subject. Though not expressly recognized in the Maryland Code or in our prior cases as a type of relationship which creates a duty of care, evidence in the record suggests that such a relationship involving a duty or duties would ordinarily exist, and certainly could exist, based on the facts and circumstances of each of these individual cases. * * *

IV. *The Special Relationships*

A. *The Consent Agreement*

* * *

By having appellants sign the Consent Form, both KKI and appellants expressly made representations, which, in our view, created a bilateral contract between the parties. At the very least, it suggests that appellants were agreeing with KKI to participate in the research study with the expectation that they would be compensated, albeit, more or less, minimally, be informed of all the information necessary for the subject to freely choose whether to participate, and continue to participate, and receive promptly any information that might bear on their willingness to continue to participate in the study. This includes full, detailed, prompt, and continuing warnings as to all the potential risks and hazards inherent in the research or that arise during the research. KKI, in return, was getting the children to move into the houses and/or to remain there over time, and was given the right to test the children's blood for lead. As consideration to KKI, it got access to the houses and to the blood of children that had been encouraged to live in a "risk" environment. In other words, KKI received a measuring tool—the children's blood. Considerations existed, mainly money, food coupons, trinkets, bilateral promises, blood to be tested in order to measure success. "Informed consent" of the type used here, which imposes obligation and confers consideration on both researcher and subject (in these cases, the parents of the subjects) may differ from the more one-sided "informed consent" normally used in actual medical practice. * * *

B. *The Sufficiency of the Consent Form*

* * *

A reasonable parent would expect to be clearly informed that it was at least contemplated that her child would ingest lead dust particles, and that the degree to which lead dust contaminated the child's blood would be used as one of the ways in which the success of the experiment would be measured. The fact that if such information was furnished, it might be difficult to obtain human subjects for the research, does not affect the need to supply the information, or alter the ethics of failing to provide such information. A human subject is entitled to *all* material information. * * * The "informed" consent was not valid because full material information was not furnished to the subjects or their parents.

* * *

D. *The Federal Regulations*

A duty may be prescribed by a statute, or a special relationship creating duties may arise from the requirement for compliance with statutory provisions. [F]ederal regulations have been enacted that impose standards of care that attach to federally funded or sponsored research projects that use human subjects. [ ] * * * [The court excerpts 45 C.F.R. § 46.116 which is reproduced, *supra*.]

* * *

In the case of Whitlock v. Duke University, 637 F.Supp. 1463 (M.D.N.C. 1986), affirmed by, 829 F.2d 1340 (4th Cir. 1987), the [Court] decided that in determining what duty a researcher owes to a subject of nontherapeutic experimentation, it would analyze a duty consistent with 45 C.F.R. section 46.116. [ ] That court held that a researcher has a duty to inform the subject of *all* risks that are *reasonably foreseeable*. *Whitlock* involved a subject who suffered organic brain damage from decompression experiments. The District Court ultimately held (and was affirmed by the Court of Appeals for the Fourth Circuit) that although a heightened duty existed between a researcher and an adult research participant requiring the researcher to disclose all foreseeable risks, in *Whitlock* there was no evidence presented that the risk of organic brain damage was foreseeable.

That result is clearly distinguishable from the present cases, where the risks associated with exposing children to lead-based paint were not only foreseeable, but were well known by KKI * * *. Moreover, in the present cases, the consent forms did not directly inform the parents that it was possible, even contemplated, that some level of lead, a harmful substance depending upon accumulation, might contaminate the blood of the children.

Clearly, KKI, as a research institution, is required to obtain a human participant's fully informed consent, using sound ethical principles. It is clear from the wording of the applicable federal regulations that this requirement of informed consent continues during the duration of the research study and applies to new or changing risks. * * *

* * *

V.   The Ethical Appropriateness of the Research

* * *

Researchers cannot ever be permitted to completely immunize themselves by reliance on consents, especially when the information furnished to the subject, or the party consenting, is incomplete in a material respect. A researcher's duty is not created by, or extinguished by, the consent of a research subject or by IRB approval. The duty to a vulnerable research subject is independent of consent, although the obtaining of consent is one of the duties a researcher must perform. All of this is especially so when the subjects of research are children. Such legal duties, and legal protections, might additionally be warranted because of the likely conflict of interest between the goal of the research experimenter and the health of the human subject, especially, but not exclusively, when such research is commercialized. There is always a potential substantial conflict of interest on the part of researchers as between them and the human subjects used in their research. If participants in the study withdraw from the research study prior to its completion, then the results of the study could be rendered meaningless. There is thus an inherent reason for not conveying information to subjects as it arises, that might cause the subjects to leave the research project. That conflict dictates a stronger reason for full and continuous disclosure.

* * *

* * * Practical inequalities exist between researchers, who have superior knowledge, and participants "who are often poorly placed to protect themselves from risk." [ ] "[G]iven the gap in knowledge between investigators and participants and the inherent conflict of interest faced by investigators, participants cannot and should not be solely responsible for their own protection." [ ]

VI. Parental Consent for Children to Be Subjects of Potentially Hazardous Nontherapeutic Research

The issue of whether a parent can consent to the participation of her or his child in a nontherapeutic health-related study that is known to be potentially hazardous to the health of the child raises serious questions with profound moral and ethical implications. What right does a parent have to knowingly expose a child not in need of therapy to health risks or otherwise knowingly place a child in danger, even if it can be argued it is for the greater good? * * * We have long stressed that the "best interests of the child" is the overriding concern of this Court in matters relating to children. * * *

To think otherwise, to turn over human and legal ethical concerns solely to the scientific community, is to risk embarking on slippery slopes, that all too often in the past, here and elsewhere, have resulted in practices we, or any community, should be ever unwilling to accept.

* * *

[The court describes several cases involving the donation of organs or tissue from a minor child or incompetent to a family member.]

What is of primary importance to be gleaned in [these transplantation] cases is not that the parents or guardians consented to the procedures, but that they first sought permission of the courts, and received that permission, before consenting to a nontherapeutic procedure in respect to some of their minor children, but that was therapeutic to other of their children.

In the case sub judice, no impartial judicial review or oversight was sought by the researchers or by the parents. [Emphasis in original.] * * *

* * *

VII. Conclusion

We hold that in Maryland a parent, appropriate relative, or other applicable surrogate, cannot consent to the participation of a child or other person under legal disability in nontherapeutic research or studies in which there is any risk of injury or damage to the health of the subject.

We hold that informed consent agreements in nontherapeutic research projects, under certain circumstances can constitute contracts; and that, under certain circumstances, such research agreements can, as a matter of law, constitute "special relationships" giving rise to duties, out of the breach of which negligence actions may arise. We also hold that, normally, such special relationships are created between researchers and the human subjects used by the researchers. Additionally, we hold that governmental regulations can create duties on the part of researchers towards human subjects out of which "special relationships" can arise. Likewise, such duties and relationships are consistent with the provisions of the Nuremberg Code.

The determination as to whether a "special relationship" actually exists is to be done on a case by case basis. [ ] The determination as to whether a special relationship exists, if properly pled, lies with the trier of fact. We hold that there was ample evidence in the cases at bar to support a fact finder's determination of the existence of duties arising out of contract, or out of a special relationship, or out of regulations and codes, or out of all of them, in each of the cases.

* * *

RAKER, Judge, concurring in result only:

* * *

I cannot join in the majority's sweeping factual determinations that the risks associated with exposing children to lead-based paint were foreseeable and well known to appellees and that appellees contemplated lead contamination in participants' blood; that the children's health was put at risk; that there was no complete and clear explanation in the consent agreements that the research to be conducted was designed to measure the success of the abatement procedures by measuring the extent to which the children's blood was being contaminated and that a certain level of lead accumulation was anticipated; that the parental consent was ineffective; that the consent form was insufficient because it lacked certain specific warnings; that the consent agreements did not provide that appellees would provide repairs in the event of lead dust contamination subsequent to the original abatement measures; that the Institutional Review Board involved in these cases abdicated its responsibility to protect the safety of the research subjects by misconstruing the difference between therapeutic and nontherapeutic research and aiding researchers in circumventing federal regulations; that Institutional Review Boards are not sufficiently objective to regulate the ethics of experimental research; that it is never in the best interest of any child to be placed in a nontherapeutic research study that might be hazardous to the child's health; that there was no therapeutic value in the research for the child subjects involved; that the research did not comply with applicable regulations; or that there was more than a minimal risk involved in this study. I do not here condone the conduct of appellee, and it may well be that the majority's conclusions are warranted by the facts of these cases, but the record before us is limited. Indeed, the majority recognizes that the record is "sparse." The critical point is that these are questions for the jury on remand and are not properly before this Court at this time.

* * * I cannot join the majority in holding that, in Maryland, a parent or guardian cannot consent to the participation of a minor child in a nontherapeutic research study in which there is *any* risk of injury or damage to the health of the child without prior judicial approval and oversight. Nor can I join in the majority's holding that the research conducted in these cases was *per se* inappropriate, unethical, and illegal. Such sweeping holdings are far beyond the question presented in these appeals, and their resolution by the Court, at this time, is inappropriate. I also do not join in what I perceive as the majority's wholesale adoption of the Nuremberg Code into Maryland state tort law. * * *

Accordingly, I join the majority only in the judgment to reverse the Circuit Courts' granting of summary judgments to appellees.

Notes and Questions

1. Should the federal regulations be enforceable in litigation by participants in research, or should the government retain exclusive enforcement authority? If a private right of action for the enforcement of the federal regulations is desirable, should Congress or the state legislature enact legislation, similar to that relating to private actions for the violation of nursing home standards as described in Chapter 2 that would provide for statutory damages in the absence of physical harm or for punitive damages? For analysis of *Kennedy Krieger* and the liability issue in the context of genetic research, see Larry Palmer, Genetic Health and Eugenics Precedents: A Voice of Caution, 30 Fla. St. L. Rev. 237 (2003).

2. *Kennedy Krieger* is only one of several private lawsuits brought in the past few years against research institutions for violation of standards in research. See, e.g., Diaz v. Tampa General Hospital, 2000 WL 1682918 (M.D. Fla. 2000) in which the court approved a $3.8 million settlement of claims that the physicians and hospital, pursuant to an IRB-approved protocol, administered a drug designed to improve maturation in the lungs of infants at risk of premature birth. There was no allegation that any person suffered physical harm. For a detailed description of the facts of *Diaz*, see Stephen Hanlon and Robyn Shapiro, Ethical Issues in Biomedical Research: Diaz v. Hillsborough County Hospital Authority, 30 Human Rights 16 (2003), describing one patient who allegedly was given the consent form after the administration of Demoral or morphine and was told to consent or the "baby would die." For a description of other lawsuits, see A. Dembner, Lawsuits Target Medical Research Patient Safeguards, Boston Globe, August 12, 2002, A–1; 11 BNA Health Law Reporter 1434 (reporting on a settlement of a lawsuit against the University of Oklahoma involving melanoma research); 11 BNA Health Law Reporter 1269 (reporting on a suit filed against a hospital in Massachusetts over a gene therapy protocol); D. Wilson and D. Heath, Class Action Filed Against "The Hutch," Seattle Times, March 27, 2001, A–1 (describing suit filed against Hutchison Cancer Center, researchers, and a for-profit joint venturer); see discussion of the lawsuit involving Jesse Gelsinger, below. See also, Cook County v. Chandler, 538 U.S. 119, 123 S.Ct. 1239, 155 L.Ed.2d 247 (2003), in which researcher filed a *qui tam* action against research institute and hospital alleging that they defrauded the government, *inter alia*, by failing to abide by human subject protection regulations and in which the primary legal issue resolved thus far is the question of the application of the False Claims Act to county government. On remand, the District Court denied the County's attorneys access, under HIPAA, to patients' records desired for defense of the action. Chandler v. Hektoen Institute for Medical Research, 2003 WL 22284199 (N.D. Ill. 2003). For discussion of the application of the False Claims Act to research, see P.E. Kalb and K.G. Koehler, Legal Issues in Scientific Research, 287 JAMA 85 (2002); Daniel J. Powell, (Note) Using the False Claims Act as a Basis for Institutional Review Board Liability, 69 U. Chi. L. Rev. 1399 (2002).

While increased enforcement by OHRP, described earlier, and increased risk of liability create pressure on IRBs and research institutions to control research and constrain researchers, these entities also run the risk of being sued by researchers whose research is limited. For example, the Pennsylvania Supreme Court upheld a jury verdict in favor of a researcher, reducing the amount of the award to $2.9 million. In that case, the researcher claimed that the University failed to follow its own procedures before sanctioning him for research misconduct. Ferrer v. University of Pennsylvania, 573 Pa. 310, 825 A.2d 591 (2002).

The case law is quite underdeveloped in this area with almost all of the suits ending in settlements, some confidential. How do you advise researchers about the scope of the liability risk? How can that risk be reduced?

3. The court is very critical of "in house" IRBs. Increasingly, private, free-standing organizations are providing IRB services directly to researchers through contract. Is it likely that these entities are more or less independent than IRBs within the research organization? See, David Foroter, Independent Institutional Review Boards, 32 Seton Hall L. Rev. 513 (2002).

4. Although the Court denied the University's motion for reconsideration, it issued a per curiam opinion stating the following:

> In the Opinion, we said at one point that a parent "cannot consent to the participation of a child . . . in nontherapeutic research or studies in which there is any risk of injury or damage to the health of the subject." As we think is clear from Section VI of the Opinion, by "any risk," we meant any articulable risk beyond the minimal kind of risk that is inherent in any endeavor. The context of the statement was a non-therapeutic study that promises no medical benefit to the child whatever, so that any balance between risk and benefit is necessarily negative. As we indicated, the determination of whether the study in question offered some benefit, and therefore could be regarded as therapeutic in nature, or involved more than that minimal risk is open for further factual development on remand.

Does this statement clarify or confuse the situation? See, Loretta Kopelman, Pediatric Research Regulations Under Legal Scrutiny: Grimes Narrows Their Interpretation, 30 J.L. Med. & Ethics 38 (2002), arguing that the key issue in *Grimes* is the interpretation of "risk" as used in the regulations and that *Grimes* was correct in application to the particular protocol at issue. But see, Lainie Friedman Ross, In Defense of the Hopkins Lead Abatement Studies, 30 J.L. Med. & Ethics, 50 (2002), arguing that the court misinterpreted the regulations in a way that would make important research impossible.

5. Was the court correct in its conclusion that the study could not be done under the federal regulations? HHS regulations provide supplementary protection to children who are research subjects. These regulations divide research upon children into three categories: "research not involving greater than the minimal risk;" "research involving greater than minimal risk but presenting the prospect of direct benefit to the individual subjects;" and "research involving greater than minimal risk and no prospect of direct benefit to individual subjects, but likely to yield generalizable knowledge about the subject's disorder or condition." 45 C.F.R. §§ 46.401–46.409. "Minimal risk" is defined in § 46.102(i), above.

Where there is more than minimal risk but the research will also benefit the child, the risk must be justified "by the anticipated benefit to the subjects" (unleavened by any benefit that society may derive), and "[t]he relation of the anticipated benefit to the risk [must be] at least as favorable to the subjects as that presented by available alternative approaches." 45 C.F.R. § 46.405. Non-therapeutic research involving more than minimal risk may be approved only if there is a "minor" increase over minimal risk, the "experiences" that accompany the research are those that the child-subjects are likely to undergo anyway, and the research is aimed at a disorder or condition actually suffered by the subject. 45

C.F.R. § 46.406. The regulations require the consent (called "permission" in the regulations) of one parent before a child may participate in research, although the permission of both parents (if they are reasonably available) is required before a child becomes a subject in non-therapeutic research involving greater than minimal risk.

The regulations also require that "the IRB shall determine that adequate provisions are made for soliciting the assent of the children, when in the judgment of the IRB the children are capable of providing assent." 45 C.F.R. § 46.408. The IRB is required to consider the age, maturity, and psychological state of the subjects when determining whether the children are capable of assenting, and the IRB is entitled to make a determination of the propriety of requiring subject assent on either a protocol-by-protocol or child-by-child basis. Id.

The majority opinion appears to require that prior court approval be sought in any non-theraputic research involving children. Does this make sense? To what other groups might this requirement be applied? Should public, extra-institutional review be required for all non-therapeutic research?

6. Federal policy concerning research with children as participants is not monolithic. In fact, several programs are in place to encourage pediatric pharmaceutical research. See, for example, Karena Cooper, Pediatric Marketing Exclusivity—As Altered by the Best Pharmaceuticals for Children Act of 2002, 57 Food & Drug L.J. 519 (2002), describing the federal regulations that provide pharmaceutical companies with incentives to test drugs on children; Randall Baldwin Clark, Speed, Safety, and Dignity: Pediatric Pharmaceutical Development in an Age of Optimism, 9 U. Chi. L. Sch. Roundtable 1 (2002), arguing that the restrictions on research with children are incompatible with the 2002 Act. See also, Michelle Oberman and Joel Frader, Dying Children and Medical Research: Access to Clinical Trials as Benefit and Burden, 29 Am. J.L. Med. 301 (2003).

Note on Regulations Restricting Research on Other Vulnerable Populations

The history of experimentation with human subjects is rife with illustrations of the tendency to victimize the most vulnerable populations, whether they be poor, rural African American men in Tuskegee; concentration camp prisoners in Nazi Germany; mentally impaired children in Willowbrook State Hospital; or many others. Still, our society has a love-hate relationship with medical research. While we may distrust researchers, especially where they are financially motivated as discussed in the next note, we also love the newest technology and the newest drugs and have great optimism about progress.

Why might any individual want to offer himself as a "human guinea pig," if for reasons other than compensation or pure altruism? Why does the NIH run a publicly accessible website posting all of its current research protocols? If you had cancer and proven treatments were ineffective, would you want to participate in the test of a new drug? Why would a person with HIV but without health insurance want to participate in a research protocol?

Does the protection of particular groups, such as children or women or the mentally impaired always work for good? Or, can it have undesirable consequences? As you read above, the exclusion of children has had an impact on research testing the effect of drugs on children as compared to adults.

Women

The exclusion of women from participation as subjects for research presents another example. The regulations that worked that exclusion did not focus on all women, but the impact of excluding women who could be pregnant or become pregnant during the course of the study had the effect of excluding nearly all adult women.

Federal regulations governing research severely limit fetal research and research involving pregnant women as subjects. Generally, such research cannot be conducted unless all appropriate studies on animals and "nonpregnant individuals" is completed; the purpose of the research is to meet the health needs of the subject (either the pregnant woman or the fetus); the risk is minimized; those who are engaged in the research "will have no part in ... any decisions as to the timing, method, and procedures used to terminate the pregnancy [or] determining the viability of the fetus ...;" and there will be no change in the abortion procedure "solely in the interest" of the research. In addition, "[n]o inducements may be offered to terminate pregnancy ..." for the purpose of doing research upon the fetus. 45 C.F.R. § 46.206.

The regulation also divides research on a fetus into that done *in utero* and that done *ex utero*. Research cannot be done upon a fetus *in utero* unless the purpose of the medical intervention is therapeutic and the risk to the fetus is minimized, or, alternatively, the risk to the fetus is minimal (as defined by the regulations) and "the purpose of the activity is the development of important biomedical knowledge which cannot be obtained by other means." 45 C.F.R. § 46.208. An *ex utero* fetus which may be viable cannot be employed as a research subject except in very narrow circumstances. A viable *ex utero* fetus is treated as a child under the regulations.

Pregnant women may be employed as subjects only if the research is therapeutic and the risk to the fetus is minimized, or the risk to the fetus is minimal, as defined by the regulation. 45 C.F.R. § 46.207. Whether the research is done on a pregnant woman, a fetus *in utero,* or a fetus *ex utero*, before the research is conducted the researcher must obtain the consent of both the mother and the father of the fetus unless the treatment is therapeutic for the mother, the father's whereabouts cannot be reasonably ascertained or he is not reasonably available, or the pregnancy is the result of rape. 45 C.F.R. § 46.208.

The fetal protection regulations have had an adverse impact on the inclusion of women in research and clinical trials. Exclusionary "protective" policies meant that there was almost no research using women subjects examining how life-threatening conditions such as cancer or heart disease behaved in the female body as compared to the male body and almost no research on the effectiveness and safety of pharmaceuticals on other than your standard male body. Beginning in 1983, the NIH began to encourage research on women and produced a 1985 study that documented the impact of the exclusion of women from research. In 1986, NIH issued guidance to grantees stating that NIH policy encouraged the inclusion of women (and minorities) in NIH-funded research. Subsequent studies of the impact of that policy statement concluded, however, that research protocols were still excluding women. In 1994, NIH issued new regulations requiring that protocols include women and minorities as subjects. See Sarah K. Keitt, Sex & Gender: The Politics, Policy, and Practice of Medical Research, 3 Yale J. Health Pol'y L. & Ethics 253 (2003); Barbara Noah, The Participation of Underrepresented Minorities in Clinical Research, 29 Am. J. L. & Med. 221 (2003); NIH Office of Research on Women's Health, http://www4.od.nih.gov/orwh.

Prisoners

Since 1978, federal regulations have severely limited research using prisoners as human subjects. Such research is permitted only to study incarceration and its consequences or problems (like hepatitis, alcoholism or sexual assault) particularly affecting prisoners as a class. In a wide range of cases, even that research is permitted only after the Secretary of DHHS has consulted with appropriate experts in the field and given notice of the intent to carry out the research in the Federal Register.

When prisoners are to be used as subjects, the research must be approved by an IRB that is independent of the prison, and which includes at least one prisoner or prisoner representative. That IRB can then approve the research only if prisoners are given no advantages because of their participation in the study, if the risks are the kind that unincarcerated subjects would be willing to undertake, if the subjects are equitably selected, if participation will have no effect on parole decisions (and the prisoner knows this), and if there is adequate provision for follow up. 45 C.F.R. §§ 46.301 through 46.306.

Are there good reasons for providing prisoners with so much regulatory protection from research? Some say the regulations go too far, and that we should permit prisoners to discharge their debt to society by becoming research subjects if they wish to do so. See Sharona Hoffman, Beneficial and Unusual Punishment: An Argument in Support of Prisoner Participation in Clinical Trials, 33 Ind.L.Rev. 475 (2000). See also Allen Hornblum, Acres of Skin: Human Experiments at Holmesburg Prison (1998). For judicial consideration of these issues, see Bailey v. Lally, 481 F.Supp. 203 (D.Md.1979)(claim that prison conditions were so bad and inducements to participate in research so great that consent could not be voluntary, and thus violated prisoners' constitutional rights); People v. Gauntlett, 134 Mich.App. 737, 352 N.W.2d 310 (1984)(sex offender could not be forced to undergo experimental "chemical castration" as a condition of probation).

Mentally Impaired Individuals

The incidence of Alzheimer's Disease and other forms of dementia typically associated with advanced age is expected to grow at a rapid rate with the aging of our population. The suffering from this constellation of disorders, as well as other mental impairments, is serious; and research that will help prevent, manage, or cure these conditions holds out some hope. This research at some point requires subjects who themselves suffer from dementia and who are not capable of consenting to research. Once again, we see the conundrum. Unlike the situation with children and prisoners, however, no federal regulations provide guidance in the appropriate application of the federal regulations, including the provisions for consent by the subject's legal representative, to this population.

Several episodes drew attention to research with mentally impaired persons, including the invalidation of state regulations that allowed such research within certain circumstances. See T.D. v. New York State Office of Mental Health, 91 N.Y.2d 860, 668 N.Y.S.2d 153, 690 N.E.2d 1259 (1997). The National Bioethics Advisory Commission issued a report in 1998 addressing the appropriate standards for research. (Research Involving Persons with Mental Disorders That May Affect Decisionmaking Capacity). In addition, Maryland and New York undertook studies to develop proposed legislation and regulation. A few other states have legislation addressing consent for research. See, Diane E. Hoffman & Jack Schwartz, Proxy Consent to Participation of the Decisionally Impaired in Medical Research—Maryland's Policy Initiative, 1 J. Health Care L. & Pol'y 123, 125–27 (1998). The NBAC and state initiatives are similar in many respects.

Recommendations include that IRBs require an independent assessment of decisionmaking capacity of particular individuals, finding that relying on personnel associated with the protocol would provide inadequate protection to subjects. A second issue is the identification of the appropriate substitute decisionmaker, and on what basis (i.e., substituted judgment or best interests) the decision should be made. Finally, most of the proposed guidelines address the question of whether the scope of the substituted consent should be limited in the same risk terms as it is for research with children. Rebecca Dresser, Dementia Research: Ethics and Policy for the Twenty–First Century, 35 Ga.L.Rev. 661 (2001).

Note on Conflicts of Interest in Research

The court in *Kennedy Krieger* repeated several times in its opinion that Johns Hopkins was a "compensated researcher," clearly implying that its interests were influenced by financial gain. The issue of financial conflicts of interest in research is one of the most prominent issues in research oversight today.

The issue rose to public attention with the death of Jesse Gelsinger and the subsequent lawsuit filed against the University of Pennsylvania, the research physician, and the bioethicist who had consulted with the IRB in its approval of the protocol. Jesse was 18 years old and had a liver disorder that was under control. Under the research protocol, physicians inserted a virus, based on the cold virus, to deliver genetic material with the hope that this genetic therapy would cure the disease. An FDA investigation after the death revealed a number of breaches of federal regulations including continuing with the protocol after four patients had suffered serious reactions; failing to notify the FDA of the adverse events, contrary to a specific agreement between the University and the FDA; and altering consent forms, without the required approval of the FDA, to eliminate information that monkeys subjected to the intervention had died. (Because the protocol involved genetic therapy it had been subjected to heightened review at the FDA itself as a condition of approval.) Rick Weiss and Deborah Nelson, Penn Settles Gene Therapy Suit, Washington Post, Nov. 4, 2000, 2000 WL 25426175.

Financial conflicts of interest on the part of both the researcher and the University attracted the most public attention, however. Although reports vary in details, it appears that the University gave Genovo, a private corporation, the exclusive rights to patent the results from the researcher's laboratory. The University also allowed the researcher to control up to 30% of Genovo stock, a company he founded, in an exception to the University's conflict of interest guidelines. The University would receive $21 million to support the research, and the University owned stock in Genovo. The University had received legal counsel, covering research regulation issues, from an outside law firm in arranging the tripartite financial relationship. Pennsylvania Biotechnology Researcher Negotiates Corporate Funding, Philadelphia Inquirer, Feb. 27, 2000.

Gelsinger's lawsuit was quickly resolved by a confidential settlement. Informal reports indicate that the settlement was about $5 to $10 million.

Public discussion of financial conflicts in research sometimes speaks in terms of unethical people doing unethical things. The root of the growth of financial conflicts of interest in research, however, is both more complicated and more interesting. Although concern over financial conflicts of interest in research have been noted for over a decade, the increase in financial conflicts of interest, in fact, are a predictable result of a change in federal policy designed to promote the positive goal of more rapid movement of research results from laboratories and protocols to medical use for patients.

In 1980, Congress enacted the Bayh–Dole Act (35 U.S.C. § 200) and un-leashed the entrepreneurial spirit of researchers and their institutions. This federal statute transferred property rights in the products of federally-funded research to the researchers and their institutions. The Act encouraged researchers to form for-profit companies for the development and marketing of the products of research. Rather than allowing the results of federally-funded research to gather dust, the transfer of property rights to the researchers themselves would get the results into the hands of entities able to develop and market products for medical treatment. Universities developed "technology transfer" offices to capitalize on this opportunity. Universities and researchers sought patents and entered into joint ventures to license the patent or developed companies to develop the products or conduct further research. Universities usually use tech transfer proceeds to fund medical education and research, offsetting revenue reductions in their clinical activities due to managed care and Medicare changes.

An additional pressure producing financial conflict of interest is the fact that support for research has shifted significantly with much more research on phar-maceuticals being supported directly by industry. Competition for this industry financing has intensified as new actors have entered the research field. In 1991, 80% of funded pharmaceutical research took place in academic medical centers for example; but in 1998, only 40% occurred in academic medical centers.

We not only have a conflict of interest on the part of researchers, we have a conflict of policy in the federal laws applying to research. How should those policies be weighed against each other? Are these financial conflicts of interest new to research, or are they similar to the conflicts already recognized?

All research with human subjects has an embedded conflict of interest. Human beings participating in research are not to be treated as mere instru-ments; they retain their essential human dignity. At times, the duty to protect the subject comes into direct conflict with the desire to produce new knowledge for the good of all. Particularly in the setting where the physician is engaging both in the treatment of a patient and in research, this conflict is deep and not always handled effectively. The primary risk in this traditional conflict is the risk to the patient/subject in favor of the benefits of research.

Financial conflicts of interest certainly present a risk that the researcher will endanger the participant. Studies of financial conflicts of interest, however, indicate that these conflicts also may endanger the validity of the results of research. A meta-analysis of quantitative studies on the effectiveness of drugs concluded that the studies showed "a statistically significant association between industry sponsorship and pro-industry conclusions." Justin Bekelman, *et al.*, Scope and Impact of Financial Conflicts of Interest in Biomedical Research, 289 JAMA 454 (2003).

The FDA, NIH, and the Public Health Service, as well as several private associations such as the American Society of Clinical Oncology, have developed policies on conflicts of interest. (See, e.g., 42 C.F.R. § 50.604; 21 C.F.R. § 54.2.) Essentially, all of these regulations require that the research organization have a written policy; that there be disclosure of conflicts to the institution; that there be an internal review mechanism; and that conflicts be "managed," "reduced," or "eliminated," as appropriate. HHS issued guidance on this issue. The guidance is not directive, however, and consists mostly of questions and points the institution ought to consider. 68 Fed. Reg. 15456 (March 31, 2003).

Problem: Conflicts or Not?

Consider the following two questions as an attorney advising a university about conflicts of interest policy.

1.   Should all or some financial conflicts of interest be disclosed to patients? Which conflicts need to be disclosed, if any? If you require disclosure, is the following form, used in the Gelsinger protocol, adequate? If not, how would you change it?

> Please be aware that the University of Pennsylvania, Dr. James M. Wilson, (the Director of the Institute for Human Gene Therapy) and Genovo, Inc. (a gene therapy company in which Dr. Wilson holds an interest) have a financial interest in a successful outcome from the research involved in this study.

2.   Should the following protocols be approved by your IRB or should your conflicts policy prohibit the research? If you believe it can go forward but with specific limitations, what would they be?

> a.   The sponsor of the study would pay the institution $2500 per person enrolled and an additional $2500 if the person remains enrolled through the conclusion of the study.

> b.   A nurse coordinator has invested $5,000 in a publicly traded pharmaceutical corporation that owns most of the drugs tested in her unit.

> c.   The researcher and university co-own a patent on a particular medical device, which they have licensed to a company in which the researcher holds a 25% interest. The device needs to be tested as part of the FDA approval process. The principal investigator on the protocol is the researcher, and the research would be done at the university hospital as well as other hospitals. The company is providing the financial support for the research.

> d.   A protocol covers a clinical trial of a new medication for inflammation. The principal investigator for the protocol is on the speakers' bureau for the pharmaceutical firm that is funding the protocol and receives a fee of $1500 for every presentation she gives at any conference in relation to any research she does. Last year, she received $18,000 for such presentations.

> e.   A university is courting a biotech firm for a major donation for a new research building. The university's development office has asked researchers whose research has been supported by the firm to make a presentation on the importance of the new building at the meeting at which the firm will be asked for a donation. The associate provost for research is a member of the fundraising committee.

> f.   An untenured faculty member is in his last year before tenure. He has had difficulty in getting publishable results from his research either because he has had problems in enrolling or retaining subjects or because his results have been largely negative. The protocol currently under review by the IRB is probably his last chance.

For further discussion, see Biomedical Research: HHS Direction Needed to Address Financial Conflicts of Interest (GAO–02–89); Robert Gatter, Walking the Talk of Trust in Human Subjects Research: The Challenge of Regulating Financial Conflicts of Interest, 52 Emory L.J. 327 (2003) and Greg Koski, Research, Regulations, and Responsibility: Confronting the Compliance Myth–A Reaction to Professor Gatter, 52 Emory L.J. 403 (2003); Mark Barnes and Patrik S. Florencio, Financial Conflicts of Interest in Human Subjects Research: The Problem of Institutional Conflicts, 30 J. L. Med. & Ethics 390 (2002); and Karen Jordan, Financial Conflicts of Interest in Human Subjects Research: Proposals for a More

Effective Regulatory Scheme, 60 Wash. & Lee L. Rev. 15 (2003). See also Trudo Lemmens and Paul Miller, The Human Subjects Trade: Ethical and Legal Issues Surrounding Recruitment Incentives, 31 J. L. Med. & Ethics 398 (2003).

D. REFORMING THE SYSTEM TO PROTECT RESEARCH PARTICIPANTS

The Institute of Medicine, commissioned by HHS, assessed the current system for protecting research subjects. The IOM Committee on Assessing the System for Protecting Human Research Participants issued the report excerpted below, edited by D. D. Federman, et al., in 2003.

RESPONSIBLE RESEARCH: A SYSTEMS APPROACH TO PROTECTING RESEARCH PARTICIPANTS* EXECUTIVE SUMMARY.

* * *

Statement of the Problem

[A] fact that has repeatedly confounded this committee's deliberations is the lack of data regarding the scope and scale of current protection activities. This absence of information seriously handicaps an objective assessment of protection program performance and needs and the development of useful policy directions. Nonetheless, the evidence is abundant regarding the significant strains and weaknesses of the current system, and this committee has reached the conclusion that major reforms are in order.

First, significant doubt exists regarding the capacity of the current system to meet its core objectives. Although all stakeholders agree that participant protection must be of paramount concern in every aspect of the research process, a variety of faults and problems in the present system have been noted. The common finding is that dissatisfaction with the current system is widespread.

Second, it has been shown that IRBs are "under strain" and "in need of reform" [ ]. The complexity of the issues, the variability in the research settings, the limitations of funding options, the demands of investigators and participants for access to research, and the accountability for institutional compliance have magnified and complicated IRBs' responsibilities. This heavy burden has made it difficult both to recruit knowledgeable IRB members and to allow them sufficient time for the necessary ethical reflection.

Third, the existing regulatory framework ... cannot adequately respond to the complex and ever-changing research environment, with weaknesses related to gaps in authority, structure, and resources. ...

* * *

The specific structure of a protection program is secondary to its performance of several essential functions. These functions include:

1) comprehensive review of protocols (including scientific, financial conflict of interest, and ethical reviews),

2) ethically sound participant-investigator interactions,

3) ongoing (and risk-appropriate) safety monitoring throughout the conduct of the study, and

4) quality improvement (QI) and compliance activities.

Refocus Institutional Review Board Mission on Ethical Review of Protocols

* * *

... The Institutional Review Board (IRB), as the principal representative of the interests of potential research participants, should focus its full committee deliberations and oversight primarily on the ethical aspects of protection issues. To reflect this role, IRBs should be appropriately renamed within research organizations' internal documents that define institutional structure and policies. The committee suggests the name "Research Ethics Review Board" (Research ERB).

From this point forward in this report, the term "Research ERB" will be used in the context of the committee's envisioned HRPPP [Human Research Participant Protection Program], and the term "IRB" will be reserved for comments regarding the existing protection framework.

All members of the Research ERB should have a core body of knowledge, and a critical mass of the membership, either scientist or nonscientist, should possess a specialized knowledge of human research ethics. The research organization's goal should be to create or associate with a Research ERB in which unaffiliated members, nonscientists, and those who represent the local community and/or the participant perspective comprise at least 25 percent of the membership [ ]. Although the committee recognizes that identifying this increased proportion of willing and able unaffiliated and nonscientist individuals will be difficult and that they will require additional training, the proportional shift is important to the integration of the participant or community and could help insulate Research ERBs from potential conflicts of interest at the organizational level.

Further, as modern IRBs have tended to become larger and to reflect a broader range of scientific expertise, some IRB deliberations have tended to be dominated by the scientific perspective, increasing the potential to marginalize the perspectives of nonscientist members and those who focus on ethics-based concerns [ ]. Therefore, the refocused Research ERB's deliberative objective should aim for consensus rather than majority control [ ]. No protocol should be approved without three-quarters of the voting members concurring. Just as a vote of unanimity would effectively give a veto to a single dissenting committee member, allowing a simple majority to approve a protocol in the face of substantial minority opinion can too easily suppress responsible ethical opinions.

Distinguish Scientific, Conflict of Interest, and Ethics Review Mechanisms

The scientific and ethical review of protocols should be equally rigorous. Therefore, each review requires distinct, although overlapping, expertise. Research ERBs that are constituted to emphasize the ethical dimensions of protocol review should not be expected to have a primary membership with the range of knowledge and skills needed to adequately assess the scientific and technical merits of every protocol under their purview. Although the in-depth scientific evaluation of proposals is fundamental to the comprehensive ethics review of any protocol, the Research ERB need not conduct the initial scientific review. Instead, summaries of the scientific review should be submitted to the Research ERB as a component of its ethics-focused deliberations.

Furthermore, there is a need to ensure that no financial or other interests on the part of the investigator, research organization, or the Research ERB (as a body or as individual members) will distort the conduct of research with human participants. While there are non-financial self-interests intrinsic to the pursuit of research questions, the frequency and complexity of potential financial conflicts of interest in research are expanding, and the federal government and relevant professional and industry groups should continue to consider their potential ramifications and pursue rigorous policies for handling them [ ]. A process for scrutinizing potential financial conflicts of interest in any protocol is vital to the subsequent evaluation of participant risks and benefits by the Research ERB [ ].

Despite the need for review from three distinct perspectives (scientific, ethical, and financial conflict of interest), the interrelated nature of these perspectives requires that a *single* body be vested with the authority to make final protocol determinations and be accountable for those determinations. This body is and should remain the Research ERB. The focused reviews of scientific merit and potential financial conflicts of interest should inform the ethics review process for each protocol [ ].

* * *

Recognize and Integrate Participant Contributions

[P]articipants and their representatives should be meaningfully included in the review and oversight of research to ensure that pertinent concerns are heard and that researchers conduct studies that meet participant needs [ ]. . . .

Revitalize Informed Consent

Informed consent should be an ongoing process that focuses not on a written form or a static disclosure event, but rather on a series of dynamic conversations between the participant and the research staff that should begin before enrollment and be reinforced during each encounter or intervention. Multidisciplinary approach should be tailored to individual differences in participant education and learning capabilities.

* * *

The informed consent conversation(s), as well as the written consent document, should not be obscured by language designed mainly to insulate the institution from liability. Rather, the process should ensure that participants clearly understand the nature of the proposed research and its potential risks and benefits to them and society.

* * *

Compensate Participants for Research–Related Injury

Despite decades of discussion on the ethical obligation to compensate participants for research-related injury, little information is available regarding the number of such injuries and the cost of providing compensation for them [ ]. In the face of real potential for diminished public trust in the research community, providing reasonable compensation for legitimate instances of research harm is critical to restoring credibility.

* * *

The responsibility for no-fault compensation programs should fall initially on the institution or organization accountable for conducting the research, and its terms should be specified in the documentation accompanying the participant's agreement to participate. . . .

Enhance Safety Monitoring

The safety of research volunteers must be guaranteed from the inception of a protocol, through its execution, to final completion and reporting of results. Continual review and monitoring of risk-prone studies is needed to ensure that emerging information has not altered the original risk-benefit analysis. Therefore, risk-appropriate mechanisms are needed to track protocols and study personnel; provide assurances that data are valid and collected according to applicable practices . . .; and ensure that participants' safety, privacy, and confidentiality are protected throughout a study. Protection measures should be monitored by various means at all levels to ensure that consent has been properly given and that all adverse events have been identified and appropriately reported by the investigator to the relevant institutional body, sponsor, and federal agency(ies).

* * *

Manage Potential Conflicts of Interest

Confidence about the current system of participant protection is undermined by the perception that harm to research participants may result from conflicts of interest involving the researcher, the research organization, and/or the research sponsor. This concern is particularly acute regarding financial conflicts of interest, as the relationships between the academic and private research enterprises continue to evolve. Therefore, mechanisms for identifying, disclosing, and resolving conflicts of interest should be strengthened, especially those involving financial relationships [ ].

* * *

In the committee's view, because the Research ERB lacks the necessary resources or authority to ensure the appropriate management of potential conflicts of interest, the responsibility for assessing and managing financial conflicts of individuals (investigators, research staff, and Research ERB members) should lie with the research organization [ ]. Likewise, organizations should ensure that an independent, external mechanism is in place for the evaluation of potential institutional conflicts [ ]. In both instances, conflict of interest information should be communicated in a timely and effective manner to the Research ERB, which should make the final assessment with regard to ensuring participant protections.

* * *

Notes and Questions

1.   What are the biggest changes in the current IRB system recommended by the Institute of Medicine Committee? Is it a bold proposal that would substantially reform the system, or a mere tinkering with the current system?

2.   Who can institute the changes that have been recommended? Which would require Congressional action; which could be done by federal administrative agencies; and which could be accomplished by changes at local institutions? If you were in-house counsel at a research university would you advise them to adopt these arguably more active and most probably more expensive processes?

3.   The IOM Committee recommended, in text not included in the excerpt, that federal regulation and oversight extend to virtually all research with human participants in the United States, even research that is privately funded and conducted at research centers that receive no government funding of any kind. Is that extension of federal regulatory authority warranted as a matter of policy? Does the federal government have authority to regulate research in this way? The state of Maryland, after the *Kennedy Krieger* litigation began, enacted a statute that requires that all research with human subjects in that state comply with the federal regulations. It also added a requirement that IRB minutes be available to the public. Md. Code, Health–General, § 13–2001 *et seq.* Review the federal regulations: May the state regulate research in this way? Is it advisable to do so?

4.   The IOM Committee emphasizes, elsewhere in its report, the development of an "ethical research culture" at the institution. How does this differ from compliance with legal requirements? What role, if any, would the organization's lawyer play in such a culture? How would you go about creating an "ethical research culture?" Are there any academic policies, such as basing tenure and salary increases on success in funded research, that would need to be altered?

5.   Most regulation and scholarship concerning the enforcement of ethical and legal standards for research focus on the role of the IRBs or the physician-investigator. But see, Arlene David, *et al.*, The Invisible Hand in Clinical Research: The Study Coordinator's Critical Role in Human Subjects Protection, 30 J. L. Med. & Ethics 411 (2002). If study coordinators, typically a staff-level position held by a nurse or similar professional on an employment-at-will basis, are the last, best defense against research abuses, how might an institution encourage or discourage the fulfillment of that role?

III.   INTERNATIONAL REGULATION OF RESEARCH INVOLVING HUMAN SUBJECTS

The Nuremberg Code has been restated and expanded several times since that judgment was rendered. The most significant elaboration on the Nuremberg Code is the Declaration of Helsinki, first promulgated by the World Medical Association in 1964 and periodically updated and amended. The World Medical Association consists of representatives from most of the world's organized national medical associations; the American Medical Association is the representative from the United States. Amidst considerable controversy over the increasing use of third world populations as subjects in research conducted and funded by first world institutions, the World Medical Association adopted this version of the Declaration in 2000.

DECLARATION OF HELSINKI, ETHICAL PRINCIPLES FOR MEDICAL RESEARCH INVOLVING HUMAN SUBJECTS

As adopted in 1964 and amended in 1975, 1983, 1989, 1996 and 2000.

A. INTRODUCTION

* * *

3. The Declaration of Geneva of the World Medical Association binds the physician with the words, "The health of my patient will be my first consideration," and the International Code of Medical Ethics declares that, "A physician shall act only in the patient's interest when providing medical care which might have the effect of weakening the physical and mental condition of the patient."

* * *

8. Medical research is subject to ethical standards that promote respect for all human beings and protect their health and rights. Some research populations are vulnerable and need special protection. The particular needs of the economically and medically disadvantaged must be recognized. Special attention is also required for those who cannot give or refuse consent for themselves, for those who may be subject to giving consent under duress, for those who will not benefit personally from the research and for those for whom the research is combined with care.

9. Research Investigators should be aware of the ethical, legal and regulatory requirements for research on human subjects in their own countries as well as applicable international requirements. No national ethical, legal or regulatory requirement should be allowed to reduce or eliminate any of the protections for human subjects set forth in this Declaration.

B. BASIC PRINCIPLES FOR ALL MEDICAL RESEARCH

* * *

13. The design and performance of each experimental procedure involving human subjects should be clearly formulated in an experimental protocol. This protocol should be submitted for consideration, comment, guidance, and where appropriate, approval to a specially appointed ethical review committee, which must be independent of the investigator, the sponsor or any other kind of undue influence. This independent committee should be in conformity with the laws and regulations of the country in which the research experiment is performed. The committee has the right to monitor ongoing trials. The researcher has the obligation to provide monitoring information to the committee, especially any serious adverse events. The researcher should also submit to the committee, for review, information regarding funding, sponsors,

institutional affiliations, other potential conflicts of interest and incentives for subjects.

* * *

15.   Medical research involving human subjects should be conducted only by scientifically qualified persons and under the supervision of a clinically competent medical person. The responsibility for the human subject must always rest with a medically qualified person and never rest on the subject of the research, even though the subject has given consent.

16.   Every medical research project involving human subjects should be preceded by careful assessment of predictable risks and burdens in comparison with foreseeable benefits to the subject or to others. This does not preclude the participation of healthy volunteers in medical research. The design of all studies should be publicly available.

17.   Physicians should abstain from engaging in research projects involving human subjects unless they are confident that the risks involved have been adequately assessed and can be satisfactorily managed. Physicians should cease any investigation if the risks are found to outweigh the potential benefits or if there is conclusive proof of positive and beneficial results.

18.   Medical research involving human subjects should only be conducted if the importance of the objective outweighs the inherent risks and burdens to the subject. This is especially important when the human subjects are healthy volunteers.

19.   Medical research is only justified if there is a reasonable likelihood that the populations in which the research is carried out stand to benefit from the results of the research.

* * *

22.   In any research on human beings, each potential subject must be adequately informed of the aims, methods, sources of funding, any possible conflicts of interest, institutional affiliations of the researcher, the anticipated benefits and potential risks of the study and the discomfort it may entail. The subject should be informed of the right to abstain from participation in the study or to withdraw consent to participate at any time without reprisal. After ensuring that the subject has understood the information, the physician should then obtain the subject's freely-given informed consent, preferably in writing. If the consent cannot be obtained in writing, the non-written consent must be formally documented and witnessed.

23.   When obtaining informed consent for the research project the physician should be particularly cautious if the subject is in a dependent relationship with the physician or may consent under duress. In that case the informed consent should be obtained by a well-informed physician who is not engaged in the investigation and who is completely independent of this relationship.

24.   For a research subject who is legally incompetent, physically or mentally incapable of giving consent or is a legally incompetent minor, the investigator must obtain informed consent from the legally authorized representative in accordance with applicable law. These groups should not be included in research unless the research is necessary to promote the health of

the population represented and this research cannot instead be performed on legally competent persons.

25. When a subject deemed legally incompetent, such as a minor child, is able to give assent to decisions about participation in research, the investigator must obtain that assent in addition to the consent of the legally authorized representative.

26. Research on individuals from whom it is not possible to obtain consent, including proxy or advance consent, should be done only if the physical/mental condition that prevents obtaining informed consent is a necessary characteristic of the research population. The specific reasons for involving research subjects with a condition that renders them unable to give informed consent should be stated in the experimental protocol for consideration and approval of the review committee. The protocol should state that consent to remain in the research should be obtained as soon as possible from the individual or a legally authorized surrogate.

27. Both authors and publishers have ethical obligations. In publication of the results of research, the investigators are obliged to preserve the accuracy of the results. Negative as well as positive results should be published or otherwise publicly available. Sources of funding, institutional affiliations and any possible conflicts of interest should be declared in the publication. Reports of experimentation not in accordance with the principles laid down in this Declaration should not be accepted for publication.

C. ADDITIONAL PRINCIPLES FOR MEDICAL RESEARCH COMBINED WITH MEDICAL CARE

28. The physician may combine medical research with medical care, only to the extent that the research is justified by its potential prophylactic, diagnostic or therapeutic value. When medical research is combined with medical care, additional standards apply to protect the patients who are research subjects.

29. The benefits, risks, burdens and effectiveness of a new method should be tested against those of the best current prophylactic, diagnostic, and therapeutic methods. This does not exclude the use of placebo, or no treatment, in studies where no proven prophylactic, diagnostic or therapeutic method exists.

30. At the conclusion of the study, every patient entered into the study should be assured of access to the best proven prophylactic, diagnostic and therapeutic methods identified by the study.

31. The physician should fully inform the patient which aspects of the care are related to the research. The refusal of a patient to participate in a study must never interfere with the patient-physician relationship.

32. In the treatment of a patient, where proven prophylactic, diagnostic and therapeutic methods do not exist or have been ineffective, the physician, with informed consent from the patient, must be free to use unproven or new prophylactic, diagnostic and therapeutic measures, if in the physician's judgement it offers hope of saving life, re-establishing health or alleviating suffering. Where possible, these measures should be made the object of research, designed to evaluate their safety and efficacy. In all cases, new information should be recorded and, where appropriate, published. The other relevant guidelines of this Declaration should be followed.

Problem: The African and Asian AIDS Trials

The roles of international research organizations, and American researchers doing research abroad, were called into question as a consequence of a series of perinatal HIV transmission studies done in Africa and Asia in the mid–1990s. There is a particular need for treatment for HIV-positive pregnant women in some African and Asian countries, where the HIV infection rate is far higher than it is in most of the developed world. There are more than a half million HIV infected babies born each year, most in the developing world. The United Nations has put a high priority on finding some genuinely feasible way of dealing with this increasingly pervasive problem.

As a general matter, without treatment, between 17% and 25% of pregnant women who are infected with HIV will give birth to an HIV-positive baby, although that figure may be even higher in the developing world. In the United States, an HIV-positive mother will be offered therapy of a combination of drugs, including AZT, during her last six months of pregnancy and intravenous medication during delivery. A c-section is often recommended if the mother has been taking AZT. The baby then will be treated for six weeks after birth. This protocol, which decreases the transmission rate to about 8%, is too expensive (at more than $500) for use in developing countries, where needles are usually re-used and risk infection. The United Nations AIDS program, along with the United States National Institutes of Health, the Centers for Disease Control and others, sponsored research in which mostly impoverished HIV-positive women in poor countries were randomized to a few different relatively inexpensive courses of treatment. Some women were also randomized to a placebo. While the consent of those who participated in the study was sought by the investigators, it was not always provided in writing, and, given the alternative—no treatment at all—some believe that it was inherently coerced consent. The purpose of the research was to find some less expensive and safe way of treating HIV-positive pregnant women in very poor countries; of course, the beneficiaries of the research could include the HIV-positive pregnant women (and third party health care payers) in the United States and the rest of the developed world, too.

Do you think that the research was properly done? Was it done consistently with the Declaration of Helsinki? Was this appropriate research likely to save hundreds of thousands of lives, or was it another example of the developed world imposing a burden (here, of medical research) on the poor and on people of color? Does it make any difference to your analysis that the research ultimately found that some (but not all) of the shorter, cheaper, less invasive protocols were almost as good (but not quite as good) as the current protocol used in the United States? For one summary account of the studies, see L. Altman, Spare AIDS Regime Is Found To Reduce Risks To Newborns, New York Times, February 2, 1999, at A–1.

Notes and Questions

1.　Is the Declaration of Helsinki consistent with the Nuremberg Code? With the federal regulations? How do they vary? Which is likely to be more effective as a practical guide to those engaged in research involving human subjects?

2.　Some proposals to change the Declaration in 1999 proved too controversial, and were ultimately rejected by the Association at their 2000 meeting. Probably the most vigorously discussed proposal was one that would have permitted scientists to test new treatments against "the best diagnostic, prophylactic or therapeutic method *that would otherwise be available* [to the subject]." If this language had been adopted, impoverished subjects without any access to medical care could have been given ineffective treatment (or a placebo); without it, arguably, those subjects would have to be afforded the best alternative treatment available to anyone, anywhere in the world. As one advocate for the change pointed out, a "plain meaning" approach to the current regulation would prohibit Indian drug companies carrying out drug research in India. He cited the research that led to the development of Oral Rehydration Therapy (ORT). This treatment, which has saved millions of lives, could never have been developed in Bangladesh if the trials had had to compare ORT to intravenous treatment. S. Eckstein, Ethical Issues in International Health Research Programme, 10 Dispatches (2) 2,14 (2000). This issue remained the subject of lively debate internationally, and in 2002 the World Medical Association adopted a footnote "clarification" of paragraph 29 of the Declaration:

> The WMA hereby reaffirms its position that extreme care must be taken in making use of a placebo-controlled trial and that in general this methodology should only be used in the absence of existing proven therapy. However, a placebo-controlled trial may be ethically acceptable, even if proven therapy is available, under the following circumstances:
>
> -Where for compelling and scientifically sound methodological reasons its use is necessary to determine the efficacy or safety of a prophylactic, diagnostic or therapeutic method; or
>
> -Where a prophylactic, diagnostic or therapeutic method is being investigated for a minor condition and the patients who receive placebo will not be subject to any additional risk of serious or irreversible harm.

3.   Another 1999 proposed change would have allowed for oral, rather than written, informed consent, when the risk to the subject is "slight" and when the medical procedure to be used is "customarily used in the practice of medicine without documentation of consent." Would this attempt at streamlining research bureaucracy be worth the additional risk to research subjects?

4.   What changes, if any, would you make to the Declaration? Is it too strict, thus limiting research too severely, or is it too liberal, allowing research that is inappropriate? For an account of some of the issues raised in the vigorous debate over the 1999 amendments and the 2000 redraft, see R. Levine, The Need to Revise the Declaration of Helsinki, 341 NEJM 531 (1999); T. Brennan, Proposed Revisions to the Declaration of Helsinki—Will They Weaken the Ethical Principles Underlying Human Research, 341 NEJM 527 (1999); and B. Loff and J. Black, The Declaration of Helsinki and Research in Vulnerable Populations, 172 Med. J.Aust. 292 (2000).

Chapter 7

DISTRIBUTIVE JUSTICE AND THE ALLOCATION OF HEALTH CARE RESOURCES—THE EXAMPLE OF HUMAN ORGAN TRANSPLANTATION

I. INTRODUCTION

Despite the debate over whether a workable concept of "necessary" health care can be developed and the acknowledged fact that more health care is sometimes worse than less health care, our society still struggles over the basic principles that underlie the uneven distribution of and unequal access to health care services in the U.S. We do not find similar debates over other goods and do not often ask whether the distribution of automobiles or abflexers or lack of access to Caribbean cruises is "just."

Some argue that health care has a special status because it is the sine qua non of life as a human being. Without some measure of health, without "normal species functioning," in the words of philosopher Norman Daniels, meaningful life is simply impossible. We cannot speak of giving people the opportunity to participate in life in our society without, at the least, some minimal level of health. Further, we cannot expect citizens to meet their civic duties unless we assure them of the health to do so. Others argue that the need for health care is different from the need for other goods or services because the need is unfairly distributed throughout the society. Essentially, people who take this position argue that those who are sick have been dealt a bad hand in life, and adequate health care levels the playing field for the sick in relation to the healthy. Further, some argue, we all benefit by the general good health of the rest of society, so we should be willing to commit our social resources to attain this end. The rest of us will be less subject to disease if others are healthy, and our economy will generate more for all of us if the work force is healthy. Finally, some argue that we have a moral duty to address the suffering that is caused to our fellow man by ill health. This last argument may be restated: we are offended to see pervasive illness in our society, and our sensibilities are best served by assuring that everyone has adequate health care.

Libertarians accuse those who seek to redistribute health resources of unjustified paternalism. People can make their own choices about whether to spend their money on medical treatment, pharmaceuticals, travel, or fast cars.

What we are really trying to do, they may argue, is just redistribute wealth. If that is the goal, we ought to give the poor additional resources and let them spend those resources as they feel will best allow them to fully participate in society. Some may spend it on health care, to be sure, but others may reasonably decide that it ought to be spent on education, clothing, or other goods and services in which there is a tremendous disparity among members of our society. There is a very helpful account of the reasons that health care might be different from other kinds of goods and services, and a response to each of those arguments, in Einer Elhauge, Allocating Health Care Morally, 82 Cal. L. Rev. 1452 (1994). One of the earliest and most oft-cited theories regarding the application of the principle of distributive justice to health care resources is found in Norman Daniels, Just Health Care (1985). See also Normal Daniels et al., Is Equality Bad for Our Health? (2000). For a general introduction to this issue, see Tom Beauchamp and James Childress, Principles of Medical Ethics 326–394 (5th ed. 2001).

There is a wide range of approaches to distributive justice that might be applied to health care (and to anything else of which there is a scarce supply). One approach, the libertarian market approach, would accept the current distribution of resources as a general matter, and allow for a change only if willing participants in the market were to trade for one. Under this approach, anyone who wants more health care or more health insurance than that person has now should be able to buy it from any willing seller, but the government should not redistribute resources from those who now have those resources to those who do not have them. Such a redistribution would constitute an unjust taking of resources from those who have earned them to those who have been unwilling or unable to be productive or have chosen to spend their resources for other purposes.

In contrast, theories of distributive justice, when applied to health care, do permit or require some redistribution of resources. An egalitarian and communitarian theorist, at the other extreme from the libertarian marke-teers, might argue that justice requires equality and that all members of society should be provided with the same health care. This theory, whatever merits it might have in providing for the distribution of housing or clothing, for example, does not make much sense when applied to the distribution of health care because individuals' needs vary so substantially from one to another across the society. Those who take the communitarian approach are more likely to distribute health care so that each person has access to the same range of health care resources whenever those resources are required. Many national health care systems outside of the United States are based, at least in part, on this "equal opportunity" theory.

There are a number of approaches to distributive justice that fall in between the pure market theory of the libertarians and the pure equality models of the egalitarians and communitarians. Virtually all of these ap-proaches depend upon the identification of a package of basic services that would be made available to every person within the society. In addition, under most of these theories, individuals could purchase more health care (directly or through insurance) if they wished to do so and could afford it. The health resources included in such a package of basic services could be defined as a "minimum package," that is, the resources required by those in the society with the least health care needs. Alternatively, every person could be provided a "generally adequate package," which would include the resources required by most people in society. Each person could also be provided something greater than that—perhaps a package sufficient to provide for the health care needs of nearly all members of society.

The socially guaranteed package of health care services could also vary from group to group within society. In the United States, children, the elderly, those with end-stage renal disease and pregnant women are entitled, as a general matter, to more socially guaranteed services than are most others. Further, a plan which provides a package of basic services could also provide that some people deemed less worthy by the society—those who put their health at risk through their own conduct, for example, or those who are not employed—would be entitled to fewer services than those deemed worthy by the society.

Of course, it is not so easy to decide what, exactly, ought to be in the package of basic services, or even how that package should be defined. Should it be defined in terms of particular goods and health care services, in terms of prospective patient desires, in terms of needs defined by primary care physicians, or in some other way? Some kinds of services—for example, mental health services or infertility services—are deemed to be necessary by some people and to be inessential luxuries by others. The development of such a package of basic health care services that is available to every person has been fundamental to most efforts at systematic health care reform in the United States over the past several years; the difficulty in defining such a package may be one reason such reform has failed.

Injustice in the distribution of health care resources may manifest itself in many different ways. While some are concerned by any differential access to health resources, many people are especially concerned by what appear to be particularly invidious distinctions based on race and gender in the distribution of those resources. There is little question that African Americans have less access to many kinds of health care than do Whites, even after adjusting for differences in income. Similarly, the poor, people in rural areas, women, and other minorities may be provided with less access to health care—especially high tech and expensive health care—than their richer, urban, male nonminority counterparts. A series of studies show substantial differences in access to health care by race. These are cited and discussed in Chapter 8. See also David Barton Smith, Health Care Divided: Race and Healing a Nation (1999).

Do you think that there is some reason to distribute health care through a mechanism other than the market? What theory of distributive justice would you apply to the distribution of health care resources? How would you address the evidence that suggests that the poor, members of racial minorities, women, and people in rural areas have less access to health care than do others? Ultimately, is there any way to determine whether a particular health care distribution is fair, or, for that matter, whether a health care system is a fair or just system? What is the baseline for making such determinations? Is it possible, for example, to apply universal standards of fairness to the many different and diverse communities in the United States, or to the wide range of societies across the globe?

While the issue of fairness arises in a host of contexts, the rest of this chapter will investigate the issue of the just distribution of health care resources by focusing on the distribution of organs for transplant rather than the reform of the health care system as a whole. Because organs suitable for transplant are scarce, and because there often is no adequate alternative to the transplant, they put the issue of the just and proper distribution of health care in stark relief.

ALLOCATION AND RATIONING

Through allocation, a society determines how much of its resources to devote to a particular purpose: for example, how much money should be allocated to Medicare or Medicaid as compared to education or defense; within Medicare or Medicaid, how much should be allocated to dialysis or transplantation as compared to long-term care; how much federal support should be devoted to medical research and for which diseases or conditions; how many long-term care or hospital facilities should a state approve through its certificate-of-need program?

Through rationing, a society decides which individuals get the particular resources available. In the United States, ability to pay is the dominant means through which we distribute available health care resources. But for some few resources, we have created nearly universal entitlement (as the Medicare program has done with dialysis and kidney transplantation for any person with end-stage renal disease) but experience a shortage of resources (e.g., human kidneys for transplant). For other resources, we maintain intentional shortages in order to contain consumption, as may be the case with state control of the supply of nursing homes or with publicly funded health services. Finally, there may be resources that are price-controlled, where patients are required to pay something for the service but where they are not allowed to offer more dollars and, in effect, bid against one another. This final situation describes the distribution of solid organs in the U.S. In these cases, non-market means are developed to ration health care resources.

Obviously, allocation decisions affect rationing decisions: if more resources are allocated to a particular purpose or legal restrictions on supply are removed, rationing may become less pressing or less frequent. Rationing decisions also affect allocation decisions: uncomfortable public rationing decisions may stimulate a greater allocation to increase the supply of the scarce resources.

Allocation and rationing decisions often treat the loss of human life differently, with greater tolerance for "statistical lives" lost and much less tolerance for the loss of "identifiable lives." A classic scenario illustrates the difference: cost-sensitive decisions concerning mine safety that increase the statistical risk of death are accepted even when the predicted loss is quite precise and clear, while at the same time the expense of rescue is of very little concern when an individual miner is trapped in a collapsed mine. Under the concepts discussed earlier, allocation deals mostly with statistical lives, while rationing most often deals with identifiable lives. Whether the individual has a name, a face and a personality or is just a number may alter decisions.

Many processes can be used to allocate or ration health care resources. As already noted, the U.S. relies on the market for the rationing of most, but not all, health care resources. A second option is to allocate resources and establish rationing rules through a political process. Allocation decisions are often made through political processes including federal and state budgeting processes. "Aresponsible" or "black box" committees that are not required to provide reasons for the selection of one recipient over another and that cannot be subject to effective public scrutiny may be used to ration scarce resources. Expert panels may ration scarce resources and may do so under a mantle of scientific or medical or financial expertise. Bureaucratic organizations also shield rationing decisions from broad public scrutiny. For a classic and influential analysis of allocation and rationing over several contexts, see Guido Calabresi and Philip Bobbitt, Tragic Choices (1970).

The advent of managed care and certain other cost containment devices has stimulated debate over whether or how extensively and on what principles medical professionals and health care institutions should become involved in rationing care among patients. Rationing health care "at the bedside" is a substantial departure from the physician's traditional role as determined advocate for each individual patient. Are physicians in the best position to ration care among patients? How might their decisions differ, if at all, from black box committees or bureaucracies, for example? Will physician decisions be more or less reviewable than decisions by others? What impact would such a change in role identification have on physician-patient relationships? See, Mark A. Hall, Rationing Health Care at the Bedside, 69 N.Y.U.L. Rev. 693 (1994); David Mechanic, Professional Judgment and the Rationing of Medical Care, 140 Penn. L. Rev. 1713 (1992); Edmund D. Pellegrino, Rationing Health Care: The Ethics of Moral Gatekeeping, 2 J. of Contemp. Health L. & Pol. 23 (1986); E. Haavi Morreim, Balancing Act: The New Medical Ethics of Medicine's New Economics (Boston: Kluwer Acad. Pub. 1991); Susan M. Wolf, Health Care Reform and the Future of Physician Ethics, 24 Hastings Center Rep. 28 (1994).

By what criteria should health care services be rationed? During the 1960s, before hemodialysis became widely available, the Seattle Artificial Kidney Center was reported to have selected patients for hemodialysis partially on the basis of " ... age and sex of patient; marital status and number of dependents; income; net worth; emotional stability, with particular regard to the patient's capacity to accept treatment; educational background; the nature of the occupation; past performance and future potential; the names of people who could serve as references." Shana Alexander, They Decide Who Lives, Who Dies, 53 Life 102–104 (Nov. 9, 1962) as quoted in Maxwell Mehlman, Rationing Expensive Lifesaving Medical Treatments, 1985 Wisc. L.Rev. 239, 256.

Should more "neutral" standards be used to ration scarce health care resources? What standards would be neutral? Are medical indications relating to survivability with and without the treatment neutral standards? Would a lottery or a "first come-first served" system be more acceptable? How should the pool for these latter two methods be defined: should it be geographically defined; should it matter whether the patient is a resident of the state or of the United States; who should decide where the line starts and who is allowed to get in line?

II. RATIONING OF SCARCE HUMAN ORGANS

Problem: Selecting an Organ Transplant Recipient

You are awakened in the middle of the night by an urgent phone call from an administrative staff member of the large urban teaching hospital that you represent. The hospital is a transplant center. The hospital has encountered the following problem.

For the last few weeks, two patients have been under treatment at the hospital for acute liver failure. One, James Patterson, is a 65–year-old retired CEO of a major computer software company. He has two children, a 40–year-old daughter with a child of her own and a 24–year-old son. James is an alcoholic and has been in and out of the hospital for the past few years for problems secondary to his alcoholism. Although he has been through detoxification programs several times, he always has returned to his drinking. This time, though, he has abstained from alcohol for more than six months and so meets the minimum criterion for former alcoholics for liver transplant. James is active in his church and is a financial supporter of the local university athletics department. He is still on his employer's health insurance plan, which has a cap on transplant coverage. The second patient is Antonia Friedman, a 30–year-old attorney with two children, ages 2 and 4. She is an active member of the local city council and has contributed generously in the past year to the hospital's building fund. She recently was exposed to Hepatitis A, which has quickly destroyed most of her liver. Friedman has full coverage health insurance. Within the last week both patients have taken a turn for the worse, and both will die within the next few weeks if they do not receive a liver transplant.

A few hours ago, a patient was admitted to the hospital with massive head trauma caused by an automobile accident. The patient is now brain dead, but is being kept on life support systems to preserve his organs for transplantation. The liver is undamaged, and it will be donated for transplantation. Tissue matching shows that it is an acceptable organ for either Patterson or Friedman. Patterson's physician was the first to list his patient on the transplant list, which he did three days earlier than did Friedman's physician.

Who should receive the organ and why? Assume that the hospital is prohibited under federal funding requirements from discrimination on the basis of gender, race, age or disability. How would such a prohibition operate in this situation?

See, V.H. Schmidt, Selection of Recipients for Donor Organs in Transplant Medicine 23 J. Med. & Philosophy (1998); United Network for Organ Sharing, Policy 3.6; M. Benjamin, Transplantation for Alcoholic Liver Disease: The Ethical Issues 3 Liver Transplantation & Surgery 337 (1997); Alvin H. Moss & Mark Siegler, Should Alcoholics Compete Equally for Liver Transplantation? 265 JAMA 1295 (1991); Carl Cohen, et al., Alcoholics and Liver Transplantation? 265 JAMA 1299 (1991).

Suppose instead that Antonia Friedman is a convicted felon serving 25 years for money laundering or health care fraud. Who should receive the liver? See, Limited Organ Supply Raises Allocation Concerns, Ethics Forum, Am.Med.News, July 1, 2002, for a debate between two medical ethicists over the issue (available at www.ama-assn.org/amednews/2002/07/01/prca701.htm); and Jessica Wright, Medically Necessary Organ Transplants for Prisoners: Who is Responsible for Payment? 39 B.C. L. Rev 1251 (1998). For a summary of the controversy over a heart transplant provided to a prisoner in California, see American Political Network: American Health Line, November 9, 2001; January 31, February 5, August 1, December 19, 2002.

Note: The Organ Procurement Transplant Network

The National Organ Transplant Act (NOTA) requires the Department of Health and Human Services (HHS) to establish an Organ Procurement Transplant Network (OPTN) through which the retrieval, distribution and transplantation of human organs is organized. HHS contracts with the United Network for Organ Sharing (UNOS), a private nonprofit organization, for the management of the federal OPTN.

In a 1993 study of the national organ procurement and distribution system, the General Accounting Office found that nearly every Organ Procurement Organization was noncompliant with UNOS policy on at least one factor for distribution of organs. GAO, Organ Transplants: Increased Effort Needed to Boost Supply and Ensure Equitable Distribution of Organs (April 1993). In the face of continued concern, HHS promulgated new regulations in 1999. Through these new regulations, the federal government took a more active role in determining how organs should be allocated. After the 1999 rule, UNOS no longer enjoyed the deference that had been accorded to its policies; however, the regulation does allow OPTN, and thus UNOS, to propose policies that must be agreed upon by an HHS oversight committee. From the standpoint of the federal government, the new regulation is intended to ensure consistency between OPTN policies (as implemented by UNOS) and the NOTA. See 64 Fed. Reg. 16296 codified at 42 C.F.R. pt. 121 (1998); Special Section: Organ Transplantation: Sharing Policy and Keeping Public Trust, 8 Cambridge Quarterly (1999).

The 1999 regulation establishes standardized criteria for placing patients on transplant waiting lists and for distribution of donated organs. The regulation also sets standards for the availability of organ transplant data. The Institute of Medicine of the National Academy of Sciences published a report evaluating the new HHS rule. Assessing Current Policies and the Potential Impact of the DHHS Final Rule (1999). The report is generally favorable toward the 1999 regulation and quite supportive of increased federal oversight of OPTN.

1. Geographic Distribution of Organs

Prior to the 1999 regulation, UNOS policy was to retain organs in the geographic area where they were harvested if a patient with the appropriate medical status was in that area. Under that system, geographic disparities in the length of wait time occurred. Median waiting times by region varied considerably. The median wait time for a liver, for example, ranged from 20 to 78 days in Region 3, while the wait in Region 9 amounted to 279 to 443 days. 59 Fed. Reg. 46482, 46486 (September 8, 1994). Similar variations existed for other organs as well. The geographic priorities meant that a transplantable organ harvested in Region 3 would stay in Region 3 as long as there was a qualified patient in that region even if patients with a more urgent need or who present marginally better survival waited in other regions. The rationale behind the old UNOS policy was to reduce organ preservation, improve organ quality and survival outcomes, reduce the costs incurred by the patient, and increase access to transplantation by increasing interest in donation. The purpose of the new rule is to make the most effective use of organs by allocating them to the most medically urgent and appropriate patients. With the exception of thoracic organs which are still allocated locally, regionally, and then nationally, all other organs are now allocated based on medical urgency rather than geography. See P.A. Ubel & A.L. Caplan, Geographic Favoritism in Liver Transplantation: Unfortunate or Unfair? 339 NEJM 1322 (1998). Because organs are now allocated according to medical urgency rather than strictly geographically, the HHS hopes wait times will become less disparate throughout the country.

2. *Listing Patients for Transplantation*

Individual private physicians and hospitals decide who gets on the UNOS computer registry and when. Patients receive priority points for the length of time they have been on the list, among other criteria, so getting on the list earlier rather than later is quite significant. Once a patient is on the waiting list, the patient data is placed in the UNOS national databank and the patient's medical status places them in line for an organ. Under UNOS Policy 3.6.3, for example, position on the liver wait list is based on a point system which combines both how long a patient has been on the list and the patient's medical status.

There had been wide variability in patient listing practices for heart, lung, and liver transplant programs around the country. For this reason, UNOS developed specific national policies for patient listing for the differing types of transplants including liver, kidney, thoracic organ, intestine, and pancreas, as well as a general policy for those organs not specifically addressed. Under the 1999 HHS regulation, the policies are to be reviewed by the Advisory Committee on Organ Transplantation which advises the Secretary of HHS. See http:www.organdonor.gov/acot.html

An expose of listing practices at the University of Illinois and University of Chicago hospitals revealed that physicians there may have exaggerated their patients' medical condition to move them up higher on the list and pump up the volume of liver transplants performed at those facilities. The federal government pursued the issue after a whistleblower faculty member filed a law suit. The hospitals involved denied all of the allegations and made financial settlements with the government, with Illinois paying the largest amount of $1 million. A Man of Principle, Chicago Tribune Magazine, Jan. 25, 2004 (2004 WL 65046062).

Psychosocial factors traditionally have played a large role in considering which patients receive donated organs. In 1999, UNOS expressed concern over the use of non-medical transplant candidate criteria. UNOS Ethics Committee, General Considerations in Assessment of Transplant Candidacy. The Committee, however, justified the use of certain non-medical criteria based on the shortage of available organs for transplantation. With organs in such short supply, UNOS believes the best potential recipients should be identified based on both medical and non-medical criteria. Examples of non-medical criteria currently used by physicians and other health care providers include organ failure caused by behavior, compliance/adherence, repeat transplantation, and alternative therapies. According to the UNOS Ethics Committee, the non-medical criteria by which transplant candidates are evaluated should be constantly reassessed and modified to reflect changes that occur in technology, medicine, and other related fields and should be examined for excessive subjectivity. www.unos.org/Resources/bioethics.asp?index=4

3. *Zero Antigen Mismatch and Disparate Impact by Race*

Zero antigen mismatch occurs when a recipient patient and a donated kidney have no antigen mismatches, even though all six antigens on which kidneys and recipients would be matched for a "perfect match" may not have shown up in testing a particular kidney. A partial match occurs when a mismatch for one or more of the six antigens has been detected.

UNOS policy requires that if there is a patient anywhere in the nation with a zero antigen mismatch with the available kidney, that kidney must be given to the patient with the zero antigen mismatch. A zero antigen mismatch with an available kidney is a ticket to override distribution to any local or regional patients with less than zero antigen mismatch. Where there is partial antigen match, UNOS policy favors patients with a higher degree of partial antigen match over others who are otherwise in the same category. Prior to the 1999 HHS regulation, geographically-based policy preferred transplantation in a patient in the same locale or region as the donor.

Data indicate that the priority for zero antigen mismatch has a disparate impact by race on recipient patients, however. African Americans may be disadvantaged in the rationing of kidneys by the zero antigen mismatch standard and by the partial match standard because antigens are distributed differently among different racial groups.

African–American transplant candidates constituted 36.5% of the kidney waiting list in 2002 and whites comprised 54.1%. In the same year, whites received, for example, 64.3% of kidneys from deceased donors, while African Americans received 29.1%. In 1998, the numbers were 66.3% and 27.2%, respectively. OPTN, Annual Report 2003. At the same time, end-stage renal disease is much more prevalent among African Americans, occurring at nearly four times the rate of the white population.

In 1995, white donors provided 90% of kidneys available for transplant, but in 1998 whites accounted for only 76% of the transplantable kidneys. This change is attributed to the increased efforts of UNOS and other organizations to increase organ donation awareness. However, to level off the zero antigen mismatch standard the donation rate for African Americans would have to increase five times over the current rate for African Americans and four times over the current rate for white donors.

The antigen match problem also exists within the preference for higher degree of match where only a partial match is found. Transplantation is significantly more likely to succeed where there is a perfect six-antigen match. Data on zero antigen mismatch also show significantly better survival rates. In contrast, partial antigen match shows much smaller differences in survival rates across differences in the numbers of antigens matched. Data from 2001 indicated one-year survival rates for cadaveric kidney transplants of 86.1% for mismatch of 5 antigens; 87.5% for 4; 89.2% for 3; 90.4% for 2; and 91.4% when there is only 1 mismatch. UNOS 1999 Annual Report (September 1999). Are these differences significant?

Although the antigen match policy is based on increased survival, kidney-recipient selection policies do not uniformly prefer survivability. For example, "presensitized" patients, who have previously received a kidney that failed within a short time after transplant, receive priority. Presensitized patients have priority for transplant even though the presensitization caused by the earlier transplant diminishes the chances for successful transplant significantly. UNOS altered its kidney antigen mismatch policy in May, 2003. By February, 2004, it appeared that the change had increased transplants for minority recipients by 7%. New Policy Helps Minorities in Need of Kidneys, Chicago Tribune, Feb. 5, 2004 (2004 WL 67384149).

A similar allocation issue arises when the transplant candidate is HIV-positive, but not in the terminal stages of the disease. UNOS policy states that asymptomatic HIV-positive patients should not necessarily be excluded from organ transplantation; however, the actual practice at transplant centers diverges from this policy. Some argue that HIV-positive patients should be eligible for transplants even if their outcomes were worse than HIV-negative patients. They point to the priority established for patients with prior failed transplants and the availability of transplants for persons with hepatitis C and diabetes, who have lesser survival rates, as evidence that relative efficacy is not the only value at play. See Halpern, Ubel, and Caplan, Solid–Organ Transplantation in HIV-infected Patients, 347 NEJM 284 (July 25, 2002):

> There are two distinct ethical questions about efficacy: Does the transplantation benefit the individual patients? Would it benefit other patients more? ... The second question—concerning relative efficacy—is rarely addressed in the distribution of plentiful resources, but there is strong moral basis for posing this question when scarce resources are being allocated. We do not ask whether elderly persons should receive antihypertensive therapy, even though the benefits of long-term treatment are greater for younger persons.

Should we confine our arguments about relative efficacy to the question of organ transplantation; or should the same question be applied to most health care services? While it is hard to argue that transplantable solid organs are not scarce, can you argue that other types of medical interventions are also scarce?

Problem: Setting Priorities

There has been increasing pressure on the scarce supply of transplantable organs raising questions about whether survivability should be adopted as the sole criterion for selecting the candidate for transplantation. If survivability were to be the over-arching standard, which of the current policies discussed above would have to be altered?

Do you agree that policies should be consistent in terms of an absolute priority for relative efficacy? If not, what values might lead us to conclude otherwise? If you do favor departures from relative efficacy, under what terms would you accept them? Whom would you authorize to make those departures? The physician in deciding to list the patient? The individual transplant centers? UNOS? HHS? A "black box" committee?

There is wide variation in transplant survival rates among hospitals doing transplants. Should this variation be added to the calculation of who gets priority for transplant with organs shifted away from transplant centers with poorer records?

How would you resolve the policy issues in regard to these standards if you were the Secretary of HHS, a member of Congress, or UNOS?

See Ian Ayres, Laura G. Dooley, Robert S. Gaston, Unequal Racial Access to Kidney Transplantation, 46 Vand. L. Rev. 805 (1993); Benjamin Mintz, Analyzing the OPTN Under the State Action Doctrine—Can UNOS Organ Allocation Criteria Survive Strict Scrutiny? 28 Colum. J.L. & Soc. Probls. 339 (1995).

Problem: State or Federal Control?

The HHS 1999 regulation attempts to eliminate the disparity in median wait times among various geographic regions. Several states, however, have enacted laws which favor intra-state distribution by placing restrictions on out-of-state organ transfers. In effect, these state laws attempt to perpetuate the policy as it was before the promulgation of the regulations:

La. Rev. Stat. Ann. § 17:2353

[I]n the event an anatomical gift is made in the state of Louisiana of any vascular organ for transplantation purposes, if the donor does not name a specific donee and the organ is deemed suitable for transplantation to an individual, the vascular organ shall be donated to the Louisiana-designated organ procurement organization. Said organization shall use its best efforts to determine if there is a suitable recipient in the state.

* * *

[T]he Louisiana-designated organ procurement organization may only transfer a vascular organ to an out-of-state organ procurement organization or suitable out-of-state recipient for transplantation if either:

(a) A suitable recipient in the state of Louisiana cannot be found in a reasonable amount of time.

(b) The Louisiana-designated organ procurement organization has a reciprocal agreement with the out-of-state procurement organization [governing organ sharing between Louisiana and that state].

Assume you are on the staff of a U.S. Senator from a state that has a statute rejecting the national uniform distribution of organs. The Senator has asked you to develop a position paper on whether the HHS policy on national distribution should be overturned legislatively. Do you support federal or state control for organ allocation policy? Is the federal government making allocation political by stepping in and taking more control? Should UNOS, as a private corporation and an expert in the field, be able to establish policies without federal governmental oversight? See Dulcinea Grantham, Transforming Transplantation: The Effect of the Health and Human Services Final Rule on the Organ Allocation System, 35 U.S.F.L. Rev. 751 (2001); Roderick T. Chen, Organ Allocation and the States: Can States Restrict Broader Organ Sharing? 49 Duke I.J. 261 (1999); Laura E. McMullen, Equitable Allocation of Human Organs: An Examination of the New Federal Regulation, 20 J. Legal Med. 405 (1999).

III. INCREASING THE SUPPLY OF ORGANS FOR TRANSPLANTATION: THE IMPACT OF LEGAL RESTRAINTS

For most health care services and goods scarcity could be resolved if enough funds were provided. Funding also has an effect on the availability of organ transplantation: access to funding certainly determines whether an individual will receive a transplant and funding can support research to maximize the success of human organ transplants or the use of non-human organ sources. In the case of organ transplantation, however, even unlimited funding will not resolve the shortage of human organs available for transplantation. In 2002, there were 14,774 kidney transplants; 5,329 liver transplants, and 2,155 heart transplants. By comparison in 1995, there were 11,807 kidney transplants; 3,923 liver transplants; and 2,361 heart transplants (UNOS Scientific Data Registry, September 7, 1999). The number of reported deaths on the waiting list in 2002 increased, with 3,674 dying on the kidney wait list; 1,884 on the liver list; and 1,774 on the heart list, despite the increase in the number of transplants performed. Comparative figures for 1995 were 1,520 for kidneys; 804 for livers; and 770 for hearts. Demand continues to outstrip supply. On May 21, 2000, 69,728 organs were needed for patients listed, compared to 43,854 in 1995.

As you analyze the statutes and case law presented below, consider the values implied in the law relating to the procurement of human organs for transplantation and the impact on supply.

NEWMAN v. SATHYAVAGLSWARAN

United States Court of Appeals, Ninth Circuit, 2002.
287 F.3d 786.

Parents, whose deceased children's corneas were removed by the Los Angeles County Coroner's office without notice or consent, brought this 42 U.S.C. § 1983 action alleging a taking of their property without due process of law. The complaint was dismissed by the district court for a failure to state a claim upon which relief could be granted. We must decide whether the longstanding recognition in the law of California, paralleled by our national common law, that next of kin have the exclusive right to possess the bodies of their deceased family members creates a property interest, the deprivation of which must be accorded due process of law under the Fourteenth Amendment of the United States Constitution. We hold that it does. * * *

* * *

Robert Newman and Barbara Obarski (the parents) each had children, Richard Newman and Kenneth Obarski respectively, who died in Los Angeles County in October 1997. Following their deaths, the Office of the Coroner for the County of Los Angeles (the coroner) obtained possession of the bodies of the children and, under procedures adopted pursuant to California Government Code § 27492.47 as it then existed, removed the corneas from those bodies without the knowledge of the parents and without an attempt to notify them and request consent. The parents became aware of the coroner's actions in September 1999 and subsequently filed this § 1983 action alleging a deprivation of their property without due process of law in violation of the Fourteenth Amendment.

II. PROPERTY INTERESTS IN DEAD BODIES

[T]he Supreme Court repeatedly has affirmed that "the right of every individual to the possession and control of his own person, free from all restraint or interference of others," [ ] is "so rooted in the traditions and conscience of our people," [ ] as to be ranked as one of the fundamental liberties protected by the "substantive" component of the Due Process Clause. [ ] This liberty, the Court has "strongly suggested," extends to the personal decisions about "how to best protect dignity and independence at the end of life." [ ] The Court has not had occasion to address whether the rights of possession and control of one's own body, the most "sacred" and "carefully guarded" of all rights in the common law, [ ] are property interests protected by the Due Process Clause. Nor has it addressed what Due Process protections are applicable to the rights of next of kin to possess and control the bodies of their deceased relatives.

A. History of Common Law Interests in Dead Bodies

* * *

Many early American courts adopted Blackstone's description of the common law, holding that "a dead body is not the subject of property right." [ ] The duty to protect the body by providing a burial was often described as flowing from the "universal ... right of sepulture," rather than from a concept of property law. [ ] As cases involving unauthorized mutilation and disposition of bodies increased toward the end of the 19th century, paralleling the rise in demand for human cadavers in medical science and use of cremation as an alternative to burial, [ ] courts began to recognize an exclusive right of the next of kin to possess and control the disposition of the bodies of their dead relatives, the violation of which was actionable at law. Thus, in holding that a city council could not "seize upon existing private burial grounds, make them public, and exclude the proprietors from their management," the Supreme Court of Indiana commented that "the burial of the dead can [not] ... be taken out of the hands of the relatives thereof" because "we lay down the proposition, that the bodies of the dead belong to the surviving relations, in the order of inheritance, as property, and that they have the right to dispose of them as such, within restrictions analogous to those by which the disposition of other property may be regulated." [ ] * * *

B. Interests in Dead Bodies in California Law

[The court traces the history of California law concerning the disposition of dead bodies. California courts referred to "quasi-property" rights in cases disputing the handling of cadavers, including cases in which the courts held that civil litigants had no right to demand an autopsy; next-of-kin could exclude the decedent's friends from the funeral; and permitted an action for retaining organs after autopsy.]

C. The Right to Transfer Body Parts

The first successful transplantation of a kidney in 1954 led to an expansion of the rights of next of kin to the bodies of the dead. In 1968, the

National Conference of Commissioners on Uniform State Laws approved the Uniform Anatomical Gift Act (UAGA), adopted by California the same year, which grants next of kin the right to transfer the parts of bodies in their possession to others for medical or research purposes. [ ] The right to transfer is limited. The California UAGA prohibits any person from "knowingly, for valuable consideration, purchas[ing] or sell[ing] a part for transplantation, therapy, or reconditioning, if removal of the part is intended to occur after the death of the decedent," Cal. Health & Safety Code § 7155, as does federal law, 42 U.S.C. § 274e (prohibiting the "transfer [of] any human organ for valuable consideration"). * * *

In the 1970s and 1980s, medical science improvements and the related demand for transplant organs prompted governments to search for new ways to increase the supply of organs for donation. [ ] Many perceived as a hindrance to the supply of needed organs the rule implicit in the UAGA that donations could be effected only if consent was received from the decedent or next of kin. [ ] In response, some states passed "presumed consent" laws that allow the taking and transfer of body parts by a coroner without the consent of next of kin as long as no objection to the removal is known. [ ] California Government Code § 27491.47, enacted in 1983, was such a law.

III. DUE PROCESS ANALYSIS

"[T]o provide California non-profit eye banks with an adequate supply of corneal tissue," S. Com. Rep. SB 21 (Cal.1983), § 27491.47(a) authorized the coroner to "remove and release or authorize the removal and release of corneal eye tissue from a body within the coroner's custody" without any effort to notify and obtain the consent of next of kin "if ... [t]he coroner has no knowledge of objection to the removal." The law also provided that the coroner or any person acting upon his or her request "shall [not] incur civil liability for such removal in an action brought by any person who did not object prior to the removal ... nor be subject to criminal prosecution." § 27491.47(b).[2]

* * *

In two decisions the Sixth Circuit, the only federal circuit to address the issue until now, held that the interests of next of kin in dead bodies recognized in Michigan and Ohio allowed next of kin to bring § 1983 actions challenging implementation of cornea removal statutes similar to California's. *Whaley v. County of Tuscola*, 58 F.3d 1111 (6th Cir. 1995)(Michigan); *Brotherton v. Cleveland*, 923 F.2d 477 (6th Cir. 1991)(Ohio). * * *

The supreme courts of Florida and Georgia, however, have held that similar legal interests of next of kin in the possession of the body of a deceased family member, recognized as "quasi property" rights in each state, are "not ... of constitutional dimension." *Georgia Lions Eye Bank, Inc. v. Lavant*, 255 Ga. 60, 335 S.E.2d 127, 128 (1985); *State v. Powell*, 497 So.2d 1188, 1191 (Fla. 1986)(commenting that "[a]ll authorities generally agree that the next of kin have no property right in the remains of a decedent"). The

2. For body parts other than corneas, California adopted the 1987 version of the UAGA authorizing transfer when no knowledge of objection is known and after "[a] reasonable ef- fort has been made to locate and inform [next of kin] of their option to make, or object to making, an anatomical gift." Cal. Health & Safety Code § 7151.5(a)(2).

Florida Supreme Court recently rejected the broad implications of the reasoning in *Powell* distinguishing that decision as turning on a balance between the public health interest in cornea donation and the " 'infinitesimally small intrusion' " of their removal. *Crocker v. Pleasant*, 778 So.2d 978, 985, 988 (Fla. 2001)(allowing a § 1983 action to go forward for interference with the right of next of kin to possess the body of their son because "in Florida there is a legitimate claim of entitlement by the next of kin to possession of the remains of a decedent for burial or other lawful disposition").

We agree with the reasoning of the Sixth Circuit and believe that reasoning is applicable here. Under traditional common law principles, serving a duty to protect the dignity of the human body in its final disposition that is deeply rooted in our legal history and social traditions, the parents had exclusive and legitimate claims of entitlement to possess, control, dispose and prevent the violation of the corneas and other parts of the bodies of their deceased children. With California's adoption of the UAGA, Cal. Health and Safety Code § 7151.5, it statutorily recognized other important rights of the parents in relation to the bodies of their deceased children—the right to transfer body parts and refuse to allow their transfer. These are all important components of the group of rights by which property is defined, each of which carried with it the power to exclude others from its exercise, "traditionally . . . one of the most treasured strands in an owner's bundle of property rights." [ ]

* * *

Nor does the fact that California forbids the trade of body parts for profit mean that next of kin lack a property interest in them. The Supreme Court has "never held that a physical item is not 'property' simply because it lacks a positive economic or market value." [ ]

Because the property interests of next of kin to dead bodies are firmly entrenched in the "background principles of property law," based on values and understandings contained in our legal history dating from the Roman Empire, California may not be free to alter them with exceptions that lack "a firm basis in traditional property principles." [ ] We need not, however, decide whether California has transgressed basic property principles with enactment of § 27491.47 because that statute did not extinguish California's legal recognition of the property interests of the parents to the corneas of their deceased children. It allowed the removal of corneas only if "the coroner has no knowledge of objection," a provision that implicitly acknowledges the ongoing property interests of next of kin.

* * *

* * * The property rights that California affords to next of kin to the body of their deceased relatives serve the premium value our society has historically placed on protecting the dignity of the human body in its final disposition. California infringed the dignity of the bodies of the children when it extracted the corneas from those bodies without the consent of the parents. The process of law was due the parents for this deprivation of their rights.

* * *

The scope of the process of law that was due the parents is not a question that we can answer based on the pleadings alone. This question must be addressed in future proceedings.

* * *

We do not hold that California lacks significant interests in obtaining corneas or other organs of the deceased in order to contribute to the lives of the living. Courts are required to evaluate carefully the state's interests in deciding what process must be due the holders of property interests for their deprivation. [ ] An interest so central to the state's core police powers as improving the health of its citizens is certainly one that must be considered seriously in determining what process the parents were due. [ ] But our Constitution requires the government to assert its interests and subject them to scrutiny when it invades the rights of its subjects. Accordingly, we reverse the district court's dismissal of the parents' complaint and remand for proceedings in which the government's justification for its deprivation of parents' interests may be fully aired and appropriately scrutinized.

Notes and Questions

1. Many states have statutes similar to that at issue in *Newman*. For example, some states allow for the removal of any organ without consent after an attempt to contact the family is made. See, e.g., Haw. Rev. Stat. § 327–4 and Idaho Code § 39–3405. Other states allow for the removal of corneas or specified other tissue without an attempt to notify family when there is no objection known. See, e.g., Mo.Stat. § 58–770, Ark. Code § 12–12–320, and Colo. Rev. Stat. § 30–10–621, which allow for the removal of the pituitary gland under such circumstances. Should the type of tissue involved be relevant to whether consent is required? Is the attempt to contact family, even if unsuccessful, significant? Morally? Legally? If the family has religious objections to "mutilation" of the body, is an attempt to notify adequate? See, e.g., Carrie Pearson O'Keeffe, (Note) When an Anatomical "Gift" Isn't a Gift: Presumed Consent Laws As an Affront to Religious Liberty, 7 Texas Forum on Civil Liberties and Civil Rights 287 (Fall 2002).

2. The Ninth Circuit leaves open the possibility that the State could justify its taking of the corneas. Of course, that won't happen in this case because of the amendment discussed below. How could the State justify its taking of the corneas without consent? Does it matter that some of the tissue taken is used for research instead of transplantation? That some is used for cosmetic surgery instead of life-saving surgery? Would legislation that required only a reasonable attempt to contact next-of-kin as opposed to actual consent, as does the Uniform Anatomical Gift Act, satisfy due process requirements?

3. The California legislature had amended the statute at issue in *Newman* prior to the Ninth Circuit's consideration of this case. As noted by the Court:

> In 1998, § 27491.47(a)(2) was amended to require that the coroner obtain written or telephonic consent of the next of kin prior to removing corneas. The Committee Report accompanying that change in law argued that "existing law governing corneal tissue removal does not adequately reflect the importance of obtaining the consent of a decedent's next-of-kin.... [A]natomical gifts are ... 'gifts' and ... the removal of corneal tissue without the consent of a decedent's next-of-kin violates the legally recognized principle that ... an individual's right to make or decline to

make an anatomical gift [is] passed on to the next-of-kin." S. Com. Rep. S.B. 1403 (1998).

Did the legislature strike the right balance on the second try, or should it have stood behind its original legislation? What are we balancing in presumed consent? Respect for dead bodies? Respect for families? Preservation of life and health?

4.   Presumed consent, which is the common term for the reliance on known objection in the statute at issue in California, proceeds from the premise that there is some interest in the surviving family (or the decedent) in the cadaver. Is that interest worth preserving in the face of the large numbers of individuals who would benefit from transplantation? Or, should cadavers be considered "commons" available for public use? See, e.g., Aaron Spital, Conscription of Cadaveric Organs for Transplantation: Neglected Again, 13 Kennedy Institute of Ethics Journal 169 (2003), arguing that no regime that relies on autonomy will be able to meet the need for organs. For an analysis of individual control of body parts under the mainstream theories of legal thought, see Guido Calabresi, An Introduction to Legal Thought: Four Approaches to Law and to the Allocation of Body Parts, 55 Stan. L. Rev. 2113 (2003). See also, Note, "She's Got Bette Davis Eyes: Assessing the Nonconsensual Removal of Cadaver Organs under the Takings and Due Process Clauses," 90 Colum. L. Rev. 528 (1990).

5.   *Newman* focuses on the rights of the family rather than the rights of the decedent. Is that the proper focus in dealing with cadavers? If you are tempted to say that cadavers have no rights, how do you explain the UAGA's emphasis on pre-mortem anatomical gift documents? If cadavers have no rights (or if people have no right to govern the disposition of their bodies upon their death), would you support compliance with a pre-mortem gift document over the surviving family's objection, as does the UAGA? See, e.g., Aaron Spital, Mandated Choice: A Plan to Increase Public Commitment to Organ Donation, 273 JAMA 504 (Feb. 8, 1995), describing the common practice of deferring to family override.

6.   The UAGA requires that the patient or family be informed of the opportunity to donate organs upon admission to the hospital or after the patient's death. It had been hoped that such "routine inquiry" or "required request" mandates would increase the number of organs donated. That has not been the case. Why do people refuse at the point of the death of a family member? Some facilities have found that who asks the family makes a difference. See e.g., Pulling Together, UNOS Update, July/August 1996, at p. 10, reporting on comparative donation rates for requests made by doctors, nurses or bereavement staff in ascending order in terms of positive response.

7.   Before the decision in *Newman,* the LA County coroner's office discontinued the practice of harvesting corneas without consent after a series of news articles demonstrated that the practice had a disproportionate impact on people of color. In LA at the time, 80% of autopsies were performed on African–American or Latino individuals and only 16% on whites. Ralph Frammolino, Harvest of Corneas at Morgue Questioned, L.A.Times, Nov. 2, 1997. Would this data alter your analysis of the advisability of non-consensual organ harvesting or reliance on presumed consent? See, Michele Goodwin, Rethinking Legislative Consent Law, 5 DePaul J. Health Care L. 257 (2002) and Deconstructing Legislative Consent Law: Organ Taking, Racial Profiling and Distributive Justice, 6 V.J.L. & Tech. 2 (2001).

8.   The UAGA allows the donor to designate a recipient and some believe that this provision can incentivize more donations. LifeSharers is a non-profit organization that has set up a national network to facilitate the designation of recipients of organs donated upon death. Its web site states:

If you or a loved one ever need an organ for a transplant operation, chances are you'll die before you get it. You can improve your odds by joining LifeSharers. Membership is free. LifeSharers is a non-profit voluntary network of organ and tissue donors. LifeSharers members promise to donate upon their death, but they give fellow members first access to their organs and tissue. As LifeSharers members, you and your loved ones will have access to organs and tissue that otherwise may not be available to you. As the LifeSharers network grows, more and more organs and tissue may become available to you—if you are a member.

LifeSharers argues that a membership network in which members get priority for organs donated by members is justified because "it's not fair to give organs to non-donors when there are donors who need them. But people who have agreed to donate their organs when they die get only about 30% of the organs transplanted in the United States." In order to qualify for priority for LifeSharers-donated organs, an individual must be a member for 180 days prior to transplantation. LifeSharers organs that are not suitable for any LifeSharers member would be used for anyone on the transplant list. As of April 2004, LifeSharers claimed over 2200 members. See http://www.lifesharers.com/. Should LifeSharers be encouraged? See, Adam J. Kolber, A Matter of Priority: Transplanting Organs Preferentially to Registered Donors, 55 Rutgers L. Rev. 671 (2003); Michael T. Morley, (Note) Increasing the Supply of Organs for Transplantation Through Paired Organ Exchanges, 21 Yale L. and Pol'y Rev. 221 (2003).

9. Life-sustaining organs may be removed only from persons who have died. Chapter 4 presents the current legal standard for determination of death, the whole brain death standard, which was adopted in part to allow for removal of organs while the person is still attached to a ventilator so that the organs remain oxygenated and transplantable. That chapter also describes efforts to expand the legal standard for determination of death in order to increase the supply of organs.

Note: Market Solutions to Organ Shortages

The UAGA prohibits the sale for "valuable consideration," of "an organ, tissue, eye, bone, artery, blood, fluid, or other portion of the human body" . . . "if removal is . . . intended to occur after the death of the decedent." The Act specifies that "valuable consideration does not include reasonable payment for the removal, processing, disposal, preservation, quality control, storage, transportation, or implantation of a part." Federal law provides that it is illegal for "any person to knowingly acquire, receive, or otherwise transfer any human organ for valuable consideration for use in human transplantation if the transfer affects interstate commerce." The federal statute defines human organ as "human (including fetal) kidney, liver, heart, lung, pancreas, bone marrow, cornea, eye, bone, and skin or any subpart thereof." Federal law provides that "valuable consideration" does not include "reasonable payments associated with the removal, transportation, implantation, processing, preservation, quality control, and storage of a human organ or the expenses of travel, housing, and lost wages incurred by the donor of a human organ in connection with the donation . . .". 42 U.S.C.A. § 274(e). How does the sale of blood, semen, and ova proceed under with these statutes? Is the sale of these items different in kind from the sales prohibited under the UAGA or the federal act?

Could an unemployed living kidney donor be paid "lost wages" for the time spent on the removal of the organ and recovery? What should the hourly rate for organ transplantation be? If the donor earns minimum wage, is that the amount that should be paid? Should the lawyer-donor and the cook-donor be paid differently for the same labor? Are ova donors, who are paid several thousand dollars, being paid for their ova or for expenses or for their time? Should this compensation be allowed? Required? Regulated?

The state of Pennsylvania enacted legislation to establish a public trust fund that would supply funds to families of decedents who donated organs. Payments would be limited to $3,000 and could be used to cover funeral expenses and incidental expenses borne by the family in relation to the donation. 20 Pa.C.S.A. § 88622. Because of concerns that the NOTA prohibits such payments, the plan dropped coverage for funeral expenses and decided to cover only incidental expenses such as food, lodging and transportation for the family. See discussion in John Zen Jackson, When It Comes to Transplant Organs, Demand Far Exceeds Supply, New Jersey Law Journal, December 16, 2002.

In light of the prohibition on sales and the requirement of consent, is the scarcity of human organs any less a result of policy decisions than is the scarcity of other health care services or goods? If it could be proven that allowing the sale of non-life-sustaining organs (such as a single kidney or a part of the liver) by living persons or the sale of any organs by or on behalf of the estate (or creditors) of cadavers would substantially increase the number of organs available, would you support legalization of such sales? If so, under what circumstances?

Historically, the legal boundaries established in the UAGA and in the NOTA have been strong enough to deter the development of a market system even though there are legal gaps that give some room for such a market. Support for financial incentives for "donation" seems to be increasing, however. In June, 2002, the American Medical Association House of Delegates adopted a report from the Association's Council on Ethical and Judicial Affairs (CEJA) recommending that financial incentives for the donation of cadaveric organs be tested on an experimental basis. Cadaveric Organ Donations: Encouraging the Study of Motivation, Report of the Council on Ethical and Judicial Affairs, available in proceedings of the 2002 Annual Meeting of the AMA posted on the AMA's web site at www.ama-assn.org. The AMA has supported limited financial incentives for cadaveric organ donation since 1993. (See, Financial Incentives for Organ Donation, Policy E–2.15, AMA Policy Database, available on the AMA web site.) The more recent report recommends rigorous study of the impact of certain financial incentives under the following circumstances: consultation and advice is sought from the population to be studied; written protocols with sound study design are approved by institutional review boards and are available to the public; incentives are modest and set at the lowest level that can reasonably be expected to increase donations; no study should include payment to living donors and should be limited to cadaveric organs only; organs so donated should be allocated by UNOS under medical need standards so that the purchasing of specific organs does not occur.

Major concerns about moving to a market in human organs include the commodification and demeaning of the human body; the desperation of the poor which would undermine autonomy and consent for the sale; and the disparate impact on poor populations who would become objects for the rich. It is also feared that the introduction of financial incentives would destroy altruistic donations, increasing the expense of transplants, and would introduce elements of fraud undercutting any boundaries that might be set. The counterweights to these arguments include the need for life-saving organs; respect for human individualism and autonomy; and recognition that there is wealth being made in the current transplant industry that is not shared with the donors.

Do the limitations in the AMA proposal respond to these concerns? Do you think that ultimately the sale of organs will be legalized? If so, what limitations do you expect to see, if any? Would the form of compensation or incentive make a difference; i.e., are tax credits or discounted insurance premiums or donations to charities in the name of the organ source more acceptable than direct payments?

For a good discussion of these issues from an ethical perspective, see the March 2003 issue of the Kennedy Institute of Ethics Journal, including, Robert Veatch, Why Liberals Should Accept Financial Incentives for Organ Procurement; Amitai Etzioni, Organ Donation: A Communitarian Approach; and Jeffrey P. Kahn, Three Views of Organ Procurement Policy: Moving Ahead or Giving Up? For more, see, David Kasserman, Markets for Organs: Myths and Misconceptions, 18 J. Contemp. Health L. & Pol'y 567, 568 (2002); David J. Rothman, Ethical and Social Consequences of Selling a Kidney, 288 JAMA 1640 (2002); James F. Blumstein, The Use of Financial Incentives in Medical Care: the Case of Commerce in Transplantable Organs, 3 Health Matrix 1 (1993); Gregory S. Crespi, Overcoming the Legal Obstacles to the Creation of a Futures Market in Bodily Organs, 55 Ohio St. L.J. 1 (1994); and Julia D. Mahoney, The Market for Human Tissue 86 Va.L.Rev. 169 (March 2000).

Problem: Organ Donation From an Adolescent

Laurel Singer, aged sixteen, has been brought to General Hospital with extremely serious injuries she suffered while diving from the river bluffs nearby. Efforts by the ambulance emergency medical technicians and the emergency room doctor to resuscitate her have failed. She has died. Laurel's friends have tried to call her parents, but they are on vacation somewhere in Australia. In looking for other contacts, they have come across her driver's license. Laurel signed the organ donor card on the back of her driver's license.

Assume that the following provisions of the UAGA have been adopted in your state:

§ 2. (a) An individual who is at least 18 years of age may (i) make an anatomical gift, (ii) limit an anatomical gift to one or more purposes, or (iii) refuse to make an anatomical gift.

(h) An anatomical gift that is not revoked by the donor before death is irrevocable and does not require the consent or concurrence of any person after the donor's death.

§ 3. (a) Any member of the following classes of persons, in the order of priority listed, may make an anatomical gift of all or a part of the decedent's body for an authorized purpose, unless the decedent, at the time of death, has made an unrevoked refusal to make that anatomical gift: (1) the spouse of the decedent; (2) an adult son or daughter of the decedent; (3) either parent of the decedent; (4) an adult brother or sister of the decedent; (5) a grandparent of the decedent; and (6) a guardian of the person of the decedent at the time of death.

§ 4. (a) The coroner may release and permit the removal of a part from a body within that official's custody, for transplantation or therapy, if:

(1) the official has received a request for the part from a hospital, physician, surgeon, or procurement organization;

(2) the official has made a reasonable effort, taking into account the useful life of the part, to locate and examine the decedent's medical records and inform persons listed in Section 3(a) of their option to make, or object to making, an anatomical gift;

(3) the official does not know of a refusal or contrary indication by the decedent or objection by a person having priority to act as listed in Section 3(a);

(b) If the body is not within the custody of the coroner, the local public health officer may release and permit the removal of any part from a body in the local public health officer's custody for transplantation or therapy if the requirements of subsection (a) are met.

§ 8. (a) The time of death must be determined by a physician or surgeon who attends the donor at death or, if none, the physician or surgeon who certifies the death. Neither the physician or surgeon who attends the donor at death nor the physician or surgeon who determines the time of death may participate in the procedures for removing or transplanting a part unless the document of gift designates a particular physician or surgeon.

§ 11. (a) A hospital, physician, surgeon, coroner, local public health officer, enucleator, technician, or other person, who acts in accordance with this Act or with the applicable anatomical gift law of another state or attempts in good faith to do so is not liable for that act in a civil action or criminal proceeding.

May a surgeon remove Laurel's transplantable organs? Under the UAGA, what must the doctor do in order to proceed? If the parents arrive after the surgery has been completed and they object to the harvesting of the child's organs, do they have any action against the emergency room doctor, the surgeon, or the hospital? How far does the good faith immunity provision of the UAGA extend? Would the hospital and surgeon be entitled to summary judgment on the parents' claim under this immunity clause? What would the parents' damages be if they did have a claim?

There have been a surprising number of cases filed against hospitals and transplant centers for actions taken in the harvesting of organs. See, for example, Schembre v. Mid–America Transplant Assn., 2003 WL 21692986 (Mo.App. E.D. 2003), denying summary judgment in favor of the defendant because negligence of the nurse in procuring an organ is a question of fact; Sattler v. Northwest Tissue Center, 110 Wash.App. 689, 42 P.3d 440 (2002), holding that the question of good faith in the immunity provision precluded summary judgment where the surviving husband claimed that he had authorized harvesting of bone and skin but not the eyes and the hospital's agent claimed that he had; Perry v. Saint Francis Hospital, 886 F.Supp. 1551 (D.Kan. 1995), holding the hospital liable. See also, Jacobsen v. Marin General Hospital, 192 F.3d 881 (9th Cir. 1999), holding that the hospital was not liable for negligence in a failed effort to reach next of kin; Ramirez v. Health Partners of Southern Arizona, 193 Ariz. 325, 972 P.2d 658 (Ct.App. 1998), where the hospital was held to have immunity. See also Rahman v. Mayo Clinic, 578 N.W.2d 802 (Minn.App. 1998).

Note: Organs from Living Donors

Living donors who are legally competent may donate (but not sell) non-life-sustaining organs and frequently do so for family members in need. Some transplant centers also have seen an increase in the number of persons who offer to donate a nonvital organ to anyone who needs it. See, Lainie Friedman Ross, Solid Organ Donation Between Strangers, 30 J.L. Med. & Ethics 440 (2002), for a discussion of the ethical issues arising in this type of intervivos donation. Although ethical issues relating to coercion and consent arise in any intervivos donation, especially those within families, legal issues arise primarily when the donor is legally incompetent or when the donor refuses consent. The principles discussed in these cases are the same as those that govern many medical treatment decisions for incompetent patients.

In Strunk v. Strunk, 445 S.W.2d 145 (Ky. App. 1969), for example, the court decided that it would permit a kidney to be removed from an incompetent ward of the state upon petition of his mother, for the purpose of being transplanted into the body of his brother who was dying of a kidney disease. In its holding, the court concluded that the court should decide in the same manner as the incompetent would if he were capable. In addition, the court stated that the best interests of the incompetent brother were served by allowing the transplant, because in donating a kidney to save his brother's life, the incompetent brother's mental well-being was ensured.

The court in Guardianship of Pescinski, 67 Wis.2d 4, 226 N.W.2d 180 (1975), explicitly rejected the "substituted judgment" rule of *Strunk* in favor of examining whether the organ donation was in the "best interests" of the incompetent. In *Pescinski*, the court concluded that there was "absolutely no evidence here that any interests of the ward will be served by the transplant." The court appeared to base its conclusion on Pescinski's mental illness which was characterized by "marked indifference" and "flight from reality." The court described the lack of a relationship between Pescinski and his sister who needed the kidney. Would *Pescinski* have been decided differently if the facts were the same as those in *Strunk?* See, John Robertson, Organ Donations by Incompetents and the Substituted Judgment Doctrine, 76 Colum.L.Rev. 48 (1976); Michael T. Morley, (Note) Proxy Consent to Organ Donation by Incompetents, 111 Yale L.J. 1215 (2002).

In *Strunk*, a sibling donor for the needy brother already existed. What if he had not? Could his parents have deliberately conceived another child to be an organ donor for him? In 1989, the parents of Anissa Ayala, who suffered from leukemia and needed a bone marrow transplant, decided to have another child. Although they hoped that the new sibling could donate bone marrow to Anissa, they realized that there was only a one in four chance she would be a match. Anissa's sister, Marissa, was born in 1990, and she qualified as a match. She was physically able to donate marrow at six months. Extracting bone marrow for transplantation can be risky and painful. Should the hospital require court approval before proceeding, or is this the kind of decision parents should ordinarily make for their children? How should the court rule in the case of an infant donor? The results of a survey of 15 of the 27 bone marrow transplant centers indicate that at least forty children have been conceived for the purpose of bone marrow donation to a sibling (as described in Vicki G. Norton, Unnatural Selection: Nontherapeutic Preimplantation Genetic Screening and Proposed Regulation, 41 U.C.L.A. L. Rev. 1581 (1994)). See also, Curran v. Bosze, 141 Ill.2d 473, 153 Ill.Dec. 213, 566 N.E.2d 1319 (1990), for decision refusing order for blood testing of toddlers for potential transplant to half-sibling. Teena–Ann Sankoorikal, Using Scientific Advances to Conceive the "Perfect" Donor: The Pandora's Box of Creating Child Donors for the Purpose of Saving Ailing Family Members, 32 Seton Hall L.Rev. 583 (2002).

A different issue arose in Head v. Colloton, 331 N.W.2d 870 (Iowa 1983), in which the court considered whether a person in need of a bone marrow transplant could have access to hospital records that would reveal the identity of a potential matched donor. "Mrs. X" was on the hospital's bone marrow registry solely because she had been tested for potential donation of blood platelets to a family member of hers. The opinion states that "through a series of conversations with a staff member," the plaintiff learned of the existence of this potential donor. The hospital had followed its own procedure to determine whether Mrs. X was willing to be a donor by contacting her by letter with a follow-up phone call in which general questions were used to determine her willingness to donate. The procedure prohibited revealing the existence of a particular person in need. Mrs. X responded to the hospital that she was not interested in being a donor. Plaintiff sued asking that the hospital either tell Mrs. X of his specific need or be required to give his attorney access to Mrs. X's identity so that the attorney could tell her. The court denied the request, holding that the record was confidential.

Why would the hospital have established the procedure it did for contacting potential bone marrow donors? Why would the hospital refuse to tell Mrs. X that she was a match for a specific individual needing a bone marrow transplant? If we tend to treat "statistical lives" differently than "identifiable lives," shouldn't Mrs. X have been informed of the need? How does an approach to Mrs. X differ, if at all, from the situation faced by an individual to give an organ for a family member? How does it differ from "required request?" The case turned on the legal issue of confidentiality. How was the confidentiality of Mrs. X's records affected by Mr. Head's request that the hospital approach her? See, Mark F. Anderson, Encouraging Bone Marrow Transplants From Unrelated Donors: Some Proposed Solutions to a Pressing Social Problem, 54 U. Pitt. L. Rev. 477 (1993).

Chapter 8

PUBLIC HEALTH AND BIOTERRORISM

I. INTRODUCTION TO PUBLIC HEALTH LAW

BARRY LEVY, TWENTY–FIRST CENTURY CHALLENGES FOR LAW AND PUBLIC HEALTH (1999)

32 Ind. L. Rev. 1149.

PUBLIC HEALTH

I am often asked, "What is public health?" I respond by describing typical daily activities that have been impacted by public health to make our lives safer and more healthful: drinking clean (and often, fluoridated) water, eating more nutritious meals (even with "Nutrition Facts" printed on packages of processed foods), driving safer and less polluting cars, regularly exercising, working in safer and more healthful workplaces, and, for many of us, having access to high quality, comprehensive health care, including preventive clinical services. All of this, and more, is the result of public health. Public health has accounted for about twenty-five of the thirty years of increased life expectancy in the United States since the turn of the century. Most people take all of this for granted—unless there is an outbreak of disease, an increase in the occurrence of some disease or injury, an outbreak of domestic or community violence, or a natural disaster.

When public health is most successful, public health activities—in public health practice, education, research, policy development and implementation, and administration and finance—are all almost invisible.

As stated in a landmark report of the Institute of Medicine in 1988, public health is "what we, as a society, do collectively to assure the conditions in which people can be healthy." It takes a society to practice public health—not just public health professionals. * * *

THE LAW

Laws concerning public health, at the national, state, and local level, are designed primarily to protect and promote health, and, at the same time, to ensure the rights of individuals. In various situations, different laws take precedence. Public health legal powers derive from the United States Constitution and the state constitutions. Many states have reasonably well-defined codes of public health that provide a basis for public health practice. Many state and local health officers are not fully aware of all the public health powers that they have—powers that can enable them to take necessary actions. For example, in a city in Massachusetts recently, the public health council realized existing laws enabled it to take actions to support a needle exchange program to prevent transmission of HIV and other pathogens. Many public health laws are enacted and enforced under the state's police powers—something that can cut both ways. Many of us public health professionals do not see ourselves as police officers; indeed when we come across as police officers, we may be undermining the public trust that is so essential for our work.

A prominent textbook on public health [Douglas Scutchfield and C. William Keck, Principles of Public Health Practice (1997)] outlines eight areas of public health law:

1. *Environmental Health Laws.*—These deal with food, workplace safety, wastewater disposal, and air pollution. Issues often arise concerning right of entry and compensation—not only compensation to victims who may have been harmed, but also compensation to those whose property may have been taken as a result of public health measures.

2. *Laws and Regulations on Reporting (Surveillance) of Disease and Injury.*—These enable public health workers to track disease, to identify disease outbreaks, to identify disturbing disease and injury trends, and to provide the basis for intervention to control disease and injury. Many of these laws and regulations transcend an individual's or a patient's right to privacy. Even though physicians are mandated to report specific diseases and injuries of public health importance, most do not; much disease and injury reporting rests on reporting from state laboratories or other sources of data.

3. *Laws Pertaining to Vital Statistics.*—Birth and death records provide an important basis for much public health work, despite frequent inaccuracies, especially in the cause of death recorded on death certificates.

4. *Disease and Injury Control.*—These laws often focus on prevention of disease and injury at the community level. Many policies and programs on such issues as tobacco and alcohol control—like preventing teenagers from drinking and smoking—pertain to this area of public health law.

5. *Involuntary Testing.*—These laws provide a basis to determine disease prevalence, such as prevalence of HIV/AIDS in a given community, and to identify those who need treatment or restriction from work. In many jurisdictions, food handlers are tested on a regular basis to determine if they have certain infections that might be spread through food preparation.

6. *Contact Tracing.*—Voluntary in nature, contact tracing has proven to be a very effective and efficient way of controlling diseases, such as tuberculosis and sexually transmitted diseases. It played an important role in the worldwide eradication of smallpox.

7. *Immunization and Mandatory Treatment.*—The book *How Can I Help? [ ]* describes a dramatic episode in India during the smallpox eradication campaign: An international immunization team invaded a household in the middle of the night to forcibly vaccinate a family against their will. This

episode raises many interesting legal, sociocultural, and public health questions. In the United States and many other countries, laws that mandate certain immunizations exempt people who have religious objections to immunizations. We need also recognize that even safe and efficacious immunizations can be fatal to some people who receive them. Approximately one in a million people who receive polio vaccine may actually contract and die from polio.

8. Personal Restrictions.—Public health authorities have the right to restrict a person carrying salmonella bacteria from working as a food handler. In the past, public health workers often quarantined people who had contagious diseases of public health significance, such as tuberculosis, before effective drugs were available. Quarantine is a form of isolation; while we believe that we are well beyond the age of quarantine, some people believe that we will need to quarantine in the future those infected with resistant infectious agents that pose public health threats. While quarantine is seldom used in the United States today, Cuba has quarantined (isolated from the rest of society) people infected with HIV.

Notes

1. Which of these eight areas of Public Health Law have contributed most substantially to the health of the American public? While most public health officials have pointed to the first—environmental health policies—each of the others has made a substantial contribution to public health over the past century. Most public health activities—like restricting an infected person from working as a food handler—will fit in two, three, or more of these categories.

2. What makes an issue a "public health" issue? Is the quality of the gene pool a public health issue? The widespread use of alternative medicines? Tobacco? Gun violence? Domestic violence? What difference does it make whether an issue is characterized as a public health issue? Are we more likely to defer to governmental decisions, and more likely to accept governmental intrusions on individual liberties, where the public health is involved?

3. Another approach to public health law is provided by Lawrence Gostin, who defines public health law as "the legal powers and duties of the state to assure the conditions for people to be healthy (e.g., to identify prevent and ameliorate risks to health in the population) and the limitations on the power of the state to constrain the autonomy, privacy, liberty, proprietary, or other legally protected interests of individuals for the protection or promotion of community health." Professor Gostin goes on to suggest "five essential characteristics of public health law:"

Government: Public health activities are a special responsibility of the government.

Populations: Public health focuses on the health of populations.

Relationships: Public health addresses the relationship between the state and the population (or between the state and individuals who place themselves or the community at risk).

Services: Public health deals with the provision of population-based services grounded on the scientific methodologies of public health (e.g., biostatistics and epidemiology).

Coercion: Public health authorities possess the power to coerce individuals and businesses for the protection of the community, rather than relying on a near universal ethic of voluntarism.

Lawrence Gostin, Public Health Law: Power, Duty Restraint (2000), at 4.

4. In the article excerpted above, Dr. Levy also quotes Article 25 of the Universal Declaration of Human Rights:

Everyone has a right to a standard of living adequate for the health and well-being of [oneself] and [one's] family, including food, clothing, housing and medical care and necessary social services, and the right to security in the event of unemployment, sickness, disability, widowhood, old age or other lack of livelihood in circumstances beyond one's control.

Is this a principle of public health?

5. Lawrence Gostin's public health textbook, supra note 3, provides an exceptional account of the breadth of public health law, and an excellent bibliography as well. See also Lawrence Gostin, Scott Burris and Rita Lazzarini, The Law and the Public's Health: A Study of Infectious Disease Law in the United States, 99 Colum. L. Rev. 59 (1999). For interesting historical and Constitutional approach to these issues, see Wendy Parmet, From Slaughter–House to Lochner: The Rise and Fall of the Cosnstitutionalization of Public Health, 40 Am. J. Leg. Hist. 476 (1996). For a good account of the international public health issues, see Roger Detels et al., eds., Oxford Textbook of Public Health (4th ed. 2004).

Problem

As a legislator in your state, you have become very concerned about obesity in the population, and you are worried about the long range consequences of this condition on the vitality of the public. In particular, you have become concerned about the proliferation of fast food sites that offer economical but very high fat foods. You are also disturbed by the relatively unhealthy foods available at the public schools, most of which have contracts with beverage companies to run their vending machines and snack bars, and by the disappearance of mandatory physical education requirements at the high school level.

Is the problem of obesity a "public health" problem, or simply a problem for some individuals? Is it a matter oF personal responsibility, unrelated to the obligations of the law? Would it make any difference if you classified obesity as a "public health" problem? What legal responses might be available to the state legislature to address this problem?

Do you feel the same way about tobacco or school violence or "extreme sports" as public health problems?

II. THE CONSTITUTIONAL FOUNDATION OF PUBLIC HEALTH LAW

JACOBSON v. MASSACHUSETTS

Supreme Court of the United States, 1905.
197 U.S. 11, 25 S.Ct. 358, 49 L.Ed. 643.

[The Revised Laws of that Commonwealth, c. 75, § 137, provide that "the board of health of a city or town if, in its opinion, it is necessary for the public health or safety shall require and enforce the vaccination and revaccination of all the inhabitants thereof and shall provide them with the means of free vaccination. Whoever, being over twenty-one years of age and not under guardianship, refuses or neglects to comply with such requirement shall forfeit five dollars."

* * *

Proceeding under the above statutes, the Board of Health of the city of Cambridge, Massachusetts, on the twenty-seventh day of February, 1902, adopted the following regulation: "Whereas, smallpox has been prevalent to some extent in the city of Cambridge and still continues to increase; and whereas, it is necessary for the speedy extermination of the disease, that all persons not protected by vaccination should be vaccinated; and whereas, in the opinion of the board, the public health and safety require the vaccination or revaccination of all the inhabitants of Cambridge; be it ordered, that all the inhabitants of the city who have not been successfully vaccinated since March, 1, 1897, be vaccinated or revaccinated."] [Ed. Note: This description is reprinted from the syllabus of the Court.]

MR. JUSTICE HARLAN, after making the foregoing statement, delivered the opinion of the court.

We pass without extended discussion the suggestion that the particular section of the statute of Massachusetts now in question [ ] is in derogation of rights secured by the Preamble of the Constitution of the United States. Although that Preamble indicates the general purposes for which the people ordained and established the Constitution, it has never been regarded as the source of any substantive power conferred on the Government of the United States or on any of its Departments. Such powers embrace only those expressly granted in the body of the Constitution and such as may be implied from those so granted. Although, therefore, one of the declared objects of the Constitution was to secure the blessings of liberty to all under the sovereign jurisdiction and authority of the United States, no power can be exerted to that end by the United States unless, apart from the Preamble, it be found in some express delegation of power or in some power to be properly implied therefrom. [ ]

We also pass without discussion the suggestion that the above section of the statute is opposed to the spirit of the Constitution. * * * We have no need in this case to go beyond the plain, obvious meaning of the words in those provisions of the Constitution which, it is contended, must control our decision.

What, according to the judgment of the state court, is the scope and effect of the statute? What results were intended to be accomplished by it? These questions must be answered.

* * *

The authority of the State to enact this statute is to be referred to what is commonly called the police power—a power which the State did not surrender when becoming a member of the Union under the Constitution. Although this court has refrained from any attempt to define the limits of that power, yet it has distinctly recognized the authority of a State to enact quarantine laws and "health laws of every description;" indeed, all laws that relate to matters completely within its territory and which do not by their necessary operation

affect the people of other States. According to settled principles the police power of a State must be held to embrace, at least, such reasonable regulations established directly by legislative enactment as will protect the public health and the public safety. [ ] It is equally true that the State may invest local bodies called into existence for purposes of local administration with authority in some appropriate way to safeguard the public health and the public safety. The mode or manner in which those results are to be accomplished is within the discretion of the State, subject, of course, so far as Federal power is concerned, only to the condition that no rule prescribed by a State, nor any regulation adopted by a local governmental agency acting under the sanction of state legislation, shall contravene the Constitution of the United States or infringe any right granted or secured by that instrument.
* * *

We come, then, to inquire whether any right given, or secured by the Constitution, is invaded by the statute as interpreted by the state court. The defendant insists that his liberty is invaded when the State subjects him to fine or imprisonment for neglecting or refusing to submit to vaccination; that a compulsory vaccination law is unreasonable, arbitrary and oppressive, and, therefore, hostile to the inherent right of every freeman to care for his own body and health in such way as to him seems best; and that the execution of such a law against one who objects to vaccination, no matter for what reason, is nothing short of an assault upon his person. But the liberty secured by the Constitution of the United States to every person within its jurisdiction does not import an absolute right in each person to be, at all times and in all circumstances, wholly freed from restraint. There are manifold restraints to which every person is necessarily subject for the common good. On any other basis organized society could not exist with safety to its members. Society based on the rule that each one is a law unto himself would soon be confronted with disorder and anarchy. Real liberty for all could not exist under the operation of a principle which recognizes the right of each individual person to use his own, whether in respect of his person or his property, regardless of the injury that may be done to others. * * * The good and welfare of the Commonwealth, of which the legislature is primarily the judge, is the basis on which the police power rests in Massachusetts[ ].

Applying these principles to the present case, it is to be observed that the legislature of Massachusetts required the inhabitants of a city or town to be vaccinated only when, in the opinion of the Board of Health, that was necessary for the public health or the public safety. The authority to determine for all what ought to be done in such an emergency must have been lodged somewhere or in some body; and surely it was appropriate for the legislature to refer that question, in the first instance, to a Board of Health, composed of persons residing in the locality affected and appointed, presumably, because of their fitness to determine such questions. To invest such a body with authority over such matters was not an unusual nor an unreasonable or arbitrary requirement. Upon the principle of self-defense, of paramount necessity, a community has the right to protect itself against an epidemic of disease which threatens the safety of its members. * * * Smallpox being prevalent and increasing at Cambridge, the court would usurp the functions of another branch of government if it adjudged, as matter of law, that the mode adopted under the sanction of the State, to protect the people at large, was arbitrary and not justified by the necessities of the case. We say necessities of the case, because it might be that an acknowledged power of a local community to protect itself against an epidemic threatening the safety of all, might be exercised in particular circumstances and in reference to particular persons in such an arbitrary, unreasonable manner, or might go so far beyond what was reasonably required for the safety of the public, as to authorize or compel the courts to interfere for the protection of such persons. * * * There is, of course, a sphere within which the individual may assert the supremacy of his own will and rightfully dispute the authority of any human government, especially of any free government existing under a written constitution, to interfere with the exercise of that will. But it is equally true that in every well-ordered society charged with the duty of conserving the safety of its members the rights of the individual in respect of his liberty may at times, under the pressure of great dangers, be subjected to such restraint, to be enforced by reasonable regulations, as the safety of the general public may demand.

* * *

Looking at the propositions embodied in the defendant's rejected offers of proof it is clear that they are more formidable by their number than by their inherent value. Those offers in the main seem to have had no purpose except to state the general theory of those of the medical profession who attach little or no value to vaccination as a means of preventing the spread of smallpox or who think that vaccination causes other diseases of the body. What everybody knows the court must know, and therefore the state court judicially knew, as this court knows, that an opposite theory accords with the common belief and is maintained by high medical authority. We must assume that when the statute in question was passed, the legislature of Massachusetts was not unaware of these opposing theories, and was compelled, of necessity, to choose between them. It was not compelled to commit a matter involving the public health and safety to the final decision of a court or jury. It is no part of the function of a court or a jury to determine which one of two modes was likely to be the most effective for the protection of the public against disease. That was for the legislative department to determine in the light of all the information it had or could obtain. * * * Upon what sound principles as to the relations existing between the different departments of government can the court review this action of the legislature? If there is any such power in the judiciary to review legislative action in respect of a matter affecting the general welfare, it can only be when that which the legislature has done comes within the rule that if a statute purporting to have been enacted to protect the public health, the public morals or the public safety, has no real or substantial relation to those objects, or is, beyond all question, a plain, palpable invasion of rights secured by the fundamental law, it is the duty of the courts to so adjudge, and thereby give effect to the Constitution. [ ]

Whatever may be thought of the expediency of this statute, it cannot be affirmed to be, beyond question, in palpable conflict with the Constitution. Nor, in view of the methods employed to stamp out the disease of smallpox, can anyone confidently assert that the means prescribed by the State to that end has no real or substantial relation to the protection of the public health and the public safety. Such an assertion would not be consistent with the experience of this and other countries whose authorities have dealt with the disease of smallpox. [The Court then summarizes the history of vaccination in Europe and America.]

* * *

Since then vaccination, as a means of protecting a community against smallpox, finds strong support in the experience of this and other countries, no court, much less a jury, is justified in disregarding the action of the legislature simply because in its or their opinion that particular method was— perhaps or possibly—not the best either for children or adults.

* * *

We are not prepared to hold that a minority, residing or remaining in any city or town where smallpox is prevalent, and enjoying the general protection afforded by an organized local government, may thus defy the will of its constituted authorities, acting in good faith for all, under the legislative sanction of the State [by refusing to be vaccinated]. If such be the privilege of a minority then a like privilege would belong to each individual of the community, and the spectacle would be presented of the welfare and safety of an entire population being subordinated to the notions of a single individual who chooses to remain a part of that population. * * * The safety and the health of the people of Massachusetts are, in the first instance, for that Commonwealth to guard and protect. They are matters that do not ordinarily concern the National Government. So far as they can be reached by any government, they depend, primarily, upon such action as the State in its wisdom may take; and we do not perceive that this legislation has invaded by right secured by the Federal Constitution.

Before closing this opinion we deem it appropriate, in order to prevent misapprehension as to our views, to observe * * * that the police power of a State * * * may be exerted in such circumstances or by regulations so arbitrary and oppressive in particular cases as to justify the interference of the courts to prevent wrong and oppression. Extreme cases can be readily suggested. Ordinarily such cases are not safe guides in the administration of the law. It is easy, for instance, to suppose the case of an adult who is embraced by the mere words of the act, but yet to subject whom to vaccination in a particular condition of his health or body, would be cruel and inhuman in the last degree. We are not to be understood as holding that the statute was intended to be applied to such a case, or, if it was so intended, that the judiciary would not be competent to interfere and protect the health and life of the individual concerned.

MR. JUSTICE BREWER and MR. JUSTICE PECKHAM dissent [without opinion].

Notes and Questions

1. This oft-cited case established the foundation for public health regulation that came during the ensuing century. While it plainly recognizes the authority of the state to exercise its police powers by imposing public health restrictions on willing and unwilling citizens (and others), it does leave some questions open. It provides that the legislature (or others, with powers properly delegated from the legislature) may make judgments on scientific questions relating to public health.

However, the state may not act "by regulations so arbitrary and oppressive in particular cases as to justify the interference of the courts to prevent wrong and oppression." When will the state cross this line? The Court says that, "Extreme Cases can readily be suggested," but it doesn't actually suggest them. Can you identify these cases?

2. The Jacobson case was not the first vaccination case to be litigated in the federal courts. In Wong Wai v. Williamson, 103 F. 1 (N.D.Cal.1900) the Circuit Court faced an action by Wong Wai, "a subject of the emperor of China, residing in the city and county of San Francisco," seeking to enjoin the city from enforcing a resolution of the board of health that prohibited Chinese residents from traveling outside of the city without proof that they had been inoculated with the "Haffkine Prophylactic," which was thought to provide immunization against bubonic plague. The resolution applied only to those of Chinese extraction, although there was no evidence that they were any more likely than other to be subject to the plague. The Circuit Court recognized the public health authority of the city, but also recognized that there were limits to the exercise of this police power.

> The conditions of a great city frequently present unexpected emergencies affecting the public health, comfort, and convenience. Under such circumstances, officers charged with the duties pertaining to this department of the municipal government should be clothed with sufficient authority to deal with the conditions in a prompt and effective manner. Measures of this character, having a uniform operation, and reasonably adapted to the purpose of protecting the health and preserving the welfare of the inhabitants of a city, are constantly upheld by the courts as valid acts of legislation, however inconvenient they may prove to be, and a wide discretion has also been sanctioned in their execution. But when the municipal authority has neglected to provide suitable rules and regulations upon the subject, and the officers are left to adopt such methods as they may deem proper for the occasion, their acts are open to judicial review, and may be examined in every detail to determine whether individual rights have been respected in accordance with constitutional requirements.

> * * *

> In the light of these well-established principles [that provide that public health measures must have an appropriate relationship with the ends they seek to serve], the action of the defendants as described in the bill of complaint cannot be justified. They are not based upon any established distinction in the conditions that are supposed to attend this plague, or the persons exposed to its contagion, but they are boldly directed against the Asiatic or Mongolian race as a class, without regard to the previous condition, habits, exposure to disease, or residence of the individual; and the only justification offered for this discrimination was a suggestion made by counsel for the defendants in the course of the argument, that this particular race is more liable to the plague than any other. No evidence has, however, been offered to support this claim, and it is not known to be a fact. This explanation must therefore be dismissed as unsatisfactory.

103 F. at 12–15. The Court went on to find that the actions of the board of health violated not only "the express provisions of the constitution of the United States, in several particulars, but also of the express provisions of our several treaties with China and of the statutes of the United States." 13 F. at 23.

3. The Court suggests that it may be improper to apply the Massachusetts statute and the Cambridge order to an adult whose health would be placed at risk by vaccination, even though the only exception in the statute is for children whose health would be at risk. Could an adult with some legitimate health concerns about vaccination forgo it? Would this be a matter to be determined by the Board of Health, or by the courts?

4. In a long historical footnote, the Court traces the history of vaccination from the "first compulsory act" in England in 1853. In fact, as early as 1827 the city of Boston required vaccination for school attendance, and in 1855 the Massachusetts became the first state with required childhood vaccination laws associated with school attendance. The laws were fairly common by the end of the nineteenth century, but, for political and other reasons, they were not regularly enforced. Some were limited to application when there was a public health threat in the community, and some courts recognized religious defenses to the obligation to be vaccinated. See Rhea v. Board of Education, 41 N.D. 449, 171 N.W. 103 (1919). Today all states provide for exemptions when the vaccination would threaten the health of the child, all but two allow for religious exemption (although the nature of those exemptions varies from state to state), and just under half the states allow for an exemption on "moral" or other grounds. Are states Constitutionally required to have religious exemptions? If a state has a religious exemption, should that legislation also permit a "moral" exemption?

The immunizations children must have to be enrolled in school is a matter of state law, but, as a general matter, states adopt the Centers for Disease Control (CDC) list. In order to keep some kinds of federal funding, the states now must make an effort to enforce their own immunization laws. This issue is not entirely a scientific one, though, and vaccine manufacturers do lobby state legislatures to have their own products included on the mandatory list.

5. While the health value of continued required immunization is now well established, those who fear government conspiracies have often had special concerns about vaccinations. It is unclear just why this has become a political issue as well as a public health issue, but it is not hard to find those who oppose vaccination with missionary zeal. The CDC, the World Health Organization, and other organizations have joined together to refute several myths about vaccination that sometimes scare parents into seeking exemptions. For a full list of the most common arguments against vaccination and the refutation of each, see the CDC's pamphlet designed for primary care providers, 6 Common Misconceptions about Vaccinations and How to Respond to Them, http://www.cdc.gov/nip/publications/6mishome.htm. For an excellent account of this issue, and the basis for much of these notes, see James Hodge Jr., School Vaccination Requirements: Legal and Social Perspectives, 27 NCSL State Legislative Report, No. 14 (August 2002). For a an excellent overview of the issue and a clever proposal to finesse the opposition to immunization while respecting individuals' liberties, see Ross Silverman, No More Kidding Around: Restructuring Childhood Immunization Exceptions in Insure Public Health Protection, 12 Ann. Health L. 277 (2003).

6. Of course, there are side effects to vaccination, and some are very serious. While we are all safer if everyone is vaccinated, the safest possible course of action is to assure that everyone else's child is vaccinated, and yet not have your own child vaccinated. If everyone else is immunized, there is no chance you will be subject to the disease, whether or not you are immunized. Is it an altruistic decision to decide against seeking an exemption from a required immunization law? Is there any way to avoid this version of the prisoner's dilemma without eliminating all exemptions?

7.   Compensation for injuries that arise out of immunization is specifically addressed in the National Vaccine Injury Compensation Program, 42 U.S.C. sections 300aa–10 through 34. This statute may be unique in providing that attorneys must inform potential plaintiffs in vaccine injury cases of the existence of the law and the remedy it provides:

> It shall be the ethical obligation of any attorney who is consulted by an individual with respect to a vaccine-related injury or death to advise such individual that compensation may be available under the program for such injury or death.

42 U.S.C. section 300aa–10(b). For an excellent history of the liability litigation-induced vaccine shortages that gave rise to this no-fault compensation scheme and its predecessors, see Elizabeth Scott, The National Childhood Vaccine Injury Act Turns Fifteen, 56 Food & Drug L.J. 351 (2001).

8.   How does the Jacobson case affect other kinds of public health regulation? Does it place limits on the efforts of states to limit pollution? Maintain vital statistics? Do involuntary disease testing? Engage in contact tracing? Impose mandatory treatment, quarantine, or isolation? Do genetic screening?

Problem

You are the legal counsel to the school district in Midvale, Alabama. The Code of Alabama § 16–30–1 requires certain immunizations as a condition of school attendance. Exemptions to this provision are found in the following section:

§ 16–30–3. Exemptions

The provisions of this chapter shall not apply if:

(1) In the absence of an epidemic or immediate threat thereof, the parent or guardian of the child shall object thereto in writing on grounds that such immunization or testing conflicts with his religious tenets and practices; or

(2) Certification by a competent medical authority providing individual exemption from the required immunization or testing is presented the admissions officer of the school.

First grader Miranda Black's parents, who resent the heavy burden of government, have decided that they will not submit to any immunization requirement. They reason that Miranda should not have to shoulder the public health value of immunization by risking the side effects of the immunization. Her doctor will not provide the "certification" that the school authorities want because there is no medical reason for her to avoid immunization, and thus her parents have submitted to the school authorities a statement that "compulsory immunization violates our Christian view that the government cannot make us do anything." School health officials are concerned because there were four cases of whooping cough in Midvale during the last year—up from two the year before, and one the year before that. They attribute the increase to the increasing number of people who have obtained exemptions. The school officials have asked you how they should react to the request that Miranda be exempt.

III. FORCED TREATMENT, ISOLATION AND QUARANTINE

One public health technique that has been employed since contagion was understood (and, perhaps paradoxically, before) is separating those who may be contagious from those who are to be protected. Those who are ill are generally said to be "isolated" from others, while those who have been exposed, but have not yet become ill (and who may never become ill) are said to be put in "quarantine" for the incubation period of the relevant disease. These techniques—which require a direct and severe limitation on the liberty of people who have violated no law—have been used to protect the community from a wide range of diseases, from plague to smallpox. Until the beginning of the twentieth century most quarantine was implemented through orders given by public health officials under statutes that gave them authority to act whenever they decided that the public health required it. Very little process, if any, was given to those very few patients who were quarantined or isolated, and the quarantine or isolation—which could be in the patient's house, in a hospital or in another institution of some sort—lasted until the one locked up was no longer a public health threat. In many states, the only way one quarantined or isolated could seek judicial relief was through a petition for a writ of habeas corpus.

While statutes authorizing quarantine and isolation were rarely invoked since the due process revolution of forty years ago, in states where the issue arose courts grafted Constitutional due process requirements on to the broad statutory grants of authority given public health agencies. In the 1980s a few states modernized and updated their quarantine statutes out of a concern that they would eventually be invoked to address the issue of HIV and AIDS, although, fortunately, they were never used for that purpose in the United States. Very recently the increase in drug resistant strains of tuberculosis have given rise to a new round of state revisions of quarantine and isolation statutes. One example of a new statute, enacted in 2000, follows.

Tuberculosis Control Units
Ohio Code §§ 339.80–89 (2003)

* * *

§ 339.80. Investigation of reported cases

When a county or district tuberculosis control unit receives a report * * * of a confirmed or suspected case of tuberculosis, the unit shall conduct an investigation that includes personal contact with the individual with tuberculosis. The investigation shall commence not later than three working days after the unit receives the report.

§ 339.81. Confidentiality of information, data, reports

Any information, data, and reports with respect to a case of tuberculosis that are furnished to, or procured by, a county or district tuberculosis control unit or the department of health shall be confidential and used only for statistical, scientific, and medical research for the purpose of controlling tuberculosis in this state. No physician, hospital, or other entity furnishing information, data, or reports pursuant to this chapter shall by reason of such furnishing be deemed to have violated any confidential relationship, be held to answer for willful betrayal of a professional confidence, or be held liable in damages to any person.

§ 339.82. Responsibilities of individual with active or communicable tuberculosis

Except as provided [in the section on spiritual treatment, below], all of the following apply to individuals with tuberculosis:

(A) (1) An individual who has been diagnosed as having active tuberculosis shall complete the entire tuberculosis treatment regimen prescribed for the individual by a physician. The regimen prescribed shall include a course of antituberculosis medication, recommendations for management of tuberculosis, and instructions for following contagion precautions to prevent the spread of tuberculosis.

(2) If an individual fails to take prescribed antituberculosis medication in accordance with division (A)(1) of this section, the county or district tuberculosis control unit shall establish a procedure under which the individual is required to be witnessed ingesting the antituberculosis medication by individuals designated by the unit. The individual shall take the medication in accordance with the procedure.

(B) An individual with communicable tuberculosis who is not hospitalized or otherwise confined shall not attend any public gathering or be in any public place that the county or district tuberculosis control unit determines cannot be maintained in a manner adequate to protect others from the spread of the disease. An individual with communicable tuberculosis who cannot be maintained outside of a hospital in a manner adequate to protect others from the spread of the disease shall submit to hospitalization and remain hospitalized.

(C) An individual with active tuberculosis who intends to travel or relocate shall notify the county or district tuberculosis control unit. The unit shall notify the Ohio department of health when an individual with active tuberculosis relocates. The department shall notify the tuberculosis control unit of the tuberculosis control district to which the individual intends to travel or relocate or the appropriate public health authority of the state to which the individual intends to travel or relocate.

§ 339.83. Notice to individual not in compliance

When a county or district tuberculosis control unit becomes aware that an individual with active or communicable tuberculosis is not in compliance with [this section], the unit shall inform the individual that [the law] requires compliance and that the unit may issue an * * * compelling the individual to comply.

§ 339.84. Order compelling compliance

If an individual fails to comply with [this Act], the county or district tuberculosis control unit may issue an order compelling the individual to comply.

§ 339.85. Injunction against violation of order

If an individual fails to comply with an order * * *, the county or district tuberculosis control unit may apply to the probate court of the appropriate county for an injunction prohibiting the individual from continuing to violate the unit's order. If the tuberculosis control unit believes that an individual's failure to comply with its order involves an immediate danger to the public health, the unit may request that the court issue an injunction without granting the individual an opportunity for a prior hearing or that the court hold an expedited hearing on the matter.

§ 339.86.   Court order for detention of noncomplying individual

(A) If an individual fails to comply with an injunction issued * * *, the county or district tuberculosis control unit may request that the probate court of the appropriate county issue an order under which the unit is granted the authority to detain the individual in a hospital or other place to be examined or treated for tuberculosis. In the request, the unit shall provide the following information:

(1) The name of the individual;

(2) The purpose of making the request for detention;

(3) An individualized assessment that contains a description of the circumstances and behavior of the individual that constitutes the basis for making the request;

(4) A recommendation for the length of time that the individual should be detained;

(5) A recommendation of a hospital or other place to be used for the detention.

(B) The court may issue an order for detention for an initial period of not more than one hundred eighty days. At the end of the initial period of detention, the court shall review the case and may extend the order for subsequent periods of not more than ninety days. At the end of each subsequent period of detention, the court shall review the case. When the court receives satisfactory evidence that the individual subject to the order no longer has active tuberculosis, the court shall terminate the order for detention.

(C) An individual who has been detained under this section may provide the tuberculosis control unit with the names, addresses, and telephone numbers of relatives and friends to be notified of the detention, and the unit shall notify all or a reasonable number of those individuals. An individual who has been detained shall not be subject to forcible administration of antituberculosis medication. The individual may, at any time, submit a request to the tuberculosis control unit to be released from detention.

During any proceeding pertaining to an individual's detention or proposed detention, the individual has the right to be represented by counsel. If the individual is indigent, the individual may apply for court-appointed counsel. The court may appoint counsel for the individual if it determines that the individual is indigent.

§ 339.87.   Emergency detention order

(A) When a tuberculosis control unit has reasonable grounds to believe that an individual who has, or is suspected of having, active tuberculosis poses a substantial danger to the health of other individuals, the tuberculosis control unit may issue an emergency detention order directing a sheriff or other law enforcement officer to remove the individual to a hospital or other place to be examined and treated for tuberculosis.

(B) Not later than the end of the third business day after detention of an individual under division (A) of this section, the tuberculosis control unit shall apply to the probate court of the county from which the individual was removed for a detention order * * *.

§ 339.88. Expenses of detention

The expenses incurred for detention * * * shall be paid by the individual detained or if the individual is indigent, by the board of county commissioners of the county from which the individual was removed. * * *

§ 339.89. Spiritual treatment in lieu of medical treatment

[The preceding sections] do not require a person to undergo testing, medical treatment, or detention in a hospital or other place for treatment if the person, or, in the case of a child, the child's parents, rely exclusively on spiritual treatment through prayer, in lieu of medical treatment, in accordance with a recognized, religious method of healing. The person may be quarantined or otherwise safely isolated in the home or another place that is suitable to the health of the person and has been approved by the tuberculosis control unit as a place that provides appropriate protection to other persons and the community.

Notes and Questions

1. Does the Ohio law properly balance the public health interest of the community and the personal civil liberties of those who might have tuberculosis? Is the statute legally sound? Is it medically sound—i.e., is it likely to actually lead to the delivery of appropriate medical care to those who have tuberculosis but refuse treatment? Might the prospect of the application of the statute drive some potential patients underground? What would be the public health consequences if that were to happen?

2. What procedures are Constitutionally required before a person with a communicable disease can be forced to accept treatment, or be isolated or quarantined? Would the processes be different for those who are merely required to undergo treatment, those who are isolated in their own homes, those who are quarantined in a hospital, and those who are locked up in a jail for the criminal offense of failing to comply with a public health order? For each attribute of the quarantine and isolation process listed below, apply the *Mathews v. Eldridge*, 424 U.S. 319, 96 S.Ct. 893, 47 L.Ed.2d 18 (1976) balancing test and evaluate (1) the importance of the individual's interest (here, in being free of unwanted treatment, isolation or quarantine), (2) the risk that there will be an erroneous determination unless the additional procedure is afforded, and (3) the public interest in forgoing that procedure (including the interest in quick and efficient resolution of the matter).

3. What kind of notice should be required before an order of isolation or quarantine is issued? Given the liberty interest that is at stake, is it ever appropriate to issue an order of isolation or quarantine without giving the respondent an opportunity to appear? Given the public health interest that is at stake, is it necessary to notify the respondent before an order is issued? Is it always necessary to have a pre-isolation or pre-quarantine hearing, or is a hearing shortly after the order is implemented sufficient?

If a hearing is required before a person is isolated or quarantined, what rights must be afforded the respondent at such a hearing? Must it be before a judge, or may a public health officer issue the order? Is the respondent entitled to counsel? Is the state obliged to provide counsel if the respondent cannot afford to hire one? Is the respondent entitled to present evidence? Must she be able to subpoena witnesses? If she needs expert medical testimony (that she poses no public health danger, for example) but she is indigent, must the state pay for her expert witness? May the respondent be required to testify against herself?

Who bears what burden of proof at the hearing? If the state initially bears the burden of proof, must it prove each element necessary to obtain an order by a preponderance of the evidence (this is a civil case, after all), by clear and convincing evidence (this might be analogous to a civil commitment proceeding, where this standard is required under *Addington v. Texas*, 441 U.S. 418, 99 S.Ct. 1804, 60 L.Ed.2d 323 (1979)), or beyond a reasonable doubt (this does result in a loss of liberty, much like a criminal case)? After the state meets its initial burden, may the burden be shifted to the respondent to show that he is no longer subject to isolation or quarantine before he can be released?

Must there be an opportunity for appeal? Must a patient who, after being in quarantine, suddenly is willing to comply with a treatment regimen, be able to seek review of his isolation or quarantine? Must the state regularly prove that continuing quarantine and isolation is appropriate? Should isolation and quarantine orders automatically expire after a certain amount of time? How long? How often should there be review of those who have been isolated or quarantined?

Must the medical and legal proceedings be kept confidential? As a matter of common law? Under the HIPAA privacy regulations? Does this mean that the hearing must be closed to the public and the record sealed? Can the information still be used for purposes of contact tracing—i.e. to find others who may have contacted the disease from the respondent? For particular other purposes? What are they?

Different states give a very wide range of different answers to almost all of these questions. Because quarantine and isolation are so infrequently imposed, there has been little litigation to determine the process that are Constitutionally required. Of course, the United States Constitution is not the only source of process in these cases. Process will also be determined by state constitutions, which may impose greater procedural requirements than the United States Constitution, state statutes, and state rules (including rules of procedure and rules of evidence). For a good account of the underlying social issue, see Sheila Rothman, Living in the Shadow of Death: Tuberculosis and the Social Experience of Illness in American History (1994). For a useful legal analysis, see Rosemary Reilly, Combating the Tuberculosis Epidemic: The Legality of Coercive Treatment Measures, 27 Colum. J. L. & Soc. Prob. 101 (1993), and Lawrence Gostin, The Resurgent Tuberculosis Epidemic in the Era of AIDS, 54 Md. L. Rev. 1 (1995).

Problem

You are a public health official who has been appointed as chief of a tuberculosis control unit in one county in Ohio. You have learned that Cristina Gonzalez, a ten year old child who lives with her parents, is now being treated for an active and highly communicable form of tuberculosis. Because there is no other apparent source of the disease, the child's pediatrician has reported that she believes that the child may have contracted the disease from her uncle, Jesus Chavez, who recently moved in with Cristina's family after leaving a part of Honduras with a particularly high rate of tuberculosis infection. Cristina told the pediatrician that her uncle had a very heavy cough and that he sometimes had some trouble breathing when he walked up the stairs.

Cristina's parents have told you that Mr. Chavez does not have proper immigration documents, and that he is very frightened about meeting with any authorities. He once sought treatment at the local public hospital, where he was denied care and treated very rudely; he would never go back, under any circumstances. The Gonzalezes have also told you that any attempt to find Mr. Chavez in the Gonzalez home would force him to move to another relative's house, and that he would not agree to any treatment that is imposed by the authorities. The Gonzalezes have suggested to the public health authorities that they should not worry about the case, because Mr. Chavez was planning to move back to Honduras in the next few months anyway.

What can you do under the Ohio statute? What should you do?

IV. BIOTERRORISM AND PUBLIC HEALTH

THE MODEL STATE EMERGENCY HEALTH POWERS ACT
As of December 21, 2001.

(A Draft for Discussion Prepared by The Center for Law and the Public's Health at Georgetown and Johns Hopkins Universities For the Centers for Disease Control and Prevention).

* * *

Section 104 **Definitions.**

(a) "Bioterrorism" is the intentional use of any microorganism, virus, infectious substance, or biological product that may be engineered as a result of biotechnology, or any naturally occurring or bioengineered component of any such microorganism, virus, infectious substance, or biological product, to cause death, disease, or other biological malfunction in a human, an animal, a plant, or another living organism in order to influence the conduct of government or to intimidate or coerce a civilian population.

* * *

(h) "Isolation" is the physical separation and confinement of an individual or groups of individuals who are infected or reasonably believed to be infected with a contagious or possibly contagious disease from non-isolated individuals, to prevent or limit the transmission of the disease to non-isolated individuals.

* * *

(m) A "public health emergency" is an occurrence or imminent threat of an illness or health condition that:

    (1) is believed to be caused by any of the following:

        (i) bioterrorism;

        (ii) the appearance of a novel or previously controlled or eradicated infectious agent or biological toxin;

        (iii) [a natural disaster;]

        (iv) [a chemical attack or accidental release; or]

        (v) [a nuclear attack or accident]; and

    (2) poses a high probability of any of the following harms:

        (i) a large number of deaths in the affected population;

(ii) a large number of serious or long-term disabilities in the affected population; or

(iii) widespread exposure to an infectious or toxic gent that poses a significant risk of substantial future harm to a large number of people in the affected population.

* * *

(*o*) "Quarantine" is the physical separation and confinement of an individual or groups of individuals, who are or may have been exposed to a contagious or possibly contagious disease and who do not show signs or symptoms of a contagious disease, from non-quarantined individuals, to prevent or limit the transmission of the disease to non-quarantined individuals.

* * *

ARTICLE IV. DECLARING A STATE OF PUBLIC HEALTH EMERGENCY

Section 401 **Declaration**. A state of public health emergency maybe declared by the Governor upon the occurrence of a "public health emergency" as defined in Section 1–104(m). Prior to such a declaration, the Governor shall consult with the public health authority and may consult with any additional public health or other experts as needed. The Governor may act to declare a public health emergency without consulting with the public health authority or other experts when the situation calls for prompt and timely action.

* * *

Section 403 **Effects of declaration**. The declaration of a state public health emergency shall activate the disaster response and recovery aspects of the State, local and inter-jurisdictional disaster emergency plans in the affected political subdivision(s) or geographical area(s). Such declaration authorizes the deployment and use of any forces to which the plans apply and the use or distribution of any supplies, equipment, and materials and facilities assembled, stockpiled, or available pursuant to this Act.

(a) **Emergency powers**. During a state of public health emergency, the Governor may:

(1) Suspend the provisions of any regulatory statute prescribing procedures for conducting State business, or the orders, rules and regulations of any State agency, to the extent that strict compliance with the same would prevent, hinder, or delay necessary action (including emergency purchases) by the public health authority to respond to the public health emergency, or increase the health threat to the population.

(2) Utilize all available resources of the State government and its political subdivisions, as reasonably necessary to respond to the public health emergency.

(3) Transfer the direction, personnel, or functions of State departments and agencies in order to perform or facilitate response and recovery programs regarding the public health emergency.

(4) Mobilize all or any part of the organized militia into service of the State. An order directing the organized militia to report for active duty shall state the purpose for which it is mobilized and the objectives to be accomplished.

(5) Provide aid to and seek aid from other states in accordance with any interstate emergency compact made with this State.

(6) Seek aid from the federal government in accordance with federal programs or requirements.

* * *

Section 404 **Enforcement**. During a state of public health emergency, the public health authority may request assistance in enforcing orders pursuant to this Act from the public safety authority. The public safety authority may request assistance from the organized militia in enforcing the orders of the public health authority.

Section 405 **Termination of declaration**. [may be by executive order of the Governor, by majority vote of both houses of the state legislature, or, automatically, after 30 days, unless it is renewed by the Governor].

* * *

ARTICLE V. SPECIAL POWERS DURING A STATE OF PUBLIC HEALTH EMERGENCY: MANAGEMENT OF PROPERTY

* * *

Section 502 **Access to and control of facilities and property—generally**. The public health authority may exercise, for such period as the state of public health emergency exists, the following powers concerning facilities, materials, roads, or public areas—

(a) **Use of materials and facilities**. To procure, by condemnation or otherwise, construct, lease, transport, store, maintain, renovate, or distribute materials and facilities as may be reasonable and necessary to respond to the public health emergency, with the right to take immediate possession thereof. Such materials and facilities include, but are not limited to, communication devices, carriers, real estate, fuels, food, and clothing.

(b) **Use of health care facilities**. To require a health care facility to provide services or the use of its facility if such services or use are reasonable and necessary to respond to the public health emergency as a condition of licensure, authorization or the ability to continue doing business in the state as a health care facility. The use of the health care facility may include transferring the management and supervision of the health care facility to the public health authority for a limited or unlimited period of time, but shall not exceed the termination of the declaration of a state of public health emergency.

* * *

Section 505 **Control of health care supplies**. [This section provides that the public health authority may procure, distribute and ration health care supplies.]

Section 506 **Compensation**. The State shall pay just compensation to the owner of any facilities or materials that are lawfully take nor appropriated by a public health authority for its temporary or permanent use under this Article according to the procedures and standards set forth in Section 805 of this Act. Compensation shall not be provided for facilities or materials that are closed, evacuated, decontaminated, or destroyed when there is reasonable cause to believe that they may endanger the public health pursuant to Section 501.

* * *

ARTICLE VI. SPECIAL POWERS DURING A STATE OF PUBLIC HEALTH EMERGENCY: PROTECTION OF PERSONS

Section 601 **Protection of persons**. During a state of public health emergency,the public health authority shall use every available means to prevent the transmission of infectious disease and to ensure that all cases of contagious disease are subject to proper control and treatment.

* * *

Section 603 **Vaccination and treatment**. During a state of public health emergency the public health authority may exercise the following emergency powers over persons as necessary to address the public health emergency—

(a) **Vaccination**. To vaccinate persons as protection against infectious disease and to prevent the spread of contagious or possibly contagious disease.

    1. Vaccination may be performed by any qualified person authorized to do so by the public health authority.

    2. A vaccine to be administered must not be such as is reasonably likely to lead to serious harm to the affected individual.

    3. To prevent the spread of contagious or possibly contagious disease the public health authority may isolate or quarantine, pursuant to section 604, persons who are unable or unwilling for reasons of health, religion, or conscience to undergo vaccination pursuant to this Section.

(b) **Treatment**. To treat persons exposed to or infected with disease.

    1. Treatment may be administered by any qualified person authorized to do so by the public health authority.

    2. Treatment must not be such as is reasonably likely to lead to serious harm to the affected individual.

    3. To prevent the spread of contagious or possibly contagious disease the public health authority may isolate or quarantine, pursuant to section 604, persons who are unable or unwilling for

reasons of health, religion, or conscience to undergo treatment pursuant to this Section.

* * *

Section 604 **Isolation and quarantine**.

(a) **Authorization**. During the public health emergency, the public health authority may isolate * * * or quarantine * * * an individual or groups of individuals. This includes individuals or groups who have not been vaccinated, treated, tested, or examined * * *. The public health authority may also establish and maintain places of isolation and quarantine, and set rules and make orders. Failure to obey these rules, orders, or provisions shall constitute a misdemeanor.

(b) **Conditions and principles**. The public health authority shall adhere to the following conditions and principles when isolating or quarantining individuals or groups of individuals:

(1) Isolation and quarantine must be by the least restrictive means necessary to prevent the spread of a contagious or possibly contagious disease to others and may include, but are not limited to, confinement to private homes or other private and public premises.

(2) Isolated individuals must be confined separately from quarantined individuals.

(3) The health status of isolated and quarantined individuals must be monitored regularly to determine if they require isolation or quarantine.

(4) If a quarantined individual subsequently becomes infected or is reasonable believed to have become infected with a contagious or possible contagious disease he or she must promptly be removed to isolation.

(5) Isolated and quarantined individuals must be immediately released when they pose no substantial risk of transmitting a contagious or possibly contagious disease to others.

(6) The needs of persons isolated and quarantined shall be addressed in a systematic and competent fashion, including, but not limited to, providing adequate food, clothing, shelter, means of communication with those in isolation or quarantine and outside these settings, medication, and competent medical care.

(7) Premises used for isolation and quarantine shall be maintained in a safe and hygienic manner and be designed to minimize the likelihood of further transmission of infection or other harms to persons isolated and quarantined.

(8) To the extent possible, cultural and religious beliefs should be considered in addressing the needs of individuals, and establishing and maintaining isolation and quarantine premises.

(c) **Cooperation**. Persons subject to isolation or quarantine shall obey the public health authority's rules and orders; and shall not go beyond the isolation or quarantine premises. Failure to obey these provisions shall constitute a misdemeanor.

* * *

Section 605 **Procedures for isolation and quarantine**. During a public health emergency, the isolation and quarantine of an individual or groups of individuals shall be undertaken in accordance with the following procedures. [this section then provides for temporary isolation and quarantine without notice, for a petition to continue isolation or quarantine, a formal hearing and the issuance of an order, appeal rights, actions for relief from isolation or quarantine, the right to bring actions for breaches of the condition requirements for isolation or quarantine, the right to counsel and the consolidation of cases where is is efficient to do so.]

* * *

Section 804 **Liability**.

(a) **State immunity**. Neither the State, its political subdivisions, nor, except in cases of gross negligence or willful misconduct, the Governor, the public health authority, or any other State or local official referenced in this Act, is liable for the death of or any injury to persons, or damage to property, as a result of complying with or attempting to comply with this Act or any rule or regulations promulgated pursuant to this Act during a state of public health emergency.

(b) **Private liability**. [Private parties acting within the terms of this Act] shall not be civilly liable for causing the death of, or injury to, any person or damage to any property except in the event of gross negligence or willful misconduct.

Section 805 **Compensation**.

(a) **Taking**. Compensation for property shall be made only if private property is lawfully taken or appropriated by a public health authority for its temporary or permanent use during a state of public health emergency declared by the Governor pursuant to this Act.

* * *

LAWRENCE O. GOSTIN, THE MODEL STATE EMERGENCY HEALTH POWERS ACT: PUBLIC HEALTH AND CIVIL LIBERTIES IN A TIME OF TERRORISM

13 Health Matrix 3 (2003).

Safeguarding the public's health, safety, and security took on new meaning and urgency after the attacks on the World Trade Towers in New York and the Pentagon in Washington, D.C. on September 11, 2001. On October 4, 2001, a Florida man named Robert Stevens was diagnosed with inhalational anthrax. The intentional dispersal of anthrax through the U.S. postal system in New York, Washington, Pennsylvania and other locations resulted in five confirmed deaths, hundreds treated, and thousands tested. The potential for new, larger, and more sophisticated attacks have created a sense of vulnerability. National attention has urgently turned to the need to rapidly detect and react to bioterrorism, as well as to naturally occurring infectious diseases.

In the aftermath of September 11th, the President and the Congress began a process to strengthen the public health infrastructure. The Center for Law and the Public's Health (CLPH) at Georgetown and Johns Hopkins Universities drafted the Model State Emergency Health Powers Act (MSEH-PA or the "Model Act") at the request of Centers for Disease Control and Prevention (CDC) and in collaboration with members of national organizations representing governors, legislators, attorneys general, and health commissioners. Because the power to act to preserve the public's health is constitutionally reserved primarily to the states as an exercise of their police powers, the Model Act is designed for state—not federal—legislative consideration. It provides responsible state actors with the powers they need to detect and contain a potentially catastrophic disease outbreak and, at the same time, protects individual rights and freedoms. Thirty-six states and the District of Columbia have introduced legislative bills based on the MSEHPA; thirty-nine states and the District of Columbia have enacted or are expected to shortly enact a version of the Model Act. Despite its success in many states, the Model Act has become a lightening rod for criticism from both ends of the political spectrum. It has galvanized public debate around the appropriate balance between personal rights and common goods.

* * *

RE–THINKING THE PUBLIC GOOD

American values at the turn of the 21st century fairly could be characterized as individualistic. There was a distinct orientation toward personal and proprietary freedoms and against a substantial government presence in social and economic life. The attacks on the World Trade Center and Pentagon and the anthrax outbreaks reawakened the political community to the importance of public health. Historians will look back and ask whether September 11th, 2001 was a fleeting scare with temporary solutions or whether it was a transforming event.

There are good reasons for believing that resource allocations, ethical values, and law should transform to reflect the critical importance of the health, security and well being of the populace. It is not that individual freedoms are unimportant. To the contrary, personal liberty allows people the right of self-determination, to make judgments about how to live their lives and pursue their dreams. Without a certain level of health, safety, and security, however, people cannot have well-being; nor can they meaningfully exercise their autonomy or participate in social and political life.

My purpose is not to assert which are the more fundamental interests: personal liberty or health and security. Rather, my purpose is to illustrate that both sets of interests are important to human flourishing. The Model State Emergency Health Powers Act was designed to defend personal as well as collective interests. But in a country so tied to rights rhetoric on both sides of the political spectrum, any proposal that has the appearance of strengthening governmental authority was bound to travel in tumultuous political waters.

* * *

GEORGE J. ANNAS, BLINDED BY BIOTERRORISM: PUBLIC HEALTH AND LIBERTY IN THE 21ST CENTURY

13 Health Matrix 33 (2003).

* * *

In Blindness, Nobel Prize laureate Jose Saramago chronicles the quarantining of the first victims of a plague of blindness. We meet many people who become blind in Saramago's novel, including an opthamologist, a one-eyed man with an eye patch, and a man born blind. Saramago reminds us that we are all blind in one way or another, and that there are many things about ourselves and our society that we can't or won't see. The quarantine itself turns out to be isolating, inhumane, and degrading; the interned blind being portrayed by themselves and others as pigs, dogs, and "lame crabs." Soldiers stand guard, and shoot anyone trying to escape, mostly out of fear that they themselves might become infected by the blindness virus.

Of course many Americans were temporarily blinded on September 11 by the smoke and debris in the terror attacks on the World Trade Center and the Pentagon. And even after the smoke cleared, fear and anger fueled a desire for revenge and a quest for security. The security quest seemed even more urgent following the anthrax attacks through the mail. Fear generated responses that in retrospect appear overzealous, potentially counterproductive, and unnecessarily destructive of human rights. This is easier to see after almost two years have elapsed since 9/11, especially in the area of bioterrorism.

* * *

THE "MODEL" STATE EMERGENCY HEALTH POWERS ACT

In the immediate aftermath of 9/11 and the subsequent anthrax attacks, hospitals, cities, states, and federal officials began developing or revisiting plans for future biological attacks. The federal response almost immediately emphasized stockpiling drugs and vaccines that could be used to respond to a future attack, especially one involving smallpox. Other initiatives have proposed enhancing the public health infrastructure of the country (especially its ability to monitor emergency department diagnoses and pharmacy sales of relevant drugs), and the training of first responders to recognize and treat the diseases most likely to be caused by a bioterrorist attack (such as anthrax, smallpox, and plague). Major efforts are also underway to improve coordination and communication among local, state, and federal officials responsible for emergencies, and to more clearly delineate lines of authority involving "homeland security." All of these are reasonable and responsible steps our government should take.

On the other hand, planning for mass quarantine and forced vaccination—likely with investigational vaccines—are unreasonable steps that are more likely to foster public panic and distrust than to be effective in a real emergency. Mass quarantine was a staple of public health from the 14th century to the early 20th century, and its implementation has been historically justified by labeling those groups quarantined as not only dangerous but almost diabolical. As historian-physician Howard Markel has put it:

History teaches us that society has no shortage of means available to dehumanize and minimize so-called undesirable groups of people. The grave risks of this minimization process are magnified when combined with the threat of contagious disease. It is at this moment that rhetorical scapegoating may be transformed into a mentality of quarantine. Not only does the infectious disease become the 'enemy' but, so, do the human beings (and their contacts) who have encountered the microbe in question. A common symptom of the quarantine mentality is to do everything possible to prevent the spread of an epidemic, often at the neglect of the human or medical needs of those labeled contagious. [Howard Markel, QUARANTINE!: East European Jewish Immigrants and the New York City Epidemics of 1892, 185–86 (1997)].

* * *

Constitutional rights need not be compromised for effective public health intervention. But even if policy makers were unconcerned with restricting civil liberties, such a strategy as that outlined in the model act would be counterproductive. This is because the proposal is likely to undermine public trust in public health, trust that is absolutely essential to containing panic in a bioterrorist-induced epidemic. Unlike 1900, for example, we now have 24 hour a day news television, the internet, cell phones, and automobiles. These make effective large-scale quarantine impossible unless the public is convinced that it is absolutely necessary to prevent the spread of fatal disease and is fairly and safely administered. Making it a crime to disobey a public health officer, for example, will only increase public distrust in that it proclaims that public officials cannot provide valid reasons for their actions. Former Senator Sam Nunn, who played the president in the Dark Winter [bioterrorism practice] exercise, accurately observed after it was over: "There is no force on earth strong enough to get 250 million Americans to do something they do not believe is in their own best interests or that of their families."

The necessity for maintaining public trust and confidence also means that the argument that in a public health emergency there must be a tradeoff between effective public health and protecting civil rights is simply wrong. As the AIDS epidemic has demonstrated, the promotion of human rights can be essential to deal effectively with an epidemic. Public health officials recognized early that draconian mandatory HIV screening measures, for example, would simply help drive the epidemic underground where it would spread faster and wider. Likewise, draconian quarantine measures seem most likely to create public panic that will encourage people to avoid public health officials and physicians rather than seek them out. In this regard, protection of civil liberties is a core ingredient to successfully responding to a bioterrorist attack. Treating our fellow citizens as the enemy, and using police tactics or martial law to force treatment and isolate them, is much more likely to cost lives than to save them. This is one reason why there has not been a large-scale quarantine in the U.S. since World War I, and why bioterrorism experts doubt that a mass quarantine could be effective.

* * *

The planned use of arbitrary force by Americans against Americans is un-American, even if done in the name of public health. No American physician should be forced to do anything to a patient that the physician does not believe is in the patient's best interests, and even then only with the patient's consent. No American soldier should be forced to take experimental drugs and vaccines; and no American citizen should be forced to take any drug or vaccine, or to be quarantined against their will, when any other less restrictive alternative is available. America is strong because its people are free, and to be both moral and effective public planning for war and public health emergencies must be based on respecting freedom and trusting our fellow citizens. Rather than adopt the tactics of repressive totalitarian regimes, the United States should lead the world in proclaiming a new, global public health, based on transparency, trust, and science, and most importantly, based on respect for human rights.

Notes

1. The MSEHPA also includes provisions that require public health emergency planning by the state governments, the collection of data on pathogens and those who bear them, public health tracking, information sharing, the disposal of potentially dangerous waste and human remains, medical examination and testing, the protection of health information, the emergency licensing of health care professionals, access to mental health services, and the financing of the actions required by the Act itself. Good or bad, it is the most comprehensive model act dealing with these issues. The Turning Point Model Public Health Act, a more general model act that addresses many of the issues raised in MSEHPA, will soon be available.

2. There are several arguments made against the adoption of the MSEHPA. First, George Annas, among others, argues that there should be a federal response, not a state-by-state response, to bioterrorism, and that we need an appropriate federal reaction, not a set of fifty different state statutes. Do you agree? Would the federal government have the power to take the kinds of actions authorized by MSEHPA, or are these entirely within the police powers of the states?

3. Most of the other arguments directed to the MSEHPA are based in a concern that civil liberties—both personal and economic—are improperly sacrificed to the maintenance of security. Do you think that the Act gives governors too much power? Is there a way for that power to be shared with the legislatures, or is legislative action necessarily too unwieldy to be of use in a true emergency? Is the argument that the MSEHPA improperly concentrates power in the hands of a few people inconsistent with the argument that we need a federal, rather than a state, approach to this issue?

4. How do you imagine that the MSEHPA would be applied in practice? Suppose you were governor of a state in which several cases of smallpox had been discovered at one hospital. Would you invoke the Act? What difference would it make if you did? Are there parts of the Act you would not employ? Would it make a difference if the cases of smallpox were coincident with a large explosion, possibly the result of terrorism, in a large city in another state? What additional information would you need to make these decisions, and how would you get it?

5. There is a great deal that has been written about bioterrorism and its legal consequences. Particularly helpful resources can be found in the footnotes to both the Gostin and Annas articles found in the excellent first issue of volume 13 of Health Matrix (2003). For critiques of the Model Act, see Ken Wing, Policy

Choices and Model Acts: Preparing for the Next Public Health Emergency, 13 Health Matrix 71 (2003), Wendy Parmet, Quarantine Redux: Bioterrorism, AIDS and the Curtailment of Individual Liberty in the Name of Public Health, 13 Health Matrix 85 (2003), Edward Richards, Terry O'Brien and Katharine C. Rathbun, Bioterrorism and the Use of Fear in Public Health, 34 Urban Lawyer 685 (2002), and David Reich, Modernizing Local Responses to Public Health Emergencies: Bioterrorism, Epidemics and the Model State Emergency Health Powers Act, 19 J. Contemp. Health L. & Pol. 379 (2003). For an international approach, see David Fidler, Public Health and International Law: Bioterrorism, Public Health and International Law, 3 Chi. J. Int. L. 7 (2002).

*

Index

References are to Pages

ABORTION
Distinguished from contraception, 85–87
Freedom of Access to Clinic Entrances Act, 83–85
Informed Consent Requirements, 54
Legal status, 50–87
Parental consent and notification requirements, 76–77
"Partial birth" abortion, 68–74, 80–83
State regulation of medical procedures, 77–78
"Undue burden" test, 57–68, 74–75

ACQUIRED IMMUNE DEFICIENCY SYNDROME (AIDS)
See also Americans with Disabilities Act (ADA); Rehabilitation Act
International research, 450–451

ADVANCE DIRECTIVES
Durable powers of attorney for health care decisions, 292–294
Living wills, 291–292
Patient Self Determination Act, 298
Pre-mortem document of gift of organs, 467, 469–471
Uniform Health Care Decisions Act, 283–291
Values history form, 327

ALCOHOLISM
Organ transplants, 455–456

ALLOCATION OF HEALTH CARE
Generally, 453–455
Organ transplantation, 455–461

AMERICANS WITH DISABILITIES ACT (ADA)
Genetics, 164–197, 197–199

ANENCEPHALIC INFANTS
Generally, 220–233
Application of Emergency Medical Treatment and Active Labor Act (EMTALA), 229–234
As organ donors, 220–229

ARTIFICIAL INSEMINATION
Determination of heirs, 115
Donor (AI–D), 110
Homologous (AI–H), 109
Legal relations of parties, 113–116
Potential liability of parties, 115
Process, 109

ASSISTING SUICIDE
See Physician Assisted Death

AUTONOMY
Defined, 240–242

BABY DOE
See Right To Die; Newborns

BABY SELLING
See Surrogacy

BENEFICENCE
Defined, 240–242

BIOETHICS
General principles, 4–27

BIOTERRORISM
See Public Health

BRAIN DEATH
See Death

CAESAREAN SECTION
Forced, 132–139

CEREBRAL PALSY
Right to die, 218–222

CLONING
Generally, 153–159

COMPETENCY
Generally, 274–282

CONFIDENTIALITY
Donor registry, 472
Genetics, 188–195

CONSOLIDATED OMNIBUS BUDGET RECONCILIATION ACT OF 1985 (COBRA)
See Emergency Treatment and Labor Act

CONTRACEPTION
Distinguished from abortion, 85–87
Legal status, 49–50

DEATH
Brain death, 177–184
    Anencephalic infants, 220–238
    Definition, 212–216
    Homicide, 216–218
Determination for purposes of organ donation, 220–238
Higher brain death, 218–220
Religious perspective, 237–238

501

DECISIONAL CAPACITY
See Competency

DISABILITIES
See Americans with Disabilities Act (ADA);
    Genetics; Rehabilitation Act

DISCRIMINATION
See Americans with Disabilities Act, Civil
    Rights Acts, Race and Health; Staff
    Privileges

DISEASE
Defining, 185–186

DISTRIBUTIVE JUSTICE
    Generally, 451–455
And organ transplants, 451–461

DO NOT RESUSCITATE ORDERS
Generally, 295–298

DURABLE POWERS OF ATTORNEY
See Advance Directives; Right to Die

DUTY TO PROTECT THIRD PARTIES
Duty to warn of inheritable medical conditions,
    190–195

EGG TRANSFER
See In Vitro Fertilization

ELVIS
Proof that he lives in St. Louis, 502

EMBRYO TRANSFER
See In Vitro Fertilization

EMERGENCY MEDICAL CARE
See Emergency Medical Treatment and Labor
    Act (EMTALA)

**EMERGENCY MEDICAL TREATMENT AND
    LABOR ACT (EMTALA)**
Application to newborns, 228–232

EMPLOYMENT–AT–WILL
And ethical research culture, 446

EMPLOYMENT DISCRIMINATION
    See also Americans with Disabilities Act
        (ADA); Rehabilitation Act
Genetics, 164–165
HIV/AIDS, 197–200

EMTALA
See Emergency Medical Treatment and Labor
    Act

END OF LIFE TREATMENT
See Right to Die; Physician Assisted Death

EUTHANASIA
See Physician Assisted Death

EXPERIMENTATION
See Research Involving Human Subjects

FAMILY
Alternative definitions and reproductive possi-
    bilities, 107–109
Authority to consent to medical treatment,
    296–297
Confidentiality of genetic information within,
    187–195
Duty to warn of inheritable medical conditions,
    190–195

FEDERAL MEDICAL PRIVACY STANDARDS
    Se also Health Insurance Portability and
        Accountability Act (HIPAA)
Exceptions regarding duty to warn and duty to
    report, 194–195
Genetic information, 195

FETAL MATERNAL CONFLICT
See Fetus

FETAL MATERNAL DECISION MAKING
See Fetus

FETUS
Abuse and neglect law, 168–169
Application of civil remedy to pregnant woman
    to protect fetus, 168–169
Application of criminal law to pregnant wom-
    an, 169–171
Civil commitment of pregnant woman to pro-
    test fetus, 171–172
Constitutional recognition, 39–41
Development, 36–39
Employer "Fetal Protection" policies, 172–173
Forced C–Sections, 166–167
Guardians for, 173–181
Potential conflict with mother, 159–181
Research upon fetal tissue, 437–438

FUTILITY
Choosing futile medical care, 309–311

GENETICS
    Generally, 182–187
Confidentiality, 190–195
Databases, 206–209
Duty to warn of genetic conditions, 190–195
Employment discrimination, 197–200
Eugenics, 183
Gene therapy, 186, 439
Genetic information defined, 187–188, 189
Genetic screening, 197–200, 206
HIPAA, 194–195, 197
Human experimentation, 200–206, 439
Human Genome Project described, 182–183
Illness defined, 183–185
Insurance, 187–190, 196–197
Patents, 205–206
Pharmacogenomics, 186
Population genomics, 185–186
Property, 200–206
Race and ethnicity, 174, 185–186, 206
Reproductive decision making, 195–196, 206

GESTATIONAL SURROGACY
See Surrogacy

GUARDIANSHIP FOR FETUS
Generally, 173–181

HEALTH INSURANCE
Eligibility and rate-setting regarding genetic conditions, 187–190, 196–197

HEALTH INSURANCE PORTABILITY AND AC-COUNTABILITY ACT OF 1996 (HIPAA)
Genetics, 194–195, 197

HIPPOCRATIC OATH
Text, 27–28

HIV/AIDS
See Acquired Immune Deficiency Syndrome (AIDS)

HUMAN EXPERIMENTATION
See Research Involving Human Subjects

HUMAN GENOME PROJECT
See Genetics

HUMAN REPRODUCTION
See also Artificial Insemination; Genetics; In Vitro Fertilization; Surrogacy
Overview of Sexual Reproduction, 105–107

IMMUNIZATION
Constitutional Issues, 476–483

INFORMED CONSENT
See also Right to Die
Abortion, 76–77
Duty to disclose
Conflicts of interest in experimentation, 439–442, 445, 446
Family consent laws, 295–298
Genetic databases, 206–209
Inter-vivos organ donation, 471–472
Listing in donor registry, 471–475
Presumed consent for DNA databases, 206–209
Presumed consent for organ donation, 462–468
Research involving human subjects, 419–434, 444–446

INSTITUTIONAL LIABILITY
Research entities, 424–435

INSTITUTIONAL REVIEW BOARDS (IRBS)
See also Research Involving Human Subjects
Generally, 368–385

IN VITRO FERTILIZATION
See also Genetics
Cost, 117
Legal relations of parties, 118–125
Process, 116–118
Status of parents, 118–125
Status of unimplanted embryos, 126–129

ISOLATION
See Public Health

JEHOVAH'S WITNESS
Refusal of blood transfusion, 270–275

JOINT COMMISSION ON ACCREDITATION OF HEALTHCARE ORGANIZATIONS (JCAHCO)
Research entity accreditation, 424

LIVING WILLS
See Advance Directives; Right to Die

MAIMONIDES
Doctor's Prayer, 28–29

MARIJUANA
See Medical Marijuana

MEDICAL MARIJUANA
Generally, 399–409

MEDICAL RECORDS
See also Confidentiality
Genetic information, 190–194
Use in DNA databases, 206–209
Use in research, 414, 416–417

MERCY KILLING
See Physician Assisted Death

NATIONAL COMMITTEE ON QUALITY AS-SURANCE
Accreditation of research entities, 424

NATIONAL ORGAN TRANSPLANT ACT (NOTA)
See Organ Transplantation

ORGAN PROCUREMENT TRANSPLANT NET-WORK
See Organ Transplantation

ORGAN TRANSPLANTATION
Alcoholism, 455–456
Allocation, 455–461
Designated donees, 467
Living donors, 471–472
Federalism concerns, 460–461
Liability for retrieval, 471
Life sharers, 467–468
Living donors, 471–472
Market, 468–469
National Organ Transplant Act (NOTA), 456–457, 460–461, 468–469
Non–heart beating donors, 195–197
Organ distribution policies, 457–461
Organ Procurement and Transplantation Network (OPTN), 459–461
Personal consent, 466
Presumed consent, 462–468
Prisoners as recipients, 456
Property rights, 462–466
Race, 458–460, 467
Required request, 467
Uniform Anatomical Gift Act, 462–471
United Network for Organ Sharing (UNOS), 456–460

PAIN MANAGEMENT
Intractable pain acts, 396–397
Medical Marijuana, 397–409
Pain relief statutes, 397–398
Pain Relief Promotion Act, 398

"PARTIAL BIRTH" ABORTION
See Abortion

PATIENT SELF DETERMINATION ACT
See Advance Directives

PERSISTENT VEGETATIVE STATE
Patient decision making, 301–305

PERSONHOOD
Attributes, 31–39
Common law recognition, 44–46
Constitutional recognition, 39–41
Definition, 32–33
Distinguished from doghood, 31
Physical development, 36–39
Statutory recognition, 41–44

PHYSICIAN ASSISTED DEATH
Constitutional status, 366–381
Death With Dignity Act (Oregon), 388–395
Kevorkian, 381–383
Netherlands practice, 383–387
Opposition of medical groups, 387
State legislative action, 388–395, 397

PRESIDENT'S COMMISSION FOR THE STUDY OF ETHICAL PROBLEMS IN MEDICINE AND BIOMEDICAL AND BEHAVIORAL RESEARCH
Described, 413–414

PRINCIPLES OF MEDICAL ETHICS
AMA text, 29–30

PUBLIC HEALTH
Generally, 473–475
Bioterrorism, 489–498
Immunization, 476–483
Isolation, 484–488
Model State Emergency Health Powers Act, 489–494
Quarantine, 484–488

QUARANTINE
See Public Health

RACE AND HEALTH
Distributive justice, 453
Genetics, 185–186, 206, 207–208
Organ transplantation, 458–460, 467
Principle of justice, 453
Research involving human subjects, 413–414, 438

RATIONING
Generally, 453–455
Organ transplantation, 455–461

RESEARCH INVOLVING HUMAN SUBJECTS
Accreditation, 424
AIDS trials in Africa and Asia, 450–451
Bayh–Dole Act, 440
Children as subjects, 424–436
"Common Rule," 422
Conflict of interest for medical researcher, 427, 439–442, 444–446
Consent to research, 419–434, 442–443, 445–446
Data safety monitoring, 423–445
Declaration of Helsinki, 359–363
Emergency medicine research, 424
Ethical review boards, 443–444
Federal regulations, 412–424, 431
Fetal protection, 437–438

RESEARCH INVOLVING HUMAN SUBJECTS
—Cont'd
Genetic research, 200–209
History, United States, 412–414
Institute of Medicine recommendations, 442–446
Institutional Review Boards (IRBs), 414–446
    Generally, 414, 417–419, 424–434
    Contractual IRBs, 435
    Membership, 417–418, 422
    Reform, 442–447
International research, 447–452
Mentally impaired persons as subjects, 438–439
Minorities as research subjects, 413–414, 438
Nazi experimentation, 410
Nuremberg code, 410–412
Office of Human Research Protection, 423–424
Private litigation, 424–435
Research upon children, 379–380
Research upon fetuses, 379–380
Research upon prisoners, 380–381
Research upon stored tissue, 169
Therapeutic misconception, 422–423
Tuskegee Syphilis Study, 413–414
Willowbrook State Hospital Study, 413
Women as research subjects, 436–438
Pregnant women as research subjects, 437–438

RIGHT TO DIE
    See also Advance Directives; Autonomy; Beneficence; Competency; Death; Persistent Vegetative State; Physician Assisted Death
Active and passive conduct, 305–306
Advance directive, 250–296
Best interest test, 298–303
Children, 342–352
Clear and convincing evidence standard, 312–336
Competent patients, 258–298
Constitutional status, 244–257
Countervailing state interests, 265–268
Durable power of attorney for health care decisions, 292–294
Family consent laws, 296–297
Family members disagree, 308–333
Futile medical care, 309–311
Incompetent patients, 298–341
Jehovah's Witnesses refusal of blood transfusion, 270–274
Judicial process, 312–336
Living wills, 291–292
Newborns, 352–366
Nutrition and hydration, 307–308
Ordinary v. Extraordinary treatment, 306–307
Patient Self Determination Act, 298
Persistent vegetative state, 268–269
Physician assisted death, See General Index
Profoundly retarded patient, 337–441
Religious basis for decision, 257–258, 269–274
State law bases, 268–269
Substituted judgment, 300–309
Transfer to a state with more favorable laws, 256–257
Uniform Health Care Decision Act, 283–291
Vegetative state, See Persistent Vegetative State

SERIOUSLY ILL NEWBORNS
See Right to Die

STERILIZATION
Developmentally disabled, 87–89
Eugenic purposes, 87–91
Incentives, 90
Legal status, 87–96

SUBSTITUTED JUDGMENT
See also Right to Die
Organ donation, 468–471

SUICIDE AND ASSISTING SUICIDE
See Physician Assisted Death

SURROGACY
As baby selling, 136
Constitutional implications, 133
Cost, 129
Enforceability of contract, 131–133
Fraud, 145–155
Gestational surrogacy, 129–134
Gestational mother different from ovum
source, 137–142
History, 129
Legal status, 130–153
Process, 129–130

SURROGACY—Cont'd
Uniform Parentage Act provisions, 150–153

UNITED NETWORK FOR ORGAN SHARING
See Organ Transplantation

WARDEN OF THE EMBRYO FREEZER
His special dilemma, 99

WRONGFUL BIRTH
See also Wrongful Conception; Wrongful
Life
Damages, 95–97, 100–103
Defined, 85–98, 99–100
Distinguished from wrongful conception, 93–95
History, 99–104

WRONGFUL CONCEPTION
See also Wrongful Birth; Wrongful Life
Damages, 100–103
Defined, 99–100
Distinguished from wrongful birth, 95–97,
99–100
History, 99–104

WRONGFUL LIFE
See also Wrongful Birth; Wrongful Concep-
tion
Damages, 100–103
Defined, 99–100

†